FILM and the ARTS in SYMBIOSIS

FILM and the ARTS in SYMBIOSIS

A RESOURCE GUIDE

Edited by

Gary R. Edgerton

GREENWOOD PRESS

New York • Westport, Connecticut • London

791.43
F4872

Library of Congress Cataloging-in-Publication Data

Film and the arts in symbiosis.

88-11204

  Bibliography: p.
  Includes index.
  1. Moving-pictures and the arts. I. Edgerton,
Gary R. (Gary Richard), 1952-
PN1995.25.F53   1988   791.43'01   87-8465
ISBN 0-313-24649-1 (lib. bdg. : alk. paper)

British Library Cataloguing in Publication Data is available.

Library of Congress Catalog Card Number: 87-8465
ISBN: 0-313-24649-1

First published in 1988

Greenwood Press, Inc.
88 Post Road West, Westport, Connecticut 06881

Printed in the United States of America

The paper used in this book complies with the
Permanent Paper Standard issued by the National
Information Standards Organization (Z39.48-1984).

10 9 8 7 6 5 4 3 2 1

CONTENTS

Contents

PREFACE

This resource handbook is designed to take a first systematic look at the key relationships that exist between motion pictures and eleven other traditional or communication arts. This book is, of course, not the first publication in which film has been considered in tandem with other arts or media, especially in regard to literature, theater, and television. This effort is, however, a beginning inquiry into outlining the abundant interconnections that are now present in the media arts environment with respect to the movies, instead of just focusing on one symbiotic union.

A major intent of this project is to highlight and promote the interdisciplinary tradition that composes the movie discipline as a whole. Consequently, this anthology relies on the multifaceted nature that has always characterized film studies; and in turn, work by scholars who have studied or taught American Studies, Art, Broadcasting, Communication, English, Mass Media, Music, Photography, Popular Culture, Liberal Studies, and Theater are pulled together for ready access in one volume. The book is therefore arranged to reflect those various interests and areas of overlap that are apparent each year at the many academic conferences that address the study of motion pictures from scores of diverse and provocative vantage points.

From the start, it was undertood that our approach to film and the process of symbiosis would be exploratory since much of the writing in this relatively new research area is rapidly evolving. Each author became involved in the project because of a previous interest and background in the specific topic that he or she agreed to investigate further for this text. Likewise, it was assumed that the individual contributors would shape their respective chapters according to their own strengths and expertise, while always being cognizant of just a few parameters in order to ensure a certain degree of consistency in style and agenda.

First of all, each chapter is composed of five broad sections: a brief introduction; a history and development; styles and genres of interaction; a brief bibliography or review of the literature; and a selective filmography. The one ground rule for the historical overview is that at least four areas of symbiosis be acknowledged: craftsmanship and technology; business and economics; society and culture; and art. The assumption behind this stipulation is that developments occuring in one of these arenas typically affect the others, and vice versa.

Moreover, it was understood from the outset that this multileveled or systems approach would be tempered in execution by two factors. To begin with, the relevancy of each one of these four levels of symbiotic interaction varies with each specific media pairing. For example, business and industry will not be as crucial for motion pictures and painting as it is for movies and television. In this same way, artistic symbiosis is just beginning to emerge for motion pictures and the new media, while film and theater have been sharing aesthetics for nearly a century.

Second, it was presumed that the interests and predisposition of each particular author would clearly determine which levels of interaction were accorded more or less attention in the individual chapters. The intended strategy, therefore, was for each author to remain as mindful as possible of balancing the topic area with concerns and agenda items for all four levels of interaction as he or she judged appropriate.

Next, the styles and genres of interaction section is intended to outline the most prominent themes that arise as each symbiotic union is considered. This recap of issues is again meant to be multileveled in conception. In addition, the annotated bibliographies and filmographies were selectively determined as a means of highlighting the key sources in each topic area. In this way, the anthology is designed to function not only as an introductory handbook to these eleven symbiotic pairings, but also as a reference guide for researchers and students who wish to investigate further these specific media relationships through what is already available in print, film, video, and audio recordings. The information in each of the filmographies is also adapted to fit the particular case at hand; for instance, the availability of old-time radio plays is addressed in the chapter on movies and radio, while pertinent recordings are indicated in the listing for film and classical music.

As a starting point for the broader issue of media symbiosis, it was agreed from the beginning that each author would shade his or her unit of analysis toward American film, although certainly not to the total exclusion of international motion pictures. Of course, influences from outside the United States have always been crucial in shaping the business, art, culture, and technology of motion pictures here. As a matter of focus and manageability, however, much of what is discussed in the book has a bias in favor of the American milieu. The hope is that future research will extend the purview of publications involving the area of media symbiosis further into the international sphere.

With the completion of this anthology, a debt of gratitude is owed to a great many people. First of all, Marilyn Brownstein of Greenwood Press encouraged the book's development. She and Cynthia Harris offered both guidance and advice throughout its growth and evolution.

A very special thank you is given to the ten contributors who not only gave their time and expertise to the project but also offered many valuable comments, suggestions, and questions that helped clarify the focus and direction of the text. The effort and participation of all the authors was an invaluable help for me along the way.

During the past eight years, my interest in the whys and wherefores of mass media symbiosis has been fueled by conference, classroom, and informal discussions and debates with a number of teachers, colleagues, and students. Of special note, I would like to thank Carolyn Anderson, Rod Carveth, Vern Cronen, Rob Faulkner, Marty Norden, Maury Shelby, Dick Stromgren, and Rick Vincent at the University of Massachusetts; Ray Browne, Leslie Dick, Jack Estes, Brent Greene, Geoff Hammill, Kathy Merlock Jackson, Kwok Wha Lau, Pat McCarthy, Mike Marsden, Lori Murphy, Jack Nachbar, George Plasketes, Dave Ostroff, Cathy Pratt, Arvind Singhal, Denise Trauth, and Esther Ching-Mei Yau at Bowling Green; and Fred White and Ed Worteck at Goucher. I would like also to extend my sincere gratitude to the faculty development committee at Goucher College for supporting a summer's worth of my research and writing on this project by the awarding of an Elizabeth Nitchie Fellowship. Thanks also to Marty Norden for preparing the index.

The staffs at the Library of Congress, Motion Picture, Broadcasting, and Recorded Sound Division; the Museum of Broadcasting; the Museum of Modern Art, Film Department and Video Archives; and the National Archives and Records Service were all most helpful in aiding various authors with research and review of audiovisual materials for this volume. I would also like to acknowledge the help and enthusiasm of Bill Schurk at the audio archives of the Popular Culture Library at Bowling Green State University.

Finally, my deepest thanks and appreciation go to my wife, Nan, for her constant understanding and support. As always, she contributed wise and welcome recommendations and advice throughout the course of the project.

FILM and the ARTS
in
SYMBIOSIS

1

INTRODUCTION

GARY R. EDGERTON

Relationships among the media might be described in biological terms as symbiotic. They interrelate in complex ways that in the long run often turn out to be mutually beneficial. They use each other's material and talent, invest in each other's stocks, and benefit from each other's technological development.
—Sydney W. Head[1]

THE TRANSFORMATION OF ART AND CULTURE IN AMERICA DURING THE COMMUNICATION REVOLUTION

I must study politics and war, that my sons may have liberty to study mathematics and philosophy, geography, natural history and naval architecture, navigation, commerce, and agriculture, in order to give their children a right to study painting, poetry, music, architecture, statuary, tapestry, and porcelain.
—John Adams in a letter to Abigail Adams, 1780

The above timetable by the man who would become America's second president offers a certain amount of insight into the way the arts developed in the United States. As noted by Adams, the first priority of the colonies, and later the new nation, was understandably survival. His idea was that the next generation would take on the task of building up the young republic's commercial well-being and stability by its accomplishments in farming and industry. Finally, their children would then be in the position to cultivate, and could be afforded the luxury of cultivating, the fine arts.

The condition of progress which is implied by this scenario more or less came to pass, although Americans in the late nineteenth century never really embraced the finer arts in just the same way as Europeans traditionally had. What interested these Americans the most was another kind of aesthetic impulse which was frankly more practical and utilitarian, and this attitude which led to a redefining of the role and function of art in the United States was already flourishing during the days of Adams.

The influence of the fine arts was not readily apparent in the thirteen colonies, with the noticeable exception of a handful of thriving seaports, such as Boston and Philadelphia, which were open to the constant flow and influx of all sorts of ideas and people, some carrying with them the skills and vestiges of the European artistic tradition. On the whole, however, the means of communication were slow in early America, and communities were ordinarily isolated. This general state of affairs did not mean that there was no art in the young country; in fact, early America was already developing its own aesthetic traditions out of its need for survival and its vigorous, plain, coarse, and materialistic culture.

The arts that manifested themselves most clearly in the colonial period were not necessarily of the fine and liberal variety presumably presided over by the proverbial muses. Instead, most Americans of this period were much more inclined either to be practitioners of the manual arts or to appreciate the efforts of so-called manual artists: carpenters, potters, smiths, brick masons, and painters. The artistic watchword is probably more craftsmanship than anything else, as the examples that remain today of unpretentious and tasteful furniture, simple though elegant silverware, and crude but vital portraits painted by scores of anonymous, itinerant limners, all reflect an inherent tendency to blend the aesthetic with the materialistic and the practical. This is the artistic impulse that the United States would carry into its third and fourth generations in the late nineteenth century. And these circumstances also provided a foundation on which the communication revolution would begin to emerge along with the second generation's push and concern with commerce and industry.

Communication was actually the youngest and most invisible of four major forces or revolutions that transformed the face of America during the middle and late nineteenth century. The first and probably most formidable was the industrial revolution, which resulted in the rise of several key developments: large-scale automation appeared, as did a society of mass labor and attitudes of mass consumption. Why was this growing industrialism important for the arts and communication media in America? First of all, the arts in the United States became highly technical, commercialized, and even more popular than ever.

The emerging media arts were also based on a wedding of humans and machines. This fact was evidently consistent with the more technical and utilitarian attitude that had been apparent now for generations in the manual arts tradition of this country; these new media arts can be viewed as an extension of this American tendency to blend the practical with the aesthetic. Finally, these new mass communication arts eventually demanded large amounts of money to manufacture and distribute their messages. Likewise, the growing print and electronic-based media industries eventually borrowed and standardized assembly-line production, wholesaling, and retailing methods for the rest of the American industrial sector in the late nineteenth century and early twentieth century as their way of more effectively reaching the fresh and burgeoning phenomenon of the mass audience.

What in fact provided this conflux of human resources that made this new phenomenon possible was a subsequent urban revolution. From 1870 to 1890 the total U.S. population doubled. Villages became towns, and towns became cities. From 1860 to 1910 the population of Philadelphia tripled, New York quadrupled, and Chicago increased twenty times to two million inhabitants. The key here, of course, is immigration. The number of immigrants actually declined after the Civil War, but exploded soon afterwards.

By 1910, therefore, one-third of the U.S. population was foreign-born. In fact, from 1900 to 1910 one million immigrants a year were pouring into America during the growth and spread of big-city newspapers, the prehistory of radio, and the birth of the movies. The very texture of life in the United States was changing in two fundamental ways. First, ethnics were challenging the primacy of the WASP establishment. In 1860 only one percent of the American population was foreign-born; by 1910 this figure increased to 38 percent. Second, between 1900 and 1920 the U.S. farm population began its wholesale move to the cities. To put this trend into perspective, 50 percent of the American population were farmers in 1880; by 1922 only 10 percent were farmers.

Why, then, are the related issues of immigration and urbanization significant to the development of the communication arts and media in America? In the first place, a consumer population was now centralized. Also, media arts such as the movies and radio were inexpensive entertainment, and accessible to the literate and illiterate alike. The socializing potential of these emerging communication arts cannot be underestimated, as together they served to blend the diverse character of the American melting pot by contributing to an ever-present top layer of shared popular culture, albeit this stratum at the time was only skin-deep.

All in all, for most Americans the meaning of art—fine, popular, and folk— began to merge boundaries and evolve. Critics of the new media arts would later argue that this rising popular culture adversely affected the elite and folk arts in the United States by both distracting their audiences and absorbing their source material as if these forms were its own. Upon inspection, however, neither argument holds up in the face of subsequent developments. The specter of the ignorant, mass audience never materialized, except in the minds of elitist critics. The boundaries between levels of art clearly became more obscure, although the essential character of fine, popular, and folk culture flourished with their respective audiences throughout the course of the late nineteenth century and into the twentieth century as well.

Moreover, fine, popular, and folk arts have always borrowed a variety of materials from all kinds of different sources. The difference with the emerging media arts were their unprecedented public posture; when film imitated compositional or lighting stylistics from the traditions of painting, for example, or annexed themes for its soundtracks from the annals of classical or folk music, these aesthetic appropriations were visible for any one of millions who cared to notice. The subsequent effect of motion picture art on setting and structure in both the serious novel and the stage play was no less profound, but was visible to a smaller number of people.

Two provocative patterns remain though: the borrowing or symbiotic exchange between the fine, popular, and folk arts has indeed been beneficial for American culture as a whole by broadening the exposure of every aesthetic level, encouraging many to seek out and experience the original forms, and making some headway in breaking down the class barriers that are inherent in the social predilection for stratifying art and culture. In this way, the symbiotic process itself serves a democratizing function.

Second, the new communication technologies of the last century, such as film, records, radio, television, and video, actually served to speed up and facilitate artistic and media symbiosis by their transmitting and recording capabilities. The technologies themselves transcended the usual material distinctions between different arts and media, and in turn allowed an extraordinary degree of aesthetic, structural, and thematic crossover that was simply impossible before the industrial revolution.

One central irony involving the ideological content that was packaged in motion pictures and on the radio from the outset, though, is the fact that as the United States moved from a rural to an urban society, the ethos and values that were most apparent in print, on the screens, and over the airwaves of America's media arts remained typically rural. Village virtues, like love and neighborliness, and the ever-present myth of individualism still permeated the characters and stories in pulp novels, staged melodramas, the movies, and later on the radio, even as the real operating philosophies of the modern American marketplace developed another set of values.

Social Darwinism and American Pragmatism were the fuels that drove the third major convulsion that transformed the social fabric of the United States in the nineteenth century: an economic revolution. This particular force, in fact, emerged in large part from the conditions created by the American Civil War. As has been characteristic during the last 125 years of the U.S. economy, profits increase in times of war. There were fewer than one thousand millionaires in all of America prior to 1860, but by 1865 there were more than ten thousand. In general terms, the United States at this point entered a period of unprecedented economic growth which lasted for the next several decades.

Indeed, from 1865 to 1875 Americans began to feel a sense of total identification with their nation which is usually symptomatic of a country that is approaching some degree of public fulfillment. This feeling of unbounded optimism and unawareness of limits was prefigured in 1855, and probably most elegantly articulated, in the poetics of Walt Whitman: "The United States themselves are essentially the greatest poem." The bard's "spirit responds to his country's spirit. . . . he incarnates its geography and natural life and rivers and lakes."[2]

A change had indeed taken place after 1865. No longer was the representative

American a poet or intellectual like Whitman, or Emerson, or Thoreau. The last three decades of the nineteenth century saw the emergence of another kind of prototype: a Morgan, a Carnegie, a Vanderbilt, and the quintessential U.S. big businessman and tycoon, John D. Rockefeller. In 1860 the United States was a country of small enterprise; and although the myth of Jeffersonian America and a condition of laissez-faire never really existed in any purified form in the United States, at least what these abstractions represented offered some semblance to the reality of the pre–Civil War social structure. By 1870, however, the pretence that these conceptual models existed in America could no longer stand the test of any type of rigorous analysis.

Henry James once said that Americans came out of the Civil War "tasting of the tree of knowledge." A similar loss of innocence and metaphoric fall from grace is certainly evident in the new philosophies that the American people were then embracing. Social Darwinism was a theory brought to the United States in the late 1860s by Englishman Herbert Spencer. According to this theory, American society was a Darwinian jungle in which the superior gained power: the strong, self-made man proved himself the fittest to survive in this anarchistic, social universe. The proponents of industrial capitalism understandably embraced this notion since it afforded their success an almost divine justification, while failure became a moral symbol of personal inadequacy. It also wasn't long before these ideas were popularized and disseminated through the new mass media in the United States in forms like Andrew Carnegie's *Gospel of Wealth* and the many stories written by Horatio Alger.

Social Darwinism, therefore, provided Americans with a strict and distorted yardstick by which to measure themselves; in other words, those who failed in the marketplace ultimately had no one to blame but themselves. With so much at stake, it is easy to see how Charles S. Peirce and William James, Henry's older brother, later developed the philosophy of American Pragmatism. This line of reasoning held that truth and virtue were relative to their time and place. This theory soon found itself popularized as well in the much-used adage "the ends justify the means."

Consequently, Social Darwinism and American Pragmatism provided voice for not only the unleashed vigor and vitality of the domestic marketplace during the last three decades of the nineteenth century, but also many of the shortcomings that have, at times, plagued U.S. business, politics, and also the industry of mass communication during the past one hundred years. For instance, telegraphy, telephony, motion pictures, the electrical manufacturing, recording, and broadcasting industries, all were subject to control by internal monopolies and trusts early in their respective developments. Obviously, even the culture industries were captive to attitudes of winning at all costs, periods of unrestricted competition, and elements of exploitation and dehumanization in the workplace.

The nation as a whole in the late nineteenth century and early twentieth century even went through an era of escalating manifest destiny, which in turn led to the premise that God was on the side of America, directing her actions. In the aforementioned *Gospel of Wealth*, steel tycoon Andrew Carnegie proposed two central assumptions that were grounded in this idea confirming the watchfulness and blessing of the Divine. The first notion was "the stewardship of the elite," which purported that God was raising up a core of elite men to lead and rule in the socioeconomic arena. This concept was then closely followed with the argument of divine justification, or the belief that not only do these men deserve to earn vast amounts of wealth, but their superior abilities and intellect also make them best able to demonstrate where and how their money will do the most good.

As a result of these suppositions, the American money magnates became philanthropists; and in the process, all their previous actions were accorded the stamp of divine sanction. For example, Carnegie himself built over twenty-five hundred libraries around the world and established the Carnegie Corporation of New York with an endowment of $125 million to support educational projects. He retired to a Scottish castle in 1901 after selling out his controlling interest in the U.S. Steel Corporation. This polite Victorian gentleman never really understood the logic behind the criticisms that were subsequently lodged against him for being one of the worst of all the robber barons from this period of American history.

In retrospect, therefore, never before or since has politics been so dwarfed by economics in the United States as it was during the last quarter of the nineteenth century. Mark Twain called the era the Gilded Age and described it as "an age of excesses and contrasts, materialism and individualism, optimism and speculation, and an ever-widening gap between poverty and riches." The Gilded Age was surely a time that generated the capital necessary for the growth of America's new media arts and the corresponding culture industries that supported their inventions and subsequent commercial realization and acceptance.

This era was also dominated by a whole new social phenomenon of American "nouveau riche" and the trappings of their opulence and unbounded consumption. In the 1870s and 1880s, the money barons built mansions and castles of Gothic, Oriental, and Romanesque architecture which were decorated with all varieties of towers, domes, columns, and stained-glass windows. By 1890 the rich had moved out of the cities, and away from the thousands of incoming ethnics to various retreats, such as Newport, Rhode Island; Kennebunkport, Maine; and Ashfield, Massachusetts.

The machinations and indulgences of the so-called robber barons gave a certain tone and quality to life and culture in the United States. In a sense, these highly successful Americans were trying to buy a higher, more European-defined style of culture, because in their rise to power they had lost sight of what they were as a people before the Civil War. In this sense, the nouveau riche in the United States began looking elsewhere for an identity which would mesh more smoothly with their added wealth and status.

From a cultural perspective, therefore, most of the rich and educated in America continued to depend on Europe for direction in drama, music, and all the other fine arts through the turn of the century. Most serious theaters in the United States performed only European plays. Symphony orchestras, which began to appear and be sponsored by major U.S. cities during the Gilded Age, limited their repertoire almost entirely to European composers. A strong tradition was even establishing itself in American painting, although many of the more accomplished artists such as James McNeill Whistler and John Singer Sargent left for added direction and influence in Europe. A few men of letters, most notably Henry James, also became expatriates.

The key here is that by the 1890s, in a traditionally utilitarian culture that was growing even more materialistic, the fine arts simply had little impact on the lives of most Americans. The middle, working, and new immigrant classes in the United States found their entertainment at circuses, vaudeville shows, local taverns, and the new professional sports. These people also clamored for a degree of aesthetic fulfillment by attending to the emerging media arts. Pulp novels and barnstorming melodramas had been popular for years. After 1895 Americans could enter a nickelodeon and lose themselves at the movies for five cents admission. And then after 1922 they could sit alone, or gather with the family in the living room, and listen to America's most famous entertainers on the radio.

As noted before, the last and most subtle force that was also shaping America after the Civil War was a revolution in communication. Recreation and leisure time was evolving in the United States at the turn of the century in a number of provocative ways. First of all, hard-fought and slowly developing improvements in the conditions of labor, along with a shorter workweek, allowed leisure time to become more democratized. In this way, America's proverbial common man and woman were developing life-styles that afforded them more time for art and entertainment. Although the average person in the United States had the equivalent of only a fourth-grade education by 1900, dictating the aesthetic and cultural styles would no longer be the sole domain of the wealthy, the highly educated, and the nouveau riche.

In turn, middle- and working-class Americans brought their traditions of utilitarianism to their love of and excitement about the media arts. The same American impetus that had blended aesthetic with practical inclinations in the manual arts during the colonial period gave a similar vitality to the mechanical arts during the industrial revolution. Like the manual arts before them, photography, the phonograph, and the motion picture all retained a sense of craftsmanship, and more important, a function. With the corresponding influences of the industrial and economic revolutions, the purpose of the new mechanical art objects went beyond furnishing and servicing the household as was the case with the manual arts. Film and records would instead be used to make money for the newly emerging culture industries. Where else but in the United States would such a large-scale commercializing and redefining of the arts and culture be possible?

George Eastman with his Kodak film and Thomas Edison with his phonograph and kinetoscope were both entrepreneurs and cultural forces that were cut from a much different cloth than what was familiar in the traditions of West European art. In general, most Americans would never be comfortable with aesthetic notions that championed "art for art's sake," while the more modern and self-reflexive European styles in painting, sculpture, dance, music, theater, and the novel seemed seriously at odds with the social and cultural forces that were emerging chaotically from the United States of the nineteenth century.

American art and culture was neither inclined toward nor ready to produce a Matisse, a Picasso, a Stravinsky, or an Ibsen. Instead, the media and performing arts in the United States concentrated on the vitality of the pulp detective, the movie Western, the musical comedy onstage, and blues, ragtime, and jazz. At first, of course, most people here and abroad failed to recognize in such styles and genres the substance of art. Inherited standards such as truth, beauty, and timelessness interfered with any such recognition; the commercial nature of the media arts further compounded the confusion. Soon craftsmen such as D. W. Griffith, however, developed artistic identities. The artistry of Scott Joplin became available through piano rolls and sheet music; Louis Armstrong introduced jazz to a wider audience by making records; and Charlie Chaplin's genius on film made him the most recognizable person in the world by the late teens.

It is no coincidence, in fact, that the United States finally made an artistic contribution of international significance with the vitality and power of its movies. Film embodied those contradictions that converged uneasily with the confluence of the industrial, urban, economic and communication revolutions. This medium was at once technical and aesthetic; formulaic in content and still absorbingly meaningful to millions; always commercial, and sometimes even liberating. Soon American jazz recordings would also have a profound influence on classical musicians in Europe, especially in France. The irony here, of course, is that though the communication arts emerged in the second and third decades of the twentieth century as the most widespread, pervasive, and influential aesthetic forces in the history of American art and culture, the prior appearance of these media had not been taken seriously by any more than a handful of resolute art lovers and aficionados in either the United States or Europe.

The fine arts, on the other hand, continued to achieve little connection with the everyday lives of most people in the United States. American, French, and Russian filmmakers, critics, and theorists next began to assert themselves in the teens and twenties and to ask questions that reflected an entirely different aesthetic sensibility and landscape: Did film art have to be "true" and "beautiful"? If not, what was the function of art anyway? And what should be the relationship between film art and reality? The new media arts were already having their effect on traditional assumptions about art and culture both domestically and overseas.

By the turn of the century, therefore, the traditions of the manual arts had long given way to the mechanical arts, which in turn would soon be eclipsed by the even newer electronic arts. Motion pictures operated as a sort of bridge between the older mechanical technologies of the nineteenth century and the emerging electronic world of radio, records, television, and video. The recording and transmitting capabilities of all these media arts enabled them to borrow freely from each other and to appropriate additional source material from both the fine and folk arts. In turn, these communication technologies had the ability to transform seemingly alien styles and conventions into variations all their own.

In fact, as the more popular, mechanical, and electronic arts matured in the twentieth century, these media also demonstrated the surprising capacity of encompassing some of those qualities that were once typically associated only with the fine arts, namely, self-reflexivity and the individualized expression of an artist's vision or worldview. The process of aesthetic and media symbiosis evidently had come full circle as elite strains of painting, theater, the novel, poetry, and music, all showed the profound effects and influence of America's ubiquitous media environment by the mid-twentieth century.

As a result of their mutual involvement, the elite as well as the media arts have expanded beyond their original borders. What could be more American than using various high technologies as a means of facilitating the crossover between strains of fine, popular, and folk art, making the results accessible to millions, and earning money in the process? The media arts and their seemingly unlimited symbiotic potential have indeed redefined the scope, purposes, and boundaries of art and culture in the United States over the course of the last century. These mass communication technologies have imbued art, culture, and entertainment in America with a truly national flavor and sweep. In addition, their influences worldwide have at times been even more radical and complex.

FILM: THE SYNTHETIC ART

Anything that happens in life that can be seen or heard can be recorded on film. . . . The "art" of film, then, bridges the older arts rather than fitting snugly into the preexisting spectrum. . . . The earliest film experimenters "did" painting on film, "did" the novel, "did" drama, and so forth, and gradually it became evident which elements of those arts worked on filmic situations and which did not. . . . The neutral template of film was laid over the complex systems of the novel, painting, drama, and music to reveal new truths about certain elements of those arts. . . . for the last hundred years the history of the arts is tightly bound up with the challenge of film.

—James Monaco[3]

In this anthology, the primary units of analysis are the forms and channels of contemporary art. The authors represented herein make little distinction between fine, folk, or popular media arts, at least in terms of differentiating carefully between these various modes. Much of what is published in media studies in general, and film studies in particular, highlights who produced the work; how the work is coded, and what it expresses; who attends to the work, and to what effect; or how the work affects or influences society and culture.

In a related vein, the researchers in this book firmly root their attention on a different but complimentary set of agenda items: How do the arts interrelate in the media environment of the twentieth century? How have communication technologies, especially motion pictures, affected our attitudes toward art and entertainment? What are the various levels on which media symbiosis actually occurs? And how do certain mass communication media (during one era film and radio, and now television and video) influence the character and function of other arts and media, and ultimately direct the subsequent course of symbiotic development? These are obviously not easy questions, but the authors' intentions in what follows are to begin formulating ways to address and explain these issues and problems.

Martin Norden's chapter on "Film and Painting" begins the anthology's series of eleven case studies which are intended as in-depth introductory overviews of specific symbiotic pairings involving motion pictures with other arts and media. At the outset, Norden contrasts what is traditionally considered a fine art with a popular art and asserts that the relationship between painting and the cinema, "is at best a minor one" when compared with the interconnections between the movies and "other expressive forms such as theater and literature." Having thus put film and painting's symbiotic union into perspective, Norden then emphasizes examples of visual design and consciously avoids the usual pitfall of merely listing painterly movements and corresponding film styles.

Professor Norden argues that the aesthetic interchange between painting and film art is far more subtle than what is typically apparent by the mere act of cataloging common examples as he sets out to discuss and explain three levels of interaction: "clear-cut influences, likely influences, and coincidental but still noteworthy similarities." In the process, he covers a great deal of useful ground by combining examples from Hollywood features, international classics, the experimental cinema, and the documentary tradition in a presentation and analysis that touches upon various art movements, visual aesthetics, artists and their filmed biographies, and the cultural impact of certain painters and avant-garde filmmakers.

In his chapter on "Film and Photography," Charles Berg outlines how the motion picture is a technical and conceptual extension of photography. He simultaneously deals with both historical issues and the matter of styles and genres in three overview sections entitled "the cinematic apparatus," "photography as subject matter," and "photography as theoretical paradigm." In the process, Berg touches on aspects of technology, culture, and shared aesthetics in tracing a coordinated and symbiotic interchange that has remained vital for more than one hundred years. As Professor Berg points out, this union has proceeded naturally since the industrial revolution, and has resulted in a crosssover of inventors, artists, mechanics, and generic forms, like the photographic compilation film.

Richard Shale researched and wrote the chapter "Film and the Graphic Arts." In this context, he covers animated cartoons, comic strips, comic books, and to a lesser degree, movie posters and advertising art. Professor Shale aptly points out that the comics have had a profound influence on filmmakers as varied and diverse as Alain Resnais, George Lucas, Federico Fellini, and the Marx Brothers. His discussion deals with shared aesthetics, such as angles, shot types, lighting effects, and editing strategies. Shale also highlights aspects of technological development, competition, and exploitation in both the newspaper and movie industries involving the use of comic strips and their heroes as content, and the outrage and subsequent movement towards suppression that have periodically swelled up in certain sectors of American culture against both comic books and motion pictures. The crossover between comics, cartoons, and the movies offers a long-standing and intriguing case of how the popular arts share and enrich each other's standing as entertainment forms, businesses, and social forces.

Carolyn Anderson next investigates the profilic and enduring research area "Film and Literature." Focusing on the interrelations between prose fiction from North American novelists and movies grounded in the Hollywood tradition, Anderson's comprehensive overview emphasizes aspects of aesthetics and culture, and to a lesser degree, she explains how the business exigencies of reaching the "presold audience" virtually guarantee that approximately 30 percent of American motion pictures be based on best-selling novels. Professor Anderson also develops four important and provocative themes in her styles and genres of interaction section: generic content shared between these media; writers who have worked in both forms; the adaptation process; and the aesthetic similarities and differences in regard to literary and filmic narrativity, structure, and technique.

The symbiotic crossover between "Film and Theater" is at least as prolonged and intense as what is outlined in the chapters on literature and motion pictures. Gregory Waller interweaves issues and insights about aesthetics, craftmanship, business, and culture in his discussion about the complex and century-old interplay between the stage and screen. The author relies on examples derived from both the United States and Europe, as he intersperses representative works culled from the highbrow, lowbrow, and middlebrow theater and film worlds.

In the process, Professor Waller thoroughly addresses those questions that are crucial in laying the groundwork for understanding this important symbiotic relationship: What has been the influence of both avant-garde and traditional stage aesthetics on the development of film storytelling, acting methods, mise-en-scène, lighting, and vice versa? What has been the role that theatrical artists have played in the development of film art, and vice versa? How have Hollywood and Broadway cooperated and competed over the years? And how have the stories, characters, and conventions of each medium served as source material for the other?

In his chapter on "Film and Classical Music," Royal Brown extends this anthology's exploration into the cinema's multifaceted and synthetic character by shifting attention to the realm of aural design. At the outset he asserts the "drama enhancing potential" of film music and identifies the precedent of incidental music in the theater. Although Brown acknowledges examples from both Hollywood and the international cinema, he provides an intriguing and comprehensive analysis of the contribution of classical music scores to the development of American film art. In this way, Professor Brown concludes that the Hollywood system, in spite of its long history of controls and tampering, has produced an incredible number of soundtracks that beautifully complement their movies, stand up well musically, and reveal strong individual styles. He moreover investigates these various styles of film music and ends his chapter by examining the ways in which film music has been designed to interact with both the visual and verbal languages of the cinema.

As a companion piece to the previous chapter, Gary Burns next examines those strains of musical influence that affected and merged with the movies from the vantage point of popular culture. He traces the interactions of "Film and Popular Music" from the nearly simultaneous invention of the phonograph and motion picture technology to the more recent video explosion. Professor Burns emphasizes how film quickly became associated with popular music, even in the so-called silent era, and develops themes that relate to aspects of technological, business, and aesthetic symbiosis. He analyzes the interplay of popular musicians, record companies, and filmed musicals from the days of Tin Pan Alley to the present emergence and maturation of rock and roll.

Although popular music is both a performing and a recording art, radio brings the anthology squarely into the sphere of the electronic or mass media arts. In my exploration of "Film and Radio," I try to identify which levels of interaction are most prominent during each stage of symbiosis. In this way, it becomes apparent that technology, business and economics, aesthetics, and then sociocultural impact, in that order, are the dominant levels in which movies and radio interrelated and enriched the prospects of each other from the turn of the century to the 1950s.

The history of their relationship is also unique in the fact that both communication arts shared a position of primary technological, economic, aesthetic, and social influence over America's other mass media for almost the entire decade of the 1940s; never before or since has such a seemingly equal and complementary relationship existed between two of the mass electronic arts in the United States. Finally, the specific case of film and radio during the last thirty-five years also points to the fact that mass media symbiosis has become a much more complex and entangled process since World War II. In the example of radio and movies, for instance, the symbiotic equation now includes print, records, television, and video as fundamental and interconnecting parts of a much larger, overlapping media process.

William Lafferty next oulines the growing pains and eventual maturation of commercial TV and the American movie business in "Film and Television." Television in this chapter means TV in the traditional sense: networks, affiliates, and independent stations. The author hones in predominantly on the 1940 through 1960 time frame and explains in detail how the technology of TV developed in the United States, Great Britain, and Europe; how Hollywood eventually learned to adapt itself to the new and unprecedented influence of the domestic television industry; and how the interchange of genres, programming conventions, and aesthetics increased in frequency and success between the two media throughout the 1950s. Professor Lafferty's styles and genres of interaction section is particularly concerned with the fertile symbiosis that took place in this era between TV and movies (as well as radio) in story types, style, and technique.

In "Film and Video Art," Edward Small begins with a brief introduction and the styles and genres of interaction section as a means of laying the groundwork for the later historical overview. Small thus offers a beginning definition for the genre of avant-garde production which conceives of the independent video movement as an evolutionary extension of the traditions of the experimental mode of filmmaking.

Professor Small presents and explains eight technostructural characteristics which avant-garde film and video art share with each other along the lines of technology, aesthetics, cultural aims, and economic priorities. He then argues that there exists an "intrinsic bonding" between "film's mechochemical and video's electronic constructions" which results in a symbiotic form, "cinevideo." Professor Small concludes that video art is "the latest connection in the long, long thread of inspiration stretching back through experimental film, photography, painting, sculpture, right to the roots of art history."

Bruce Austin deals with video in a much different sense in the following chapter on "Film and the New Media." In many quarters, the so-called new video technologies are reshaping the way we think about both TV and film. As Austin points out, there are dozens of new media, but he primarily concentrates on those forms that are most closely aligned with recent developments in the American motion picture industry, namely, pay-television and home video.

Professor Austin begins by investigating film's relations to STV, basic and premium cable, videodiscs, and videocassettes over the broad areas of shared technology, economic competition, social impact, and to a lesser degree, common aesthetics. He further asserts that symbiosis with the new media is actually redefining how we talk about the film medium itself, as well as how we perceive the inner workings of the movie industry. He concludes by arguing that this process of symbiosis ultimately affects what visual entertainment is produced, who will view these movies, under what circumstances, and for what reasons. Clearly, of all the symbiotic combinations that are considered in this anthology, the relations between film and the new media are the most fluid and indefinite at present.

While encouraged with our first step into the topic area of media symbiosis, all the authors represented within this anthology would be the first to admit that our explorations of how film and the other arts and media interrelate are just a beginning. Next steps for writing about symbiosis can take a number of provocative directions. First, more thinking can help refine how we describe and analyze levels of interaction. Which levels are most important during each particular phase of the symbiotic process? Moreover, do any common trends surface between a number of symbiotic groupings? Is a theory of media symbiosis possible, or is each case study so idiosyncratic that very few common patterns are evident?

Next, the nexus points between arts and media other than just those covered in this book should be investigated as well. As pervasive as has been the influence of motion pictures during the twentieth century, television has been even more commanding and potent in its effect on the growth and development of the other artistic, mechanical, and electronic channels of communication. Although always acknowledged, TV's contributions to the contemporary media environment in general, and the symbiotic process in particular, certainly need to be explained in greater detail. Last, much more work remains to be done in extending the examination of symbiosis into the international arena. This broader unit of analysis will raise the additional levels of cross-cultural and political interaction into the forefront of the present dialogue involving media symbiosis.

As an aid for continued research, a number of reference books and pamphlets are particularly useful as a means of locating the appropriate primary source material in the media arts. The following entries fall into two broad categories: directories that list (1) the major research archives and libraries in the mass communication arts and (2) the availability of film and video rentals, including all the specific works that are referred to in the chapters within this anthology.

1. Bukalski, Peter J., Compiled by Fay C. Schreibman. *Factfile #15—Broadcast Television: A Research Guide.* Los Angeles: American Film Institute Education Services, 1983, pp. 39–54. This pamphlet has a number of extremely helpful sections. There is an introduction that outlines tips on how to approach a special library or archive. Next, the authors list ten special libraries or information centers specializing in broadcast television, seventeen academic archives of national significance, and the whereabouts of the NBC, CBS, ABC, and PBS archives. There is also information on relevant state and local historical societies, public libraries, and suggestions on locating programs if they are not presently in an archive or library.

2. *Educational Film/Video Locator of the Consortium of University Film Centers and R. R. Bowker.* 2 vols. 3d ed. New York: R. R. Bowker, 1986. 3,600 pages. This book lists over 48,500 films and videocassettes that are available for rent from various colleges and universities across the United States. The movies and tapes are cross-referenced according to subject heading, producer, and distributor.

3. Godfrey, Donald G., ed. *A Directory of Broadcast Archives.* Washington, D.C.: Broadcast Education Association, 1983. 90 pages. This pamphlet lists the name, sponsor, types of holdings, and accessibility of the collection for fifty-eight American and thirteen Canadian and British archives or study centers for broadcasting and video materials. This guide also includes in an appendix the addresses for thirty-seven smaller collections across the United States.

4. Heintze, James R. *Scholars' Guide to Washington, D.C.: Audio Re-*

sources—Sound Recordings in the Arts, Humanities, and Social, Physical, and Life Sciences. Washington, D.C.: Smithsonian Institution Press, 1985. 395 pages. This book outlines the location and describes the holdings of literally hundreds of collections and organizations in the nation's capital devoted in one way or another to audio materials, including libraries, archives, manuscript repositories, museums, data banks, broadcasting organizations, research centers, U.S. government agencies, record stores, radio stations, and colleges and universities.

5. Kupferberg, Audrey E., "Film Archives," in Maltin, Leonard, ed. *The Whole Film Sourcebook.* New York: New American Library, 1983. pp. 197–229. This valuable reference book has a chapter on film archives. Short descriptions of fourteen of the most important archives in the United States and addresses of seventy-six international film study centers and repositories are listed.

6. Limbacher, James L. *Feature Films: A Directory of Feature Films on 16mm and Videotape Available for Rental, Sale, and Lease.* 8th ed. New York: R. R. Bowker, 1985. 734 pages. This reference work is the most up-to-date sourcebook devoted to the commercial rental of motion pictures. Each citation includes the film's name, year of release, a full set of credits, format, length, and distributor(s). In addition, the 26,000 motion pictures are cross-listed according to subject and director. The names and addresses of all the important domestic distributors and a relevant bibliography are also included.

7. Rowan, Bonnie. *Scholar's Guide to Washington, D.C.: Film and Video Collections.* Washington, D.C.: Smithsonian Institution Press, 1980. 283 pages. Although this reference work is beginning to get out of date, it is still a valuable starting place for finding the wealth of motion picture and video material that is available in Washington, D.C., at various archives, libraries, universities, and government agencies. The text also includes an excellent guide by David Culbert on how to do research at the National Archives and Records Center, along with his critical bibliography on film and video studies.

8. Schlosser, Anne G. *Factfile #11—Film/Television: A Research Guide.* Washington, D.C.: American Film Institute Education Services, 1977. pp. 3–13. This pamphlet contains the names, addresses, hours, and a brief description of holdings for seventeen film research libraries, four university film study centers, three film studio research libraries, six television research libraries, five university television study centers, and two network research libraries.

9. Smart, James R. *Radio Broadcasts in the Library of Congress, 1924–1941.* Washington, D.C.: Library of Congress, 1982. 149 pages. This valuable resource book catalogs the name of the show, the performers, the station, network, length of time, and the date (if available) of tens of thousands of broadcasts during the birth and maturation of network radio in America. The programs, which are available at the Broadcasting and Sound Recording Division of the Library of Congress, are listed in chronological order for easy reference.

10. Weaver, Kathleen, Richard Prelinger, and Linda J. Artel. *Film Programmer's Guide to 16mm Rentals.* 3d ed. Albany, Calif.: Reel Research, 1980. 320

pages. Because of the enormous flux and company turnover that has occurred in the distribution of 16-mm films over the past five years, this helpful guide is quickly falling out of date. Nevertheless, it has comprehensive listings for fiction films, documentaries, early cinema offerings, and newsreels. In addition, the titles are indexed at the end according to their directors.

NOTES

1. Sydney W. Head, *Broadcasting in America: A Survey of Television and Radio*, 3d ed. (Boston: Houghton Mifflin, 1976), p. 482.

2. Walt Whitman, Preface (1855) to the first edition, *Leaves of Grass*, ed. Harold W. Blodgett and Scully Bradley (1965; repr. New York: W. W. Norton, 1968), pp. 709, 711.

3. James Monaco, *How to Read a Film: The Art, Technology, Language, History, and Theory of Film and Media*, rev. ed. (New York: Oxford University Press, 1981), p. 20.

2

FILM AND PAINTING

MARTIN NORDEN

INTRODUCTION

The relationship of film and painting stresses the importance of visual design more than any other media linkage. Indeed, visual design—which includes composition, perspective, color, lighting, settings, texture, and other elements that play a part in the shaping of visual imagery—is the very heart of the film-painting connection. Yet, as we shall see, the relationship goes beyond the obvious visual appeal of each medium to encompass distinct ways of looking at the world, such as expressing certain artistic impulses and attacking (or defending) various social phenomena. These similarities and others will serve as this chapter's foci of investigation.

It is important to note at the outset, however, that film's relationship with painting is at best a minor one, particularly if we compare it with film's relationships with other expressive forms such as theater and literature. Film analyst Charles Eidsvik has gone as far as to argue that film's visual sense derives mainly from theater and photography, with painting providing only a negligible influence on the "look" of film.[1] In addition, it is difficult to ignore the related view that painting is primarily a fine art and film a popular art—a familiar dichotomy stressing such areas of difference as creative purposes, modes of reproduction, and audiences.

Significant functional and physical differences between the media also cannot go overlooked. Most films tell stories while paintings do not (at least not in the conventional sense) but instead explore arrested moments in time. Related to this functional difference is a physical one: the media's capabilities for portraying motion. A strong artistic impulse to represent movement has existed ever since primitive people painted running beasts on their cave walls millennia ago, yet the painterly image, of necessity, must remain static; motion, the sine qua non of cinema, can only be implied in painting. As noted by film director Joseph von Sternberg, "The ablest painter, sensitive as he is to a single canvas, is helpless to control that ever-shifting, mobile canvas of the motion picture."[2]

Despite these and other differences, film and painting have enjoyed a symbiotic relationship for many years. As Parker Tyler has asserted, "There has always been commerce, more or less conscious, between painting and the film."[3] Examples of interchange between the two media abound, and they range from the clear-cut influence of various modernist art movements on the avant-garde cinema of the 1920s to art documentaries and Hollywood's occasional big-budget "biopix" of famous painters during the 1950s and 1960s. The high number of examples illustrating the various facets of the film-painting relationship dictated the following strategy for the next two parts of this chapter: the Historical Development section outlines the major art movements and relevant films within a historical framework, while the Themes and Issues section examines their form and content at greater length. Discussions of paintings, films, and art movements that may seem all too brief in the former section are usually more fully realized in the latter.

HISTORICAL DEVELOPMENT

The union of painting and film is nearly as old as cinema itself and initially appeared in the form of painted canvas backdrops for films. A year after the Frenchmen Auguste and Louis Lumière produced the first films in 1895, their countryman George Méliès was already designing and painting sets for the fantasies and historical films that became his specialties. By 1897 Méliès had built the world's first film studio on his property at Montreuil, France, where he designed many sets for his films. Film stock was comparatively insensitive to light back then, and with special lighting equipment virtually nonexistent, Méliès and other pioneers had to find ways of taking maximum advantage of sunlight to make their films. Méliès constructed his studio largely of glass for this purpose, and painted the backgrounds he designed on large (approximately ten feet by twelve feet) flat canvases that could be easily maneuvered to receive the full effect of the sun's rays. Following the conventions governing the creation of theatrical settings, Méliès gave his flat backdrops the illusion of depth by relying on trompe l'oeil techniques. His desire for painterly control over his settings even extended to the set floors, which he covered with canvases painted to duplicate the looks of various types of flooring materials.

Méliès's set designs contributed as much to the special magic of his films as his celebrated trick effects, and it is likely he had been attempting to mimic certain painterly compositions in his backdrops. Film historian Léon Barsacq has observed a possible influence by the paintings of Douanier Rousseau on the look of such Méliès fantasies as *A Midsummer Night's Dream* (1901) and *The Kingdom of the Fairies* (1903). Among other similarities, Rousseau's paintings and Méliès's films featured bold colors that harmonized well and strangely outfitted characters that somehow rarely seemed ridiculous as they interacted amid bizarre settings.[4]

Méliès's films were instantly popular with audiences, and their success was not lost on several rival film companies. Later in 1897, Charles Pathé and Léon Gaumont began making films heavily indebted to the Méliès canon, particularly in their use of painted sets as backgrounds for both fantastic and realistic films. Unlike the Méliès company, these larger film concerns could afford to hire set designers such as Maurice Fabrège and Hugues Laurent, who had already gained fame for their similar work in the theater and opera worlds. Film's painted-set tradition had now gone "big time."

By today's standards, the painted sets look hopelessly flat, stagey, and artificial, but audiences of that era were moved by their apparent authenticity. As Hugues Laurent noted of the work of fellow designers Gaston Dumesnil and Henri Menessier, "it was impossible not to believe one was in the intended location" painted on their canvases.[5]

As audiences became more sophisticated, however, they demanded a greater realism in the backgrounds of the films they watched. The years 1908 to 1914 saw a steady rise in the use of plywood doors and molding, furniture, and other three-dimensional objects in set design, culminating in the first film set constructed entirely of plywood in 1914. World War I temporarily halted film production in France, and by the time it resumed, constructed sets had largely supplanted their painted counterparts. In later years, a smattering of films such as the German Expressionist classic *The Cabinet of Dr. Caligari* (1919) and Jean Cocteau's Surrealistic *Blood of a Poet* (1930) resurrected the painted-set technique by using painted canvases to reflect the inner states of their lead characters, but the number of such films was too low to signal a major comeback of the tradition.

With the development of new forms of artificial lighting and more light-sensitive film stocks well under way by this time, commercial filmmakers continued their move toward greater realism by experimenting with different forms of lighting that suggested a greater sense of three-dimensionality. Cecil B. deMille, remembered as Hollywood's early maestro of sin, sex, and spectacle, is also credited with developing the style of illumination known as "Rembrandt Lighting" in film while working for Jesse Lasky and Samuel Goldwyn during the 1910s. Wishing to avoid the flat, uniform lighting common to just about all films up to that time, deMille experimented with side lighting, resulting in pronounced light and shadowy areas reminiscent of the Dutch master's seventeenth-century paintings. DeMille's chiaroscuro lighting created dramatic effects, but some people in the business had a hard time accepting it. According to Jesse Lasky's autobiography, Goldwyn was so befuddled by the unusual lighting in deMille's *The Warrens of Virginia* (1915) that he wired Lasky to let him know he would have difficulty selling a film in which the actors' faces were frequently obscured by darkness. Lasky relayed the message to deMille, who thought it over a few moments before giving his legendary reply: "Tell him it's Rembrandt lighting." In classic capitalistic fashion, Goldwyn immediately raised the rental rates for the film.[6]

The rise of realism in the popular arts, exemplified by the changing view on set design and lighting in commercial films, coincided with an inverse move toward greater abstraction in the fine arts. Though diametrically opposed, these movements—especially as expressed in film and painting—were unquestionably related; they were among the manifold results of the industrial revolution begun during the 1800s. The rise of still photography and other new technologies, many of which led directly to the development of cinema, had a profound effect on many painters. Still photography and its cinematic offspring largely displaced the art world's representational function by manifesting an objectivity and veracity which even the most accomplished painters had difficulty matching. Numerous painters moved away from a belief in a strict fidelity to nature and a divinely ordered universe and started interpreting the world around them in different ways. Some, like the Cubists and the Futurists, rendered objects and movements semi-abstractly by fragmenting and then recombining them. Others, like the Expressionists and the Surrealists, gave their art an "altered state of consciousness" quality. Still others—the Dadaists—relied on random juxtapositions of objects and contexts and the frequently unexpected, even shocking images that ensued to form the backbone of their work. Ushered in by Impressionism, a mid–nineteenth-century art movement coinciding with the development of cinema's immediate ancestors, the modernist movements rocked the art world during the first three decades of the twentieth century. All found expression not only in painting (arguably their premiere medium) but in film as well.

One major trait shared by many artists engaged in the new art forms is that they frequently crossed over into a variety of media. Typically, artists who created paintings also wrote poetry and music, performed plays, and/or made films. For example, Fernand Léger, the French painter of Cubist and Futurist works, helped design similar sets for Marcel L'Herbier's *L'Inhumaine* (1923) and made his own Futurist film, *Ballet Mécanique* (1923). The Russian filmmaker Dziga Vertov, who wrote Futurist poetry as a teenager, made a number of Futurist films, most notably, *The Man with the Movie Camera* (1929). Premiere Dadaists such as Marcel Duchamp, Man Ray, Francis Picabia, and Hans Richters eagerly embraced film as the latest in a series of media outlets for the strange blend of whimsy, anarchy, and chance that characterized their work. Though he made no films, Theo van Doesburg, a tireless art promoter and major force in "De Stijl" (the Dutch variant of Geometric Abstractionism which translates simply as "The Style"), was so impressed with Hans Richter's abstract film of moving rectangles, *Rhythmus 21* (1921), that he arranged for its screening at the Théâtre Michel in Paris. Clearly, the zest with which pre-Depression artists explored the new art movements knew few media boundaries.

The arrival of the Depression and World War II signaled a major decline in the film-painting relationship. Some filmmakers moved away from abstract artistry to deal directly with pressing, social, political, and economic issues in their films. Others found it a challenge to make any films at all, such as Hans Richter, whose work was decried by the Nazis as decadent art. Oskar Fischinger, Len Lye, and Norman McLaren were among the exceedingly few filmmakers who

continued experimenting with abstract, painterly designs during the turbulent
1930s and 1940s.

With the exceptions of the short films of Fischinger, Lye, and McLaren, the
major interactions between film and painting during the post-Depression and
World War II years took place within feature-length narrative films. In Europe
during the 1930s and mid–1940s, such otherwise diverse directors as Jean Renoir,
Carl Theodor Dreyer, and Sergei Eisenstein made leisurely paced films whose
visual images were virtual homages to certain painterly styles. During the same
years, Hollywood demonstrated its interest in painting in a very different fashion;
the Disney studio meticulously created animated films whose background imagery rivals Impressionism (or, in the case of *Fantasia* [1940], Expressionism),
while other studios produced occasional melodramatic movies that focused on
the devastating effects of blindness on the lives and careers of fictional painters.

The years immediately following World War II are often characterized as an
age of intense interest in human psychology,[7] and Hollywood filmmakers contributed to the spirit of the era by producing movies that examined the behavior
and inner struggles of their lead characters. Such movies occasionally featured
dream sequences highly reminiscent of the Surrealist paintings of the 1920s and
1930s. At the same time, Hollywood sometimes used painted portraits of people
as major story elements, occasionally in a supernatural vein.

During a period stretching from the late 1940s to the mid–1960s, Hollywood
filmmakers and European documentarists shared a strong interest in depicting
the life and work of famous painters such as Michelangelo, Rubens, Toulouse-
Lautrec, Van Gogh, and Picasso. The high point of this interest occurred in
September 1956, when New York City's Plaza Theatre and the Metropolitan
Museum of Art joined forces in a mutually beneficial effort: the museum loaned
one of Van Gogh's most famous paintings—the 1888 *L'Arlesienne*— to the
theater for the world premiere of *Lust for Life*, Hollywood's sensitive treatment
of the tormented artist's life. In return, the museum received more than $5,000
raised at the premiere for its student fellowship program. In an age of turmoil
and uncertainty, the timeless and soothing qualities of art held a strong appeal
for filmmakers, who may have wanted to reassure themselves and the world that
fine art had indeed survived the carnage of World War II and also to help it
reexert its civilizing influences. Other filmmakers, aware of Cold War pressures,
may have desired to make films on politically neutral subjects, or at least subjects
whose integrity was unassailable. Still others may have wanted to combat the
new medium of television and its assumed lowbrow appeal. Whatever the reasons, the resulting films are generally quite striking, as are the contemporaneous
films of Norman McLaren. At a time when Abstract Expressionism—best exemplified by the splattery "action paintings" of Jackson Pollack—was gaining
prominence, McLaren continued his singular filmmaking work of hand-painting
abstract designs directly on clear film stock.

The 1960s were also a period marked by the rise of "pop art," when artists
such as Andy Warhol not only created pop paintings and sculptures but a host

of films as well. "Op art," pop art's companion movement, also found cinematic expression in the form of "flicker films"—experimental films featuring the use of rapidly edited shots of solid black and solid white.

On the narrative-film front, filmmakers continued to invoke past painting styles on an intermittent basis in movies from the 1960s well into the 1980s. In addition, a descendant of the painted-set tradition called *matte painting* reached maturity during the 1960s and remains a frequently employed technique in Hollywood movies. Usually listed in film credits under the general label of "Special Optical Effects," the matte-painting process is the art of painting a scene to look like a large photograph of a given environment but with key areas of the painting (the "matte") left blank. After the artist finishes the painting, other filmmakers will optically insert live-action scenes into the blank areas of the matte to create a composite image. If the matte is done well, the audience should be unable to determine where the painting ends and the live-action areas begin. Ironically, if the painting looks too much like a painting, the audience will be distracted and the effect ruined. Like so many other aspects of "movie magic," the matte painting aspires to invisibility.

Albert Whitlock is Hollywood's premiere creator of matte paintings, which have played a part in such otherwise disparate films as *North by Northwest* (1959), *Colossus: The Forbin Project* (1970), *Oklahoma Crude* (1973), *The Sting* (1973), *Mame* (1974), *Earthquake* (1974), *The Wiz* (1978), and *Dune* (1984). Working with oil-base paints and sheets of plate glass measuring several feet, Whitlock will meticulously paint highly realistic background scenes called for in the script that cannot be photographed in a cost-efficient way. In other words, Whitlock's matte paintings are particularly useful in films in which it would be either costly to construct full-sized artificial settings or difficult to film in actual settings, such as historical films, fantasies, and disaster epics. In *Oklahoma Crude*, for example, the filmmakers needed several shots of period oil derricks to give a better sense of the film's era and setting: the early wildcatting days in Oklahoma. After several failed attempts to build replicas of the oil wells, the filmmakers hired Whitlock to create several matte paintings which included the derricks in the background. The final version of the film contains four Whitlock matte shots, and they are the film's only shots that contain complete views (i.e., long shots) of the oil wells.

This anecdote illustrates the unfortunate way that many movie producers have regarded matte painting: as an afterthought or a stopgap measure. Whitlock has described his job as "darning and mending" holes in movies,[8] and even today the matte painting is not held in high esteem. With audiences unaware of the best matte paintings, Whitlock and his peers continue to pursue their art in considerable obscurity.

As we move through an age of unprecedented visual communication, the mutual influences of film and painting continue to be felt. An example may be found in the recent convergence of fine art and popular art. *Time* art critic Robert Hughes lamented in 1985 that high art used to be a retreat from the mass culture offerings of film, TV, and other media. This assumption no longer holds true, Hughes argued, since the immediacy, brevity, disconnectedness, and frequent blandness of the mass media have had a strong impact on the way many painters view the world and render that view on canvas.[9]

STYLES AND GENRES OF INTERACTION

Before we begin exploring the relationship of film and painting in greater depth, a caveat is in order. In some instances, there is a year-by-year matchup of painterly movements and film styles, often with the same people involved in both media. Such instances are the easiest to deal with in terms of identifying connections between painting and cinema. Other times, however, the influence of one medium on the other may not have manifested itself until years later; in certain cases, the presumed influence may not be an influence at all but merely a reflection of similar concerns. In the interest of avoiding ad hoc pitfalls, I have endeavored in the following discussions to distinguish between clear-cut influences, likely influences, and coincidental but still noteworthy similarities.

In his article "The Film Sense and the Painting Sense," Parker Tyler argued that the movie camera follows one of two trends in its relationship with the world of art: it may animate works of art, or it may de-animate life into the "still" terms of painting.[10] As the following discussions will make clear, Tyler's dichotomy, articulated in the 1950s, holds up quite well.

The development of cinema's predecessors during the middle part of the nineteenth century coincided with the rise of Impressionism, a painterly style that signaled a shift away from a predominantly religious view of the world and occupies the middle ground between classical and modernist styles. Impressionist paintings reflect a strong interest in the beauty of nature and in the way light falls on objects. Through small, dense brush strokes and brighter, richer colors, Impressionist painters such as Pierre-August Renoir, Claude Monet, and Camille Pissarro gave a light, feathery quality to their works.

Two distinct qualities of Impressionism exist, often in the same paintings: a love of nature and a fascination with technology. Impressionist artists frequently portrayed upper-class city folk enjoying the pleasures of the French countryside (picnicking, rowing down a river, etc.) or explored the breathtaking beauty of city gardens—even haystacks—lit in a variety of ways. Yet the industrial revolution kept creeping into the movement, mainly with its emphasis on trains, bridges, and the freedom of movement from the congestion of the city to the pleasures of the country that they suggested.

Art critics quickly denounced and ridiculed Impressionist paintings when they were first publicly exhibited in the late 1860s and early 1870s, and audiences did not widely appreciate them until this century. For these and other reasons, the influence of Impressionism on film did not appear until years later.

The most obvious example of a filmmaker following an Impressionist tradition is Jean Renoir, the second son of Impressionist painter Pierre-August Renoir.

Shortly before his death in 1919, the elder Renoir told his son that he had spent his life painting the same three or four pictures over and over; interestingly, the younger Renoir was later to say the very same thing about his films: that he had spent his artistic career refining only a handful of themes and motifs. Included among them were themes also explored by his father and other Impressionist painters, such as a love for nature and its sense of beauty and freedom.

Renoir began making films in 1925 with money inherited from his father. Out of the many films he made, the one that best illustrates the legacy of Impressionism is *A Day in the Country* (1936). Set in the countryside outside Paris, the film quickly introduces a fairly well-to-do Parisian merchant and his mother, wife, daughter, and prospective son-in-law about to enjoy "a day in the country." Their "day" is replete with fishing, boating, and picnicking in the picturesque French countryside, and includes Laurel and Hardy-esque fishing scenes involving the father and future son-in-law, and romantic encounters of the mother and daughter with a satyr-like oarsman and his moody companion.

With its portrayal of different classes and its obvious love of nature, the film bears a strong resemblance to many Impressionist paintings of the 1860s and 1870s. An example is *Oarsmen at Chatou*, painted by Renoir's father in 1879. Chatou was a popular recreational place in the country for upper-class people, and in this painting, an upper-class man and woman stand on a bank overlooking the Seine River. They are watched by two oarsmen, one of whom stands on the bank, his legs straddling the end of a docked rowboat, while the other sits in the boat's midsection. They exhibit a trace of impatience as they wait for the upper-class couple to make up their minds, and it is an attitude similar to the sense of detachment that the oarsmen display toward the Parisian family during the early passages of *A Day in the Country*. The film is also similar to Monet's 1868 painting, *On the Seine at Bennecourt*, which features an upper-class woman out in the country, seated high on a river bank overlooking the Seine while a rowboat rests in the foreground.

The influence of Impressionism on film extends all the way from the 1930s to today. Albert Whitlock, the best-known of film's matte painters noted earlier, has likened his work to Impressionism; considering his strong concern with the way that light falls on objects, it is an apt analogy.[11] In addition, the sensitivity of film stock to light, which reached new heights during the mid–1970s, allowed filmmakers to work with candlelit scenes and other low-lighting conditions. The resulting films frequently had a softness reminiscent of the Impressionist style coupled with an Impressionistic-minded love of nature. They include Stanley Kubrick's *Barry Lyndon* (1975), Terrence Malick's *Days of Heaven* (1978), and Roman Polanski's *Tess* (1979). The latter film serves well as a case in point. It overflows with soft-focus imagery, particularly in the early scenes between Tess and Alec, such as the boating scene and the now-famous "strawberry-eating" scene in the D'Urberville arbor. Interestingly, Polanski subtly altered his film's visual style once the dishonored Tess has returned home from the D'Urbervilles; as Tess gathers hay and performs sundry other farm chores, the style shifts from a Monet-like Impressionism to the romanticized treatment of rural life often found in the works of the sixteenth-century Flemish painter Pieter Brueghel.

Art historians have generally credited Impressionism with setting the stage for the appearance of Cubism, Futurism, and the other modernist art movements of the first three decades of the twentieth century. Of these latter movements, Cubism—originated circa 1906 by Pablo Picasso and Georges Braque—is perhaps the most important artistic force in this century. Its stress on the underlying structures of objects and its intense interest in fragmentation and recombination have had an enormous impact on a variety of media, film most assuredly included.

At first blush, Cubism appears only tenuously connected with film of any kind. Indeed, one may argue that few films, avant-garde or otherwise, bear any significant resemblance to either the typically static Cubist subjects—portraits, still lifes, landscapes—or their semi-abstract treatment as manifested in the classic works of Picasso and Braque.

Though the subjects of Cubism and film may have differed radically, their *treatment* provided some conceptual common ground. Cubist paintings often present their subjects from multiple viewpoints, a characteristic found in most films. A Cubist portrait painter might show the top, front, and side of a human head all at once, a task a filmmaker could just as easily accomplish by editing together shots of the head taken from different camera angles. The major difference, of course, is that the painting would show the different viewpoints simultaneously, whereas the film would show them consecutively. Yet the general practice of breaking down objects into smaller chunks and reassembling them into new wholes is similar in both media.

Cubism appeared at a time when cinema, no longer regarded as a plaything or scientific curiosity, was becoming a big business (complete with its first monopoly in 1908) and a "cinematic language" was in its rudimentary stage. The half-minute runs of the camera that constituted entire films in 1895 had given way to ten-to-twelve-minute films consisting of long shots, medium shots, and close-ups, often taken from a variety of angles. Edwin S. Porter and D. W. Griffith were among the vanguard of experimenters who so structured their films, and their articulations occurred at about the same time that Picasso and Braque were treating their Cubist works. While it is difficult to determine whether the filmmakers and the Cubists knew of each other's work, they clearly shared an interest in presenting the world in a fragmented, restructured way. Just as filmmakers sought to liberate their medium from the conventions of theater by stressing those things theater has difficulty accomplishing (such as shifting perspectives), the Cubists wanted to free their work from classical painting styles. Practitioners in both media avoided single, fixed perspectives, preferring instead to place their viewers in a more omniscient position by "opening up" their vision.

In addition to its relationship with film, Cubism shared a link with the latter medium through its progeny. Cubism is generally recognized as the progenitor of numerous other twentieth-century art movements, and many of them are directly related to developments in the avant-garde and documentary fields of film. Art historian Sarah Newmeyer's discussion of Cubism's pervasiveness is typical:

Important in and of itself as a separate art movement, Cubism's transcendent importance lies in the train of art development it set in motion and of which it was the immediate or the underlying cause. Whether these new movements—Futurism, Suprematism, Abstractionism, etc.—came as action or reaction, Cubism was their catapulting force, and their effects have virtually permeated twentieth-century living in the form of architecture, furniture, industrial, typographical, and many other fields of design such as jewelry, textiles, and chinaware. Everything that has modern shape or pattern in the world we live in today has the roots of its design in the original Cubist determination to discover and *uncover*, to rearrange or even to disarrange the essential form that underlies outward appearance.[12] (emphasis in original text)

Newmeyer's list can easily be amended to include cinema in general and avant-garde cinema in particular, as several of Cubism's related "isms"—Futurism, Precisionism, Suprematism—bear close similarities in their specialized ways to various types of cinema. The film medium has been well-suited to representing the modernistic concerns of a variety of Cubist progeny, as we shall see.

Of the three offshoots of Cubism studied here, Futurism was the first to appear. The 22 February 1909 edition of the French newspaper *Le Figaro* announced the movement's birth in the form of a Futurist manifesto written by the Italian poet Filippo T. Marinetti and endorsed by several Italian painters, including Umberto Boccioni, Gino Severini, and Giacomo Balla. A portion of their proclamation read:

We will sing the love of danger, the habit of energy and boldness. . . . We will extol aggressive movement, feverish insomnia, the double-quick step, the somersault, the box on the ear, fisticuffs. We will declare that the splendor of the world has been enriched by a new beauty—the beauty of speed. A racing motor-car, its frame adorned with great pipes like snakes with explosive breath—a roaring motor-car that seems to run on shrapnel is more beautiful than the Victory of the Samothrace.[13]

In a follow-up manifesto, the painters themselves dealt more directly with their proposed techniques, as indicated in these excerpts:

The gesture we seek to represent on canvas will no longer be an arrested movement . . . all is in a state of flux, of headlong change . . . objects in movement multiply themselves endlessly and become distorted as they overflow each other like vibrations launched into space and weaving through it. Thus a trotting horse has not four legs but twenty and their movements are triangular.[14]

In brief, the Futurists and the Cubists were both interested in the process of fragmentation and recombination, but the former artists were much more concerned with movement, speed, and dynamism. While the Cubists presented stationary objects from multiple viewpoints simultaneously, the Futurists wished to show stages of action concurrently, similar to the effects achieved in multiple-exposure photography. In terms of their form, Cubist paintings exude considerable energy, but they seem downright tranquil next to their "feverish" Futurist offspring.

The Futurists combined their desire to depict movement, especially violent movement, with a sharp interest in the excitement and turbulence of modern city life and the dynamics of machinery. Futurism unquestionably reflected the Machine Age brought about by the tremendous strides in science and technology from the mid-nineteenth century through the first decades of the twentieth, and its powerful imagery had a wide-ranging impact. An example of an artist so influenced by the movement is the American painter Joseph Stella, who attended a Futurist exhibition in London in 1912. During the year following his return to the states he painted his famous *Battle of Lights, Coney Island*, which depicts furious abstract movement amid the setting of the famous Brooklyn amusement park. In 1917 he painted another Futurist-inspired work: *Brooklyn Bridge*, full of energized angles and strong contrasts. Similar expressions by other artists found their way into France and the USSR.

Since film was obviously a child of the technological revolution, it should come as no surprise to learn that the Futurists saw great artistic possibilities in the fledgling medium. On 11 September 1916, Marinetti, Balla, and other Futurists proclaimed their concern for the theatrical direction film was then taking and offered their prescription in a manifesto called "The Futurist Cinema," segments of which follow:

At first look the cinema, born only a few years ago, may seem to be Futurist already, lacking a past and free from traditions. Actually, by appearing in the guise of theatre without words, it had inherited all the most traditional sweepings of the literary theatre. Consequently, everything we have said and done about the stage applies to the cinema. Our action is legitimate and necessary in so far as the cinema up to now has been and tends to remain profoundly passéist, whereas we see in it the possibility of an eminently Futurist art and the expressive medium most adapted to the complex sensibility of a Futurist artist. . . . The cinema, being essentially visual, must above all fulfill the evolution of painting, detach itself from reality, from photography, from the graceful and solemn. It must become anti-graceful, deforming, impressionistic, synthetic, dynamic, free-wording.[15]

Though the Futurists who penned this manifesto made precious few films (one of them being the 1916 effort, *Vita Futurista*, which no longer exists), numerous films made by other filmmakers during the 1920s and beyond exhibit Futurism's concern for movement, machines, and the dynamism of urban life. One of the earliest and most famous examples of this trend is the French film *Ballet Mécanique* (1923), which was largely the responsibility of Fernand Léger. Art historians have frequently linked Léger with the Cubists, but his post–World War I paintings often show a decidedly un-Cubist preoccupation with machine-like shapes. This tendency was perhaps a reflection of his experiences in World War I as a member of the French Transport Corps, and it continued to find expression in his paintings up to his death in 1955. It also played a significant role in his *Ballet Mécanique*, a film which, as art historian Edward Aiken has argued, deserves a Futurist label instead of the Cubist one commonly ascribed to it.[16] The consistent themes of the film—"the humanization of objects and the mechanization of humans,'' as noted by avant-garde film critic P. Adams Sitney—are prime Futurist concerns.[17] The film is laden with close-ups of machine parts and kitchen items such as gelatin molds, funnels, and dishware coming to life through rapid editing, occasionally fragmented by a prismatic lens. The film's most famous segment—the "looping" or reiteration of a shot of a lower-class woman ascending a flight of stairs—underscores the machine-like, repetitive qualities of working-class lives. Léger did add a conspicuous Cubist touch to his otherwise machine-oriented film by starting and ending it with an animated Cubist rendition of Charlie Chaplin. Perhaps Chaplin was returning the favor in his feature-length film *Modern Times* (1936) during a famous scene when a conveyer belt pulls his "Little Tramp" character around cogs and gears inside a huge assembly-line machine.

Sergei Eisenstein's *The Battleship Potemkin* (1925) is world-famous for its compositions and editing techniques, and it is quite likely that Futurism influenced the Russian filmmaker to some degree. Early in the film, for instance, a sailor on board the *Potemkin* is washing dishes when he comes across a plate inscribed with the words "Give Us This Day Our Daily Bread.'' Eisenstein had the sailor break the plate in a rage, presumably to show the latter's (if not the former's) anger with the inefficacy of religion on the ship. Instead of filming the sailor's act in a single shot, however, Eisenstein broke the action down in a series of very quick, almost subliminal, shots from different angles. This style of editing, which heightened the power of the scene, is markedly similar to the Futurist way of fragmenting action in a painting. The film also bears the mark of Futurism during its final act, which contains many close-ups of furiously moving parts of the ship's engine as the *Potemkin* mutineers prepare to defend themselves against the czarist fleet bearing down on them.

Other filmmakers of the time recognized the suitability of their medium to the presentation of moving machine parts and incorporated this and other aspects of Futurism into many of their works. For example, Marcel L'Herbier's *L'Inhumaine* (1923) not only has rapidly edited shots of a car's engine and wheels but also features extravagant Futurist-Cubist sets designed by Léger and Alberto Cavalcanti. Fritz Lang's *Metropolis* (1927) is replete with mechanical motifs, from its opening montage of hyperkinetic machine parts to the creation of a female robot who leads members of a city's working class in a revolt. With these features, along with its portrayal of the workers as machine-like automotons, *Metropolis* unquestionably owes a debt to Futurism. Joris Ivens's *The Bridge* (1928) and Shirley Clarke's much later *Bridges-Go-Round* (1958) share a concern for the lines of force inherent in bridges that Joseph Stella explored in his Futurist treatment of the Brooklyn Bridge, described above. Clarke's description of her own film as a study of "the patterns made by bridges in space, their massive power, and the particular quality of motion that is given to bridges when moving in relation to them" is a Futurist-sounding statement just as applicable to the Ivens film and the Stella painting.[18]

Two groups of film in particular reflect Futurism's dual concerns of machinery and fast-paced urban life: the "city symphonies" and the works of the Russian filmmaker Dziga Vertov. The city symphonies were films that depicted the daily rhythms of large industrial cities in pre-Depression Europe. Walter Ruttmann's *Berlin: Symphony of a Big City* (1927), the most famous of the symphonies, works especially well as an embodiment of the twin Futurist concerns; in addition to showing the hectic pace of a typical "day in the life" of Berlin (accomplished in part through fast editing, shots of busy streets often filmed from moving vehicles, and shots of hyperactive businessmen), *Berlin* is heavy with close-ups of machine parts, such as those of telephones and typewriters, which Ruttman occasionally presented in a multi-image, kaleidoscopic fashion. Another city symphony, *Nothing but the Hours* (1926) focuses on the dawn-to-dusk activity of Paris. Directed by Alberto Cavalcanti, the Brazilian émigré who also helped design the Futurist-Cubist settings for *L'Inhumaine*, the film reflects concerns similar to those of *Berlin*.

The films of Dziga Vertov also exhibit Futurist-inspired concepts. Futurism had reached Russia by the mid–1910s, where a teenaged Vertov, already developing a heady interest in technology, found himself coming under its spell. He wrote Futurist poetry and experimented with technological marvels of the time: first, audio recording; then, motion-picture cameras. The latter innovation completely fascinated him, and during the early 1920s, he mixed Futurist and Bolshevik principles with his notions on the new medium. The result was the creation of his "Cinema-Eye" theory, which he put into practice with the production of a film entitled, appropriately enough, *Cinema-Eye* (1924). As cinema historian Albert Leong has noted, the film "incorporated two principles which were to remain at the center of Vertov's cinema: the power of technology, hence the superiority of the mechanical camera-eye to the human eye; and movement, as the very nature, not only of the mechanics of the machine, but of the whole social and physical universe."[19] Vertov strongly developed these and other Futuristic concerns (such as the classic analysis-and-synthesis pattern developed by the Cubists and the Futurists, which he realized masterfully through rapid editing) in his own city symphony, *The Man with the Movie Camera* (1929). Ostensibly about Moscow, *The Man with the Movie Camera* is more significantly a film about the nature of film. Vertov employed split screens, slow motion, fast motion, freeze frames, superimpositions, and unusual camera angles in his film to show that the camera eye could see things differently (and better, by implication) than the human eye. A mechanical subject—the camera itself— becomes the star of the film as it explores buildings, trains, steel girders, and printing presses, among other subjects, with a dazzling virtuosity before it literally takes a bow (via animation) on its tripod before an appreciative audience at the film's end.

If Futurism was strongly concerned with the cult of the machine, then surely two of its spiritual progeny in the avant-garde filmmaking world of the 1950s and 1960s are Bruce Conner and Kenneth Anger. In at least three films, Conner and Anger were just as intrigued as the Futurists with machines: Conner's *A Movie* (1958), and Anger's *Scorpio Rising* (1963) and *Kustom Kar Kommandos* (1965).

The Conner film is similar to the Futurist films cited earlier in that it features fast-paced editing, but unlike some of these other works, *A Movie* consists primarily of a mix of disparate newsreel footage made up of long and medium-long shots. The subjects of *A Movie*, however, are frequently related to machinery and other forms of technology: racing cars, motorcycles, sunken (and sinking) ships, warplanes, bizarre bicycles, submarines, the undulating Tacoma suspension bridge, the Hindenburg zeppelin, atomic bomb blasts. One theme that emerges from *A Movie* is that the union of human aspirations and technology often results in destruction in one form or another.

The Anger films are different from *A Movie* and the other films discussed here in terms of pacing; instead of fast cutting, Anger often used lingering tracking shots. Through this approach, however, one can sense the way Anger (or at least the way his characters) felt about the mechanical subjects of *Scorpio Rising* and *Kustom Kar Kommandos*—motorcycles and customized cars, respectively—by the way his camera lovingly, even worshipfully, "caresses" them, sometimes in intimate close-up. (A similar and probably noncoincidental camera-caress of a motorcycle also appears in the 1969 film *Easy Rider*.) Though different in technique, these films share with *A Movie* the Futurist interest in machines and the rotten fruits of the Machine Age, specifically decadence and destruction.

A second offspring of Cubism, and one that shared an interest with Futurism in the urban environment but offered far different interpretations, is Precisionism. Precisionism was primarily an American movement during the 1920s and 1930s, and its practitioners were mainly interested in depicting architectural landscapes through strong, sharp geometrical figures. Their major concern was the presentation of city buildings in a pristine, personless, timeless, and passionless way. In place of the dynamism of city life depicted in Futurist paintings and films, the Precisionists offered just the opposite: mammoth urban structures devoid of human activity, standing in mute testament to the hardness and coldness of modern life. The most prominent Precisionists were Charles Sheeler and Charles Demuth, who painted such works as *Church Street El* (1920) and *Classic Landscape* (1931), and *Modern Conveniences* (1921) and *Business* (1921), respectively.

A number of avant-garde films manifest Precisionism's objective and impersonal approach to big-city buildings. One obvious example is a film on which Sheeler himself worked, along with Paul Strand, entitled *Manhatta* (1921). This film, the first American avant-garde film ever made, is based on a Walt Whitman poem on the subject of New York. In the film, lines of Whitman verse are intercut with beautifully composed but static shots of various Manhattan buildings. As with the classic Precisionist paintings, *Manhatta* shows no human beings; it is instead a photographic essay comprised of geometric patterns formed by buildings.

Another film which bears a Precisionist influence is Robert Flaherty's *24 Dollar Island* (1925). This film also eschews human beings as subjects and instead focuses on various architectural details of Manhattan structures. Flaherty's extensive use of the telephoto lens, which enabled him to pick up such details, also had the Precisionistic effect of flattening the details as well as the buildings themselves.

The city symphonies, discussed primarily in Futurist terms, also owe a debt to Precisionism. The early morning sequence of *Berlin* serves well as a case in point, since much of it consists of static shots of buildings without human activity. The scenes of this sequence are meant to represent the city while it sleeps and are a prelude to the furious activity of a typical day in Berlin, but as a unit they also represent another ''photographic essay'' of city buildings, one quite beautiful and rather clearly modeled after the Precisionist approach to the urban landscape.

A discussion of avant-garde films that exhibit Precisionist tendencies would not be complete without mention of a more recent film that might well be regarded as filmic Precisionism taken to its limit: Andy Warhol's *Empire* (1964). This unique film, which owes as much to Minimalism as to Precisionism, consists soley of a single, static, eight-hour run of the camera, featuring the Empire State Building in long shot. Unlike the Precisionist paintings and like-minded films discussed above, the subject of *Empire* is shown within the context of time; the sky darkens eventually, lights come on in the building, etc. Otherwise, the film is a veritable homage to the Precisionist movement and demonstrates, if nothing else, the intolerability of real time in film.

The third and final scion of Cubism studied here is sandwiched chronologically between Futurism and Precisionism but is much more abstract than either: Suprematism. The movement was founded in 1913 by Kasimir Malevich, a Russian who from 1910 to that time created paintings that were generally Cubist in nature. They were similar to Léger's with respect to form and color, though they did not demonstrate an interest in machine shapes. In 1913, however, Malevich abandoned the Cubist semi-abstract techniques in favor of an approach which eliminated all reference to objective reality. He became interested solely in pure geometry, and his earliest Suprematist works consisted entirely of black squares or circles on white backgrounds. He took his new movement to the limit in 1918 with a composition entitled *White on White*, which was made up of a white square on a white background. His later works consisted of various configurations of such basic geometric forms as circles, squares, and rectangles, some in color.

It may be tempting to write off Malevich and his one-man movement as something of an aberration, but he and other practitioners of Geometric Abstractionism (of which Suprematism is sometimes considered a form) such as the

Dutch artists Piet Mondrian and Theo van Doesburg have affected a variety of other artists and concerns. For example, their works have exerted a significant influence on newspaper and magazine layout and design.

Cinema is another area which shows the mark of Suprematism, though Malevich himself obscured Suprematism's relationship with film by railing against the photographic and naturalistic limitations of the new medium.[20] Though Malevich viewed film as a limited means of artistic expression, others who followed his lead in exploring geometric shapes, were not nearly as shortsighted; indeed, a number of the earliest avant-garde films reflect a similar interest in the geometric purity of Suprematism, most notably the so-termed absolute films of the German artist Hans Richter. In particular, his Rhythmus film series—*Rhythmus 21* (1921), *Rhythmus 23* (1923), and the no longer extant *Rhythmus 25* (1925)—bear striking similarities to the earliest Malevich efforts. *Rhythmus 21*, for example, consists of squares and rectangles moving via animation against a neutral background. While much has been made of the relationship between Richter's Rhythmus films and music, one can hardly overlook the prominent resemblances between the films and the Suprematist paintings.

The colorful geometric films of Oskar Fischinger are also related to Suprematism and its concerns. Fischinger's experimentation with animated geometric figures in Germany in the early 1920s eventually led to the creation of films such as *Circles* (1933), *Allegretto* (1936), *An Optical Poem* (1937), and *Radio Dynamics* (1941). All of these works exhibit pure geometric shapes as their prime concern, which Fischinger usually presented in vivid color and synchronized to big-band jazz or classical music.

A connection more conceptual in nature exists between Suprematism and the avant-garde cinema with respect to the much later "flicker films," including *Arnolf Rainer* (1960) by Peter Kubelka, *The Flicker* (1966) by Tony Conrad, and portions of *Report* (1965) by Bruce Conner. Related to the optical art, or "op art," movement of the 1960s, flicker films (or flickering portions of films) consist of black and white frames which alternate in random or structured patterns. As the Malevich paintings usually feature a geometric shape in tonal contrast to another one (i.e., the rectangle formed by the canvas) at the same time, the flicker films feature a similar tonal contrast of geometric shapes (i.e., the rectangles formed by the film frame), but this contrast occurs only over time. It is a point similar to the one made earlier concerning Cubism and film (i.e., Cubist paintings show multiple viewpoints simultaneously, while most films offer them consecutively). Depending on the length of the shots, the black and white frames in actual projection may appear as a rapidly pulsating grayish blur tinged with subjective color, but their conceptual similarity with the Suprematist paintings remains intact.

A kind of intermediary link between Suprematism and flicker films may be found in Joseph Anderson and Edward Small's *Alpha Mandala* (1972), a film which consists of a large, flickering white circle set off against a black background. Though the filmmakers were primarly concerned with exploring the effects of flickering films on audiences, *Alpha Mandala* nevertheless shares with the early Suprematist works the classic simplicity of design, geometric purity, and strong tonal contrast between subject and field.[21]

An art movement that developed concurrently with Cubism and its descendants in Europe is Expressionism. Of its various manifestations, the Teutonic version is the most famous and engendered a brief revival of the painted-set tradition. Primarily a visual movement, Expressionism extended to all the arts in Germany. The sharp, contrasty angles and bold diagonal lines of Expressionist painting were well represented in the most famous of the Expressionist films, Robert Wiene's *The Cabinet of Dr. Caligari* (1919), in which the audience views the world through the eyes of a madman. Its settings look as if they were lifted directly out of an Expressionist art gallery; stark, angular light streaks and shadows zigzag through both the interior and exterior settings to help characterize the bizarre subjective experience. *Caligari*'s set designers (including Hermann Warm, who stated that "films must be drawings brought to life"),[20] created many of the film's lighting effects by painting light and dark areas directly on the walls and floors of the studio sets. Though the designers may have based their actions on sheer economy (it being less expensive to paint the jagged light patterns than to bring in special lighting equipment), the resulting painted patterns complement the actors' costuming, makeup, and movement to create an overall Expressionist style.

For all its fame, *The Cabinet of Dr. Caligari* was one of only a few Expressionist films to use painted sets in so radical a manner and to rely on them so heavily. Subsequent Expressionist filmmakers tended to favor three-dimensional sets over the more flattened environments of *Caligari*, sending film's painted-set tradition into yet another hiatus.

Another movement that helped undermine the conventional notions of truth, goodness, beauty, and transcendence as reflected in art was Dada, which arose shortly after World War I. Founded by Tristan Tzara, Dada emphasized the random juxtaposition of objects and the comic anarchy that often ensues. Dada's practitioners were displaced intellectuals disillusioned with the war and dissatisfied with the directions taken by modern society and its art forms. In a strong spirit of dissent, they felt that if art had a right to exist, its opposite—anti-art, or expressions based on sheer chance—also had a right to exist. As Tzara proclaimed in his 1922 "Lecture on Dada," everything in the world occurs in an irrational manner. The Dadaists wanted to abolish all things logical and conventional as well as the connectedness of things, which they tried to accomplish in their works by cutting off everyday objects from their conventionalized meanings and placing them in unexpected contexts.

A widespread movement (it had branches in New York, Paris, and Zurich, among other cities), Dada featured more crossover artists than any other new art movement. Tzara, Hans Arp, Max Ernst, Richard Huelsenbeck, Hugo Ball,

Marcel Duchamp, Man Ray, Kurt Schwitters, Hans Richter, Francis Picabia, and many other Dadaists worked in a wide variety of arts, creating paintings, poems, plays, ballets, sculptures, and films.

Dada found expression in such playfully nihilistic films of the time as Man Ray's ironically titled *Return to Reason* (1923), which bizarrely juxtaposes springs, buttons, nails, and tacks with a dancing naked woman, and Hans Richter's *Ghosts Before Midday* (1927), in which normally inanimate objects such as collars, guns, and coffee cups revolt against their human owners while under the spell of ghosts (suggested by a set of derbies flying about in unison).

In 1924, René Clair directed what became the best-known of the Dadaist films, *Entr'acte*. Its title translating as "intermission," *Entr'acte* was one of the first collective efforts of the Dadaists. Written by Francis Picabia and scored by Erik Satie (the music no longer survives, unfortunately), the film included Satie, Man Ray, and Marcel Duchamp among its actors. *Entr'acte* premiered in December 1924 in Paris, during the intermission of a Dadaist ballet also written by Picabia entitled *Relâche*, which means "no show."

Clair included numerous bizarre touches in this short avant-garde film. For example, he occasionally cut away to a slow-motion shot of a ballerina, filmed from such an extremely low, worm's-eye perspective that all the audience sees of her are her legs and billowing skirt. (Clair obtained the shot by having the ballerina dance on a sheet of glass while he filmed from below.) Later in the film, Clair brought his camera up to a higher level to reveal that the ballerina was not a "she" but a "he": a bearded male dancer in a tutu. Other strange elements of the movie include cigarettes forming themselves via animation into a structure resembling the Parthenon, and actors Marcel Duchamp and Man Ray playing chess on a rooftop before their chess board metamorposes into the Place de la Concorde.

The highlight of this Dadaist romp is a funeral procession sequence featuring a camel-drawn hearse, which commences shortly after a man wielding a rifle kills another fellow on whose shoulder a pigeon has landed. The mourners—several dozen upper-class people, a few of whom had thrown streamers at the church and eaten some of the hearse's trimmings—follow the hearse on foot. What little dignity the affair has is shattered in short order when the hearse becomes disconnected from the camel and goes out of control. The erstwhile dignified mourners chase after it, first in slow motion, then eventually in fast motion. A supposedly legless man who has been propelling himself in a cart, seeing that he cannot keep up with the others, stands up and runs after them.

The "sham cripple" is perfectly in keeping with the remainder of the film. He is not really a cripple, and the dead man is not really dead; the latter happily springs from his coffin with a theatrical flourish following the runaway-hearse scene. With a wave of his magic wand, he makes the casket and each of the half-dozen or so people around him disappear, before turning the wand on himself and disappearing. He later reappears by crashing through the movie's The End sign to playfully inform the audience that the film is not over yet. With its crazy chase and other absurd touches, the film owes as much to Dada as it does to Mack Sennett's Keystone Kops movies, which delighted the Dadaists to no end with their anarchy.

As the Dada movement started burning itself out during the early 1920s, many of its practitioners became Surrealists. Indeed, one wag has suggested that Surrealism was Dada reborn with a program. Strongly influenced by the writings of Sigmund Freud, the Surrealists were mainly concerned with depicting dream states and other altered-consciousness states, and would often employ automatism (the mental act of releasing the unconscious mind from the control of the conscious) to achieve the free expression of the unconscious mind.

The most famous of the Surrealist painters, Salvador Dali, occasionally dabbled in film with predictably bizarre results. Dalie and fellow Spaniard Luis Buñuel plumbed their unconscious minds for imagery that eventually went into their famous eye-opening short subject, *Un Chien Andalou* (1929). Dali in particular seemed eager to use *Un Chien Andalou* to lash out at contemporary bourgeois society and its love of abstract art, as this quotation indicates:

The film produced the effect that I wanted, and it plunged like a dagger into the heart of Paris as I had foretold. Our film ruined in a single evening ten years of pseudo-intellectual post-war advance-guardism. That foul thing which is figuratively called abstract art fell at our feet, wounded to the death, never to rise again, after having seen "a girl's eye cut by a razor blade"—this was how the film began. There was no longer room in Europe for the little maniacal lozenges of Monsieur Mondrian.[23]

Un Chien Andalou is laden with grotesque and preposterous imagery: a woman's underarm hair transplants itself on a man's face; the protagonist tows an ungainly collection of items, including two priests and two grand pianos loaded with dead donkeys, while pursuing a woman; ants emerge from a hole in a human hand. With scenes like these along with the film's most famous moment—through the artifice of editing, a man (Buñuel himself) slices open a woman's eyeball to begin the film—*Un Chien Andalou* still has the power to shock and repel uninitiated audiences.

Man Ray, who made the Dadaistic *Return to Reason*, also made several Surreal films, including *Emak Bakia* (1926) and the better-known *L'Etoile de Mer* (1928). The latter film, based on a poem by Robert Desnos, features a mysterious affair between a man and a woman interspersed with symbolic sexual images occasionally presented in a multiscreen format, such as starfish tentacles and a collapsing chimney. Other films of the time relying on an extensive use of dreamlike imagery include Jean Cocteau's *Blood of a Poet* (1930) and Germaine Dulac's *The Seashell and the Clergyman* (1927), based on a script by Antonin Artaud.

As the world entered the Depression and Hollywood its Golden Age, American commercial filmmakers began exploring the film-painting relationship in several different ways. One trend consisted of those occasional Hollywood films that examined the traumatic effects of blindness on the careers of fictional painters.

In 1939 the Paramount company produced William Wellman's *The Light That Failed*, a melodrama based on the Rudyard Kipling novel. It stars Ronald Coleman as Dick Heldar, a British war correspondent in the Sudan whose head injury forces him to change careers. He chooses painting and quickly becomes famous for his realistic paintings of Sudanese war scenes. As his successes grow, so do his frequent headaches and his eyes' sensitivity to light, and he eventually learns that his degenerating optic nerve will leave him totally blind within a year. After managing to befoul all his interpersonal relationships, a despondent and blind Heldar returns to the Sudan as a war correspondent (having lied about his vision) and is killed in battle almost immediately.

Another example of this trend is *Dead Man's Eyes*, a 1944 Universal "B" film directed by Reginald LeBorg. Lon Chaney, Jr., played Dave Stuart, an artist engaged to the daughter of a wealthy patron of the arts. While painting another woman's portrait, Stuart accidentally dabs acetic acid on his eyes, causing great damage to them. A doctor tells him his only hope is a corneal transplant, and his prospective father-in-law—ever sympathetic to the arts—quickly has his will rewritten to include a provision that, in the event of his death, his corneas are to be given to Stuart. When the fellow is murdered shortly thereafter, Stuart becomes a suspect amid three or four others but is later vindicated. With the transplant a success, Stuart is able to resume his career amid wedding-bell bliss.

Another tendency among Hollywood films of the time is the use of portraits, especially full-length ones, as major story elements, and examples are many. The portraits of Baskerville ancestors provide major clues to Sherlock Holmes (Basil Rathbone) in a faithful, atmospheric retelling of Arthur Conan Doyle's classic of mystery and detection, *The Hound of the Baskervilles* (1939). The portrait of the deceased title character of Alfred Hitchcock's *Rebecca* (1940) dominates its gothic setting and eventually inspires the film's nameless young heroine (Joan Fontaine) to dress like Rebecca in a misguided effort to please her new husband. Writer-director Albert Lewin based his *The Picture of Dorian Gray* (1945) on Oscar Wilde's story abou the growing decadence of a handsome young man, whose portrait ages while he himself remains youthful. William Dieterle's *Portrait of Jennie* (1948) retells the story by Robert Nathan about a mysterious and mesmerizing woman who models for a painter. Alfred Hitchcock's *The Paradine Case* (1948), about a woman accused of murdering her blind husband, features the use of a full-length portrait of the deceased, painted only a week before his death. The portrait is the only visual image of him throughout the film. Since the audience never sees the blind character except by way of the portrait, it in a sense is "blind," too—a bit of Hitchcockian whimsy, perhaps.

A third Hollywood trend of the time is a legacy of 1920s Surrealism: the portrayal of characters' dream states. By far the most famous example of this tendency is the celebrated collaboration of Alfred Hitchcock and Salvador Dali in the making of *Spellbound* (1945). In this film, a psychiatrist (Ingrid Bergman) tries to analyze the dreams of an amnesiac wanted for murder (Gregory Peck). Interspersed with his verbal recollections of his dreams are segments of a Dali-designed dream sequence. Hitchock described his interest in obtaining Dali's services in these terms.

I was determined to break with the traditional way of handling dream sequences through a blurred and hazy screen. I asked [David] Selznick if he could get Dali to work with us and he agreed, though I think he didn't really understand my reasons for wanting Dali. He probably thought I wanted his collaboration for publicity purposes. The real reason was that I wanted to convey the dreams with great visual sharpness and clarity, sharper than the film itself. I wanted Dali because of the architectural sharpness of his work. Chirico has the same quality, you know, the long shadows, the infinity of distance, and the converging lines of perspective. But Dali had some strange ideas; he wanted a statue to crack like a shell falling apart, with ants crawling all over it, and underneath, there would be Ingrid Bergman, covered by the ants! It just wasn't possible. My idea was to shoot the Dali dream scenes in the open air so that the whole thing, photographed in real sunshine, would be terribly sharp. I was very keen on the idea, but the producers were concerned about the expense. So we shot the dream in the studios.[24]

In the final version of the film, the dream sequence is divided into four parts. Among its highlights are a series of painted eyes cut by a pair of scissors (reminiscent of the eye-slashing scene in the Buñuel-Dali film, *Un Chien Andalou*) and a faceless man standing on a rooftop holding a droopy wheel akin to the melting clocks in Dali's most famous painting, *The Persistence of Memory*.

The postwar years were marked by several new trends: Hollywood's big-budget treatments of famous painters, and European documentaries on similar topics. One of the earliest examples of the former tendency is John Huston's Oscar-winning *Moulin Rouge* (1952), a biography of the nineteenth-century Parisian painter Henri Toulouse-Lautrec. After buying the screen rights to Pierre LeMure's 1951 best-seller on the artist, Huston immediately found himself beset by difficulties, not the least of which was the way to deal with the height of the leading character; due to a childhood fall and glandular difficulties, Toulouse-Lautrec grew no taller than four feet and eight inches. Huston solved the problem by having his star, José Ferrer, walk about on well-padded knees while keeping the lower portion of the actor's body out of camera range. Toulouse-Lautrec's associates and paintings also posed problems, since the diminutive artist preferred the company of prostitutes and music hall performers and often included them in his paintings. Hollywood's Production Code people insisted that Huston play down the prostitution angle in Toulouse-Lautrec's life and work, so Huston left it up to the audience's imagination by letting the paintings speak for themselves.

Another outstanding example of Hollywood's interest in famous painters is Vincente Minnelli's *Lust for Life* (1956), an extravagant MGM production based on Irving Stone's biography of Vincent Van Gogh. Filmed on the actual Dutch and southern French locales where Van Gogh worked, the film focuses mainly on the artist's loneliness, anguish, and complete dedication to his art. It covers his life from his early experiences as an evangelist in a Belgian mining district to his suicide at the age of thirty-seven, and generates a considerable tension between the dark, insecure, sick painter and his sunny, bright paintings. The film, which features powerful performances by Kirk Douglas as Van Gogh; Anthony Quinn as his mentor, Paul Gauguin; and James Donald as Van Gogh's sympathetic brother, earned unanimous praise from the critics.

The mid–1960s saw the production of several other lavish biographies of painters, but the minigenre by then had entered a state of decline. In 1965 Carol Reed directed *The Agony and the Ecstasy*, based on Irving Stone's novel about the stormy relationship of Michelangelo and Pope Julius II. The Pope (Rex Harrison) had commissioned the famous Florentine artist (Charlton Heston) to paint frescoes on the walls and ceiling of the Sistine Chapel, but Michelangelo took years to become properly inspired before finishing the job. The film's strongest points are its detailing of the process by which Michelangelo transferred his sketches to the interior surfaces of the chapel, and the reverence with which it treats its subjects. Though visually stunning, the film is vitiated considerably by its relative lack of dramatic conflict and its unflattering portrayal of Michelangelo the human being.

Similar problems plagued the Italian-French co-production of *El Greco* (1986), shot in Spain. A visually sumptuous but largely plotless movie centering on the life of the sixteenth-century painter, *El Greco* is not much more than a vehicle for Mel Ferrer, who co-produced the film, wrote its music, and played the title role.

Documentary filmmakers of the time shared their narrative counterparts' interest in the lives and work of famous artists, and the resulting art documentaries occupy a middle ground between mainstream documentaries and experimental films. The most prolific of the art documentarists is Alain Resnais. In 1947 the twenty-five-year-old Resnais made a half dozen short 16-mm films on relatively obscure painters that nonetheless were his personal favorites: Lucien Coutard, Felix Labisse, Hans Hartung, Oscar Dominguez, Cesar Domela, and Max Ernst. He called the films ''visits'' (e.g., *Visit with Lucien Coutard, Visit with Felix Labisse*), and pleased with their outcomes, he expanded his filmic interests to include better-known artists in 1948 and 1950 with *Van Gogh* and *Gauguin*, respectively.

The prize-winning *Van Gogh* remains the more important of the two films. (Critics and Resnais himself consider *Gauguin* a failure, and precious little information exists on it.) *Van Gogh* is noteworthy as Resnais' first 35-mm film, the criticism it generated, and the issues that emerge from it. Made in collaboration with Gaston Diehl and Robert Hessens, *Van Gogh* features an extensive use of camera movement and editing in its presentation of Van Gogh's paintings. André Bazin's description of the film suggests the movement employed by Resnais:

Here the director has treated the whole of the artist's output as one large painting over which the camera has wandered as freely as in any ordinary documentary. From the ''Rue d'Arles'' we climb in through the window of Van Gogh's house and go right up to the bed with the red eiderdown.[25]

Resnais and his collaborators came under considerable criticism for their alleged disservice to Van Gogh's paintings. Responding to the criticism, Resnais stated that he and his fellow filmmakers viewed the short film as an experiment:

It concerns itself, in effect, with finding out if painted trees, painted houses, can, in a narrative, thanks to the montage of the cinema, serve to take the place of real objects, and if, in this case, it is possible to substitute for the spectator, and almost without his knowledge, the internal or interior world of an artist, a world such as is revealed by photography.[26]

In both this film and his 1950 documentary *Guernica*, a cinematic rendering of Picasso's famous painting depicting the horrors wreaked by the Spanish Civil War, Resnais began juxtaposing images of the past with those of the present. The comparisons and the tension that arose from them became so fascinating for Resnais that he used them as major elements in many of his later films (*Hiroshima, Mon Amour* [1959] and *Last Year at Marienbad* [1961] are perfect examples), even after his interest in art documentaries had waned.

The Italian filmmaker Luciano Emmer also made a considerable number of art documentaries, and Resnais has openly acknowledged the influence of Emmer's work on his own early films.[27] Emmer's best-known work is *Goya* (1952), in which the filmmaker portrayed the world as viewed by the Spanish painter during the late 1700s and early 1800s. Emmer frequently attempted to animate the characters in Goya's paintings and etchings through panning and accelerated editing; a painted scene of a bullfight, for example, might be broken down into an orchestrated series of pans and quick shots to resemble a cinematic rendering of a real bullfight.

Art films by other directors of the time manifested similar techniques. *Rubens* (1948), by Henri Storck-Haesaerts, combines a presentation of the Flemish artist's world with an exploration of his paintings and pays partiuclar attention to his preoccupation with circular motions. In like fashion, the American film *Grandma Moses* (1950) mixes scenes of Anna Mary Robertson's life in the country with similar view from her paintings, thus implying the sources of her inspiration.

The best known of all art documentaries of the period is *The Titan* (1950), the American version of Kurt Oertel's 1940 Swiss film, *Michelangelo*, shot in Italy. The main reason for its anonymity until after World War II was Oertel's poor choice for the first country in which to distribute his film: Nazi Germany, where the documentary had been confiscated and held for years by the United States Alien Property Custodian. Through the efforts of Robert Flaherty and others, an English-language version of the film called *The Titan*, narrated by Frederic March, was released in 1950.

The Titan shows no humans but instead focuses on various historic Italian locations to give a sense of the environment in which the great Florentine artist lived and worked. These scenes are then punctuated with dramatic shots of Michelangelo's frescoes, sculptures, and other works, such as his treatments of human anatomy in *The Last Judgment* on a wall of the Sistine Chapel. Under frequently shifting lighting conditions, the camera panned across (and, in the case of sculptures, around) the works and injected them with a new vitality.

The year 1956 marked the emergence of a different kind of art film: *The Mystery of Picasso*. The documentary was directed by Henri-Georges Clouzot, whose stated intention was "to grasp that secret mechanism which guides the creative artist through his perilous adventure."[28] Unlike the other art documentaries discussed in this chapter, *The Mystery of Picasso* examines the process by which paintings are created and actually shows an artist at work. The seventy-five-minute film follows Pablo Picasso, then seventy-four, as he created paintings at his Cannes studio. Occasionally Clouzot placed his camera directly behind Picasso's semitranslucent canvas to record the artist's brush strokes from a unique perspective. Typical scenes from the film show Picasso with his back to the camera as he contemplated a wall-sized blank canvas. Moments later, we see him beginning work on the canvas, aided by assistants while perched on a ladder. Later the film shows him appraising the finished work. While the film obviously cannot show the inner workings of the artist's mind during the creative act, it does at least give a sense of the process by which he worked. The film also suggests the evolution of a painting, since Picasso frequently began with a rough sketch and then proceeded to overlay a series of variations of the sketch on it with brush and pen. The result is not unlike the effect achieved in an art film on the work of Henry Matisse, as noted by Parker Tyler:

In a documentary on Matisse, we are shown how the artist developed his conception of a head in a series of sketches from a quasi-naturalistic version to the final form. This was done by superimposing the finished sketches transparently so that an illusion of organic evolution was obtained. . . . In the case of Matisse's head the element of *mutation* is added.[29] (emphasis in original text)

Over the years, a number of filmmakers have demonstrated an interest in incorporating and expanding on famous painterly styles in their works, but outside a biographical or documentary format. Indeed, this has been going on ever since the days of Georges Méliès. For example, fellow filmmaker (and magician) Orson Welles based the "looks" of his first two features on two very different painterly styles. Certain aspects of his *Citizen Kane* (1941) resemble Expressionist paintings, such as its early exterior views of Xanadu and the painted canvases that constitute the high walls of the Thatcher Library. On the other hand, *The Magnificent Ambersons* (1942), set around the turn of the century, evokes a nostalgia for a lost era by featuring a high number of compositions that take their inspiration from nineteenth-century Currier and Ives prints.

Another example is Carl Theodor Dreyer, who developed his own variant of "Rembrandt Lighting" in *Day of Wrath*, made in Denmark in 1943 during the Nazi occupation. Its story focuses on witch-hunting during the Middle Ages, but the film is better remembered today for its baroque illumination. Judging from the chiaroscuro lighting that characterizes scene after scene in *Day of Wrath*, Dreyer rather clearly modeled his imagery after paintings of the period by Rembrandt and others. As Siegfried Kracauer has observed, "It is as if old Dutch masters had come to life."[30]

The great Russian filmmaker and theorist Sergei Eisenstein came under attack from many quarters for his *Ivan the Terrible, Part 1* (1945). Apart from its political ramifications (its lead character being a prerevolutionary figure and a czar at that), the film was criticized for its many static, tableau-like compositions. In analyzing this film, Parker Tyler had detected references to the abstract paintings of Eisenstein's contemporary and countryman Vasily Kandinsky in many of *Ivan*'s scenes. Tyler attributed the compositions to Eisenstein's early experience designing abstract-geometric stage sets.[31]

A wide range of more recent narrative films have likewise drawn on specific painterly styles and compositions. Luis Buñuel, never known for subtlety in his attacks on the Catholic Church, consciously modeled a beggars' feast after Leonardo da Vinci's *The Last Supper* in his *Viridiana* (1961). Herbert Ross's *Pennies from Heaven* (1981) owes much of its Depression-era look to the thirties and forties urban paintings of American artist Edward Hopper. For example, one late-night scene involving several people seated at the cafe counter, filmed through the cafe's plate glass windows, is modeled directly after Hopper's most famous painting, *Nighthawks* (1942). Another 1981 film, *Superman II*, features a giant Cubist-like device capable of playing back recorded messages, which the Man of Steel operates in his Fortress of Solitude.

As the relationship of film and painting matures and new connections between the media emerge, there is always a question of how far to go when discussing the influence of one movement or person on another and the extent of that influence; if taken far enough, such speculation could lead to all sorts of theoretical permutations. Suffice it to say that no matter how one looks at the various facets of the film-painting relationship, it is clear that the considerable number of interactions between film and painting are substantial and varied, and stretch from the very beginning of film's history through today.

NOTES

1. Charles Eidsvik, *Cineliteracy: Film among the Arts* (New York: Random House, 1978), pp. 159–60.

2. Josef von Sternberg, *Fun in a Chinese Laundry* (New York: Macmillan, 1965), p. 322.

3. Parker Tyler, "The Film Sense and the Painting Sense," *Art Digest* 15 February 1954:10.

4. Léon Barsacq, *Caligari's Cabinet and Other Grand Illusions: A History of Film Design* (Boston: New York Graphic Society, 1976), p. 8.

5. Cited in ibid., p. 9.

6. The entire anecdote is recounted in Kenneth Macgowan, *Behind the Screen: The History and Technique of the Motion Picture* (New York: Dell, 1965), pp. 168–69.

7. For a summary of this view, see Martin F. Norden, "America and Its Fantasy Films, 1945–1951," *Film and History* 12 (February 1982): 1–11.

8. Cited in Tom Greene, "The Art of the Matte: Dissolving Albert Whitlock," *Filmmakers Newsletter* 7 (October 1974): 29.

9. Robert Hughes, "Careerism and Hype amidst the Image Haze," *Time* 17 June 1985: 79–80.

10. Tyler, "The Film Sense," p. 10.

11. Cited in Greene, "The Art of the Matte," p. 28.

12. Sarah Newmeyer, *Enjoying Modern Art* (New York: New American Library, 1955), pp. 142–43.

13. Cited in ibid., p. 149.

14. Ibid., p. 150.

15. Cited in Malcolm Le Grice, *Abstract Film and Beyond* (Cambridge, Mass.: MIT Press, 1977), pp. 10, 12.

16. Edward A. Aiken, "Léger's *Ballet mécanique* and Futurism" (Paper presented to the Society for Cinema Studies, March 1978).

17. Cited in Audio Brandon Films, *16 mm International Catalog* (Mount Vernon, N.Y.: Audio Brandon Films, 1978), p. 526.

18. Cited in David Curtis, *Experimental Cinema* (New York: Dell, 1971), p. 158.

19. Cited in Audio Brandon catalog, p. 486.

20. Sergei Eisenstein, *Film Form: Essays in Film Theory*, ed. and trans. Jay Leyda (New York: Harcourt, Brace & World, 1949), p. 79 (editor's note).

21. For a story of *Alpha Mandala* and its effects, see Edward S. Small and Joseph D. Anderson, "What's in a Flicker Film?" *Communication Monographs* 43 (March 1976): 29–34.

22. Cited in Siegfried Kracauer, *Theory of Film: The Redemption of Physical Reality* (New York: Oxford University Press, 1960), p. 39.

23. Salvador Dali, *The Secret Life of Salvador Dali*, trans. Haakon Chevalier (London: Vision Press, 1968), p. 212.

24. Cited in François Truffaut, *Hitchcock*, rev. ed. (New York: Simon & Schuster, 1984), pp. 163, 165.

25. André Bazin, *What Is Cinema?*, vol. 1, trans. Hugh Gray (Berkeley: University of California Press, 1967), p. 166.

26. Cited in John Francis Kreidl, *Alain Resnais* (Boston: Twayne, 1978), pp. 38–39.

27. Ibid., p. 41.

28. Cited in "Two Painters, Two Pictures," *New York Times* 22 July 1956: pt. 6, p. 51.

29. Tyler, "The Film Sense," p. 12. After being out of circulation for nearly twenty-five years, *The Mystery of Picasso* was revived in 1986 when the Samuel Goldwyn Company began distributing the film to theaters across the country.

30. Kracauer, *Theory of Film*, p. 81. Kracauer noted other films whose visual style is heavily indebted to paintings from the era covered in them, incuding Jacques Feyder's *Carnival in Flanders* (1935), Renato Castellani's *Romeo and Juliet* (1954), Teinosuke

Kinugasa's *Gate of Hell* (1954), and the Czech film *The Emperor and the Golem* (1955). A *New York Times* reviewer wrote of the latter film that "nearly every scene suggests a period painting brought to life." See Kracauer, Theory of Film, p. 82.

31. Tyler, "The Film Sense," pp. 11–12.

SELECTED BIBLIOGRAPHY

Most of the attention paid to the relationship of film and painting has been in the form of books and articles on avante-garde film. Malcolm Le Grice's *Abstract Film and Beyond* and David Curtis's *Experimental Cinema* are both brief but dense historical surveys of avant-garde film, and both pay particular attention to the roles that artistic movements (mostly Impressionism, Cubism, and Futurism in the former, Dada and Surrealism in the latter) played in the shaping of this film form. Standish D. Lawder's *The Cubist Cinema* covers similar territory but in more depth and is capped with an exhaustive treatment of Fernand Léger's Futurist film masterpiece, *Ballet Mécanique*. Udo Kultermann's largely pictorial *Art and Life* briefly traces the ancestry of 1960s art (including film and television) to some of the modernist movements of the 1920s. David Bordwell's *French Impressionist Cinema* closely examines the form and content of thirty-six French avant-garde films en route to constructing a paradigm of the genre. The comparison of Maya Deren's well-known avant-garde film *Meshes of the Afternoon* with early attempts at Surrealist film-making stands out amid several filmmaker–art movement examinations in P. Adams Sitney's *Visionary Film*.

A special issue of *Post Script* devoted to the general topic of "Modernism" contains two essays of direct relevance to the issues discussed in this chapter. "Reflections on Dada and the Cinema" by Edward A. Aiken examines the early history of Dadaist involvement in filmmaking, while "Films that 'Never Transcend the Realm of Art' " by Elizabeth Jones focuses on the place of film pioneers D. W. Griffith, Sergei Eisenstein, and Dziga Vertov within the general Modernist movement.

The information culled from a range of articles from other journals helped flesh out this chapter. Parker Tyler's "The Film Sense and the Painting Sense" studies the way the motion picture camera acts as interpretive instrument, whether animating paintings through movement and editing or de-animating movie scenes by emphasizing famous (but obviously inanimate) painterly styles. Tom Greene's "The Art of the Matte" is primarily an interview with Albert Whitlock, in which the matte-painting expert discusses his techniques. Martin F. Norden's "The Avant-Garde Cinema of the 1920s" examines the connections between avant-garde film and three derivatives of Cubism: Futurism, Precisionism, and Suprematism. Robert Bruce Rogers's "Cineplastics" (a term borrowed from the famous art historian Elie Faure) explores "motion painting" as the latest in a series of art styles consisting of Impressionism, Post-Impressionism, Cubism, Expressionism, and Plastic Abstractionism. Rogers examines exemplars of cineplastics, such as the hand-painted films of Len Lye and Norman McLaren and the more traditionally photographed works of Hans Richter.

Several famous film theorists have also examined the film-painting relationship. André Bazin's *What Is Cinema?*, vol. 1, contains a brief essay entitled "Painting and Cinema." It focuses mainly on short documentaries that deal with artists or paintings that appeared shortly after World War II, such as *Van Gogh* and *Guernica*. His general thesis concerning the film on art is that "however you look at it the film is not true to the painting," the main reason for which is that a second art medium (film) profoundly changes the first through different color values and angles, camera movement, etc.

Siegfried Kracauer expresses similar views in his *Theory of Film*. He examines a film genre that lies somewhere between the avant-garde film and the documentary: the film on painting and the other plastic arts. Like Bazin, Kracauer believes that such films should faithfully render the output of an artist's career or even show the process by which a painting is created. What such film should *not* do, however, is become artworks themselves by fragmenting the paintings (cutting off the borders, for example) or creating collages of the paintings through the editing process. Both he and Bazin believe that paintings in film should be treated like complete physical objects, and that filmmakers should avoid interpreting them through such techniques as camera movement and tight close-ups of various parts of the canvas.

Several general-interest film books round out this select bibliography. Charles Eidsvik's *Cineliteracy* contains a brief but provocative section on film and painting, in which he contends that painting has had minimal impact on narrative film. John Francis Kreidl's *Alain Resnais* offers a spare recapitulation of the famed French director's early art documentaries. The first chapter of Léon Barsacq's *Caligari's Cabinet and Other Grand Illusions* offers a discussion of the painted-set tradition established by French filmmakers during the medium's salad days before audiences demanded a greater veracity in film set design.

Books and Articles

Aiken, Edward A. "Reflections on Dada and the Cinema." *Post Script: Essays in Film and the Humanities* 3 (Winter 1984): 5–19.

Barsacq, Léon. *Caligari's Cabinet and Other Grand Illusions: A History of Film Design.* Boston: New York Graphic Society, 1976.

Bazin, André. *What Is Cinema?.* vol. 1. Trans. Hugh Gray. Berkeley: University of California Press, 1967.

Bordwell, David. *French Impressionist Cinema: Film Culture, Film Theory, and Film Style.* Dissertations on Film series. New York: Arno Press, 1980.

Curtis, David. *Experimental Cinema.* New York: Dell, 1971.

Eidsvik, Charles. *Cineliteracy: Films Among the Arts.* New York: Random House, 1978.

Greene, Tom. "The Art of the Matte: Dissolving Albert Whitlock." *Filmmakers Newsletter* 7 (October 1974): 28–32.

Jones, Elizabeth. "Films That 'Never Transcend the Realm of Art.' " *Post Script: Essays in Film and the Humanities* 3 (Winter 1984): 20–33.

Kracauer, Siegfried. *Theory of Film: The Redemption of Physical Reality.* New York: Oxford University Press, 1960.

Kreidl, John Francis. *Alain Resnais.* Twayne's Theatrical Arts Series. Boston: Twayne, 1978.

Kultermann, Udo. *Art and Life.* Trans. John William Gabriel. New York: Praeger, 1971.

Lawder, Standish D. *The Cubist Cinema.* New York: New York University Press, 1975.

Le Grice, Malcolm. *Abstract Film and Beyond.* Cambridge, Mass.: MIT Press, 1977.

Norden, Martin F. "The Avant-Garde Cinema of the 1920s: Connections to Futurism, Precisionism, and Suprematism." *Leonardo: Journal of the International Society for the Arts, Sciences, and Technology* 17, no. 2 (1984): 108–112.

Rogers, Robert Bruce. "Cineplastics: The Fine Art of Motion Painting." *Quarterly of Film, Radio, and Television* 6 (1951–1952): 375–87.

Sitney, P. Adams. *Visionary Film: The American Avant-Garde, 1943–1978.* 2d ed. New York: Oxford University Press, 1979.

Tyler, Parker. "The Film Sense and the Painting Sense." *Art Digest* 15 February 1954: 10–12, 27–28.

SELECTED FILMOGRAPHY

The Agony and the Ecstasy (USA 1965). Twentieth Century-Fox. Directed and produced by Carol Reed. Screenplay by Philip Dunne. With Charlton Heston, Rex Harrison, Diane Cilento.

Ballet mécanique (France 1923). Synchro-Ciné. Directed by Fernand Léger. With Kiki.

The Battleship Potemkin (USSR 1925). First Studio of Goskino. Directed and screenplay by Sergei Eisentein. With Alexander Antonov, Vladimir Barsky.

Berlin: Symphony of a Big City (Germany 1927). Directed by Walter Ruttmann. Produced by Karl Freund. Screenplay by Karl Freund, Walter Ruttmann, and Carl Mayer.

The Cabinet of Dr. Caligari (Germany 1919). Decla-Bioscop. Directed by Robert Wiene. Produced by Erich Pommer. Screenplay by Carl Mayer and Hans Janowitz. With Werner Krauss, Conrad Veidt, Lil Dagover.

Un Chien Andalou (France 1929). Directed and produced by Luis Buñuel. Screenplay by Luis Buñuel and Salvador Dali. With Pierre Batcheff, Simone Mareuil, Luis Buñuel.

A Day in the Country (France 1936). Directed and screenplay by Jean Renoir. Produced by Pierre Braunberger. With Gabriello, Sylvia Bataille, Georges Darnoux, Jane Marken.

Entr'acte (France 1923). Les Ballet Suédois. Directed by René Clair. Produced by Rolf de Maré. Screenplay by Francis Picabia and René Clair. With Erik Satie, Marcel Duchamp, Man Ray.

Lust for Life (USA 1956). Metro-Goldwyn-Mayer. Directed by Vincente Minnelli. Produced by John Houseman. Screenplay by Norman Corwin. With Kirk Douglas, Anthony Quinn, James Donald.

The Man with the Movie Camera (USSR 1929). VUFKU (Ukraine). Directed and screenplay by Dziga Vertov.

Michelangelo (Switzerland 1940). Directed by Kurt Oertel. Reedited and rereleased by Richard Lyford as *The Titan* in 1950.

The Mystery of Picasso (France 1956). Filmsonor. Directed, produced, and screenplay by Henri-Georges Clouzot. With Pablo Picasso.

Spellbound (USA 1945). Selznick International. Directed by Alfred Hitchcock. Produced by David O. Selznick. Screenplay by Ben Hecht. With Ingrid Bergman, Gregory Peck, Leo G. Carroll.

Van Gogh (France 1948). Directed by Alain Resnais.

3

FILM AND PHOTOGRAPHY

CHARLES BERG

INTRODUCTION

The intertwined histories of film and photography spring from man's age-old desire to record his passage through this mortal coil, a desire motivated by the need to rationalize man's existence through the creation and contemplation of images "reflecting" upon his uniquely human character, experiences, and feelings.

This impulse to document, and to thereby leave a trace of his passage for himself as well as for future generations, is most clearly evident through an examination of the history of painting. From the ancients who depicted the saga of the hunt on the walls of the caves at Altamira and Lascaux to nineteenth-century landscape painters like Constable and Turner, the story of painting, as E. H. Gombrich so brilliantly illustrates in his *Art and Illusion*, can be understood as nothing less than a chronicle of man's ardent quest to achieve as full and faithful a rendering of life as possible.[1]

The desire to "capture" reality has not been restricted to painting. Indeed, the most potent aesthetic tradition in Western civilization centers on the notion of *mimesis*, or imitation. Derived from Aristotle's *Poetics*, the mimetic ideal has informed the evolution of drama, the subject of Aristotle's investigations, as well as literature and the graphic arts.[2]

When man's genius turned to things industrial in the nineteenth century, it is not surprising that much attention was given to the eternal dream of transcribing nature. But in an era devoted to the practical application of new discoveries in chemistry and physics, the recording of reality was seen as a task to be accomplished through mechanical, rather than artistic, means.

HISTORIC OVERVIEW—THE CINEMATIC APPARATUS

During the nineteenth century, the efforts of artists, regardless of medium, to imitate reality were eclipsed by rapid developments in photography and, then, cinematography. Indeed, at the technological level, film can be viewed as a direct extension of photography.

However, in examining the key components necessary for a viable cinematic apparatus—the term used here to refer to the gamut of technical, economic, and cultural elements required for the complex system we now comonly refer to as *film, the cinema,* or *the movies*—it is also necessary to point to developments that took place either before or beyond the formal history of photography itself.

The camera, though inextricably tied to photography, actually predates the first photographic imprints by at least several centuries. In 1589 John Babtista Porta described what Leonardo da Vinci would later call the *camera obscura,* or darkened chamber. A completely light-tight room save for a few rays allowed to pass through a small hole, the camera obscura projected inverted reproductions of scenes outside the room onto the wall opposite the aperture, or opening. While proving itself a helpful aid to artists attempting more accurate portrayals of scenes from life, variations in the design of the camera obscura were made by scientists such as the astronomer Johannes Kepler to study the heavens.[3]

In the seventeenth century Athanasius Kirchner, a Jesuit mathematics professor, claimed to have invented what he called the *magick lantern*. By using an artificial light source, a candle, and a concave mirror to intensify the projection of images drawn onto slides, the magic lantern became a standard part of scientific demonstrations. And in later modifications, including the addition of a lens to sharpen the focus, the magic lantern enjoyed considerable success as a novelty included in the shows of itinerant entertainers.

Though antedating photography and film, the camera obscura and magick lantern would figure as key elements in the photochemical media by virtue of their status as forerunners of the modern camera and projector. In addition, the development of magic lantern techniques helped initiate speculations about the nature of visual perception.

Specifically, sequences of images were drawn on glass lantern slides configured as either horizontal strips or circular discs. This, in turn, led to the organization of information presented by lantern-lectures in sequential series akin to present-day slide shows. On one occasion, two interrelated images were rapidly alternated, thereby producing sensations of movement. This phenomenon, a result of the fusion of "after-images," created illusions such as a sleeping man being suddenly haunted by a monstrous nightmare. The scientific explanation for the delightful entertainment achieved by such comic slip slides was called *persistence of vision*, a concept formalized in a presentation made to the British Royal Society by Peter Mark Roget in 1824.[4]

The concept of persistence of vision was soon adapted to a host of mechanical toys that offered a wide array of kinetic diversions. One of the earliest and easiest to manufacture was the Thaumatrope. Devised in 1825 by Dr. John Paris of London, the Thaumatrope consisted of two drawings, say a bird and a cage, on opposite sides of a stiff paper disc. When the disc was spun by strings attached to each side, the two drawings seemed to merge, thereby creating the illusion of a bird in its cage. Though the bird quivered a bit, the Thaumatrope produced an essentially static impression. It did, however, because of its great popularity, spur other inventive efforts.

Plateau of Brussels introduced his Phenakistiscope in 1832. Using as many as sixteen drawings depicting an object in motion mounted at the end of a slotted metal disc attached to a handle, the Phenakistiscope produced illusions of movement when the viewer held the spinning device up to a mirror and peered through the sixteen slots synchronized with the drawings. Though there was no camera, film, projection, or screen, the Phenakistiscope was significant for having produced the first moving pictures and, indeed, the first animated cartoons.

The Zoetrope, or Wheel of Life, was an improved variation on the sequential motion principle exploited by the Phenakistiscope. An upright pasteboard drum employing strips of sequential drawings showing an object in motion, the Zoetrope permitted a viewer to "see" a monkey jumping over a fence or a juggler juggling by gazing through slots cut into the top part of the rotating drum. With an ever-expanding library of strips of animated actions, the Zoetrope became the most popular nineteenth-century parlor toy utilizing the phenomenon of afterimage retention.

Another important nonphotographic landmark involved the development of a machine designed to project Phenakistiscopic drawings. Engineered by Baron Franz von Uchatius in 1853 for the Austrian army, this pioneering projector was commissioned for the purposes of military instruction.[5]

By the middle of the nineteenth century, then, a practical understanding of the principle of persistence of vision had manifested itself in the development of such varied devices as the Thaumatrope, Phenakistiscope, Zoetrope, and Uchatius's projector. The first shutters, in the form of viewing slots punched into either discs or drums, had appeared. Also, there was the discovery that a rate of sixteen images per second was necessary for achieving an illusion of continuous movement. Indeed, moving pictures, at least in the form of primitive animation, had become a reality. The cinematic apparatus, however, was still missing one key technical element. That, of course, was photography.

Photography, "a chemical and physical process that gives nature the ability to reproduce itself," as one nineteenth-century savant described it, was first demonstrated by Nicéphore Niépce in 1816.[6] Using metal plates coated with photosensitive silver salts, the Frenchman captured the tonal gradations of various landscapes, Unfortunately, Niépce's Heliographs were fuzzy in detail. Also, they held their images only briefly before fading to black. Some way of stopping or "fixing" the photochemical reaction of the silver salts was needed.[7]

In 1837, Louis Jacques Mandé Daguerre, another Frenchman, succeeded in creating clear and permanent images on burnished metal plates called Daguerrotypes. "The mirror with a memory," exclaimed Oliver Wendell Holmes.[8] About the same time in England, William Henry Fox Talbot devised paper negatives in what proved to be the prototype of reversal paper printing.

Europeans and Americans, fascinated with the technological offspring of Daguerre and Talbot, created a huge demand for photographic services and products. By 1850, a booming industry catering to the public's seemingly insatiable desire for photographs had appeared.

Daguerre's innovation was successfully exploited in the form of the popular nineteenth-century *tintype*, before being relegated to obsolescence. Talbot's negatives, on the other hand, proved more significant in that they led directly to George Eastman's Kodak camera and, then, to the modern motion picture.

Photography, like other mechanical marvels of the new industrial age, seized the imaginations of nineteenth-century artists, scientists, and thinkers. It is not surprising, then, that so much inventive and speculative energy was devoted to "making motion out of stills."

One of the earliest attempts in creating "moving photographs" took place in Philadelphia, where in 1861 Coleman Sellers photographed a sequence of stills showing his two children playing. Because each phase of the action, a child hammering, had to be posed to accommodate the extended shutter openings required for proper exposure, Sellers's pioneering effort can be regarded as the first example of pixilation, the process of animating human subjects at a rate of one or several frames per take.[9]

In 1870, again in Philadelphia, Henry Renno Heyl elaborated on Sellers's procedure to produce brief motion pictures made from posed stills. Among his subjects were a waltzing couple and an acrobat. Having met the challenge of matching such nuances of the action as the flutters of the folds of the dancer's skirt, Heyl next turned his attention to the presentation of his carefully posed efforts.

Whereas Sellers affixed his photographs to a paddle-wheel device somewhat similar to the riffle-book, whose bent-back pages present a parade of passing pictures. Heyl turned to a modified version of Uchatius's projector. By mounting a series of eighteen photographs on a disk and rotating them in front of a bright light while a shutter exposed each phase of the action in sequence, Heyl, according to contemporary reports, was able to satisfy an audience of some 1,500 when he first displayed his "motion pictures" in 1870.[10]

Heyl, by linking sequences of moving photographs with a projector, demonstrated the special pleasures of viewing motion pictures in the company of an audience. Sellers's device, in contrast, provided diversion for only a solitary viewer. Therefore, Heyl deserves credit for establishing the concept of movie-going as a group, rather than an individual, entertainment. Finally, in terms of exhibition, the experience of watching a motion picture by Heyl was closer to the experience of going to a play or a concert, whereas the experiencing of Sellers's motion picture was more akin to reading a book where the individual controls the pace and subject matter of the experience.

Though the presentations of Sellers and Heyl technically qualify as motion pictures, it was a photographer by the name of Eadweard Muybridge who systematically photographed subjects in unposed, natural motion. And though partially shrouded in confusion, contradiction, and lack of documentation, like so many of film's early landmark events, the story of Muybridge's cinematic rendering of a racehorse deserves to be told.

Muybridge, an Englishman plying his trade as an itinerant photographer in nothern California, was commissioned by Leland Stanford, the former governor of California, to aid in a study of a horse's gait. Though popular accounts of the incident claim that Stanford was motivated by a $25,000 wager on whether a horse ever had all four feet off the ground simultaneously (it did, as Muybridge was to prove), it seems more likely that Stanford undertook the study as a breeder and trainer of fine horses.

Muybridge, working at Stanford's Palo Alto horse ranch during the period 1872–1879, finally achieved the photographic proof sought by Stanford by setting up a battery of twelve still cameras along the rail of the governor's training track. By attaching strings to each camera's shutter and stretching his string across the track, Muybridge captured the critical phases of a horse's gait which proved that, indeed, there is a moment in a horse's stride when all four hooves are off the ground.

During the next twenty years, largely under Stanford's patronage as well as that of the University of Pennsylvania, Muybridge continued to perfect his multiple camera technique. The number of cameras was increased, faster or more light-sensitive film was used, and a grid of white vertical lines against a black background was added to chart the actions of his subjects more precisely. From horses, Muybridge moved to elephants, tigers, dancers, wrestlers, hurdlers, and nude runners. Muybridge's photographs were widely published and the photographer enjoyed great popularity as a lecturer on the topics of animal locomotion and motion photography.

For his lectures, Muybridge initially projected his photographs as silhouettes through a magic lantern. Later, he mounted the photos on a Phenakistiscopic disc. And though his devise was a modification of Uchatius's Projecting Phenakistiscope, Muybridge coined the term *Zoopraxiscope* (life-constructing viewer) for his own machine. By combining projection with his photographs, Muybridge thrilled audiences with illusions of movement which were reenactments from life itself.[11]

Muybridge's contributions to the evolution of the motion picture were critical. Instead of posed stills in the manner of Sellers and Heyl, Muybridge presented systematic and instantaneous photographs of sequential stages of unposed, natural motions. He was also the first to project such work in public exhibitions that ranged from scientific societies to the Chicago World's Fair of 1893.

The use of motion photography as a scientific tool, thanks to Muybridge's successes, inspired further experiments. Etienne Jules Marey, a prominent Parisian physiologist, after helping host a presentation by Muybridge in 1882, developed what he called the Photographic Gun. The barrel of the gun was actually the housing for the lens, while the circular chamber, instead of bullets, held a photographic glass plate. The plate rotated twelve times during a single second of shooting, producing twelve exposures arranged around the plate.

Marey's Chronophotographs, when projected on the Phenakistiscope, produced fluid analyses of birds in flight, falling cats, and human activities such as jumping, running, and fencing. In 1888 Marey brought photography to the brink of motion pictures by replacing the glass plate with paper roll film. Significantly, Marey demonstrated and explained his methods to Thomas Alva Edison at the Paris Exposition of 1889.[12]

Edison, the Wizard of Menlo Park and America's archetypal inventor-entrepreneur, was very much aware of motion photography. "In the year 1887," Edison recalled, "the idea occurred to me that it was possible to devise an instrument which should do for the eye what the phonograph does for the ear, and that by a combination of the two all motion and sound could be recorded and reproduced simultaneously."[13] In 1888, Edison met with Muybridge to discuss combining the phonograph, which Edison had invented in 1877, with Muybridge's photographs and projector. Edison also delegated one of his top aides, William Kennedy Laurie Dickson, to the task of developing a photograph camera.[14]

At about the same time, George Eastman was in the process of perfecting a flexible film base. Instead of coating the photosensitive emulsion on a glass plate or paper roll, Eastman began applying his emulsions to a base made of celluloid, a material strong, transparent, and yet flexible. This was the material that made still photography an amateur medium accessible to virtually everyone in the middle class.

In 1889 Eastman's new Kodak camera and film combination was advertised as embodying "the only system of continuous film photography" where "you press the button and we do the rest." For the sum of two dollars, one could purchase a roll of Eastman's celluloid which yielded one hundred exposures.[15]

Dickson, realizing the importance of Eastman's rolls of flexible film, redirected his inventive efforts from a camera based on an emulsion-coated cylinder modeled after the phonograph, to a camera designed to accommodate the new celluloid strips. The Kinetograph, patented in 1891, marked the culmination of the enterprise of Edison's motion picture project supervised by Dickson.

Edison's West Orange, New Jersey, factory soon produced the Kinetoscope, a peephole viewer that allowed a single person to witness brief half-minute snippets of filmed actions. There were a few natural wonders such as Niagara Falls, but the majority of subjects were staged bits of theatrical business such as dancing, juggling, clowning, and even primitive slapstick comedy. Introduced in 1893 at the Chicago World's Fair, the Kinetoscope soon became a prime attraction at amusement parlors in both America and Europe.

In order to supply the new nickel-in-the-slot market, Dickson constructed a studio, the Black Maria. Built on a revolving track to follow the sunlight necessary for proper film exposure, the cleverly designed Black Maria had the distinction of being the very first motion picture studio.

Edison, with his stable of inventive assistants and widespread business network, should have been preeminent during the first phase of the film era. However, he failed to envision the motion picture's commercial promise. In one of the major blunders in an otherwise illustrious career, Edison failed to pay out the $150 necessary to patent the Kinetograph and Kinetoscope outside the United States. As a result, inventor-entrepreneurs in Europe as well as in the United States scrambled to develop their own cameras.

Edison compounded his problems in commercially exploiting motion pictures by ignoring the projection of his motion pictures for too long. Content with collecting nickels from the battery of Kinetoscopes in place by 1894, Edison shunned projection until pressed by would-be competitors. Prodded by the success of the Lumière Brothers who unveiled their Cinématographe in Paris on December 28, 1895, the Wizard's business advisors persuaded Edison to manufacture the Edison-manufactured machine was marketed as another Edison invention under the name of Vitascope.[16]

Debuting on 23 April 1896 at Koster and Bial's Music Hall, a vaudeville house located in New York's Herald Square, the Vitascope projected dancing girls, waves breaking, and scenes from Charles Hoyt's play *A Milk White Flag*. The screening, sandwiched between the live acts of Koster and Bial's regular vaudeville bill, was an immediate hit. A glowing review in the *New York Dramatic Mirror* concluded by stating, "The Vitascope is a big success, and Mr. Edison is to be congratulated for his splendid contribution to the people's pleasure."[17]

The exhibition of the Lumières' Cinématographe and Edison's Vitascope mark the successful evolution and combination of elements necessary for a viable cinematic apparatus, an apparatus that can be regarded as a direct technological extension of photography. And though the two media have developed separate and distinct histories based on divergent cultural, social, and aesthetic functions, film and photography have continued to share common technological concerns having to do with ever-improving emulsions and equipment ranging from lenses to light meters. That kind of detailed technological history, however, is another story.

HISTORIC OVERVIEW—PHOTOGRAPHY AS SUBJECT MATTER

Photographs, photographic conventions, and photographers have figured prominently in the development of the three major approaches to film—documentary, experimental, and narrative.

The documentary approach, with its mission to record and reveal reality, though having roots in the scientific investigations of animal locomotion carried out by Muybridge and Marey, commenced at the dawn of the film age with the short, single-shot films of Louis and August Lumière. The sons of a prosperous portrait photographer-turned-manufacturer, the Lumière Brothers helped their father build the family business in Lyons, France, into Europe's leading supplier of photographic products, second internationally only to Eastman's plant in Rochester, New York.

Though the two brothers were inventors who patented their work in both their names, it was Louis who actually invented the Cinématographe. His ingenious camera, which could also double as a printer and projector, was light in weight, easy to use, and was handcranked. Edison's camera, in contrast, was a hundred times heavier than the Cinématographe and was dependent on electricity.

While the Lumières' camera could go out into the world to catch life on the run, Edison's bulky camera demanded that life be brought to it, in the Black Maria, to perform. Technology, then, directly influenced subject matter. So while Edison presented a parade of vaudevillians and thus put cinema on its course as a medium of entertainment, the Lumières presented vignettes from life itself and established the precedent of film as a recorder of life's passing scene.[18]

Following their initial successes with scenes from life in France, the Lumières sent a number of *operateurs* out across the globe. By late 1896, a cadre of one-man film units was fascinating audiences with scenic views shot by other Lumière operators from around the world, as well as with scenes that had been shot locally. Erik Barnouw, in his masterful history *Documentary*, sums up the reactions of those early audiences by noting that "The familiar, seen anew in this way, brought astonishment."[19]

Significantly, most of the operators trained by the Lumières had backgrounds in still photography. Their familiarity with the problems of exposure, composition, and printing gave them the experience necessary for their new roles as cinematographers. It is not surprising, then, that the surviving scenic views shot by the Lumières' agents are of very high technical quality in terms of focus, exposure, and composition.[20]

At the turn of the century, as the motion picture was taking its first steps as a medium with a destiny of its own, the development of an industrially based, mass culture was taking place on other formats. In journalism, mass circulation newspapers were made possible by improved technology, and abetted by the yellow journalism of such newspaper tycoons as Pulitzer and Hearst whose papers competed with lurid accounts of death, dishonor, and disaster. And though the technical means had not yet been perfected for using photographs, turn-of-the-century newspapers were heavily illustrated with drawings, charts, and cartoons.[21]

The circulation wars between Hearst and Pulitzer reached a climax with the Spanish-American War of 1898, a conflict fanned, in large part, by the excesses of yellow journalism. When the battleship *Maine* was blown up in Havana harbor, America declared war along with the newspapers. With the public's appetite for war stirred to a frenzy, there was not only a demand for words about the battle but a demand for images as well. Enterprising filmmakers attempted to fill the void.

Albert E. Smith and J. Stuart Blackton, two of the founders of the pioneering Vitagraph studio, in response to exhibitors' clamorings for Cuban coverage, sent a crew to Havana. Smith, much to his delight, found a young Theodore Roosevelt willing "to halt his march up San Juan Hill and strike a pose."[22] But because of difficulties in shooting actual combat footage, Smith and Blackton decided that they needed something a bit more spectacular. They therefore concocted a table-top battle of Santiago Bay with explosions, the sinking of cardboard ships into an inch-deep bay, and profuse billows of cigar smoke. When intercut with the shots of Roosevelt, the staged naval engagement, in spite of its obvious deceit, was nonetheless accepted by contemporary audiences as the real thing.[23]

Vitagraph's coverage of the Spanish-American War is noteworthy for several reasons. First, it established the motion picture as a journalistic medium, a function that would become institutionalized by the film industry as the newsreel.[24] It also indicated film's potential for capitalizing on topical events, a phenomenon that manifested itself not only in newsreels and documentaries but in feature films as well.

The classic gangster films produced by Warner Brothers in the early 1930s, for example, were directly inspired by the banner headlines of the day trumpeting mob mayhem and murder. And though photojournalism had made a major impact on both newspapers and magazines by the 1920s, it turned out that the sensational stills found in print only stimulated a greater desire for motion pictures of the same objects, in both documentary and fictive forms.

The home movie is an equally significant filmic tradition that owes its inspiration to photography. Even before Eastman had made his Kodak camera available to the public in the 1880s, relatively inexpensive portrait photography had made it possible for the common man to "freeze" himself for posterity. With the arrival of the motion picture, this impulse to chart and preserve the stuff of the common man can be seen in the Lumières' still-charming *Feeding the Baby* (1895), film's first home movie.

Because 35-mm motion pictures were just too costly for the average person, home movies did not become a large-scale phenomenon until the 1930s and 1940s, when 16-mm and 8-mm gauges were introduced to the marketplace as amateur formats. Today, the home movie tradition thrives because of relatively cheap and accessible super–8 and electronic video systems.

The use of photographs as subject matter for motion pictures has a long history. In dramatic films, a cutaway or insert of a picture of a loved one has become a narrative convention functioning to concretize the object of a character's affection. Even in an early silent film such as D. W. Griffith's *Birth of a Nation* (1915), the strategy worked perfectly to establish Ben Cameron's infatuation with Elsie Stoneman due to Griffith's adroit intercutting between a daguerreotype of the attractive young woman and a reaction shot of the obviously smitten young man.

In the documentary, photographs have served an even more important role thanks to *City of Gold* (1957), an Academy Award–winning short made by the National Film Board of Canada. By animating a collection of over two hundred eight-by-ten-inch glass-plate negatives photographed in 1898 by A. E. Haig at the height of the Klondike gold rush, and combining them with an intimate narration and a poignant musical score, directors Colin Low and Wolf Koenig created a masterpiece that inspired a new genre, the photographic compilation film.

Among the notable offspring spawned by *City of Gold* are *The Real West* (1961), narrated by Gary Cooper and chronicling westward expansion during the 1880s and 1890s, and its sequel, *End of the Trail* (1965), narrated by Walter Brennan and telling the same story but from the viewpoint of the American Indian. Produced for the National Broadcasting Company by Donald Hyatt, both films were compiled from tens of thousands of photographs.[25]

Photographic archives were raided, not just in the United States but around the world. In a category of documentaries that Barnouw labels "prosecutor," photographic evidence was assembled into films that give chilling proof of the atrocities committed during World War II. In Europe, souvenir photo albums left by dead Nazis included grizzly reminders of the Nazi reign of terror as well as family snapshots. Barnouw asks, "Were they kept with nostalgia, or pride?" In any case, these photographs formed the substance of the award-wining *Fleisher's Album* (1962), directed by Janusz Majewski, and *The Every-Day Life of Gestapo Officer Schmidt* (1963), by Jerzy Ziarnik, both of Poland.[26]

Photographers also have figured importantly in the documentary. Joris Ivens, the Dutch documentarist, supervised the Amsterdam branch of his family's photographic business before directly *The Bridge* (1928) and *Rain* (1929), two poetic or impressionistic studies that reflected the pictorial values of the then popular art photography movement. Other photographers who saw film as a logical extension of their work in art photography included Man Ray, an American working in Paris whose *Emak Bakia* (1927) was structured around shimmering light patterns produced by rotating objects, and Ralph Steiner, an American whose H_2O (1929) was an undulating montage of water images.[27]

In the 1930s, another group of photographers came to the fore of the American documentary film. But, in contrast to the aesthetic concerns of the photographers-turned-filmmakers of the 1920s, such noted photographers as Ralph Steiner, Paul Strand, and Willard Van Dyke were now galvanized by the challenging social and economic issues brought on by the Great Depression. Art was out, social advocacy was in.

Film and Photo Leagues were formed in the major cities to create support for projects designed to document the shantytowns, strikes, protests, and foreclosures that troubled the nation during the period 1930–1932. With the election of Franklin D. Roosevelt, visual documentations expanded to include treatments that suggested solutions, rather than just problems. *Hands* (1934), a short film by Ralph Steiner and Willard Van Dyke, exemplified this more upbeat approach by dramatizing the relief efforts of the Works Project Administration through a study of hands. Sponsored and distributed by Pathé, the film used a problem-solution design through a progression running from idle hands to hands at work and then to hands putting money back into circulation, money earned in government relief projects.[28]

Perhaps the most significant use of documentary photographers-cinematographers during the Depression came in 1935, when Ralph Steiner, Paul Strand, and Leo Hurwitz were engaged by director Pare Lorentz for *The Plow That Broke the Plains* (1936), a project of the Resettlement Administration, one of Roosevelt's New Deal social agencies. In spite of protests from Hollywood over the federal government's involvement in filmmaking, artistic differences between Lorentz and his premier cinematographers, and severe budgeting difficulties, the film not only got made but received enthusiastic responses from both critics and audiences. A chronicle of the extreme problems that hit the midwestern states largely because of high winds, drought, and erosion, *The Plow That Broke the Plains* stirred discussion and action on such programs as soil conservation and resettlement. The film's success spurred production plans for *The River* (1937), which dealt with flood control and hydroelectric power, and used the talents of cinematographers Willard Van Dyke and Floyd Crosby. [29]

Photographers have played an equally important role in the development of the experimental film. Man Ray, the expatriate American painter and photographer, made films in Paris during the 1920s, not for financial gain but as part of his artistic vision and output.

As a photographer, Ray developed a unique technique for creating images without using a camera by placing various objects directly on a piece of film and then exposing them to light. When developed, his prints, or rayograms, revealed silhouetted outlines of such objects as pins, tacks, and springs. In *Return to Reason* (1925), a three-minute film, Ray used animated rayograms, Dadaistic mobiles, and images of a nude torso in an abstract work that suggested film could be successfully exploited as an artistic medium of personal expression.

In *Emak Bakia* Ray included points of light shot deliberately out of focus, a prism lens that yielded angular refractions, various superimpositions, and a shot of a woman's legs repeated four times. Though perhaps frustrating for someone looking for either a story or a clear organizing premise, *Emak Bakia* still delights with its iconoclastic wit and visual bravura while at the same time reflecting the work then being created by experimental photographers. [30]

A more recent film directly tied to photography is *La Jetée* (1962). A thirty-minute love story set against the horrors of a subterranean post-atomic holocaust society, French director Chris Marker tells his story with stark black-and-white photographs instead of live action cinematography. The juxtaposition of the high-contrast photos and the perplexed and oppressed voice of Marker's troubled hero make *La Jetée* one of the most original and disturbing films ever produced. [31]

Photographic conventions developed during the nineteenth century influenced visual strategies deployed by the silent film's first wave of directors and cameramen. In fact, during the silent film period of 1895–1927, one of the most common terms used to refer to motion pictures was "photoplay." And one of the earliest and most successful motion picture fan magazines was entitled *Photoplay*.

It is appropriate to mention that before the photoplay, there was the "picture play," a term coined by the enterprising American showman Alexander Black.

In 1894 and 1985, Black put drama on the screens of the lyceum circuit in the form of hour-and-a-half to two-hour picture plays that he wrote and photographed. Specifically, Black showed about three hundred lantern slides as he recited an accompanying story from a lectern positioned next to the screen. Each scene was shot from an angle approximating the position of a choice seat in the center of a theater's orchestra section.

In picture plays such as *Miss Jerry* (1894), Black used the distinguished politician Chauncey M. Depew, who would later become a U.S. senator from New York. Black, more significantly, because of his desire to present rather elaborate narratives, anticipated what would become the standard running time of the feature-length film.[32]

Black also reflected the photographic convention of composing his subjects in full-figure framings. His characters were shot head to toe with plenty of headroom as well as footroom, a practice employed almost without exception until D. W. Griffith started directly at Biograph in 1908. The rational for this compositional dictum was the belief that audiences wanted to get the full value of their admission fees and therefore wanted to see *all* of the actors' physical features.

The full-figure convention was also supported by the influence of the theater where, indeed, the whole actor was always on view. It is not surprising, then, that Griffith had to battle the front office at Biograph over his realization of the dramatic and narrative potentials of intercutting within a scene, where full-figure establishing shots would alternate with medium shots and close-ups. After many stormy confrontations, Griffith finally made his point. And in the process of weaning film away from such photographic and theatrical conventions, Griffith became cinema's most innovative and influential director.[33]

Another photographic technique that proved more of a liability than an asset was the iris shot. An iris, an essentially circular frame, was used extensively throughout the first half of the silent period to isolate a character or object essential to the drama. Eventually, the insert or cut-in to a close-up replaced the iris as a means of providing visual emphasis.

The main problem with the iris stemmed from its inability to enlarge the subject that it isolated, a problem solved by the close-up. Also, abrupt transitions from the standard rectangular frame to the iris and back again tended to disrupt a film's overall visual continuity.

The influence of photography on film production was, then, a mixed blessing. While the pioneer moviemakers certainly benefited from a technical knowledge of photography and darkroom procedures, still photography, along with theater, did impede the development of film's unique abilities to manipulate space and time. "As it escaped the proscenium," observes film historian John Fell, "the development of film technique likewise required a developing awareness of how film space differed from still images."[34]

Another dimension of the relationship between film and photography concerns film's use of photographers as well as cinematographers as dramatic subjects.

In *The Cameraman* (1928), a wonderful Buster Keaton vehicle directed by Edward M. Sedgwick, Keaton plays a tintype photographer who graduates, after a series of hilarious misadventures, to the status of newsreel cameraman.[35]

Another silent film about film is *The Man with the Movie Camera* (1929). Directed by Soviet documentarist Dziga Vertov, and starring his brother Mikhail Kaufman as the intrepid cameraman of the title, this landmark film is a virtual encyclopedia of cinematic techniques involving cinematography as well as editing.[36]

One of the most profound films dealing with photography is *Blow-Up* (1967). Directed by Michelangelo Antonioni and starring David Hemmings as a highly successful fashion photographer, *Blow-Up*, while entrancing at the surface with its gaudy focus on the swinging London of the 1960s, is ultimately a philosophical probe posing such questions as What is reality? What is illusion? What is truth? While offering no specific solutions, Antonioni's film is provocative in that it points these questions not only at life but at the nature of photography and film as well.[37]

HISTORIC OVERVIEW—PHOTOGRAPHY AS THEORETICAL PARADIGM

Photography's intrinsic capacity to hold a mirror up to nature has been the critical backdrop against which theorizing about the film medium has taken place.

Indeed, the mimetic impulse has been photography's dominant principle, not just in terms of theory but in terms of practice as well. From the pioneering work of Louis Jacques Mandé Daguerre and Henry Fox Talbot on up to the present day, photographers have instinctively understood their basic mission as the faithful reproduction of reality.

Mathew B. Brady's Civil War photographs, the street scenes of Alfred Stieglitz, the portraits by Edward Steichen, Charles Strand's cityscapes, and the documentary revelations of Depression-era photographers Walker Evans, Dorothea Lange, Margaret Bourke-White, and Gordon Parks exemplify photographic mimesis, as do such historical-critical terms as "naturalistic photography," "straight photography," and "documentary photography."[38]

Also significant is the largely unchronicled story of the amateur photographer, ever devoted to reproducing slices of everyday life through snapshots, from the beginnings of the Kodak era in the late 1880s up to the Polaroid era of the past twenty years.

While mimetic or realistic concepts have been central to photographic theory and practice, it should be pointed out that many photographers have actively mediated their work through deliberate manipulations of the image either with the camera or in the darkroom. At one extreme are the cameraless prints of Man Ray, his rayogram silhouettes. More common interventions, however, have been accomplished through the use of defocusing, filters, special lenses, variations in exposure, and framing, all of which can be brought into play either when shooting, printing, or enlarging.

Also, the arranging of the stuff of life through posing, or mise-en-scène, has been important to photographic expressionists who view their medium as an artistic arena amenable to the creation of personal, subjective visions. Here stand such recent photographic formalists as Aaron Siskind, Minor White, and Otto Steinert.[39]

The impact of photography and its aesthetics on theorizing about film has been focused almost exclusively, to borrow Siegfried Kracauer's provocative phrase, on photography as a medium offering nothing less than "the redemption of physical reality."[40]

Kracauer, perhaps the leading exponent of cinematic realism, speaks of the motion picture's *filmic* qualities as being centered, like those of photography, on spatial and compositional concerns. The prime elements of the motion picture, then, are photographic in nature and involve the unstaged, the accidental, the big, the small, the light, the dark, and the like. Kracauer, while extremely helpful in elucidating film's spatial dimension, falls short in his treatment of film's temporal dimension. Significantly, Kracauer's *Theory of Film* provides exhaustive coverage of most of film's formative elements but does not devote a single chapter to editing.[41]

J. Dudley Andrew, in his masterful overview *The Major Film Theories*, divides classical film theory into two opposing camps—the formative or expressionist and the realist or photographic.[42] Similarly, theorists Gerald Mast and Marshall Cohen split film's theorists into realists and antirealists. "Kracauer," they note, "insists that it is the clear obligation and the special privilege of film, a descendent of still photography, to record and reveal, and thereby redeem, physical reality."[43]

Mast and Cohen make an important distinction between Kracauer, a first-generation realist, and André Bazin and his second-generation realist disciples. Whereas Kracauer insists on the unique, documentary-like realism of cinema, Bazin conceptualized film's realism as being essentially mythic rather than photographic. Bazin, then, seemed to suggest a kind of spiritual realism rather than the literal realism advocated by Kracauer.[44]

The basic problem with Kracauer's insistence that the raw material of filmmakers should be reality itself is its extreme narrowness. Most other theorists, including the second-generation realists of the Bazin school, ask, quite reasonably, "Why should filmmakers restrict themselves only to unmediated physical reality?" To do so would be to dismiss the masterworks of directors such as Sergei Eisenstein, Josef von Sternberg, Jean Cocteau, and Orson Welles. It would mean dismissing animation, experimental films, and those documentaries calling upon dramatic reenactments of actual events. And it would mean calling into question virtually all narrative films since almost all dramatic films embody some combination of realist as well as expressionist elements.[45]

In spite of the tremendous problems raised by Kracauer's constricted view,

Kracauer has nonetheless proved valuable in articulating an important position that works efficiently when applied to appropriate works such as cinema verité documentaries. Also, Kracauer's position has been important in that it has provided a catalyst for provoking, in the best of dialectic traditions, fresh theorizing about film's special nature, including those aspects which are unique to the motion picture and those which share functional properties with other media such as photography.

CONCLUSION

Photography and film have enjoyed a set of rich, interactive relationships which have resonated along technological, cultural, economic, and theoretical lines. Indeed, film can be regarded as a logical extension of nineteenth-century photography in that it elaborated upon photography's technological base as well as upon the nineteenth-century dream of mechanically reproducing as complete a spectrum of reality as possible.

Today, as technology continues to evolve, the concerns and possibilities raised by both photography and film are being extended even further. And while the photochemical media of photography and film will undoubtedly continue to develop, they will be augmented and modified by the new electronic media of video and holography.

NOTES

1. E. H. Gombrich, *Art and Illusion: A Study in the Psychology in Pictorial Representation* (1960; repr. Princeton: Princeton University Press, 1969), pp. 3–30.

2. Gerald Mast and Marshall Cohen, "Film and Reality," in *Film Theory and Criticism: Introductory Readings*, ed. Mast and Cohen, 2d ed. (New York: Oxford University Press, 1979), p. 1.

3. Kenneth Macgowan, *Behind the Scenes: In History and Techniques of the Motion Picture* (New York: Delacorte Press, 1965), p. 40.

4. John L. Fell, *A History of Films* (New York: Holt, Rinehart and Winston, 1979), pp. 4–5.

5. Macgowan, *Behind the Screen*, p. 39.

6. Ibid.

7. Ibid., p. 42.

8. Ibid., p. 43.

9. Fell, *A History of Films*, pp. 6–7.

10. Macgowan, *Behind the Screen*, p. 45.

11. Gerald Mast, *A Short History of the Movies*, 4th ed. (New York: Macmillan, 1986), pp. 12–13.

12. Fell, *A History of Films*, p. 7.

13. Thomas A. Edison in the foreword to Antonia Dickson and W.K.L. Dickson's *History of the Kinetograph, Kinetoscope and Kineto-Phonograph* (1895; repr. New York: Arno Press, 1970), p. 4.

14. Macgowan, *Behind the Screen*, p. 69.

15. Ibid., p. 66.

16. Mast, *A Short History of the Movies*, p. 22.

17. The 2 May 1896 review is cited by Fell, *A History of Films*, p. 14.

18. Erik Barnouw, *Documentary: A History of the Non-Fiction Film* (New York: Oxford University Press, 1974), pp. 4–5.

19. Ibid., p. 7.

20. This judgment is based on screenings of the Lumières' work available from the Museum of Modern Art's Circulating Film Library.

21. Joseph R. Dominick, *The Dynamics of Mass Communication* (Reading, Mass.: Addison-Wesley, 1983), pp. 80–82.

22. Albert E. Smith, *Two Reels and a Crank* (Garden City, N.Y.: Doubleday, 1952), p. 148.

23. Barnouw, *Documentary*, p. 24.

24. The seminal source of information on newsreels is Raymond Fielding, *The American Newsreel, 1911–1967* (Norman: University of Oklahoma Press, 1972).

25. Barnouw, *Documentary*, pp. 200–201.

26. Ibid., pp. 172–73.

27. For a comprehensive yet concise overview of the experimental film, see David Curtis, *Experimental Cinema: A Fifty-Year Evolution* (New York: Dell, 1971).

28. Barnouw, *Documentary*, pp. 112–13.

29. Ibid., pp. 113–20.

30. Curtis, *Experimental Cinema*, pp. 24–25.

31. Roy Armes, *French Cinema* (New York: Oxford University Press, 1985), p. 185.

32. Macgowan, *Behind the Screen*, p. 88.

33. Lewis Jacobs, *The Rise of the American Film: A Critical History* (1939; repr. New York: Teachers College Press, 1968), p. 102.

34. Fell, *A History of Films*, p. 6.

35. David Robinson, *Buster Keaton* (Bloomington: Indiana University Press, 1969), pp. 170–74.

36. Barnouw, *Documentary*, pp. 62–65.

37. For a variety of critical opinions on *Blow-Up*, see Roy Huss, ed., *Focus on Blow-Up* (Englewood Cliffs, N.J.: Prentice-Hall, 1971).

38. See Beaumont Newhall, *The History of Photography from 1839 to the Present Day*, rev. ed. (New York: Museum of Modern Art, 1964), for a comprehensive yet concise history of photography and photographic theory.

39. Ibid., pp. 197–201.

40. Siegfried Kracauer, in *Theory of Film: The Redemption of Physical Reality* (1960; repr. New York: Oxford University Press, 1965), presents an elaborate, though convoluted case for a realist film aesthetic based upon photography.

41. Gerald Mast, *Film/Cinema/Experience: A Theory of Experience* (New York: Harper & Row, 1977), p. 9.

42. J. Dudley Andrew, *The Major Film Theories: An Introduction* (New York: Oxford University Press, 1976), p. vi.

43. Mast and Cohen, *Film Theory and Criticism*, p. 2.

44. Ibid., p. 3.

45. See Andrew, *The Major Film Theories*, pp 140–45, for further discussion of the contrasting realist views of Kracauer and Bazin.

SELECTED BIBLIOGRAPHY

Andrew, J. Dudley. *The Major Film Theories*. New York: Oxford University Press, 1976.

Armes, Roy. *Film and Reality: An Historical Survey*. Baltimore: Penguin Books, 1974.

———. *French Cinema*. New York: Oxford University Press, 1985.

Barnouw, Erik. *Documentary: A History of the Non-Fiction Film*. New York: Oxford University Press, 1974.

Barsam, Richard Meran. *Nonfiction Film: A Critical History*. New York: E. P. Dutton, 1973.

Brownlow, Kevin. *The Parade's Gone By*. New York: Alfred A. Knopf, 1968.

Ceram, C. W. (pseud.) *Archaeology of the Cinema*. Trans. Richard Winston. New York: Harcourt, Brace & World, 1965.

Cook, Olive. *Movement in Two Dimensions: A Study of the Animated and Projected Pictures Which Preceded the Invention of Cinematography*. London: Hutchinson, 1963.

Curtis, David. *Experimental Cinema: A Fifty-Year Evolution*. New York: Dell, 1971.

Dickson, Antonia and W.K.L. Dickson. *History of the Kinetograph, Kinetoscope, and Kineto-Phonograph*. New York: Albert Bunn, 1895; repr. New York: Arno Press, 1970.

Dominick, Joseph R. *The Dynamics of Mass Communication*. Reading, Mass: Addison-Wesley, 1983.

Eder, Joseph Maria. *History of Photography*. Trans. Edward Epstean. 1945; repr. New York: Dover, 1978.

Everson, William K. *American Silent Film*. New York: Oxford University Press, 1978.

Fell, John L. *A History of Films*. New York: Holt, Rinehart and Winston, 1979.

Fielding, Raymond. *The American Newsreel, 1911–1967*. Norman: University of Oklahoma Press, 1972.

———, ed. *A Technological History of Motion Pictures and Television*. Berkeley: University of California Press, 1967.

Gombrich, E. H. *Art and Illusion: A Study in the Psychology of Pictorial Representation*. 1960; repr. Princeton, N.J.: Princeton University Press, 1969.

Huss, Roy, ed. *Focus on Blow-Up*. Englewood Cliffs, N.J.: Prentice-Hall, 1971.

Jacobs, Lewis. *The Rise of the American Film: A Critical History*. 1939; repr. New York: Teachers College Press, 1968.

Jenkins, Reese V. *Images and Enterprise: Technology and the American Photographic Industry, 1839–1925*. Baltimore: Johns Hopkins University Press, 1975.

Kracauer, Siegfried. *Theory of Film: The Redemption of Physical Reality*. 1960; repr. New York: Oxford University Press, 1965.

Le Grice, Malcolm. *Abstract Film and Beyond*. Cambridge, Mass.: MIT Press, 1977.

MacCann, Richard Dyer, ed. *Film: A Montage of Theories*. New York: E. P. Dutton, 1966.

MacDonnell, Kevin. *Eadweard Muybridge: The Man Who Invented the Moving Picture*. Boston: Little, Brown, 1972.

Macgowan, Kenneth. *Behind the Screen: The History and Techniques of the Motion Picture*. New York: Delacorte Press, 1965.

Mast, Gerald. *Film/Cinema/Movie: A Theory of Experience*. New York: Harper & Row, 1977.

————. *A Short History of the Movies*. 4th ed. New York: Macmillan, 1986.

Mast, Gerald and Marshall Cohen, eds. *Film Theory and Criticism: Introductory Readings*. 2d ed. New York: Oxford University Press, 1979.

Newhall, Beaumont. *The History of Photography from 1839 to the Present Day*. rev. ed. New York: Museum of Modern Art, 1964.

————. *Latent Image: The Discovery of Photography*. Garden City, N.Y.: Doubleday, 1967.

Quigley, Martin, Jr. *Magic Shadows: The Story of the Origin of Motion Pictures*. 1948; repr. New York: Biblo and Tannen, 1969.

Robinson, David. *Buster Keaton*. Bloomington: Indiana University Press, 1969.

Rosenblum, Naomi. *A World History of Photography*. New York: Abbeville Press, 1984.

Smith, Albert E. *Two Reels and a Crank*. Garden City, N.Y.: Doubleday, 1952.

Sontag, Susan. *On Photography*. New York: Farrar, Strauss, Giroux, 1977.

SELECTED FILMOGRAPHY

Blow-Up (Great Britain 1967). Directed by Michelangelo Antonioni.

The Cameraman (USA 1928). Directed by Edward Sedgwick. With Buster Keaton.

City of Gold (Canada 1957). Directed by Colin Low.

End of the Trail (USA 1967). Produced by Donald B. Hyatt for NBC's Project XX Series. Narrated by Walter Brennan.

Hands (USA 1934). Directed by Ralph Steiner and Willard Van Dyke.

La Jetée (France 1962). Directed by Chris Marker.

1895 Lumière Films (France 1895–1897). Produced by Auguste and Louis Lumière.

The Man with the Movie Camera (USSR 1928). Produced, directed, and edited by Dziga Vertov.

Origins of the Motion Picture (USA 1955). Produced by the United States Navy.

The Plow That Broke the Plains (USA 1936). Directed by Pare Lorentz.

Rain (Netherlands 1929). Produced and directed by Joris Ivens and Mannus Franken.

The Real West (USA 1964). Produced by Donald B. Hyatt for NBC's Project XX Series. Narrated by Gary Cooper.

4

FILM AND THE GRAPHIC ARTS

RICHARD SHALE

INTRODUCTION AND HISTORY

The graphic arts are used in all stages of filmmaking from the earliest sketches of the production designer to the finished posters which advertise the film. Within the sphere of popular entertainment are several hand-drawn media which bear a close relationship to film: the animated cartoon, comic strip, and comic book. Animation is, of course, the most obvious and significant union of the graphic arts and cinema, but comic strips and comic books are also linked symbiotically to film. (The comic book, originating in the 1930s as a collection of comic strip reprints, will be discussed later.)

The comic strip, says M. Thomas Inge, "may be defined as an open-ended dramatic narrative about a recurring set of characters, told with a balance between narrative text and visual action, often including dialogue in balloons, and published serially in newspapers."[1] Erwin Panofsky in his celebrated essay "Style and Medium in the Motion Pictures" calls the comic strip "a most important root of cinematic art."[2] Both movies and comic strips were born at the close of the nineteenth century, both are primarily pictorial, and both employ sequentially ordered individual segments, either frames or panels, for a cumulative effect. In his essay, "The Funnies, the Movies, and Aesthetics," Earle J. Coleman notes some additional similarities: both create the illusion of motion, convey an often dreamlike state, and are omnipotent in that they can do anything in any situation, unlike drama. Moreover, both movies and comics have been subjected to rather repressive moral codes of self-censorship.[3]

Many film directors have been influenced by comics. French director Alain Resnais has said, "What I know about film has been learned from comic strips as much as from the cinema—the rules of cutting and editing are the same for the comics as for the cinema."[4] Federico Fellini worked as a cartoonist and wrote comic strips before turning to film; *The White Sheik*, his first solo directorial effort, is an amusing tale involving a comic strip hero. George Lucas, whose childhood interest in comic books has been well documented, arranged with

Marvel Comics to produce a comic book adaptation of *Star Wars* three months before the film premiered. William Friedkin claims he got his inspiration for the famous chase scene in *The French Connection* from *The Spirit*, a comic book by Will Eisner. Even the Marx Brothers, notes comic art historians Bill Blackbeard and Martin Williams were inspired by the comic strips and named themselves after the fashion of Gus Mager's *Monk* strips, one of which was titled "Groucho the Monk."[5]

The symbiotic relationship between comics and film began quite early. Frederick Burr Opper, for instance, began to draw his *Happy Hooligan* strip for the Hearst papers in 1900. By January 1902 the Edison Studio was marketing a film, *The Twentieth Century Tramp*, which was subtitled "Happy Hooligan and His Airship." Winsor McCay began his strip *Dreams of a Rarebit Fiend* in 1904 and within two years the Edison Studio had a film version of that as well.[6] McCay, of course, later turned to animation and brought many of his comic strip creations to the screen.

In the first two decades of the twentieth century, the era "before Mickey," animators frequently used characters which had first been established in the comic strips. By the 1930s and 1940s the opposite seemed more common; in this golden age of animation, the popular stars such as Mickey Mouse, Donald Duck, or Bugs Bunny originated as film characters and then made the transition to comic strips or comic books.

Craftsmanship and Technology

Both the motion picture and the comic strip represented not simply new art forms but the culmination of technological achievements of the post–Industrial Revolution. Copper engraving and etching used in the eighteenth century had, for technical reasons, necessitated the separation of illustration and text. With the introduction of woodblock engraving in the nineteenth century, text and picture were reintegrated, setting the stage for the age of illustration in the United States and throughout the world.[7]

Artists found a market for their work in such popular periodicals as *Frank Leslie's Illustrated Newspaper* and *Harper's Weekly*. Within the space of half a dozen years these influential humor magazines sprang up: *Puck* (1877), *Judge* (1881), and *Life* (1883). These proved to be the training ground for a group of artists who would emerge a few decades later when the comic strip was born.

In the first half of the nineteenth century men such as Niépce and Daguerre in France were working on an entirely different technique of reproduction—photography. By the end of the 1880s George Eastman had perfected flexible roll film; his Kodak cameras ("You push the button. We do the rest.") would soon place photography in the hands of everyone.[8]

This fascination with mechanical reproduction was matched by the desire to create the illusion of movement. By the late 1870s Emile Reynaud was able to project moving images onto a screen by means of a device he called a Praxinoscope, and in a few years he was entertaining crowds at his Théâtre Optique with this precursor of cinema.[9]

Concurrent experiments in several countries in the 1880s led to a race to develop motion pictures. Film historian Jack Ellis explains: "The contestants are too numerous to mention, but the principle frontrunners in the international competition were Thomas Edison and Thomas Armat in the United States; Marey, Le Prince, and Louis and Auguste Lumière in France; Ottomar Anschütz, Max Skladanowsky, and Oskar Messter for Germany; and Friese-Greene and Robert Paul representing England."[10]

"The animated cartoon, the movie, and the comic strip," notes Pierre Cou-perie, "were born simultaneously; although each appeared independently of the other two, they embodied in three related forms the single deep-seated trend underlying the entire nineteenth century."[11] The nineteenth-century audience would soon see its demand for visual entertainment, humor, and spectacle merge with the inexorable trend toward new technology and increased industrialization.

The simultaneous development of motion pictures by several inventors would have its parallel in the birth of the comic strip: efforts in both America and Europe make it difficult to ascribe to any one person the invention of the comic strip. "The perfect analyst of the early strip," writes David Kunzle, "would have to unite the talents of the historian of politics, art, literature, and social mores; he would also be a folklorist and a criminologist." "The early comic strip," he adds, "is a broadsheet; its history is part of the history of the broadsheet, and corresponds precisely to the incidence of broadsheet activity in different cultures at different periods. Germany in the fifteenth through seventeenth centuries, Holland in the seventeenth century, England in the seventeenth and eighteenth centuries—all were strongholds of the broadsheet, and it is these countries at these times which give us our strips and picture stories."[12] But the comic strip as we know it did not emerge until the last decade of the nineteenth century.

In the early 1890s publishers in New York and Chicago began experimenting with color printing, and in April 1893 an American newspaper's first color page appeared. The honor went to the *New York Recorder*, which beat Joseph Pulitzer's *New York World* by one week. Pulitzer persisted and within a few years had perfected the color process—except for the color yellow, which resisted drying properly. To test some new driers, Charles Saalburgh, Pulitzer's color-press room foreman, chose a cartoon by Richard Outcault called "Down in Hogan's Alley" which used slum residents to satirize current events. As comic strip historian Stephen Becker explains, "One of the residents of Hogan's Alley was a gap-toothed, jug-eared urchin who wore what looked like a white nightgown. Saalburgh chose that nightgown as the test area for his tallow-drying yellow. The results astonished not only Saalburgh, but Pulitzer himself, most of New York City, certainly Outcault, a rival publisher named William Randolph Hearst, and ultimately the entire world of journalism."[13] The immense popularity of the Yellow Kid, as Outcault's character came to be called, led to a bidding war for his creator's services and ultimately the phrase "yellow journalism," which such rivalry exemplified.

By World War I the principal characteristics of both comic strips and motion pictures were in place. In the previous decade director D. W. Griffith had perfected film syntax and had advanced nearly all aspects of film technique. The success of his two-and-a-half-hour *Birth of a Nation* in 1915 had swept aside the remaining arguments that audiences would not sit through a film which ran over an hour. The animation industry experienced similar advances. Raoul Barré, a French-Canadian animator, invented a "peg" system for registering drawings and a "slash" system to eliminate the need to redraw stationary objects. Earl Hurd and J. R. Bray patented, in 1914 and 1916 respectively, a process using celluloid, whose transparency eliminated the necessity of redrawing backgrounds and nonmoving parts for each frame.[14] Many popular comic strips of the time, such as Bud Fisher's *Mutt and Jeff* and Sidney Smith's *Old Doc Yak*, were adapted to the screen, though some stars, such as Felix the Cat, originated as animated characters and later moved to newsprint.

The 1920s represent a period of growth and maturation for both media. For film, the key development was the conversion to sound in the late 1920s. The Disney Studio, founded in 1923, released in 1928 its first sound cartoon, *Steamboat Willie*, starring a new character named Mickey Mouse, who immediately became popular and made the transition to comic strip in January 1930.[15]

In addition to sound, the perfection of three-strip Technicolor revolutionized the animation industry. Disney's *Flowers and Trees* (1932) was the first film to use the new color process, and for his willingness to gamble on the new Technicolor, Disney was granted exclusive rights to it for three years. By the mid–1930s all of the major studios had switched to color for their cartoons. Another technical innovation pioneered by Disney and Ub Iwerks was the multiplane camera, a device which placed the animation cells onto different levels to create the illusion of depth.

Business and Economics

By the mid–1890s the technology to produce color comics was in place. In the coming decades the historical development of the comic strip would be shaped less by technological innovation than by the intense rivalry of newspaper tycoons such as Joseph Pulitzer and William Randolph Hearst (whose drive for higher circulation was fictionalized in Orson Welles's film *Citizen Kane*.)[16]

Hearst had in 1895 purchased the moribund *New York Morning Journal* (once owned by Albert Pulitzer, Joseph's brother) and had immediately set out to improve the paper's sagging popularity. He soon discovered that comics were an effective way to build circulation. He hired Richard Outcault away from Pulitzer and began a color supplement, advertised in typical Hearstian prose as "eight pages of polychromatic effulgence that make the rainbow look like a lead pipe."[17] Outcault, rehired by Pulitzer, then by Hearst, finally ended up at James

Gordon Bennett's *New York Herald*, where in 1902 he created his most famous character, Buster Brown.

Joining Outcault in the Hearst stable was James Swinnerton, who came from Hearst's *San Francisco Examiner*, and Rudolph Dirks, who created in 1897 one of history's longest running strips, *The Katzenjammer Kids*. Like Outcault, Dirks had sold cartoons to *Judge* and *Life*. As Bill Blackbeard and Martin Williams have pointed out, *The Katzenjammer Kids* combined for the first time strip continuity and speech balloons.[18] When Dirks went on vacation, Hearst hired someone else to do the strip. Dirks sued and was awarded the rights to the characters but not the title. Hearst hired Harold Knerr to continue *The Katzenjammer Kids* while Dirks began *Hans and Fritz* (later titled *The Captain and the Kids*) for a Hearst rival. Both strips remained popular for the next sixty years.

The high salaries paid by the newspaper magnates and the promise of a new medium for art and humor lured many artists from *Puck* and other humor magazines. Within a few years of the appearance of the Yellow Kid, such magazine cartoonists as Outcault, Dirks, and Frederick Opper moved to newspapers. "This exodus," notes Rick Marschall, "naturally had a profound effect on magazine humor and depleted its artistic ranks; in the final analysis it was largely responsible for the death of the magazines."[19]

Comic strips had grown increasingly popular by the end of the first decade of the twentieth century, and syndicates formed to handle their nationwide distribution. In 1915 Hearst formed the International Film Service, an animation studio, to exploit the comic strip characters, such as Krazy Kat, Happy Hooligan, and the Katzenjammer Kids, licensed to his King Features Syndicate. These cartoons were released as part of Hearst's weekly newsreel. Gregory LaCava was in charge of production, and the animators included Walter Lantz, Grim Natwick, I. Klein, Frank Moser, Jack King, and Ben Sharpsteen, all of whom left a significant mark on animation history.[20]

Though there had been reprint collections of comic strips published in the 1920s, the comic book as we know it was not born until 1933, when Eastern Color Printing Company published ten thousand copies of *Funnies on Parade*, a giveaway premium for Proctor and Gamble. Max C. Gaines, a salesman for Eastern Color, believed that other advertisers would buy such books for premiums, and so *Famous Funnies: A Carnival of Comics* and *Century of Comics*, also reprints of Sunday newspaper strips, were published in quantities of 100,000 to 250,000.[21] Within two years publishers had joined with the major comic strip syndicates to offer several titles of reprinted strips.

The golden age of comic book history began in 1938 with the appearance of Superman in *Action Comics* No. 1. By 1943, only a decade after their first appearance, comic books had achieved astonishing popularity. According to Pierre Couperie, "Their monthly sales amounted to 18,000,000 copies—ten times more than the combined sales of *Life*, *Reader's Digest*, and *Saturday Evening Post*—and constituted one-third of total magazine sales."[22]

The audience for comic books differed in age from the readership of comic strips. ''Strips,'' note Dick Lupoff and Don Thompson, ''are written and published for the people who buy newspapers—adults—and comic books are slanted toward and produced for the people who buy them—kids.''[23] Despite this distinction in audience, the most popular characters enjoyed exposure in both media.

By 1941 over 160 comic book titles were being published.[24] The writers of the popular superhero, spy, and crime-fighter comics often drew their inspiration from such pulp magazines as *Weird Tales* and *Amazing Stories*. In his history of the pulps, Ron Goulart draws an interesting distinction between those magazines and comics: ''The interiors of the pulps were, visually, a letdown, and you actually had to read the stories to get anywhere near the thrills promised by the cover. Later, comic books, somewhat like buffered aspirin, cut down on the time it took for the action to get from the page to the brain—and they took away much of the pulps' audience.''[25]

Nowhere was the cross-pollination between comic books, comic strips,and film more evident than in the production of movie serials during the mid–1930s and 1940s. The same adventure heroes who battled adversity in the comic strips and comic books made an easy and rapid transition to the motion picture screen. Universal, the studio most involved in the production of serials, adapted Alex Raymond's *Flash Gordon* in 1936, and the result, said one critic, was ''far and away the best serial ever made.''[26] Universal also filmed *Buck Rogers* and later adapted two other strips by Raymond—*Jungle Jim* and *Secret Agent X–9*. Republic and Columbia were the other studios most actively producing serials, and in the 1940s they looked increasingly to the comics for material to adapt. Republic filmed Chester Gould's *Dick Tracy* as well as comic book superheroes *Captain Marvel* and *Captain America*. Republic's *Jungle Girl* serial was successful enough that Fawcett Publications created a comic book based on the title character. Columbia's serials based on comics included *Mandrake the Magician*, *Terry and the Pirates*, and *Superman*. The Fleischer Studio also produced a series of animated Superman cartoons.

Superman's popularity has remained strong into the 1980s. The success of *Superman*, a 1978 feature starring Christopher Reeve, led to *Superman II* in 1980 and *Superman III* in 1983 and prompted Hollywood to turn again to comic books and strips for material. More than a dozen film adaptations of comics characters have appeared in the last decade, and most of these films bear little resemblance to the serials and low-budget adaptations of decades past. Larger budgets have enabled filmmakers to achieve higher production values and often impressive special effects. In 1979 *Flash Gordon* and *Buck Rogers in the 25th Century* returned to the movie screen, this time not as serials but as major features, but this renaissance of comic characters has by no means been restricted to science fiction or costumed superheroes.

Robert Altman's live action version of *Popeye* (1980) starred Robin Williams as Elzie Segar's spinach-loving sailor. *Conan the Barbarian*, starring Arnold Schwarzenegger as the Marvel Comics hero, appeared in 1982, and a sequel, *Conan the Destroyer*, followed in 1984. Harold Gray's comic strip *Little Orphan*

Annie became the basis for a hit Broadway musical in 1979; John Huston directed the film version in 1982. *Greystoke: The Legend of Tarzan, Lord of the Apes* added in 1984 yet another chapter in the lengthy and durable screen career of Edgar Rice Burroughs's most famous creation. Not all adaptations, however, have depended upon long-established characters. Howard the Duck, who had begun as a Marvel Comics character in the mid–1970s, emerged as a movie star of sorts in the summer of 1986.

In a related vein, movie posters and allied forms of advertising art offer quite a different, yet significant, connection between film and the graphic arts. In the earliest days of motion pictures, elaborate posters were not yet necessary; the novelty of the new medium was sufficient. Stars and directors were seldom if ever identified by name, so the early posters stressed only the studio name and story line of the film.

As films and audiences grew more sophisticated, the necessity of identifying the stars became apparent. Producers had long resisted such a development, knowing that the fame resulting from name identification would tip the balance of bargaining power to the actors. By the time Griffith's *Birth of a Nation* appeared in 1915, the star system had become firmly established, and the content of the movie poster changed to accommodate the public's thirst for names and faces.

The poster artists, writes film historian David Robinson, succeeded ''in creating a medium that was unique: loud, brash, vulgar, braggart, using the human form as a provocation and the letters of the alphabet as a violence, declaring an irrepressible and irresistible vitality, making intoxicating use of form and composition and rhythm.''[27]

The golden age of the Hollywood movie poster coincided with the studio era—the mid–1920s to the mid–1950s. Though the stars and even some directors became famous, the poster artists, who were for the most part studio employees, labored in anonymity. Graphic style was prescribed by the image of the studio and the star. ''Only the comedy films seemed to have permitted stylistic flexibility,'' notes Robinson. ''To have caricatured to the slightest degree the great romantic and dramatic stars would have been an impermissible sacrilege.''[28]

Posters were not the only form of graphic art used to lure patrons into the movie theaters. Newspaper ads and especially lobby cards were also extensively employed. As the name implies, lobby cards were displayed in the foyers of theaters to entice passersby. Distributed in sets of eight to sixteen, these lobby cards first measured eight by ten inches but were soon standardized at eleven by fourteen inches. Though most of the films they advertised were shot in black and white, lobby cards were always done in color. What mattered was not accuracy but the sense of excitement the cards created.

Society and Culture

Until the emergence of the adventure strip in the late 1920s, the comic strip, as its name implies, was primarily devoted to comedy and fantasy. The rich tradition of American humor, especially satire, carried on in the nineteenth century by such writers as Mark Twain, Artemus Ward, and Petroleum V. Nasby, took on a new vigor with the birth of the newspaper comic strip. Ernest Brennecke, writing in *Century Magazine* in 1924, observed that "The funny paper has . . . become not only a faithful reflection of the tastes and ethical principles of the country at large; it is also manifestly an extremely powerful organ of social satire. The *daily block of cinema-squares* is the medium through which the vices of man are held up for all to see [emphasis mine]."[29] Nearly a decade later *Fortune Magazine* looked back on the early strips and saw them as

a form of crude but vigorous satire at a time when American literature in general was saccharine and imitative. The meaner and littler aspects of American life and character were lampooned in the funnies long before Sinclair Lewis discovered *Main Street* or *Babbitt* . . . [T]aking their material from the life they observed around them, the comic-strip artists presented a series of extremely pointed (and fundamentally ill-natured) comments on the American public, which promptly roared with laughter and came eagerly back for more."[30]

Because comic strips run for years, our perception of them and their effect on us tend to be cumulative. "The characters in the funnies and comics," says Arthur Asa Berger, "have a 'history,' so to speak—and their activities become more meaningful the more we are acquainted with this history, the longer we've been following the strip, or the heroes. We sort of 'know them,' and they become a part of us, in a way. Since the strips are eternal (often continuing after the originator dies) they are one of the few things that we carry with us from childhood to our old age"[31]

The comic strip artists enriched not only our tradition of humor but our vocabulary as well. Film historian Terry Ramsaye says that the word "movies" gained popularity because of its frequent use in the comics.[32] H. L. Mencken, himself no stranger to humor, listed in his monumental study *The American Language* some of the expressions which originated in comic strips. To Elzie C. Segar, the creator of Popeye, Mencken ascribed the invention of words such as "goon" and "jeep." Phrases such as "heebie jeebies," "hotsy-totsy," and "horse feathers" sprang from the pen of Barney Google's creator, Billy DeBeck. "The comic strip artist," notes Mencken, "has been a very diligent maker of terse and dramatic words." Citing such novelties as "zowie," "socko," "plop," "wow," and "grrr," he concludes that "their influence upon the general American vocabulary must be very potent."[33]

The rise of the newspaper syndicates in the early part of the twentieth century gave comic strip artists widespread national fame, but such exposure came with a price. Faced with the need to appeal simultaneously to the whole country, no artist could now afford to offend large segments of society. Not only did the strips have to be approved by the syndicate chiefs, but local editors could also pull any strip which offended community standards.

Because their methods of distribution were unlike those of comic strips, films and comic books would react to the cries for censorship in a different way. Fearful of outside interference, especially from the government, the motion picture industry in 1930 had written a self-censoring Production Code to govern the content of movies. From 1934 (when it began to be strictly enforced) to the 1960s (when it was finally replaced by the ratings systems), the Production Code profoundly affected the movies. Even the animation industry did not escape the strict tenets of the code. One animated star who was affected was Betty Boop. Leonard Maltin summarizes the changes her character quickly underwent: "Her body was immediately covered up; gone was the garter, the short skirt, the decolletage. The lechers who once lusted for Betty were retired and replaced by such all-American accoutrements as a dog and a cute nephew. Betty became a bachelor girl with no interest in men whatsoever."[34]

Public concern over the content of comic books came two decades after the establishment of the Motion Picture Production Code. In April 1954 a growing concern over comics culminated in the publication of *The Seduction of the Innocent*, a book by child-psychiatrist Fredric Wertham, who blamed virtually all of the ills of youth on comic strips. That same month a U.S. Senate Sub-committee on Juvenile Delinquency held hearings on the evils of comics.

In response to this outcry and to diffuse the threat of possible legislation, several comic book publishers created the Comics Code Authority, by their own admission "the most stringent code in existence for any communications media."[35] The shake-up in the comics industry following these events brought to a close the Golden Age of comic book history.

Dell, which published comic book adaptations of the animated stars of Disney, Warner Brothers, MGM, and Universal, refused to join the Comics Code signatories and instead made a "Pledge to Parents" that "Dell Comics are good comics." Instructive because it reveals the limits imposed by self-censorship is a passage from the "Hints On Writing for Dell Comics," written in 1954:

Avoid sophisticated and adult themes such as psychoanalysis. . . . We avoid showing or mentioning the following items: anything dealing with minority races, politics, religion, labor, suicides, death, afflictions (such as blindness), torture, kidnapping, blackmail, snakes, sex, love, female villains, crooked lawmen or heavies of any race other than the white race. At all times keep the stories *clean* and in *good taste*. Don't make fun of the law or portray law officials as stupid, dull-witted, or cruel. Try to avoid atom bombs, Communists, and international intrigue generally.[36]

The storm over Wertham's book and government scrutiny passed, and by 1956 the Silver Age of comics began with the introduction of a new, more realistic kind of superhero. Marvel Comics creations such as the *Fantastic Four*, *The Amazing Spider-Man*, *The Hulk*, and *X-Men* in the early sixties spurred a resurgence in comic book popularity. The introduction of underground "comix" such as *Zap* in 1967 signaled the erosion of taboos such as those listed by Dell Comics only a dozen years earlier.

After a mid–1970s slump, comics again experienced a jump in popularity in the 1980s. Some new comic books, such as *Camelot 3000*, *American Flagg*, and *Rōnin*, aimed for an older audience and took on a darker tone. "The world of adult comics is full of downers," says Professor Benjamin DeMott; "the tone aimed at, in general, is knowing cynicism, and the feelings evoked are, more often than not, grim, self-taunting and hopeless." He concludes that "the deep, broad-based cynicism expressed in adult comics has not been a norm in this country's working class youth; its advent could have a powerful impact on politics and culture."[37]

Art

The works of animators, comic strip artists, and comic book creators form a significant body of twentieth-century art which is only now beginning to be studied and appreciated. Richard Outcault; Rudolph Dirks; James Swinnerton, whose *Little Bears* is often listed as the first comic; and Frederick Burr Opper, whose *Happy Hooligan* ranked among the most popular of the early strips, are major figures who shaped a new art form. George Herriman's *Krazy Kat* ran from 1910 to 1944 and remains perhaps the most celebrated comic strip of all time. Its abstract fantasies, surreal landscapes, and whimsical language were unique.

Winsor McCay occupies a significant place at the forefront of both comic strip creators and animators. As an artist, says Judith O'Sullivan, "McCay transformed the serpentine line and irrational color of art nouveau by an absolute command of perspective and an interest in motion. Through successive imagery and the addition of verbal content in the balloons, he created a compelling visual narrative, an altogether personal vision of the turn of the century's international style."[38] His comic strip *Little Nemo in Slumberland*, begun in 1905, employed dreamlike plots and graphic experiments with perspective and angle which foreshadowed both the surrealist movement and the fluid action he would later create in his animation. McCay's animated film *Gertie the Dinosaur*, released in 1914, gave the medium its first real cartoon star.

Expanding the forms established by these pioneers was a new group of comic strip artists who emerged in the 1930s. Milton Caniff, who cites the films of Alfred Hitchcock as an influence, used "camera" angles and tonal details to create mood in *Terry and the Pirates* and *Steve Canyon*. He and Will Eisner pioneered the use of chiaroscuro in comic strips, similar to the *film noir* lighting in movies of the 1940s. Hal Foster, who created the *Tarzan* strip in 1929, and Burne Hogarth, who took over the strip in 1937, were especially gifted stylists. Other significant artists who contributed new styles and approaches to the medium in the 1930s and 1940s were Alex Raymond, who created the *Flash Gordon* strip; Al Capp, whose *Li'l Abner* added a new chapter to American folklore and satire; Walt Kelly, whose *Pogo* became one of the most popular strips of the postwar era; and Floyd Gottfredson, who drew the Mickey Mouse comic strips for over forty years.

As far back as the silent era, painters had turned to film to explore its possibilities as an abstract art form. Freed from the constraints imposed by commercial cinema, such artists as Hans Richter, Viking Eggeling, and Oskar Fischinger experimented with color and design to create avant-garde animated films. Len Lye in Great Britain and Norman McLaren in Canada pioneered the technique of drawing directly on film to create short motion pictures which required no camera.

Movie posters were often a showcase for innovative design, though poster artists outside the United States seemed to enjoy greater opportunities for graphic experimentation and stylistic freedom than the American artists employed by the major studios. At the turn of the century, French artist Jules Cheret created many posters which celebrated the earliest efforts of such film pioneers as the Lumière Brothers. In Russia in the 1920s and 1930s artists such as Alexander Rodchenko and the Stenburg Brothers created an impressive body of work.

In Great Britain in the 1940s and 1950s S. John Woods, himself a graphic designer, assembled a group of artists who created notable posters which advertised the films of the Ealing Studio. Bevis Hillier, who has written extensively on the history and art of posters, offers the following perspectives: "I would think it fair to suggest that the Ealing posters have a higher place in the canon of world poster art (certain that of the *film* poster art) than Ealing films occupy in movie history."[39]

East European countries such as Poland and Yugoslavia created in the postwar years a tradition of bold experimentation in graphic styles, and this was soon reflected in the animated films emerging from Zagreb and Warsaw in the 1960s. The gifted Polish animator Jan Lenica observed in 1957 that "the poster is a sort of primer from which the reading and understanding of painting may be learned, helping the onlooker to become accustomed to the forms and language of art."[40]

Film poster artists were charged with a specific task—namely, to attract the attention of the moviegoing public. That they sometimes aspired to and achieved more than this goal is evident from the impressive body of poster artwork which has been collected and preserved.

STYLES AND GENRES

Comic strips fall into two formats: the joke-a-day and the continuity strip. The former is commonly used for the humor strips (which dominated the medium's first three decades); the latter is identified most with the adventure strips which began in the 1930s, though its origins are much earlier. Clare Briggs' short-lived *A. Piker Clerk* (1903–1904) used a day-to-day continuity, as did C. W. Kahles' *Hairbreadth Harry* (begun in 1906) and Harry Hershfield's *Desperate Desmond* (1910–1912).

Though Roy Crane's *Wash Tubbs* (1924) was a notable precursor, the adventure strip was really established with the arrival of two strips which premiered on the same day—January 7, 1929: *Tarzan*, by Hal Foster, and *Buck Rogers*, by Phil Nowlan and Dick Calkins. These adventure strips required skillful plotting and bold graphics to sustain the necessary dramatic mood, and many strip artists turned to the movies for inspiration. Angles, close-ups, and lighting effects common to the filmmaker's vocabulary now appeared in the comic pages. Pierre Couperie credits Milt Caniff with performing this cinematic style: "His most justly famous creation, 'Terry and the Pirates,' was begun in October, 1934, and, after the inevitable trial-and-error period, finally found its definitive style. Alternating between the pen and the brush, Caniff became a master in the use of skillful illumination, elaborate chiaroscuro effects, and violent black-and-white contrasts, thereby endowing his narrative with a characteristic atmosphere which it shares with the films of that period."[41]

Four panels seem to be the standard for daily strips, though this is often disregarded, especially in recent years when strips have been considerably reduced in size on the comics page. Will Eisner, another artist especially gifted in the cinematic style, was one of the first to exploit the flexibility of the panels. One large panel with many details might be used for a dramatic impact or to slow down the movement of the strip; several narrow panels would speed the action, achieving the same effect filmmakers did with rapid cutting. Characters who burst through panel boundaries could add a sense of depth. Some artists, however, notably Jules Feiffer, have dispensed entirely with panel boundaries.

The use of color, so significant in the birth of the comic strip, paradoxically seems less necessary for strips than for either comic books or films. Weekday black-and-white strips were introduced in the Hearst papers in the early 1900s. Hearst's *New York Evening Journal* began the first full daily page of comics on January 31, 1912. Explains Bill Blackbeard and Martin Williams, "Initially made up of four large daily strips, including Herriman's *Family Upstairs* and Harry Hershfield's *Desperate Desmond* (a continuing cliff-hanger), the Hearst page expanded to five, then six, and finally nine daily strips through the teens and early twenties . . . By the 1930s, comic strips by the daily pageful and Sunday color section collections were to be found in most American and Canadian newspapers."[42]

With the shift in popularity from humor to adventure strips in the 1930s, the term "comic strip" became something of a misnomer. David Kunzle points out that only in the English language is the strip designated as comic. The Germans say *bildergeschichte* (picture story); the French, perhaps most accurately, call it a *bande dessinée*, or "drawn strip."[43] The Italian term, *fumetto* (literally "puff of smoke"), refers to the speech balloons, but this term, too, is imprecise. Though it is the predominant method for indicating dialogue, the speech balloon is not a necessary component of the comic strip. For *Tarzan* and later *Prince Valiant*, Hal Foster printed a narrative text with his drawings rather than using balloon dialogue. Carl Anderson's *Henry* was a "silent" strip which used no speech at all.

Comic strip artists have drawn upon many art traditions. The surrealist element of Winsor McCay and George Herriman's strips has already been noted. In the early years especially, occasional strips were drawn by artists who later gained fame as painters. Lyonel Feininger, for example, drew a strip briefly for the *Chicago Tribune* in 1906, sending his work to them from Europe. George Luks, one of the Eight, or Ashcan School, took over drawing the Yellow Kid when Richard Outcault switched publishers.

The tradition of caricature is very strong in comic strip art, especially in the strips of Al Capp and Walt Kelly, who in *Li'l Abner* and *Pogo* lampooned politicans and other notable figures, a tradition carried on today in Garry Trudeau's *Doonesbury*.

Comic strips may also be divided into genres according to their content. Animal strips are typified by *Krazy Kat*, *Felix the Cat*, and *Mickey Mouse*. Most are joke-a-day strips, though the latter, drawn by Floyd Gottfredson, was an adventure continuity narrative from its debut in 1930 to the 1950s when pressure from the distributor King Features forced the artist to switch to a daily joke format. One of the most famous animal strip characters is Pogo, who debuted as a comic book character in 1943 and moved to newspapers in 1948.

Kid strips have been popular since the creation of *The Katzenjammer Kids* in 1897. Percy Crosby's *Skippy*, begun in 1928, influenced later comics kids such as Charlie Brown and Dennis the Menace. Girl strips were particularly popular in the 1920s. Among the best known were Cliff Sterrett's *Polly and Her Pals* (begun in 1912), Martin Branner's *Winnie Winkle* (1920), and Russ Westover's *Tillie the Toiler* (1921).

The adventure strips included crime-fighting narratives such as Chester Gould's *Dick Tracy*, science fiction such as *Flash Gordon* and *Buck Rogers*, and the costumed superheroes whose exploits in comic books were quickly adapted to newspapers and movie screens.

Among the most durable and popular of all comic strip genres is the domestic strip. George McManus's *Bringing Up Father* began in 1913 to chronicle the marital struggles of Maggie and Jiggs. Chic Young's *Blondie*, begun in 1930, remains after half a century one of the most popular strips in the world. Unique among comic strips is *Gasoline Alley*, a domestic strip which uses continuity rather than the joke-a-day more common to the genre. Begun in 1919 by Frank King, taken over by Dick Moores, and drawn now by Jim Scancarelli, *Gasoline Alley* follows real time. Over the past six decades, its characters have aged at the same rate as its readers.

Comic strips have had the greatest flexibility of content and have embraced the widest number of genres. Comic books share many of these genres, with particular emphasis on the costumed superhero. Animated cartoons have been less flexible and have focused, as did the early comic strips, primarily on humor.

Most animated films, that is, those created one frame at a time, employ some form of graphic art, though some, such as puppet films, do not. Cel animation, a method by which the image is drawn on transparent celluloid, is by far the most common technique employed by animators and has been in use since 1914 when the process was patented by Earl Hurd. Other techniques include drawing-on-film, ink-on-glass, silhouette or cutout, and sand animation. The latter uses a layer of sand illuminated from below; light and dark areas are then created by manipulating the depth of the sand. Pinscreen animation, practiced by only a few artists, requires a specially constructed screen filled with hundreds of thousands of pins which may be pulled out or pushed in. Side lighting and the different height of the pins create a shadowy effect not unlike a charcoal drawing which moves.

Cel animation is done either by the straight-ahead method, in which each successive frame carries the action forward, or by the key-pose-and-in-between method, in which the animator sketches first the key poses or extreme positions of the action and an assistant or in-betweener fills in the connecting poses.

Among the most significant animated films of the silent era was Winsor McCay's *Gertie the Dinosaur*, released in 1914. May film histories erroneously list *Gertie* as the first animated cartoon. "With all its impact," says Leonard Maltin, "it might as well have been. Many men who started working in animation during the teens were inspired to do so by this one film. One might say that *Gertie* launched an entire industry"[44]

If *Gertie* launched the animation industry, then Walt Disney steered it through its golden age. Beginning in the late 1920s, the Disney Studio released two influential cartoon series: one was based on Mickey Mouse, Disney's first animated star; the other, called *Silly Symphonies*, relied on music rather than on established characters. Disney's artists created short films that transformed simple gags into well-constructed plots revolving around the personality of the star character. In doing so they elevated two standards of the industry and influenced all animators who came after them. The highly successful *Three Little Pigs*, released in 1933, is an example of personality animation at its best.

In the 1930s and 1940s most of the major Hollywood studios opened animation departments, and their animators strived to imitate the Disney style. MGM with such characters as its popular pair Tom and Jerry, and Warner Brothers with Bugs Bunny, Porky Pig, Tweetie Pie, and Sylvester capitalized on the concept of personality animation and raised it to heights comparable with Disney.

Since the standard length of cartoon shorts was about seven minutes, Disney's feature-length *Snow White* in 1937 was seen as a gamble, but its success paved the way for a succession of now classic, animated Disney features. The Fleischer Studio released the feature-length *Gulliver's Travels* in 1939, but most studios had neither the budget, the talent, nor the inclination to move beyond the short cartoon.

In the mid–1940s the founding of a new studio, United Productions of America (soon shortened to UPA), heralded some stylistic changes. UPA departed from the Disney method, which painstakingly attempted to imitate real animals and movement, and created looser, more carefree graphics. *Time* magazine described the new style as "simple but highly stylized; bold line drawings, understated motion, striking color and airy design in the spirit of modern poster art, caricatured movements and backgrounds as well as figures."[45]

The UPA style would have considerable influence around the world, especially on a group of former newspapermen and cartoonists in Yugoslavia who founded the Zagreb Studio. The Zagreb animators and their counterparts in other European countries such as Poland rejected both the Disney style of anthropomorphism and the concept that cartoons were made for children. The common characteristic of these Zagreb cartoons is a complete absence of dialogue or spoken commentary. The films are usually short, pungent, and satiric explorations of the human condition. They captured worldwide attention in the 1960s, by which time nearly all of the Hollywood studios had closed their animation departments and abandoned the production of short films.

Influenced by UPA and Zagreb, animators in the 1960s turned increasingly to the use of less realistic characters and textured, abstract surfaces instead of meticulously detailed backgrounds. This stylized animation should not be confused with limited animation, a cost-cutting method which reduced the number of drawings per minute and eliminated all unnecessary movement and detail. With limited animation the nuances found in personality animation were lost, and the picture became secondary to the soundtrack.

Since the end of the golden age of animation in the 1950s, innovations in the style and content of animated films have depended increasingly on independent animators or on those working for government-sponsored agencies such as the National Film Board of Canada.

The content and style of animated films, comic strips, and comic books have changed considerably during this century. Among the changes has been the erosion of the boundaries separating them. The most popular characters, for example, frequently appear in more than one of these media. The relationship of these popular graphic arts to motion pictures and the influence each has had on the other has been considerable.

NOTES

1. M. Thomas Inge, "The Comics As Culture," *Journal of Popular Culture* 12, no. 4 (Spring 1979): 631. For additional definitions, see Stephen Becker, *Comic Art in America* (New York: Simon and Schuster, 1959), p. 3; and David Kunzle, *The Early Comic Strip: Narrative Strips and Future Stories in the European Broadsheet from c. 1450 to 1825* (Berkeley: University of California Press, 1973), pp. 1–8.

2. Quoted in Daniel Talbot, ed., *Film: An Anthology* (Berkeley: University of California Press, 1959), p. 17.

3. Earle J. Coleman, "The Funnies, the Movies, and Aesthetics," *Journal of Popular Culture* 18, no. 4 (Spring 1985): 90–91.

4. Quoted in Edward Murray, *Fellini the Artist* (New York: Frederick Ungar, 1976), p. 9.

5. Bill Blackbeard and Martin Williams, eds., *Smithsonian Collection of Newspaper Comics* (Washington, D.C.: Smithsonian Institution Press, 1977), p. 53.

6. Kemp Niver, *The First Twenty Years* (Los Angeles: Locare Research Group, 1968), p. 24.

7. See Jerry Robinson, *The Comics: An Illustrated History of the Comic Strip* (New York: G. P. Putnam's Sons, 1974), p. 19; and Pierre Couperie et al., *A History of the Comic Strip* (New York: Crown, 1968), p. 17.

8. Jack Ellis, *A History of Film*, 2d ed. (Englewood Cliffs, N.J.: Prentice-Hall, 1985), p 22; and James Monaco, *How To Read a Film* (New York: Oxford University Press, 1981), pp. 55–56.

9. Ellis, *A History of Film*, pp. 13–14.

10. Ellis, p. 22.

11. Couperie, p. 9.

12. Kunzie, *The Early Comic Strip*, pp. 6, 4.

13. Becker, *Comic Arts*, p. 10.

14. Leonard Maltin, *Of Mice and Magic: A History of American Animated Cartoons* (New York: New American Library, 1980), pp. 9–12.

15. See appendix A of Cecil Munsey, *Disneyana: Walt Disney Collectibles* (New York: Hawthorn, 1974), pp. 325–27, for a chronology of Disney comic strips.

16. See W. A. Swanberg, *Citizen Hearst* (New York: Bantam, 1971), pp. 89–99, for an account of the Hearst-Pulitzer newspaper war.

17. Becker, *Comic Art*, p. 14.

18. Blackbeard and Williams, *Smithsonian Collection of Newspaper Comics*, p. 330.

19. Rick Marschall, "A History of Newspaper Syndicates," in *World Encyclopedia of Comics*, ed. Maurice Horn, vol. 2 (New York: Chelsea House, 1976), p. 708.

20. Maltin, *Of Mice and Magic*, p. 156.

21. M. Thomas Inge, "A Chronology of the Development of the American Comic Book," in *The Comic Book Price Guide*, ed. Robert Overstreet (New York: Harmony, 1985), p. A–73.

22. Couperie, p. 73.

23. Dick Lupoff and Don Thompson, *All In Color For a Dime* (New Rochelle, N.Y.: Arlington House, 1970), p. 17.

24. Inge, "Chronology," p. A–74.

25. Ron Goulart, *Cheap Thrills: An Informal History of the Pulp Magazines* (New Rochelle, N.Y.: Arlington House, 1972), p. 15.

26. Qutoed in Lupoff and Thompson, *All In Color*, p. 202.

27. Quoted in John Kobal, *Fifty Years of Movie Posters* (New York: Bounty Books, 1973), p. 3.

28. Quoted in Kobal, p. 6.

29. Quoted in Blackbeard and Williams, *Smithsonian Collection of Newspaper Comics*, p. 55.

30. Quoted in Blackbeard and Williams, p. 278.

31. Arthur Asa Berger, "Comics and Culture," *Journal of Popular Culture* 5, no. 1 (Summer 1971): 168–69.

32. Quoted in H. L. Mencken, *The American Language, Supplement I* (New York: Alfred A. Knopf, 1962), p. 373.

33. Mencken, *Supplement I*, p. 333; and H. L. Mencken, *The American Language*, 4th ed. (New York: Alfred A. Knopf, 1965), p. 189.

34. Maltin, *Of Mice and Magic*, pp. 101–102.

35. Inge, "Chronology," p. A–75.

36. Tom Andrae, "The Expurgated Barks," in (Carl Barks, ed.) *Carl Barks Library of Walt Disney's Uncle Scrooge*, (1985) vol. 3 (Scottsdale, Ariz.: Another Rainbow Publishing), p. 522.

37. Benjamin DeMott, "Darkness at the Mall," *Psychology Today* 18, no. 2 (February 1984): 48, 52

38. Judith O'Sullivan, "In Search of Winsor McCay," *AFI [Quarterly] Report* 5, no. 2 (Summer 1974): 7.

39. Quoted in David Wilson, *Projecting Britain: Ealing Studios Film Posters* (London: BFI Publishing, 1982), p. vii.

40. Quoted in introduction to Tadeusz Kowalski, *The Polish Film Poster* (Warsaw: Filmowa Agencja Wydawnicza, 1957), no pagination.

41. Couperie, p. 63.

42. Blackbeard and Williams, *Smithsonian Collection of Newspaper Comics*, p. 16.

43. Kunzle, *The Early Comic Strip*, p. 1.

44. Maltin, *Of Mice and Magic*, p. 5.

45. Quoted in Maltin, p. 324.

SELECTED BIBLIOGRAPHY

The investigation of the relationship between film and the popular graphic arts has been made easier in recent years by a growing body of scholarship covering the fields of animation, poster art, comic strips, and comic books. Several publishers have reprinted early comic strips and comic books, making the task of primary research considerably easier, and many articles on comic art which originally appeared in hard-to-find fanzines have been collected and reprinted.

A useful starting point is M. Thomas Inge's bibliographic essay on "Comic Art," which forms chapter 4 in the *Handbook of American Popular Culture*, volume 1, edited by Inge. His outline of the history and criticism of the field is full of helpful references, and his citations will guide the researcher to the major collections. His bibliography, now slightly dated, includes a section on anthologies and reprints. Since most reprints list the strip creator as author, a researcher would do well to look first under the names of the original artists such as Milt Caniff, Ale Raymond, or Walt Kelly.

In "The Aesthetics of the Comic Strip," one of several essays in a special issue of the *Journal of Popular Culture* (Spring 1979) on "The Comics as Culture," Robert C. Harvey identifies and discusses four elements useful for analyzing comic strips: narrative breakdown, layout, panel composition, and style. Earle J. Coleman's "The Funnies, the Movies, and Aesthetics" is also helpful for its thoughts on methodology and definition. The author explores the aesthetic relationship between film and comic art and calls for an application of traditional art theory to cartoon comic books and strips. In "The Comic Strip and Film Language" Francis Lacassin argues that such "cinematic" techniques as close-ups, medium shots, and high and low angles appeared in comic strips well before the birth of motion pictures.

Two sources which provide the historical precedents for comic art are William Murrell's two-volume *History of American Graphic Humor* and E. H. Gombrich's *Art and Illusion:*

A Study in the Psychology of Pictorial Representation. Gombrich's chapter "The Experiment of Caricature" specifically delineates the ancestry of the comic strip.

John Geipel's *The Cartoon: A Short History of Graphic Comedy and Satire* identifies the comic strip as the slang of graphic art and provides a chronology tracing the cartoon from the fifteenth century through the eighteenth-century masters such as Hogarth, Rowlandson, and Gillray to the 1970s.

A recent addition to the field by the creator of *The Spirit* is Will Eisner's *Comics and Sequential Art*. An outgrowth of his course at New York's School of Visual Arts, the book focuses on the graphic nature of comic art. Additional sources on graphic art are listed in James J. Best's *American Popular Illustrations: A Reference Guide*.

In the 1980s animation has increasingly attracted the attention of film scholars, and an extensive body of useful texts now exists. The logical embarkation point for any voyage into animation literature is Thomas W. Hoffer's *Animation: A Reference Guide*, which expands considerably the material in his bibliographic essay on "Animation" in volume 1 of the *Handbook of American Popular Culture*. Hoffer's historical outline, extensive annotated bibliography, and seven appendices offer the scholar numerous directions to pursue and must be considered essential reading.

An interesting primary source is John Randolph Bray's "Development of the Animated Cartoon." Bray, a pioneer in the history of animation, is not bashful about promoting his own importance, yet his vantage point if not his conclusions makes the piece worth reading.

The best history of early animation is without question Donald Crafton's *Before Mickey: The Animated Film 1898–1928*, a fascinating and meticulously researched examination of the medium's first three decades. Crafton's extensive bibliography is a gateway to further work in this period, which most animation histories treat rather cursorily.

Complementing Crafton's study of the silent era is Leonard Maltin's *Of Mice and Magic: A History of American Animated Cartoons*. This excellent survey, organized by studio, is followed by over one hundred pages of studio filmographies and a glossary. His fifty-page chapter on Disney, for example, is insightful and thorough.

Gerald and Danny Peary's *The American Animated Cartoon: A Critical Anthology*, is a collection of essays, some never before published, organized by studio with emphasis on Disney and Warner Brothers. Highlights include John Canemaker's essays on Winsor McCay and John Bray, Greg Waller's on Disney, and such arcana as Disney's "friendly" testimony before the House Un-American Activities Committee in 1947.

Less helpful histories are Donald Heraldson's *Creators of Life: A History of Animation* and Ralph Stephenson's *Animated Film*. The latter, though marred by errors, is of some value for its emphasis on European animators. John Halas and David Rider's *The Great Movie Cartoon Parade* is an awkwardly oversized paperback, mostly pictorial and of little value to the researcher.

Bruno Edera's *Full Length Animated Films* details the surprisingly large number of feature animations, though one must remember that many of the best animators never worked in the long form. Jeff Lenburg's *The Great Cartoon Directors* covers eight directors including Ub Iwerks, Walter Lantz, Dave Fleischer, and several of the Warner Brothers stalwarts. A bibliography would have been helpful; however, filmographies of the eight are included.

Researchers who wish to explore the effects of World War II on animation will find detailed production credits and plot summaries in Michael Shull and David Wilt's *Doing Their Bit: Wartime American Animated Short Films, 1939–1945*. Richard Shale's *Donald*

Duck Joins Up: The Walt Disney Studio During World War II, a history of that studio's considerable involvement with the U.S. government during the war years, includes several appendices listing Disney's government films and an extensive annotated bibliography.

By far the best animation journal is the regrettably now defunct *Funnyworld: The World of Animated Films and Comic Art*, edited by the knowledgeable Mike Barrier. The twenty-two issues published between October 1966 and April 1981 contain a wealth of information, interviews, and reviews.

The production techniques of animators are explained in Roy Madsen's *Animated Film: Concepts, Methods, Uses*; John Halas and Roger Manvell's *Technique of Film Animation*; and Kit Laybourne's *The Animation Book*. The latter is profusely illustrated and covers alternatives to cel animation such as clay, sand, and computer techniques.

An unusual book which demonstrates clearly the similarities of comic and film art is James Morrow and Murray Suid's *Moviemaking Illustrated: The Comicbook Filmbook*. Panels from Marvel Comics are used to illustrate principles of filmmaking such as camera angles, shot composition, editing, and lighting.

John Canemaker's *The Animated Raggedy Ann and Andy: An Intimate Look at the Art of Animation, Its History, Techniques, and Artists* recounts the making of Richard Williams's less than successful 1977 feature based on Johnny Gruelle's famous characters.

Several books have focused on specific studios. Will Friedwald and Jerry Beck's *Warner Brothers Cartoons* is an extended filmography which provides production credits and plot synopses for the animated films made by that studio between 1929 and 1969.

Leslie Cabarga's *The Fleischer Story* is the only full-length study of the studio which gave us Betty Boop, Popeye, and the animated Superman. Unfortunately, the book has no index or bibliography, and the filmography is impossibly arranged. Many illustrations, photos, and press clippings are reproduced, but the layout is crowded and unappealing. The reader is directed to *Funnyworld* No. 21, which contains a review of Cabarga's book by Michael Dobbs.

Only a few foreign animation studios have received book-length attention. Ron Holloway's *Z Is For Zagreb* introduces the Yugoslavian animators responsible for elevating the Zagreb Studio to worldwide prominence in the 1960s. Two works by Roger Manvell, *The Animated Film, With Pictures from the Film Animal Farm by Halas and Batchelor* and *Art and Animation: The Story of the Halas and Batchelor Animation Studio 1940/ 1980*, offer insights into Britain's most famous animation team. Neither book has much text, though the latter has a bibliography and complete filmography.

There are surprisingly few studies of individual animators. *Tex Avery: King of Cartoons* and *The Walter Lantz Story: With Woody Woodpecker and Friends*, both by Joe Adamson, provide close looks at two major figures in the field. A recent addition by an animator whose career *is* a history of the medium is Shamus Culhane's *Talking Animals and Other People: The Autobiography of One of Animation's Legendary Figures*. Valliere T. Richard's *Normal McLaren, Manipulator of Movement, The National Film Board Years, 1947–1967* is far less helpful. The paragraph-length explanations of McLaren's films are marred by an astounding number of intrusive footnotes which, unfortunately, speak more to the derivative nature of the work than to any depth of research.

Walt Disney is, arguably, the most significant individual in animation history, and, not surprisingly, his studio and the films produced there have attracted considerable interest among film historians. Richard Schickel's *The Disney Version: The Life, Times, Art, and Commerce of Walt Disney* generated much discussion and controversy when published two years after Disney's death. Schickel attempted to debunk some of the mythology

surrounding Disney (much of it studio-generated), but unfortunately the book was riddled
with errors and wrongheadedness. Despite the mistakes and negativism, Schickel provided
considerable insight into American popular culture and compiled a useful bibliography.
An updated version published in 1985 includes a new chapter called "Disney Without
Walt."

Two other books focus on Disney as an individual. Bob Thomas's *Walt Disney: An
American Original* emerged in 1976 as the definitive biography. *Disney's World*, published in 1985 by veteran biographer Leonard Mosley, nicely complements Thomas's
earlier work.

Three works focus on the artistic aspects of the studio. Robert Feild's *Art of Walt
Disney*, published in 1942, was the first serious attempt to define Disney's method and
technique. Christopher Finch's *Art of Walt Disney: From Mickey Mouse to the Magic
Kingdoms* is a large, copiously illustrated volume which includes sections on animation,
live action films, and the two theme parks. By far the most impressive and detailed
account of the studio's method is *Disney Animation: The Illusion of Life* by Frank Thomas
and Ollie Johnston. The authors, two of Disney's "Nine Old Men," are veteran animators
who worked on every important animated feature from *Snow White* (1937) until their
retirement in 1978. The very substantial text and stunning illustrations provide a complete
education in personality animation.

Leonard Maltin's *The Disney Films* is the best source of information on the individual
features. The first edition devoted a two- to three-page essay to each film produced by
the studio during Walt's lifetime. However, the updated edition, which carries the study
from 1967 through *Splash* (1984), reduces this treatment to credits and a one- or two-
sentence plot summary.

Music has been an important part of Disney films since the days of *Steamboat Willie*.
A detailed case study of how a musical soundtrack is constructed is Ross B. Care's
"Threads of Melody: The Evolution of a Major Film Score—Walt Disney's *Bambi*."

Essential reading for anyone who strongly imagines that the Disney Studio was interested only in making films is Cecil Munsey's *Disneyana: Walt Disney Collectibles*. This
history of Disney character merchandising is particularly useful in tracing the relationship
between films and the comic strips and books spun from them.

Disney's most famous characters form their own library. David Bain and Bruce Harris'
Mickey Mouse: Fifty Happy Years, Marcia Blitz's *Donald Duck*, and *Walt Disney's
Donald Duck: Fifty Happy Years of Frustration* are largely pictorial and nonscholarly
yet often contain nuggets of interest and should not be overlooked. Blitz's book, for
example, is suprisingly informative.

The increased interest in popular culture in the last two decades which has fueled
scholarly interest in film has also led to several significant histories and general reference
works on comic art. Comic strips have received far more scholarly attention than comic
books, perhaps because the latter are a newer field and are perceived to be aimed exclusively toward children.

The history of the comic strip, or "pre-history" to use the author's term, is covered
in detail in David Kunzle's *The Early Comic Strip: Narrative Strips and Picture Stories
in the European Broadsheet from c. 1450 to 1825*. As the subtitle indicates, this first of
a proposed two volumes stops well before the emergence of the comic strip as we know
it today. Particular significance is placed on the English artist William Hogarth, whom
the author calls by far the most important figure for the four centuries covered by the

book. Kunzle's eight-page introduction is particularly recommended for its attempt to define the comic strip and address the concerns of its historians.

The seminal work in the comic strip genre is Martin Sheridan's *Comics and Their Creators*, first published in 1942. Biographical sketches of strip artists make this history especially valuable. Coulton Waugh's *The Comics* followed in 1947. The author, a former strip artist whose eye trouble forced him to quit the profession, focuses primarily on comic strips and devotes only the final chapter to comic books.

Stephen Becker's *Comic Art in America*, which appeared in 1959, is a broad history of the medium, covering, as a subtitle indicates, "the Social History of the Funnies, the Political Cartoons, Magazine Humor, Sporting Cartoons, and Animated Cartoons." Though some depth is sacrificed to gain this breadth, Becker's study is still essential reading.

Another comprehensive, essential book is *A History of the Comic Strip*, co-authored by Pierre Couperie, Maurice Horn, and several others. Unlike Becker's study, this volume offers an international perspective.

The early 1970s saw a marked increase in comic strip literature. Judith O'Sullivan's *The Art of the Comic Strip* is a catalog for a 1971 art exhibit, which, despite its relatively short length, include a useful text and thirty-five pages of biographies of strip artists which nicely complement and update the profiles found in Martin Sheridan's earlier work.

The Steranko History of Comics is a multivolume project which focuses on the costumed superheroes. Volume 1 covers Superman, Batman, Captain America, and others, while volume 2 covers Captain Marvel. Four additional volumes are proposed. James Steranko, himself a comic artist, cites the influence of the pulp magazines on the origin of the costumed superhero. The text is substantial, but a researcher would be far better served had the volumes included an index and a table of contents.

Two prominent strip artists who have made substantial contributions to the field are Jerry Robinson, creator of *still life* and *Flubs & Fluffs*, and Mort Walker, creator of *Beetle Bailey*. Robinson's *The Comics: An Illustrated History of Comic Strip Art* offers in addition to the readable text and reprints, over a dozen brief essays by prominent artists such as Milt Caniff, Hal Foster, Chic Young, and Walt Kelly. Laced with anecdotes, Walker's *Backstage at the Strips* is a fascinating account of the craft and behind-the-scenes work of a cartoonist.

Any understanding of the history of the comic strip depends upon a grasp of the origins and workings of the newspaper syndicates. Two concise explanations are Boyd Lewis's "The Syndicates and How They Grew" and Richard Marschall's "A History of Newspaper Syndicates."

Horn's contributions to comic art literature could fill a small bookshelf. The two-volume *World Encyclopedia of Comics* contains nearly nine hundred pages of alphabetical entries covering artists and characters, six appendices, seven indexes, several essays, and a world chronology of comic art which runs from 1734 to the present. Horn has also edited the *World Encyclopedia of Cartoons*, which follows a similar format. Its almost eight hundred pages include five appendices and five indexes.

Horn's *Seventy-Five Years of the Comics*, a catalog from a 1971 exhibit at the New York Cultural Center, is mostly reprints, though the sixteen pages of text offer a condensed overview of the comic art. More specialized is Horn's *Comics of the American West*, in which he explores how comic books and strips have contributed to the mythology of the west.

For references to comic art literature in other countries, see Wolfgang Kempkes's

International Bibliography of Comics Literature. The citations, printed in both English and German, are arranged first by category such as technical aspects or readership, and then by country within each category.

Social and cultural historians have contributed many essays on comic art. *The Seven Lively Arts*, a collection of essays by Gilbert Seldes, an early champion of popular culture, contains "The 'Vulgar' Comic Strip" and "The Krazy Kat That Walks By Himself," both written in 1924.

Film scholars who are accustomed to turning to Robert Warshow for his classic essays on Westerns and gangster films may recall that Warshow also wrote on the comics, "Woofed With Dreams," a 1946 essay on Krazy Kat, and "Paul, the Horror Comics, and Dr. Wertham," a 1954 piece on his eleven-year-old son's fascination with EC Comics, are both collected in *The Immediate Experience.*

Two additional collections are *The Funnies: An American Idiom*, edited by David Manning White and Robert H. Abel, and *The Comic-Stripped American* by Arthur Asa Berger. Berger contends that "Comics must always be studied in conjunction with history" (p. 14.) and subtitles his book "What Dick Tracy, Blondie, Daddy Warbucks, and Charlie Brown Tell Us About Ourselves." An earlier, condensed version of Berger's observations may be found in his essay "Comics and Culture," which introduces a special in-depth section on comics in the Summer 1971 *Journal of Popular Culture.*

The greatest difficulty faced by historians of comic art is accessiblity to the original work. Happily for the scholar, public interest in nostalgia has prompted many publishers to issue collections of the better known strips. *The Hyperion Library of Classic American Comic Strips*, edited by Bill Blackbeard, offers, for example, twenty-two volumes of some of the earliest and most significant daily and Sunday strips such as Cliff Sterrett's *Polly and Her Pals*, Harry Hershfield's *Abie the Agent*, and Ed Wheelan's *Minute Movies.* The definitive study of this artist is Mike Barrier's *Carl Barks and the Art of the Comic Book*, one of the few books devoted to a single comic book artist.

The Smithsonian Collection of Newspaper Comics, edited by Bill Blackbeard and Martin Williams, also reproduces, often in color, many of the classic early strips. See " 'The Family Upstairs' Moves Back In" for Mike Barrier's review of this collection. Barrier later co-edited with Williams a companion volume *A Smithsonian Book of Comic-Book Comics*, which reproduces thirty-two complete stories, among them the first appearances of Superman, Batman, and Pogo.

Most books on specific strip characters are largely pictorial and nonscholarly, yet they should not be discounted as source material. If the strip has been popular enough to warrant a collection, the character has likely appeared in comic book or film form as well. As a rule, these collections include the characters' first appearances.

Dean Young (son of creator Chic Young) and Rick Marschall's *Blondie and Dagwood's America* is typical of the genre and consists of reprints. The bibliography includes a list of Blondie comics, children's books, radio and television shows, and a filmography of the Blondie movies which ran from 1938 to 1950. For more on the Bumstead family's screen career, see Judith Cornes's "Living With Father: Remembering the Blondie Films."

Among the more impressive of these reprinted collections is Jerry Robinson's *Skippy and Percy Crosby*. Crosby's strip ran from 1925 to 1945 and exerted, says Robinson, a greater influence than any other strip of its genre. The author combines a biography of Crosby with a text which argues that Skippy was the prototype for Dennis the Menace and Charlie Brown.

Two of the most popular strips to emerge since World War II are *Pogo* and *Peanuts*, and both have spawned much commentary and several volumes of reprints. The origin and development of Pogo are best discovered in Walt Kelly's *Ten Ever-Lovin' Blue-Eyed Years With Pogo 1949–1959*.

The Graphic Art of Charles Schulz, a 1985 museum catalog, includes panel reprints, a discourse on the artistic quality of Schulz's drawing, and several appreciative essays by such authors as Bill Mauldin, M. Thomas Inge, Umberto Eco.

Burne Hogarth's *Tarzan of the Apes* falls into a different category in that the drawings which make up the book are not reprints but new art. Hogarth, one of the medium's most technically gifted artists, drew the *Tarzan* strip from 1937, when he replaced Hal Foster, to 1950. Accompanying the new art is a lengthy and instructive essay, "The Magic of Burne Hogarth" by Maurice Horn. Thomas A. Pendleton's "Tarzan of the Papers," divides Hogarth's work into three periods and offers a detailed comparison of Hogarth's and Foster's interpretation of the character.

Other scholarly treatments of individual comic strip artists include Thomas W. Hoffer's "From Comic Strips to Animation: Some Perspectives on Winsor McCay" and Judith O'Sullivan's "In Search of Winsor McCay" from the *AFI [Quarterly] Report*'s Summer 1974 special issue on animation. Laurence E. Mintz's excellent essay "Fantasy, Formula, Realism, and Propaganda in Milton Caniff's Comic Strips" thoroughly examines the work of one of the medium's true masters and is a model of comic art scholarship.

Arthur Asa Berger's *Li'l Abner: A Study in American Satire*, published in 1970, was the first book-length study devoted to a single comic strip character. Recently published are *Krazy Kat: The Art of George Herriman* by Patrick McDonnell et al. and *Krazy Kat's Kreator: A Biography of George Herriman* by Bill Blackbeard and Rick Marschall.

The first book devoted to comic book (as opposed to comic strip) characters was Jules Feiffer's *The Great Comic Book Heroes*, published in 1965. The adventures of thirteen costumed superheroes including Superman, Batman, Wonder Woman, and Captain Marvel are reprinted and supplemented with about fifty pages of text. Les Daniels's *Comix: A History of Comic Books in America* followed six years later and also consisted mainly of reprints. The thoughtfully organized text identifies turning points in the medium's history and concludes with a chapter on underground comics.

The evolution of comic book content is perceptively examined in Clinton R. Sanders's "Icons of the Alternate Culture: The Themes and Functions of Underground Comix"; Max J. and Joey Skidmore's "More Than Mere Fantasy: Political Themes in Contemporary Comic Books"; Benjamin DeMott's "Darkness at the Mall."

Reference works on comic books, in addition to Maurice Horn's *World Encyclopedia of Comics* mentioned earlier, include *Crawford's Encyclopedia of Comic Books*, which carries a chronology of comic art development and an index, and Michael L. Fleisher's *Encyclopedia of Comic Book Heroes*, an eight-volume set which examines the same costumed superheroes covered by Jules Feiffer.

Particularly useful is Robert M. Overstreet's *Comic Book Price Guide*, which is updated yearly (the 1985–1986 volume is the fifteenth edition) to provide price guidelines for collectors. The book is of considerable value to researchers for its alphabetical listing of all comics and for essays such as M. Thomas Inge's "A Chronology of the Development of the American Comic Book."

Dick Lupoff and Don Thompson have edited two separate anthologies of comic book literature. Lupoff's *All In Color For a Dime* appeared in 1970 and included eleven essays;

Thompson's *The Comic-Book Book* followed four years later. Both volumes are recommended.

Marvel Comics have received extensive coverage in Stan Lee's *Origins' of Marvel Comics* and *Son of Origins of Marvel Comics*. Both books are mostly reprints. The former covers such Marvel creations as the Fantastic Four, Spider Man, and Thor; the latter examines, among others, X-Men and the Silver Surfer.

Much more useful because it is primarily text rather than reprinted comic material is Will Jacobs and Gerald Jones's *The Comic Book Heroes: From the Silver Age to the Present*. The authors focus on Marvel and DC Comics and detail the history of comics from 1956 through the mid–1970s slump to their resurgence in the 1980s.

Denis Gifford's *Happy Days: One Hundred Years of Comics* is not about comics as we usually define them but is a collection of covers of British comic magazines. The century to which the title refers is 1874, when James Henderson's *Funny Folks* first appeared, to 1974.

Comic book characters who have been accorded book-length coverage are, as one might expect, the superheroes whose exploits have been recorded in several media. *The Collected Works of Buck Rogers in the 25th Century*, edited by Robert C. Dille (son of syndicate head John F. Dille, who was instrumental in creating the strip), includes, in addition to many reprints, the script of the first Buck Rogers radio broadcast and an explanation of the various Sunday page formats to which artists must adapt their strips.

Nelson Bridwell, an editor for DC Comics, has published *Batman: From the Thirties to the Seventies* and *Superman: From the Thirties to the Eighties*. The Batman volume is superior, though neither is particularly useful to scholars. A better book on the man from Krypton is Gary Grossman's *Superman: Serial to Cereal*.

The movie serials, which form such a significant convergence of film and comic art, are examined in two volumes: Jim Harmon and Donald Glut's *The Great Movie Serials: Their Sound and Fury* and Raymond William Stedman's *The Serials: Suspense and Drama by Installment*. The latter is larger by almost two hundred pages and includes an extensive bibliography which the Harmon and Glut study lacks. Stedman includes radio and television serials as well as movies, and this expanded scope is welcome since many of the newspaper chains which originated comic strips also owned radio stations and adapted the strip characters to radio serials.

Roy Kinnaird's *Fifty Years of Serial Thrills* indexes every film serial made between 1912 and 1956—over five hundred titles in all. More than half date from the silent era, and of these fewer than two dozen survive Chris Steinbrunner's "The Four-Panelled, Sock-Bang-Powie Saturday Afternoon Screen," found in Lupoff and Thompson's *All In Color For a Dime*, offers yet another look at movie serials.

Movie posters differ considerably in form, content, and purpose from comic books and strips, but they nonethless form a category of popular graphic expression which, like comic art, shares a symbiotic relationship with film. The most thorough treatment of the subject is Gregory Edwards's *The International Film Poster*, which offers a useful and substantial text, beautiful color reproductions, an index, and a bibliography.

The Movie Poster Book, by Stephen Schapiro and David Chierichetti, lacks an index or bibliography and has a very short text, but the excellent color reproductions make the volume worth examining. A similar treatment is John Kobal's *Fifty Years of Movie Posters*, which has a fine introduction by film historian David Robinson. Kobal has also co-edited with V. A. Wilson *Foyer Pleasure: The Golden Age of Cinema Lobby Cards*.

Foreign poster artists have also received attention from the historians. *The Polish Film*

Poster by Tadeusz Kowalski includes a brief introduction by Polish animator Jan Lenica. Mildred Constantine and Alan Fern's *Revolutionary Soviet Film Posters* reproduces over seventy examples including many from non-Soviet films such as Stroheim's *Foolish Wives* and Keaton's *Sherlock Jr.* David Wilson's *Projecting Britain: Ealing Studios Film Posters* gathers samples of poster art commissioned by the studio famous for its charming comedies.

Recent additions to the genre include *Movie Posters: The Paintings of Batiste Madalena* and "Film in a Frame," a brief pictorial essay in the November 1985 *American Film* which reproduces the artwork of the French poster artist Jean Mercier, who began designing for film in 1924.

While movie posters often achieve respect as works of art, other forms of motion picture publicity, such as newspapers ads, stress the more utilitarian nature of graphic design. At least three books are devoted to this commercial aspect of movie advertising. *Movie Gallery: A Pictorial History of Motion Picture Advertisements . . . Great Movies, Great Stars 1920–1970s*, apparently self-published by Emil Noah, Jr., has no text but simply black-and-white reproductions of ads crammed onto each page. A similar approach is used in Malcolm Vance's *The Movie Ad Book*, which has a minimal two pages of text in each of a dozen chapters. A far better treatment is *Those Great Movie Ads* by Joe Morella, Edward Z. Epstein, and Eleanor Clark. The authors divide advertisements into "genres" such as logos, schmeer ads, and "the director-as-star." In the midst of the somewhat cluttered black-and-white reproductions is an eleven-page essay on "A Brief Look at Movie Advertising."

Books and Authors

Abbot, Lawrence L. "Comic Art: Characteristics and Potentialities of a Narrative Medium." *Journal of Popular Culture* 19, no. 4 (Spring 1986): 155–76.

Adams, John Paul and Rick Marschall. *Milton Caniff: Rembrandt of the Comic Strip.* Endicott, N.Y.: Flying Buttress Publications, 1981. 62 pp.

Adamson, Joe. *Tex Avery: King of Cartoons.* New York: Popular Library, 1975. 237 pp.; bibliog.

———. *The Walter Lantz Story: With Woody Woodpecker and Friends.* New York: G. P. Putnam's Sons, 1985. 240 pp.

AFI [Quarterly] Report 5, no. 3 (Summer 1974). Special issue on animation.

Andrae, Tom. "Moved By the Spirit." *Funnyworld* No. 21 (Fall 1979): 20–27.

Bain, David and Bruce Harris. *Mickey Mouse: Fifty Happy Years.* New York: Harmony, 1977. 255 pp.; bibliog.

Barrier, Mike. *Carl Barks and the Art of the Comic Book.* New York: M. Lilien, 1981. 227 pp.; bibliog.

———. " 'The Family Upstairs' Moves Back In." *Funnyworld* No. 19 (Fall 1978): 45–48.

Barrier, Michael and Martin Williams, eds. *A Smithsonian Book of Comic-Book Comics.* Washington, D.C.: Smithsonian Institution Press; New York: Harry N. Abrams, 1981. 336 pp.; bibliog.

Becker, Stephen. *Comic Art in America.* New York: Simon and Schuster, 1959. 387 pp.; indexed.

Berger, Arthur Asa. "Comics and Culture." *Journal of Popular Culture* 5, no. 1 (Summer 1971): 164–78.

————. *The Comic-Stripped American*. New York: Walker and Company, 1973. 225 pp.

————. *Li'l Abner: A Study in American Satire*. New York: Twayne, 1970. 191 pp.; indexed, bibliog.

Best, James J. *American Popular Illustrations: A Reference Guide*. Westport, Conn.: Greenwood Press, 1984.

Blackbeard, Bill, ed. *The Hyperion Library of Classic American Comic Strips*. 22 vols. Westport, Conn.: Hyperion Press, 1977.

————. *Krazy Kats and Gibson Girls: A Bibliography of American Comic Art in the Twentieth Century*. New York: Garland, 1984.

Blackbeard, Bill and Rick Marschall. *Krazy Kat's Kreator: A Biography of George Herriman*. New York: Holt, Rinehart and Winston, 1985.

Blackbeard, Bill and Martin Williams, eds. *Smithsonian Collection of Newspaper Comics*. Washington, D.C.: Smithsonian Institution Press; New York: Harry N. Abrams, 1977. 336 pp.; indexed, bibliog.

Blitz, Marcia. *Donald Duck*. New York: Harmony, 1979. 256 pp.; bibliog.

Bray, John Randolph. "Development of the Animated Cartoon." *Moving Picture World* 21 July 1917: 3–7.

Bridwell, Nelson. *Batman: From the Thirties to the Seventies*. New York: Bonanza Books, 1971. 388 pp.

————. *Superman: From the Thirties to the Eighties*. New York: Crown, 1983. 384 pp.

Cabarga, Leslie. *The Fleischer Story*. New York: Nostalgia Press, 1976. 183 pp.

Canemaker, John. *The Animated Raggedy Ann and Andy: An Intimate Look at the Art of Animation, Its History, Techniques, and Artists*. Indianapolis: Bobbs-Merrill, 1977. 292 pp.; indexed, bibliog.

————. "Elfriede! On the Road With Mrs. Oskar Fischinger." *Funnyworld* No. 18 (Summer 1978): 4–14.

Care, Ross B. "Threads of Melody: The Evolution of a Major Film Score—Walt Disney's *Bambi*." In *Wonderful Inventions: Motion Pictures, Broadcasting, and Recorded Sound at the Library of Congress*. Ed. Iris Newsom. Washington, D.C.: Library of Congress, 1985: 80–115.

Chute, David. "The Great Frame Robbery." *Film Comment* 18, no. 5, September-October 1982: 13–17.

————. "Keeping Up With the Jones." *Film Comment* 21, no. 6, December 1985: 14–15.

Coleman, Earle J. "The Funnies, the Movies, and Aesthetics." *Journal of Popular Culture* 18, no. 4 (Spring 1985): 89–100.

Constantine, Mildred and Alan Fern. *Revolutionary Soviet Film Posters*. Baltimore: Johns Hopkins University Press, 1974. 97 pp.; indexed, bibliog.

Corliss, Richard. "Warnervana." *Film Comment* 21, no 6, December 1985: 11–13, 16–19.

Cornes, Judith. "Living With Father: Remembering the Blondie Films." *American Classic Screen* 6, no. 1 (1982): 25–28.

Couperie, Pierre, Maurice Horn, et al. *A History of the Comic Strip*. Trans. Eileen B Hennessey. New York: Crown, 1968. 256 pp.; indexed.

Crafton, Donald. *Before Mickey: The Animated Film 1898–1928*. Cambridge, Mass.: MIT Press, 1982. 413 pp.; indexed, bibliog.

Crawford, Hubert H. *Crawford's Encyclopedia of Comic Books*. Middle Village, N.Y.: Jonathan David, 1978. 438 pp.; indexed.

Culhane, Shamus. *Talking Animals and Other People: The Autobiography of One of Animation's Legendary Figures*. New York: St. Martin's Press, 1986. 379 pp.; indexed, bibliog.

Daniels, Les. *Comix: A History of Comic Books in America*. New York: Outerbridge and Dienstfrey, 1971. 198 pp.; indexed, bibliog.

DeMott, Benjamin. "Darkness at the Mall." *Psychology Today* 18, no. 2 (February 1984): 48–52.

Dille, Robert C., ed. *The Collected Works of Buck Rogers in the 25th Century*. New York: A & W Publishers, 1977. 288 pp.

Edera, Bruno. *Full Length Animated Feature Films*. New York: Hastings House, 1977. 196 pp.; indexed, bibliog.

Edwards, Gregory. *The International Film Poster*. Salem, N.H.: Salem House, 1985. 224 pp.; indexed, bibliog.

Eisner, Will. *Comics and Sequential Art*. Tamarac, Fla.: Poorhouse Press, 1985. 154 pp.; indexed.

Feiffer, Jules. *The Great Comic Book Heroes*. New York: Bonanza Books, 1965. 189 pp.

Feild, Robert. *The Art of Walt Disney*. New York: Macmillan, 1942. 290 pp.; indexed.

"Film in a Frame." *American Film* XI, no. 2, November 1985: 39–41.

Finch, Christopher. *The Art of Walt Disney: From Mickey Mouse to the Magic Kingdoms*. New York: Harry N. Abrams, 1973. 458 pp.; indexed.

Fleisher, Michael L. *Encyclopedia of Comic Book Heroes*. 8 vols. New York: Collier, 1976.

Friedwald, Will and Jerry Beck. *Warner Brothers Cartoons*. Metuchen, N.J.: Scarecrow Press, 1981. 271 pp.; indexed.

Funnyworld: The World of Animated Films and Comic Art. Ed. Mike Barrier. No. 1 (October 1966) to No. 22 (April 1981).

Geipel, John. *The Cartoon: A Short History of Graphic Comedy and Satire*. New York: A. S. Barnes, 1972. 185 pp.; bibliog.

Gifford, Denis. *Happy Days: One Hundred Years of Comics*. London: Jupiter Books, 1975. 128 pp.; bibliog.

Gombrich, E. H. *Art and Illusion: A Study In the Psychology of Pictorial Representation*. New York: Pantheon Books, 1961. 466 pp.; indexed bibliog.

Goulart, Ron. *The Adventurous Decade*. New Rochelle, N.Y.: Arlington House, 1975. 224 pp.; indexed.

———. *The Great Comic Book Artists*. New York: St. Martin's Press, 1986. 144.

The Graphic Art of Charles Schulz. Oakland, Calif.: Oakland Museum, 1985. 128 pp.; bibliog.

Grossman, Gary. *Superman: Serial to Cereal*. New York: Popular Library, 1976. 188 pp.

Halas, John and Roger Manvell. *The Technique of Film Animation*. New York: Hastings House, 1973. 360pp.; indexed, bibliog.

Halas, John and David Rider. *The Great Movie Cartoon Parade*. New York: Bounty Books, 1976. 120 pp.; indexed.

Harmon, Jim and Donald Glut. *The Great Movie Serials: Their Sound and Fury*. Garden City, N.Y.: Doubleday, 1972. 384 pp.; indexed.

Harrison, Randall. *The Cartoon: Communication to the Quick*. Beverly Hills, Calif.: Sage Publications, 1981. 151 pp.; indexed, bibliog.

Harvey, Robert C. "The Aesthetics of the Comic Strip." *Journal of Popular Culture* 12, no. 4 (Spring 1979): 640–52.

Heraldson, Donald. *Creators of Life: A History of Animation*. New York: Drake, 1975. 298 pp.; bibliog.

Hoffer, Thomas W. *Animation: A Reference Guide*. Westport, Conn.: Greenwood Press, 1981. 385 pp.; indexed, bibliog.

————. "From Comic Strips to Animation: Some Perspectives on Winsor McCay" *Journal of the University Film Association* 28, no. 2 (Spring 1976): 23–32.

Hogarth, Burne. *Tarzan of the Apes*. New York: Watson-Guptill, 1972. 154 pp.

Holloway, Ron. *Z Is For Zagreb*. South Brunswick, N.J.: A. S. Barnes, 1972. 127 pp.; indexed.

Horn, Maurice. *Comics of the American West*. New York: Winchester Press, 1977. 224 pp.; indexed, bibliog.

————. *Seventy-Five Years of the Comics*. Boston: Boston Book and Art, 1971. 109 pp.; bibliog.

————, ed. *World Encyclopedia of Cartoons*. 2 vols. New York: Gale Research, 1980. 787 pp.; indexed, bibliog.

————, ed. *World Encyclopedia of Comics*. 2 vols. New York: Chelsea House, 1976. 898 pp.; indexed, bibliog.

Inge, M. Thomas. "A Chronology of the Development of the American Comic Book." *The Comic Book Price Guide*. Ed. Robert M. Overstreet. 15th ed. New York: Harmony, 1985. A–73–A–75.

————. "Comic Art." *Handbook of American Popular Culture*. Ed. M. Thomas Inge. 3 vols. Westport, Conn.: Greenwood Press, 1979–1981. 1: 77–102.

Jacobs, Will and Gerald Jones. *The Comic Book Heroes: From the Silver Age to the Present*. New York: Crown, 1985. 292 pp.; indexed.

Kelly, Walt. *Ten Ever-Lovin' Blue-Eyed Years with Pogo 1949–59*. New York: Simon and Schuster, 1959. 288 pp.

Kempkes, Wolfgang. *International Bibliography of Comics Literature*. New York: R. R. Bowker, 1971. 213 pp.; indexed.

Kinnaird, Roy. *Fifty Years of Serial Thrills*. Metuchen, N.J.: Scarecrow Press, 1983. 210 pp.; indexed.

Knight, Arthur. "UPA, Magoo, and McBoing Boing." *Art Digest* 26 (1 February 1952): 22.

Kobal, John. *Fifty Years of Movie Posters*. New York: Bounty Books, 1973. 175 pp.

Kobal, John and V. A. Wilson. *Foyer Pleasure: The Golden Age of Cinema Lobby Cards*. New York: Delilah Communications, 1983. 158 pp.

Kowalski, Tadeusz. *The Polish Film Poster*. Warsaw: Filmowa Agencja Wydawnicza, 1957. 141 pp.

Kunzle, David. *The Early Comic Strip: Narrative Strips and Picture Stories in the European Broadsheet from c. 1450 to 1825*. Berkeley: University of California Press, 1973. 471 pp.; indexed, bibliog.

Lacassin, Francis. "The Comic Strip and Film Language." Trans. David Kunzle. *Film Quarterly* 26, no. 1 (Fall 1972): 11–23.

Laybourne, Kit. *The Animation Book*. New York: Crown, 1979. 272 pp.; indexed, bibliog.

Lee, Stan. *Origins of Marvel Comics*. New York: Simon and Schuster, 1974. 254 pp.

————. *Son of Origins of Marvel Comics*. New York: Simon and Schuster, 1975. 249 pp.

Lenburg, Jeff. *The Great Cartoon Directors*. Jefferson, N.C.: McFarland, 1983. 147 pp.; indexed.

Lewis, Boyd. "The Syndicates and How They Grew." *Saturday Review* 11 December 1971: 67–69.

Lupoff, Dick and Don Thompson, eds. *All In Color For a Dime*. New Rochelle, N.Y.: Arlington House, 1970. 263 pp.

McDonnell, Patrick, et al. *Krazy Kat: The Art of George Herriman*. New York: Harry N. Abrams, 1986. 624 pp.

McLuhan, Marshall. *Understanding Media*. New York: McGraw-Hill, 1964. 359 pp.

Madsen, Roy. *Animated Film: Concepts, Methods, Uses*. New York: Interland, 1969. 234 pp.; indexed bibliog.

————. *Of Mice and Magic: A History of American Animated Cartoons*. New York: New American Library, 1980. 470 pp.; indexed.

Manvell, Roger. *The Animated Film: With Pictures from the Film Animal Farm by Halas and Batchelor*. London: Sylvan Press, 1954. 63 pp.

————. *Art and Animation: The Story of the Halas and Batchelor Animation Studio 1940/1980*. New York: Hastings House, 1980. No pagination; bibliog.

Marschall, Richard. "A History of Newspaper Syndicates." *World Encyclopedia of Comics*. Ed. Maurice Horn. 2 vols. New York: Chelsea House, 1976. 2: 721–27.

Mintz, Laurence E. "Fantasy, Formula, Realism, and Propaganda in Milton Caniff's Comic Strips." *Journal of Popular Culture* 12, no. 4 (Spring 1979): 653–80.

Morella, Joe, Edward Z. Epstein, and Eleanor Clark. *Those Great Movie Ads*. New York: Garland Books, 1972. 320 pp.

Morrow, James and Murray Suid. *Moviemaking Illustrated: The Comicbook Filmbook*. Rochelle Park, N.J.: Hayden, 1973. 150 pp.; indexed.

Mosley, Leonard. *Disney's World*. New York: Stein and Day, 1985. 330 pp.; indexed.

Movie Posters: The Paintings of Batiste Madalena. Intro. Judith Katten. New York: Harry N. Abrams, 1985. 64 pp.

Munsey, Cecil. *Disneyana: Walt Disney Collectibles*. New York: Hawthorn, 1974. 385 pp.; indexed.

Murrell, William. *A History of American Graphic Humor, vol. 2: 1865–1938*. New York: Macmillan, 1938. 271 pp.; indexed, bibliog.

Noah, Emil, Jr. *Movie Gallery: A Pictorial History of Motion Picture Advertisements . . . Great Movies, Great Stars 1920–1970s*. Fort Lauderdale, Fla.: Noah Communications, 1980. 384 pp.

O'Brien, Richard. *The Golden Age of the Comic Book 1937–1945*. New York: Ballantine, 1977. 231 pp.; bibliog.

O'Sullivan, Judith. *The Art of the Comic Strip*. College Park: University of Maryland Department of Art, 1971. 95 pp.; bibliog.

————. "In Search of Winsor McCay." *AFI [Quarterly] Report* 5, no. 2 (Summer 1974): 4–9.

Overstreet, Robert M., ed. *The Comic Book Price Guide*. 15th ed. New York: Harmony, 1985. 448 pp.

Peary, Gerald and Danny Peary, eds. *The American Animated Cartoon: A Critical Anthology*. New York: E. P. Dutton, 1980. 310 pp.; indexed, bibliog.

Pendleton, Thomas A. "Tarzan of the Papers." *Journal of Popular Culture* 12, no. 4 (Spring 1979): 691–701.

Reitberger, Reinhold and Wolfgang Fuchs. *Comics: Anatomy of a Mass Medium.* Trans. Nadia Fowler. Boston: Little, Brown, 1972. 264 pp.

Richard, Valliere T. *Norman McLaren, Manipulator of Movement, The National Film Board Years, 1947–1967.* Toronto: Associated University Presses, 1982. 128 pp.; indexed, bibliog.

Robinson, Jerry. *The Comics: An Illustrated History of Comic Strip Art.* New York: G. P. Putnam's Sons, 1974. 256 pp.; indexed.

———. *Skippy and Percy Crosby.* New York: Holt, Rinehart and Winston, 1978. 155 pp.

Sanders, Clinton R. "Icons of the Alternate Culture: The Themes and Functions of Underground Comix." *Journal of Popular Culture* 8, no. 4 (Spring 1975): 836–52.

Schapiro, Stephen and David Chierichetti. *The Movie Poster Book.* New York: E. P. Dutton, 1979. 95 pp.

Schickel, Richard. *The Disney Version: The Life, Times, Art, and Commerce of Walt Disney.* rev. ed. New York: Simon and Schuster, 1985. 449 pp.; indexed, bibliog.

Seldes, Gilbert. *The Seven Lively Arts.* New York: A. S. Barnes, 1962. 306 pp.

Selling Dreams: British and American Film Posters 1890–1976. N.p.: Welsh Arts Council, n.d. 84 pp.

Shale, Richard. *Donald Duck Joins Up: The Walt Disney Studio During World War II.* Ann Arbor, Mich.: UMI Research Press, 1982. 185 pp.: indexed, bibliog.

Sheridan, Martin. *Comics and Their Creators.* Boston: Robert T. Hale, 1942. 304 pp.; indexed.

Shull, Michael and David Wilt. *Doing Their Bit: Wartime American Animated Short Films, 1939–1945.* Jefferson, N.C.: McFarland, 1986.

Skidmore, Max J. and Joey Skidmore. "More Than Mere Fantasy: Political Themes in Contemporary Comic Books." *Journal of Popular Culture* 17, no. 1 (Summer 1983): 83–92.

Smith, Conrad. "The Early History of Animation: Saturday Morning TV Discovers 1915." *Journal of the University Film Association* 29, no. 3 (Summer 1977): 23–30.

Stedman, Raymond William. *The Serials: Suspense and Drama by Installment.* 2d ed. Norman: University of Oklahoma Press, 1977. 574 pp.; indexed, bibliog.

Stephenson, Ralph. *Animated Film.* New York: A. S. Barnes, 1973. 206 pp.; indexed, bibliog.

Steranko, James. *The Steranko History of Comics.* 2 vols. Reading, Penn.: Supergraphics, 1972.

Theisen, Earl. "History of the Animated Cartoon." *Journal of the Society of Motion Picture Engineers* 29, no. 3 (September 1933): 239–49.

Thomas, Bob. *Walt Disney: An American Original.* New York: Simon and Schuster, 1976. 379 pp.; indexed.

Thomas, Frank and Ollie Johnston. *Disney Animation: The Illusion of Life.* New York: Abbeville Press, 1981. 575 pp.; indexed.

Thompson, Don and Dick Lupoff, eds. *The Comic-Book Book.* New Rochelle, N.Y.: Arlington House, 1974. 360 pp.

Vance, Malcolm. *The Movie Ad Book*. Minneapolis: Control Data Publishing, 1981. 160 pp.; indexed.

Walker, Mort. *Backstage at the Strips*. New York: Mason/Charter, 1975. 311 pp.; indexed.

Walt Disney's Donald Duck: Fifty Happy Years of Frustration. Tucson, Ariz.: HP Books, 1984. 96 pp.; bibliog.

Warshow, Robert. *The Immediate Experience: Movies, Comics, Theatre, and Other Aspects of Popular Culture*. New York: Atheneum, 1974. 282 pp.

Waugh, Coulton. *The Comics*. New York: Macmillan, 1947. 360 pp.; indexed.

White, David Manning and Robert H. Abel, eds. *The Funnies: An American Idiom*. New York: Free Press of Glencoe, 1963. 304 pp.; bibliog.

Wilson, David. *Projecting Britain: Ealing Studios Film Posters*. London: BFI Publishing, 1982. 67 pp.; indexed.

Young, Dean and Rick Marschall. *Blondie and Dagwood's America*. New York: Harper and Row, 1981. 144 pp.; bibliog.

SELECTED FILMOGRAPHY

The following animated films have been selected to illustrate a wide range of historical periods, nationalities, studios, graphic styles, and production techniques such as cel, sand, collage, and pinscreen animation. The list is meant to be representative rather than definitive.

The Adventures of Prince Achmed (German 1926). Made by Lotte Reiniger.

Animal Farm (Great Britain 1955). Made by John Halas and Joy Batchelor.

Animated Cartoons: The Toy That Grew Up (USA 1946). Made by Roger Leenhardt.

Aucassin and Nicolette (Canada 1975). Made by Lotte Reiniger.

Ballet Mécanique (France 1924). Made by Fernand Léger.

Before Mickey (Various Countries and Dates). Compilation of early animated films; an approximately two-hour, companion videotape to Crafton's book of the same title. Available through MIT Exhibits, 28 Carleton Street, Cambridge, MA 02142.

Begone Dull Care (Canada 1949). Made by Norman McLaren.

Cohl Animation Program (France 1909–1912). Made by Emile Cohl, and includes *Fantasmagorie* (1909), *Les Râteleiers (The Dentures)* (1909), *The Automatic Moving Company* (1910), and *Professor Bonehead Is Shipwrecked* (1912).

Colour Box (Great Britain 1935). Made by Len Lye.

Composition in Blue (German 1935). Made by Oskar Fischinger.

Dreams of a Rarebit Fiend—The Pet (USA 1917). Made by Winsor Mccay.

Duck Amuck (USA 1953). Made by Chuck Jones.

Ego (Italy 1969). Made by Bruno Bozzetto.

The Eye Hears, The Ear Sees (Canada 1970). Made by Gavin Miller. Documentary on the career of Norman McLaren.

Ersatz (Yugoslavia 1961). Made by Dusan Vukotic (at Zagreb).

Fabulous Fleischer Folio (USA 1934–1940). Made by Dave Fleischer. Ten of the classic Fleischer Studio "Color Classics."

Fantasia (USA 1940). Made by Walt Disney Studio.

Farmer Alfalfa's Wayward Pup (USA 1917). Made by Paul Terry.

Frank and Ollie: Four Decades of Disney Animation (USA 1978). Disney footage by
    master animators Frank Thomas and Ollie Johnston.
Frank Film (USA 1973). Made by Frank Mouris.
Games of Angels (Les Jeux Des Anges) (Poland 1964). Made by Walerian Borowczyk.
Gerald McBoing Boing. (USA 1951). Made by Robert Cannon.
Gulliver's Travels (USA 1939). Made by Dave Fleischer (for Paramount).
Humorous Phases of Funny Faces (USA 1906). Made by J. Stuart Blackton.
Hunger (Canada 1974). Made by Peter Foldes.
International Tournée of Animation (Yearly compilation of the world's best animation
    assembled in cooperation with Association Internationale de Film d'Animation.
    Programs average 100–120 minutes. *The 17th Tournée* (1982) departed from the
    usual format to showcase the best of the National Film Board of Canada's forty-
    two years of artistry.
Is My Palm Red? (USA 1933). Made by Dave Fleischer. (Betty Boop)
Krazy Kat Program #1 (USA 1917). Made by G. Hamilton and Frank Moser, and
    includes *Krazy and Ignatz at the Circus*, *Krazy and Ignatz Discuss the Letter
    "G"*, and *He Made Me Love Him.*
The Light Fantastic (Canada 1974). Made by Rupert Glover and Michael Patenaude.
    This film is a detailed retrospective of the National Film Board of Canada.
Masque of the Red Death (Yugoslavia 1970). Made by Pavao Stalter and Vladimir Jutrisa
    (at Zagreb).
Milestones for Mickey (USA 1928–1940). Made by the Disney Studio, and includes *Plane
    Crazy* (1928), *The Band Concert* (1935), *Mickey's Service Station* (1935), *Thru
    the Mirror* (1936), and *The Sorcerer's Apprentice* sequence from *Fantasia* (1940).
Milestones in Animation (USA 1928–1937). Made by the Disney Studio, and includes
    Steamboat Willie (1928), *Skeleton Dance* (1929), *Flowers and Trees* (1933), *The
    Three Little Pigs* (1933), and *The Old Mill* (1937).
Mindscape (France 1976). Made by Jacques Drouin.
Motion Painting #1 (Germany 1947). Made by Oskar Fischinger.
Moving Pictures: The Art of Jan Lenica (USA 1975). Made by Richard Rogers.
Musical Poster #1 (Great Britain 1940). Made by Len Lye.
Otto Mesmer and Felix the Cat (USA 1978). Made by John Canemaker, and includes
    excerpts from five vintage Felix cartoons.
The Owl Who Married a Goose: An Eskimo Legend (Canada 1974). Made by Caroline
    Leaf.
Popeye [the Sailor] Meets Sinbad [the Sailor] (USA 1936). Made by Dave Fleischer.
Quasi at the Quackadero (USA 1975). Made by Sally Cruikshank.
Remembering Winsor McCay (USA 1976). Made by John Canemaker.
Rythmus 21 (Germany 1921). Made by Hans Richter.
Snow White and the Seven Dwarfs (USA 1937). Made by the Disney Studio. (Supervising
    Director was David Hand.)
The Street (Canada 1976). Made by Caroline Leaf.
Symphonie Diagonale (German 1921). Made by Viking Eggeling.
The Tell Tale Heart (USA 1953). Made by T. Parmalee at UPA.
Walking (Canada 1969). Made by Ryan Larkin.
What's Opera Doc? (USA 1957). Made by Chuck Jones.
The Wild Hare (USA 1940). Made by Tex Avery.
Yellow Submarine (Great Britain 1968). Directed by George Dunning. Screenplay by Lee
    Minoff, Al Brodax, Jack Mendelby, and Erich Segal.

5

FILM AND LITERATURE

CAROLYN ANDERSON

INTRODUCTION

Process and product, verb and noun, indefinite and definite, the word "film" appears uncomfortably, but not infrequently, in tandem with "literature." As a medium, the cinema's true equivalent is not literature, but print; as a narrative art, film can be considered a form of literature; as commercial entertainment, movies seem something else entirely.[1] Despite its lack of symmetry, the phrase "film and literature" strikes a chord of recognition strong enough and invites comparisons sensible enough to merit its continued use.

In considering the vast topic of literature and film over a period of almost a century, I have limited my discussion of literature to prose fiction of developed length (novels) written by North American authors, while expanding notions of the literary to include novels of varying degrees of artistic ambition and success. All films discussed are narrative features produced by North American companies (with one exception). Narrowing ever more, I have drawn most of my film samples from the Hollywood tradition. In addition to these restrictions, I have shaped this chapter around examples of the most obvious relationship between literature and film adaptations. As a process, adaptation provides insights into differences and similarities between forms and also calls attention to the social-political-cultural milieu in which these works are produced. Studio executives estimate that roughly 30 percent of contemporary American movies are based on novels; that in the last fifty years approximately 80 percent of best-sellers have been made into films; that three-fourths of the Academy Awards for Best Picture have gone to adaptations and that three-fourths of those pictures were adaptations of novels and short stories.[2] Best-seller lists and Oscars are not sensitive measures of artistic worth, but they are important indicators of cultural influence and economic power.

This chapter is divided into a section on the historical development of the relationship between literature and film, a discussion of styles and genres of interaction, a summary of the extensive scholarship on the topic, and a list of the films and novels discussed. Across sections, a focus on adaptations persists. A risk in emphasizing adaptations is the natural tendency to regard the original work as the sacred text. The more beloved the source, the stronger the urge to evaluate the adaptation with a lover's vocabulary: to regard one as faithful, another as a betrayal. (The same emotional response is a common reaction to the reverse adaptation process of the novelization.) Even when the calmer tones of description are evoked, the source is more often seen as standard than as raw material. A viewer's experience of an adaptation is conditioned not only by the film itself, but by the reading that has preceded (and even followed) its viewing.

Some find it helpful to classify general levels of correspondence. Geoffrey Wagner, for example, charts three principal manners—transposition, commentary, and analogy. In a transposition a novel is directly given on the screen with the minimum of apparent interference''; analogy films ''take but the merest hints from their source''; the commentary falls between these two extremes.[3] These classification systems can function either as judgments or as a basis for generalizations about the adaptation process. The forty-three pairs of novels and films described in this chapter are not grouped according to Wagner's scheme, but the examples add support to his claim of narrative fidelity as the dominant correspondence. The typical kinds of changes that occur in adaptations (condensation of plot and character; emphasis on dialogue and action; attention to emotion rather than reflection; a heightening of [already high] love interest; a pull toward the happy ending, and so forth) and the typical rationales for those changes (the transference of a nontechnological form to a form highly dependent on technology; the formal constraints and opportunities of a visual medium, conceptions of the film audience, exigencies of the marketplace, and so forth) are best understood by an examination of specific adaptations. The goal here is not to confirm or challenge the conventional wisdom about *inherent* qualities of literature and film, but to describe *realized* qualities and thus chart the symbiotic relationship between the two media in its most concrete form.

HISTORICAL DEVELOPMENT

Tracing the historical development of the complex relationship between film and literature over a period approaching a century helps one to see how deep and how various are the connections that bind these media one to another. As cultural products, shaped by artistic, social, technological, and economic concerns, the movies and the novels of each historical period have mirrored and molded their time.

Silent Film, 1895–1926

By the turn of the century, American moviemakers and audiences had discovered film's ability to bring new life to familiar stories. In 1903 American Mutoscope Company produced *Sherlock Holmes Baffled* and Edwin S. Porter directed an adaptation of *Uncle Tom's Cabin* for Edison. Before the silent era ended, there would be three more film versions of Harriet Beecher Stowe's immensely popular novel. Although many of the earliest moviegoers were illiterate, most of these viewers participated in cultures with rich storytelling traditions. The simple action stories, romances, and comedies of the one- and two-reelers fed a developed appetite for narrative and also forged a link between genre film and pulp fiction, and more and more immigrants learned to read English. The popularity of serial novels coincided with an interest in serialized films (e.g., *The Perils of Pauline*). Between 1907 and 1911 the Patents Company often distributed multireel films in serials of one reel a week, a practice some exhibitors subverted by holding reels and then projecting them as a single bill.

Longer foreign imports attracted a more educated and more affluent American audience in the early teens. Although the short-lived *film d'art* movement (1908–1912) has been rightly criticized for its pretentious and static adaptations of classical novels and plays, the success of these European productions with middle-class American audiences encouraged domestic companies to support the production of features (films of five reels or more). Although American companies had always been dependent on literary works for source material—often with ludicrous results, such as the one-reel versions of Dickens's novels—a feature-length format provided a far more amenable cinematic form for the complexities of characterization and plot development that novel adaptations required. No individual shaped this new cinematic form more than D. W. Griffith; no film shaped the nation's view of cinema's narrative power more than Griffith's *The Birth of a Nation* (1915). The literary source for America's first cinematic masterpiece was a mediocre, albeit best-selling, novel of the Civil War era, *The Clansman* (1905). At the intermission of the New York premiere of *The Birth of a Nation*, author Thomas Dixon responded to audience enthusiasm by taking the stage to declare the film superior to both his original novel and his stage adaptation which had played at the same Liberty Theater. Dixon said he would have permitted only the son of a soldier and a Southerner to direct a movie based on his work. Griffith then described his goal: "to place pictures on a par with the spoken word as a medium for artistic expression appealing to thinking people."[4] Working from a complicated script that existed only in his head, Griffith satisfied his goal. So innovative was his achievement that existing exchanges refused to distribute the three-hour film, which demanded a forty-piece orchestra. Griffith and Mutual president Harry Aitken formed their own company to distribute what became the most widely seen, and praised, production of its time. The film's cost, admission price, publicity campaign, length of run, box-office receipts (and defalcation of receipts) were all unprecedented.

Despite Griffith's creativity in constructing new filmic methods of storytelling, he depended heavily on precedents from popular nineteenth-century novels and melodramas for his sentimental notions of characterization and thematic conflict. Through parallel editing, Griffith developed a dynamic cinematic form for contrasting good and evil and making rescues emotional experiences. A son of a soldier and a Southerner, Griffith accepted Dixon's villains and his assumption of white supremacy. Protests against the film's racism came from various quarters, particularly the newly organized National Association for the Advancement of Colored People (NAACP). Although attempts to obtain injunctions against exhibition were largely unsuccessful, pressure against the film resulted in the deletion of some of its most objectionable parts. Formal protests in cities throughout the country served as a rallying point for the NAACP and brought the issue into the public arena.[5] President Woodrow Wilson, a college friend of Dixon's, retracted his (alleged) description of Griffith's film as "like writing history with Lightning," but *The Birth of a Nation* permanently changed the nation's attitute toward film.

Many of Griffith's innovative techniques and reactionary attitudes were continued in the 1920 production of *The Last of the Mohicans*. Co-directors Maurice Tourneur and Clarence Brown took advantage of the visual splendor of the West (shooting on location at Big Bear Lake and Yosemite Valley); they created a narrative that moved fluidly between exciting action scenes and moments of tender lyricism, between the particular and the abstract; they used light and shadow as symbolic motif in contrasting good and evil nonwhites; they told a romantic story that played to the audience's fascination with the horror of miscegenation. Griffith himself had adapted James Fenimore Cooper's popular tale into a Biograph one-reeler, *Leatherstocking* (1909). The 1920 version demonstrated what great technical advances had been made in a decade. Also, by placing Cora, the white woman who loves the noble Uncas, at the moral center of the film, French director Tourneur added a layer of complexity to the classic American adventure novel.[6]

The moral nobility of Cooper's heroes contrasted strongly with the essential brutishness of *McTeague* (1899). The deep pessimism of Frank Norris's naturalistic novel set it against the grain of popular literature and film, while simultaneously making it appealing to one of the silent era's most individualistic directors, Erich von Stroheim. It began as a project for Goldwyn Pictures, but by the time von Stroheim completed his forty-two-reel, ten-and-one-half-hour adaptation, his employer was Metro-Goldwyn-Mayer; and his nemesis from Universal, Irving Thalber, had become executive producer. Ordered to shorten *McTeague*, von Stroheim, then a friend, made substantial cuts, but still not satisfied with the length, the studio edited and released a ten-reel, two-and-one-half-hour version titled *Greed* (1924).

Even in its truncated form (which von Stroheim disowned), *Greed* remains a remarkable example of naturalist narrative.[7] Von Stroheim exploited the cinema's potential for building symbolic meaning from details accurately presented. Shooting entirely on location (in San Francisco, Death Valley, and the California Hills), von Stroheim emphasized the deterministic connections that existed between characters and their environment. Rather than depending on the crosscut or subjective cut as did Griffith, von Stroheim relied on deep focus photography and long takes for creating meaning within, rather than between, frames.

For some, *Greed* has served as the quintessential example of studio commercialism and corporate insensitivity to artistic expression; for others, *Greed* demonstrates the absurd self-indulgence of translating a complicated novel, line by line, into cinematic form. Many think MGM exaggerated the film's costs and its losses as justification for seizing editorial control. Most agree that *Greed*, albeit diminished, is one of the silent era's most complex and most powerful films.

Two other films produced by MGM in the mid–1920s—*Ben-Hur* (1925) and *The Scarlet Letter* (1926)—indicate the range of projects supported by the studio most committed to adaptation. *Ben-Hur* exemplifies the economic madness a studio will endure in pursuit of adapting a best-seller to the screen. *Ben-Hur: A Tale of the Christ* (1880), by Lew Wallace, had broken all publishing records. A subsequent theatrical tour became the most profitable production in theatrical history.[8] Much to the producer's surprise, a 1907 movie version of *Ben-Hur* precipitated the first breach of copyright case in film history. By 1921 the rights had changed hands and the price had escalated to an astonishing one million dollars. The following year, MGM negotiated for an unprecedented equal division of profits in exchange for film rights.

A long, wasteful shooting began in Italy. The making of the picture became the topic of Hollywood gossip, speculation, and jokes. The leading man and director were both replaced, yet problems with the unwieldy production continued. Cast and crew were recalled to California, where the Circus Maximus was rebuilt and the chariot race was reshot, photographed by forty-two cameras before the largest crowd ever assembled for a film. That remarkable sequence, edited from 200,000 to 750 feet, and the equally spectacular battle at sea were the highlights of what became a great popular success (although not profitable to MGM, which had spent more than $4,000,000 on the epic). The film was far less successful at presenting the religious mysticism of the novel.

The 1926 MGM production of *The Scarlet Letter* was not the first film version of Nathaniel Hawthorne's 1850 tale of guilt and pride, but the fourth. Still, the studio treated the project with the respect befitting a classic by casting Lillian Gish as its star and assigning the production to a director with an international reputation, Victor Sjostrom. The Swedish director, renamed Seastrom by the studio, was a master of subtle cinematography and seemed well suited to interpreting the novel's brooding themes. Hawthorne's exquisite visual sense is well served by the cool, organized beauty of the film. *The Scarlet Letter* is about the concealment of emotion, about the suppression of sensuousness; however, the film does not always resist making those emotions visible, and sentimental. In what had already become typical Hollywood style, the adaptation solves the mysteries of the characters' lives; it flattens the ambiguities central to Chillingworth and Dimmesdale. Mark W. Estrin argues that the use of titles necessarily moves the film to melodrama, "since the fuller context and accompanying distancing by the narrator had been stripped away."[9] Nevertheless, Gish projects both the fragility and the inner strength of Hester. Her sensitive performance is one of the most moving of the silent era.

The Studio Era, 1927–1946

Although the role of the screenwriter was limited in the silent era, it consisted of more than just writing intertitles. Most of the early one- and two-reelers were improvised from story ideas, a practice that continued into comedy features. Studio writers, many of them women, developed gags, designed narrative structures, and, later, wrote full scenarios for dramatic features. When silent productions became more elaborate, the studios began what became a tradition of hiring well-known journalists and novelists.[10] The introduction of sound intensified the studios' dependence on professional writers. With that dependence went the promise of huge salaries for produced screenplays. In 1941 Bennett Cerf, the publishing head of Random House, wrote, "The thing an author wants most from his publisher these days is a letter of introduction to Darryl Zanuck."[11] James Agee, John Dos Passos, William Faulkner, F. Scott Fitzgerald, Ernest Hemingway, John Steinbeck, and Nathanael West were among the respected writers who worked on at least one screenplay. Despite the money and notoriety offered the screenwriter, "behind his back he was called a hack and considered a necessary nuisance."[12] The Hollywood process of contract employment, with its office assignments, decisions by committee, and rigid scheduling, deprived screenwriters of artistic autonomy. The tragic deaths of Fitzgerald and West, only a day apart, brought attention to Hollywood's "appalling record of talent depraved and wasted."[13]

Many novelists have felt their talents were wasted by the studios, but Theodore Dreiser made his disappointments the grounds for litigation against Paramount. Dreiser had sold the silent screen rights to his sprawling two-volume novel *An American Tragedy* to Famous Players the year after its publication. Four years passed, years that saw Famous Players reorganized into Paramount, the introduction of talkies, and the Great Depression. By 1930 there was pressure on the studio not to make a film based on a bleak novel that was an ironic inversion of the Horatio Alger myth. Dreiser threatened to sue. Paramount paid him additional money for the sound rights and, surprisingly, hired Soviet filmmaker Sergei Eisenstein (and Ivor Montagu) to write the screenplay. Less surprisingly, the Eisenstein-Montagu script—which maintained that the protagonist was essentially innocent—was rejected. Paramount executive B. P. Schulberg labeled the script "a monstrous challenge to American society."[14] Paramount then assigned Josef von Sternberg to make a quick, low-budget version. Unlike von Stroheim, von Sternberg had no reverential attitude toward the naturalistic novel. Like von Sternberg's other projects, *An American Tragedy* became a story of erotic obsession more than social determinism. The strong-willed director later recalled, "I eliminated the sociological elements, which, in my opinion, were far from being responsible for the dramatic action with which Dreiser had concerned himself."[15]

The first important literary figure to challenge the studio's insensitivity in adaptation, Dreiser took legal action to stop exhibition, claiming the film outraged his book.[16] New York Justice Graham Witschief ruled that the film was a faithful transcription. Still, Paramount added seven scenes and begged Drieser to endorse the film in its new form, which he refused to do. Ever outrageous, von Sternberg suggested in retrospect, "Actually Mr. Dreiser's attorneys made a mistake in not calling on me to be a witness for Mr. Dreiser, for I would have agreed with him. Literature cannot be transferred to the screen without a loss of its values; the visual elements completely revalue the written word."[17]

When Twentieth Century-Fox purchased the screen rights to John Steinbeck's critical and popular success *Grapes of Wrath*, the studio was "contractually bound to preserve the theme of the novel."[18] Although some critics argue that the point of the movie (individual acceptance) was exactly opposite the call to social revolution in the novel.[19] Steinbeck himself was pleased with the adaptation. Another contrast to Dreiser's situation was the rapidity of the adaptation and production process, despite similar warnings that the subject matter was depressing, if not inflammatory. The best-seller had been condemned, banned, and burned. Opposition was particularly well organized in California. Nevertheless, studio head Darryl Zanuck purchased the rights within a month of the 1939 publication and assigned four outstanding talents to the picture: writer Nunnally Johnson, director John Ford, cinematographer Gregg Toland, and actor Henry Fonda. Working under the false title *Highway 66*, the clandestine project was rushed through production and premiered within less than a year of the novel's publication. It was greeted with extraordinarily good reviews and became Fox's most profitable picture in a bad year (1940) for the studio. By 1940 the Depression was safely behind the country and, therefore, could be confronted by Hollywood. The film version of *The Grapes of Wrath* treats the epic migration of the Dust Bowl farmers in sentimental terms, presenting the plight of the Joads as a social problem amenable to reformist solution. Ford emphasizes the family relationships, turning Tom and Ma into archetypes and diluting the impact of the historical moment. Still, Toland's camera work shares many of the pictorial qualities and much of the emotional power of the documentary films of Pare Lorentz and the photographs of Dorothea Lange, Walker Evans, and Margaret Bourke-White. In one of his most memorable performances, Fonda projects the deeply felt moral anger that charges through Steinbeck's novel.

During the Depression, Hollywood made considerable efforts to avoid subjects like the destruction of Dust Bowl farms and to present a respite to the nation's problems. Musicals and romances with happy endings were standard fare. So, too, were nostalgic adaptations of lastingly popular novels. "In the aftermath of wars or depressions, books and films idealizing the domestic sphere. . . . find an especially receptive market."[20] Set in the Civil War period, Louisa May Alcott's *Little Women* offered a model of cooperation and optimistic self-sufficiency to Depression audiences. The 1933 version of Alcott's sentimental masterpiece was produced by RKO, the smallest of the major studios and one with a penchant for literary adaptations. The director, George Cukor, remembered for his outstanding ensemble direction of actresses, urged the studio to feature a performer who would later collaborate with Cukor on many films and become RKO's major star of the 1930s—Katharine Hepburn. Hepburn played the semiautobiographical part of Jo with the combination of spunk and glamour that would characterize her screen persona. Alcott had been educated at home by her father, Bronson Alcott, with some instruction by Thoreau and Emerson. She later supported many of her father's experiments in communal living with the profits from her novels. In the 1933 film of *Little Women*, the family as "little commonwealth" is less social experiment than it is the locus of domestic action. Jo's independence and financial success are displayed as temporary strategies, necessary in her father's absence and then abandoned to her romance with the fatherly Professor Bhaer.

Literary adaptations in the thirties reached their romantic apex in 1939 with two MGM productions both (at least partially) directed by Victor Fleming: *The Wizard of Oz* and *Gone With the Wind*. Both are opulent, spectacularly entertaining products of the studio system at its most efficient, constructing beautifully crafted fairy tales. Both were showcases for the then new three-color Technicolor process, but both have remained popular with audiences for decades.

The Wizard of Oz is based on fourteen best-selling books about Oz (from *The Wonderful Wizard of Oz* [1900] to *Glinda of Oz*) [1920]) written by L. Frank Baum. Ostensibly for children, the series is a serious and delightful American fairy tale about the dream of escape. Baum knew that "fantasy works by a combination of wonder and fear, joy and nightmare."[21] MGM built on that knowledge, constructing a musical fantasy that remains charming. The daring choice of black-and-white photography to make visible the drabness of Dorothy's life in Kansas is but one of Fleming's inventive decisions. Far less daring is the "adult" happy ending of the film, which (unlike Baum's conclusion) asks us to dismiss Dorothy's adventures as a dream. Yet the longing in Judy Garland's trembling voice as she tearfully repeats "There's no place like home" at the end of the film questions such a rational dismissal of the somewhere over the rainbow.

By the end of the 1930s, film subjects had shifted from the classics to recent best-sellers. No 1930s novel better fit the label "best-seller" than Margaret Mitchell's *Gone With the Wind*. Independent producer David O. Selznick bought the rights to the enormously popular romance and worked on its production for three years. He insisted that the script follow the plot and language of the novel as closely as possible, declaring that readers of the book would be annoyed by any changes in the movie version. F. Scott Fitzgerald, one of the many who worked on the script, wrote of the experience: "Do you know . . . I was absolutely forbidden to use any words except those of Margaret Mitchell, that is, when new phrases had to be invented one had to thumb through as if it were Scripture and check out phrases of hers which would cover the situation!"[22] Selznick outwrote all the writers associated with the project and then agreed to produce the film for MGM, so that he could cast contract star Clark Gable as the roguish Rhett Butler.

The mixture of daring and Victorian moralism in the novel made it an incredible success of great cultural significance. That mixture was exploited in the film with equally successful results. Scarlett O'Hara and Rhett Butler shocked and delighted audiences with their unabashed opportunism. Mitchell's ornate style, her blend of fairy tale and historic reconstruction, her creation of romantic characters set in a period of great upheaval—all these characteristics lent themselves to dramatic spectacle. The structural and thematic parallels between *Birth of a Nation* and *Gone With the Wind* are unmistakable. As with the Griffith classic, the four-hour MGM epic has its intermission at the return from Civil War; part 2 presents the Reconstruction. Some of the episodes set in Atlanta, for instance the sequence of the wounded and dying in the Station Plaza and the flight from the burning city, have a visceral power equal to Griffith's achievements in visual storytelling.

The studio era was a time when many of America's best novelists worked in Hollywood, but only once were the talents of two future Nobel laureates joined in a single project. On a hunting trip Howard Hawks boasted to his friend Ernest Hemingway that a good movie could be made of the author's worst novel, which, according to the director, was *To Have and Have Not*.[23] Hawks proceeded to buy the screen rights (which Hemingway had previously sold to Howard Hughes) and assigned veteran screenwriter Jules Furthman to write the screenplay. The Furthman version followed the novel (itself three short stories stitched together) in depicting insurrection and smuggling in Cuba. When Hawks submitted the script for government approval (a typical procedure during the war years), he met with objections. Therefore, he decided to situate the film in wartime Martinique and brought in a Warners writer who had been working on an unproduced screenplay about the anti-Vichy French—William Faulkner.[24]

Between 1932 and 1954 Faulkner spent a total of four years in California and worked on about forty-eight films, eighteen of which reached the screen. Faulkner's screenplay for *To Have and Have Not* (1944) created the characters as they were *before* the action of the novel. Despite Faulkner's skill at formal literary innovation, he did not exploit Hemingway's experiments with form and point of view in his adaptation. The scenario is a straightforward action romance; the tone of the film, which is easygoing and intrinsically sociable, is far more reminiscent of Hawks's movies than it is of the work of Hemingway or Faulkner. The protagonist, Henry Morgan, played by Humphrey Bogart, is a combination of Hawksian hero, Hemingway code hero, and an extension of the persona Bogart created in *Casablanca* the year before. Once again, Bogart is the uncommitted man who joins the struggle, finding commitment to war the answer to his inner dilemmas. The sparks generated by the offscreen romance of Bogart and co-star Lauren Bacall added excitement to this audience-pleaser. The Grosset and Dunlap tie-in edition of the (heretofore minor) novel went through three printings during the period in which *To Have and Have Not* was in general release.[25]

Hollywood in Transition, 1947–1965

The first full year of peacetime after World War II—1946—was Hollywood's most profitable year. That success was followed by an abrupt decline that continued and deepened for a decade. One of many indications of the sudden loss of confidence was the near evacuation of the writers' buildings at the studios. In 1946 Paramount had approximately thirty-five writers and twenty-two contract writers; in 1947 only seven writers remaining, a mere two on contract, which led Raymond Chandler to write "They say Hollywood is really a shambles. . . . The atmosphere is hysterical."[26] Reasons for the hysteria included the 1948 U.S. Supreme Court divestiture order,[27] the House Un-American Activities Committee (HUAC) Hearings on subversive influences within the film industry, and the growing competition for audience attention and loyalty from foreign imports and the burgeoning American television industry.

Predictably, a combination of timidity and experimentation darts through the films of this anxious era. The adaptations of two wartime novels—*From Here to Eternity* and *The Naked and the Dead*—illustrate that tension. Both provided the security of the best-seller, yet each novel had presented a critical portrait of the authoritarian character of the military man. The adaptation of *From Here to Eternity* (1953) used the characters' discontent to move the narrative, yet the film version obfuscated author James Jones's fundamental critique of the social system. An enormous financial success and the winner of eight Oscars, *From Here to Eternity* titillated American audiences with scenes of unusual sexual frankness, yet it ultimately confirmed traditional middle-class values. The strong, selfish sergeant (played by Burt Lancaster) not only survives, but thrives. The film ends with the attack on Pearl Harbor and, according to Brandon French, a retreat into two fantasy worlds: for men, it "is a perfect fantasy retreat to the good old days of World War II, a celebration of the event which provided them with an honorable escape from domestic life. . . . The end of the movie is also a fantasy of retreat for women, back to wartime when they were free to memorialize their failed affairs of the past as ideal romances, and to fantasize the fulfillment of their romantic ideals in the future. . . . "[28] Yet, as French points out, the last shot of the film indicates that the central female character, Karen (Deborah Kerr), has recognized the other woman's romantic lie. The recognition is subtle, but available for audience members ready to see it.

Although *From Here to Eternity* was awarded the 1951 National Book Award, its literary reputation never equaled that of *The Naked and the Dead*, the 1948 novel that launched Norman Mailer's career. Nevertheless, the adaptation of Mailer's novel took a decade to reach the screen and then was not given the prestige film treatment accorded to *From Here to Eternity*. *The Naked and the Dead* tells an adventure story of a military operation on a Pacific Island, and through inset biographical sketches of the main characters, it also offers a critique of American society. The film adaptation, directed by Raoul Walsh, follows the codes of the adventure film, disregarding the filmic possibilities of the time machine interludes from the novel. With Aldo Ray as the coarse Sergeant Craft, the film version has a raucous directness that is both its strength and its weakness. Mailer himself dismissed the film: "*The Naked and the Dead* was one of the worst movies ever made. If it had been just a little worse than that it would have come out the other end and been extraordinarily funny, a sort of pioneer classic of pop art . . . but the picture was finally not bad enough.''[29]

After the aggressive optimism of most of the films of the Depression and war years, the earnest postwar ''social consciousness'' films were considered pioneering. Throughout the late 1940s and early 1950s the studios generated hundereds of films that dealt melioristically with social issues. Nearly one-third of the films produced in Hollywood in 1947 had a ''problem'' content of some sort.[30] One of the best of this cycle and probably the best adaptation of a Faulkner novel was *Intruder in the Dust* 1949. MGM had purchased the screen rights within a month of the novel's publication.[31] Production control had just passed to Dore Schary, a liberal who strongly supported the project.[32] Clarence Brown, a Southerner who, as a young man, had witnessed blacks shot and killed in a race riot, regarded the film as a kind of payment of conscience. The film narrative, like the novel, is told from the point of view of a young boy, with most of the movie presented as an extended flashback, yet in the film, the boy repudiates the bigotry of his community, rather than accepting it. The script by Ben Maddow (the poet David Wolff) rejects Faulkner's concept of the ''Black man's burden'' and, instead, argues that Lucas Beauchamp's refusal to accept second-class citizenship is appropriate and admirable.

Faulkner had recommended certain places in Oxford, Mississippi, for the location shooting and even did some uncredited revision of the script, although he left town during much of the filming. He thought it was a good picture. Schary himself suggested the sentimental final line, ''There goes our conscience.'' He insisted that this explicitly stated moral be placed where the moral in a cautionary tale would be, at the end. Louis B. Mayer had quite another reaction to the assertive pride so eloquently expressed by Juano Hernandez (in his first movie role). The MGM studio head found Lucas ''too uppity'' and said the picture would be a financial failure, which it was.[33]

Intruder in the Dust is a touching, beautifully crafted movie melodrama whose sense of racial equity was ahead of its time. In many ways, this version of Faulkner's most accessible novel is the most faithful of the many Faulkner adaptations, yet even in this case, Bruce Kawin's claim holds true that ''Having seen the films but not read the novels, the audience would have little respect for Faulkner, little knowledge of him.''[34]

In 1940 *Native Son* was the first Book-of-the-Month Club selection by a black writer. The following year Orson Welles and John Houseman staged a successful Broadway version of the tragic story of Bigger Thomas, a black chauffeur who accidentally kills a white woman. Despite this pattern of success and despite author Richard Wright's description of ''How Bigger Was Born'' in largely cinematic terms, the fear that Hollywood would drastically alter the anger of *Native Son* and thus diminish its power kept Wright from accepting lucrative bids for the screen rights to his best-seller.[35] Instead, Wright agreed to director Pierre Chenal's offer to shoot the film in France, Wright's postwar home. Governmental pressure aborted that production effort. The film was eventually made in Argentina in 1951 with the support of a Uruguayan producer. When the actor who had played Bigger in the Broadway version became ill during shooting, Wright (who had no acting experience) replaced him, with unfortunate results. Misfortune continued.

Even though Wright and Chenal had softened the screenplay considerably, the New York State Board of Censors demanded cuts of over a half hour; the states of Pennsylvania, Wisconsin, and Ohio barred exhibition entirely. The Ohio board said the "film contributes to racial misunderstanding, presenting situations undesirable to the mutual interests of both races . . . undermining confidence that justice can be carried out and presenting racial frictions at a time when all groups should be united against everything that is subversive."[36] The trial court denied the distributor's petition. On appeal, the Supreme Court of Ohio affirmed the denial; however, the U.S. Supreme Court found the Ohio censorship law vague and indefinite and reversed the Ohio courts.[37] *Native Son* could be shown, but few saw it.

A decade after *Native Son*, filmmakers who wanted to explore the frustrations of ghetto life honestly still felt it necessary to go outside the studio system. In 1964 independent producer Frederick Wiseman and director Shirley Clarke released a poignant adaptation of Warren Miller's novel *The Cool World*. Wiseman had purchased the screen rights to Miller's first-person account of teenage gang activity for $500. The production followed the low-budget pattern of what might be called the New York school of social realism. Clarke shot on location in Harlem, using mostly nonprofessional actors and postdubbing the sound. The result is a film of great spontaneity and emotional power. In a reversal of the Hollywood pattern, the ending of the screen version is much less hopeful than Miller's novel, which has the teenage narrator speaking from a juvenile correction home where he had found some sense of self-worth. A critical success in the independent circuit, *The Cool World* played "something like 175 dates in the first eighteen months," which to an independent like Clarke was doing "very, very well."[38]

Exodus (1960) seems to be the antithesis of spunky, independent films like *The Cool World*. Running 220 minutes, released in Panavision 70, made on a huge budget, filmed in studios and in the Middle East, based on Leon Uris's popular novel about the Israeli fight for independence, *Exodus* is an entertaining adventure film, packed with incident and remarkable characters played by stars. Still, *Exodus* was not thoroughly ingrained in 1950s conservatism, for producer-director Otto Preminger hired Dalton Trumbo to write the screenplay, Trumbo's first under his own name since 1947 when he was blacklisted as a result of his refusal to testify at the HUAC hearings. In the mid–1940s Trumbo was Hollywood's highest paid writer (possibly excepting Ben Hecht).[39] One of the imprisoned Hollywood Ten, Trumbo continued to write under various pseudonyms and, as Robert Rich, won an Oscar for best screenplay in 1956 for *The Brave One*. Trumbo's screenwriting tended toward the turgid, and he was quite at home with message-spectaculars like *Exodus*.

Giant (1956) was another message-spectacular that embodied the ambivalence of the time toward nascent civil rights. A classically styled epic of clear moral confrontation in the new West, *Giant* examines the growth of a dynasty. Edna Ferber's popular novel had enraged many Texans and created national interest in the saga of the Benedict family.[40] The film version pitted Rock Hudson and James Dean against each other in a struggle for the admiration of Elizabeth Taylor and the audience. Representing old wealth, Bick Benedict (Hudson) at first seems overbearing and bigoted. He has none of the sensitivity of his ranch hand Jett Rink (Dean). However, thirty years later, Rink has become entirely corrupted by his oil fortune; he is the prototype of the vulgar millionaire. In contrast, Benedict has earned his wife's respect and epitomizes the principle of noblesse oblige. He personally fights for the rights of his Mexican daughter-in-law and represents the "right-minded land baron," the "proponent of controlled progress."[41] Dean had already become a youth cult figure when *Giant* went into production. His tragic death (at twenty-four) before the release of the picture created a special aura of anticipation around the film, and a particular curiosity about the corruption of Jett Rink.

The fears of the 1950s, sometimes spilling into paranoia, found intensified expression in the horror and science fiction genres. A wide assortment of phobias could be contained in these allegories of terror. Two haunting adaptations— *Night of the Hunter* (1955) and *The Innocents* (1961)—demonstrate the era's fascination with the nature of evil. Neither of these imaginative films limits itself to generic conventions, but both build on the codes of the horror film. Each in its own way (*Night of the Hunter* with its tonal shifts, *The Innocents* with its commitment to ambiguity) indicates future directions for both literature and film.

The film *Night of the Hunter* is a highly stylized gothic horror story in which a mad preacher pursues two innocent children after marrying and murdering their mother. The plot comes from an unexceptional Davis Grubb novel; the exceptional treatment of the material is the result of the detailed screenplay by James Agee (his last)[42] and the direction of Charles Laughton (his first and last).

Robin Wood recognized Laughton's audacity: "The entire film is pitched on the borderline of absurdity."[43] Robert Mitchum plays with rabid intensity the fraudulent preacher with the letters L-O-V-E and H-A-T-E tattooed on his fingers. His pursuit of the children through the swamp, at once particular and mythic, is memorably photographed by Stanley Cortez. Just as sex is presented as the source of evil, the ever asexual Lillian Gish appears as the angel of mercy who saves the innocents in a fairy-tale ending. *Night of the Hunter* flaunts its stylization with romantic and comic daring.

In contrast, *The Innocents*, directed by Jack Clayton, turns on the subtle ambiguity central to the brilliant work of Henry James. Taking its story and its tone from the novella *The Turn of the Screw*, *The Innocents* suggests connections between evil and sexuality, but innocence and guilt remain unknowable. Jeanne Thomas Allen has wisely noticed that "the eerie, often unidentifiable soundtrack" carries the "best approximation of the novella's essential ambiguity."

Uncertainty builds because sounds are not only unidentifiable in themselves, but also "ambiguous as to the film's code system" which it develops "for music, echo effects, exaggerated volume, and electronic sound."[44] Sounds sometimes merge into each other, sometimes are heard simultaneously. In *The Innocents* Clayton walked the line between ambiguity and confusion that would become a central path for filmmakers of the next decade.

Contemporary Trends, 1966–Present

Among the many connections between literature and film in the United States have been the bonds of support for and the bonds of resistance to public and private attempts to influence literary and filmic content. Public efforts to suppress distribution/sale/exhibition of books and movies have taken various forms, from local and state censorship boards to federal customs offices. The most successful private ordering has come from the Catholic Church, which issues an Index of Forbidden Books and—through the Legion of Decency, established in the 1930s—rates movies according to their moral content. The film industry itself, always alert to threats of federal control, has implemented various types of self-regulation and self-labeling, from the inauguration of the Hays Office in 1922 through the introduction of the Production Code in 1930 to the installation of the Motion Picture Association of America (MPAA) classification system in 1968. Various publishing houses and distributors (e.g., Grove Press, Joseph Burstyn), organizations (e.g., the American Civil Liberties Union), and individual attorneys (e.g., Ephraim London, Edward de Grazia) have been key figures in the contemporary struggle for First Amendment protection for books and films. The censorship history of *Tropic of Cancer* reflects that struggle.

Tropic of Cancer, Henry Miller's first book, was published in Paris in 1934. Reaction was immediate: the book became an international sensation, banned in all English-speaking countries. Defying the twenty-seven-year-old ban, Grove Press released an American edition in 1961. Litigation promptly developed in twenty-one states.[45] The expenses incurred to defend *Tropic of Cancer* left the small publishing house on the edge of financial disaster, but publisher Barney Rossett continued his strong support of sexual frankness and radical politics, both in publishing (e.g., *The Evergreen Review*) and film distribution (e.g., *Titicut Follies*) through the 1960s and after.

In the late 1950s, the U.S.Supreme Court began to consider the constitutional issues posed by governmental restraints on "obscene" expression. In *Grove Press v. Gerstein* (1964), the Supreme Court for the first time decided that a specific novel (*Tropic of Cancer*) was not obscene and was entitled to constitutional protection from suppression for the entire nation.[46] In 1970 when a film version was made of Miller's autobiographical novel, large chunks of the sexually explicit prose were moved directly into Rip Torn's voice-over narration, and many scenes of sexual activity were visualized. The MPAA classified the film "X—no one under 17 admitted," but there was no legal attempt to suppress exhibition of material that had been the source of intense controversy in the early 1960s.

The same year—1970—a film based on John Updike's sexually explicit *Rabbit, Run* was released. The rights to *Rabbit, Run* had been purchased by director Jack Smight shortly after its publication in 1960. Unable to find financial backing for production, Smight had to borrow money to renew the rights in the mid–1960s. Finally, he convinced Warners to finance a production of Updike's tale of a man on the run. Although Updike has said that he originally wrote *Rabbit, Run* "in the present tense in a sort of cinematic way" and "thought of it as *Rabbit, Run: A Movie*,"[47] his complicated use of stream of consciousness to create Harry "Rabbit" Angstrom's perceptions of his past, his present, and his dreams turned out to be as unfilmable as Faulkner. Updike's precise, controlled style, his unusual blend of naturalism and spiritualism, and his subtle characterizations were lost in an adaptation so clumsy that Smight tried to get his name removed from the credits. Warners (unsuccessfully) marketed the film by linking it to other "explosive" films of the late 1960s, but did not exhibit it in the East until 1974.

In contrast to the fate of *Rabbit, Run*, the adaptation history of *The Godfather* is a dream scenario. The staggering success of the various *Godfather* projects has shaped how Hollywood conceives, produces, and markets films. Paramount, working on a plan of one big hit a year in the 1960s, bought the film rights to *The Godfather* on the basis of one hundred pages of Mario Puzo's manuscript.[48] The studio decided to groom *The Godfather* for the hit slot. Francis Ford Copppola was not the studio's first choice for the directorial assignment (Peter Yates and then Costa-Gavras refused the offer), but he proved a brilliant choice. Before the first film opened (in 1972, not at Christmas 1971, as originally planned), Puzo's (1969) novel had sold one million hardback and twelve million paperback copies. Coppola's film version exceeded even studio expectations, breaking the domestic box-office record set by *The Sound of Music* (1965). The sequel, *Godfather II* (1974), goes significantly beyond where the novel leaves off in terms of character action, and, even more than the first film, goes beyond the original novel in the sophistication of its narrative structure. Coppola skillfully moves the sage of the Corleone family both forward and backward in time, using chronological juxtaposition as social analysis. Far less popular than its predecessor, the dark sequel challenges the romance of American success. *Godfather II* "does not compare a success with failure, but shows how the success of the Corleones leads directly and inevitably to the failure."[49] *The Godfather* series fully realized its status as popular myth when the two films were reedited (by Barry Malkin) and broadcast as a three-part, nine-hour (including commercials and credits) miniseries on NBC-TV in November 1977. Coppola's analytic juxtapositions were sacrificed to the smooth logic of chronological storytelling in *Mario Puzo's the Godfather: The Complete Novel for Television*. By the late 1970's the dynastic novel had found a new home.

Not only has television become the producer of popular literary sagas that adapt so well to the expansive possibilities of the miniseries, but television, particularly public television, has eagerly grasped the role of keeper of the classics. The serious contemporary novel of fairly limited narrative scope is still more likely to move to the large screen. Three such films from the 1970s— *Deliverance* (1972), *One Flew Over the Cuckoo's Nest* (1975), and *Who'll Stop the Rain?* (1978)—illustrate a range of authorial collaboration, translation success, and audience acceptance.

Deliverance combines poetry and adventure in an allegorical tale of a canoe trip that takes four city men into the center of a dangerous and beautiful natural world. Author James Dickey wrote the screenplay and even plays a minor role in the film (as the sheriff, his face locked in a threatening grin, who questions the men after they leave the river and their dead), but director John Boorman nevertheless ends the film with its protagonist, Ed Gentry, in a nightmare of regret and fear. In Dickey's novel, Gentry, despite and perhaps because of the deaths he witnessed and caused, has been brought back to life—delivered.[50] Gentry's psychological journey, which is the core of the novel, has been replaced by an emphasis on events rendered with great visual power by cinematographer Vilmos Zgismond: the shocking rape of Bobby Trippe, Lewis Medlock's grotesque injury in the rapids, Gentry's stalking and killing of the mountain man who may have been an innocent. Burt Reynold's star presence tilts the film. He plays Medlock, the natural hunter, with such aggressive bravado that the part and the attitude can be read either as 1940s hero or 1970s caricature.

Although both the novel and the film of *Deliverance* were popular, their success was minor compared to *One Flew Over the Cuckoo's Nest*, a nonconformist's bible in the 1960s and a winner of four major Oscars (Best Picture, Director, Actor, and Actress) in 1975. Adapted into a successful Broadway play in 1963, Ken Kesey's novel took more than a decade to reach the screen. Kesey himself wrote a screenplay, but it was rejected; he bitterly dismissed the changes in the filmed version, primarily the shift in narrative perspective from Chief Bromden to Randle McMurphy.[51] Changed, too, were both the cartoon quality of the mock Gospel novel and its mordant satire. Czech director Milos Forman softened Kesey's satire and replaced Bromden's hallucinations with the concrete world of location shooting—at the Oregon State Hospital. Still, the film tapped the enormous anti-institutional sentiment, especially among the young, that had partly accounted for the book's success. As the prophet of natural passion, McMurphy sacrifices himself and redeems the Chief. But first, McMurphy— played with great zest by Jack Nicholson—awakens all the inmates to the joys of anarchy. McMurphy's ingenious opposition to the cruelty and sterility of officialdom, as embodied by Big Nurse, delighted audiences, eager to embrace the Szazian view that mental illness is a myth from which one can escape in slow motion.

One of Kesey's band of Merry Pranksters in the 1960s[52] was Robert Stone, who wrote one of the best novels of the 1970s, *Dog Soldiers*. Not only was Stone familiar with the domestic drug scene, but he had been a correspondent in Vietnam in 1971, the time in which his novel is set, and knew how decidedly unmerry international drug traffic could be. Using as his basic story line the adventure tale of John Converse, an embittered journalist in Saigon who smuggles a load of heroin into the United States, Stone created a haunting story of the physical and moral consequences of a vicious, immoral war. *Dog Soldiers* won the National Book Award in 1974. Soon after, independent producer Herb Jaffe purchased the film rights. Stone himself worked on two scripts for a year, but he was unable to translate the daring mixture of interior and exterior narration in his novel. Jaffe considers the predicament common: "You always have that problem with a novelist who adapts his own novel. The odds are . . . that it's not going to work. There are rare times when it *really* works, but those are unusual occasions when the guy has a movie in mind in the first place."[53] Judith Rascoe, a friend of Stone's, wrote the final script, changing Marge Converse, the journalist's wife, into an innocent partner in the drug smuggling and shaping her relationship with soldier of fortune Ray Hicks into a far more traditional romance than the blunt desire for dope and sex found in Stone's novel. Directed by Karel Reisz and titled *Who'll Stop the Rain?*, the film is, despite some softening, still a grim look at people on the margin of a cruel and greedy society. Even Hicks's former guru, Dieter, cannot stop the violent destruction that has become as natural as rain. In 1978 the scars of Vietnam were still fresh; few Americans wanted to see movies that would make those wounds visible.

In 1969 the Wall Street Journal quoted one story editor as stating that "more than 80% of the movies made today are adaptations of literary material."[54] Despite the probable exaggeration in this claim and despite the fact that original screenplays have fluctuated in relative number and importance throughout the last two decades, there has been consistent commercial interest in the "presold audience." More than ever, adaptation is a commercial process, recycling best-selling books into box-office successes. Large corporations began acquiring movie studios in 1962 (when Music Corporation of America purchased Universal), and by the end of the decade they were scrambling to buy publishing houses. Media conglomerates often approach adaptations as the multiple packaging of a single property. There is no better example of this symbiotic process than *The Deep* (1977).

James Monaco regards *The Deep*, not *Close Encounters of the Third Kind*, as "the real secret to Columbia's success in 1977."[55] An unremarkable film by most standards, the pirate melodrama was the sixth highest grossing film of the year. What was remarkable about *The Deep* was its marketing campaign, orchestrated by producer Peter Guber over a two-year period. The film was presold by Peter Benchley's follow-up novel to *Jaws*. The book was first published in hardcover, then in paperback. Excerpts and condensations appeared in magazines. Guber himself wrote *Inside "The Deep"*, a behind-the-scenes account that went on sale two days before the simultaneous opening of the film at 800 theaters. For a month before the opening, Guber, Benchley, director Peter Yates, and the stars blanketed the talk-show circuit. A merchandising campaign, with products ranging from a poster of Jacqueline Bisset in a wet T-shirt to a see-through blue vinyl soundtrack album was mounted to advertise the film and also to sell tie-ins (mostly manufactured by companies owned by Columbia). Guber is known as one of the best promoters in Hollywood. His approach to "packaging a concept" has influenced contemporary publishing and filmmaking.

Just as the studios have lost their individual identities, so, too, have the publishing houses. The absorption of Alfred A. Knopf into Random House in 1960 set the tone for mergers that begot mergers. Besides mergers, the most important recent trend in publishing has been the emergence of the bookstore chain. Those trends were combined in 1984 when K-mart Corporation, the nation's second largest retailer, purchased Waldenbooks, the nation's second largest bookstore chain. Publishing, like movie production, is focusing more and more attention on fewer and fewer products. Agents, often lawyers by training and negotiators by instinct, are increasingly powerful weavers of "the deal fabric."[56] Part of the deal for a film adapted from a novel is a reissue of the novel, usually with production stills and a large promotional campaign. For big films with original screenplays, novelizations are often part of the economic package. The creation of books based on films dates back to such early successes as *Son of the Sheik* (1926) and *King Kong* (1932), but a complicated web of current economic circumstances encourages the practice.[57] The 1982 novelization of *E. T.: The Extraterrestrial*, which sold millions of copies, has led to mounting criticism of the kinds of books being published as paperback lists increasingly dominate book sales.

One of the effects of the corporate takeovers is the added pressure on paperback houses to devote ever-larger amounts of time and money to category sales. These sales are closely linked to market research studies and the advertising of new "lines" created as their consequence.[58] Three contemporary novels—*The Shining*, *Rumble Fish*, and *The Color Purple*—each a popular example of a different fiction category, illustrate how film adaptations in the 1980s have attempted (with varying degrees of success) to exploit and expand the notion of category sales. In each case, the film director had no developed association with the particular fiction category.

Stephen King's pulp gothics have frightened and entertained millions of American readers. It is difficult to imagine a sensibility more alien to King's direct popular appeal than that of Stanley Kubrick, arguably the coolest, most abstract of all contemporary American directors. Shot mostly in the EMI-Elstree studios outside London, *The Shining* project occupied the reclusive Kubrick for more than three years. A provocative trailer first appeared the Christmas before the film's 1980 summer release. In dramatic, mysterious contrast to the frenzied edition of most trailers, the preview for *The Shining* was a single shot of the elevator doors in an empty hotel lobby. As the camera stares, what looks like blood begins seeping, then gushing, from the closed doors. The blood swells in volume to the point that it carries heavy furniture along in its surge toward the camera, toward those who wait in the theater to be engulfed in a tale of horror.

But Kubrick's film never engulfs the audience. *The Shining* is as enigmatic as its trailer. Despite the terrifying content, the passion in the film is all directed toward the dry elevations of modernism. Far less interested in character and incident than in technical virtuosity and metaphysics, Kubrick has designed an elaborate sructure to ponder—alone, if need be—the immortality of evil and the centrality of authorship.

Francis Coppola's adaptation *Rumblefish* (1982) is another example of a director trying to push an essentially adolescent novel into a more complex form. S. E. Hinton, who began publishing fiction at seventeen, writes novels for teenagers, the largest moviegoing audience and the most reluctant readers. Nevertheless, Hinton's novels are extremely popular with young adults, many of whom never read best-sellers. *Rumble Fish*, which concerns a confused teenager's misplaced respect for his older brother, is typical of her compassionate stories of ordinary, and often disappointing, relationships. Coppola latched his operatic energy onto Hinton's simple story. The result is a visually experimental film that constantly reaches for symbolic effect. Despite the imaginative casting of Dennis Hopper as the father and Mickey Rourke as Motorcycle Boy and the use of four fine young actors with considerable teenage followings—Matt Dillon, Nicholas Cage, Vincent Spano, and Christopher Penn—Coppola's *Rumblefish* lacks the basic concern for adolescents' feelings that makes Hinton's fiction important to teenagers.

The Color Purple (1985) is an exemplar of the successful crossover movie. Director Steven Spielberg and scenarist Menno Mayjes have taken the story of the emotional and sexual growth of an abused child–woman, written by a black feminist, and turned it into a national crowd-pleaser. Alice Walker's novel was no stranger to success (winning both the Pulitzer Prize and the National Book Award; selling over a million copies) nor to controversy (sparking protests for its negative presentation of black men and its celebration of lesbian love), but Spielberg's film version moved *The Color Purple* into another arena of celebrity and debate. The tie-in edition of the novel topped the national paperback sales charts soon after the film's winter holiday release; the movie was nominated for Best Picture and numerous other awards. Its release intensified the never dormant debate about the effects of negative portrayals of black family life and provoked picket lines by groups such as the Coalition Against Black Exploitation.[59]

In Walker's novel, a reader follows Celie's dramatic metamorphosis from battered child to proud, self-sufficient woman through a series of letters. Most of them are from Celie to God; some follow her adult correspondence with her beloved sister Nettie, who becomes a missionary in Africa. These are necessarily restricted, private views of the world, understandable and powerful on those limited terms. In the first part of the film, Celie is presented as both object and mediator of the audience's vision. Celie remains near the heart of the enacted events, but the film soon abandons her voice-over and moves into a seemingly omniscient ''present,'' with its implication of expanded viewpoint. Still, there is no expansion of understanding beyond Celie's in the novel. The simplicity remains, and is softened by a sentimentality that sometimes spills into light comedy. The central dynamic for Celie's change in the novel—the power of sisterhood—is transmuted into a generalized notion of the redemptive power of love. Despite the abuse inflicted on the characters, a visual sweetness permeates the film and prepares one for the series of emotional reconciliations that end the family saga. Spielberg's *The Color Purple* illustrates the strengths and the weaknesses of popular visual storytelling; it displays the possibilities and the problems of adapting an alternative literary voice to the conventionality of mainstream moviemaking.

STYLES AND GENRES OF INTERACTION

Within and across historical periods, film and literature have been linked by a common interest in genre content, by individuals who have worked in both forms, by an appropriation of the activities of the other medium as story material, and by a shared concern with narrative structure.

Westerns

Western novels have been popular in America since the middle of the nineteenth century. Three Western novels adapted into films—*The Virginian, Shane,* and *Little Big Man*—indicate how the genre has accommodated itself to the attitudes of various periods. Owen Wister's *The Virginian* topped the best-seller lists in the year of its publication (1902). "Generally, [*The Virginian*] is credited with beginning the twentieth-century western craze. More than any other book, it stands as the transition between the dime novel and the modern literary and cinematic western."[60] Dedicated to Theodore Roosevelt, the novel has enjoyed continued popularity. If affirmed the traditional frontier virtues in the wake of the growing obsolescence of those virtues; it gave classic formulation to the Western myth just as the reality of the Western frontier was ending.[61] The East-West conflict which moves the plot is resolved by a synthesis of American traditions: The Eastern schoolmarm, Molly, marries the Virginian, thus accepting the code of the West. Played by Gary Cooper in the 1929 film version, the Virginian became the prototypical Western hero: ideally brave, handsome, honorable, and chivalrous.

Several decades later, no such marriage of differences seemed possible. Written in 1949 and filmed in 1953, *Shane* carries "the antithesis between success and honor to its inevitable conclusion: the destruction or exile of the hero from the developing town, which can no longer permit the explosions of individual will and agression."[62] No matter how longingly the young boy calls out for his hero to "come back," Shane must ride on. Unwilling to be absorbed in the domestic or social world, the Western hero is fated to be an outsider, albeit a romantic one. Told from the point of view of a young boy (as remembered in the novel, as "lived" in the film), *Shane* is unabashedly mythic. Director George

Stevens pushed the genre's iconography to symbolic extremes, identifying Shane with the natural world and creating a visual allegory of good and evil.

The burden of Western fiction is to determine whether the coming of civilization is good or ill.[63] The novel *Little Big Man* rejects the absolutism of such a choice and takes a contemporary position of general skepticism; the film version holds another attitude popular in the early 1970s—it turns cowboys into villains, Indians into heroes. "Both [Thomas] Berger [the novelist] and [Arthur] Penn [the director] take aim at the standard legends of the West; but while Penn is the idealistic debunker, taking sides with the Indians against the white invaders of the frontier, Berger is the cynical revisionist, whose earthy skepticism spares no one, Indian or white, from full participation in the corruption and vulgarity of the cutthroat times."[64] Berger's amoral picaresque saga turns on an irony quite foreign to the Western tradition. Although it has moments of bawdy comedy, Penn's film teems with moral outrage. He puts white murderousness at the center of his narrative and presents the Cheyenne as an idealized alternative to the materialism, narrow-mindedness, and cruelty of white society. Stressing the parallel between the Indians and the Vietnamese, Penn makes the Washita River Massacre the dark climax of the film. He presents Jack Crabb, the 121-year-old narrator, as an absurd hero, eternally out of step, reactive rather than active, yet a survivor who can "correct" the tall tale of the West.

Hard-boiled Fiction/*Film Noir*

Edmund Wilson called them "poets of the tabloid murder,"[65] a fitting oxymoron for writers who published in the pulp magazine *Black Mask* yet earned the respect of European intellectuals. They moved their hard-boiled stories into film and shaped a style dubbed *film noir* by French critics (using Marcel Duhamel's *Serie Noire* books as an analogue). Dashiell Hammett, James M. Cain, and Raymond Chandler were the best of this breed of California-based writers. Their vision of a dark, corrupt world can be seen in their stories, their screenplays, and in three sample *films noirs* adopted from their novels: *The Maltese Falcon* (1941), *Double Indemnity* (1944), and *Lady in the Lake* (1947). The influence of Hammett, Cain, and Chandler on popular prose and Hollywood movies has reached far beyond their individual collaborations.

In *The Maltese Falcon*, Hammett presents the definitive treatment of the American private detective. Sam Spade is a deceiver in a righteous cause, a moral man skillfully operating in an immoral world. The 1941 film version, directed by John Huston and starring Humphrey Bogart, made Spade an embodiment of the Hemingway hero, a romantic figure who remains true to his own code. Spade's journey into darkness does not corrupt him: he is able to turn the woman he loves over to the police. Bogart's cool toughness and Huston's hard, precise directorial style capture the tone of Hammett's fiction.[66]

All three of these novels are told in the first person, but in *Double Indemnity* it is not the figure of light who tells the story, but one of the murderers. In the film version, a bleeding Walter Neff, who has been shot by his co-conspirator and lover, dictates his confession into a tape recorder. The events then appear as an extended flashback. This break with the linear tradition of Hollywood storytelling establishes a fatalistic mood and provides an opportunity for Neff to comment cynically on the irreversible patterns of desire, transgression, and self-punishment that form this story. The knowing, laconic voice-over became a staple of *film noir*. Evidence of betrayal by the woman, always a strong possibility in this misogynistic genre, is present from the beginning, so a particular sense of doom surrounds the smug playfulness of the first encounters between Neff (Fred MacMurray) and Phyllis (Barbara Stanwyck). One of the trademarks of hard-boiled fiction is its rich urban vulgate. Screenwriter Raymond Chandler took Cain's story and added a series of aggressive verbal exchanges between Walter and Phyllis. Their banter is full of innuendo and the fresh rhythms of a witty, sleazy couple on the make. Alan Spiegel's superb reading of *Double Indemnity* includes this judgment: "Of its cold, hard, dark, flavorful kind, there is nothing better."[67]

Lady in the Lake (based on a Chandler novel constructed out of several short stories) takes the sense of individual perception central to hard-boiled fiction and attempts to translate it into cinematic terms. The result is a radical stylistic departure: almost all of *Lady in the Lake* is shot with a subjective camera. In the prologue, the tough private-eye narrator Phillip Marlowe speaks facing the camera: "You'll see it just as I saw it. You'll meet the people; you'll find the clues. And maybe you'll solve it quick and maybe you won't." Thereafter, Marlowe (Robert Montgomery) is seen on only three more occasions when he directly addresses the audience, several times when he passes a mirror, and in the last scene (which was dictated by the studio). Other characters speak directly into the camera as if addressing Marlowe. The preview audience for *Lady in the Lake* wanted to *see* the leads kiss in a traditional closing embrace, so MGM demanded that Montgomery (who also directed the film) include a final shot that violates all his earlier dogged attempts to present only Marlowe's viewpoint.[68] Montgomery's severe experiment in first-person point of view necessitated basic alterations in set design, acting, shooting, and editing. *Lady in the Lake* did not change mainstream visual storytelling; however, its failures provide important clues regarding the position of the film spectator in the text.

The Hollywood Novel

Nancy Brooker Bowers defines the Hollywood novel as "an American regional fictional genre that features characters who work in the film industry either in Hollywood or with a Hollwyood production company on location."[69] When she expands the genre to include other novels about film activities (independent productions, film festivals, and so forth), her list of novels written in English or translated into English in the 1912–1982 period swells to nearly seven hundred entries. Clearly, the film industry has been a compelling topic for novelists, many of whom have worked in the industry. Their dreams and disappointments shape the love-hate relationship with Hollywood that festers at the center of many of these novels. Those complex relationships go through still more permutations when the novels are adapted into films. The struggle for power that often moves the narratives is mirrored in the dynamics of the adaptation process. The result is often a curious self-loathing presented as entertaining exposé. Since the climate for recrimination was particularly ripe in the 1970s, it is not surprising that an unusually high number of films critical of the movie colony were produced in that decade. Some adaptations reached back more than a generation for their despair, most notably the long-awaited film versions of *The Day of the Locust* (1975) and *The Last Tycoon* (1976).

The Day of the Locust was published in 1939, the year before Nathanael West's death in an automobile accident. West registered a disappointment in *The Day of the Locust* that went far beyond the personal with a savage, comic brilliance that is yet to be equaled by another Hollywood novel. He used the bizarre life of the movie industry to focus on the dangerous, explosive boredom and essential meaninglessness that he thought endemic throughout American society. His story of a brutal and mindless world is told through the eyes of a young set designer whose collage "The Burning of Los Angeles" imagines the destructive potential of the "locusts"—the crowds drawn to Hollywood/California by dreams of money and fame. Teased and cheated, the frustrated "extras" turn into a rioting, murderous mob.

West worked in Hollywood writing screenplays the last five years of his life. His prose style, characterized by roving, panoramic descriptive techniques and short, episodic scenes, actually predates his script work, but it is a style generally considered cinematic.[70] Consequently, *The Day of the Locust* adapted easily to the screen at the structural level; however, West's use of metaphor and his perceptive analysis of the crowd's fury elude the filmmakers, resulting in a film that is "satirical and spectacular," but, unlike West's novel, "not deeply serious."[71]

Despite their considerable difference in personal and literary styles, West and F. Scott Fitzgerald are often mentioned in the same breath, as Hollywood casualties. Fitzgerald died before he finished *The Last Tycoon*, but he left a remarkable account of the problems besetting the "last" Hollywood producer with a sense of moral and social responsibility. Patterned on the meteoric career of Irving Thalberg, the boy wonder at MGM in the 1920s and 1930s, Fitzgerald's story of Monroe Stahr uses the interior exhaustion and the decline in leadership in the studio system as emblematic of the breakdown of the American dream itself. Fitzgerald, himself drawn to Hollywood as moth to flame, used the teenage daughter of a rival producer as his primary narrator. Her adolescent infatuation with Stahr limits her viewpoint, so Fitzgerald shifted perspective to other characters, using a style that might be described as crosscutting.[72] The screen adaptation unfortunately joined a screenwriter renowned for subtle understatement, Harold Pinter, and a director associated with passionate overstatement, Elia Kazan. The resulting film is a limp, yet obvious, look at historic Hollywood.

Even more lethargic is the film adaptation (1972) of Joan Didion's *Play It As It Lays*. Didion, who co-wrote the script with her husband John Gregory Dunne, presents a deeply depressing view of people on the fringes of the movie colony, filtered through the disintegrating consciousness of a cult film star, played by Tuesday Weld. The alienated actress continually drives the Los Angeles freeways, haunted by memories, tormented by fears of a failing marriage and a doomed career. Her journey through the Hollywood–Beverly Hills–Malibu area is a trip into Babylon, with insanity and death the only forms of escape. The satiric bite of Didion's novel has been flattened in a film overcome by its own angst.

In spirited contrast, *The Stunt Man* (1980) is a flamboyantly funny movie about paranoia and the fine art of filmic deception. Based on a relatively unknown novel by Paul Brodeur, the movie begins by following a fugitive on the run and never slows down. As Eli Cross, the egotistical, manipulative, ultimately enigmatic director, Peter O'Toole sparkles with comic intensity. The fugitive who becomes a stuntman rarely knows where the lines between reality and illusion are drawn, but he is sure that the satanic director is drawing them. The poster/T-shirt design for *The Stunt Man* summarizes the film's operating attitude: a horned, tailed Eli Cross claims from his director's chair: "If God could do the tricks we can do, he'd be a happy man."

Narrative Structure

As storytellers, novelists and filmmakers share a common body of narrative techniques, but before and beyond the level of craft, they share and help shape attitudes and patterns of cognition—ways of thinking about time, space, and being. Many have noted the influence of the cinematic imagination on the modern novel, pointing out literary parallels to montage editing (time shifts, fragmentation, episodic structure), camera angles and focus (changes in perspective or point of view), establishing shots and pans (survey of a physical setting), zooms and close-ups (close attention to detail), fades and dissolves (overlapping story lines), and so forth, emphasizing what Wayne C. Booth sees as a basic distinction between novelists who tell and novelists who show.[73] The desire to show, however, was precinematic. Speigel argues convincingly that Conrad's stated ambition (in 1897) to make his readers *see* flowed from an increasingly common narrative desire to unite "image and concept . . . visual fact and value."[74] Griffith described his goal for *The Birth of a Nation* in words almost identical to Conrad's. Speigel traces this shared desire of storytellers to show *and* tell to the development of the "concretized novel," seeing Flaubert as the seminal figure, "who drew together the dramatizing and visualizing tendencies of his immediate predecessors

(Balzac, Dickens, Gogol, Hawthorne) and presented them with a definitive form.''[75] Claude-Edmonde Magny makes a similar argument when she writes,

The great lesson the American novel learned from the movies—that the less one says the better, that the most striking artistic effects are those born of the juxtaposition of two images, without any commentary, and that the novel, no more than any other art, should not say too much—was very well understood by Hemingway, Faulkner, and Steinbeck. But Stendhal, Balzac, and the naturalists had anticipated it: long before the twentieth century, they had already invented the journalistic novel.[76]

The movies have also taught novelists lessons about the plasticity of time-space relationships. Each subsequent generation of American novelists, ever more immersed in the Film Age, has explored ways of organizing and fragmenting narrative time and space. An irony emerges: the novels considered most cinematic (for example, the work of Faulkner and John Dos Passos) are often the most unfilmable. Three contemporary adaptations, all based on novels that are relatively experimental in narrative structure and particularly interested in exploring time-space relationships, illustrate the hesitancy of commerical cinema to exploit the time-space potential of the medium.

As Joseph Heller himself acknowledges, *Catch–22* employs a structural pattern developed by Faulkner whereby a complicated narrative is told largely in terms of fragments and the slow feeding of interrupted episodes.[77] Chronological time, in its usual sense, is meaningless, replaced by what is often called psychological time. ''Things happen'' more than once, sometimes more than twice. One of the intended effects of this technique is a feeling of timelessness. The looping potential of film would seem especially amenable to a spiral structure.[78] Nevertheless, the film version of *Catch–22* (1970) resists structural innovation. It accommodates Heller's surreal black comedy within a traditional narrative framework that is esssentially chronological and ''logical'' in its plotting. One important exception should be noted. Although the film does not mention Heller's often repeated phrase, ''Snowden's secret,'' director Mike Nichols, through visual repetition and extension, reveals Snowden's primal secret: the discovery of death.

Slaughterhouse-Five by Kurt Vonnegut, Jr., shares aspects of setting (World War II), tone (black comedy), and structural design (episodic, repetitive) with *Catch–22*. *Slaughterhouse-Five* is the story of an eternal innocent, unstuck in time, who learns to accept his essential powerlessness over life, which is simply a series of moments randomly strung together, some bad, some good. The tale is told with an aggressive randomness that challenges traditional notions of narrative causality. Vonnegut brackets his novel with an autobiographical frame in which he discusses writing a (this) book about the destruction of Dresden.[79] The modernist bracket does not appear in the film *Slaughterhouse-Five* (1972). As usual in the illusionary cinema, the story seems to tell itself. Director George Roy Hill and screenwriter Stephen Geller take the novel's fragmentary, nonsequential episodes and divide most of Billy's life into three recognizable periods: Billy as a German prisoner of war, as a family man and optometrist in suburbia, and as movie star Montana Wildhack's lover in the human zoo on the planet Tralfamadore. The movie traces each stage chronologically as a series of events; each period progresses to an obvious climax.[80] Editor Dede Allen intercut Billy's time trips, so that the three periods interrupt each other, yet they never blend. The result is a multilinearity that provides a complicated, yet still conventional, variant of narrative progression. The movie plays with the topic of time-space distortion while presenting Billy's time tripping less as random movement in time and space than as a zany past, present, and future.

E. L. Doctorow's novel *Ragtime* employs a formal structure that seeks to link two historical eras—the one with which the book deals (pre–World War I America) and the other from which the book emerges (1970s America). The narration continually reminds the reader of the vantage point of the present in understanding the truth about the past, while it audaciously links historical personages and fictional characters (for example, Emma Goldman and Younger Brother) and puts real people into wildly imaginative situations (Freud and Jung in the Tunnel of Love). *Ragtime* is a novel about the contradictions in the lazy, volatile age it depicts, but it is also about ways of seeing, about the distortions involved in historical and aesthetic expression. One of the illusionists in the novel is Tateh, an immigrant turned movie entrepreneur. His story charts the growing influence of the cinema—its promises and its lies. Like many modern novelists, Doctorow uses the temporal cutting of the cinema to create a spatial patterning of temporal relations. Doctorow treats time "not as a chronological sequence, but as a network. . . . It is as though the whole era were laid out on a grid, events given meaning according to their spatial, rather than temporal, relation to other events."[81]

When producer Dino De Laurentiis fired director Robert Altman from the *Ragtime* adaptation project, there was a general sigh of disappointment from many admirers of the novel who had thought the creator of *Nashville* (1975) was the one American director who would have the irreverence, wit, and imagination to bring Doctorow's panorama alive on the screen. The situation and its resulting disappointment remind one of the burdens of expectation—both commercial and artistic—that surround any adaptation of a popular and well-respected novel. Milos Forman's film (1981) rejects any overt modernist attention to the act of narrative construction. Instead, the film concentrates on the contradictions within the period setting. A motif of a waltzing couple swirls through the story, in opposition to the ragtime music at the center of the life of the black piano player Coalhouse Walker, Jr. After an opening credit sequence that pictures the waltzers, a newsreel projected on a movie screen with musical accompaniment by Walker introduces many of the characters and themes of Doctorow's amazing novel. For those ready to see the point, the playful mixture of the historic and the fictive immediately suggests the control the modern director has over history. For other audience members, the newsreel could function simply as an eye-catching introduction to the characters in a complicated and moving story. As novel and as film, *Ragtime* illustrates and celebrates an "exchange" between the two art forms.[82]

NOTES

I gratefully acknowledge the research assistance of Mara Tripp and Lee Murphy and a critical reading of the manuscript by Tom Benson.

1. See Raymond Durgnat's essay "Outtakes," in *Film and/as Literature*, ed. John Harrington (Englewood Cliffs, N.J.: Prentice-Hall, 1977), p. 259. Cf. Gerald Mast, *Film/Cinema/Movie* (New York: Harper & Row, 1977).

2. Patricia Holt, "Turning Best Sellers into Movies," *Publishers Weekly* 22 October 1979: 36–40. Charles Eidsvik makes a strong and provocative argument for moving film criticism "Toward a 'Politique des Adaptations' " in Harrington, pp. 27–37.

3. Geoffrey Wagner, *The Novel and the Cinema* (Cranbury, N.J.: Fairleigh Dickinson University Press, 1975), pp. 222, 230.

4. Richard Schickel, *D. W. Griffith: An American Life* (New York: Simon & Schuster, 1984), pp. 275–76, bases his account on a description from *Moving Picture World*, 13 March 1915.

5. See Thomas Cripps, *Slow Fade to Black: The Negro in American Film 1900–1942* (New York: Oxford University Press, 1977), pp. 41–69, for a detailed account of organized resistance to *The Birth of a Nation*.

6. Jan-Christopher Horak, "Maurice Tourneur's Tragic Romance," in *The Classic American Novel and the Movies*, ed. Gerald Peary and Roger Shatzkin (New York: Frederick Ungar, 1977), pp. 10–19.

7. For a full history of the film, see Herman G. Weinberg, *The Complete "Greed"* (New York: Arno, 1972).

8. I depend on Kevin Brownlow's carefully researched discussion of the film, pp. 385–414, in *The Parade's Gone By . . .* (Berkeley: Ballantine Books, 1968).

9. Mark W. Estrin, " 'Triumphant Ignominy' on the Screen," in *The Classic American Novel*, ed. Peary and Shatzkin, p. 27. Also see Julian Smith, "Hester, Sweet Hester Prynne—*The Scarlet Letter* in the Movie Market Place," *Literature/Film Quarterly* 2 (1974): 100–09.

10. See "Scenario," pp. 269–278 in Brownlow.

11. Bennett Cerf, *Hollywood Reporter* 9 January 1941: 3.

12. William Froug, *The Screenwriter Looks at the Screenwriter* (New York: Macmillan, 1972), p. xiii.

13. Edmund Wilson, *The Boys in the Back Room: Notes on California Novelists* (San Francisco: Colt Press, 1941), p. 72.

14. Sergei Eisenstein, "Dickens, Griffith, and the Film Today," in *Film Form: Essays in Film Theory*, trans. and ed. Jay Leyda (New York: Harcourt, Brace, 1949), p. 196. In *With Eisenstein in Hollywood* (New York: International Publishers, 1969), pp. 110–120, Ivor Montague describes the aborted collaboration and includes the Eisenstein scenario (appendix 2). See also Keith Cohen, "Eisenstein's Adaptation," in *The Classic American Novel*, ed. Peary and Shatzkin, pp. 239–56; and James Lundquist, *Theodore Dreiser* (New York: Frederick Ungar, 1974), pp. 20–25.

15. Josef von Sternberg, *Fun in a Chinese Laundry: An Autobiography* (New York: Collier Books, 1972), p. 46.

16. See Edward Murray, *The Cinematic Imagination: Writers and the Motion Pictures* (New York: Frederic Ungar, 1972), pp. 116–23.

17. Von Sternberg, p. 259.

18. Russell Campbell, "Trampling Out the Vintage: Sour Grapes," in *The Modern American Novel and the Movies*, ed. Gerald Peary and Roger Shatzkin (New York: Frederick Ungar, 1978), p. 109.

19. Warren French, who provides the most complete analysis of the adaptation in *Filmguide to "The Grapes of Wrath"* (Bloomington: Indiana University Press, 1973), is of this opinion. Cf. George Bluestone, *Novel into Film* (Baltimore: Johns Hopkins University Press, 1957), pp. 147–69; and Morris Beja, *Film & Literature* (New York: Longman, 1979), pp. 107–117.

20. Kate Ellis, "Life with Marmee: Three Versions," in *The Classic American Novel*, ed. Peary and Shatzkin, p. 62. For the text of the screenplay, see Lorraine Nobel, ed., *Four-Star Scripts: Actual Shooting and How They Are Written* (Garden City: Doubleday Duran, 1936).

21. Janet Juhnke, "A Kansan's View," in *The Classic American Novel*, ed. Peary and Shatzkin,. p. 169. Also see Aljean Harmetz, *The Making of "The Wizard of Oz"* (New York: Alfred A. Knopf, 1977).

22. Andrew Turnbell, ed., *The Letters of F. Scott Fitzgerald* (New York: Scribner, 1963), p. 284. For full accounts of the complicated production, see Gavin Lambert, *GWTW: The Making of "Gone with the Wind"* (Boston: Little, Brown, 1973); Roland Flamini, *Scarlett, Rhett, and a Cast of Thousands: The Filming of "Gone with the Wind"* (New York: MacMillan, 1975); and Richard Harwell, ed., *Gone With the Wind as Book and Film* (Columbia, South Carolina: University of South Carolina Press, 1983).

23. Gene D. Phillips, *Hemingway and Film* (New York: Frederick Ungar, 1980), p. 50.

24. In *Faulkner and Film* (New York: Frederick Ungar, 1977), Bruce F. Kawin places Faulkner in the project from the outset. His version of the hunting trip (based on a personal interview with Hawks) has Hemingway saying, "You can't make a picture out of [*To Have and Have Not*]," and Hawks retorting, "OK, I'll get Faulkner to do it. He can write better than you can anyway" (p. 109). See Murray, p. 154, and Kawin, p. 69. Also, see William Rothman, "To Have and Have Not Adapted a Novel," in *The Modern American Novel*, ed. Peary and Shatzkin, pp. 70–79; Robin Wood, "To Have (Written) and Have Not (Directed)," in *Movies and Methods*, ed. Bill Nichols (Berkeley: University of California Press, 1976), pp. 297–305; and Frank M. Laurence, *Hemingway and the Movies* (Jackson: University of Mississippi Press, 1981), pp. 82–113.

25. Phillips, *Hemingway and Films*, p. 59. For more recent examples of the effect of adaptations on book sales, see Michael Blowen, "How the Movie Sells the Book," *Boston Globe* 12 January 1986: B1, 7.

26. Personal correspondence to James Sandor, 14 September 1947, quoted in William Luhr, *Raymond Chandler and Film* (New York: Frederick Ungar, 1982), p. 8. The information on Paramount writers is from the same letter.

27. *United States v. Paramount Pictures, Inc., et al.*, 334 U.S. 131 (1948), at 166.

28. Brandon French, *On the Verge of Revolt: Women in American Films of the Fifties* (New York: Frederick Ungar, 1978), pp. 59–60. Cf. Donald Spoto, *Camerado: Holly-*

wood and the American Man (New York: W. W. Norton, 1978), pp. 35–39. Spoto considers the film "a gallery of classic male portraits" (p. 36).

29. Norman Mailer, "Naked Before the Camera," in *The Modern American Novel*, ed. Peary and Shatzkin, p. 187. Mailer realizes, "A novelist sells his work to Hollywood not in order that the work shall survive the translation, but to purchase time for himself ..." (p. 188).

30. David A. Cook, *A History of Narrative Film* (New York: W. W. Norton, 1981), p. 401.

31. Kawin, *Faulkner and Film*, p. 40.

32. E. Pauline Degenfelder, "Rites of Passage: Novel to Film," in *The Modern American Novel*, ed. Peary and Shatzkin, p. 184. I rely on Degenfelder and Kawin for production details. Also see Dorothy B. Jones, "William Faulkner: 'Novel Into Film,' " *Quarterly of Film, Radio and Television* 8 (Fall 1953); 51–71.

33. Nora Sayre, *Running Time: Films of the Cold War* (New York: Dial Press, 1982), p. 47.

34. Kawin, *Faulkner and Film*, p. 66.

35. Part of the essay, which first appeared in the Saturday Review, is quoted in Peter Brunette, "Two Wrights, One Wrong," in *The Modern American Novel*, ed. Peary and Shatzkin, pp. 131–32. Brunette, in turn, has relied on Michel Fabre, *The Unfinished Quest of Richard Wright* (New York: William Morrow, 1973), for many production details.

36. Quoted in Edward De Grazia and Roger K. Newman, *Banned Films: Movies, Censorship and the First Amendment* (New York: R. R. Bowker, 1982), p. 342. Wright was a member of the Communist party when he wrote *Native Son*.

37. *Superior Films v. Department of Education, Classic Pictures v. Department of Education*, 112 N.E. sd 311 (1953); *Superior Films, Inc. v. Department of Education of Ohio*, 346 U.S. 587 (1954).

38. Shirley Clarke, "Symposium on Distribution of the Independent Cinema," *Film Culture* 42 (Fall 1966): 51.

39. Richard Corliss, *Talking Pictures: Screenwriters in the American Cinema* (New York: Penguins, 1974), p. 256. See also Dalton Trumbo, *Additional Dialogue: The Letters of Dalton Trumbo, 1942–1962* (New York: M. Evans; distributed in association with Lippincott, 1970). In 1971 Trumbo directed an adaptation of his own novel, *Johnny Got His Gun*.

40. Ferber comments on the book's reception and the making of the film version in her second autobiography, *A Kind of Magic* (New York: Doubleday, 1963).

41. Joan Mellon, *Big Bad Wolves: Masculinity in the American Film* (New York: Pantheon Books, 1977), p. 234.

42. Available in James Agee, *Agee on Film* (New York: McDowell, Oblensky, 1958). Agee died in May 1955 and never saw the completed picture.

43. Robin Wood, "Charles Laughton on Grubb Street, " in *The Modern American Novel*, ed. Peary and Shatzkin, p. 208.

44. Jeanne Thomas Allen, "Turn of the Screw and the Innocents: Two Types of Ambiguity," in *The Classic American Novel*, ed. Peary and Shatzkin, p. 139. The soundtrack examples are all Allen's. Also see James W. Palmer, "Cinematic Ambiguity: James's *The Turn of the Screw* and Clayton's *The Innocents*," *Literature/Film Quarterly* 5 (1977): 198–215.

45. I rely on De Grazia and Newman, *Banned Films*, pp. 107–110, for the litigation details.

46. Some of the many cases involving Miller's novel are *Besig v. U.S.*, 208. F. 2d 142 (1953); *Yudkin v. Maryland*, 182 A. 2d 798 (1962); *Grove Press Inc. v. Gerstein*, 378 U.S. 577 (1964). The decisions in these cases, and others involving *Tropic of Cancer*, have been collected in Edward De Grazia, *Censorship Landmarks* (New York: R. R. Bowker, 1969) pp. 233–35, 449–69, 508.

47. Updike, quoted in Jane Howard, "Can a Nice Novelist Finish First?" *Life* 4 November 1966: 88. I depend on Gary Seigel, "Rabbit Runs Down," in *The Modern American Novel*, ed. Peary and Shatzkin, pp. 247–55, for production details.

48. Production details are from Michael Pye and Lynda Myles, *The Movie Brats: How the Film Generation Took Over Hollywood* (New York: Holt, Reinhart & Winston, 1979).

49. John Hess, "*Godfather II*: A Deal Coppola Couldn't Refuse," in *Movies and Methods*, ed. Nichols, p. 85. Hess sees the film as a successful critique of capitalism. Cf. David Thomson, *Overexposures: The Crisis in American Filmmaking* (New York: William Morrow, 1981), pp. 283–97.

50. See Janes F. Beaton, "Dickey Down the River," in *The Modern American Novel*, ed. Peary and Shatzkin, pp. 293–306; and Michael Dempsey, "*Deliverance*/Boorman: Dickey in the Woods," *Cinema* 8, no. 1 (1973): 10–17.

51. Seth Cagin and Philip Dray, *Hollywood Films of the Seventies* (New York: Harper & Row, 1984), p. 234. Also see Molly Haskell, "Kesey Cured: Forman's Sweet Insanity," in *The Modern American Novel*, ed. Peary and Shatzkin, pp. 266–71.

52. Tom Wolfe provides an account of Kesey's messianic role in the Pranksters' LSD experiments in *The Electric Kool-Aid Acid Test* (New York: Bantam Books, 1968).

53. Herb Jaffe in Stephen Zito, "*Dog Soldiers*: Novel into Film," *American Film* September 1977: 10.

54. As quoted in Holt, "Turning Best Sellers into Movies," p. 40. Holt considers the figure inflated, but indicative of the situation in 1969, which was followed by drastic cuts in inventory shortly thereafter.

55. James Monaco, *American Film Now*, rev. ed. (New York: New American Library, 1984), p. 25. Details of the marketing of the *The Deep* are all from Monaco.

56. See Thomas Whiteside, *The Blockbuster Complex* (Middletown, Conn.: Wesleyan University Press, 1981), especially pp. 64–79.

57. See Michael Barsom, "Now Playing at a Bookstore Near You," *American Film* April 1985: 50–53, 73.

58. Janice A. Radway, *Reading the Romance: Women, Patriarchy, and Popular Literature* (Chapel Hill: University of North Carolina Press, 1984), pp. 35–36.

59. See Frances M. Beal, "The Purple Comes Through, But Not the Black," *Frontline* 20 January 1986: 18.

60. John G. Cawelti, *Adventure, Mystery and Romance: Formula Stories as Art and Popular Culture* (Chicago: University of Chicago Press, 1976), p. 215.

61. Joseph F. Trimmer, "Three Treks West," in *The Classic American Novel*, ed. Peary and Shatzkin, p. 190.

62. Cawelti, *The Six-Gun Mystique* (Bowling Green: Bowling Green University Popular Press, 1971), p. 65. Also see Jack Schaefer, *Shane: The Critical Edition*, ed. James C. Work (Lincoln: University of Nebraska Press, 1984), which includes collected comment on both novel and film.

63. James K. Folsom, *The American Western Novel* (New Haven: New Haven College and University Press, 1966), p. 31.

64. Mark Bezanson, "Berger and Penn's West: Visions and Revision," in *The Classic American Novel*, ed. Peary and Shatzkin, pp. 273–74. Also see John W. Turner, "*Little Big Man*: The Novel and the Film, A Study of Narrative Structure," *Literature/Film Quarterly* 5 (1977): 154–63.

65. Edmund Wilson, Classics and Commercials: A Literary Chronicle-of-the-Forties (New York: Farrar, Straus & Giroux, 1962), p. 21.

66. Cf. Virginia Wright Wexman, "The Transfer from One Medium to Another: *The Maltese Falcon* from Fiction to Film," *Library Quarterly* 45 (1975): 46–55.

67. Alan Speigel, "Seeing Triple: Cain, Chandler and Wilder on *Double Indemnity*" in *Film/Literature*, ed. George E. Toles (Winnipeg: University of Manitoba Press, 1983), p. 83.

68. I rely on Luhr, *Raymond Chandler and Film*, for production history notes.

69. Nancy Brooker Bowers, *The Hollywood Novel and Other Novels About Film, 1912–1982: An Annotated Bibliography* (New York: Garland, 1985), p. ix. Also see Terry Curtis Fox, "The Hollywood Novel," *Film Comment* 21, no. 12 (1985): 7–13; and James Robert Parish and Michael R. Pitts, *Hollwyood on Hollywood* (Metuchen, N.J.: Scarecrow Press, 1978).

70. For a survey of comment on the cinematic texture of West's novels, see Murray, pp. 212–16.

71. Sidney Gottlieb, "The Madding Crowd in the Movies," in *The Modern American Novel*, ed. Peary and Shatzkin, pp. 85–106. Also see Joan Zlotnik, "*The Day of the Locust*, a Night at the Movies," *Film Library Quarterly* 6, no. 1 (1974): 22–26; and Andrew C. Bobrow, "John Schlesinger and 'The Day of the Locust,' " *Filmmakers Newsletter* 8, no. 9 (1975): 28–32.

72. See Murray, chap. 14, especially pp. 202–205, for a discussion of Fitzgerald's cinematic imagination. For comment on the adaptation, see Irene Kahn Atkins, "Hollywood Revisited: A Sad Homecoming," *Literature/Film Quarterly* 6 (1977): 105–11; and Charles Silver and Mary Corliss, "Hollywood Under Water: Elia Kazan on *The Last Tycoon*," *Film Comment* 13, no. 1 (1977): 40–44.

73. Wayne C. Booth, *The Rhetoric of Fiction* (Chicago: University of Chicago Press, 1965).

74. Alan Speigel, *Fiction and the Camera Age: Visual Consciousness in Film and the Modern Novel* (Charlottesville: University Press of Virginia, 1976), p. xiii. Conrad's remark is from the preface to *The Nigger of the "Narcissus"*, in *A Conrad Argosy* (New York: Doubleday, 1942), p. 83. In *Film and the Narrative Tradition* (Norman: University of Oklahoma Press, 1974), John L. Fell presents a strong argument for a growing concern, throughout the nineteenth century, for a spatially and temporally complex kind of storytelling.

75. Speigel, *Fiction and the Camera Age*, p. xiii.

76. Claude-Edmonde Magny, *The Age of the American Novel: The Film Aesthetic of Fiction Between Two Wars* (Originally published, 1948), trans. Eleanor Hockman (New York: Frederick Ungar, 1972), p. 48.

77. Joseph Heller, "On Translating *Catch–22* into a Movie," in *A Catch–22 Casebook*, ed. Frederick Kiley and Walter McDonald (New York: Doubleday, 1973), p. 361. Also see Fred H. Marcus and Paul Zall, "*Catch–22*: Is Film Fidelity an Asset?" in Fred H.

Marcus, *Film and Literature: Contrasts in Media* (Scranton: Chandler, 1971), pp. 127–36.

78. Bruce F. Kawin, *Telling It Again and Again: Repetition in Literature and Film* (Ithaca: Cornell University Press, 1972, argues that the Kierkegaardian principle of repetition is the generating principle of both film and modern literature.

79. See Linda Dittmar, "Fashioning and Re-fashioning: Framing Narratives in the Novel and Film," in *Film/Literature*, ed. Toles, pp. 189–203, for a lucid discussion of bracketing.

80. Stephen Dimco, "Reconciliation: *Slaughterhouse-Five*—the Film and the Novel," *Film Heritage* 8, no. 2 (Winter 1972–1973): 1–12.

81. Anthony B. Dawson, "*Ragtime* and the Movies: The Aura of the Duplicable," in *Film/Literature*, ed. Toles, p. 205. Dawson, in turn, depends on Joseph Frank, "Spatial Form in the Modern Novel," *Sewanee Review* 53 (1945): 221–40, 433–56, 643–53.

82. In *Film and Fiction* (New Haven: Yale University Press, 1979) Keith Cohen develops the notion of "exchange."

SELECTED BIBLIOGRAPHY

Since the teens, there has been a steady and, at times, rushing stream of published speculation about the relationship between literature and film. Although George Bluestone's *Novels into Film* (1957) deserves its reputation as the seminal work in English on the topic, Bluestone's was not the first dissertation comparing media. Several books and hundreds of articles by theorists, critics, and moviemakers had addressed the topic prior to 1975. Sergei Eisenstein's influential comparisons of literary and cinematic techniques were available to English readers in 1949, but Claude-Edmonde Magny's analysis of the film aesthetic of fiction (published in France in 1948) was not reissued in English until 1972. Throughout the 1960s, many American academics trained in departments of literature turned their attention to media trait theories. By 1973 interest in comparative analysis was sufficient to create and support an academic journal devoted to a continuing discussion of the topic: *Literature/Film Quarterly*. During the 1970s several publishing companies, particularly Frederick Ungar, supported numerous book-length studies on film-literature reciprocity.

The extensive writing on the relationship between literature and film might be divided into eight categories. I shall limit my examples to a few partial citations and then list full citations of the books mentioned and other relevant books and articles at the end of this section. (1) *Annotated bibliographies.* Jeffrey Egan Welsh has compiled the most comprehensive literature review to date. He lists 1,235 entries, including dissertations. Nancy Brooker Bowers traces a particular variant of symbiosis in her annotated bibliography of over 700 works of fiction about filmmaking. (2) *Single-authored textbooks for film/literature courses.* Morris Beja and Stuart Y. McDougal have both shaped texts around numerous adaptation examples. Many introductory film texts devote a chapter to literature and film. Charles Eidsvik's *Cineliteracy* stands between those extremes of attention to cross-media comparisons. (3) *General anthologies.* Collections such as the traditional anthology of reprinted essays edited by John Harrington or the more contemporary sampling edited by George E. Toles provide a range of opinion and critical method. (4) *Specific anthologies.* A number of collections of pieces about single adaptations have been organized by origin and era of the original novels (e.g., *The Modern American Novel and the Movies*, ed. Gerald Peary and Roger Shatzkin). The anthology *Stories in*

Film, ed. by William Kittredge and Steven M. Krauzner, gathers together pieces on adaptations based on short stories. (5) *Extended case studies*. Lillian Ross's wry account of the filming of *The Red Badge of Courage (Picture)* has never been equaled for its penetrating look at the politics of adaptation. Also recommeded are monographs published by Indiana University Press on individual films (e.g., Warren French's *Filmguide to "The Grapes of Wrath"* and Carolyn Geduld's *Filmguide to "2001: A Space Odyssey"*). (6) *Critical studies of single authors/screenwriters*. Novelists who played dual roles in the adaptation process have been the focus of a cluster of critical biographies (e.g., Bruce F. Kawin's *Faulkner and Film* and Aaron Latham's *Crazy Sundays: F. Scott Fitzgerald in Hollywood*). Richard Corliss has written an important survey of the work of Hollywood screenwriters, many of whom were (and are) novelists and adapters. (7) *Economic analyses*. Thomas Whiteside's *Blockbuster Complex* presents an overview of the economic connections between the publishing and filmmaking industries. Patricia Holt's articles for *Publishers Weekly* have regularly provided insight into marketplace realities in the 1980s. (8) *Critical studies of general narrative patterns*. Although there has been a tradition of interest in narratology (the study of narrative structure), scholarship in this area has intensified since the mid–1970s. The cogent writing of Seymour Chatman stands at the center of this work. David Bordwell, Keith Cohen, John L. Fell, Bruce F. Kawin, Frank McConnell, Bruce Morrissette, and Alan Speigel are among the scholars who are currently contributing to sophisticated comparative analysis of the structures of literary and cinematic discourse.

Books and Articles

Asheim, Lester. "From Book to Film: A Comparative Analysis of the Content of Novels and Motion Pictures Based Upon Them." Ph.D. diss., University of Chicago, 1950.

————. "From Book to Film: Summary." *Quarterly of Film, Radio, and Television* 6 (1952): 258–73.

Beja, Morris. *Film & Literature*. New York: Longman, 1979.

Bluestone, George. *Novels into Film*. Baltimore: Johns Hopkins University Press, 1957.

Bordwell, David. *Narration in the Fiction Film*. Madison: University of Wisconsin Press, 1985.

Bowers, Nancy Brooker. *The Hollywood Novel and Other Novels About Film, 1912–1982: An Annotated Bibliography*. New York: Garland, 1985.

Boyum, Joy Gould. *Double Exposure: Fiction into Film*. New York: Universe, 1985.

Caws, Mary Ann. *Reading Frames in Modern Fiction*. Princeton, N.J.: Princeton University Press, 1985.

Chatman, Seymour. *Story and Discourse: Narrative Structure in Fiction and Film*. Ithaca: Cornell University Press, 1978.

Conger, Syndy M. and Janice R. Welsch, eds. *Narrative Strategies: Original Essays in Film and Prose Fiction*. Macomb: Western Illinois University Press, 1980.

Corliss, Richard. *Talking Pictures: Screenwriters in the American Cinema*. New York: Penguin,1974.

DeMarco, Norman. "Bibliography of Books on Literature and Film." *Style* 9, no. 4 (1957): 593–607.

Dick, Bernard. "Authors, Auteurs, and Adaptations: Literature as Film/Film as Literature." *Yearbook of American Comparative and General Literature* 27 (1978): 72–76.

Eidsvik,Charles. "Toward a 'Politique des Adaptations.' " *Literature/Film Quarterly* 3, no. 3 (1975): 255–63. [Also reprinted in Harrington, pp. 27–37.]

———. *Cineliteracy: Film Among the Arts.* New York: Random House, 1978.

Eisenstein, Sergei. "Dickens, Griffith, and the Film Today." In *Film Form: Essays in Film Theory.* Trans. and ed. Jay Leyda. New York: Harcourt, Brace, 1949: 195–255.

Enser, A. G. S., ed. *Filmed Books and Plays: 1928–1974.* Orlando, Fla.: Academic Press, 1974.

Fadiman, Regina K. *Faulkner's "Intruder in the Dust": Novel into Film.* Knoxville: University of Tennessee Press, 1977.

Fell, John L. *Film and the Narrative Tradition.* Norman: University of Oklahoma Press, 1974.

French, Warren. *Filmguide to "The Grapes of Wrath."* Bloomington: Indiana University Press, 1973.

Froug, William. *The Screenwriter Looks at the Screenwriter.* New York: Macmillan, 1972.

Geduld, Carolyn. *Filmguide to "2001: A Space Odyssey."* Bloomington: Indiana University Press, 1973.

Geduld, Harry M., ed. *Authors on Film.* Bloomington: Indiana University Press, 1972.

Goodwin, James. "Literature and Film: A Review of Criticism." *Quarterly Review of Film Studies* 4, no. 2 (1979): 227–46.

Harrington, John, ed. *Film and/as Literature.* Englewood Cliffs, N.J.: Prentice-Hall, 1977.

Horton, Andrew and Joan Magretta, eds. *Modern European Filmmakers and the Art of Adaptation.* New York: Frederick Ungar, 1981.

Jinks, William. *The Celluloid Literature.* Encino, Cal.: Glencoe Press, 1971.

Kawin, Bruce F. *Telling It Again and Again: Repetition in Literature and Film.* Ithaca: Cornell University Press, 1972.

———. *Faulkner and Film.* New York: Frederick Ungar, 1977.

———. *Mindscreen: Bergman, Godard, and First-Person Film.* Princeton, N.J.: Princeton University Press, 1978.

Kittredge, William and Steven M. Krauzner, eds. *Stories into Film.* New York: Harper Colophon Books, 1979.

Klein, Michael and Gillian Parker, eds. *The English Novel and the Movies.* New York: Frederick Ungar, 1981.

Latham, Aaron. *Crazy Sundays: F. Scott Fitzgerald in Hollywood.* New York: Viking Press, 1971.

Laurence, Frank M. *Hemingway and the Movies.* Jackson: University of Mississippi Press, 1981.

Luhr, William. *Raymond Chandler and Film.* New York: Frederick Ungar, 1982.

Luhr, William and Peter Lehman. *Authorship and Narrative in the Cinema: Issues in Contemporary Aesthetics and Criticism.* Toms River, N.J.: Capricorn, 1977.

Magny, Claude-Edmonde, *The Age of the American Novel: The Film Aesthetic of Fiction Between the Two Wars (1948).* Trans. Eleanor Hockman. New York: Frederick Ungar, 1972.

Marcus, Fred H. *Short Story/Short Film.* Englewood Cliffs, N.J.: Prentice-Hall, 1977.

————. *Film and Literature: Contrasts in Media*. Scranton: Chandler, 1971.

McConnell, Frank. *The Spoken Seen: Film and the Romantic Imagination*. Baltimore: Johns Hopkins University Press, 1975.

————. *Storytelling and Mythmaking: Images from Film and Literature*. New York: Oxford University Press, 1979.

McDougal, Stuart Y. *Made into Movies: From Literature to Film*. Niles, Ill.: Holt, Rinehart, and Winston, 1985.

Mendilow, A. A. *Time and the Novel*. Atlantic Highland, N.J.: Humanities Press, 1965.

Miller, Gabriel. *Screening the Novel: Rediscovered American Fiction in Film*. New York: Frederick Ungar, 1980.

Monaco, James. *American Film Now: The People, the Power, the Money, the Movies*. rev. ed. New York: New American Library, 1984.

Morrissette, Bruce. *Novel and Film: Essays in Two Genres*. Ed. James R. Lawler. Chicago: University of Chicago Press, 1985.

Murray, Edward. *The Cinematic Imagination: Writers and the Motion Pictures*. New York: Frederick Ungar, 1972.

Peary, Gerald and Roger Shatzkin, eds. *The Classic American Novel and the Movies*. New York: Frederick Ungar, 1977.

————. *The Modern American Novel and the Movies*. New York: Frederick Ungar, 1978.

Pendo, Stephen. *Raymond Chandler on Screen: His Novels into Film*. Metuchen, N.J.: Scarecrow Press, 1976.

Phillips, Gene D. *Hemingway and Film*. New York: Frederick Ungar, 1980.

Richardson, Robert. *Literature and Film*. Bloomington: Indiana University Press, 1969.

Ross, Harris. "A Selected Bibliography of the Relationship of Literature and Film." *Style* 9, no. 4 (1975): 564–92.

Ross, Lillian. *Picture*. New York: Avon, 1952.

Ruchti, Unrich and Sybil Taylor. *Story into Film*. New York: Dell, 1978.

Schneider, Harold W. "Literature and Film: Marking Out Some Boundaries." *Literature/Film Quarterly* 3, no. 1 (1975): 30–44.

Sontag,Susan. *Against Interpretation*. New York: Dell, 1972.

Spiegel, Alan. *Fiction and the Camera Age: Visual Consciousness in Film and the Modern Novel*. Charlottesville: University Press of Virginia, 1976.

Toles, George E., ed. *Film/Literature*. Winnipeg: University of Manitoba Press, 1983.

Wagner, Geoffrey. *The Novel and the Cinema*. Cranbury, N.J.: Fairleigh Dickinson University Press, 1975.

Welch, Jeffrey Egan. *Literature and Film: An Annotated Bibliography, 1909–1977*. New York: Garland Publishing, 1981.

Whiteside, Thomas. *The Blockbuster Complex: Conglomerates, Show Business and Book Publishing*. Middletown, Conn.: Wesleyan University Press, 1981.

Wicks, Ulrich. "Literature/Film: A Bibliography." *Literature/Film Quarterly* 6 (Spring 1978): 135–43.

SELECTED FILMOGRAPHY AND THE ADAPTED NOVELS

An American Tragedy (USA 1931). Paramount. Directed by Josef von Sternberg. Screenplay by Josef von Sternberg and Samuel Hoffenstein.
   An American Tragedy by Theodore Dreiser (Sun Dial Pres, 1925).

Ben-Hur (USA) 1925). MGM. Directed by Fred Niblo. Screenplay by Bess Meredyth
    and Carey Wilson.

Ben-Hur: A Tale of the Christ by Lew Wallace (Harper & Row, 1880).

The Birth of a Nation (1915). Epoch Producing Corporation. Directed by D. W. Griffith.
    Screenplay by D. W. Griffith and Frank Woods.

The Clansman by Thomas Dixon, Jr. (Grosset & Dunlap, 1905).

Catch–22 (USA 1970). Paramount. Directed by Mike Nichols. Screenplay by Buck Henry.

Catch–22 by Joseph Heller (Simon & Schuster, 1961).

The Color Purple (USA 1985). Warner Brothers. Directed by Steven Spielberg. Screen-
    play by Menno Meyjes.

The Color Purple by Alice Walker (Harcourt Brace Jovanovich, 1982).

The Cool World (USA 1964). Wiseman Film Company. Directed by Shirley Clarke.
    Screenplay by Shirley Clarke and Carl Lee.

The Cool World by Warren Miller (Little, Brown, 1959).

The Day of the Locust (USA 1975). Paramount. Directed by John Schlesinger. Screenplay
    by Waldo Salt.

The Day of the Locust by Nathanael West (Acunian Press, 1939).

The Deep (USA 1977). Columbia. Directed by Peter Yates. Screenplay by Peter Benchley
    and Tracy Keenan Wynn.

The Deep by Peter Benchley (Doubleday, 1976).

Deliverance (USA 1972). Warner Brothers. Directed by John Boorman. Screenplay by
    James Dickey.

Deliverance by James Dickey (Dell, 1970).

Double Indeminity (USA) 1944). Paramount. Directed by Billy Wilder. Screenplay by
    Billy Wilder and Raymond Chandler.

Double Indemnity by James Cain (Avon, 1942).

Exodus (USA 1960). United Artists. Directed by Otto Preminger. Screenplay by Dalton
    Trumbo.

Exodus by Leon Uris (Doubleday, 1958).

From Here to Eternity (USA 1953). Columbia. Directed by Fred Zinnemann. Screenplay
    by Daniel Taradash.

From Here to Eternity by James Jones (Scribner, 1951).

Giant (USA 1956). Warner Brothers. Directed by George Stevens. Screenplay by Fred
    Guiol and Ivan Moffat.

Giant by Edna Ferber (Doubleday, 1952).

The Godfather (USA 1972). Paramount. Directed by Francis Ford Coppola. Screenplay
    Mario Puzo and Francis Ford Coppola; and *The Godfather II* (USA 1974). Par-
    amount. Directed by Francis Ford Coppola. Screenplay by Francis Ford Coppola
    and Mario Puzo.

The Godfather by Mario Puzo (Putnam, 1969).

Gone With the Wind (USA 1939). MGM. Directed by Victor Fleming, George Cukor,
    and Sam Wood. Screenplay by Sidney Howard.

Gone With the Wind by Margaret Mitchell (Macmillan, 1936).

The Grapes of Wrath (USA 1940). Twentieth Century-Fox. Directed by John Ford.
    Screenplay by Nunnally Johnson.

The Grapes of Wrath by John Steinbeck (Viking, 1939).

Greed (USA 1924). MGM. Directed and Screenplay by Erich von Stroheim. Titles by
    June Mathis.

McTeague by Frank Norris (Doubleday & McClure, 1899).

The Innocents (USA 1961). Twentieth Century-Fox. Directed by Jack Clayton. Screenplay by William Archibald and Truman Capote.

The Turn of the Screw by Henry James (Scribner, 1898).

Intruder in the Dust (USA 1949). MGM. Directed by Clarence Brown. Screenplay by Ben Maddow.

Intruder in the Dust by William Faulkner (Random House, 1948).

Lady in the Lake (USA 1947). MGM. Directed by Robert Montgomery. Screenplay by Steve Fisher.

The Lady in the Lake by Raymond Chandler (Grosset & Dunlap, Knopf, 1943).

The Last of the Mohicans (USA 1920). Associated Producers. Directed by Maurice Tourneur and Clarence Brown. Screenplay by Robert A. Dillon.

The Last of the Mohicans by James Fenimore Cooper (Norton, 1826).

The Last Tycoon (USA 1976). Paramount. Directed by Elia Kazan. Screenplay by Harold Pinter.

The Last Tycoon, An Unfinished Novel by F. Scott Fitzgerald (Scribner, 1941).

Little Big Man (USA 1970). Hiller-Stockbridge. Directed by Arthur Penn. Screenplay by Calder Willingham.

Little Big Man by Thomas Berger (Dial, 1964).

Little Women (USA 1933). RKO. Directed by George Cukor. Screenplay by Sarah Y. Mason and Victor Herrman.

Little Women: Or Meg, Joe, Beth and Amy [two parts] by Louisa May Alcott (Little, Brown, 1868, 1869).

The Maltese Falcon (USA 1941). Warner Brothers. Directed and Screenplay by John Huston.

The Maltese Falcon by Dashiell Hammett (Modern Library, 1931).

The Naked and the Dead (USA 1958). RKO. Directed by Raoul Walsh. Screenplay by Denis Sanders and Terry Sanders.

The Naked and the Dead by Norman Mailer (New American Library, 1948).

Native Son (USA 1951). Produced by Walter Gould. Directed by Pierre Chenal. Screenplay by Pierre Chenal and Richard Wright.

Native Son by Richard Wright (Harper & Row, 1940).

Night of the Hunter (USA 1955). United Artists. Directed by Charles Laughton. Screenplay by James Agee.

Night of the Hunter by Davis Grubb (Harper & Row, 1953).

One Flew Over the Cuckoo's Nest (USA 1975). Fantasy Films. Directed by Milos Forman. Screenplay by Lawrence Hauben and Bo Goldman.

One Flew Over the Cuckoo's Nest by Ken Kesey (Viking, 1962).

Play It as It Lays (USA 1972). Universal. Directed by Frank Perry. Screenplay by Joan Didion and John Gregory Dunne.

Play It as It Lays by Joan Didion (Pocket Books, 1970).

Rabbit, Run (USA 1970). Warner Brothers. Directed by Jack Smight. Screenplay by Howard B. Kreitsek.

Rabbit, Run by John Updike (Alfred A. Knopf, 1960).

Ragtime (USA 1981). Paramount. Directed by Milos Forman. Screenplay by Michael Weller.

Ragtime by E. L. Doctorow (Random House, 1975).

Rumblefish (USA 1982). Universal. Directed by Francis Ford Coppola. Screenplay by S. E. Hinton and Francis Ford Coppola.

   Rumble Fish by S. E. Hinton (Delacourte, 1975).

The Scarlet Letter (USA 1926). MGM. Directed by Victor Sjostrom (Seastrom). Screenplay by Frances Marion and Victor Sjostrom.

   The Scarlet Letter by Nathaniel Hawthorne (Houghton Mifflin, 1850).

Shane (USA 1953). Paramount. Directed by George Stevens. Screenplay by A. B. Gutherie, Jr.

   Shane by Jack Schaefer (Amsco, 1949).

The Shining (USA 1980). Warner Brothers. Directed by Stanley Kubrick. Screenplay by Stanley Kubrick and Diane Johnson.

   The Shining by Stephen King (Doubleday, 1977).

Slaughterhouse-Five (USA 1972). Universal. Directed by George Roy Hill. Screenplay by Stephen Geller.

   Slaughterhouse-Five; or, the Children's Crusade, a Duty Dance with Death by Kurt Vonnegut, Jr. (Dell, 1969).

The Stunt Man (USA 1980). Melvin Simons Productions. Directed by Richard Rush. Screenplay by Lawrence B. Marcus.

   The Stunt Man by Paul Brodeur (Grove, 1970).

To Have and Have Not (USA 1944). Warner Brothers. Directed by Howard Hawks. Screenplay by Jules Furthman and William Faulkner.

   To Have and Have Not by Ernest Hemingway (Scribner, 1937).

Tropic of Cancer (USA 1970). Paramount. Directed by Joseph Strick. Screenplay by Joseph Strick and Betty Botley.

   Tropic of Cancer by Henry Miller (1934; Grove, 1961).

The Virginian (USA 1929). Paramount. Directed by Victor Fleming. Screenplay by Edward E. Paramore, Jr., and Howard Estabrook.

   The Virginian by Owen Wister (Grosset & Dunlap, 1902).

Who'll Stop the Rain? (USA 1978). United Artists. Directed by Karel Reisz. Screenplay by Judith Rascoe and Robert Stone.

   Dog Soldiers by Robert Stone (Houghton Mifflin, 1974).

The Wizard of Oz (USA 1939). MGM. Directed by Victor Fleming. Screenplay by Noel Langley, Florence Ryerson, and Edgar Allan Woolf.

   The Wonderful Wizard of Oz by L. Frank Baum (G.M. Hill, 1900).

6

FILM AND THEATER

GREGORY WALLER

INTRODUCTION

In the diverse, diffuse field of film's symbiotic relationship with other arts and other twentieth-century media of communication, no single process of interaction has been more widely discussed and is more significant than film's ongoing interaction with theater. To chart, even in an abbreviated, provisionary way, the historical course and the aesthetic, economic, and cultural ramifications of the relationship between stage and screen requires that we take into account the following, often interrelated, concerns:

1. the competition and the cooperation between the film industry and the commercial theater, especially the major American film studios' economic relationship with vaudeville and the legitimate theater (Broadway);

2. the role that theater personnel have played in the development of the movies—most notably actors and playwrights, but also directors, choreographers, producers, and set designers;

3. the influence of both the avant-garde and the traditional theater on the pictorial style, dramatic conventions, and narrative structure of film as evidenced in acting methods, techniques of lighting, set design, mise-en-scène, and blocking, and assumptions concerning the treatment of characterization, plot, and dialogue;

4. the long-standing reliance of filmmakers on stage productions as a source of material to be filmed, the "canning" and adaptation of stage plays, and the American film industry's appropriation and revision of theatrical genres and subgenres like the melodrama, musical, domestic comedy, farce, and the psychological drama;

5. the attempt to incorporate motion pictures into theatrical performance and the influence of film techniques on drama and stagecraft, particularly in the avant-garde, experimental theater;

6. the image of the world of the theater and of theatricalism in general in film, and, conversely, the representation of the movies and of Hollywood in stage plays; and

7. the role of theater as comparison point in defining the cultural status of film as art and popular entertainment.

These topics are by no means of equal importance, and they pose quite different problems to the researcher. Keeping in mind the difficulty in assessing the nature and extent of artistic and economic influence and in sorting out complex casual relationships, let us trace in broad outline the history of the interaction between film and theater and indicate the kind of issues raised by this symbiotic relationship.

HISTORICAL DEVELOPMENT

As Jeanne Thomas Allen argues, "the emergence of film in late nineteenth-century America was closely tied to the mass theatrical entertainments from which it was launched as a business and as a mass art."[1] When the Edison Company sought readily available and commercially appealing subject matter for the motion picture loops that were to be shown on Edison's kinetoscope (a peep-show like machine which allowed for the individual viewing of extremely brief motion pictures), W. K. L. Dickson immediately turned to the wealth of material available on the New York stage—vaudeville acts, scenes from stage comedies, dance routines from Broadway musicals, and so on.[2] The most widely publicized of Edison's films, *The Kiss* (1896), was in fact a re-creation by actors John C. Rice and May Irwin of a climactic moment from *The Widow Jones*, a successful Broadway musical. And when the Edison Company in 1896 introduced Vitascope, a projection system that allowed for the public viewing of film, *The Kiss* was, according to Charles Musser, the "most popular film on Vitascope programs."[3]

During the first decade of motion-picture history, adaptations and visual records of stage performances—like Edwin S. Porter's film of the ever-popular theatrical version of *Uncle Tom's Cabin* in 1903—remained an important part of the industry's increasing output, which soon also included re-created historical scenes, proto-newsreel footage, and narrative episodes. In a more general sense, the popular theater's tradition of low comedy, spectacle, and melodrama served as the model and the backdrop for virtually all of the early attempts to use film for narrative purposes. For example, Georges Méliès's highly successful trick films, farcical comedies, and films of fantastic adventures were rooted in nineteenth-century stage spectacles like the melodramatic "féerie," which combined acrobatics, mime, illusionist tricks, and elaborately mounted, technically sophisticated sets.[4]

The popular theater not only provided the first filmmakers with suitable subject matter and proven methods of dramatic narrative, it also served as a market for film, particularly in the United States. Less than a year after the Lumière Brothers held their first screening for a paying, public audience in December 1895, New Yorkers were able to see projected motion pictures as part of the program in vaudeville theaters. Such a move to integrate film into a theatrical performance (as one in a series of basically independent acts) was in keeping with vaudeville's policy of incorporating "visual novelties of all sorts: pantomime, shadowgraphy, puppetry, *tableaux vivants*, and lanternry," among others.[5] Trick films in the Méliès manner, "living newpspapers," and other short films remained an often important part of the typical vaudeville program for the next several years. Robert C. Allen concludes that in addition to the fact that vaudeville circuits "effected the rapid national diffusion of the motion picture and gave it a huge national audience," vaudeville's traditional "demand for novelty . . . encouraged cinematic experimentation."[6]

With the success of films like *The Great Train Robbery* (1903) and the emergence of storefront motion-picture theaters (nickelodeons) beginning in 1905, the film industry competed more directly with the popular theater for the increasing middle-class family audience. Film triumphed over vaudeville in part because of the motion pictures' reduced distribution costs and standardized production and because film was more amenable than vaudeville acts to protection under patent and copyright laws.[7] The commercial interaction between film and vaudeville, however, lasted well into the teens. Promoted by exhibitors like William Fox (later founder of Fox Film Corporation) and Marcus Loew (later founder of Loew's chain of cinemas and partner in MGM), so-called small-time vaudeville, which featured a relatively equal mix of live acts and films, flourished between 1909 and 1915. The feature-length films that began to appear in 1912–1913 found a particularly good market in small-time vaudeville, which succeeded in attracting a middle-class audience. The popularity of feature films led to the opening of ornate motion picture "palaces" that were modeled on the marketing and exhibition strategies of small-time vaudeville. Feature-length motion pictures were, needless to say, the principal attraction offered by the picture palace, though live acts continued to appear as an introductory or supplemental part of the show in many large movie theaters until the introduction of the sound film in the late 1920s.[8] (Interestingly, in the late 1930s some attempt was made by movie exhibitors to offer bills that combined a feature film with a streamlined version of a Broadway play.)[9]

The aesthetic and economic interplay and competition between stage and screen did not end, however, with the displacement of traditional vaudeville by the movies and the transformation of small-time vaudeville into the picture palace system of exhibition, for what came to be known as the legitimate theater (or simply Broadway) also felt the effects of the expanding motion-picture industry. Most significant in this regard was the *film d'art* movement, an attempt to wed stage and screen that would strongly influence the development of both theater and film in America. In 1908 the Société Film d'Art was formed in Paris to film stage productions starring actors and utilizing other stage personnel (like scenery designer Emile Bertin) from the Comédie Française. The goal of this enterprise was to tap the middle-class audience and to confer some degree of cultural legitimacy upon the movies. The company's first effort, *The Assassination of the Duc de Guise* (1908), met with critical acclaim and box-office success. Filmed against the backdrop of stage sets with each shot centered before the action at medium or medium-long distance (thereby providing the viewer with the facsimile of what would be a prime viewpoint before the proscenium arch in a legitimate theater), *The Assassination of the Duc de Guise* became the model for a spate of film versions of stage productions. Pathé, Gaumont, and other major French film companies quickly began offering comparable highbrow theatrical productions, and what later film historians call the *film d'art* movement spread throughout Europe. One immediate effect of *film d'art* was to bestow a certain degree of cultural prestige on the new medium. Jay Leyda, for instance, writes that the first such production to be exhibited in Russia "was received with rapture . . . swelling the film audience with new devotees from the respectable classes, who now conferred dignity and artificiality upon the cinema."[10] The *film d'art* movement reached a peak of sorts in 1912 when Mounet-Sully, a leading French actor, appeared in *Oedipus Rex* and Sarah Bernhardt in *La Dame Aux Camelias* and *Queen Elizabeth*.

Editorials in *Scribner's*, the *Moving Picture World*, and other periodicals advised American studios to follow the French lead and "make films of notable stage plays."[11] The *film d'art* movement became a force in the American film industry when Adolph Zukor secured the distribution rights for *Queen Elizabeth* and formed the Famous Players Film Corporation in partnership with Broadway producer Daniel Frohman. (*Queen Elizabeth* premiered with great success at Loew's theaters in New York City as part of a film-vaudeville program.) In 1912 Famous Players released *The Prisoner of Zenda*, the first in a spate of film adaptations of Broadway productions starring theatrical headliners. Famous Players went so far as to hire Wilfred Buckland from David Belasco's theatrical company to serve as art director for its films, further strengthening the link between the emerging feature film and the American stage.

Other companies immediately followed suit, includng United Pictures, which offered "canned" versions of the Broadway productions of William Brady and the Schuberts, and the Lasky Feature Play Corporation, founded by Jesse Lasky, Cecil de Mille, and Samuel Goldfish (later Goldwyn). In 1913 Marc Klaw and Abraham Erlanger, major theatrical booking agents and producers, joined with the Biograph Company (for whom D. W. Griffith had begun his film career) in a venture called the Protective Amusement Company with plans to market film versions of 104 hit plays. During 1914, this company released twenty-six "Well-known Plays in Motion Pictures"—including drawing-room comedies and several melodramas that had been produced for the stage by Belasco. Faced with a poor critical and box-office response—in part because of their choice of plays and their attempt to charge the same admission price as for legitimate theater productions—Klaw and Erlanger did not complete their planned series of "Extraordinary Film-Plays."[12] Zukor and Lasky proved to be much more astute, and Famous Players merged with Lasky's company in 1916 to form the Lasky–Famous Players Corporation, the forerunner of Paramount Studios. In the famous players movement, with its connections to small-time vaudeville, we can see the Hollywood studio system beginning to take shape.

Though no examples of *film d'art* remain intrinsically interesting today, this movement drew attention to issues that would continue to be of great importance in film history: the role of adaptations, the nature of acting for stage and screen, and the desire to "raise" the movies (and the mass movie audience) through an alliance with other, well-established forms of art. Moreover, Zukor's promotion of "famous plays" and "famour players" directly affected both Broadway and the film industry. The fact that movie exhibitors could charge a relatively low admission price for a standardized product (often featuring well-known stage perfomers) helped cause the drop in theatrical touring companies from 236 per week in 1910 to 34 per week in 1920.[13] The decline of the road probably also affected the makeup of the theater audience nationwide, as the movies attracted erstwhile patrons of the popular theater, including the urban working class and the inhabitants of towns and cities no longer serviced by touring companies. Such changes led Jack Poggi to speculate that "the theater probably became somewhat *less* democratic (in a sense) after the triumph of the movies."[14] With legitimate stages across the nation being turned into movie houses, the New York City theater became increasingly important to the industry. Broadway flourished, and the cost of mounting a production became more and more expensive, leading to the "hit-flop syndrome."[15] Films like *Queen Elizabeth* and the activities of the first generation of movie magnates were crucial in bringing about these and other fundamental changes in the American theater industry.

In addition, the commercial success of *Queen Elizabeth*, *The Prisoner of Zenda*, *The Count of Monte Cristo* (1913), and other American-made film versions of well-known stage performances prompted many film producers to follow Zukor's lead and hire famous players from the legitimate theater. "Actor-snatching"—as drama critic Walter Prichard Eaton dubbed it in 1915—was the most visible sign of an exodus that also saw playwrights and producers accept the high salaries offered by the film industry in the teens.[16] (Of at least equal significance were the many performers who moved from vaudeville and the music hall to film, including actors, dancers, and such prominent screen comics as Charlie Chaplin, Buster Keaton, and, later, W. C. Fields, Mae West, and the Marx Brothers.) Spurred by open competitive bidding among film companies searching for proven dramatic product, the average price paid for the screen rights to a successful Broadway play rose from $2,000 in 1913 to $50,000 in 1919, fundamentally altering the economics of the American legitimate theater and linking the fate of Broadway to the money of Hollywood.[17] (To some extent the impulse behind the famous players movement never entirely disappeared. Leyda describes how twenty-five "film recordings of complete theatre productions" by premiere Russian stage companies were released during 1952–1953.[18] Also related to this movement is Ely Landau's American Film Theatre project, which sponsored in the early 1970s a series of films "derived from notable productions of stage plays," including *Rhinoceros* and *The Iceman Cometh*.)[19]

While the early *film d'art* movement may have failed even as canned drama, since, in William K. Everson's words, Zukor's productions "were totally inadequate and even harmful records of the stars they sought to immortalize,"[20] these films had a substantial effect on the course of commercial filmmaking. For example, the fact that these adaptations were conceived of and explicitly advertised as vehicles for Sarah Bernhardt and other famous players helped promote the rise of the star system in the film industry. And a number of stage actors, directors, and producers who began working in film during this period would leave their mark on the new medium. Among the Broadway actors Zukor hired for the movies were Mary Pickford and Douglas Fairbanks, soon to become the foremost movie stars of the silent period. Most significantly, *Queen Elizabeth* and the subsequent highly publicized examples of filmed theater were feature-length films, and as such they surely contributed to the industry's wide-scale adoption and promotion of the feature-film format between 1912 and 1915.

Praised at the time for attempting to "raise the level of Cinematography"[21] and for promoting the "general uplift" of the mass audience,[22] the alliance of stage and screen promoted by Zukor and Lasky was condemned by Vachel Lindsay (*The Art of the Moving Pictures*), Gilbert Seldes (*An Hour with the Movies and the Talkies*), and many other film critics and historians who saw the *film d'art* movement as a prime instance of the sort of "stage blight" that threatened the evolution of any uniquely cinematic art.[23] Indeed, set against the bombastic performances and retrogressive, uninteresting visual style of static filmed dramas like *Queen Elizabeth*, the achievement of D. W. Griffith's Biograph shorts and his epic feature films becomes even more impressive (much as Edwin S. Porter's *The Great Train Robbery* benefits substantially when set against Porter's stage-bound film version of *Uncle Tom's Cabin*). However, to understand the history of film simply as a heroic struggle for freedom from the influence of the stage is to overlook the fact that many of the films of both Porter and Griffith—like a great many other films of the silent period—have strong links to the nineteenth-century popular theater's tradition of spectacle and melodrama. The career of Griffith quite clearly demonstrates this point, for this universally acclaimed filmmaker came to the movies after having tried his hand at stage acting and playwriting (his melodramatic play, *The Fool and the Girl*, closed after two weeks). Far from rejecting his theatrical heritage, Griffith paid $175,000 in 1920 for the screen rights to the decidedly old-fashioned melodrama *Way Down East*, which became his most commercially successful film after *Birth of a Nation*.

The influence of the Victorian theater on the first generation of filmmakers went well beyond the sale of screen rights and the popularity of adaptations. Along with comic strips, dioramas, stereographs, and dime novels, suspenseful and spectacular melodramas form the nineteenth-century narrative tradition from which the movies emerge.[24] As early as 1910, Horace M. Kallen, writing in the *Harvard Monthly*, identified film as a "force in the field of theatre . . . that will vindicate and perhaps re-establish on its pristine eminence, the discarded and abased melodramas."[25] Many of Griffith's films could be seen as precisely this type of reestablishment, and in less pristine and polished form the plot structures, character types, and methods for creating suspense in stage melodrama pervade the first generation of narrative films, which came to promote a comparable system of moral and ideological values. This extremely significant link between film and theater is thoroughly explored in A. Nicholas Vardac's *Stage to Screen: Theatrical Method from Garrick to Griffith*. Vardac argues that the nineteenth-century stage was dominated by an increasing demand both for greater "photographic" realism in staging (as in the productions of Henry Irving, David Belasco, and Steele MacKaye) and for romantic, spectacular, suspenseful subject matter (as in the melodramas of Dion Boucicault or in pantomime spectacles). Furthermore, this predominantly pictorial theater often relied on what Vardac calls "filmic devices"—crosscutting between two lines of action, a chronological narrative, dissolves from one scene to the next, and visualized dream sequences, for example. Thus when Porter made *The Great Train Robbery*, he "merely translated into the idiom of the motion-picture camera the mid-century aims and methods of the melodrama branch of this graphic theatre of realism and romance." And Griffith with *The Birth of a Nation* fully achieved the "cinematic ideal" toward which "the pictorial theatre had been striving . . . during the entire span of the nineteenth century."[26] While *Stage to Screen* proposes two contradictory theses—(1) that the movies are a logical step in the evolution of theater and (2) that the nineteenth-century stage is simply second-rate pre-cinema or proto-cinema—Vardac conclusively demonstrates the historical continuity and the important correspondences between the silent film and the Victorian stage.

During the silent period, film had an equally noteworthy and far more symbiotic relationship with a much different type of theater—the experimental "new stagecraft" that defined itself in opposition both to nineteenth-century aspirations and to the stylishness of the commerical theater. For example, the Italian Futurist movement had close ties to the cinema, as evidenced not only by the 1916 film, *Vita Futurista*, and the manifesto of the same year, "The Futurist Cinema," but also by the prominent role of film in the futurists' stage performances. Filippo Tommaso Marinetti's influential statement, "The Variety Theatre" (1913), specifically called for the inclusion of motion pictures as one of the key "performance elements" in the futurist theater, since the movies "enrich" the variety theater "with an incalculable number of visions and otherwise unrealizable spectacles."[27] In *Futurist Performance*, Michael Kirby notes how the emphasis on simultaneous action in certain futurist plays "undoubtedly derived in part from an attempt to parallel in stage terms the way in which motion pictures moved instantaneously from one locale to another."[28] From the Italian Futurists through the wave of equally revolutionary movements in the late teens and 1920s, the avant-garde incorporated, influenced, and was influenced by the cinema. By the early 1930s, a critic surveying the "cinematographic tempo" of Leon Schiller's productions at the Polish Theater in Warsaw (an effect "attained by projecting quick light on single fragments of scenes") could proclaim with some justification that the most significant trend in the experimental theater of the previous decade was the interest in mixed-media performances and the attempt to "obliterate" the "boundary of film and theatre."[29] This interplay between stage and screen proved to be particularly rich and influential in postwar Germany and Soviet Russia.

The relationship between film and theater in Weimar Germany went well beyond the oft-cited fact that the painted shadows and nightmarish décor in *The Cabinet of Doctor Caligari* (1919) closely resemble the type of sets employed in expressionist stage productions. (Proponents of "pure" cinema have long bemoaned Caligari's intentional artifice and theatricality.) Adaptations of classical and modern drama—including F. W. Murnau's film of *Tartuffe* (1925), a cinematic rendering of Georg Kaiser's *From Morn to Midnight* (1920), and, most notably, G. W. Pabst's adaptations of Wedekind (*Pandora's Box* [1928]) and Brecht (*The Threepenny Opera* [1931])—figured prominently in the first "golden age" of the German cinema. Conversely, avant-garde plays showed the influence of the movies by incorporating film sequences, as in Yvan Goll's *The Immortal One* (1920), or by attempting to imitate a cinematic style, as in Walter Hasenclaver's *Humanity*, which has been called "the most extreme form of the Expressionist reduction of language and its approximation to pure pantomime and silent film."[30]

The most important link between stage and screen in Germany during this period lies in the pervasive influence of famed theater director Max Reinhardt. On two noteworthy occasions, Reinhardt personally tried his hand at filmmaking: at the height of the *film d'art* movement, he directed films of two plays, and in 1935 he co-directed *A Midsummer Night's Dream* for Warner Brothers. More important, from Reinhardt's company in the late teens came many of the most internationally acclaimed German film actors of the 1920s, including Elisabeth Bergner, Emil Jannings, and Conrad Veidt, as well as directors like Paul Wegener, Paul Leni, and Ernst Lubitsch. Films as otherwise dissimilar as Wegener's *The Golem* (1920) and Lubitsch's *Madame Dubarry* (1919), notes film historian Lotte Eisner, borrow from Reinhardt's innovative chiaroscuro lighting effects and masterful staging of crowd scenes. Eisner argues that the "decorative stylization" of Fritz Lang's films also derives to a great extent from Reinhardt's stage productions. With the success of Lang, Leni, and Lubitsch in Hollywood, the influence of Reinhardt's lighting and staging techniques extended even further.[31]

Other, more experimental branches of the new stagecraft in Weimar Germany promoted the motion picture's role as component of and inspiration for any truly modern theater. Thus the Bauhaus group's call for a "total" theater that would, as Laszlo Moholy-Nagy put it in 1924, utilize projected motion pictures and would be equipped with highly mechanized "moveable space constructions . . . in order to bring certain action moments on the stage into prominence, as in film 'close-ups'."[32] Throughout the 1920s in productions like *Rasputin* (1927), Erwin Piscator experimented with the combination of live actors and film as he expanded the technical resources of the stage and developed his ideas about "Epic theater" at the Volksbühne in Berlin. Through the plays, productions, and theoretical writings of Bertolt Brecht—who worked with Piscator during the

1920s—the methods and assumptions of Epic theater would in turn help shape the course of modern political filmmaking as well as leftist film theory in the 1970s and 1980s.[33]

The interplay between film and theater was at least as equally significant in Russia during the 1920s as it was in Weimar Germany. Like Piscator, Vsevolod Meyerhold not only used film in his influential productions of the 1920s, but with "mobile constructions, moving walls, pivoting screens, as well as a revolving stage . . . he aimed at creating a continuity on stage comparable to the cinema."[34] (Before the revolution Meyerhold had directed at least three films, including an adaptation of *The Picture of Dorian Gray*.) Meyerhold, in fact, demanded nothing less than the "cinematification" of the theater, and like countless avant-garde artists of the period he found inspiration in and recognized his own artistic affinities with Chaplin's comedies.[35] Meyerhold's experiments with "bio-mechanical" training of actors, constructivist set design, open-air collective spectacles (like *The Storming of the Winter Palace* in 1920), and *commedia dell'arte* performances all would have a major influence on the Soviet cinema, most directly on the films and critical writings of Sergei Eisenstein.

Unlike V. I. Pudovkin, director of *Mother* (1926) and *The End of St. Petersburg* (1927), who adopted Stanislavsky's system for training actors and championed the naturalist tradition of the Moscow Art Theatre, Eisenstein found inspiration in avant-garde stagecraft and in non-Western theater like the Kabuki and the Chinese theater of Mei Lon Fang.[36] His career, as the title of an often-reprinted autobiographical essay makes clear, led Eisenstein "Through Theater to Cinema," and he repeatedly emphasized the correspondences between his work for the stage and screen. Behind *Strike* and *The Battleship Potemkin* lay Eisenstein's experiences as a student of Meyerhold and a set designer and director of agit-prop productions at the Proletcult Theater and The Factory of the Eccentric Actor, a Futurist workshop theater. (Sergei Yutkevich, Grigori Kostinstev, and a number of other directors and scenarists who would figure prominently in the Soviet film of the 1920s and 1930s shared Eisenstein's background in the avant-garde theater.) Eisenstein's first film, *Glumov's Diary*, was shown as part of the Proletcult's production of *Enough Simplicity in Every Wise Man* (1923), and he began working on *Strike* soon after staging *Gas Masks* in the Moscow Gas Works. "Montage of Attrctions," Eisenstein's 1923 manifesto calling for a new method of theatrical production based on the "montage of 'real matters' " and influenced by the circus, the music-hall, and the motion picture, sets forth the cinematic method he was to explore in his films and his critical writings of the 1920s. From his experiences with Meyerhold and agit-prop theater through his production of Wagner's *The Valkyrie* at the Bolshoi Theater in 1940, Eisenstein's unflagging interest in all manner of stagecraft (and particularly the non-Western and avant-garde theater) remained one of the strongest influences on his career in film.

Interestingly, few of the innovative avant-garde films produced in France during the 1920s bore the traces of the new stagecraft—one notable exception being *La Coquille et La Clergyman* (1928), which was directd by Germaine Dulac from a scenario by Antonin Artaud, Surrealist playwright, actor, and theorist. However, George Méliès's early films and the *film d'art* movement had established an important bond between stage and screen in the French film industry that continued with the commercial success of film versions of popular melodramas during and after World War I. Richard Abel suggests that this genre of bourgeois melodrama was reshaped and transformed by Abel Gance in films like *J'Accuse* (1919).[37] At the same time, André Antoine, who had been so important in promoting naturalist drama at his Théâtre Libre and Théâtre Antoine, began directing films for the Société Cinématographiques des Auteurs et Gens des Lettres. Through his insistence on location filming and naturalistic acting and subject matter, Antoine helped introduce a new realism to commercial French film. Perhaps the most interesting link between stage and screen in France during the 1920s was the cinematic reworking of popular boulevard comedies by, among others, René Clair (*The Italian Straw Hat* [1928], from Eugene Labiche's farce) and Jean Renoir (*Tire au Flanc* [1929], from a long-running vaudeville comedy).[38]

Although there was little direct or indirect interaction between film and the American noncommercial theater of the 1920s—like the Provincetown Players and the Theatre Guild—the links between Hollywood and Broadway remained strong even as the American film industry began to be influenced by the innovations of European avant-garde film and theater (principally through the influx of talent from the German film industry, led by Lubitsch and Murnau). Though it has often been claimed that Hollywood silent films of the 1920s bore the traces of "theatricalism" and that Broadway productions of the same period were being mounted with an eye toward Hollywood, such assertions are difficult to prove. Equally conjectural is Poggi's suggestion that once "the movies took over from the theater certain practices in manufacturing plays to suit (and shape) the taste of a mass audience," the playwright addressing a New York City audience in the 1920s "could be more daring in both form and subject matter."[39] What is apparent is that the film industry continued to hire personnel from the theater, to offer adaptations of classic and modern drama (*Kismet* [1920], *What Price Glory?* [1926]), and to place increased emphasis on the function of the art director, whose responsibilities include overseeing the designing of sets and costumes—an important aspect of both theatrical and film production. In fact, as Léon Barsacq notes in *Caligari's Cabinet and Other Grand Illusions: A History of Film Design*, a number of highly influential set designers and art directors—including Georges Méliès and the German expressionist designer, Hermann Warm—came to film with much stage experience.

The economic interaction between Hollywood and Broadway in the years immediately before the introduction of the sound film is more easily documented. Screen rights remained a valuable commodity—the sentimental hit *Abie's Irish Rose*, for example, sold for $300,000 and a percentage of the film profits—oftentimes determining whether a theatrical production would be profitable or not. In hopes of eliminating open bidding and cutting the cost of screen rights, film companies began financing Broadway productions. From the 1919–1920 season, when it acquired Charles Frohman's theatrical producing company, Lasky–Famous Players backed legitimate stage productions as part of what Adolph Zukor called his company's "search for dramatic material."[40] More significantly, in 1925 William Fox (then head of Fox Film Corporation) announced plans to finance a number of plays in return for a share of profits and an option to buy the screen rights. Defenders of the theater quickly warned that under the Fox plan plays would be produced solely because of their potential value as movie material and that Hollywood would thereby corrupt and lower the artistic standards of the legitimate stage. Playwrights were less concerned with the danger of compromising their talents by writing for a film-financed theater than with the money they would lose if Fox and the theatrical producers managed to circumvent the practice of competitive bidding for screen rights.

In December 1925 the playwrights formed the Dramatists Guild and demanded a fifty-fifty split with producers on screen rights, which were to be sold by open, competitive bidding. Eventually Broadway producers agreed to these demands, and in April 1926 the Guild signed the Minimum Basic Agreement (MBA), which included several provisions specifically addressing the question of screen rights. The ratification of the MBA caused Fox to drop his plan to finance Broadway productions, and more important, it altered the course of the American Theater. The conflict and agreement had, for example, reduced the power of the producer and emphasized the role of organized labor and collective bargaining in the commercial theater. In Robert McLaughlin's words, "the adoption of this production contract, in short, was one of the important organizational and economic adjustments of any magnitude the theatre has ever had to make. The procedures involved in producing a Broadway play today are, in most aspects, the same as they were after April 1926."[41] And these procedures arose, to a great extent, because of Broadway's relationship to Hollywood during the silent film era.

During the transformation of the American film industry from the silent to the sound film between 1926 and 1929, Hollywood's reliance on the commercial theater was more pronounced than ever during the heyday of the famous players movement. Among the principal subjects of the more than one thousand short sound films Lee De Forest produced between 1923 and 1927 were vaudeville acts and scenes from current plays. Like De Forest's Phonofilms, many of Warner Brothers' first short Vitaphone synchronized sound films were also recordings of theatrical performers, including Al Jolson, the most renowned vaudeville star in America, who was featured in *The Jazz Singer* (1927). Adapted from a Broadway play and—like countless subsequent movie musicals—offering an inside view of the world of the stage, *The Jazz Singer* was perhaps the single film that most convincingly sold the public and the studios on the sound film. As part of its massive retooling for the production and exhibition of talkies, the film industry began a highly visible talent raid, hiring vaudeville performers and actors, directors, playwrights, and composers from Broadway, while at the same time studios like Paramount and MGM planned to begin shooting on New York sound stages.[42] Faced with these much-publicized developments, most film critics rallied to the defense of the "pure" art of the silent film and condemned the talkie as, in Richard Watts, Jr.'s words, "a pale, inadequate reflection of the stage, lacking the virtues of both cinema and theater."[43]

By 1929 Hollywood's demand for Broadway talent had slackened appreciably, and California was again the undisputed center of studio activity. The enormous influence of the stage on the early sound film, however, was immediately apparent in, for example, the prominent role of theatrical personnel in the film industry and the many adaptations of plays—like Paramount's first all-talkie, *Interference* (1928), which included a spoken prologue by theatrical producer Daniel Frohman. Other revealing signs of the times: Douglas Fairbanks and Mary Pickford teamed for the first time in *The Taming of the Shrew* (1929), and hallowed stage actor George Arliss became for a brief period what one critic called "the mouthpiece for the new medium" in prestigious box-office successes like *Disraeli* (1929).[44] Despite the great number of Broadway performers who failed to make any mark in the movies, Hollywood's look eastward yielded a number of important finds, including the Marx Brothers, who came to the movies via adaptations of their Broadway hits, *The Cocoanuts* (1929) and *Animal Crackers* (1930), and Paul Muni, who was recruited by William Fox from the Yiddish Art Theater. The stage also provided the performers, the composers, and even the setting and subject for MGM's first all-talkie, *Broadway Melody* (1929), which won the Academy Award for best picture and initiated a vogue for movie musicals and operettas. Roger Dooley notes that during 1929 and 1930, "almost every successful musical comedy and operetta of the '20s was filmed," including *Whoopee* (1930), co-produced by Samuel Goldwyn and Florenz Ziegfeld and choreographed by Busby Berkeley in his first film work.[45] In fact, it is within the generic framework of the musical—from *Forty-Second Street* (1933) to *All That Jazz* (1979)—that Hollywood has most often offered its image of the legitimate theater.

The popularity of the sound film exacerbated certain problems that had faced the commercial theater since at least the teens: the further decline of the road and the increased dominance of the hit/flop syndrome. While Hollywood's search for suitable talkie material led to higher average prices for screen rights (and thus to the theater's ever-greater economic dependence on the sale of screen rights), the studios again sought to circumvent competitive bidding by backing Broadway productions. By 1935 Hollywood financing affected approximately one-fourth of all new productions, and playwrights and drama critics once again feared that the theater would be adversely affected by the influence of the film industry with its eye toward a mass audience and its strict censorship code. Under pressure from the Dramatists Guild, the MBA was revised in 1936 to give playwrights greater control over the sale of screen rights and a larger share of the profits. For the next five years Hollywood refused to back plays—explaining, in part, why the number of Broadway productions during this period fell by almost half. The film studios began returning to the business of theatrical production in 1940 when the Dramatists Guild and the League of New York Theatres entered into a new agreement that allowed for the preproduction sale of screen rights in exchange for film financing.[46]

Hollywood's sometimes frantic search for stage-trained personnel during the first years of the sound film inevitably affected the New York theater. Famed actors and vaudeville headliners were of course the most visible object of the movies' talent raid, but McLaughlin notes that "in 1929 it was estimated that seventeen [stage] directors were contracted full time to major film studios.";[47] Perhaps most important, movie money attracted successful dramatists like Sidney Howard and Charles MacArthur in the early 1930s, and before them, Ben Hecht and Preston Sturges, who became two of the foremost screenwriters in the history of American film. Such losses did drain the theater of important talent, even if certain actors and writers continued to work in both film and theater.[48] The same trend continued through the decade, affecting both Broadway and innovative noncommercial companies like the Group Theater and the Mercury Theater, which provided the movies with talent on the order of Elia Kazan and Orson Welles.

In addition to the direct effects of the major studios' employment of theatrical personnel and involvement in financing plays, the film industry influenced the New York theater in another important but less easily documented way: Hollywood (as glamorous and superficial environment, mass entertainment industry, standardized product) served as negative exemplum against which the noncommercial theater could measure its own aesthetic sophistication and political commitment and against which Broadway could see itself as the site of cosmopolitanism, cultural prestige, and entertainment-become-art. The relationship between stage and screen in America of the 1920s and 1930s cannot be reduced to any simple struggle between art and commerce, the highbrow and the lowbrow, but this relationship to a great extent informed what theater and film critics and, at times, dramatists and filmmakers had to say about art, entertainment, and culture.

Though there were few American plays that explicitly took the movies as their subject (George S. Kaufman and Marc Connelly's 1922 comic hit, *Merton of the Movies*, being one notable exception, and over fifty years later, Christopher Durang's satiric *A History of the American Film* being another), Hollywood, continuing a trend begun in the 1920s, pictured the backstage life, flamboyant personalities, and even the commercial nexus of the New York theater in a range of films, including comedies like *Twentieth Century* (1934) and *Stage Door* (1937) and, of course, what came quickly to be known as the "backstage musical" (Warner Brothers' series of *Gold Diggers* films, Paramount's *Big Broadcasts*, and so on). Such films undoubtedly helped shape popular conceptions of Broadway and, I believe, implicitly affirmed the basic affinity between the commercial theater and the American film industry in motive (the creation of profitable "entertainment") and method (a collective effort headed by the male producer/director)—even as the spectacular production numbers of choreographers like Busby Berkeley used editing and elaborate camera movement to transcend the limitations of the stage.

Backstage musicals and comedies are but one instance of Hollywood's interaction with Broadway during the 1930s, a decade characterized by what is arguably the American cinema's deepest and richest ties to the stage. In addition to the many character actors and bit players who brought their theatrical experience to their work in the movies, consider the number of stars who began their careers in the New York theater: Katharine Hepburn, Barbara Stanwyck, Joan Crawford, Irene Dunne, Bette Davis, Cary Grant, Clark Gable, James Cagney, Henry Fonda, Spencer Tracy, Fred Astaire, and Edward G. Robinson, among others. (Several of these actors, most notably Hepburn, returned to the stage at one time or another.) In addition, W. C. Fields, Mae West, and the Marx Brothers, as well as Will Rogers, Eddie Cantor, and Jimmy Durante, all came to film comedy with extensive experience in vaudeville. The presence of so many theatrically trained performers does not so much prove that the classic Hollywood sound film was stagey or derivative, but rather it begins to suggest that Broadway and Hollywood during the 1930s occupied adjacent positions on the larger continuum of popular commercial entertainment in America.[49]

Less immediately noticeable than the actors and comedians, perhaps even than the chorus-line dancers, choreographers, and composers who came to Hollywood from Broadway in the 1930s, were the stage directors at work in the movies, like Universal's horror film specialist, James Whale, and John Cromwell, director of many David O. Selznick productions. Three of these filmmakers are particularly worthy of note: Rouben Mamoulian, William Dieterle, and George Cukor. Mamoulian, after studying at the Moscow Art Theater, producing operas and operettas, and winning great acclaim for his direction of *Porgy* for the Theatre Guild in 1927, became one of the most innovative Hollywood directors of the early sound period with films like *Applause* (1929), *Dr. Jekyll and Mr. Hyde* (1931), and *Love Me Tonight* (1932). Dieterle, having trained with Max Reinhardt and worked as both an actor and director in Germany during the 1920s, co-directed *A Midsummer Night's Dream* with Reinhardt before directing the Academy Award–winning *The Life of Emile Zola* (1937) and a number of other "biopics" for Warner Brothers in the late 1930s. Unlike Mamoulian and Dieterle, Cukors's theatrical roots were squarely in the commercial New York theater, from which he was hired as a "dialogue director" for early talkies. With the success of *Dinner at Eight* (1933), Cukor became one of MGM's top-rank directors, responsible for *Camille* (1936) and a costly production of Romeo and Juliet (1936), as well as a series of adaptations of Broadway successes like *Holiday* (1938) and *The Philadelphia Story* (1940).

If one indication of the interplay between Hollywood and the American theater during the 1930s is the contribution to the movies of theater-trained personnel like George Cukor, Busby Berkeley, Ben Hecht, and Katharine Hepburn (as well as playwrights-become-screenwriters like Clifford Odets, Sidney Howard, and Charles MacArthur), equally important is the vast number of films adapted from plays. *Dinner at Eight*, for example, was based on a successful Broadway play, as was *The Women* (1939)—also diected by Cukor—and the winner of the 1938 Academy Award for best picture, Frank Capra's *You Can't Take It With You*. (Even John Ford tried his hand at transposing plays for the screen with *Mary of Scotland* [1936] and *The Plough and The Stars* [1936].) The 1930s also saw adaptations of the works of virtually every major American playwright of the period, including Eugene O'Neill's *Anna Christie* and *Ah, Wilderness!*, Elmer Rice's *Street Scene* and *Counsellor-at-Law*, Lillian Hellman's *The Children's Hour*, Sidney Kingsley's *Dead End* and *Men in White*, Clifford Odets's *Golden Boy*, Phillip Barry's *Holiday*, and Maxwell Anderson's *Winterset* and *The Petrified Forest*. In the early 1940s the trend continued with film versions of Robert Sherwood's *Abe Lincoln in Illinois*, Thornton Wilder's *Our Town*, Hellman's *The Little Foxes*, and Barry's *The Philadelphia Story*. Adaptations such as these helped to shape the aural style of the talkies and to define the "A" quality, prestige Hollywood production—indeed, to serve as a model of culture for the movie studios and the moviegoing public.

As Roger Dooley notes in his encyclopedic survey of Hollywood films of the 1930s, adaptations of popular plays also figured prominently in several popular film genres and subgenres of the period: most obviously in backstage musicals, musical comedies, and light operettas, but also in, for example, domestic comedies which usually dealt with middle-class family life; so-called women's pictures of infidelity and marital discord; fast-paced newspaper movies in the manner of *The Front Page* (1931); exotic melodramas about the mysterious East; drawing-room comedies of the upper classes, often based on plays by Somerset Maugham, Noel Coward, and Rachel Crothers; and microcosmic *Grand Hotel*–in styled narratives. Without question, the pre–World War II Hollywood sound film often imitated, borrowed from, and measured itself against the standards of the commercial theater of the 1920s and 1930s; our problem is how to determine the precise significance of this relationship—culturally, aesthetically, and ideologically. To this end we need a close examination of the precise way the plays I have mentioned (and a great many others) were revised and restaged for the screen, as well as a comprehensive study of the role of theatrical personnel throughout the film industry.

The interaction between film and the commercial theater in Europe after the introduction of the talkies parallels the relationship between Broadway and Hollywood during the 1930s. Actors and directors moved from stage to screen (and often from Europe to America as well, further underlining the role of stage talent in the American film industry). In Great Britain, for example, theatrical impresario-become-film producer-and-director Basil Dean established the production facilities at Ealing studios and introduced several veterans of the music-hall and variety theater circuit to the movies. These performers—most notably Gracie Fields and George Formby—came to dominate British sound film comedy of the 1930s, while stage actor Charles Laughton proved to be the main attraction in the most acclaimed British film of the decade, *The Private Life of Henry VIII* (1934). Anthony Asquith's *Pygmalion* (1938)—among the best of the many British film versions of George Bernard Shaw's plays—helped promote a tradition of respectful and culturally respectable adaptations of dramatic texts that would include, in the post–World War II period, Laurence Olivier's Shakespeare films, David Lean's adaptations of Noel Coward, and Asquith's *The Browning Version* (1951) and *The Importance of Being Earnest* (1952), and in the 1960s and 1970s, filmed versions of Robert Bolt's *A Man for All Seasons*, Dylan Thomas's *Under Milk Wood*, and of plays by Ibsen and Pinter. Stage plays also served as the basis for several of Alfred Hitchcock's early sound films (including Blackmail [1929] and a version of Sean O'Casey's *Juno and the Paycock* [1930]) and for many 1930s British musicals, which—like the more ambitious German examples of this genre from this period—shared with their Hollywood counterparts an obvious dependence on performers, composers, directors, and plot conventions drawn from the commercial theater.[50]

In France during the 1930s the continuity between the commercial theater and the talkies was most apparent in the films of Sacha Guitry and Marcel Pagnol. Author of over one hundred plays, Guitry wrote, acted in, and directed a series of films (produced between 1935 and 1957), often based on his own works. Of greater critical standing are *Marius* (1931), *César* (1936), and other adaptations Pagnol produced and/or directed from his popular plays. More interesting than the attempt by Pagnol and Guitry to use film as a means of perpetuating and disseminating the formulas of the popular stage is the role that theater plays as subject and metaphor in Marcel Carné's *Children of Paradise* (1944), Max Ophul's *Lola Montes* (1955), and in many of the films of Jean Renoir, including *Rules of the Game* (1939) and, later, *The Golden Coach* (1951), which offer what Leo Braudy has called a celebration of the theater's function as an "ever-replenishing refuge of order."[51] It is worth noting that Renoir's interest in the theater is shared by two other vastly different, internationally acclaimed filmmakers, Ingmar Bergman (particularly in *The Seventh Seal* [1957] and *Persona* [1966] and Federico Fellini (whose films from *Variety Lights* [1950] often concern the popular stage and the varieties of theatrical spectacle). Using film to depict theater and the theatrical, Renoir, Bergman, and Fellini offer what are among the most insightful explorations of the relationship between the two media.

In a much more conventional fashion Hollywood musicals of the 1940s, like *Babes on Broadway* (1941) and *Cover Girl* (1944), often took the theater as their subject, continuing the 1930s musical's interest in stage performance and show business behind the scenes. Whether played out against a backstage setting or not, 1940s musicals were strongly influenced by the commercial theater: Vincente Minnelli's *The Pirate* (1947) and Stanley Donen and Gene Kelly's *On the Town* (1949), among other films, were adapted from Broadway musicals; Jack Cole, influential chief choreographer at Columbia, was trained in the theater; and, perhaps most significant, Kelly, Donen, Minnelli, Bob Fosse, and virtually all of the key members of Arthur Freed's famed production team at MGM were recruited from the New York stage. "To work for the Freed unit was understandably the ambition of Broadway and Hollywood's musical best," John Kobal declares in his history of the genre,[52] and the series of MGM musicals from *Meet Me in St. Louis* (1944) through *An American in Paris* (1951) and *Singin' in the Rain* (1952) rank with the most successful collaborations between film and theater personnel.

The other principal Hollywood genres of the 1940s were far less indebted to the theater than was the musical. Westerns, for instance, had never had close ties to the stage, and postwar *film noir* was influenced most strongly by hard-boiled fiction. Broadway hits still served as the basis for comedies like *Arsenic and Old Lace* (1944) and *Harvey* (1950), and a series of films adapted from Lillian Hellman's plays (i.e., *Watch on the Rhine* [1943] or based on her screenplays (i.e., *North Star* [1943] helped to define Hollywood's wartime anti-fascist stance, but on the whole the film industry relied less on Broadway than it had in the 1930s. The extent to which the many former stage actors, choreographers, directors, and writers at work in Hollywood brought their assumptions about performance and drama to bear upon the movies is impossible to gauge. The importance of theater-trained personnel in American film of the 1940s is, however, undeniable—witness the Freed unit, Elia Kazan (who came to Hollywood via the Group Theater to direct social problem films in the later 1940s), and especially two extraordinary writer-directors, Orson Welles (fresh from the success of his innovative Mercury Theater productions) and Preston Sturges (having moved from playwright in the late 1920s to screenwriter in the 1930s to director in the 1940s of satiric comedies like *Sullivan's Travels* [1941] and *Miracle of Morgan's Creek* [1944].

Welles, Kazan, Cukor, and Minnelli—to cite four very different filmmakers who came to film from the theater—continued to direct films after the 1940s, and the 1950s saw veteran German playwright and stage director Douglas Sirk's series of stylized melodramas at Universal. From the 1950s to the 1980s, however, an increasing number of screenwriters and directors—including Francis Ford Coppola, Martin Scorsese, George Lucas, and Steven Spielberg—entered the American film industry via film schools, journalism, television work, and nonfiction filmmaking. (Bob Fosse is the most notable exception.) Yet the theater—particularly the New York theater—continued to serve as a major source for film actors. Perhaps the most influential (and surely the most widely noted) instance of this interaction was the role played by Elia Kazan and Lee Strasberg's Actor's Studio with its Method approach to acting derived from Stanislavsky's techniques with the Moscow Art Theater and from the work of the Group Theater in the 1930s. In 1950s films like *On the Waterfront* (1954) and *Rebel Without a Cause* (1955), Lee J. Cobb, Rod Steiger, and most important, Marlon Brando and James Dean—all products of the Actor's Studio, as were Paul Newman and Geraldine Page, among others—revolutionized screen acting. Many of the prominent members of the next generation of actors also came to film with training in the Method or at least with considerable experience in the Off-Broadway theater: Faye Dunaway, Stacy Keach, Dustin Hoffman, Al Pacino, Martin Sheen, Robert DeNiro, and Cicely Tyson; and, later, Meryl Streep, William Hurt, Christopher Walken, and Richard Gere. Even in the 1980s there still seems to be a widely perceived distinction—promoted by movie reviewers and award committees—between the bravura, demanding performance of the theater-trained actor (typically in prestige,"serious" films) and the familiar gestures and appealing photogeneity of a John Wayne or a Clint Eastwood (or most performers in genre movies). As misguided as it surely is to categorically prefer the former to the latter, such assumptions about film acting reflect the motion picture's long-standing inferiority complex in the face of the established arts and remind us of the strong influence of theater personnel in the American film industry well after the decline of the studio era.

In addition, through the 1950s Hollywood continued to make use of successful Broadway plays like *Born Yesterday*, *Dial M for Murder*, and *Witness for the Prosecution*, much as the major studios turned to the comedies of Neil Simon and to prestige stage productions like *The Miracle Worker*, *The Lion in Winter*, *The Great White Hope*, and *Equus* during the 1960s and 1970s. As the musical in the post-Freed era ran out of steam, the genre was given over to big-budget adaptations of Broadway productions like Rodgers and Hammerstein's *Oklahoma!* and *South Pacific* (a trend continued with *The Sound of Music* [1965], *Funny Girl* [1968], *The Wiz* [1978], and *Annie* [1982]. Of greater interest are the films of stage plays that served to showcase Method acting in the movies and to a large extent defined what constituted adult themes in American films of the 1950s: *All My Sons* (1948) and *Death of a Salesman* (1951) from Arthur Miller; *The Big Knife* (1955) from Clifford Odets (who also wrote the script for *Sweet Smell of Success* [1957]); *Come Back, Little Sheba* (1952) and *Picnic* (1955) from William Inge; and, above all, *The Glass Menagerie* (1950), *A Streetcar Named Desire* (1951), *The Rose Tattoo* (1955), *Cat on a Hot Tin Roof* (1958), *Suddenly Last Summer* (1959), and the other adaptations of Tennessee Williams's stage plays. (*Who's Afraid of Virginia Wolfe?* [1966] follows in this tradition.) For example, Kazan brought his New York production of *A Streetcar Named Desire* (with Marlon Brando, Karl Malden, and Kim Hunter) to the screen virtually intact, creating a film that Maurice Yacowar calls a "landmark" not only because it is "an invaluable record of a legendary production," but also because "it introduced Method acting to the mass audience" and "struck a blow for mature film making."[53] By challenging, directly and indirectly, the Legion of Decency and the film industry's Production Code, *Streetcar* and the other adaptations cited above contributed to the increased freedom of expression in American film during the 1950s, while at the same time these films perpetuated the belief that "mature film making" was in fact analogous to intimate, wordy, psychological drama concerned with repression, angst, failure, and sexual (melo)dramatics.

In a somewhat similar vein, British film in the late 1950s and early 1960s found a topical direction and a renewal of "maturity" in the social realism of John Osborne's *Look Back in Anger* and *The Entertainer*, both of which were directed on the stage and filmed by Tony Richardson and were important in establishing the British "New Cinema" movement. (In contrast, the theater seems to have had no appreciable influence on French New Wave filmmakers who emerged at the same time.) Richardson also directed adaptations of Shelagh Delaney's *A Taste of Honey* (1962), and later in his career, of *Hamlet* (1969) and Edward Albee's *A Delicate Balance* (1975). Lindsay Anderson (*If . . .* [1968], *O Lucky Man!* [1973]), the most cinematically interesting of the New Cinema directors, not only came to the feature film from a background in both documentary filmmaking and stage directing, but he has continued to work in the theater, directing, among other plays, David Storey's *In Celebration* (which he then filmed as part of the American Film Theatre project).[54] In other ways as well, the interplay between stage and screen remains important in the modern British film—in, most obviously, the number of acclaimed British actors (Alan Bates, Glenda Jackson, Albert Finney, and others) who work in both media, as well as in the fact that Peter Brook and Peter Hall, among the premiere modern British stage directors, have both filmed their own stage productions (including Brook's *Marat-Sade* [1967] and *King Lear* [1971] and Hall's *A Midsummer Night's Dream* [1968]) and also tried their hand at other types of filmmaking, such as Brook's *Lord of the Flies* (1963) and Hall's *Perfect Friday* (1970).

In addition, Harold Pinter, arguably the most significant and innovative modern British playwright, has written a number of screenplays, particularly for expatriate American director Joseph Losey's *The Servant* (1963), *Accident* (1967), and *The Go-Between* (1971). To the extent that it encompasses playwriting, screenwriting, and directing stage and film productions, Pinter's career reveals once again certain lines of continuity between film and theater. Pinter could be compared with Ingmar Bergman in this respect. Bergman began as a playwright and stage director, and as one biographer has put it, "throughout his career he has remained faithful to both the stage and the screen"—from 1963 to 1966, for example, Bergman was head of Sweden's national theater, the Royal Dramatic Theater in Stockholm.[55] In the work of Pinter and Bergman, and in the vastly different careers of German director Rainer Werner Fassbinder (who was also a playwright, stage director, and actor) and the American playwright-actor-screenwriter Sam Shepard, we can see the wealth of artistic possibilities born of the creative interaction between film and theater.

And, we might add, television as well, for Bergman and Fassbinder, among many other filmmakers, created original works for European television during the 1970s. Even during the age of television and video, there has still been much interaction between film and theater. Hollywood, as I noted earlier, has continued to utilize stage personnel and to adopt hit plays from the commercial theater— including in the 1980s, *On Golden Pond* (1981), *Amadeus* (1984), and *Agnes of God* (1985). Broadway, in turn, has continued to rely heavily on the film industry's investment in play production and the purchase of screen rights. Other areas of interaction merit further study, like, for example, the relationship between black theater in America and the "blaxploitation" film of the 1970s; the role of the prolific playwright and screenwriter, Neil Simon, in defining the course of what James Monaco has called anxiety-ridden "straight comedy"[56] and the extent to which films like *Kramer vs. Kramer* (1979) and *Terms of Endearment* (1983) are generally perceived to be "legitimate" films (versus made-for-television movies and genre films) in the same sense that Broadway since the 1920s has laid claim to being the "legitimate"—i.e., culturally respectable, adult, artistically conservative—theater.

The influence of recent American avant-garde theater on Hollywood, however, has been indirect and negligible—Sam Shepard nothwithstanding. On rare occasions an experimental Off-Broadway or an Off-Off-Broadway play has been adapted for the screen (like Shirley Clarke's independently produced film version of the Living Theater's production of *The Connection*), and a number of the principal movie actors of the 1970s and 1980s got their stage training outside the aegis of Broadway. Avant-garde theater in the second half of the twentieth century can keep its distance from commercial filmmaking (and vice versa), but this theater at its best does not pretend ignorance of the movies as social institution, narrative art, and technological medium. Surveying the relationship between film and theater in an often-reprinted 1966 article, Susan Sontag notes the extent to which "the staging of many plays"—particularly in France and Eastern Europe—"is inspired by the movies," and she identifies the "pervasive notion in both advanced cinema and theatre" of the "idea of art as an act of violence." More important, Sontag quite correctly distinguishes between "the two principal radical positions in the arts today": the demand for inclusion, for synaesthesis and the mixture of genres and media; and the demand for aesthetic purity, for the "intensification of what each art distinctively is."[57] The modern experimental theater offers examples of both positions: on the one hand, the mixed-media tradition in which projected motion pictures are incorporated into the theatrical performance, as promoted in different ways by the Futurists, Meyerhold, Piscator, the Federal Theatre's "living newspaper" productions of the 1930s, Happenings of the 1950s and 1960s, Robert Blossom's Filmstage productions, and Josef Svoboda's Laterna Magika, with its "synthesis of projected images and synchronized acting and staging"[58] and, on the other hand, the quest for "pure" theater undertaken by, for example, the Living Theater and the Open Theatre in America, Peter Brook and Eugenio Barba in Europe, and, perhaps most influentially, by Polish director Jerzy Grotowski, who called for a "poor theatre" "stripped of all that is not essential" and therefore defined by the distance it keeps from the cinema.[59] No less than mixed media, "poor theatre" is in part a response to film and another indication of the interaction between stage and screen—an interaction that has strongly influenced the evolution of both film and theater in the twentieth century.

STYLES AND GENRES OF INTERACTION

The preceding survey raises several important questions about film, theater, and the particular features of their symbiotic interaction. What, for example, characterizes the artistic "influence" of theater on film and vice versa, not only among avant-garde artists but also in the realm of mainstream, commercial art? What does the relationship between stage and screen suggest about the evolution of popular genres, most notably about the course that melodrama and comedy have taken in the twentieth century? How can we best analyze the unique aesthetic status and cultural significance of film adaptations of dramatic literature and specific stage productions? How does an awareness of the symbiotic relationship between film and theater force us to pay greater heed to the role of set and costume design, lighting, and staging techniques in the movies and to rethink the oft-repeated claim that, as one film purist put it, "the history of film as an art is that of its struggle against theatricality"?[60] Furthermore, viewing film in the context of theater highlights several fundamental aesthetic issues concerning the two media, issues that have been examined and reexamined in the many books and articles that compare stage and screen. Theater historian Allardyce Nicoll, for example, argues in *Film and Theatre* that while film demands complex, individualized characters, "the truly vital theatre deals in stock figures," for "character on the stage is restricted and sterotyped."[61] However we may judge his conclusions, Nicoll's decision to discuss the presentation of character in the two media seems justified, since the fictional feature film to a great extent shares with the more traditional forms of theater those elements of drama that Aristotle defined as plot, character, spectacle, and thought. A comparative examination of stage and screen underscores the presence of these elements in the movies—and also leads us to question precisely how these elements are utilized in specific films, genres, and film movements. To what extent is the narrative film a form of Aristotelian drama? Does or should character, as Nicoll suggests, mean something quite different onscreen than onstage? Is Siegfried Kracauer correct when he asserts in *Theory of Film* that film can and therefore should forgo the highly structured plotting of theatrical drama with its "distinct patterns of meaning" and its preoccupation with "human characters and human interrelations" in favor of episodic, "open-minded narrative" that is "permeable to the flow of life out of which it arises"?[62] Much as the emergence of the motion picture caused playwrights, stage directors, and drama critics to reconsider the terms and conditions of their art, the interaction between film and theater should lead us to reassess our understanding of the elements of drama.

In addition, comparing stage and screen becomes for Nicoll, Kracauer, Rudolph Arnheim (*Film as Art*), and V. I. Pudovkin (*Film Technique* and *Film Acting*)—as well as virtually all critics and theorists of the pre–1940 period who speculated about the new art of the movies—a means of identifying "essentially" cinematic techniques and narrative possibilities, such as the manipulation via montage and camera movement of shifting point of view and the "uniquely" cinematic capacity for what Erwin Panofsky has called the "spatialization of time" and the "dynamization of space."[63] Such discussions are worthwhile, though often they are based on a narrowly circumscribed definition of theater and a prescriptive attitude toward film.

More interesting, it seems to me, is the way a comparative study of stage and screen brings to the fore questions about representation, mimesis, illusion, and performance in art—questions, in fact, that concern the very nature and function of art. Defenders of the theater against what was known as the "movie menace" never ceased to insist on the superiority of the theater's one-of-a-kind performance and the "living"—indeed spiritual—link between stage actor and audience to the facile, illusory, mechanically derived moving image, a merely visual distraction for a mass audience. Proponents of film, conversely, praised film's seemingly effortless and boundless realism at the expense of the theater's inescapable artifice and distance from life. Distinctions between the two media are, however, far less pat. As Herbert Blau argues, the theatrical performance involves not simply the "actual" presence of the actor, but the complex weaving of artifice and presence, stage and actor, performance and audience, in a "participatory space." If film, unlike theater, does not allow us to witness what Blau calls "the actor's mortality" and "vulnerability,"[64] it offers its own form of presence in absence, its own manner of participation, its own blend of intimacy and distance. No simple model of what it means to be a spectator and no reductive understanding of the role of artifice, imitation, and representation in art seems possible when we take both film and theater, in all their diverse manifestations, into account.

NOTES

1. Jeanne Thomas Allen, "Copyright and Early Theater, Vaudeville, and Film Competition," in *Film Before Griffith*, ed. John Fell (Berkeley: University of California Press, 1983), p. 176.

2. For a complete discussion of motion picture production by the Edison Company, see Gordon Hendricks, *The Kinetoscope* (New York: The Beginnings of the American Film, 1966).

3. Charles Musser, "The American Vitagraph, 1897–1901: Survival and Success in a Competitive Industry," in *Film Before Griffith*, ed. Fell, p. 26.

4. See Katherine Singer Kovacs, "George Méliès and the *Féerie*," *Cinema Journal* 16, no. 1 (Fall 1976): 1–13.

5. Robert C. Allen, "Vitascope/Cinématographe: Initial Patterns of American Film Industrial Practice," in *Film Before Griffith*, ed. Fell, p. 148.

6. Robert C. Allen, *Vaudeville and Film 1895–1915: A Study in Media Interaction* (New York: Arno Press, 1980), pp. 75–319.

7. See Allen, "Copyright and Early Theater."

8. Allen's *Vaudeville and Film* contains by far the most complete examination of the interaction between film and small-time vaudeville.

9. See Robert McLaughlin, *Broadway and Hollywood: A History of Economic Interaction* (New York: Arno Press, 1974), pp. 137–38.

10. Jay Leyda, *Kino: A History of the Russian and Soviet Film* (New York: Collier Books, 1973), pp. 33–34.

11. "The Film and the Play," *Moving Picture World* 8 (19 February 1911): 347. For a survey of critical opinion concerning the *film d'art* movement, see Gregory A. Waller, *The Stage/Screen Debate: A Study in Popular Aesthetics* (New York: Garland Press, 1983), pp. 142–52.

12. See Kemp R. Niver, *Klaw & Erlanger Present Famous Plays in Pictures* (Los Angeles: Locare Research Group, 1976), for a more complete survey of Klaw and Erlanger's contribution to the famous players movement. Paul C. Spehr, *The Movies Begin: Making Movies in New Jersey, 1887–1920* (Newark, N.J.: Newark Museum, 1977), also includes much information about other film studios with ties to the legitimate theater during the teens.

13. McLaughlin, *Broadway and Hollywood*, p. 2.

14. Jack Poggi, *Theater in America: The Impact of Economic Forces, 1870–1967* (Ithaca, N.Y.: Cornell University Press, 1968), p. 89.

15. McLaughlin, *Broadway and Hollywood*, pp. 26–27.

16. See Walter Prichard Eaton, "Actor-Snatching and the Movies," *American Magazine* 80 (December 1915): 32–37, 58–64.

17. McLaughlin, *Broadway and Hollywood*, pp. 55–56.

18. Leyda, *Kino*, p. 401.

19. For a discussion of the American Film Theatre, see Roger Manvell, *Theater and Film* (Cranbury, N.J.: Associated University Presses, 1979), pp. 249–62.

20. William K. Everson, *American Silent Film* (New York: Oxford University Press, 1978), p. 59.

21. Robert Grau, "The Moving Picture Theatre and the Stage—A Unique Situation," *Editorial Review* 5 (November 1911): 995.

22. Robet Grau, "The 'Talking' Picture and the Drama," *Scientific American* 105 (August 1911): 156.

23. Gilbert Seldes, "The Path of the Movies," *Nation* 120 (29 April 1925): 498.

24. See John Fell, *Film and the Narrative Tradition* (Norman: Oklahoma University Press, 1974).

25. Horace M. Kallen, "The Dramatic Picture Versus the Pictorial Drama: A Study of the Influences of the Cinematograph on the Stage," *Harvard Monthly* 50 (March 1910): 25.

26. A. Nicholas Vardac, *Stage to Screen: Theatrical Method from Garrick to Griffith* (1949; repr. New York: Benjamin Blom, 1968), pp. 67, 241.

27. Filippo Tommaso Marinetti, "The Variety Theatre," in *Futurist Performance*, ed. Michael Kirby (New York: Dutton, 1971), p. 179.

28. Kirby, "Introduction," *Futurist Performance*, p. 47.

29. Zygmunt Tonecki, "At the Boundary of Film and Theatre," *Close Up* 9 (March 1932): 35.

30. Walter H. Sokel, Introduction to *Anthology of German Expressionist Drama* (Garden City, N.Y.: Anchor, 1963), p. xxxi.

31. See Lotte Eisner, *The Haunted Screen: Expressionism in the German Cinema and the Influence of Max Reinhardt* (Berkeley: University of California Press, 1969).

32. Laszlo Moholy-Nagy, ''Theater, Circus, Variety,'' in *The Theater of the Bauhaus*, ed. Walter Gropius (Middleton, Conn.: Wesleyan University Press, 1961), p. 68.

33. See, for example, Martin Walsh, *The Brechtian Aspect of Radical Cinema* (London: British Film Institute, 1981); and George Lellis, *Bertolt Brecht, 'Cahiers du Cinéma,' and Contemporary Film Theory* (Ann Arbor, Mich.: UMI Research Press, 1982).

34. James Roose-Evans, *Experimental Theatre: From Stanislavsky to Peter Brook* (London: Routledge & Kegan Paul, 1984), p. 29.

35. Vsevolod Meyerhold, ''Two Lectures'' (1930), *Tulane Drama Review* 11 (Fall 1966): 187.

36. See, for example, ''The Unexpected,'' Eisenstein's meditation on film form triggered by his encounter with Kabuki theater (reprinted in *Film Form: Essays in Film Theory* [New York: Harcourt Brace, 1949]), and his essay on Chinese theater, ''The Enchanter from the Pear Garden,'' *Theatre Arts Monthly* 19 (October 1935): 761–70.

37. See Richard Abel, *French Cinema: The First Wave, 1915–1929* (Princeton, N.J.: Princeton University Press, 1984), pp. 85–90.

38. Ibid., pp. 223–38.

39. Poggi, *Theater in America*, pp. 261, 263.

40. Quoted in McLaughlin, *Broadway and Hollywood*, p. 64.

41. Ibid., p. 83.

42. Harry M. Geduld, *The Birth of the Talkies: From Edison to Jolson* (Bloomington: Indiana University Press, 1975), and Alexander Walker, *The Shattered Silents: How the Talkies Came to Stay* (New York: William Morrow, 1979), both offer much information about the interaction between Broadway and Hollywood during the first years of the sound film.

43. Richard Watts, Jr., ''As Is,'' *Close Up* 3 (Spring 1928): 15. For a survey of opinion about the relationship between the sound film and the theater, see Waller, *The Stage/Screen Debate*, pp. 152–59. Compare Watts's comment with Charles Higham's assertion that ''the invasion of Broadway dramatists at the dawn of sound gave the American cinema its adulthood. It provided it, more or less consistently until the 1950s, with a tough, insolent mind of its own. And new directors from Broadway gave a new depth to acting'' (*The Art of the American Film* [Garden City, N.Y.: Doubleday, 1974], p. x).

44. Walker, *The Shattered Silents*, p. 157.

45. Roger Dooley, *From Scarlett to Scarface: American Films in the 1930s* (New York: Harcourt Brace Jovanovich, 1984), p. 414.

46. See McLaughlin, *Broadway and Hollywood*, pp. 114–72.

47. Ibid., p. 108.

48. For a revisionist view of the much-discussed ''corruption'' of playwright by Hollywood, see John Schultheiss, ''George Jean Nathan and the Dramatist in Hollywood,'' *Literature/Film Quarterly* 4 (1976): 13–27.

49. This point is also made, unintentionally, I think, in *The American Theatre*, a volume published by the Dial Press in 1938, which consisted of John Anderson's essay, ''The American Theatre''; Rene Fülöp-Miller's essay, ''The Motion Picture in America''; and 200 pages of photographs that suggest the affinity between Broadway and Hollywood productions in terms in set design.

50. For a discussion of non-American musicals of the 1930s, see John Kobal, *Gotta Sing, Gotta Dance: A History of Movie Musicals* (London: Hamlyn, 1983), pp. 45–87.

51. Leo Braudy, *Jean Renoir: The World of His Films* (Garden City, N.Y.: Doubleday, 1972), p. 103.

52. Kobal, *Gotta Sing, Gotta Dance*, p. 199.

53. Maurice Yacowar, *Tennessee Williams and Film* (New York: Frederick Ungar, 1977), p. 24.

54. See, for example, Lindsay Anderson, "Class Theatre, Class Film," *Tulane Drama Review* 11 (Fall 1966): 122–29.

55. Birgitta Steene, "A Biographical Note," in *Ingmar Bergman: Essays in Criticism*, ed. Stuart Kaminsky (New York: Oxford University Press, 1975), p. 3.

56. James Monaco, *American Film Now* (New York: New American Library, 1979), p. 233.

57. Susan Sontag, "Film and Theater," *Tulane Drama Review* 11 (Fall 1966): 34–37.

58. Josef Svoboda, "Laterna Magika," *Tulane Drama Review* 11 (Fall 1966): 142. See also Michael Kirby, "Uses of Film in the New Theatre," *Tulane Drama Review* 11 (Fall 1966): 49–61; and Gene Youngblood's discussion of "intermedia theatre" in *Expanded Cinema* (New York: Dutton, 1970), pp. 365–86.

59. Jerzy Grotowski, *Towards a Poor Theatre* (New York: Simon and Schuster, 1968), p. 21.

60. C. R. Jones, "Stage People and Film Things," *Cinema Quarterly* 2 (Summer 1934): 222.

61. Allardyce Nicoll, *Film and Theatre* (New York: Thomas Y. Crowell, 1936), pp. 165–66.

62. Siegfried Kracauer, *Theory of Film* (New York: Oxford University Press, 1960), pp. 219–21, 254.

63. Erwin Panofsky, "Style and Medium in the Motion Pictures," in *Film Criticism and Theory*, ed. Gerald Mast and Marshall Cohen, 3d ed. (New York: Oxford University Press, 1985), p. 218.

64. Herbert Blau, "Theater and Cinema: The Scopic Drive, the Detestable Screen, and More of the Same," *Cine-Tracts* 3, no. 4 (1981): 51, 61–62.

SELECTED BIBLIOGRAPHY

Probably the two most influential discussions of the relationship between film and theater are Erwin Panofsky's "Style and Medium in the Motion Pictures" (*Critique* 1, no. 3 [January–February 1947]) and Susan Sontag's "Film and Theatre" (*Tulane Drama Review* 11 [Fall 1966]). Both of these often-reprinted essays remain essential reading for anyone interested in the aesthetics of stage and screen. Panofsky and Sontag are, however, best understood in the context of the more than 500 books, articles, interviews, and editorials that compare film and theater as cultural institutions and artistic (or inartistic) media. In *The Stage/Screen Debate: A Study in Popular Aesthetics* (1983), I examine this material, the bulk of which was published before 1940 in a wide range of general-interest periodicals, trade magazines, and specialized journals devoted to film, theater, or literature. In addition, virtually all the major film theorists from the teens through the sixties have addressed the question of the relationship between stage and screen.

Four basic positions emerged during the preliminary years of the stage/screen debate: the argument that film, the twentieth-century art par excellence, is superior to and will supersede theater; that theater—the bastion of human and cultural values—is superior to film; that the two media should remain separate, each pursuing its own unique artistic possibilities; and that film and theater should be understood as allied, historically connected forms of art. For examples of the pro-film position, see D. W. Griffith's "The Greatest Theatrical Force" (*Moving Picture World* 85 [26 March 1927]: (408); Samuel Barron's "The Dying Theater" (*Harper's* 172 [1935]: 108–17); and V. I. Pudovkin's *Film Technique* (1929) and *Film Acting* (1933). The argument for the superiority of stage to screen is well represented by famed theater producer David Belasco's "The Movies—My Profession's Flickering Bogy" (*Munsey's Magazine* 63 [April 1918]: 593–604, and by many writings of two influential theater critics, Walter Prichard Eaton ("Class Consciousness and the 'Movies'," *Atlantic* 115 [1915]: 48–56) and George Jean Nathan (*The Theatre of the Moment* [1936]. Quite clearly, however, the stage/screen debate is dominated by the purist argument that "true" film and theater should remain separate, a position argued in Hugo Munsterberg's *The Photoplay: A Psychological Study* (1916), Gilbert Seldes's *An Hour with the Movies and the Talkies* (1929), Allardyce Nicoll's *Film and Theatre* (1936), Rudolph Arnheim's *Film as Art* (1957), Siegfried Kracauer's *Theory of Film* (1960), Edward Murray's *The Cinematic Imagination* (1972), and a range of articles from Rollin Summers's "The Moving Picture Drama and the Acted Drama" (*Moving Picture World* 3 [19 September 1908]: 211–13) and Alexander Bakshy's "The Artistic Possibilities of the Cinema" (*National Board of Review Magazine* 3 [November 1928]: 3–5) to Robert Steele's "The Two Faces of Drama" (*Cinema Journal* 6 [1966–1967]: 16–32). In contrast, many of Sergei Eisenstein's essays in *The Film Sense* (1942), *Film Form* (1949), and *Film Essays and a Lecture* (1970) explore the affinity and the historical continuity between film and theater, as do several of Harry Alan Potamkin's articles which have been reprinted in *The Compound Cinema: The Film Writings of Harry Alan Potamkin* (1977). The place of film within the larger dramatic tradition is also discussed in different ways by Dallas Bower in *Plan for Cinema* (1936) and Raymond Williams in "Film and the Dramatic Tradition" included in *Preface to Film* [1954)].

Though weighted strongly toward the post–1940 period, James Hurt's anthology, *Focus on Film and Theatre* (1974), contains a number of interesting articles and interviews and includes a selective annotated bibliography. See also the special issues of the *Tulane Drama Review* (Fall 1966) and *Études Cinématographiques* (Winter 1960) devoted to film and theater. For a more complete list of relevant works through the mid–1970s, see the bibliography in *The Stage/Screen Debate*.

Almost all the standard surveys of film history contain at least some reference to the economic and aesthetic interaction between film and theater in the period before World War I. Much more useful are a range of specialized texts: Robert C. Allen's *Vaudeville and Film, 1895–1915: A Study in Media Interaction* (1980), which uses primary evidence to study the economic interaction between film and vaudeville; many of the articles in *Film Before Griffith*, edited by John Fell (1983), which shed new light on the relationship between stage and screen during the first decade of film history; and A. Nicholas Vardac's *Stage to Screen: Theatrical Method from Garrick to Griffith* (1949) and John Fell's *Film and the Narrative Tradition* (1974), which chart the links between film and the nineteenth-century popular theater. Except for Kemp Niver's *Klaw & Erlanger Present Famous Plays in Pictures* (1976), little scholarly work has been done on *film d'art* and the famous players movement, which Robert Grau offers a contemporary account of in *The Theatre of Science* (1914).

For primary material on the interaction between film and the avant-garde theater, particularly in the 1920s, see, among many other texts, the Eisenstein essays I have already cited, *Meyerhold on Theater* (1969), and the essays and manifestos collected in *The Theater of the Bauhaus* (1961). Notable critical studies of this interaction include Huntly Carter's *The New Theatre and Cinema of Soviet Russia* (1924); Zygmunt Tonecki's "At the Boundary of Film and Theatre," *Close Up* 9 (March 1932): 31–35; Mordecai Gorelik's *New Theatres for Old* (1940); Lotte Eisner's *The Haunted Screen: Expressionism in the German Cinema and the Influence of Max Reinhardt* (1969); and Peter Wollen's study of Eisenstein's aesthetics in *Signs and Meaning in the Cinema* (1972). Several of these works also discuss attempts at incorporating motion pictures into a mixed-media performance, as does Michael Kirby in *Futurist Performance* (1971) and "The Uses of Film in the New Theatre," *Tulane Drama Review* 11 (Fall 1966): 49–61, and Gene Youngblood in *Expanded Cinema* (1970).

Most general surveys of avant-garde theater, like Kenneth Macgowan's *The Theatre of Tomorrow* (1921) and James Roose-Evans's *Experimental Theatre: From Stanislavsky to Peter Brook* (1984), note the influence of film on the "new stagecraft," just as many studies of the commercial theater, like Jack Poggi's *Theater in America: The Impact of Economic Forces, 1870–1967* (1968) and Ethan Mordden's *The American Theatre* (1981), pay some attention to the relationship between Broadway and Hollywood. Of particular interest in this regard is Robert McLaughlin's *Broadway and Hollywood: A History of Economic Interaction* (1974), an invaluable study of the ties between the film industry and the commercial theater in America.

The interaction between Broadway and Hollywood also figures prominently in Alexander Walker's *The Shattered Silents: How the Talkies Came to Stay* (1978) and Harry Geduld's *The Birth of the Talkies* (1975). The introduction of the sound film generated in the late 1920s and 1930s a heated controversy about the relationship between stage and screen that is reflected in, among many other texts, William de Mille's "The Screen Speaks," *Scribner's* 85 (April 1929): 367–73; Katherine Fullerton Gerould's "The Lost Art of Motion-Pictures," *Century Magazine* 118 (August 1929): 496–506; and Rudolph Arnheim's "The New Laocoon: Artistic Composites and the Talking Film" (1938; included in *Film as Art*). For a study of the theater's influence on the film musical, one of several genres that was for all purposes born with the sound film, see John Kobal's *Gotta Sing, Gotta Dance: A History of Movie Musicals* (rev. ed., 1983).

Many performers, producers, and directors who have worked in both film and theater have published autobiographies and anecdotal reminiscences and have been the subject of interviews and show-business biographies. Unless one is looking for information on a specific career, film, or stage production, this voluminous material is of only marginal interest. (Eisenstein's autobiographical essays are a notable exception.) The same is true of most comparative discussions of acting for stage and screen, like, for example, *Actors Talk about Acting* (1963). Richard A.Blum's *American Film Acting: The Stanislavski Heritage* (1984), however, suggests one fruitful line of inquiry, and Herbert Blau suggests another by examining acting in light of post-modernism and deconstructionist criticism ("Theater and Cinema: The Scopic Drive, the Detestable Screen, and More of the Same," *Cine-Tracts* 3, no. 4 [1981]: 51–64). John Schultheiss offers a balanced view of the situation of the playwright-become-Hollywood-screenwriter in "George Jean Nathan and the Dramatist in Hollywood," *Literature/Film Quarterly* 4 (1976): 13–27, which includes informative notes and a filmography.

Much critical attention has been given to the adaptation of stage plays for the screen. André Bazin's "Theater and Cinema" (reprinted in *What is Cinema?*, vol. 1 [1967]) is an oft-cited theoretical discussion of the question of adaptation in the context of Bazin's realist film theory. More traditional is Roger Manvell's *Theater and Film* (1979), which offers, to quote its subtitle, "a comparative study of the two forms of dramatic art, and of the problems of adaptation of stage plays into films." A. G. S. Enser's *Filmed Books and Plays* (1971) is the standard reference work, listing adaptations produced since the introduction of the sound film. There are a great number of critical articles that analyze specific adaptations—many of which have been published in *Literature/Film Quarterly*. Book-length studies of specific playwrights whose works have been adapted for the screen include Donald E. Costello, *The Serpent's Eye: Shaw and the Cinema* (1965), Maurice Yacowar, *Tennessee Williams and Film* (1977), and Bernard F. Dick, *Hellman in Hollywood* (1982).

The study of Shakespeare and film is something of a minor academic industry. Comparisons between film and Elizabethan theater surfaced during the silent film era, and continued in later texts like Dwight Macdonald's "Our Elizabethan Movies" (*Miscellany* 1 [December 1929]: 27–33) and Nicoll's *Film and Theatre*. Among the many studies of film adaptations of Shakespeare's drama are Robet H. Ball, *Shakespeare in Silent Film* (1968); Roger Manvell, *Shakespeare and the Film* (1971); Charles W. Eckert, *Focus on Shakespearean Films* (1972); and Jack Jorgens, *Shakespeare on Film* (1977).

SELECTED FILMOGRAPHY

The following list is by no means comprehensive; it includes only a representative selection of the many films that reflect certain aspects of the symbiotic interaction between stage and screen.

All That Jazz (USA 1979). Twentieth Century-Fox. Directed by Bob Fosse. Screenplay by Bob Fosse and Robert Alan Arthur. With Roy Scheider, Jessica Lange, Ann Reinking, Ben Vereen.

Applause (USA 1929). Paramount. Directed by Rouben Mamoulian. Screenplay by Garrett Fort. With Helen Morgan.

Broadway Melody (USA 1929). MGM. Directed by Harry Beaumont. Screenplay by James Gleason, Norman Houston, Edmund Goulding. With Charles King, Anita Page.

The Cabinet of Doctor Caligari (Germany 1919). Directed by Robert Wiene. Screenplay by Carl Mayer, Hans Janowitz. With Werner Krauss, Conrad Veidt.

Children of Paradise (France 1945). Pathé. Directed by Marcel Carné. Screenplay by Jacques Prévert. With Arletty, Jean-Louis Barrault.

Dinner at Eight (USA 1933). MGM. Directed by George Cukor. Screenplay by Francis Marion, Herman J. Mankiewicz from the play by George S. Kaufman, Edna Ferber. With Marie Dressler, John Barrymore, Lionel Barrymore.

Forty-second Street (USA 1933). Warner Brothers. Directed by Lloyd Bacon. Screenplay by James Seymour, Rian James. With Warner Baxter, Ruby Keeler, Bebe Daniels, Dick Powell.

The Italian Straw Hat (France 1928). Directed by René Clair. Screenplay by René Clair from the play by Eugene Labiche. With Albert Prejean.

The Jazz Singer (USA 1927). Warner Brothers. Directed by Alan Crosland. Scrrenplay by Alfred A. Cohn from the play by Samuel Raphaelson. With Al Jolson.

King Lear (Great Britain 1971). Directed by Peter Brook. Screenplay by Peter Brook from the play by William Shakespeare. With Paul Scofield.

The Kiss (USA 1896). Edison Company. With John C. Rice and May Irwin.

The Little Foxes (USA 1941). Samuel Goldwyn. Directed by William Wyler. Screenplay by Lillian Hellman from her play. With Bette Davis, Herbert Marshall, Teresa Wright.

Look Back in Anger (Great Britain 1959). Directed by Tony Richardson. Screenplay by Nigel Kneale from the play by John Osborne. With Richard Burton, Mary Ure, Claire Bloom.

Marius (France 1931). Directed by Alexander Korda. Screenplay by Marcel Pagnol from his play. With Raimu, Pierre Fresnay.

A Midsummer Night's Dream (USA 1935). Warner Brothers. Directed by William Dieterle and Max Reinhardt. Screenplay by Charles Kenyon and Mary McCall from the play by William Shakespeare. With Dick Powell, James Cagney, Olivia de Havilland.

On Golden Pond (USA 1981). Universal. Directed by Mark Rydell. Screenplay by Ernest Thompson based on his play. With Henry Fonda, Katharine Hepburn, Jane Fonda, Doug McKeon.

The Philadelphia Story (USA 1940). MGM. Directed by George Cukor. Screenplay by Donald Ogden Stewart from the play by Philip Barry. With Katharine Hepburn, James Stewart, Cary Grant.

The Pirate (USA 1948). MGM. Directed by Vincente Minnelli. Screenplay by Albert Hackett, Francis Goodrich from the play by S. N. Behrman. With Gene Kelly, Judy Garland.

Pygmalion (Great Britain 1938). Directed by Anthony Asquith, Leslie Howard. Screenplay by Anatole de Grunwald, W. P. Lipscomb, Cecil Lewis, Ian Dalrymple from the play by George Bernard Shaw. With Leslie Howard, Wendy Hiller.

Watch on the Rhine (USA 1943). Warner Brothers. Directed by Herman Shumlin. Screenplay by Dashiell Hammett from the play by Lillian Hellman. With Paul Lukas, Bette Davis.

Who's Afraid of Virginia Woolf? (USA 1966). Warner Brothers. Directed by Mike Nichols. Screenplay by Ernest Lehman from the play by Edward Albee. With Richard Burton, Elizabeth Taylor, George Segal, Sandy Dennis.

You Can't Take It With You (USA 1938). Columbia. Directed by Frank Capra. Screenplay by Robert Riskind from the play by George S. Kaufman, Moss Hart. With Jean Arthur, Lionel Barrymore, James Stewart, Edward Arnold.

7

FILM AND CLASSICAL MUSIC

ROYAL BROWN

INTRODUCTION

In examining the relationship between film and classical music, the first thing that one must do is to establish certain parameters for defining ''classical'' music, which is no easy task. The term ''classical'' *should* delimit a certain period dominated, in music, by Mozart, Haydn, and Beethoven, a period that shares certain aesthetic principles with other ''classical'' art, whether painting, sculpture, architecture, or literature. The term as it is commonly used, however, connotes what some might refer to as highbrow music, music that stands in opposition to the more popular forms of the art, whether songs, dance tunes, jazz, or whatever. Even here clear distinctions are difficult to make. Numerous ''classical'' composers have not only written music set to popular dance forms, whether Beethoven's *Contredanses* or Chopin's waltzes, mazurkas, and polkas, they have actually taken popular material and either used it in larger scale works or else made various arrangements of it. In fact, when one considers the amount of nonoriginal thematic material that pops up in works by composers from Bach to Bartók, one begins to have a greater appreciation for the literal meaning of the verb ''compose'': far from implying an act of pure creativity, the word suggests an art of ''putting together,'' of taking various elements—in music harmony, rhythm, form, melody, texture, instrumentation, etc.—and combining them in such a way as to produce a coherent whole.

Attempting to go a step or two beyond the ''highbrow'' designation, one might additionally qualify classical music by the complexity of its composition. Even here, there are exceptions, but not perhaps as many. Complexity can be just as much a question of the horizontal elaboration of musical structures as of the various vertical structures. There is little difficulty in spotting the complexity of a work such as Beethoven's nearly hour-long Third (''Eroica'') Symphony, where the formal structure of the first movement alone can keep the dutiful analyzer busy for months. Or consider the ingenious way in which Beethoven, in the opening of his Violin Concerto, takes the simplest of figures—an evenly repeated, five-stroke motif on the same note—and integrates it, one way or another, into almost all the material that follows in the first movement. No wonder Sir Donald Francis Tovey refers to the work as "gigantic."[1] Even a brief Chopin waltz, however, likewise reveals staggering complexities in such areas as chord structure and in the harmonic movement generated by subtle inner voicings of these chord structures. Another area of complexity, that of the full symphony orchestra, with its choruses (strings, woodwinds, brass, percussion) of contrasting timbres, has become particularly important for film scoring.

To those who are accustomed to the use of music in films, where certain cues can be as brief as two or three seconds, it might at first appear that the complexity of classical music would work against the movement of a given film. But as it happens, a figure such as the five-stroke motif in the Beethoven Violin Concerto can often be used to much greater effect in a film than can a quasi-popular song. While the same song may be briefer in its fully realized potential than the five-note motif, which needs an entire concerto movement to take on its full meaning, the five-note motif can stand on its own much better against a brief set of images than can any part of the popular song, which is tied in to all sorts of conventions, including those of the so-called four-bar phrase. The reasons for this lie in the very basis of the relationship between music and film. On the most general level, it can be said that music provides a foundation in affect for the cinema's visual images. But this foundation is nowhere nearly as specific as one might suspect. One need only consider the title theme by Erich Wolfgang Korngold for Sam Wood's 1945 *King's Row*. Korngold, misled by the film's title, composed some gloriously scintillating music filled with fanfare-like flourishes à la his well-known scores for films such as *The Adventures of Robin Hood* and *The Sea Hawk*. But "King's Row" turned out to be the name of a fictional town wherein a kind of 1940s *Peyton Place* unfurls, complete with a sadistic doctor and the possibility of some father-daughter incest. Did Korngold have to rewrite his overture? No. Does the music work for the film anyway? Absolutely. As Susanne K. Langer has pointed out, "*what music can actually reflect is only the morphology of feeling*; and it is quite plausible that some sad and some happy conditions may have a very similar morphology. This insight has led some philosophical musicologists to suppose that music conveys *general forms of feeling*, related to specific ones as algebraic expressions are related to arithmetic. . . ."[2] In other words, "music is not self-expression, but *formulation and representation* of emotions, moods, mental tensions and resolutions—a 'logical picture' of sentiment, responsive life, a source of insight, not a plea for sympathy. Feelings revealed in music are essentially *not* 'the passion, love, or longing of such-and-such an individual,' inviting us to put ourselves in that individual's place, but are presented directly to our understanding, that we may grasp, realize, comprehend these feelings, without pretending to have them or imputing them to anyone else" (p. 222). As Langer also notes, "music at its highest, though clearly a symbolic form, is an unconsummated symbol" (p. 240). In this sense, most music can also be considered to be unconsummated affect, and as such, it is ripe, as an art form, for emotional consummation, just as in the opposite sense, photographic images, being excessively "consummated" by their resemblance to the reality they have captured, are ripe for the type of de-consummation afforded by music. One can understand even further here why popular songs, in which the combination of words and music provides a certain amount of consummation, do not generally work as well for cinema. By latching onto the verbal and photographic images of its film, the *King's Row* music's swashbuckling heroism miraculously transforms itself into small-town American heroism without a single note having been changed.

The degree to which this unconsummated nature of music is essential to the classical film score can be seen in the almost total lack of sung music on the soundtrack. Although as of the 1960s the movies saw an increasing, nondiegetic use of popular songs on music tracks, a phenomenon that has had as much to do with commercially viable spin-offs as it has with changing cinematic aesthetics, the nondiegetic classical film score has remained fairly free of the human vioce and almost totally free of lyrics. One major exception to this can be found in the music penned by Hans Werner Henze, a composer much better known for his modernistic "classical" creations than for film scores, for the Alain Resnais film *Muriel* (1963), which contains several "art songs" performed by a soprano. Even here, however, director Resnais, never known for his concessions to cinematic conventions, found that he had to record the songs in such a way as to totally obscure the lyrics for the viewer-listener. The very use of the human voice, even with lyrics, can be problematic. While a composer such as David Snell was able, using Christmas carols as a point of departure, to create an appropriately moody score using only vocalizing, a cappella chorus for Robert Montgomery's 1946 *Lady In the Lake*, and while director Stanley Kubrick effectively deployed Gyorgy Ligeti's prexisting *Lux Aeterna*, again for a cappella, vocalizing chorus, to accompany the "Star Gate" sequence in *2001: A Space Odyssey* (1968), composer David Shire, when he tried to use a vocalizing soprano in the title music for Robert Wise's *The Hindenburg* (1975), found preview audiences asking where the hell the woman's voice was coming from. Shire ultimately replaced the soprano with a solo trumpet. So as not to totally stack the cards in favor of this argument, I should note that a number of the film scores by Italian composer Ennio Morricone make use of a vocalizing soprano.

The fact that audiences *can* ask where a single human voice is coming from without questioning the presence of a large symphony orchestra on that same music track says a lot about the relationship between film and classical music. Essentially, the very human presence felt through the performance of a vocalist tends to move the musical symbol one step closer toward consummation; and by moving toward consummation, the classical symbol also moves toward the universe of the diegesis. As I have already suggested, the mainstream interaction between film and nondiegetic music depends on a dialectical opposition between the unconsummatedness of the musical symbol and the consummatedness of the cinematic image(s). It stands to reason, then, that the dialectical tension between the musical and the cinematic symbol will be increasingly tightened the more the music remains on an abstract level, and dealing with abstractions—and complexity—is one of the things that classical music does best. In fact, the use of classical devices, including a full symphony orchestra, in a musical score can actually help pull the music back from the diegesis even when the cinematic images beckon it to join. Consider Merian C. Cooper and Ernest B. Schoedsack's 1933 *King Kong*. Although, following the title sequence, there have been some eighteen minutes worth of exposition without a single note of music, diegetic or nondiegetic, once Carl Denham (Robert Armstrong) and his crew begin to approach "Skull Island," Max Steiner's large, symphonic score picks up again and rarely leaves the nondiegetic music track throughout the rest of the film. In the sequence where Denham and his crew set foot for the first time on the island and witness a native ceremony, the full, nondiegetic music track continues with a cue entitled "Aboriginal Sacrifice Dance." Yet the actors playing the natives on the screen dance to the rhythms of this music, even to the point of periodic, quasi-gorilla chest-thumps in time to a strong, two-note motive in the score. Even the most naive listener, if he or she thought about it, would realize that neither the cinematic images—the only instruments we see are drums—nor the ethnic context allow us to interpret the music as diegetic. What the filmmakers were going for in this sequence was affect, not realism; where the use of genuine, native music would have added, for 1930s American audiences, a degree of consummatedness that would have cut into the affective response, the use of certain musical mythemes, such as open fourths and fifths and heavy motor rhythms, evoking an unconscious reaction of what Roland Barthes would call "nativicity," along with the complexities of the combined timbres of strings, brass, and percussion, definitely gets the emotional juices flowing. (That this "nativicity" transcends the domain of the specific diegesis can be seen in the reuse of parts of the *King Kong* score in a film such as John Ford's 1956 *The Searchers*, where the music provides affective cues vis-à-vis native Americans.) So, while a single, human voice on the music track of *The Hindenburg* can set audiences to hunting around the screen for a consummated "source," in *King Kong* even the movement of the visual images in time with the purely orchestral and therefore more unconsummated music does not fully suffice to pull Max Steiner's score into the action or even to make audiences wonder about it.

In summary of the above, then, it might be said that film's relationship to classical music depends upon (a) the tendency of classical music toward a greater degree of complexity than one generally finds in other types of music; paradoxically, this complexity allows for an easier breaking down of music's larger, more longly elaborated structures into smaller units of affective meaning than is often possible with popular music; and (b) the tendency of instrumental classical music toward a greater degree of abstractedness or unconsummatedness than one finds in other forms of music; it is this more nearly purely unconsummatedness that creates the richest dialectic with the visual language of the cinema, which, of all the arts, manifests the greatest amount of consummation. These are, of course, gross generalizations , and the more specific forms of interaction between film and classical music will be examined shortly. For the moment, however, it would be well to look at some of the historical underpinnings that led to the type of classical film score that one still hears on the music tracks of a surprisingly large number of films.

HISTORICAL DEVELOPMENT

Numerous writers on the subject have theorized on why the cinematic medium, almost from the moment of its birth—or at least once it left the kinetoscopes and the penny arcades—voraciously attached itself to music. Two principal reasons seem to emerge: (1) music was needed to cover up the noise from both the audience and the projectors, which had not yet found their way into sound-proofed booths; and (2) music was needed, psychologically, to smooth over natural human fears of darkness and silence. As Irwin Bazelon has written,

The early music makers had no desire to allow external annoyances to compete for attention with their visual product: music was their panacea for encouraging audience empathy. In their anxiety to bring about this rapport and lessen the fear of silence, they often selected musical material bordering on the ridiculous: note, for example, the countless silent films accompanied by marches, anthems, patriotic tunes, operatic melodies, and whole segments of eighteenth- and nineteenth-century symphonic repertoire, inserted without dramatic motivation to fill any and all situations.[3]

Although the use of classical music in films has by and large been dramatically motivated for many decades now, one still finds numerous silent films that have been reissued with tracks in which the music simply moves from set piece to the next with no consideration for the action (some of the scores Charlie Chaplin composed and added to some of his two-reelers, such as *The Easy Life*, fall into this category). And if one looks in strange enough areas, such as porno films, one can find scores, such as Alden Shuman's often dreamy and paradoxically climaxless strains for the 1973 *The Devil in Miss Jones*, in which the music generally functions as a kind of nonstop, wallpaper soporific (to soothe what fears one can only guess).

The key date at which a pianist probably provided musical accompaniment for a film is probably 28 December 1895, when the Lumière Brothers presented some of their short films at the Grand Café in Paris. But film music did not become film music until the music began to coordinate with the action. This, however, did not take long, and there were, in fact, ample precedents in the theater, although cinemusic practitioners did not seem to catch on to this right away. Not only did Greek tragedies have passages that were sung, but music played an important role in highlighting some of the most emotionally charged moments. More recently, there is the entire tradition of melodrama (literally drama with music), not only in the broadly based hero/villain theatrics of the nineteenth and early twentieth centuries but even in more subtle works as Goethe's *Egmont*, for which Beethoven wrote quite an elaborate score of incidental music. Hans-Christian Schmidt cites an excellent example, appropriately entitled "Melodrama,"'during which the spoken words of Egmont are punctuated and sometimes underscored by brief phrases or sostenuto chords from a string orchestra.[4] Early opera depended too strongly on the use of various set pieces to offer a valid precedent for film music. Wagnerian opera, on the other hand, has quite a bit in common with film music. For in Wagner, full themes and tiny, quasi-thematic fragments are more important both in their immediate emotional impact and in their relationship to the dramatic structure of the opera than they are to its underlying musical structure. The same can be said to a degree of Wagner's harmonic language. American composer Roger Sessions has summed up the Wagnerian phenomenon as follows:

The "dissonances" in Bach or Mozart have a significance, both "musical" and "emotional," far different from that often lent them by hearers nurtured on nineteenth- and early twentieth-century music, in which dissonances are rather individual features than organic portions of a musical line. Here the influence of the Wagnerian leit-motif—more often than not extremely short and characterized by a single harmonic or rhythmic trait— is paramount. Its introduction is often motivated by dramatic, not musical necessities and once introduced it intentionally dominates the scene, to the obliteration of what surrounds it. The musical coherence is there, to be sure—but in a passive sense; the detail is more significant than the line, and the "theme" more important than its development. It is all too seldom noted to what an overwhelming extent the reverse is the case in the earlier music.[5]

No doubt some pianists who accompanied for silent pictures began to improvise and/or plagiarize dramatically appropriate music from the outset. But by the early 1900s, a more methodical attention to the relationship between music and film began to take form. In an article immodestly entitled "The Origin of Film Music," Max Winkler describes how he was led to find a "cue-sheet" enterprise that became a substantial spoke in the wheel of the Hollywood film industry and that lasted on through the early days of the talkies:

One day in the spring of 1912 I went to one of the small movie houses that had so quickly sprung up all over town, to see one of the superb spectacles of the day. It was called WAR BRIDES and featured the exotic Nazimova in the role of a pregnant peasant woman. The king of the mythical country where Nazimova was living passed through her village. Nazimova threw herself in front of him, her hands raised to heaven. She said—no, she didn't say anything but the title on the screen announced: "If you will not give us women the right to vote for or against war I shall not bear a child for such a country."
     The king just moved on. Nazimova drew a dagger and killed herself.
     The pianist so far had done all right. But I scarcely believed my ears when, just as Nazimova exhaled her last breath, to the heart-breaking sobs of her family, he began to play the old, frivolous favorite, "You Made Me What I Am Today."
     The pianist was one of my customers and I just could not resist going backstage

afterwards and asking him why he had chosen this particular tune at that particular moment. "Why," he said, "I thought that was perfectly clear. Wasn't it the king's fault that she killed herself"[6]

The concept that Winkler ultimately came up with was to supply the film studios, for each new release (which Winkler and soon many others would screen in advance), with cue sheets of suitable music, complete with timings, which at first were taken from the immense catalog of the Carl Fischer Company, for whom Winkler originally worked. These would be immediately sent to theater managers, pianists, organists, and/or orchestra conductors around the country. Movie theaters thereby had the potential for coherent cinemusical spectacles, Winkler had himself the beginnings of a profitable business, Carl Fischer suddenly had a huge outlet for its materials, and the film industry had the makings of considerably expanded spectacles, about which more will be said presently. Around the same time, the Edison Company was sending out "Suggestions for Music" with its pictures. By 1924, Ernö Rapée was able to publish a huge volume entitled *Motion Picture Moods for Pianists and Organists*, in which short pieces, such as Mendelssohn's *Song Without Words*, Op. 102, no. 3, or Grieg's "In the Hall of the Mountain King," were numerically categorized for their suitableness to such situations as "funeral," "happiness," "railroad," "sea storm," etc. Certain pieces, such as Otto Langey's "Agitato No. 3," which, although bearing a 1916 copyright from G. Schirmer, shamelessly rips off the accompaniment from Schubert's song "Der Erlkönig," bear indications such as "Suitable for gruesome or infernal scenes, witches, etc."[7]

It should be noted that the music supplied by cue sheets, compendiums, and the like was not limited to classical music; in fact, the cues were taken from just about any source—popular, semiclassical, classical, or whatever—that, for one reason or another, struck the compiler as useful for a particular mood, scene, or sequence. Nonetheless, a large proportion of the music came from classical sources, including, of course, numerous "popular" classics, such as "Von Suppe's "Poet and Peasant" Overture, and semiclassics, such as the diverse salon pieces for solo piano, piano duet, etc., played as pastimes in comfortable living rooms. A quintessential example of the kind of thing that quickly became standard in American cinema is the "score" compiled, arranged and composed by Joseph Carl Breil (with the collaboration of the film's director) for the 1915 premiere in New York of D. W. Griffith's *Birth of a Nation*. First of all, even at this early date, the marriage of music and cinema had already shown such potential as a money-making crowd-pleaser that, in the obvious theaters and cities, entire symphony orchestras were put in the pit to accompany the images on the screen. The movies were thus transformed, at least from time to time, into the kind of all-out spectacle for which American audiences have such a strong predilection. Although Griffith refused to have the screen surrounded with the kind of décor often used to beef up the visual attraction in those days, he did outfit his ushers in Civil War Uniforms and engage not only a full symphony orchestra but a chorus as well for the gala. Harlow Hare, in a wonderful piece written for the *Boston American* on 18 July 1915,[8] offers an exhaustive rundown of the musical cues put together by Breil. The list of "classics" alone is staggering:

Von Suppe: "Light Cavalry Overture";

Weber: Overture to *Der Freischutz*;

Grieg: "In the Hall of the Mountain King," from his *Peer Gynt* incidental music;

Bellini: Overture to *Norma* (about this music, which accompanies the assassination of Lincoln, Hare wrote, "the fatal crisis of that hour can only be rendered by classical music of enormous complexity and power" [Silva, p. 38]);

Wagner: *Die Walküre* (various excerpts);

Tchaikovsky: "1812 Overture";

Wagner : Overture to *Reinzi*;

Hérold: Overture to *Zampa*;

Haydn: "Gloria," from the Mass in C.

Mixed in with these are numerous popular songs, folk tunes, marches, and anthems, not to mention a substantial amount of music by Breil himself, including a love theme described by Hare as "one of the most beautiful love themes ever invented."[9] Even here, a song such as "Comin' Thro' the Rye" was modified by Breil, who set it to a waltz meter to accompany a southern ball. About this entire process, Hare perceptively noted, "It is . . . comparable to the way European composers like Liszt, Chopin and Dvorak take the melodies of the common people, the folk music, so to speak, and combine and elaborate them with more erudite themes" (Hare, "Harlow Hare," p. 37).

Two theoretical points are worth bringing up here. First of all, the device of incorporating a song such as "Dixie" or an anthem such as "The Star-Spangled Banner" into the fabric of ongoing music to accompany a film, as Breil did for *The Birth of a Nation*, is one of the strongest trump cards a film composer and/ or arranger can play. For even the briefest recognizable snippet of such a piece (and here is where the techniques of classical composition come in) can evoke in the listener an entire political mythology. For the tune or fragment is not simply a motif incorporated into a larger musical or musico-dramatic fiber but rather stands as the kind of second-degree sign that Roland Barthes defines as "myth" in *Mythologies*.[10] Thus, for instance, all Max Steiner needed to do at the beginning of his overture for the 1939 *Gone With the Wind* was to briefly allude to "Dixie" and to set one motif to a banjo to immediately evoke what Barthes might have called "old-southicity," and this via two different types of (second-degree) musical signifiers, one thematic, the other instrumental. One of the primary functions of film music, in fact, is to mythify the cinema, to help in the transformation of moving pictures into what Joseph Campbell would call "affect images," the music already being an unconsummated affect image.[11]

Second, even at this early point in silent cinema, where lack of a music track renders impossible a permanent relationship between a given set of musical cues and the filmic action, certain attempts were made to establish a difference between diegetic and nondiegetic music. Obviously, the bulk of the music played for silent films must be considered as nondiegetic, that is, as having nothing to do with the universe inhabited by the filmic characters, even though various sound effects, both in the form of musical onomatopoeias and of more nearly direct imitations, often punctuated key moments. But in *The Birth of a Nation*, which is no doubt not the first example, we can see a more extended attempt at creating the illusion of music (often referred to as ''source'' music) coming from *within* the narrative universe. Hare describes as follows a scene from *The Birth of a Nation*:

When piquant little *Elsie Stoneman* decides to become a nurse and solace gallant wounded youths back to health . . . , her goings and comings are accompanied by a most adorable little air which she is supposed not only to sing but to pick on the banjo. In the close-ups you can see the dainty lips fashioning the words of the song and in the full figure you can see her working the banjo a little over time, while the handsome sufferer on the pillow manages to turn his head about three-quarters in order to get a look at her. (Hare, p. 38)

But improvisations, cue sheets, and compilation scores were not the only answer. In certain instances, established classical composers were turned to for original or mostly original music. The first such score appeared suprisingly early in the history of the cinema and was penned by no less a figure than French composer Charles Camille Saint-Saëns. In 1908 various efforts were being made in France (and elsewhere) to revitalize the cinema, which some people were already seeing as moribund. One of the principal French solutions was to orient the movies toward loftier subjects and to turn the cinema into a more serious art form. To accomplish this, certain companies began to seek contributions from various established artists outside of the cinema. The most notable group to do this was the so-called *Film d'Art*, which offered its first production in Paris's Charras Theater on 17 November 1908. The film was entitled *L'Assassinat du duc de Guise* (The Assassination of the Duke de Guise). Considering the sources that were tapped—the august Académie Française for Henri Lavedan, who wrote the screenplay, and the classical Comédie Française for both the director and the actors (Le Bargy, Calmettes, Albert Lambert, Gabrielle Robinne, and Berthe Bovy)—it should come as little surprise that the producers (the Lafitte Brothers) should turn to a composer of Saint-Saëns' stature. Furthermore, various compositions by Saint-Saëns—''The Swan,'' from *The Carnival of the Animals*, the second movement of the Piano Concerto No. 2, the ''Wedding Cake Caprice'' and the *Suite algérienne*—were already making regular appearances in the movie houses. It would appear that the composer took the task quite seriously. As one of his biographers has written,

At the age of seventy-three Saint-Saëns' curiosity remained unquenchable, said 'le cinéma-Qui-vous-graphe', as he baptized it, was a toy with new and entertaining possibilities. *L'Assassinat du duc de Guise* was run through scene by scene, and as the sixteenth-century plot unravelled itself he jotted down his musical ideas in the dimly lit projection theater. The suite he wrote is scored for strings, piano and harmonium. It consists of an introduction and five tableaux, with each part meticulously cued for the action of the film. The atmosphere is suitably foreboding and the incidents of the conspiracy are pointed up by the musical devices which heighten the drama.[12]

Indeed, in listening to much of the score, one often has the impression of an accompaniment for an unsung opera, while the climactic moments that back up the assassination remarkably foreshadow film-music tropes still in use. Particularly effective, too, is a lugubrious harmonium solo that underscores the post-assassination sequence, as a mirror is being held to the duke's mouth and nose to see whether he is dead.

Numerous other scores by major composers appeared in the years to follow. The same year as *L'Assassinat du duc de Guise*, Russian composer Mikhail Ippolotov-Ivanov composed an "overture" for Alexander Drankov's *Stenka Razin* which, as Jay Leyda notes, "could be performed by chorus, gramophone, piano, or orchestra."[13] Italian opera composer Pietro Mascagni scored *L'Amica* and *Rapsodia Satanica* in 1915. In France, Darius Milhaud did newsreel music and films such as Marcel L'Herbier's *L'Inhumaine* (1923); Erik Satie composed the music for René Clair's *Entr'acte*; and Arthur Honegger did original scores for Abel Gance films, *La Roue* (1924)[14] and the massive *Napoléon* (1927), for which Honegger also relied on various anthems, marches, etc. But perhaps the best of these silent film scores was penned in 1929 by Dmitri Shostakovich, who in fact had at one point earned a meager living as a silent film pianist and who apparently offered his score for *Novi Vavilon* (The New Babylon) to that film's directors, Grigori Kozintsev and Leonid Trauberg, as a thank-you present in return for a piano they had given him. The "New Babylon" of the title is a Paris department store where the film's heroine, played by Elena Kuzmina, is an exploited worker during the Franco-Prussian war, an event that led to the Paris Commune, which was of no small significance to revolutionary Russia. Shostakovich's score begins with a raucous, sparsely orchestrated cancan wholly characteristic not only of the composer's style of that period but also of a tendency in certain European classical music, such as in the works of the French group "Les Six," toward incorporating popular musical idioms into classical compositions. In addition to this, the cancan represents for the composer one of the surest ways of evoking "Parisicity." Further on, at various points in the score, Shostakovich does not fail to quote *the* cancan from Offenbach's *Orpheus in the Underworld*. There is, however, a major difference in the way Shostakovich deploys this preexisting segment of classical music. Where in compilation scores of the period a piece such as the Offenbach cancan would come in as a kind of cue, Shostakovich, who consistently avoided, in his thirty-plus film scores, the "cue" mentality, unexpectedly brings it in as a kind of Ivesian quotation in the midst of a coherently flowing, and often quite dissonant, classical score. As if this were not enough, Shostakovich, again in the manner of Ives (although it is all but impossible that Shostakovich even knew of the existence of the American composer at the time), later on contrapuntally juxtaposes his own cancan with Offenbach's, so that the listener hears the two simultaneously. At yet another moment, Shostakovich contrapuntally weds the Offenbach cancan with the French national anthem, "La Marseillaise."

One might presume that the use of such themes as the Offenbach cancan and the "Marseillaise" play their standard role in giving positive, mythic support to things Parisian and things French, much as the use of "La Marseillaise" does in Max Steiner's score for the 1942 *Casablanca*. But the mythology behind this early Soviet film differs considerably from the mythology that produced such films as *Casablanca*. And if musical scores very often tell our emotions how to "read" a given filmic sequence, in *The New Babylon* the cinematic images often tell us how to "read" the music and the "-icities" it suggests. In this case, the themes traditionally associated with France take on a negative aura: the cancans associate themselves with the department store and all the glitter and tinsel of the bourgeois patrons and owners who exploit the workers, while "La Marseillaise" takes on the negative colors of the bourgeois who seek haven at Versailles while the workers defend Paris against the attacking Prussians. More significant evokers of the Soviet mythology are three French revolutionary songs, "Ça ira," "La Carmagnole," and "L'Internationale," that also make their way into the Shostokovich score. (That these revolutionary songs from France were already serving a prototypical role in Soviet political mythology can be seen in their appearance in a very different work of music from the same period, Nikolai Miaskovsky's 1922–1923 Sixth Symphony.)

The silent film accompanied by a score from a full orchestra remains a unique form of spectacle that cannot be duplicated even in sound films with multichannel music tracks. Although this form of entertainment understandably died out with the advent of the talkies, 1980s audiences proved quite sensitive to the uniqueness of the spectacle by their enthusiastic reception of two silent classics, *Napoléon* and *The New Babylon*, that were presented in certain American (and European) cities with live orchestral accompaniment. Kevin Brownlow's reconstruction of *Napoléon*, released in 1980 by Francis Ford Coppola's Zoetrope Studio, was unfortunately accompanied by a very mediocre score newly composed by Coppola's father, Carmine, who, in the classic tradition, mingled a substantial amount of preexisting music with his own creations. Just why Arthur Honegger's original score, which, in spite of claims to the contrary, is still largely extant, was not used remains something of a mystery. Much more artistically satisfying, at least from a musical point of view, was Corinth Films' release in Paris and London in 1982 and in the New York Film Festival of 1983 of the Kozintsev-Trauberg *The New Babylon*, which, like *Napoléon*, featured a live orchestral accompaniment, in this case using the original, sharp-edged music by Dmitri Shostakovich.

Paradoxically, the advent of sound in the late 1920s momentarily cut into the progress that background music in general and classical music in particular were making. While filmed musicals (which might be described as pop cine-operettas) such as, of course, the 1927 *Jazz Singer*, were briefly all the rage, technical considerations, which in their turn helped shape a kind of realist aesthetics, by and large cut the use of nondiegetic, incidental music to almost nothing. As one author has written on the subject,

The production of these early musicals created problems and frustrations for the composer. As remarkable as it seems, the early sound films were made without benefit of re-recording, or dubbing. . . . Max Steiner, who came to Hollywood from Broadway in 1929, remembers some of the difficulties film composers faced during the infancy of sound. "In the old days one of the great problems was standard (actual) recording, as dubbing or re-recording was unknown at the time. It was necessary at all times to have the entire orchestra and vocalists on the set day and night. This was a huge expense. . . ."[15]

Obviously, this type of expense was avoided to the greatest extent possible for nonmusical films, for which an offstage orchestra likewise had to perform any nondiegetic music. Problems in the recording itself and in the overall construction of the film also helped discourage the use of the nondiegetic score; a sequence shot with music, for instance, could not be edited without destroying the musical continuity (although, lord knows, studio moguls have traditionally never shown any great concern for musical continuity), which then could not be restored without reassembling the entire crew, including the orchestra. The added presence of spoken dialogue, sound effects, etc., likewise caused, in this era that preceded even rudimentary forms of sound mixing, huge problems for the insertion of nondiegetic music: a single misplaced or overplayed tuba from the on-the-set orchestra could single-handedly destroy all the benefits of the cinema's new medium.

When musicals lost their vogue, entire music departments at the studios vanished from the scenes. Thus, one finds numerous films from the early 1930s— John Ford's 1931 *Arrowsmith*, with a "score" by Alfred Newman, is one good example—in which the composer's contributions are limited to title music and maybe one or two brief pieces of dramatic backing. Convenient aesthetics of realism dictated that most music in dramatic films be perceived as diegetic, that is, coming from a visible "source" such as a radio. Just about the only escapees in all this were quasi-silent films, such as F. W. Murnau's 1931 *Tabu*, with a nonstop score by Hugo Riesenfeld, in which the orchestra that had once occupied the theater pit was merely transplanted to the soundtrack (Charlie Chaplin's 1936 *Modern Times*, for which Chaplin himself wrote much of the music, likewise followed this practice; but this was substantially after film music had reclaimed a place in the cinema).

It did not take long, of course, for the industry to realize the affective importance of music in dramatic films. It also did not take long for the industry to develop, with the help of international accords for the standardization of sound equipment, a technology that allowed the music to be recorded separately from the film and later added to the music track. It did take a bit longer, however, for the industry to fully shape a new film music aesthetic adapted to the cinema's new medium, sound. As we have seen, the silent cinema had already begun to get original music, occasionally even closely tailored, whether diegetically or nondiegetically, to the cinematic action. Not only did preexisting classical and semiclassical continue to back up a large number of films, but it was actually demanded by certain critics and practitioners, who found it pointless to "improve" upon the works of the great masters (one can somewhat appreciate this point when listening to Joseph Carl Breil's original strains for *The Birth of a Nation*). This attitude carried over into the sound era, where perhaps its most dramatic early application can be found in Edgar Ulmer's 1934 *The Black Cat*, a weird and kinky horror film in which Bela Lugosi, who can be heard in this film speaking his native Hungarian, plays a good guy who meets a bad guy's end while Boris Karloff incarnates a Satanist with a collection of embalmed beauties in his basement. As one writer has pointed out, "Music was Ulmer's passion,"[16] and for the score adaptation, the director turned to one Heinz Roemheld, who had, among other things, been music director at Universal for a year and who later would be one of the four orchestrator-arrangers who helped Max Steiner with his gargantuan *Gone With the Wind* score. The following is a list of the various pieces that Ulmer and Roemheld raided for their score:

Liszt: Piano Sonata in B minor; *Tasso*; Hungarian Rhapsody No. 6;[17] *Les Préludes*; *Rakoczy March*.

Tchaikovsky: Romeo and Juliet; Symphony No. 6 ("Pathétique") (first and fourth movements).

Brahms: *Sapphic Ode*; Piano Rhapsody in B minor, Op. 79, no. 1.

Chopin: Piano Prelude No. 2.

Schumann: Piano Quintet in E-flat.

Schubert: Symphony No. 8 ("Unfinished").

Beethoven: Symphony No. 7, second movement.

Bach: Adagietto, from Toccata and Fugue in C major; Toccata and Fugue in D minor.

A few points are worth noting here. First of all, several of the works above are written for solo piano, or, in the case of the Schumann, for piano and string quartet, which means that Roemheld had to arrange them for orchestra, since the symphony orchestra of classical music had already become the principal medium for performance within film codes. (Only an extremely small number of classical film scores for sound films have been scored for solo instruments, and most of these have been for "art" films such as Alain Jessua's 1965 *Life Upside Down* [*La Vie à l'envers*], with a solo piano score by Jacques Loussier; Francis Ford Coppola's 1974 *The Conversation*, for which David Shire composed a mostly solo piano score; Ingmar Bergman's 1962 *Through a Glass Darkly*, which uses Bach's solo Cello Suite No. 2; or Louis Malle's 1963 *Le Feu follet*, in which two of Erik Satie's solo piano works, the first *Gymnopédie* and the first *Gnossienne*, appear at various points.) The dramatic potential of the symphony orchestra, with its numerous tone colors and its big sound, was by this time fully realized, even though less than impressive ensembles were usually assembled for film scores: for *The Black Cat*, an orchestra of only twenty-eight musicians recorded most of the music in one nine-hour session, while an organist was given his own eight-hour session. Second, although Roemheld, except for the orchestrations, did fairly straight arrangements, the diverse cues often bump into each other in ways that seem unpardonable to the standard listener of classical music. And for some reason, Roemheld decided to save his principal butchery for Tchaikovsky, whose prototypical love theme from the 1870 *Romeo and Juliet* Overture-Fantasy appears in *The Black Cat* more as a near miss than as an actual quotation. Even more outrageous, from the standard point of view, is the way in which Roemheld conflated the opening themes from the first and last movements of the 1893 Sixth Symphony to make a single suspense theme. As was the case with the silent movies, the dramatic needs of sound cinema often impose a whole new set of laws on even preexisting classical music. Finally, although the distinctions between diegetic and nondiegetic music are generally clear in *The Black Cat*—for the diegetic cues, the evil Boris Karloff sits at an organ at one point and plays the Bach Toccata and Fugue in D Minor, while, during the Black Mass, an organist seems to play the Bach Adagietto in C—in at least one instance, an apparently diegetic cue takes off on its own and functions nondiegetically. As Mandell writes, "While making small talk in the atelier, Poelzig [Karloff] turns on an art deco radio which sneaks Schubert's *Unfinished Symphony* onto the soundtrack" (p. 39). But at this same moment a very dramatic incident takes place—the ailurophobic Lugosi kills a cat, which seems to pass its soul on to the heroine—so that the Schubert music, which plays at quite a loud volume, imperceptibly leaves the diegesis to provide affective backing. Mandell describes this phenomenon as follows:

For the cat murder, Schubert's *Unfinished Symphony* was modulated to choreograph the action. The whole sequence seems to glide along with a kind of lyrical ballet rhythm, and the footage was edited to correspond with the crescendos and diminuendos. The "climax"—Poelzig's spasmodic gripping of a nude statuette as Joan and Peter embrace— is the film's most blatant statement of sexual repression. (p. 47)

Already, at this point in history, the separate recording of the music track has made the diegetic/nondiegetic distinction a matter of illusion, since rarely is any "source" music actually miked live. One can also see here an instance in which cinematic rhythms were actually subordinated to musical ones. In fact, the advent of sound had led certain artists to foresee much greater creative interplay between the visual and audio media than has actually taken place over the last fifty years:

In the early 1930s there were some interesting experiments attempted in ''sound montage.'' Sound montage is, essentially, constructing films according to the rules of music. The investigation was carried out by the German Film Research Institute in Berlin. Edmund Meisel, the composer of the music for both *Potemkin* and *October*, was actively involved in the earlier experiments of the Institute.

While the experiments were started before the advent of sound, the researchers admitted that the idea of sound montage could only be totally successful if the music could be perfectly synchronized so that the time of the cutting and time of music would correspond exactly. The sound film made this possible.[18]

But the future of classical music in film scores has not resided, for the most part, in the use of preexisting compositions. In fact, when studio head Carl Laemmle returned from vacation to find a ''classically'' score *Black Cat*, he railed against the music as noncommercial. While numerous films have, throughout the sound era, brought in snippets of classical music as part of the diegesis, few make extensive nondiegetic use of them. Composer Miklós Rózsa, in his autobiography *Double Life*, tells how Billy Wilder, for his 1945 *Double Indemnity*, ''had the idea of using a restless string figure (as in the opening of Schubert's Unfinished Symphony) to reflect the conspiratorial activities of the two lovers against the husband.''[19] The only appearance the *Unfinished Symphony* makes in *Double Indemnity*, however, is as a diegetic cue, heard as Fred MacMurray talks with Jean Heather on a hill above the Hollywood Bowl. Yet the Schubert inspiration can certainly be distinguished in the haunting transition theme Rózsa composed to link the flashback sequences with Fred MacMurray's ongoing narration. More recently, Stanley Kubrick commissioned two different original scores—the second from no less a figure than Alex North—for his 1969 *2001: A Space Odyssey*, but then switched gears and raided the classics, using excerpts from composers as diverse as Johann Strauss, Jr., and the avant-garde Gyorgi Ligeti. Kubrick's choices struck audiences, critics, and subsequent filmmakers as so appropriate that audiovisual associations, such as the dramatic opening of Richard Strauss's tone poem *Also sprach Zarathustra* with various forms of dawning, became almost instant clichés.[20] Even in 1986 one finds a close approximation of the mournful adagio from Khachaturian's *Gayne* ballet, used by Kubrick to communicate the loneliness of outer space, in James Horner's title music for the sci-fi thriller *Aliens*. Following *2001*, Kubrick has made classical compilation scores standard practice in the 1971 *A Clockwork Orange* (Beethoven, Rossini and others, much of it diegetically motivated); the 1974 *Barry Lyndon* (Handel, Schubert, et al.), and the 1980 *The Shining* (Bartók, Ligeti, et al.). Other films have made successful use of a single work of ''classical'' music. These include Swedish director Bo Widerberg's *Elvira Madigan* (1967), in which the second movement of Mozart's Twenty-First Piano Concerto provides an appropriately bittersweet backdrop for the romantic tragedy; Bryan Forbes's *The L-Shaped Room* (1963), in which the Brahms Piano Concerto No. 1 provides both poignancy and drama throughout the film; or Woody Allen's *Midsummer Night's Sex Comedy* (1982), in which the Shakespearean inspiration led director Allen to use the incidental music Felix Mendelssohn had composed for the bard's *Midsummer Night's Dream* (worth noting here is the 1935 filmic adaptation of the Shakespeare play directed by Max Reinhardt and William Dieterle, from which Erich Korngold intricately adapted all of Mendelssohn's incidental music and several other Mendelssohn works as well; at certain points, some of the lines are actually read rhythmically to the music). Allen also made highly successful use of diverse works by George Gershwin to affectly enhance the Gotham ambience of his *Manhattan* (1979). It should be noted that the appearance of classical compositions on the music track of certain popular films gave a nice boost to the sales of classical recordings, with manufacturers being able either to pawn off Mozart and Richard Strauss albums as containing the "theme from *Elvira Madigan*" or the "theme from *2001*," or to remarket already recorded classical works on "original soundtrack" albums without having to worry about royalties to a given composer. Note should also be made of the highly original use of preexisting classical music in the films of "New Wave" French director Jean-Luc Godard. One might single out the haunting, if brief, apparitions of excerpts from five different Beethoven string quartets in the 1962 short *Le Nouveau monde* and the 1964 feature *Une Femme mariée* (*A Married Woman*).

In spite of the effectiveness of such scores as the above, however, they comprise only a very small percentage of the classical music heard in sound films, which by and large have featured scores composed in diverse classical styles that will be examined in the next section. And the original music that more than any other launched the classical film score once and for all was Max Steiner's *King Kong*, penned early on in 1933 for the production by Merian C. Cooper and Ernest B. Schoedsack. Steiner, who, like many of his colleagues in film music at the time, had come to the United States from Europe, had already composed at least several substantial scores, most notably for the 1932 *Symphony of Six Million*. As the Viennese émigré told of his experiences with the latter film,

"David [O. Selznick] said, 'Do you think you could put some music behind this thing? I think it might help it. Just do one reel—the scene where Ratoff dies.' I did as he asked, and he liked it so much he told me to go ahead and do the rest. Music until then had not been used very much for underscoring—the producers were afraid the audience would ask 'Where's the music coming from?' unless they saw an orchestra or a radio or phonograph. But with this picture we proved scoring would work."[21]

But as another film composer, Fred Steiner, has noted, "it wasn't until 1933 and *King Kong* that Steiner was offered a film wherein music would play such an important role in creating and sustaining atmosphere, characterization, and pacing."[22] Music, however, was hardly an initial part of *King Kong's* artistic conception. By the time the shooting was completed, at least one studio executive who had seen footage had strong reservations and even told Steiner, the head of RKO's music department at the time, to tack on some previously composed music tracks from the company's vaults. But producer Merian Cooper, a great believer in Film music's drama enhancing potential, intervened and gave the composer free rein to come up with some appropriate music. Steiner, inspired by the film, which, as he put it, "allowed you to do anything and everything, from weird chords and dissonances to pretty melodies" (quote in Thomas, p. 115), came up with a massive score that not only backs up some seventy-five of *King Kong*'s 103 minutes but that also demanded the services of an orchestra of as many as forty-six musicians, just about twice the number that usually appeared in studio orchestras. This added some $50,000 to the film's overall cost of nearly $700,000. But the score had far-reaching effects, even inspiring Murray Spivack, the head of RKO's sound-effects department, to pitch some of the noises, from animal grunts to Fay Wray's screams, to the same level as the music that immediately followed.

King Kong greatly helped the original, classical film score become what it was and what it largely remains today: an integral component of a given motion picture's overall profile that is so expected in people's minds that nonuse often becomes noteworthy. Even when a Broadway play with no incidental music, such as the 1985 production of *Death of a Salesman*, is transferred to the screen, as in Volker Schlöndorff's made-for-TV version of the production, a musical score, which the avid theatergoer in particular might find disconcerting, adds a new dimension to the drama. And as it happens, the classical film score continues to be inspired by the film. With very few exceptions, the composer is not brought in to begin his or her work on a film until after the shooting has been completed, at which point there is generally so little time to complete the project that the producer must also call on an orchestrator or an orchestrator-arranger to fill out the score, working from the composer's more or less elaborate notations.

Certain orchestrators, such as Hugo Friedhofer, have gone on to become important film scorers. In recent years, technology has in certain cases facilitated the composer's job by allowing the director or producers to "lay down" a "scratch track"—a provisional musical score—on the rough cut of a film to give the composer a basic idea of the musical profile desired. For his offbeat *Home Movies* (1979), for instance, director Brian De Palma laid in excerpts from various Rossini compositions to inspire a Rossini-esque score from composer Pino Donaggio (some country-western music and a Beatles song also found their way to the scratch track) without actually having to "raid the classics." This same device backfired, however, in an earlier De Palma film, *Sisters* (1973). For his first (but certainly not last) tribute to Alfred Hitchcock, De Palma logically brought in composer Bernard Herrmann, who had provided music for a number of Hitchcock masterpieces, including *Vertigo*, *North by Northwest*, and *Psycho*. For the screening they had set up for the composer, De Palma and his editor, Paul Hirsch, had used cues from recordings of various Herrmann-Hitchcock collaborations on the music track. The ever irascible Herrmann, however, railed violently against the scratch track, complaining that he needed to work with the material at hand and not with music that was not specifically tailored for the particular film.[23]

With the classical, symphonic musical score established as the norm, and with Hollywood's need to produce a large number of films, the music department became an essential component of the Hollywood studio system. The music department at Warner Brothers became a model of this type of organization.[24] Many early composers, like the actors and actresses, worked under contract to the studios and found themselves under numerous restraints. Irwin Bazelon, himself a composer, offers a rather bitter picture of the system:

The film composer is a temporary employee who can be discharged for any number of reasons, including the arbitrary judgment of his employers concerning the material he supplies. A cursory examination of a contract between composer and film company gives ample evidence of the composer's employee status. Upon signing to score a picture, the artist turns over all rights to his music to the company that engages him. Under the usual Hollywood contract, the composer functions as an indentured servant; he gets paid adequately for his creative labor but does not own any part of the music after he has completed the scoring assignment. The corporate powers reserve the right to use his work as they deem necessary: they can cut it to ribbons, arrange, rearrange, edit and readapt it for whatever purpose they desire. The disproportion between the corporation's power and the composer's impotence is plain. (p. 20)

One example of this can be seen and heard in the studio's butchering that resulted in Orson Welles's *The Magnificent Ambersons* being cut down from 131 to 88 minutes. Not only did RKO perform wholesale deletions and reshoot the picture's finale to give it a happy ending, but it cut about half of composer Bernard Herrmann's original music and arrangements and added a substantial amount of newly scored (by Roy Webb) music. The most obvious example of replacement can be heard in the insipid, quasi-silent-film organ music that accompanies Joseph Cotten and Ann Baxter's walk outdoors together near the picture's conclusion. This so infuriated composer Herrmann that he had his name removed from Welles's imaginative end credits (one wonders what particular tool of the composer's trade Welles would have used as a visual synecdoche for Herrmann). But as Bazelon has also noted, film composers have, particularly as of the 1970s, begun to acquire the rights to their creations. The composer almost always remains powerless, however, as to what happens to his or her music in the film. Even as recently as 1979, in Ridley Scott's *Alien*, a snippet of composer Jerry Goldsmith's much earlier score for *Freud* (1962) was inserted into a scene where the monster's acid "blood" drips through the space ship, while Howard Hanson's "Romantic" Symphony replaced Goldsmith had scored for the end titles. Italian versions of Jean-Luc Godard's 1963 *Le Mépris* (*Contempt*) replaced Georges Delerue's mournful, symphonic music with a jazz score à la the director's earlier *À bout de souffle* (*Breathless*). Producer-director Alfred Hitchcock, totally tied in with the system at Universal, threw out two complete scores, Bernard Herrman's for the 1966 *Torn Curtain* and Henry Mancini's for the 1972 *Frenzy*. And in 1986, one could find two different versions of Ridley Scott's *Legend*: a non-American print using the original score by Jerry Goldsmith, and an American version rescored by MCA/Universal in a desperate attempt to make *Legend* more commercial, with the electronically synthesized sounds of the German group Tangerine Dream.[25] In spite of all the controls and tamperings, however, the Hollywood system has produced an incredible number of film scores that (a) beautifully complement the movies for which they were composed; (b) stand up well musically; and (c) reveal strong individual styles that remain consistent from picture to picture. Although they can be limiting, the restraints placed upon the film composer—often brief cues that leave the composer no space to develop his or her musical ideas, the frequent split-second timing of musical figures to dramatic action, imposed conservatism, etc.—can also be seen as a kind of challenge. And particularly since the 1950s, sound recordings have revealed numerous facets of film music not readily apparent when heard (often with poor sound quality) with the film.[26]

The rest of the history of classical film music lies more in the musical styles and in the various means of interaction, which will be covered in the next section, than in any basic changes in the system. Technological improvements have, of course, given music at least the potential for a more prominent role in the overall cinematic art. One of the biggest symphonic scores ever composed, for instance—Serge Prokofiev's music for Sergie Eisenstein's 1938 *Alexander Nevsky*—sounds almost ludicrous in spots on the film's terribly recorded music track and simply cannot match the much more sophisticated photographic reproduction. On the other hand, the multichannel sound systems for which a score such as John Williams's *Star Wars* (1977) was composed can actually rival, in the excellence of their sonics, the quality of the photographic images. The music tracks of certain films, such as the Disney Studios' 1940 *Fantasia*, have been rerecorded to suit the ears of modern audiences.[27] It was in the 1950s, when the cinema tried to rival television by introducing wide-screen aspect ratios and stereophonic (and even multichannel) sound, that sound began to play a more important role in the cinema; but the advances made in both recording techniques and theater reproduction systems have not been consistently applied. In video formats, technologies such as Beta Hi-Fi or stereo television have sometimes actually allowed music to dwarf, in the quality of its reproduction, the visual image. One might also mention advances in the techniques of music editing, which can often fit musical cues to a given sequence even when the latter has been edited or reedited to a timing different from that of the original musical cue. Composer Michael Small tells the story of how the music editor for Alan J. Pakula's *The Parallax View* (1974) had to play all sorts of tricks, during the climactic convention sequence, by altering the music when the marching band was offscreen so that the band would appear to move in time with the music when it was onscreen. Multitrack recording of music (particularly for television) has also in some cases taken even more creative control from the composer, since a producer who does not like a given instrument can simply order the music editor to eliminate that instrument's particular track. Finally, perhaps the most important change in film music—classical and popular alike—in recent years has been brought about by the advent of the electronic synthesizer and of various digital processors that not only can create a wide variety of timbres but can actually cannibalize acoustic timbres so that the latter can be digitally played back through the electronic instrument, whether a keyboard or a guitar. Rare is the recent musical score, even in the most solid classical style, that is not beefed up, particularly in the bass, by some sort of synthesized sound. And certain films feature scores done completely on synthesizers, thus eliminating two of the major production costs— the symphony orchestra and the reuse fees required by the American Federation of Musicians for each member of the orchestra that recorded a given score when that score is issued on a sound recording. While some of these synthesizer scores, such as the cloying music written by Greek-born composer Vangelis for the 1981 *Chariots of Fire*, are pop-oriented, others show a solid amount of classical sophistication. For Michael Crichton's 1985 *Runaway*, for instance, Jerry Goldsmith composed an all-synthesizer score that has all the earmarks of the modern "classical" style one can hear in Goldsmith scores since the 1960s. The synthesizer programming for *Runaway*, by the way, was one by the younger generation (Goldsmith's son Saul).

STYLES AND GENRES OF INTERACTION

In the examination of the styles and genres of interaction between film and classical music, three major areas present themselves. The first is the style of the music itself, which, in the "classical" film score, generally ranges from late romantic to post-modernist. The second, and most important, involves the various ways in which film music has been made, by its practitioners, to interact with both the visual and the verbal languages in the cinema. Finally, classical music has, in certain instances, taken on a major diegetic significance that needs to be explored, at least briefly.

Musical Styles

It is hardly surprising, given the Viennese origins of early Hollywood film scorers such as Max Steiner and Erich Wolfgang Korngold, and the Middle European origins of many others, such as Franz Waxman, that much of the music that accompanied early sound films had a decidedly late romantic cast to it. Such diverse composers as Wagner, Puccini, Johann Strauss, Jr., Richard Strauss, and Gustav Mahler all left their mark on melodic, harmonic, and instrumental profiles. Nondissonant if mildly chromatic harmonies, monophonic textures, broad, sweeping melodies, and lush instrumentations (often obscured by the poor audio quality of early sound recording) were the order of the day, both because of the aesthetic proclivities of the "first wave" composers as well as the tastes of both studio and music department heads, who translated their own philistine sensitivities into dollars-and-cents worries over the reactions of imaginary audiences. Miklós Rózsa, in *Double Life*, describes the music of Victor Young, Paramount's pet composer in the 1940s, as being in "The Broadway-cum-Rachmaninoff idiom, which was then the accepted style" (p. 119). Rózsa also describes the reaction of Paramount's director to his own, more dissonant music:

He once asked me why I had so many dissonances in my music. "What dissonances?" I asked. "Well, in one spot the violins are playing a G natural and the violas a G sharp. Why don't you make it a G natural in the violas as well—just for *my* sake?" When I refused he became furious—one thing you don't do in Hollywood is disagree with an executive. (p. 119)

But the romantic score had, and still has, its place. Dramatic, substantially developed melodies perfectly set the mood and provide appropriate motivic material for such romances as William Wyler's 1939 *Wuthering Heights*, with a score by Alfred Newman. Victor Fleming's *Gone With the Wind* (1939, score by Max Steiner) and Alfred Hitchcock's *Rebecca* (1940, score by Franz Waxman) are two other excellent examples. Erich Wolfgang Korngold excelled not only at writing memorable themes—Tony Thomas describes the love theme for Errol Flynn and Brenda Marshall in Michael Curtiz's *The Sea Hawk* (1940) as "about as close as any composer has come to matching Wagner's *Liebestod* [from *Tristan und Isolde*]" (p. 136)—he also had a remarkable gift for stirring the emotions with fanfarish overtures (*The Sea Hawk*, *King's Row*), rousing, Mahleresque marches (*The Adventures of Robin Hood*), and spirited action music—the combination of mise-en-scène and music during the climactic, almost dialogueless sword fight between Henry Daniell and Errol Flynn toward the end of *The Sea Hawk* is about as pure a piece of catharsis as any spectacle will ever present. Although the pure romantic score never died out—Franz Waxman's poignant and autumnal score for Martin Ritt's *Hemingway's Adventures of a Young Man* (1962), which provides almost the entire affective base for this fairly mediocre cinematization of Hemingway short stories, proves that unselfconscious romantic inspiration could still take place well into the modernist era—it enjoyed a surprising, and quite self-conscious, renaissance in the late 1970s with John Williams's score for George Lucas's *Star Wars* (1977), which owes a tremendous debt to such scores as *King's Row* or Franz Waxman's *The Horn Blows at Midnight* (1945), not to mention the likes of English composer Gustav Holst, whose orchestral suite *The Planets* (1914–1917) has been pillaged numerous times by the cinema, including *Star Wars*.[28] *Star Wars* almost single-filmedly revived the fairy-talish, heroic genre popular in the late 1930s and early 1940s, and with it the quasi-Korngold score, which one can hear in such films as Richard Donner's *Superman* (1978, score by John Williams), Robert Wise's *Star-Trek, The Motion Picture* (1979, score by Jerry Goldsmith) or Jeannot Szwarc's 1984 *Supergirl* (Goldsmith).

More modern musical styles, however, asserted themselves early on in the cinema's sound era. The silent era had already produced a sprinkling of modern scores, most notably Shostakovich's *The New Babylon*. And, early in the sound era, Hanns Eisler's very polyphonic, nontonal, small-ensemble music for Slatan Dudow's *Kühle Wampe* (1932) stands as an outstanding example not only of early sound-film-music modernism but also of Eisler's anti-cathartic theories on film music as spelled out in *Composing for the Films* (see bibliography). In the initial stages of the sound era, though, it took more bizarre pictures such as *King Kong* of James Whale's *The Bride of Frankenstein* (1935) to bring out the modernist in Hollywood's composers and to shake studio moguls momentarily out of their conservative lethargy.

Steiner's *King Kong* music, for instance, would no doubt have scandalized most concert-going audiences with its open-interval harmonies and dissonant chords, its tritone motifs, or such devices as a chromatic scale in parallel, minor-seconds (the latter is heard when the legged serpent attacks Kong in his cave). In *The Bride of Frankenstein*, Franz Waxman, although not wholly departing from the romantic tradition in his first Hollywood score, moved toward a kind of musical expressionism in which familiar patterns—dance rhythms, melodic figures, etc.—are distorted enough by bizarre instrumentations, chromatic theme-movements, etc., to throw the viewer/listener off the center of familiar musical norms. In the comically suspenseful sequence when the monster (Boris Karloff) first confronts Dr. Pretorius (Ernest Thesiger) in the latter's laboratory, for instance, Waxman underscores the action with a lugubrious, slow, triple-meter dance given an otherworldly coloration by an electric organ.

Waxman also deploys an early electronic instrument, the Ondes Martenot, during the climactic scene where the "bride" is brought to life. Waxman also used an electrically amplified violin in *Rebecca*, while Miklós Rózsa won immense notoriety by bringing in, for Hitchcock's *Spellbound* (1945), a theremin, an electronic instrument whose pitch changes are made by movement of the hand within an electric field rather than on the ersatz keyboard of the Ondes Martenot. Rózsa went on to use the theremin in Billy Wilder's *The Lost Weekend* (1945) and in Delmer Daves' *The Red House* (1947). One can also hear a more modernistic music style in Serge Prokofiev's scores for Eisenstein's *Alexander Nevsky* (1938) and *Ivan the Terrible*, Parts 1 (1945) and 2 (1945–1946). On the other hand, the film music of Dmitri Shostakovich, who died in 1975 with some thirty-five film scores to his credit, turned largely, and often unrecognizably, conservative with the advent of the sound era.

As Hollywood moved into new areas with its *films noirs*, its psychological dramas, and its crime stories of the 1940s, newer and more modern-sounding musical styles were able to take greater hold in the cinema. If early influences ranged from Wagner to Rachmaninoff, it was twentieth-century classical composers such as Béla Bartók and Paul Hindemith that now began to leave their mark on the classical film score. Strong dissonances, that anathema of music department heads and studio moguls; a greater emphasis on rhythmic figures for their own sake, whether primitivistic (as in *King Kong*) or complex; polyphonic textures (where line is pitted against line, as opposed to the less complex style of melody/accompaniment); bitonality and polytonality (where either the melody and the accompaniment are in different keys or where the different lines of a polyphonic texture create multitonal patterns); and modal and chromatic melodic writing: all of these, as well as other modernistic devices (some of which, such as polyphony and modality, paradoxically revive much older practices), came much more to the foreground in the "classical" film score, even while late romantic practices continued to flourish, sometimes within mostly modernistic scores (producer David O. Selznick actually brought in Max Steiner to add a few, more romantic cues to offset some of Franz Waxman's moody expressionism in *Rebecca*). During the 1940s, the composer who most visibly brought the classical film score into the modern era was no doubt the Hungarian-born Miklós Rózsa, who, unlike many Hollywood film scorers, has achieved a decent reputation as a concert composer as well (because of the narrative tie-in, Rózsa actually cannibalized his own 1953 Violin Concerto, composed for Jascha Heifetz, for Billy Wilder's *The Private Life of Sherlock Holmes* [1970]). Rózsa created a perfect *film noir* sound, for instance, in his prelude for Billy Wilder's *Double Indemnity* (1944), in which the modal, main theme is set in mildly dissonant, open-interval harmonies to an obsessive, dirge-like rhythm. Obsessiveness likewise dominates the preludes for such films as *A Double Life* and Jules Dassin's *Brute Force* (1947), in which fragmented, oft-repeated melodic sharps prevail over developed themes, in which wildly dissonant chords punctuate and interrupt the musical flow, often in driving, syncopated rhythms, and in which sound layering, where several different musical events are occuring simultaneously, creates a kind of complexity rare in earlier scores. One also finds various neo-classical devices, popular with numerous twentieth-century composers, in Rózsa's scores: the climactic chase sequence in Jules Dassin's *The Naked City* (1948), for example, starts off, logically enough, as a minifugue, or *fugato* (the musical term comes from the Latin word for "flight" or "running away"). The free use of dissonance, often in even less tonal contexts than one finds in Rózsa, continues to play an extremely important role in film scoring. Important examples of this can be heard in Alex North's *The Bad Seed* (1956) and *Spartacus* (1960) or such Jerry Goldsmith scores as *Freud* (1962), *Planet of the Apes* (1968), and *The Omen* (1976). The influence of Igor Stravinksy can be strongly felt in parts of the Oscar-winning score of *The Omen*, such as the choral chanting, all the way through the extremely disjointed, all-synthesizer *Runaway* (1984).

In a very different modernist vein is the music of Bernard Herrmann, who had in fact spent much of his early career introducing radio audiences to new "classical" music. From the strictly musical point of view, Herrmann's film scores offer no major surprises; indeed, the true impact of Herrmann's considerable gift to the cinema lies in his unique musico-filmic solutions and more properly belongs to the discussion on genres of interaction. Nonetheless, when one hears the doom-and-gloom opening of Orson Welles's *Citizen Kane* (1940), Herrmann's first score, or the almost static, otherworldly figures that accompany the devil, Mr. Scratch, and his companion, Belle, in Herrmann's Oscar-winning score for William Dieterle's *The Devil and Daniel Webster* (1941), one realizes that, at many key moments in his film scores, Herrmann not only freely used dissonance but dispensed almost completely with two key elements of most Western music, classical or otherwise: theme, and harmonic movement. The "nightmare waltz" one hears during the party sequence in *The Devil and Daniel Webster* is also about as pure a piece of musical expressionism as one can find. Herrmann's strong emphasis on instrumental color as a prime communicator of cinemusical affect also helped move film music away from the traditions of late romanticism.

Another composer who early on departed in important ways from the romantic tradition was David Raksin. One of the frequent devices heard in Raksin scores is constant meter changes, which represent one of the composer's solutions for coordinating music with filmic action but are also a strong trademark in much contemporary composing. A score such as Raksin's *Forever Amber* (1947) also abounds in substantial uses of counterpoint, including a passacaglia and numerous canons. Raksin is also important as one of the few film composers to make effective use of what might be called "concert jazz." Even though the main theme for Otto Preminger's *Laura* (1944) became a popular song (but then, so did the opening theme of Tchaikovsky's First Piano Concerto), its use in the film and its frequent symphonic instrumentations bring it into the same classical domain as the music of George Gershwin. Another important piece of Raksin concert jazz can be heard in his score for Joseph H. Lewis's *The Big Combo* (1955), the main theme of which, like *Laura*'s, wanders in and out of the diegesis. The jazz influence can even be heard in Raksin's complex title music for Curtis Harrington's 1971 *What's the Matter With Helen?*", which also, in a kind of nod to the avant-gardist "collage" device, briefly quotes the old pop tune "Goody Goody." Alex North's pioneering *A Streetcar Named Desire* (1951) represents another extremely important example of concert (or perhaps "symphonic") jazz.

By far the major proportion of classical film scores, even when dissonant, have stayed within the limits of Western tonality, a hierarchical system based around a "chromatic" scale of twelve tones, extracted from which a scale of seven notes containing five "whole" steps and two "half" steps provides the basis for a harmonic system in which resolution of musical conflicts becomes the basis of the listener's "active expectation."[29] The *Animal Farm* mentality applies here: all notes are equal, but within a given "key" (of which there are twelve), some notes are more equal than others. As early as the first decade of the twentieth century, however, German composer Arnold Schoenberg began to compose within a deliberately dehierarchalized harmonic idiom—generally referred to as atonal, twelve-tone, dodecaphonic, or serial, although the latter term can refer to the dehierarchalization of the other components of music as well—

in which, in both the horizontal and the vertical harmonic structures, the implied resolutions of Western tonality are abolished by a rigorous system that forces the composer to give equal attention to all twelve notes through such devices as nonreturn to a given note until the other eleven are used up or the avoidance of the more strongly tonal intervals of the third, fourth, and fifth. The resultant music is difficult for the average listener, since it tends to demand greater attention to the component musical parts of a given work rather than catching up the emotions in patterns of tension and resolution. Needless to say, atonality has never caught on in the "classical" film score.

Nonetheless, in 1929–1930, Schoenberg actually wrote an "Accompaniment to a Cinematographic Scene" (*Begleitungmusik*) intended to evoke "threatening danger, fear, and catastrophe" but not designed for a specific picture. But even though he emigrated to Los Angeles in the 1930s and became the teacher of numerous composers, including Alfred Newman, Schoenberg had but one brush with Hollywood, which Tony Thomas describes:

Schoenberg showed no interest in film music, although his fame was such that a few producers thought it might be wise to get his name on a picture. One of them was the young, shrewd, and greatly successful Irving Thalberg. In 1937 Thalberg asked Schoenberg to come to M-G-M to discuss the possibility of scoring *The Good Earth*. He was told by the producer that this film version of the Pearl Buck book was one of the studio's most artistic efforts and presented a rare opportunity for a composer. Thalberg described one scene: "There's a terrific storm going on—the wheat fields are swaying in the wind, and suddenly the earth begins to tremble. Then, in the earthquake, the girl gives birth to a baby. What an opportunity for music." Schoenberg looked at him incredulously, "With so much going on, what do you need music for?" Thalberg was puzzled by this apparent lack of interest. He then asked Schoenberg, "What would be your terms in working for us?" Replied the composer, "I will write the music and then you will make a motion picture to correspond with it." Neither Thalberg nor any other producer approached Schoenberg again. (pp. 41–42)

It is perhaps no coincidence that one of the great, early works of atonality (free, to be sure), Alban Berg's 1925 opera *Wozzeck*, and the first atonal score for a narrative, feature-length film, Leonard Rosenman's *The Cobweb* (1955), both support the narrative theme of madness, as audiences are no doubt predisposed to associate wholesale musical departure from the norm with wholesale mental departure from the norm. Rosenman's score, although composed for large orchestra, including solo piano (Schoenberg's Piano Concerto apparently played a role in the score's inspiration), makes ample use of chamberlike groupings and the polyphonic textures that are all but essential to atonal composing. Further, the main theme is built around a tone row (a series containing all twelve notes of the chromatic scale arranged in order that determines at least part of the work's thematic and harmonic profile). For all this, the score somehow retains the kind of emotion-grabbing, dramatic quality generally demanded by Hollywood, and Rosenman, much to the surprise of many, had no trouble getting the score accepted and even recorded. Much less affectively involving and no doubt more purely atonal is Pierre Barbaud's score for Nico Papatakis's *Les Abysses* (1963), whose grim narrative comes from the same true story that inspired Genet's play *The Maids*. One finds numerous atonal figures, if not systematic use of atonality, in many of the scores composed by Pierre Jansen for the New Wave melodramas of Claude Chabrol, including *La Rupture* (1970), whose dramatic, atonal main theme is played on an Ondes Martenot. A very deceptive example is David Shire's main theme for Joseph Sargent's *The Taking of Pelham One Two Three* (1974), which almost tongue-in-cheekishly juxtaposes atonal thematic figures over a very tonal jazz base line.

Other modernistic devices have likewise made their appearance from time to time in the "classical" film score. Worth noting, for instance, is the sometimes quarter-tonal score composed in 1970 for Laslo Benedek's *The Night Visitor* by Henry Mancini, who has an undeserved reputation as a strictly pop-tune composer. The use of quarter-tones—tones falling "between the cracks," so to speak, of the twelve half-tones of the Western chromatic scale—is another anti-diatonic, twentieth-century musical practice (quarter tones and other microtones have also existed for centuries in the music of certain non-Western cultures) which, unlike atonality and serialism, has caught on with very few composers, film or otherwise.[30] For *The Night Vistior*, a horror-suspense film centered—once again— around the theme of insanity, Mancini used a chamber orchestra, with no strings, that includes twelve woodwinds, an organ, two pianos, and two harpsichords; within this ensemble, one piano and one harpsichord are tuned a quarter-tone flat vis-à-vis each other. The sounds produced, very often sustained in dissonant (to say the least) chords, have quite an unearthly aura to them. An even more recent tendency in modern classical music is "minimalism," in which short, and usually very tonal, phrases are repeated numerous times, with sometimes miniscule pattern changes providing movement from one sequence to the next, thus creating a sense of stasis, reminiscent of the music of India, that counteracts tonality's built-in urges towards forward movement and resolution. One of the principle minimalists, American composer Philip Glass, has so far provided music for two films—a nonstop score for Godfrey Reggio's nonnarrative *Koyaanisqatsi* (1983), and a more conventionally cued score for Paul Schraeder's *Mishima*, a 1935 film biography of the Japanese author.

Swiss director Alain Tanner, having heard music by American minimalist Terry Riley, went backstage after the concert and told the composer that he had just written the music for his next film. "What's the film about?" asked Riley. "I don't know yet," replied Tanner, who went on to make *No Man's Land* (1985), which uses the Riley composition on the music track, out of this initial inspiration. In 1980 Ken Russell, one of the most musically aware directors ever to have shot a film, turned to nonfilm composer John Corigliano, who produced, for *Altered States*, a nontonal orchestral score filled with kinds of glissandi, tone clusters, extreme intervalic leaps and instrumental ranges, etc., that characterize certain tendencies in contemporary music. One might also single out two scores for their novel use of percussion and other bizarre instruments: Jerry Goldsmith's *Planet of the Apes* (Franklin J. Schaffner, 1968) deploys such "instruments" and instrumental effects as tuned, aluminum mixing bowls, a bass slide-whistle, a triangle stick scraped over a gong, a ram's horn, air blown through brass instruments with inverted mouthpieces, etc.; and John Williams's *Images* (Robert Altman, 1972), in which the composer uses metal sculptures by Baschet as percussion instruments (performed by Stomu Yamashta), along with a police whistle, human grunts (à la Stockhausen), etc., to evoke the schizophrenia of the heroine. Porcile (see bibliography) mentions Pierre Henry's score for Jean-Claude Sée's *Aube* (1950–1951) as the first extended *musique concrète* (in which nonmusical objects, such as creaking doors or sirens, are used to produce sounds organized, composed, into a musical work) film score.

Finally, one of the most important contributions, where film composers in certain ways actually preceded nonfilm composers, lies in the area of electric and electronic modifications of sounds and tones. As early as 1931, Rouben Mamoulian, for his *Dr. Jekyll and Mr. Hyde*, devised, apparently on his own, a sound equivalent of the transformation scene. The director has described his efforts as follows:

To accompany the transformations I wanted a completely unrealistic sound. First I tried rhythmic beats, like a heartbeat. We tried every sort of drum, but they all sounded like drums. Then I recorded my own heart beating, and it was perfect, marvelous. Then we recorded a gong, took off the actual impact noise, and reversed the reverberations. Finally we painted on the soundtrack; and I think that was the first time anyone had used synthetic sound like that, working from light to sound.[32]

Bazelon refers to Mamoulian's brief cue as pre-*musique-concrète*. (Interestingly, the film contains no other nondiegetic music, save the ambiguous reappearance of a waltz as Jekyll breaks off his engagement and the title and end music, both of which use an orchestration of Bach's Toccata and Fugue in D minor, which Jekyll also plays on an organ during the film.

For *The Devil and Daniel Webster*, Bernard Herrmann "had the overtones of C painted on the [optical track of] the negative, so that when the film is run through the projector, a phantom fundamental is produced electronically."[33] For the same picture, Herrmann also composed a series of four variations on "Pop Goes the Weasel," which were recorded separately to be used diegetically for a sequence in which the devil plays the fiddle. In the Prendergast book, David Raksin is quoted at length describing the various electric, electronic, and mechanical gimmicks—gimmicks that are now easily produced by sophisticated equipment—he devised to create the dreamy version of the film's main (and only) theme during the sequence where the Dana Andrews character keeps the vigil in Laura's apartment (see pp. 65–67). For Fritz Lang's 1948 *Secret Beyond the Door*, Miklós Rózsa "experimented with having an orchestra play their film backwards, recording it back to front on the tape, and then playing it back as

usual; the end result sounded the right way round but had an unearthly quality''
(*Double Life*, p. 132).

Numerous other examples could be cited. But perhaps the most original and
extended use of true ''electronic film'' can be found in the Fred McLeod Wilcox
Forbidden Planet (1956), with what the film's titles describe as ''electronic tonal-
ities'' composed by the husband-and-wife team of Louis and Bebe Barron, who
had already provided electronic music for various experimental films between
1949 and 1953, and who were brought into the *Forbidden Planet* project by then
MGM studio chief Dore Schary. At that time, the creation of electronic film demanded a great deal of painstaking work designing circuits, laying down various
tracks on tapes, and mixing all the diverse sounds into a coherent, musical *composition*. An extensive article on *Forbidden Planet* describes the film as follows:

The score for FORBIDDEN PLANET represents a great many circuits designed by the Barrons. These interesting compositions ranged from the hesitating
''beta beat'' of the Id monster, to the bubbly sounds associated with Bobby the
Robot. Many of the sounds that reached the screen were collages of different
circuits taped by the Barrons and stacked like building blocks—the same principle
on which the moog synthesizer now works. Some of these themes involved as
many as seven different component sounds, each representing a separate circuit.
''From the beginning, we discovered that people compared them with sounds
they heard in their dreams,'' says Barron. ''When our circuits reached the end
of their existence (an overload point) they would climax in an orgasm of power,
and die. In the film, many of the sounds seem like the last paroxysm of a living
creature.'' Some of these circuits were nameless, but a few were derived from
some of their favorite music. The theme used as night fell on Altair IV came
from a song called *Night with Two Moons*.[34]

In fact, the circuits designed by the Barrons, who used no synthesizers or traditional electronic-music techniques, were dubbed by them as ''cybernetic circuits'' because they functioned ''electronically in a manner remarkably similar
to the way that lower life-forms function psychologically.''[35]

Genres of Interaction

The ways in which film and film music (both diegetic and nondiegetic) interact,
and theories on this interaction, are so numerous that it would take an entire
book just to adequately expose the major ones. In the following discussion, only
the salient points of such an exposition will be set forth, with examples. Before
this discussion, however, I would like to address one major theoretical point,
namely the interrelationship between the opera (and, for that matter, other forms
of classical music) and the cinemusical phenomenon. As I mentioned in the
opening section of this chapter, early opera depends too much on set pieces to
offer a valid parallel with the cinemusical spectacle. A better case can be made
for establishing a parallel between the operas of Wagner, Puccini, Richard

Strauss, Alban Berg, and, perhaps, Giuseppi Verdi. But one can go much too far even here. Prendergast, for instance, offers the following argument:

If we equate the dialogue in a film to the "sung words" of opera, we can see there is little difference between opera and film. Indeed, the recitative of opera, like dialogue in a film, serves to move the plot forward. Opera, like film, tends to emphasize the separation of the drama and the music at times. In opera this separation is almost literal: the orchestra is hidden in the pit; in the sound film the orchestra is "hidden" on the sound track. In opera the stage is the most visible element and, like the screen in a film, it draws most of our attention. In opera when the stage becomes musical (as when an aria begins) the two forces of drama and music come together to form a unified force. This same sort of thing happens in films as those points where the music is allowed to speak in a forceful and contributive way. In opera, like film, when the action on stage is the most important element, the orchestra dissociates itself from the action and becomes a commentary upon it. (p. 40)

But, Prendergast's argument does not really work except in special cases, none (that I can think of) involving American composers. However, Prendergast does evoke the early scores of Korngold, Newman, and Steiner. According to David A. Cook, Eisenstein's *Alexander Nevsky* was conceived "as a opera in which Sergei Prokofiev's brilliant score would alternately complement and conflict with the film's visual rhythms."[36] Cook also suggests that *Ivan the Terrible*, Part 1, "is an operatic film with a magnificent Prokofiev score employed contrapuntally throughout" (pp. 321–22). But one of the principal reasons for this is that Prokofiev's scores were not put together according to the logic of individual cues, as most film scores are. Rather, one can hear long passages where the music is allowed to develop according to its own codes while still serving a strong dramatic function. An excellent example of this is the sequence of Tsar Ivan's near death in *Ivan the Terrible*, Part 1. For some six minutes, Prokofiev's music moves like the accompaniment to an unsung opera, with no sound effects and with Nikolai Cherkassof's very dramatic monologue functioning a great deal like sung lyrics. Even here, however, toward the end of the scored sequence, when the ailing tsar condemns his enemies to eternal damnation, the score makes an abrupt shift that has little musical logic to it. One might also cite, as operatic cinema, the example of the Sergio Leono–Ennio Morricone collaborations in the former's so-called spaghetti westerns (not to mention the 1983 *Once Upon a Time in America*), in which Morricone's expansive music-scapes complement Leone's visual lyricism in a manner that might also be called bel canto.

But the above examples represent by far the exception rather than the rule. The point is that the film composer is obliged, much less often than the opera composer, to integrate his or her dramatic devices into a broader fabric based on musical codes. If one takes the rising, parallel seconds that back up the legged serpent in Steiner's *King Kong* score and compares this figure to a somewhat similar one that accompanies Wozzeck's walking into the lake towards the end of Berg's opera *Wozzeck*, a very cinematic opera in certain senses, one finds that Berg's music, as descriptive as it is, grows naturally from the musical material that precedes it and leads logically into the musical material that follows it (all the dialogue at this point is spoken). Steiner's much briefer figure is timed to the split second to synchronize with a particular filmic event (the appearance of the serpent), and it more or less simply pops in and out of the musical score. Further, during an opera there is singing most of the time. This necessitates music that must coordinate, harmonically, rhythmically, and texturally, with some sort of melodic line.

While film composers often have to take into account the vocal range of a given actor or actress in order to leave that pitch range more or less free in the music, the spoken dialogue in a film cannot be said to interact harmonically or rhythmically with the music. In addition to this, the very necessity of singing in opera slows down the pace of the action: the forty-five-second, wordless shower sequence in *Psycho* requires a very different kind of music from the four-to-five-minute duet that would be needed in an opera just to lead up to the killing. And, of course, the film composer scores much of his or her music for sequences with little or no verbal "action." The film composer also, on the average, puts together a score in a series of short cues ranging in time from a second or two to a median length of perhaps two to three minutes. Although the cues are often linked thematically, instrumentally, etc., the film composer, unlike the opera composer, does not have to write music to get from one dramatic moment to the next, since filmic codes, unlike operatic ones, can admit long passages of unscored diegesis.

Moreover, even when a composer does put together a score that has more than the usual musical continuity, whether operatic or otherwise, there is no guarantee that what the audience hears will preserve that logic. Miklós Rózsa describes Brazilian composer Heitor Villa Lobos's experience with the film *Green Mansions* (Mel Ferrer, 1959):

I met him when he arrived in Hollywood, asked him whether he had yet seen the film, and how much time they were allowing him to write the music. He was going to see the picture tomorrow, he said, and the music was already completed. They had sent him a script, he told me, translated into Portuguese, and he had followed that, just as if he had been writing a ballet or opera. I was dumbfounded; apparently nobody had bothered to explain the basic techniques to him. "But Maestro," I said, "what will happen if your music doesn't match the picture exactly?" Villa-Lobos was obviously talking to a complete idiot. "In that case, of course, they will adjust the picture," he replied. Well, they didn't. They paid him his fee and sent him back to Brazil. Bronislau Kaper, an experienced MGM staff composer, fitted his music to the picture as best he could. (p. 69)

Rósza also describes what happened to his own score for Billy Wilder's *Five Graves to Cairo* (1943):

Afterwards, however, the usual thing happened: the film needed cutting and was handed over to the so-called music editors, whose sole basis for deciding where to cut was to find two identical notes the required number of feet apart. What this practice did to the music's continuity and logic was another matter, and they never thought to consult me in any way. Shortly after the premiere Bruno Walter remarked to me, "You had a few modulations I didn't quite understand. . . . " I had to explain that these were the work of a pair of scissors and not of the composer. (p. 120)

For John Guillermin's 1966 *The Blue Max*, Jerry Goldsmith wrote, for a climactic air battle, a seven-and-a-half-minute passacaglia and fugue that took him longer to compose than the rest of the score. Yet in the film the audience hears only the first eight measures and the last eight. Jean-Luc Godard, conceiving of a cinemusical experiment for his 1962 *Vivre sa vie* (*My Life to Live*), asked composer Michel Legrand to write the score as a theme and eleven variations, since he envisaged the film as having an equivalent to that musical structure. The director, however, ended up using but twelve measures from one of the variations for all of the film's nondiegetic cues.[37]

Even though film music uses, then, many of the basic sounds and devices of "classical" music, the film score rarely organizes these sounds and devices into the type of extended, wholly musically coherent, concert-intended work that is one of the keystones of classical composing. Because the film composer generally works within much smaller musical confines than the concert composer, and because the film composer, unlike the opera composer, must work with a preestablished dramatic, filmic text rather than having the luxury of developing an ongoing interaction between musical and dramatic logic, the film composer must rely much more strongly than the standard "classical" composer on various devices that immediately set up levels of affective meaning in the viewer/listener by paradigmaticizing the filmic material. These basic devices can be categorized as follows.

Preexisting Musical Associations

By far the most common trick of the film composer's trade is the reliance on various predispositions, both musical and extramusical, in the audiences of a given culture. Music has a number of onomatopoeias at its disposal, such as bird calls, whether the sound of a cuckoo or various other calls frequently suggested by a flute. At the opposite end of the scale, composers have devised a musical onomatopoeia for the old steam engines that used to dominate the railroads: in *King Kong*, fast, repeated sixteenth-notes in a quadruple meter played in the strings suggest the arrival of the elevated train, while a gratingly dissonant chord in the winds suggests the whistle, all of which is rather silly, since the train in question is electric and would have nothing resembling a steam-engine's whistle. And what could be more harrowing than the chaotic, totally nontonal (and, one suspects, aleatory) pizzicato-string passage used by Ennio Morricone to evoke the plague of locusts in the TV film (later theatrically released), *Moses, the Lawgiver* (1975).

On a more abstract level, one of the commonest predispositions that can be found in the Western listener lies in the distinction between the major and the minor scale modes and the harmonic colorations they produce. In the seven-note Western scale, the major mode starts off with two whole steps before the first, closer-sounding half-step is reached; in the minor mode, the second step one hears is a half-step. Whether because of cultural conditioning or because, as Leonard B. Meyer suggests, "the association between the minor mode and emotional states depicting sadness and suffering is a product of the deviant, unstable character of the mode and of the association of sadness and suffering with the slower tempi that tend to accompany the chromaticism prevalent in the minor mode . . . ," (p. 328), the minor mode traditionally evokes emotional reactions not just of sadness and suffering but of high drama as well. As one example, in *King Kong*, at the point when Ann Darrow and Jack Driscoll are escaping from Kong, the music is in the minor mode and is filled with chromatic steps in the thematic line. As soon as the hero and heroine hit the water—and are thereby saved—the same material suddenly shifts to what is heard to be the much brighter, "happier" major mode. Similarly, in Steiner's score for John Ford's *The Searchers* (1956), at the moment John Wayne wipes off his horse and obviously realizes that his brother's family will be attacked by the Comanches, what might be referred to as the homestead theme is modified from its original major-mode profile and is heard in the minor mode. In Miklós Rózsa's score for *Spellbound*, there is a remarkable similarity between the famous love theme and the suspense theme. While in the former, however, the composer uses the major mode and the very consonant intervals of the sixth and third, the latter, which is in the minor mode, starts off with a three-note, descending chromatic scale and then drops down a tritone (an augmented fourth or flatted fifth, one of the most "dissonant" intervals in Western tonality) from the opening note (the solo violin that gets Saint-Saëns's ghostly *Danse macabre* moving plays a double-step tritone and also moves up and down on this interval).

Going one step further, dissonance also tends to automatically associate itself with high drama, both because it represents a departure from the norms of consonant tonality and because of its extended passages of nonresolution. We have already seen how the narrative situation of insanity inspired extremely dissonant musical styles, whether Leonard Rosenman's atonality for *The Cobweb* or Henry Mancini's quarter tones for *The Night Visitor*. One of composer Bernard Herrmann's great contributions to film music is his extended use of nonresolving chords in apparently tonal contexts where resolution would be expected. This works particularly well in his scores for Alfred Hitchcock films, especially *Vertigo*, *North by Northwest*, and *Psycho*, in which the musical tensions between tonality and nontonality, between implied resolution and lack thereof, mirror the dialectic of the normal and the extraordinary that characterizes the work of the "master of suspense."[38] It is perhaps because of the association of extended dissonance and other modernistic devices with gloomy narratives that many of the most original and innovative film scores have been inspired by darker-hued cinema.

Other preexisting musical associations would include, for instance, the use of the waltz for love themes. From Steiner's *King Kong* (1933) through Bernard

Herrmann's *Vertigo* (1958) and beyond, the old cliché that "two hearts beat in 3/4 time" is manifested in the frequency with which a waltz beat, whether in 3/4 or 6/8, is used for love music. Wide, intervalic leaps also tend to get the emotional juices flowing. It is no accident, for instance, that three of the most striking and cinematically effective themes ever composed—Alfred Newman's "Cathy's Theme" for William Wyler's *Wuthering Heights* (1939), the "Tara" theme in Max Steiner's *Gone With the Wind* score, or Philippe Sarde's main theme for Pierre Granier Deferre's *Le Chat* (1971)—all begin with an octave leap upward, as does the song "Somewhere Over the Rainbow" from *The Wizard of Oz*. Various preexisting ethnic associations also have served the purpose of film music quite well, both in the silent and the sound era. We have already seen how themes such as "Dixie" or "La Marseillaise" have evoked immediate responses to a given ethnic group. Diverse instruments, rhythms, and other devices can also perform the same function: a guitar and/or castanets for things Hispanic (see the nightmare sequence in Bernard Herrmann's *Vertigo*; the cue also uses the rhythm of a Spanish dance, the habañera); a major-mode theme doubled in thirds also often serves the same function (see the title theme for Jerry Fielding's *The Wild Bunch*); an accordion can evoke things French, the march "Britannia Rules the Waves" things English, a mandolin things Italian (see Nino Rota's love theme for *The Godfather*), etc.

In only a slightly different vein, the children's song, to which lyrics from "nyah nyah" to "It's raining, it's pouring . . . " have been diversely applied, constantly pops up at filmic moments demanding that "childicity" be called forth (Korngold's *King's Row* and Hugo Friedhofer's score for William Wyler's *The Best Years of Our Lives* (1946) offer two examples of this). In *The Bad Seed*, Alex North bitonally incorporates the folk tune "Mon ami Pierrot," frequently used as a piano exercise for children, which creates the presence of the evil little girl before she ever appears on screen (the tune later becomes a diegetic cue as the little girl does in fact play it on the piano). Nicolas Roeg's *Don't Look Now* (1973) immediately infuses his film with the presence of the child by having Pino Donaggio's main theme played haltingly on a piano. Other, more abstract predispositions towards instrumental color and range likewise abound. High-range instruments such as the flute tend to suggest lightness, while low instruments such as the tuba just the opposite. In a Warner Brothers cartoon ("Bully for Bugs," with music by Carl Stalling) featuring Bugs Bunny as an unwilling matador, preexisting associations towards ethnicity and instrumentality are exploited through the use of the song "La Cucaracha," which is batted back and forth between a flute (Bugs Bunny) and a tuba (bull) as one of the cartoon's sequences crosscuts between the two characters. A solo snare drum playing in a march rhythm is all that is needed to evoke "militaricity"; an occasional bugle call also does no harm. In an association that goes back at least as far as Saint-Saëns's *Danse macabre*, the xylophone and various other dry-sounding percussion instruments form the backbone, as it were, of the "Duel with the Skeleton" cue in Bernard Herrmann's score for *The Seventh Voyage of Sinbad* (1958).

Herrmann also excelled at creating instrumental profiles for given films out of less obvious and immediate associations: the orchestra for the *Journey to the Center of the Earth* (1959) has no strings but includes a number of harps plus no fewer than five organs (one cathedral and four electronic); Herrmann also revived an archaic instrument called the serpent to flatulently complement the presence of one of *Journey*'s reptilian monsters. *Psycho*'s orchestra contains nothing but strings (the composer has stated that he was aiming at a musical equivalent of the film's black-and-white photography), while the rejected score for Hitchcock's *Torn Curtain* (1965) eliminated violins and violas but relied heavily on such "metallic" (as in *iron* curtain) instruments as flutes (twelve), horns (sixteen), and trombones (nine). Certain cinemusical amalgams created for a particular filmic situation have struck viewer/listeners as so fortuitous that these associations have carried over into later pictures.

I have already cited the examples from *2001* and *Star Wars*. Also worth mentioning are the famous violin shrieks, perhaps inspired both by a woman's scream and by the diegetic motif of birds, in Herrmann's *Psycho*. These are alluded to fairly literally at several points in Pino Donaggio's score for Brian De Palma's *Carrie* (1975); even more substantial portions of the *Psycho* music turn up, uncredited, in Richard Band's music for Stuart Gordon's supernatural-horror opus, *Re-Animator* (1985). In *Forbidden Planet*, one would have to attribute as one of the reasons for the success of the Barrons' electronic score the fact that it corresponds, in its machine-created sounds and in the modern technology evoked by these sounds, to our feelings of "futuricity." One can, in fact, never be sure, in watching and listening to *Forbidden Planet*, whether much of the music is intended as diegetic sounds made by the space ship, the monster, etc., or as nondiegetic backing.

Finally, more esoteric associations are also called upon from time to time. Franz Liszt's music, for diverse reasons, often evokes feelings of Hungarianicity in the listener. But Edgar Ulmer and Heinz Roemheld had other reasons for using Liszt that are not readily apparent in the music:

The opening of Liszt's *Piano Sonata in B Minor* was hammered into a satanic musical portrait for Karloff with strings and brass. Ulmer and Roemheld called it "The Devil's Sonata." Their leaning on Liszt was deliberate—not only because of the Hungarian flavor, but because Liszt's interest in the devil was intensely personal. Much of his music exploited what were regarded as infernal regions. Some musicologists contend that the *Sonata* was another of the many forays Liszt made into illustrating scenes from Goethe's *Faust*. And, in his suffering the fatal allure of women, Ulmer found him rather apropos *The Black Cat*. (Mandell, p. 48)

Liszt's "Mephisto Waltz" does not correspond to many of our preformed feelings as to how Satanicity should be evoked. But anyone who recognizes themes from that work in Jerry Goldsmith's music for Paul Wendkos's *Mephisto Waltz* (1972) will have an inside line on just what is behind the pianist's career in the film.

Schubert's *lied*, "Death and the Maiden," and the second movement of the string quartet in which the composer incorporated that song, sound lugubrious enough; but recognition of the specific piece in Hugo Riesenfeld's score will aid viewers of *Tabu* in realizing the fate in store for that film's heroine (Riesenfeld also uses Smetena's *Die Moldau*, composed to evoke the Czechoslovakian river, at a point where the music shows a ship sailing on the sea). The musically trained ear will recognize that the opening musical cue in Tom Pierson's score for Robert Altman's 1979 *Quintet* is yet one more element of the music to evoke the number 5, since the music is written in a quintuple meter (probably 5/8). Much of Pierre Jansen's very dissonant chamber-score for Claude Chabrol's *La Femme infidèle* (1968) is scored for the usual instruments of the classical trio—violin, viola, and piano—to musically suggest one of the film's primary narrative themes, the love triangle. In a brutal piece of reverse associationism, Rick Wakeman, for Ken Russell's *Crimes of Passion*, took Dvořák's so-called New World Symphony, composed in 1893 as a fond reminiscence of the Czech composer's visit to the United States, and arranged various themes from it for synthesizer (one of the first movement's principal melodies also gets transformed into a song used for a rock video within the film) to form an ironic musical complement to the picture's scathing portrait of American sexuality. The listener, however, must be aware of the original music's programmatic implications to appreciate this irony, as there is nothing terribly American sounding about the New World Symphony.

The Leitmotif

One of the principal ways in which the above, preformed associations interact with the filmic text is the transformation of certain basic elements into extratextual paradigms. With the banjo and the snippet from "Dixie" on its music track, the diegesis of *Gone With the Wind* does not remain within a particular historical moment but relates to all "things southern" from all times. With the *Psycho* violins shrieking briefly as the heroine telekinetically closes the windows of her house, *Carrie* ties in with all the deepest and darkest feelings related to the horror-suspense genre in general and to Alfred Hitchcock's special brand in particular. When the main theme suddenly looms on the music track of *The Searchers* in a minor mode, we relate our specific feelings to all the feelings of sadness and tragedy we have experienced via music. We also move synchronically ahead, intra-textually, to the moment in *The Searchers* where the paradigmatic musical presage will be syntagmatically realized in the visuals (the long shot of the burning ranch) and in the music (a fortissimo series of shifting chords in the full orchestra). But the chief tool film music has for creating intra-textual paradigms is the so-called leitmotif, or leading motif, a device that goes all the way back to the operas of Wagner and even earlier. The leitmotif lends itself particularly well to the cinema first of all because it does not depend upon a developed theme (although a developed theme *can* function leitmotivically) but rather often makes use of brief but characteristic figures that frequently last not more than a second or two. These figures, it should be noted, are sometimes taken, in the cinema, from a larger theme that is rarely heard in toto in the film outside of the titles and/or perhaps a climactic sequence.

For *Dr. No*, for instance, Monty Norman wrote a full fledged "James Bond Theme." But it takes only that mysterious, four-note, chromatic figure that sets up the melody to signal the presence of Ian Fleming's superspy (and in this instance, the leitmotif carries over from one 007 film to the next). And it takes only the first four notes of the melody itself (usually played by the high brass) to provide subsequent Bond-flick composers, especially John Barry, with another juicy leitmotif. The first few notes of the Liszt Piano Sonata serve a similar function vis-à-vis the character of Poelzig in *The Black Cat*. By appearing in various forms (major mode, minor mode, different instruments, etc., depending on the situation) each time a given character or situation (such as love) turns up or is about to turn up in the filmic narrative, the leitmotif synchronically links together these various apparitions, thus helping the film on yet another level to attain the level of myth (Claude Lévi-Strauss, referring to Wagner as "the undeniable originator of the structural analysis of myths," points out that Wagner discovered "that the structure of myths can be revealed through the musical score."[39]

In *King Kong*, the giant gorilla's presence is planted in the audience's unconscious from the outset of the film when the title music starts off with three downward, low notes that can be referred to as "Kong's motif." Later, when everybody knows that Kong is coming to get Fay Wray, the monster is made present by that same three-note motif before we ever see him. Interestingly, those same three notes are also subtly built into the film's love theme; although probably done either unconsciously or ironically by Steiner, the inclusion of Kong's motif in the love theme says a lot about the mythic parallel between the Jack Driscoll–Ann Darrow couple and the man-monster mythology evoked by the film. A score such as Erich Korngold's *The Sea Hawk* has an immensely rich motivic structure that includes not only themes and motifs for particular characters and things (Captain Thorpe's ship, the *Albatros*, can be included in the latter category) but also at least one broad theme that seems in a certain way to stand for the entire picture and that pops up in several quite varied sequences. Each of the main characters, Geoffrey Thorpe (Errol Flynn) and Doña Maria (Brenda Marshall) is associated with a theme that can be divided into two recognizable parts, one decidedly more motivic than the other. Thorpe is identified with the opening of the fanfare that begins the film and then with an extended, much more mid-range theme that grows naturally out of it. Doña Maria's first theme has as its basis a single, rising three-note figure in the high register, which leads naturally into a theme that, once again, is more extended and more mid-range (and, in this case, mildly Hispanic in flavor). During the ongoing music that underscores the couple's meeting in the palace garden, Korngold ingeniously shuffles these various themes and motifs together, often managing to switch from one to the next on shot changes without destroying the musical continuity. In the climactic love scene where Thorpe, having escaped from the Spanish galley, sneaks into Doña Maria's carriage, the music starts off with the broadly romantic *Sea Hawk* theme alluded to above. As soon as Maria says "I love you" to Thorpe, however, her three-note motif takes over, followed by her secondary theme. Then, when Thorpe begins to speak, the music switches to his secondary theme.

In cases such as these, and thousands more that one could mention, the music functions on at least two different levels: (a) it provides, as it did for silent films, a level of affect which, in the case of a score such as *The Sea Hawk* is made all the more profound by the poignancy and sweep of the music; and (b) it creates a kind of *mémoire involontaire* and a sense of active expectation within the filmic context by linking characters and situations from the filmic past to those of the filmic present while also, at certain points, paving the way for the filmic future. While in more recent film scores the emphasis has shifted more to the first of the two levels above, with one or two themes often serving a variety of functions, the leitmotif remains one of film music's most characteristic devices, the one, in fact, that most often allows the film in certain ways to behave like a work of music.

Mickey-Mousing

One particular device that is all but unique to the brand of classical music one finds in film music, precisely because its appearance in a given score depends wholly on its coordination with visual images, is that of Mickey-Mousing, the mimicking of action on the screen by what are perceived to be equivalent musical figures. The term "Mickey-Mousing" comes from the prevalent use of this particular musical gimmick in animated cartoons, where the music reinforces the comedy. Thus, when Sylvester Pussycat sneaks upstairs on his tiptoes, a rising figure in pizzicato strings sneaks up with him. If, in *King Kong*, Max Steiner abstractly suggests the arrival of Kong with his three-note leitmotif, the composer also literalizes the still unseen footsteps with low, heavy, evenly repeated chords in the brass. When Kong tickles Ann, Steiner invents a little "tickle trill" in the winds. When Jack and Ann let go of the vine and plunge into the lake below, a fast, downward figure that includes a harp glissando mimicks this fall. Towards the end of Howard Hawks's *The Big Sleep* (1946), Humphrey Bogart fires shots that cause a secondary heavy to run away in fear. As he leaps over a bush, Steiner's music, which in other parts of the score makes heavy use of a motif from *King Kong*, brings in a rapid upward and downward glissando on a xylophone to complement the action and, one would hope, to make it slightly comical. In Terence Young's *Dr. No* (1963), the first of the James Bond flicks, one sees and hears a flagrant piece of Mickey-Mousing as the tarantula crawls over 007 (slow, contrary-motion chromatic runs in the strings and clarinet) and then as Bond frenziedly whacks the beast to death (the same dissonant chord repeated each time Bond brings down his shoe). Even when the music does not exactly try to mimick the action, its split-second timing to fit an appropriate dramatic event must be seen as an extension of the Mickey-Mousing mentality.

In *The Searchers*, for instance, Steiner's dramatic chords, which are accompanied by an initial cymbal crash, start at exactly the instant when the film cuts away from John Wayne's unsheathing of his rifle to the long shot of the burning ranch. In *Wuthering Heights*, during Cathy's death scene, the second note of the motivic octave-leap that characterizes the latter's theme suddenly becomes a minor-mode chord with an added sixth as Cathy's arm drops, visually indicating her demise. Max Steiner, perhaps the most notorious of all cinemusical paper-hangers, actually invented a device, known as the "click track," that allowed metronomic beats to be put onto a soundtrack to allow for perfect synchronization with various moments of action. (Prendergast discusses synchronization in great detail with some excellent examples; pp. 237–246.)

It is difficult to come up with cogent reasons to explain away the popularity of Mickey-Mousing and split-second synchronization well into the sound era, especially in American cinema. The vulgarization of the entire filmic text that is often brought about by such devices is perhaps the one thing, more than any other, that has given the classical film score a bad name. Even in Sir Laurence Olivier's *Richard III* (1956), which much of the time features a genuinely beautiful and moving score by Sir William Walton, better known as a concert composer than as a film scorer, a few musical excesses make parts of the film almost laughable, most notably perhaps in the final sequence, where the music twitches right along with Richard's death throes. It is because of abuses such as this that one can appreciate all the more a scene such as the discovery of Annabella Smith's body by the charwoman in Alfred Hitchcock's *The Thirty-Nine Steps* (1935). Where an American film would have cut to the dead spy's body with a loud, musical chord, Hitchcock overlaps the sound of a train whistle to replace the charwoman's visualized scream and then cuts away to a shot of a train approaching the screen.

One can suppose, of course, that the continued use of excessive synchronization can be traced back to the silent era. One can also go further and rather maliciously suggest that such devices are used by the studios to increase the passivity of audiences: simply turning on the emotions with music does not suffice; audiences must be spoonfed into having exactly the right emotions at exactly the right time. Ideally, of course, the tasteful synchronization of a particularly dramatic event with musically induced affect can lead, as it tended to in Greek theater, for instance, to a particularly pure form of catharsis. And, as animated cartoons have proven, Mickey-Mousing works especially well as an enhancer of comedic affect. But its abuse, frequent in American cinema, quickly evokes the most puerile forms of melodrama, and it has played an increasingly small role in recent dramatic films, although one has only to turn on the television to find ongoing misuses.

Possibilities for Countertendencies in Narrative Film Music

As one might suspect from the above discussions, the conventional and con-ventionalized use of classical music in film scores runs counter to almost any idealized or ideological conception one might have of the cinema, whether political, aesthetic, or both. From the Marxist political point of view, for instance, the additional mythification of the cinematic image afforded by the musical practices described above is pure anathema, and it was combatted both in theory and in practice by Hanns Eisler, who proposed what amounts to a kind of alienation effect (à la Brecht) in music. From the aesthetic point of view, the musical practices described above fall right in with invisible editing, eye-line matches, the 180-degree rule, etc., in subordinating free artistic use of the various tools of the cinematic trade to support the narrative and ''correct'' reactions to such uses (see Noël Burch, Alain Robbe-Grillet, et al.). At least one film, Luis Buñuel's *Diary of a Chambermaid*, supports its artistic and political ideology by not using a single note of music, diegetic or nondiegetic. In the United States, one might cite the example of the Disney Studios' *Fantasia* (1940) as an ex-periment in coordinating image to classical music, rather than vice versa; one of the film's episodes even sets abstract figures into motion against Bach's Toccata and Fugue in D minor. Somehow, though, *Fantasia*'s image and sound amalgams, whether dinosaur heads rising to the specific cues of Stravinsky's ballet *The Rite of Spring* or nymphs and fauns running for cover during the storm from Beethoven's ''Pastorale'' symphony, manage to further support the norms rather than break with them. More subtly, Orson Welles edited the entire ''break-fast montage'' in *Citizen Kane* around Bernard Herrmann's music.

Another device that can be used to break the mold might be referred to as anti-expectation scoring, in which jaunty, major-mode themes would underscore heavy drama, slow tempi would back up fast-action sequences, etc. Perhaps the most famous example of this would be the zither music composed and performed by Anton Karas for Carol Reed's *The Third Man* (1949). But Karas's efforts might more properly be classified as a pop (or even folk) score than as a classical one. French director Jean Cocteau has speculated that Georges Auric's music for *La Belle et la bête* (1946) was scored on such a principle. But for his *Orphée* (1950), Cocteau actually took cues that Auric had composed specifically for one sequence and used them in sequences of quite a different nature, producing what the director refers to as ''accidental synchronism.''[40]

As a final example, one might consider the case of Jean-Luc Godard who, throughout most of his career, save, perhaps, the ''Dziga Vertov Group'' period, has consistently used classical music, originally scored or otherwise (or both), in such a way as to fit in with the overall profile I have referred to elsewhere as ''aesthetic distantiation.''[41] In Godard's films, classical music generally be-comes one of the editable materials to be integrated into an overall texture that includes quotations of paintings of pre-existing classical music, and of diverse literary material. For the 1965 *Pierrot le fou*, for instance, the director got from his composer, Antoine Duhamel, a set of four fully composed pieces (simply labeled as "Thème 1," "Thème 2," etc.) in the score. Godard was then able to take whatever parts of the music he wanted and insert them into the film at will. Thus, for instance, instead of a particular figure undergoing various leit-motif-type modifications, the same part of a given *"thème"* simply reappears, sometimes for only a second or two (without there being any apparent dramatic reason for this brevity), creating a feeling of obsession wholly characteristic of Godard in general and of the film in particular.

Even at the opening of *Pierrot le fou*, where the director seems to have established a fairly conventional title/title-music relationship, the music is ac-tually edited to "begin" at the end of the theme's first section; it then returns da capo to the opening. Further on in the music, as the hero (Jean-Paul Belmondo) and heroine (Anna Karina) steal a Ford Galaxy off a garage lift, Godard un-derscores the action with a scherzo-like theme by Duhamel but subverts part of the musically induced potential for catharsis by arbitrarily turning the music off, letting the tape run, and then turning it on again (this device is repeated several times). Duhamel's score, then, serves both to provide (quite strikingly, in a rather Bernard Herrmannesque way) a sort of generalized, tragically colored effect for *Pierrot le fou* and, in just the opposite sense, to fit in with numerous other elements of the film as part of a massive collage anti-cathartically suggesting a new aesthetic politics. The full, Godardian aesthetic lies in the ongoing dialectic between catharsis and alienation, and the director's use of music plays a key role in this.

Film and Classical Music: Some Narrative Implications

To conclude this overview of film and classical music, one other area of interaction between the two arts needs to be briefly examined, namely, the role played by classical music not just as a passive element within the diegesis but as an active element in narratives of certain films. Obvious examples can be found in various film biographies in which a classical composer becomes the hero of sorts. Relatively conventional examples of this would be Charles Vidor's 1945 *A Song to Remember* (Chopin), Charles Vidor and George Cukor's 1960 *Song Without End* (Liszt), William Dieterle's 1956 *Magic Fire* (Wagner), or Milos Forman's 1984 *Amadeus* (Mozart). Two more outrageous examples have sprung from the directorial vision of Ken Russell, the 1971 *The Music Lovers* (Tchaikovsky) and the totally outlandish *Lisztomania* from 1975. In all of the above examples, generous portions of the composers' music wind their way in and out of the diegesis—Morris Stoloff and Harry Sukman even won a "Scoring of a Musical Picture" award for their Liszt arrangements in *Song Without End*— while much of the Liszt one hears in *Lisztomania* is transformed into rock (it is, after all, Roger Daltry from the rock group the Who who plays Liszt).

Fictionalized classical composers and performers have also played important narrative roles in the cinema and in many cases have inspired whole or partial compositions from the film scorer. For *Citizen Kane*, Bernard Herrmann wrote an aria for an imaginary opera entitled *Salambo*, sung in the music by Kane's second wife. Herrmann produced an even more extended piece, his "Hangover Square Concerto," for John Brahm's *Hangover Square* (1945), a suspense thriller about a demented composer-pianist (Laird Cregar) who is driven by loud noises to murder women. In the film's memorable climax, Cregar is seen playing the final notes of "his" concerto as a burning mansion collapses around him.

Erich Korngold composed a brief cello concerto (later expanded for concert performance) that is performed by Paul Henreid in Irving Rapper's 1946 *Deception*, in which Bette Davis plays a concert pianist and Claude Rains a composer (ironically of the concerto performed by Henreid) in a murderous triangle. For the Michael Powell–Emeric Pressburger *The Red Shoes* (1948), British composer Brian Easdale composed one complete ballet (the "Red Shoes" ballet) and one partial one ("Heart of Fire," heard at the beginning of the film) to represent the efforts of that film's fictitious composer (Marius Goring). And just as the ballet-within-the-film, based on a Hans Christian Andersen fairy tale, mirrors the film's tragic narrative about a ballerina (Moira Shearer) torn between her love for her composer husband and her devotion to her art (and its impresario, played by Anton Walbrook), the music likewise offers a perfect musical setting for the diegetic ballet (which is cinematically expanded beyond the confines of the theatrical stage in its complete performance within the film) while also creating a large amount of quasi-nondiegetic affect, particularly at the film's conclusion, where the ballet-within-the-film and the primary filmic narrative merge as the "Red Shoes" ballet is sadly performed without the ballerina, who has committed suicide.

In a more arbitrary vein, an entire, long sequence from Bryan Forbes's *Deadfall* (1968) is structured around a "Romance for Guitar and Orchestra" composed by John Barry (who also scored the film). During this sequence, the film cuts back and forth between a concert performance of Barry's concerto (with the composer conducting) and the carefully laid-out burglary of a mansion, so that, at certain points, conductor Barry seems to be choreographing the caper while, in reverse, the elegant burglars seem to inspire the music in the concert hall. And, of course, in both versions of Alfred Hitchcock's *The Man Who Knew Too Much* (1934 and 1956), the entire narrative momentum leads to a climactic cymbal crash that is a part of a concert performance of Arthur Benjamin's "Storm Clouds Cantata," composed for the first version. If the original version offers, on the whole, the greater artistic merit than the second, the latter's concert sequence in London's Royal Albert Hall is one of the director's true tours de force. Eliminating all dialogue from the sequence, thereby forcing James Stewart and Doris Day to perform with almost silent-film mannerisms, Hitchcock effectively makes the Benjamin cantata, which Bernard Herrmann is seen conducting, function simultaneously on the diegetic and the nondiegetic levels. Worth noting, too, is the title sequence, which shows a small symphony orchestra "performing" Herrmann's overture to the film.

Classical music has also had an unfortunate tendency to join in a negative way with preexisting musical associations, since it is frequently tied in with psychoses, megalomania, elitism, and fascism throughout the history of sound films. In Fritz Lang's *M* (1930), which has no musical score per se, Peter Lorre's frightening, offscreen whistling of "In the Hall of the Mountain King" from Grieg's *Peer Gynt* incidental music can be seen as a throwback to one of the silent cinema's first instances of exploiting predispositions, even in European audiences, toward classical music (and its lovers) as being outside the "norm."

The very use of classical music in *The Black Cat* likewise reflects this predisposition. Following World War II and Nazi Germany's love affair with Wagner, it is not surprising to find prison warden Hume Cronyn using, in *Brute Force* (1947), a 78-recording of Wagner music to cover up the cries of the prisoner he is rubber hosing. Perhaps the following lines, spoken by Deborah Kerr in reference to World War I Germany as the strains of Schubert's "Unfinished" symphony (once again) from an outdoor concert make their way to the music track in Powell and Pressburger's *The Life and Death of Colonel Blimp* (1943) best sum up the fascism association:

I was thinking how odd they are, queer. For years and years they're writing and dreaming beautiful music and beautiful poetry. All of a sudden they start a war. They sink undefended ships, shoot innocent hostages, and bomb and destroy whole streets in London, killing little children. And then they sit down in the same butcher's uniform and listen to Mendelssohn and Schubert. There's something horrid about that.

In the 1977 *Rollercoaster*, the film's extortionist is seen listening on a portable cassette player to a modern classical string quartet (written for the picture by its scorer, Lalo Schifrin) before he goes out to sabotage a rollercoaster. Several of James Bond's megalomaniacal adversaries welcome 007 into their parlor to the tune of some work of classical music, occasionally even performed by the heavy. Certain recent films, though, especially (as one might expect) from abroad, have begun to give classical music a less stereotypical role, none more stylishly than Jean-Jacques Beineix's *Diva* (1983), which uses modern technology (cassette recorders) as the diegetic pretext for linking together a crime-suspense narrative and a strange love story that involves a young postal employee's infatuation with a black soprano (Wilhelmenia Wiggins Fernandez, who in real life is an opera singer but whose performance in *Diva* is nonetheless overdubbed). Although the film's score was composed by Vladimir Cosma, who composed quite a haunting, Satie-esque main theme, *Diva* centers around an aria, "*E ben, ne andro lontano,*" from a little-known opera entitled *La Wally* by Alfred Catalani. Just as self-reflective cinema often involves a film (or some other work of art, such as a still photograph) within a film, *Diva* carries self-reflexivity to the sound and music tracks, since the diva's aria in the film is just as important as a real filmic event, as it is as the tape recording made of the initial event by the postal employee.

SOME CONCLUSIONS

The cinema attached itself to classical music almost from its inception, and classical music has continued to add and adapt its codes to the cinema for almost a century. In one way, little has changed from the earliest piano accompaniments to the most recent scores for full symphony orchestra and/or for synthesizer recorded on several tracks and played back through plaster-crumbling sound systems: classical music continues to supply the movies, whether in the theater or on television, with a layer of affect that most practitioners have found an indispensable complement to visual and narrative codes.

In other ways, however, the role of classical music in film has undergone evolutions on several fronts. By the 1980s, almost all the styles of classical music from baroque through avant-garde have found their way, at one point or another, into mainstream, narrative, commercial films. Further, many of the abuses of the past, whether musical or commercial, have by and large been eliminated. Even though close synchronization still plays an important role at certain points in particular films, composers generally work within a more flexible music-film interaction than before. The click-track has, in fact, become something of a historic relic. Technological advances in sound reproduction, whether in recording, theatrical playback, or such recent innovations as Beta-Hi-Fi or stereo television, have also helped classical music to impose its presence more strongly on the cinema. Many more film scores are also becoming the object of sound recordings; at least two California-based companies, Varèse Sarabande and Southern Cross, devote most of their efforts to film-score recordings.

On the negative side, the classical film score, although it held its own quite nicely against the jazz scores that made inroads on the music track in the 1950s and 1960s (and by now have almost totally died out), has done less well against the onslaught of a film-score genre that more often than not lacks the merit of most of the jazz scores, namely, the pop-song score. Here we are not just talking about a pop tune that opens a film (such as most of the James Bond pictures) and then gives way to a classical score. The 1970s and 1980s have seen a spate of films that cram as many rock and pop stars and their music onto the music track as possible (sometimes with originally written music, others with previously released hits). This practice, of course, is designed to attract the younger audiences that have apparently become theatrical cinema's biggest customers. Sound recordings of these "scores" often include diegetic cues heard for perhaps three seconds behind a closed door; and in many instances, the so-called soundtrack album contains songs never used or intended to be used in the film. And when a classical composer also makes contributions to the film, his or her efforts often never make the soundtrack album. One also finds abuses within the domain of the classical score, frequently in the form of overscoring, less frequently in the sphere of just plain bad music (the name of Mauric Jarre comes to mind here). Excessive use of synthesizers and their sometimes saccharinely artificial timbres also represents one of the more recent plagues to hit the classical film score. On the whole, however, classical music is alive and well in the cinema, and one can only hope for continued evolution of both its styles and its genres of interaction.

NOTES

1. See Donald Francis Tovey, *Essays in Musical Analysis, 3: Concertos* (London: Oxford University Press, 1936), pp. 87–96.

2. Susanne K. Langer, *Philosophy in a New Key: A Study in the Symbolism of Reason, Rite, and Art*, 3d ed. (Cambridge, Mass.: Harvard University Press, 1957), p. 238.

3. Irwin Bazelon, *Knowing the Score, Notes on Film Music* (New York: Van Nostrand Reinhold, 1975), pp. 13–14.

4. Hans-Christian Schmidt, *Filmmusik*, Musik aktuell, Analysen, Beispiele, Kommentare 4 (Basel and London: Bärenreiter Kassel, 1982).

5. Roger Sessions, *Roger Sessions on Music, Collected Essays*, ed. Edward T. Cone (Princeton, N.J.: Princeton University Press, 1979), p. 47. The essay in question, entitled "The New Musical Horizon," dates from 1937.

6. Max Winkler, "The Origin of Film Music," *Films in Review* 2, no. 34 (December 1951); repr. in *Film Music: From Violins to Video*, ed. James L. Limbacher (Metuchen, N.J.: Scarecrow Press, 1974), pp. 16–17.

7. These examples from Rapée are all given by Schmidt in *Filmmusik*, pp. 16–18.

8. Harlow Hare, "Harlow Hare," *Boston American*, July 18, 1915, reprinted in *Focus on The Birth of a Nation*, ed. Fred Silva (Englewood Cliffs, N.J.: Prentice-Hall, 1971), pp. 36–40.

9. Silva, p. 38. The music for this is printed in Schmidt, *Filmmusik*, p. 18.

10. Roland Barthes, *Mythologies*, trans. Annette Lavers (New York: Hill and Wang, 1972), pp. 111–117.

11. See Joseph Campbell, *Myths to Live By*, (New York: Viking, 1972). The reader will, I hope, forgive me for mentioning in almost the same breath Barthes and Campbell, two mythologists with direly diverging approaches. I would maintain that certain parallels can be made; but this is not the place to elaborate on that particular subject.

12. James Harding, *Saint-Saëns and His Circle* (London: Chapman and Hall, 1965), p. 204. Saint-Saëns continues to make musical appearances in the cinema. Renoir's 1939 *La Règle du jeu* uses the *Danse macabre*, as does one of Walt Disney's "Silly Symphonies"; and in the recent *Days of Heaven* (1978), the "Acquarium" movement from *The Carnival of the Animals* pairs up particularly well with some of Nestor Almendros's shots.

13. Jay Leyda, *Kino; A History of the Russian and Soviet Film* (New York: Collier Books, 1960), p. 35.

14. Bazelon incorrectly lists Karl Grüne as the director of this film.

15. Roy M. Prendergast, *Film Music, A Neglected Art: A Critical Study of Music in Films* (New York: W. W. Norton, 1977), p. 22.

16. Paul Mandell, "Edgar Ulmer and *The Black Cat*," *American Cinematographer* 65, no. 9 (October 1984): 48.

17. Mandell incorrectly gives this as the First Hungarian Rhapsody.

18. Prendergast refers on pp. 26 and 27 to an article by Ernest J. Borneman, "Sound Rhythms and the Film: Recent Research on the Compound Cinema," *Sight and Sound* 3, no. 10 (1934).

19. Miklós Rózsa, *Double Life: The Autobiography of Miklós Rózsa* (London: Midas Books;, New York: Hippocrene Books, 1982), p. 121.

20. Perhaps the most offbeat—and funny—use of the by then famous opening bars of *Also sprach* comes in Ken Russell's sardonic *Crimes of Passion* (1984), where a friend of the hero hums the music while the hero rises from a fetal position to erection and ejaculation in his "human penis" act.

21. Quoted in Tony Thomas, *Music for the Movies* (New York: A. S. Barnes, 1973), p. 113.

22. Notes for the Entr'acte recording of Max Steiner's *King Kong* score (Chicago: Entr'acte Recording Society, ERS 6504, 1976).

23. Herrmann's argument, which he clarified in an interview I did with him in 1974 (see Royal Brown, "An Interview with Bernard Herrmann (1911–1975)," *High Fidelity* 26, no. 9, [September 1976]: 64–67), that film music must be exactly tailored to a given film is weakened by the composer's own re-use of certain cues from film to film. An entire cue in *Psycho* is actually taken from a *Sinfonietta* for Strings that Herrmann composed in 1936. This would tend to support the point made earlier in this article about film music (and music in general) providing the morphology of emotion rather than specific affect.

24. On p. 37 of his book, Prendergast presents an "organizational chart for a music department in a typical Hollywood studio of the 1930's and 40's."

25. Much of the all-synthesizer, nonvocal music created by the three-man Tangerine Dream group, which broke into film scoring in 1977 with William Friedkin's *Sorcerer*, is hard to categorize; while some of their cues lean heavily toward rock, others definitely have characteristics of classical electronic music. Although I have not seen the Goldsmith-scored version of *Legend*, it is my opinion that in this particular instance, the producers lucked out with the Tangerine Dream music, which to my ears is somewhat less corny and somewhat more original than Goldsmith's (see my review in "Film Musings," *Fanfare* 9, no. 6 [July–August 1986]: 291–92).

26. Film-music recordings can be divided into several categories: (a) the so-called original soundtrack (actually music-track) recording, which usually contains thirty to forty-five minutes worth of cues taken directly from the recording-session tapes (generally unedited). More often than not, the orchestra is the studio orchestra, conducted by the composer. Rarely does an original soundtrack album contain all the nondiegetic cues (not to mention the diegetic cues), with several cues often being joined together on a single band. The cues are also often presented in nonfilmic order so that a certain music logic is created. The original soundtrack album may also offer cues not heard in the film, or complete cues heard only partially in the film. (b) The re-recorded score. This practice, in which diverse cues from a given film are often, but not always, arranged into a concert suite, is most useful for film scores composed before the advent of the long-playing record. In certain instances, however, poor sound quality or the unavailability of tapes or mag tracks makes desirable the rerecording of a particular score. Exorbitant resuse fees demanded by the American musicians' union have also made it cheaper to rerecord

a score, such as Herrmann's *North by Northwest*, abroad rather than to bring out a recording of the original music track. (c) "Impressions" recordings. On occasion, a recording will be released, such as Warner Brothers' *Spellbound* (Miklós Rózsa), in which the basic material from a film score has been reworked in order to make it more musically presentable. Henry Mancini, who for a picture such as *Charade* often composed a fair amount of first-rate classical cues, brought out albums filled with pop tunes, most of which had little to do with the film. A number of recordings of pop-song scores from the 1970s and 1980s also fall into the "impressions" category.

27. There are those who would consider the rerecording of *Fantasia*'s music as heretical, given that the original was conducted by no less a figure than Leopold Stokowski with the Philadelphia Orchestra.

28. In 1983 British director Ken Russell set Holst's entire suite to various sets of visual images, some of them quite outrageous, in his made-for-BBC-TV *Ken Russell's The Planets*.

29. The aesthetic concept of "active expectation" is presented by Leonard B. Meyer in *Emotion and Meaning in Music* (Chicago: University of Chicago Press, 1956), one of the most important books on musical aesthetics ever published.

30. Early twentieth-century composers to use a quarter-tone system include Julián Carrillo, who as early as 1895 wrote a string quartet using quarter tones; Charles Ives; Hans Barth; and Ivan Vyshnegradsky. More recently, composers such as Pierre Boulez have integrated quarter tones into complex systems of seriality.

31. The story is told that Russell, one of whose early TV films, *Song of Summer*, is about English composer Frederick Delius, made the cast of *The Music Lovers* listen over and over to Shostakovich's *The Execution of Stephen Razin* to get them in the mood for the painful sequence on the train where the homosexual Tchaikovsky and his nymphomaniac bride confront each other sexually for the first time, even though the music heard in the film's final cut is of course all Tchaikovsky.

32. Quoted by Tom Milne in *Mamoulian* (Bloomington: Indiana University Press, 1969), p. 49n.

33. Christopher Palmer, notes for the recording "Bernard Herrmann, *The Devil and Daniel Webster*, Welles Raises Kane" (London: Unicorn Records, UNS 237, 1973).

34. Frederick S. Clarke and Steven Rubin, "Making *Forbidden Planet*," *Cinefantastique* 8, no. 2/3 (1979): 43.

35. Louis and Bebe Barron, notes for the original soundtrack recording for *Forbidden Planet* (Beverly Hills, Calif: Planet Records, PR–001, 1976[?]).

36. David A. Cook, *A History of Narrative Film* (New York: W. W. Norton, 1981), p. 317.

37. See Royal Brown, "Music and *Vivre sa vie*," *Quarterly Review of Film Studies* 5, no. 3 (Summer 1980): 319–33.

38. See Royal Brown, "Herrmann, Hitchcock, and the Music of the Irrational," *Cinema Journal* 21, no. 2 (Spring 1982): 14–49; rev. and repr. in *Film Theory and Criticism*, ed. Gerald Mast and Marshall Cohen, 3d ed. (New York: Oxford University Press, 1985), pp. 618–49.

39. Claude Lévi-Strauss, *The Raw and the Cooked: Introduction to a Science of Mythology: I*, trans. John and Doreen Weightman (New York: Harper and Row, 1969), p. 15.

40. See Jean Cocteau, *Cocteau on the Film: Conversations with Jean Cocteau Recorded by André Fraigneau*, trans. Vera Traill (New York: Dover, 1972), pp. 71–74.

41. See Royal Brown, "Jean-Luc Godard: Nihilism Versus Aesthetic Distantiation," in *Focus on Godard*, ed. Royal S. Brown (Englewood Cliffs, N.J.: Prentice-Hall, 1972), pp. 109–22.

SELECTED BIBLIOGRAPHY

Bibliographies

Gorbman, Claudia. "Bibliography on Sound in Film" (see section 3, "Music"). *Yale French Studies* 60, no. 1, *Cinema/Sound* (1980), pp. 278–86.

Marks, Martin. "Film Music: The Material, Literature, and Present State of Research." *Notes: Quarterly Journal of the Music Library Association* 36, no. 2 (December 1979): 282–325.

Sharples, Win, Jr. "A Selected and Annotated Bibliography of Books and Articles on Music and the Cinema." *Cinema Journal* 17, no. 2 (1978): 36–67.

Wescott, Steven D. *A Comprehensive Bibliography of Music for Film and Television.* Detroit Studies in Music Bibliography 54. Detroit: Information Coordinators, 1985. 432 pages, indexed.

Books and Selected Articles

Bazelon, Irwin. *Knowing the Score, Notes on Film Music.* New York: Van Nostrand Reinhold, 1975.

Berg, Charles Merrell. *An Investigation of the Motives for and Realization of Music to Accompany the American Silent Film.* New York: Arno, 1976.

Brown, Royal S. "Herrmann, Hitchcock, and the Music of the Irrational." *Cinema Journal* 21, no. 2 (Spring 1982): 14–49; rev. and repr. in *Film Theory and Criticism, Introductory Essays*, ed. Gerald Mast and Marshall Cohen. 3d ed. New York: Oxford University Press, 1985: 618–49.

———. "Music and *Vivre sa vie.*" *Quarterly Review of Film Studies* 5, no. 3 (Summer 1980): 319–33.

Cinéma et musique (1960–1975). Ed. Alain Lacomb. Special issue of *Ecran* 39 (September 1975). Contains a survey of scores from 1960 to 1975, several interviews, articles on jazz, soul music, and pop music in the cinema, and a brief *Dictionnaire* of film composers.

Colpi, Henri. *Défense et illustration de la musique dans le film.* Lyons: SERDOC, 1963.

Eisler, Hanns. *Composing for the Films.* New York: Oxford University Press, 1947; repr. Freeport, N.Y.: Books for Libraries Press, 1971. Translation and modification of the work *Komposition für den Film* by Eisler with Theodor Adorno. The original version was published in 1969 by Rogner and Berhard in Munich.

Evans, Mark. *Soundtrack: The Music of the Movies.* Cinema Studies Series. New York: Hopkinson and Blake, 1975; repr. New York: Da Capo, 1979.

Film Music Notes (later *Film Music* and *Film and TV Music*). Periodical devoted to film music from 1941 to 1957.

Gallez, Douglas. "The Prokofiev-Eisenstein Collaboration: *Nevsky* and *Ivan* Revisited." *Cinema Journal* 17, no. 2 (1978): 13–35.

———. "Theories of Film Music." *Cinema Journal* 9, no. 2 (1970): 40–47.

Gorbman, Claudia. "Narrative Film Music." *Yale French Studies* 60, no. 1, *Cinema/ Sound* (1980): 183–203.

Limbacher, James L., ed. *Film Music: From Violins to Video*. Metuchen, N.J.: Scarecrow Press, 1974. A selection of brief articles and comprehensive, but incomplete and inaccurate, indexes

———. *Keeping Score: Film Music 1972–1979*. Metuchen, N.J.: Scarecrow Press, 1981. A 519-page update of the above, with additions and corrections.

Manvell, Roger and John Huntley. *The Technique of Film Music*. Focal Press Library of Communication Techniques. London: Focal, 1957. 2d ed., rev. and expanded by Richard Arnell and Peter Day. New York: Hasting House, 1975.

Milano, Paulo. "Music in the Film: Notes for a Morphology." *Journal of Aesthetics and Art Criticism* 1, no. 1 (1941): 89–94.

Morton, Lawrence. "The Music of *Objective: Burma*." *Hollywood Quarterly* 1 (1946): 378–95. Cue-by-cue analysis of the Franz Waxman score.

Porcile, François. *La Musique à le'écran*. Paris: Editions du Cerf, 1969.

Prendergast, Roy M. *Film Music, A Neglected Art: A Critical Study of Music in Films*. New York: W. W. Norton, 1977.

Rózsa, Miklós. *Double Life: The Autobiography of Miklós Rózsa*. New York: Hippocrene Books; London: Midas Books, 1983.

Schmidt, Hans-Christian. *Filmmusik, Musik aktuell, Analysen, Beispiele, Kommentare 4*. Basel and London: Bärenreiter Kassel, 1982. Includes a two-disc album of examples.

Steiner, Fred. "Herrmann's 'Black and White' Music for Hitchcock's *Psycho*." *Film Music Notebook* 1, nos. 1–2 (1974): 28–36 and 26–46.

Steiner, Max. "Scoring for Film." In *We Make the Movies*. Ed. Nancy Naumburg. New York: W. W. Norton, 1937: 216–38.

Sternfeld, Frederick. "Copland as a Film Composer" [*The Heiress*]. *Musical Quarterly* 37 (1951): 161–75.

———. "Miklós Rózsa's score for *The Strange Love of Martha Ivers*." *Hollywood Quarterly* 2 (1947): 242–51.

———. "Music and the Feature Films" [Friedhofer's score for *The Best Years of Our Lives*]. *Musical Quarterly* 33 (1947): 517–32.

Thomas, Tony. *Music for the Movies*. New York: A. S. Barnes, 1973.

SELECTED FILMOGRAPHY

This list represents an arbitrary culling of the more than one-hundred films mentioned in this article and is based, with two exceptions, on the availability of recordings; in no way should it be construed as a "best of" anything, as many important composers and scores have been neglected (as they have been in the body of this discussion). Even though only the most recent release has been indicated in most cases, many of the recordings listed are out of print or soon will be. Key: OST: Original Soundtrack. RR: Re-recording.

The Adventures of Robin Hood (USA 1938). Directed by Michael Curtiz. Composed by Erich Korngold. Recordings: (a) Symphonic Suite conducted by Korngold, narrated by Basil Rathbone (repr. on Delos DEL/F 25409); (b) RR score (Varèse Sarabande 704.180); (c) RR score excerpts on *The Sea Hawk* (RCA Red Seal LSC 3330) and *Captain Blood* (RCA Red Seal ARL1–0912).

Alexander Nevsky (USSR 1938). Directed by Sergei Eisenstein. Composed by Serge Prokofiev. Diverse recordings of the concert suite.

Alien (USA 1979). Directed by Ridley Scott. Composed by Jerry Goldsmith. Recording: OST (Twentieth-Century-Fox T 593).

Aliens (USA 1986). Directed by: James Cameron. Composed by: James Horner. Recording: OST (Varèse Sarabande STV 81283).

Altered States. (USA 1980). Directed by: Ken Russell. Composed by: John Corigliano. Recording: OST (RCA Red Seal ABLI–3983).

The Best Years of Our Lives. (USA 1946). Directed by: William Wyler. Composed by: Hugo Friedhofer. Recording: RR (Entr'acte EDP 8101).

The Birth of a Nation (USA 1915). Directed by: D. W. Griffith. Composed by: Joseph Carl Breil. Recording: excerpts of Breil's music (Label X, LXDR 701/2, 2 discs).

The Blue Max (USA 1966). Directed by: John Guillermin. Composed by: Jerry Goldsmith. Recording: OST (Citadel CT 7007; DC with additional music on Varèse Sarabande VCD47238).

The Bride of Frankenstein (USA 1935). Directed by: James Whale. Composed by: Franz Waxman. Recording: RR excerpts on *Sunset Boulevard* (RCA Red Seal ARLI–0708; CD: RCD1–7017) and on *New Recordings from the Films of Franz Waxman* (Varèse Sarabande 704.320).

Brute Force (USA 1947). Directed by: Jules Dassin. Composed by: Miklós Rózsa. Recording: RR of "Background to Violence" Suite (Varèse Sarabande VC 81053).

Carrie (USA 1975). Directed by: Brian De Palma. Composed by: Pino Donaggio. Recording: OST (United Artists UA-LA 716-H).

Citizen Kane (USA 1940). Directed by: Orson Welles. Composed by: Bernard Herrmann. Recording: RR (United Artists UA-LA 372-G); RR excerpts, including *Salambo* aria on *Citizen Kane* (RCA Red Seal ARL 1–0707).

The Cobweb (USA 1955). Directed by: Vincente Minnelli. Composed by: Leonard Rosenman. Recording: OST (MGM 3501).

Deadfall (USA 1968). Directed by: Bryan Forbes. Composed by: John Barry. Recording: OST (Twentieth-Century-Fox 4203).

Deception (USA 1946). Directed by: Irving Rapper. Composed by: Erich Korngold. Recording of the Cello Concerto on *Elizabeth and Essex* (RCA Red Seal ARLI–0185).

Don't Look Now (USA 1973). Directed by: Nicolas Roeg. Composed by: Pino Donaggio. Recording: OST (That's Entertainment TER 1007).

Double Indemnity (USA 1944). Directed by: Billy Wilder. Composed by: Miklós Rózsa. Recording: RR of excerpts on *Spellbound* (RCA Red Seal ARLI–0911); RR of excerpts (Polydor 2383 384).

La Femme Infidèle (France 1968). Directed by: Claude Chabrol. Composed by: Pierre Jansen.

Forbidden Planet (USA 1956). Directed by: Fred McLeod Wilcox. Composed by: Louis and Bebe Barron. Recording: OST (Planet PR–001).

Forever Amber (USA 1947). Directed by: Otto Preminger. Composed by: David Raskin. Recording: RR of suite on *Laura* (RCA Red Seal ARLI–1490).

Gone With the Wind (USA 1939). Director: Victor Fleming. Composed by: Max Steiner. Recording: numerous; best is RR on *Gone With the Wind* (RCA Red Seal ARLI–0452).

Hangover Square (USA 1945). Directed by: John Brahm. Composed by: Bernard Herrmann. Recording: Concerto on *Citizen Kane* (RCA Red Seal ARLI–0707).

Hemingway's Adventures of a Young Man (USA 1962). Directed by: Martin Ritt. Composed by: Franz Waxman. Recording: OST (Entr'acte ERS 6516ST; CD on Label X LXCD 1).

The Hindenburg (USA 1975). Directed by: Robert Wise. Music by David Shire. Recording: OST (MCA 2090).

Ivan the Terrible, Parts 1 and 2 (USSR 1945–1946). Directed by: Sergei Eisenstein. Composed by: Serge Prokofiev. Recording: Oratorio conducted by Abram Stasevich (Melodiya/Angel RB–4103, 2 discs) and by Riccardo Muti (Angel SB–3851, 2 discs).

Journey to the Center of the Earth (USA 1959). Directed by: Henry Levin. Composed by: Bernard Herrmann. Recording: RR of excerpts on *The Fantasy Film World of Bernard Herrmann* (London Phase 4 SP 44207).

King Kong (USA 1933). Directed by: Merian C. Cooper and Ernest B. Schoedsack. Composed by: Max Steiner. Recording: RR (Southern Cross SCAR 5006; CD on Southern Cross SCCD 901).

King's Row (USA 1945). Directed by: Sam Wood. Composed by: Erich Korngold. Recording: RR (Chalfont SDG 305; CD on Varèse Sarabande VCD 47203).

Koyaanisqatsi (USA 1983). Directed by: Godfrey Reggio. Composed by: Philip Glass. Recording: OST (Antilles ASTA 1).

Mishima (Japan 1985). Directed by: Paul Shraeder. Composed by: Philip Glass. Recording: OST (Nonesuch 9 79113).

The New Babylon (USSR 1928–29). Directed by: Grigori Kozintsev and Leonid Trauberg. Music by Dmitri Shostakovich. Recording: Concert suite (Columbia/Melodiya M 34502).

The Night Visitor (USA 1970). Directed by: Laslo Benedek. Music by Henry Mancini. Recording: Concert suite from OST (Citadel CT–6501).

North by Northwest (USA 1959). Directed by: Alfred Hitchcock. Composed by: Bernard Herrmann. Recording: RR (Starlog/Varèse Sarabande SV 95001; CD on Varèse Sarabande VCD 47205); RR excerpts on *Music from the Great Movie Thrillers* (London Phase 4 SP 44126).

The Omen (USA 1976). Directed by: Richard Donner. Composed by: Jerry Goldsmith. Recording: OST (Tattoo BJL1–1888).

Once Upon a Time in America (USA 1983). Directed by: Sergio Leone. Composed by: Ennio Morricone. Recording: OST (Mercury 898 697–1 M–1).

Pierrot le fou (France 1965). Directed by: Jean-Luc Godard. Composed by: Antoine Duhamel. Recording: OST (RCA [France] Ciné Music PL 37645).

Planet of the Apes (USA 1968). Directed by: Franklin J. Schaffner. Composed by: Jerry Goldsmith. Recording: OST (Project 3 PR 5023SD).

Psycho (USA 1960). Directed by: Alfred Hitchcock. Composed by: Bernard Herrmann. Recording: RR (Unicorn RHS 336; diverse reissues); concert suit on *Music from the Great Movie Thrillers* (London Phase 4 SP 44126).

Re-Animator (USA 1985). Directed by: Stuart Gordon. Composed by: Richard Band. Recording: OST (Varèse Sarabande STV 81261).

Rebecca (USA 1940). Directed by: Alfred Hitchcock. Composed by: Franz Waxman. Recording: Concert suite on *Sunset Boulevard* (RCA Red Seal ARL 1–0708).

The Red Shoes (Great Britain 1948). Directed by: Michael Powell and Emeric Pressburger.

Composed by: Brian Easdale. Recording: RR of ballet, with cuts (Odyssey 32 16 0338).

Runaway (USA 1985). Directed by: Michael Crichton. Composed by: Jerry Goldsmith. Recording: OST (Varèse Sarabande STV 81234; CD: Varèse Sarabande VCD 47221).

La Rupture (France 1970). Directed by: Claude Chabrol. Composed by: Pierre Jansen.

The Sea Hawk (USA 1940). Directed by: Michael Curtiz. Composed by: Erich Korngold. Recording: RR of excerpts on *The Sea Hawk* (RCA Red Seal LSC 3330) and *Captain Blood* (RCA Red Seal ARLI–0912).

Spartacus (USA 1960). Directed by: Stanley Kubrick. Composed by: Alex North. Recording: OST (Decca DL 9092).

Spellbound (USA 1945). Directed by: Alfred Hitchcock. Composed by: Miklós Rózsa. Recording: RR impressions (Stanyan 4021); RR excerpts on *Spellbound* (RCA Red Seal ARLI–0911).

Star Wars (USA 1977). Directed by: George Lucas. Composed by: John Williams. Recording: OST (Twentieth-Century-Fox 2T–541, 2 discs); numerous RR's of excerpts, suites, etc.

A Streetcar Named Desire (USA 1951). Directed by: Elia Kazan. Composed by: Alex North. Recording: OST (Angel S–36068).

Vertigo (USA 1958). Directed by: Alfred Hitchcock. Composed by: Bernard Herrmann. Recording: OST (Mercury Golden Imports SRI 75117); RR excerpts on *Music from the Great Movie Thrillers* (London Phase 4 SP 44126).

Wuthering Heights (USA 1939). Directed by: William Wyler. Composed by: Alfred Newman. Recording: RR (Film Music Collection FMC–6).

8

FILM AND POPULAR MUSIC

GARY BURNS

INTRODUCTION

From the almost simultaneous development of cinema and the phonograph in the late nineteenth century to the music video explosion a century later, film and music have interacted in one of the most complex and interesting cases of media symbiosis. From at least the time of Lumière's first screenings in 1895, it has been recognized that film needs music. The converse is not quite true—radio and records, not to mention concert music, got along nicely for many years without visual accompaniment of any kind. However, television eventually demonstrated that live music (the kind radio had been broadcasting for years) could benefit from pictures. Music video is now carrying the process one step further with the visualization of records. The results so far have been controversial from an aesthetic standpoint but quite successful commercially. Meanwhile, the film industry has for many years had its own ways of "illustrating" music, ranging from the production numbers in Hollywood musicals to the animated accompaniment of Beatles music in *Yellow Submarine* (1968).

This chapter focuses on the history of the interaction of film and popular music and on the genres of recordings, music, and film that have developed in the process of that interaction. The history is presented in narrative fashion, without division into major periods, but with the assumption that the major turning points occurred in the late 1920s with the arrival of synchronous sound; the early 1950s, thanks to rock and roll, television, and major structural changes in the film industry; and the 1980s, with music video, the movie soundtrack boom, and the highly developed interconnection between the film and recording industries. The discussion of genres concludes with a brief consideration of film music's functions and the theory of integration.

Writing about two media or art forms necessarily involves research in two bodies of literature. One of the most striking differences between the film and popular music publications that I have reviewed is that the latter consistently emphasises the role of blacks, Southern Americans, and the disaffected young in shaping the popular culture of the twentieth century. The literature on film, even musical film, tends to overlook the contributions of people like Dorothy Dandridge, Lena Horne, Tex Ritter, Elvis Presley, and the Beatles. This gap in the literature is a problem in itself but also indicates one way in which there has been a *lack* of symbiosis between two industries. This lack has a history all its own, largely hidden, and certainly not covered adequately in the research literature. Consideration of the film industry's "ghettoization" and exploitation of the music of blacks, Southerners, youth, and others is one of the main areas in which the present chapter is incomplete and further research is needed.

HISTORICAL DEVELOPMENT

The possiblity for music and film interacting has only existed since the invention of film, a few years after the invention of the phonograph in the late nineteenth century. Consequently, the relation between film and popular music can for the most part be traced historically as the relation between two technological and industrial systems of communication.

"Phonograph" originally referred to a cylinder player invented by Thomas Edison in 1877.[1] The operating principle of the phonograph was to use the vibration of sound waves as the driving force behind a recording stylus or needle which carved a groove in a rotating cylinder. To play back the recording, another stylus would "read" the groove and an attached diaphragm would vibrate in a manner analogous to the original sound. The diaphragm was located near the throat of a horn, which provided natural amplification for the very soft signal.

Supposedly the first recording ever made was Edison reciting "Mary Had a Little Lamb." For the first time in history, it was possible to hear a recording of one's own voice. Edison later recalled: "I was never so taken aback in my life."[2]

Edison's early plans for the exploitation of his new invention centered mainly around the spoken word and the possible business uses of recording. In an 1878 article Edison listed ten functions he foresaw for the phonograph. Leading the list was "[l]etter writing and all kinds of dictation without the aid of a stenographer."[3] The inventor went on to describe in some detail such possibilities as talking books, home recording of family members' voices, and recorded school lessons. Musical uses of the phonograph were summarized tersely in two items: "Reproduction of music" and "Music-boxes and toys."[4]

But before long, music came to overshadow other kinds of content in phonograph records. In 1887 Alexander Graham Bell and Charles Sumner Tainter introduced their "graphophone," an improved version of the phonograph. It had an electric motor (rather than a hand crank), which prevented annoying speed fluctuations in recording and playback. The next year, Edison incorporated an electric motor into his phonograph and recorded pianist Josef Hofmann, in his first serious attempt at music recording.

Although Edison was not inclined to develop records as an entertainment medium, others were, particularly the various regional subsidiaries of the North American Phonograph Company, which had been formed by businessman Jesse H. Lippincott in 1888 for the purpose of selling phonographs. Around 1890 the subsidiary companies introduced an early version of the jukebox, which promptly became the company's greatest source of profits. Jukeboxes were located in public gathering places, not in homes or offices. They served a recreational function and established popular music as the mainstay of the commercial recording industry.

Meanwhile, Edison and others were making rapid advances in motion picture technology. Although film was primarily a visual medium until the late 1920s, Edison's plans in the 1880s included combining film and the phonograph. In an 1888 document filed with the U.S. Patent Office, Edison declared "I am experimenting upon an instrument which does for the Eye what the phonograph does for the Ear. . . . "[5] He then described his kinetograph camera and kinetoscope playback device as they might be used in conjunction with a phonograph:

By gearing or connecting the Kinetograph by a positive mechanical movement, a continuous Record of all motion is taken down on the Kinetograph & a continuous record of all sounds are [sic] taken down by the phonograph. and [sic] by substituting the phonograph recording devices on the Kinetograph for a Microscope Stand & objective it becomes a Kinetoscope & by insertion of the listening tubes of the phonograph into the ear The [sic] illusion is complete and we may see & hear a whole Opera as perfectly as if actually present although the actual performance may have taken place years before.[6]

The combination device Edison referred to was known variously as a kinetograph, kinetophonograph, or kinetophone, the latter being the name under which it was sold once it was finally manufactured in 1895. The machine did unite sound and pictures, but not synchronously as Edison had planned. The kinetophone was, along with the silent kinetoscope, a coin-operated machine, similar to a jukebox except that it was designed for private viewing/listening. Apparently only forty-five kinetophones were made. The sound they played was popular music supplied by the Edison Company on cylinder: "Linger Longer Lucy," "Pomona Waltz," "Continental March," "Irish Reel," and others.[7]

At about this same time, public projection of motion pictures was getting underway in the United States and Europe. Musical accompaniment was recognized as a necessity even for some of the earliest screenings. According to Charles Hofmann, "[w]hen the Lumière brothers exhibited their first films in Paris in 1895, these films were accompanied by piano improvisations based on popular tunes. During this period George Méliès, Thomas Edison, and early filmmakers used music with their exhibitions."[8]

Film quickly became associated with popular music.[9] Initially, films had great novelty appeal and were used as part of the program in vaudeville shows and music halls, especially from 1896 to 1900. As the novelty effect wore off, films came to be used as the "chaser" at the end of the show. In the early 1900s the location of film exhibition shifted from vaudeville houses to arcades, tents, storefront theaters, and nickelodeons. As filmmakers grew more sophisticated in telling stories and began making films longer than a few minutes in length, film became able to stand on its own as a featured attraction. As Charles Berg notes, this "prompted exhibitors to provide inexpensive musical accompaniments rendered by mechanical instruments, unsynchronized phonograph recordings and insensitive pianists to neutralize distracting noises and silence and to provide continuity."[10]

After a brief disaffiliation in the early 1900s, film and vaudeville once again came together starting around 1908. By this time film was well on its way to being a big business and a well-developed art. Over the next few years, theaters became more and more the domain of films. Not only were many vaudeville theaters converted partially or entirely into movie houses, but in 1914 the first major theater built specifically for movies—the Strand—opened in New York. The Strand was a harbinger of the spectacular picture palaces to follow and a symbol of the cultural importance film had attained.

With films running to feature length, the task of providing live musical accompaniment became more demanding. As the art of film grew more mature and respectable, so did the art of film music. Camille Saint-Saëns composed a score for the 1908 Film d'Art production *The Assassination of the Duke of Guise*. D. W. Griffith took intense interest in the music that accompanied his films, notably in the case of *The Birth of a Nation* (1915), for which Griffith and Joseph Carl Breil assembled a score consisting of both classical and popular music. The film and its score were such successes that orchestral scores became common in films, especially major feature films.

One factor mitigating against the use of orchestras, however, was their expense. Exhibitors adopted various strategies to save money on the cost of musicians. The use of large orchestras was fairly well restricted to major theaters in large cities. In other locations, small ensembles or solo piano players were common. In addition, as Berg points out, "[during] the first two decades of film's existence, [musicians] were [often] overworked to the point of being expected to play from nine to twelve hours per day."[11]

Pipe organs were used in film theaters as early as 1905.[12] The Wurlitzer company introduced its first theater organ around 1912, initiating a process of technological and industrial development which soon led to the "Mighty Wurlitzer," a theatrical organ which made it possible for one musician to mimic an orchestra and create all kinds of sound effects.[13] Exhibitors liked the versatility of this organ (and its numerous competitors) and the fact that it allowed them to cut their payroll for musicians substantially.[14]

Similar economies were made where possible in the composition of musical scores. As Berg points out, many silent film scores were compilations of unoriginal material (*The Birth of a Nation* is an example). Film thus revived the tradition of the pasticcio opera of the eighteenth century.[15] Cue sheets worked on a similar principle. The first known example was a list of "Music Cues" published in 1909 in the *Edison Kinetogram*.[16] Cue sheets suggested types of music or specific compositions to be used to accompany the different scenes in a film. As the scene changed, the music would change, turning the score into a compilation of sorts no matter what music was used. Cue sheets eventually became very sophisticated and were often used in conjunction with volumes of sheet music composed and labeled according to mood. One of the earliest such volumes was published in 1913 by the Sam Fox Publishing Company.

The ability to mix classical and popular music styles freely in early film music is indicative of the musical climate around the turn of the century. At that time piano playing was quite common, especially among young women, meaning that the classical repertoire and associated music theory had at least a foothold in the general population.[17] The popular music industry was oriented toward the writer and publisher, vaudeville, and the large retail trade in sheet music. Tin Pan Alley represented the apex of these trends. Parlor songs, minstrel shows and "coon songs," novelty tunes, and patriotic numbers were among the most popular types of music around the turn of the century, but classical music also had a broad appeal. The first million-selling record was Enrico Caruso's 1903 recording of a number from Leoncavallo's *Pagliacci*. The second and third million-sellers were minstrel-type songs (1905, 1910); the fourth and fifth were Al Jolson records (1912, 1913); and the sixth was a spoken-word comedy record (1914).[18] The most obvious feature shared by this rather variegated group is the human voice, something which silent film per se could not provide. While the instrumental music that played during silent films reflected the diversity of American music as a whole, vocal music used before, between, and after films came mostly from Tin Pan Alley.

Around 1907 "song-slides" were introduced.[19] While a live singer performed, slides were projected showing the printed song lyrics. Later versions used illustrations rather than printed words. Occasionally film was used instead of slides. What this amounted to was using film to accompany music, rather than vice versa. Berg discusses several attempts to do this with classical music.[20] The main purpose in most of these cases was to break new artistic ground. When *popular* music was the starting point, added visuals were used mainly to sell the song; sheet music copies were often sold in the theater lobby. "After the Ball" and "Home Sweet Home" were two of the songs for which such films were made.[21] Song-slides and illustrative films for songs marked the beginning of an aesthetic tradition which includes production numbers in musical films, interludes in otherwise nonmusical films (eg., "Raindrops Keep Fallin' on My Head" in *Butch Cassidy and the Sundance Kid* [1969], and especially music video.

The economic function of song-slides also persisted and came to be known as song plugging. Theme songs were introduced as a way to connect the music plug directly to a feature film. Numerous cross-promotional angles were exploited. The theme song was released in sheet music form, sometimes with a picture of the film star on the cover. One or more recordings of the song would

also be released, including one sung by the film star if possible. The song would
be played before and perhaps during the film. For openings and other special
occasions, the star would appear in person at the theater to sing.[22] *Mickey* (1918)
was apparently the first film to have a title song written specifically for it.[23]
Hofmann provides numerous other examples, including *Don Juan* (1926) and
Ramona (1928) with theme songs of the same name, and *What Price Glory?*
(1926, theme song "Charmaine") and *Seventh Heaven* (1927, theme song "Diane").[24]

The song "Ramona" was given "much of the credit for the million and a
half brought in by the picture."[25] It was the biggest theme song success to date
and placed theme songs on a secure footing as a promotional device just in time
for the sound film era. In addition, "Ramona" heralded the age of the multimedia
star. Dolores Del Rio starred in the film, recorded the song, and sang it on
radio.[26] Her picture appeared on the cover of the sheet music. Although her
success as a recording artist was short-lived, she had a lengthy career in film
and on the stage.

Although music had been gradually gaining in importance as one of the in-
gredients of music, *The Jazz Singer* (1927) set off an explosion of interest in
synchronous sound, hastening the arrival of "all-talk" feature films and fore-
shadowing the flood of musicals which started in the late 1920s. *The Jazz Singer*
had already enjoyed a successful run as a stage play and was "loosely based on
[Al] Jolson's own life-story...."[27] The film built upon Jolson's star image
previously established on the stage and in recordings. As Ivor Montagu pointed
out, one major reason for the overwhelming commercial success of *The Jazz
Singer* was that "for the first time the talking-singing film was a first feature
starring a singer who, in his own field, was a unique popular (*popular*, not
classical) singing star."[28]

To encourage and capitalize upon the film's success, Brunswick Records
released Jolson's recordings of several songs from *The Jazz Singer*. As musical
films appeared by the dozens over the next few years, the three major record
companies—Victor, Columbia, and Brunswick—released hundreds of recordings
of theme songs and other music drawn from films. Movie magazines facilitated
sales of these records by establishing columns devoted to film music. One of
the first columns appeared in *Photoplay* starting in October 1929. The column
reviewed about twenty records a month, in many cases including more than one
song from the same film. Initially the column reviewed player piano rolls of
movie songs as well, but this service was eliminated after the first month.[29]

The Jazz Singer and its successors quickly made live musical accompaniment
of films obsolete. The bigger theaters continued to use live music before and
after films for many years, but despite this the arrival of sync sound had a
calamitous effect on the job market for musicians. As Berg notes, "for the
majority of musicians who had provided live music for the film there was unemployment, relocation and retraining for new jobs."[30] The theater organ, which
had previously eliminated musicians' jobs, was now itself eliminated, putting

the organists out of work. With the arrival of sound stages, musicians could no longer be employed, as they had been since around 1913, to play mood music on the set during the production of a film.[31]

Of course, the industry still needed musicians to produce its new, standardized musical soundtracks. But these jobs were all in Hollywood, which consequently became more firmly established as one of the major centers of the music industry. The change was part of what Berg called a "basic shift in the music industry's division of labor" involving "the transfer of responsibility for the sound accompaniment from the exhibitor to the producer."[32] As responsibility was transferred, so was control.

Following the success of *The Jazz Singer*, studios quickly sought to consolidate this control (and therefore their profits) by buying into the established music industry, which at that time was dominated by Tin Pan Alley. The studios concentrated on hiring the best-known Tin Pan Alley songwriters and on buying, establishing, or contracting with music publishing firms.

By the end of the twenties, Warner Brothers had purchased Witmarks, a major music publisher. Fox had contracted with the writing-publishing team of (Buddy) De Sylva, (Lew) Brown, and (Ray) Henderson for use of writers and songs in Fox films. MGM had a similar agreement, with Jack Robbins Music Company. Paramount had formed Famous Music Company as an umbrella organization for a number of established publishers including T. B. Harms, Remick's, Chappell-Harms, and Spier and Coslow. For several years starting around 1927, many of the most successful Tin Pan Alley writers worked under contract to the Hollywood studios. Besides Henderson, Brown, and De Sylva, the list included Irving Berlin, L. Wolfe Gilbert, Con Conrad, Dave Dreyer, Louis Silvers, Nacio Herb Brown, Harry Akst, and Fred Fischer.[33] As Alexander Walker notes, the film companies were eager to develop hit theme songs. The studios were interested in the publishing business "not just to protect their source of supply, but for all the extra royalties to be squeezed out of sheet-music sales, records, rolls, sound synchronisation discs, etc. . . . Possession of so many allied musical outlets was one of the reasons why the Hollywood musical flourished early and over-abundantly in the sound era."[34]

The Jazz Singer had been a trendsetting musical in a number of respects, particularly in its "backstage" plot and in the fact that it was an adaptation of a Broadway musical. In addition, *The Jazz Singer* marked a transition in the use of background music. Much of the film consisted of silent-type footage with a synchronous musical track, in essence giving the soundtrack the background role heretofore assumed by live musicians. *Don Juan* had done this same thing a year earlier without including breaks for singing numbers as *The Jazz Singer* did. By the time of *Lights of New York* (1928), usually considered the first "all-talkie," background music had been pushed firmly to the background. Although music played through much of *Lights of New York*, the film is usually not considered a musical. Thus *The Jazz Singer* helped establish the convention of the production number as functionally different from background music and as the sine qua non in the new genre known as the musical film. In many ways this was only a perpetuation of conventions already established in musical theater and silent film, but was nevertheless only one direction out of many that sound film might have emphasized.

Musicals "redefine music as singing," as Jane Feuer put it.[35] Singing was the only musical thing that was new in the films of the late 1920s. Film audiences were not used to hearing singing (or talking) during a film, but were quite accustomed to instrumental background music and sound effects. Historian John Kobal argues that "sound found no takers as long as silent films were successful; it only came into its own because of radio."[36] Whether this is true or not, it is striking that the sound film was born just as radio was developing into a national entertainment medium rivaling film in power and importance.

What John Kobal posits as a competitive relationship between film and radio actually had its symbolic side as well, particularly for stardom. Radio provided one more medium of exposure for film stars able to make the transition to sound. More importantly, radio developed stars of its own, many of whom eventually crossed over into film. The key points where film and radio intersected were drama, comedy in various forms, and music (which in most cases meant singing). The most successful crossover stars were multitalented entertainers, many of them trained in vaudeville. Bing Crosby is probably the outstanding example.

Crosby, the quintessential crooner, started in vaudeville, appeared in radio with Paul Whiteman's band from 1927 to 1929, made some records with Gus Arnheim's band for Victor in 1930, and first appeared in film with Whiteman in *King of Jazz* (1930). He became a national radio star on CBS in 1931. His success established that "[f]rom that point forward, the singer of popular songs could expect eventually to be on equal footing with the dance band."[37] Crooning was somewhat scandalous at first for its sensualness and jazz or blues inflections, but it quickly became synonymous with what we would now call mainstream pop. Crooners became fixtures in film musicals almost immediately. Crosby himself became a film star in *The Big Broadcast* (1932), the first in a series of Big Broadcast films which glamorized radio and provided film exposure for many radio stars.

The Big Broadcast series was a variation on the all-star revue and backstage formulas popular in early musicals. Revues consisted of stars-on-parade and were essentially vaudeville on film, used to promote a particular studio. *The Hollywood Revue of 1929* (MGM, 1929) was the first. It was followed by *The Show of Shows* (Warner Bros., 1929), *Paramount on Parade* (Paramount, 1930), and the aforementioned *King of Jazz* (Universal). Plot was minimal or nonexistent in the revue films.

Backstage musicals did not usually have much of a plot either, but were considered somewhat ingenious because musical numbers were incorporated into the usually predictable story. *The Broadway Melody* (1929) began a cycle of backstage musicals that did not reach fruition until a "second wave" of block-buster musicals began with *42nd Street* in 1933. This film featured the wild choreography of Busby Berkeley, who demonstrated the spectacular effects made possible by choreographing everything—dancers, sets, and the camera. Berkeley's production numbers easily provided the high points of the films they appeared in. Although the action officially took place backstage or onstage, many of his productions took off into a fantasy world bearing no resemblance to the theatrical setting where the film was supposed to be taking place. Berkeley is best remembered for his films at Warner Brothers, which included *Gold Diggers of 1933* (1933), *Footlight Parade* (1933), and *Gold Diggers of 1935* (1935).

One other major subgenre among early musicals was the operetta. The first was *The Desert Song* in 1929. It was followed quickly by many others, including Rouben Mamoulian's *Love Me Tonight* (1932) and Ernst Lubitsch's *The Love Parade* (1929) and *The Merry Widow* (1934). *The Love Parade* starred Maurice Chevalier and Jeanette MacDonald in her screen debut. These two stars, along with MacDonald's frequent co-star Nelson Eddy, were among the most popular performers in the film musicals in the 1930s. The MacDonald–Eddy partnership began in 1935 with *Naughty Marietta* and lasted through *I Married an Angel* in 1942.

In contrast to the operetta as "singer's musical" stood the "dancer's musical." Berkeley's work had shown how vital dance could be in film. Fred Astaire and Ginger Rogers took the next step and began to establish the dance musical as a star vehicle, starting with *Flying Down to Rio* in 1933. Astaire and Rogers appeared in a series of nine films through 1939, and reunited for *The Barkleys of Broadway* in 1949. Their dance routines focused on the individual and couple rather than the large chorus, and contributed to a general movement toward intimacy in musical films.

By the end of the 1930s, musicals were in their second period of decline in slightly more than a decade of existence. The first dry spell had started in 1930 and lasted until *42nd Street* in 1933. During the first "moratorium," few musicals were released. Market saturation and the Depression are generally cited as the major causes of the first lull in production of musicals. The 1933 resurgence was short-lived. According to Allen L. Woll, "[b]y 1937 the Hollywood musical was in a state of crisis. Musical films were not drawing audiences . . . Warner Brothers began to dismantle its music department . . . [In 1938] M-G-M announced that only one out of six future films would be musicals, while Columbia scheduled none in its list of future productions."[38] The Tin Pan Alley songwriters and other professionals from the music business who had migrated to Hollywood a few years earlier began to head back east in droves. Those musicals that were made used fewer chorus dancers and were generally more intimate, that is, cheaply produced.

In the 1940s additional pressures had an impact on the Hollywood musical. As World War II intensified, the foreign market for Hollywood films shrank. Antitrust actions brought an end to block-booking in 1946 and shortly thereafter forced the studios to give up their theater chains. According to Kobal, "[t]he effect of all this was a tightening of the financial reins, and a greater reliance on scripts and directors. . . . Just as the thirties had been dominated by the great stars, . . . the forties was to mark the decade of the directors. During and after the war, the two most successful genres were the 'film noir' and the musical, in both of which, to a greater degree the director was the master.''[39] The point is more valid if we include studios and producers along with directors.

MGM emerged in the forties as the most important studio for musicals. According to Jerome Delamater, ''[t]he great period of MGM musicals probably began in 1939 with Arthur Freed's productions of *Babes in Arms* and *The Wizard of Oz*.''[40] Freed went on to produce many of the most commercially successful and critically acclaimed musicals of the forties and fifties, including *Meet Me in St. Louis* (1944), *On the Town* (1949), *An American in Paris* (1951), *Singin' in the Rain* (1952), *The Band Wagon* (1953), and *Gigi* (1958).

Many significant figures in the history of the musical emerged during this period as part of the Freed-MGM coterie. Outstanding among these were directors Vincente Minnelli and Stanley Donen, performers Judy Garland, Mickey Rooney, Cyd Charisse, and Leslie Caron, and the multitalented Gene Kelly. In addition, Freed worked with established talents including Fred Astaire, Busby Berkeley, Rouben Mamoulian, and many others.

One of Freed's major contributions was to encourage original film musicals, as opposed to adaptations of Broadway productions. These resulted, as Delamater puts it, ''not in extravaganzas, but in more intimate, well-defined production numbers which grew out of the narratives, yet governed the visual and audio style of the entire film.''[41] The idea that musical numbers should ''grow out of the narrative'' is the main tenet in the theory of the ''integrated musical,'' which holds that song and story should come together symbiotically rather than interfere with each other.[42] Freed and his collaborators' sensitive handling of this integration is itself a landmark in the history of the musical.

Also working at MGM in the forties (and through the sixties) was producer Joe Pasternak, who ''specialized in the glossy boy-meets-girl-soprano films.''[43] In the thirties at Universal he had made several successful musicals starring Deanna Durbin. While at MGM he discovered Mario Lanza and became known as a popularizer of classical music. Later he made musicals with Elvis Presley and other rock stars and provided something of a historical link between rock films and classical Hollywood musicals. Pasternak's major films included *Three Smart Girls* (with Durbin, 1936) and *The Great Caruso* (with Lanza, 1951).

Other noteworthy developments in the forties included the rise of Twentieth-Century-Fox and Disney as major producers of musicals. Fox specialized in the development of female stars, especially ''Fox blondes.'' As Kobal explains, ''[t]he Fox blonde policy had begun back in the thirties, when the films of Shirley Temple, the reigning queen, were used to launch Alice Faye. When she became queen, Alice Faye did the same for Betty Grable, who did the same for June Haver, who did the same for Marilyn Monroe.''[44] Among the major musical films of these stars were *Little Miss Marker* (Temple, 1934), *Poor Little Rich Girl* (Temple and Faye, 1936), *Alexander's Ragtime Band* (Faye, 1938, also starring Ethel Merman), *Down Argentine Way* (Grable, 1940, also starring Carmen Miranda), and *Gentlemen Prefer Blondes* (Monroe, 1953, also starring Jane Russell). Disney was the major pioneer of the animated musical, beginning with the experimentation of *Steamboat Willie* (1928) and *The Three Little Pigs* (1933) and continuing through such feature films as *Snow White and the Seven Dwarfs* (1938), *Pinocchio* (1940), and *Fantasia* (1940).

Musicals related to World War II abounded in the 1940s. Warner Brothers led the way in this field and had one of the biggest successes with *Yankee Doodle Dandy* (1942), a "biopic" about George M. Cohan.[45] Also very popular in the forties was Paramount's Road series starring Bing Crosby, Bob Hope, and Dorothy Lamour. The series started in 1940 with *Road to Singapore* and lasted for another six films, ending in 1962 with *The Road to Hong Kong*.

The fifties produced "the pinnacle" of the musical genre in *Singing' in the Rain* and one of its "supreme achievements" in George Cukor's *A Star Is Born* (1954).[46] Nevertheless, this decade is generally regarded as a period of decline for the musical. Television was causing a drastic drop in movie attendance, and the TV variety program was in its heyday, giving people less reason to go out for musical/visual entertainment. Film musicals generally became less adventurous. Original screen musicals became rare, with the studios concentrating instead on Broadway adaptations (e.g., *Guys and Dolls* [1955], *Oklahoma!* [1955]) and remakes of old films (e.g., *A Star Is Born*).

More importantly, the fifties saw the beginning of rock and roll, a rebellious-sounding music that bore little resemblance to Tin Pan Alley, crooning, or show tunes. Rock and roll made its first big splash in film with *Blackboard Jungle* (1955), in which Bill Haley and His Comets sang "Rock Around the Clock" over the credits.[47] Immediately rock and roll became associated with juvenile delinquency and generational conflict, a theme that would persist in rock films.

Stylistically, early rock films did not differ much from the musical films that had come before them. Theme songs and song plugging abounded. "Rock Around the Clock" reappeared in a film of the same name in 1956. The title of Elvis Presley's first film in 1956 was changed to fit the song "Love Me Tender." Attempts were made to integrate rock musical numbers smoothly into the narrative as early as Presley's *Jailhouse Rock* in 1957. Presley's films (and many other rock films) were invariably star vehicles, extending a tradition born in the earliest days of musical films.

Important changes, long in the making, suddenly became noticeable in the relationship between film and popular music. To start with, song plugging was now, more precisely, record plugging. As early as 1920, record sales occasionally exceeded sheet music sales of some songs.[48] The phonograph, automobile, and player piano, along with the Depression, dealt severe blows to the piano industry starting in the 1930s,[49] while jukeboxes, theater organs, sound film, disc jockeys, and the use of organs and records on the radio all, at various times, eroded the job market for musicians.[50] These factors, plus the rise of the BMI (Broadcast Music, Incorporated) music licensing firm (which helped develop a new generation of popular songwriters) and the development of singing stars and hit parades, gradually made records more important than sheet music. Such 1940s and 1950s innovations as tape recording, LPs, 45-rpm records, and stereo made records even more attractive. In addition, at least part of the technical sophistication rock records would soon be known for may be attributable to sound-mixing practices in the film industry.[51]

The film and recording industries were becoming more closely related than they had ever been before. The rise of the LP format brought the success of soundtrack albums such as *Words and Music* (1948), *An American in Paris* (1951), *Oklahoma!* (1955), *Around the World in 80 Days* (film 1956, LP 1957), *Gigi* (1958), *South Pacific* (1958), *West Side Story* (1961), *Mary Poppins* (1964), *Goldfinger* (1964), and *The Sound of Music* (1965)—all of which rose to number one on the album charts.[52] Rock and roll soundtrack albums also did consistently well, especially when the film was a star vehicle for someone like Presley. Henry Mancini's soundtrack album for the TV series *Peter Gunn* (1959) was a milestone that paved the way for pop-flavored instrumental film scores including *Goldfinger*, *Doctor Zhivago* (1965), *The Good, the Bad, and the Ugly* (film 1966, LP 1968), *Love Story* (1970), and Mancini's own subsequent efforts. Mark Evans complains that

> [p]roducers were quick to jump on the bandwagon. From a business standpoint, they reached two conclusions. First, they decided that film scores could sell records. Second, they determined that these records should be oriented as much as possible toward pop music. So they made a concerted effort to find composers who would provide, not dramatic underscoring, but commercially viable pop pieces that could be exploited on records. The entrance of record company executives into the film music field changed it forever. For the first time, a key element in evaluating the worth of a score was totally divorced from the motion picture itself: Could the score sell records?[53]

Evans goes on to deplore the 1960s trend toward employment of rock stars, rather than composers, to score films. Many of these stars, Evans notes, could not even read music, and it thus became necessary to hire "take-down artists" to transcribe the stars' creations.[54]

Rock musicians generally lack the training and/or outlook of the professional film composer or the "production writer" employed to write songs for film musicals in the 1920s and 1930s. For this reason, among others, the marriage of rock and film has been based largely on the ability of film to adapt to rock. There have been relatively few good rock "scores" written specifically for films. Instead, films are often produced specifically to fit existing recordings. Alternatively, soundtracks may be constructed from "found" records that are thought to contribute the right mood or period flavor to a film.

Fitting the film to the music is a general trend which has developed along at least five rather separate avenues. First, star vehicle films have been spiced up in order to convey the energy of rock music. Richard Lester's *A Hard Day's*

Night, starring the Beatles (1964), set the standard for rock films of this sort with its combination of handheld cameras, fast editing, location shooting, and use of multiple cameras.

Second, lightweight cameras, zoom lenses, fast film, and improved microphones have made it possible to use cinéma vérité techniques in documentaries about rock concerts and rock stars. The first feature-length "rockumentary" was *The T.A.M.I. Show* (1964), the record of a 1964 concert at the Santa Monica (California) Civic Auditorium.[55] The best-known examples of this subgenre came a few years later with films such as *Monterey Pop* (1969), *Woodstock* (1970), and *Gimme Shelter* (1970).

Third, animated films have been built around rock records, starting with the Beatles' *Yellow Submarine*. Ralph Bakshi has been the major practitioner in this field (e.g., *Heavy Traffic* [1973], *American Pop* [1981]).

Fourth, rock operas have emerged as the ultimate form of concept album and a new subgenre of film, with *Tommy* (LP 1969, film 1975) and *Jesus Christ Superstar* (LP 1971, film 1973) being among the earliest examples. Rock opera films differ markedly from pop predecessors such as *The Umbrellas of Cherbourg* (1964) in that they are more firmly grounded in songs and are more presentational in their visual and narrative structure (e.g., the visual extravagance of *Tommy*, the use of choruses and the "camp" presentation of Herod in *Jesus Christ Superstar*).

Fifth, music video has arisen as the latest form of song plugging, building specifically on the tradition of song-slides and Soundies (short films or film excerpts used to promote popular records and feature films in the forties and fifties, played on a visual jukebox called a Soundie or Soundola and often shown in theaters as trailers.[56] Music video became a major ingredient of American television with the establishment of the MTV (Music Television) cable network in 1981 and has had a strong aesthetic influence on many feature films, *Flashdance* (1983) being a notable example.

Use of "found" records as the basis for a film score has been another major tendency in the rock music era. Among the trendsetters in this practice have been *The Graduate* (1967), *Easy Rider* (1969), *American Graffiti* (1973), *Coming Home* (1978), and *The Big Chill* (1983), all of which (except *Coming Home*) produced best-selling soundtrack albums.

The widespread use of rock music in films has been the major aesthetic manifestation of increased corporate interlinkage of the film and recording industries, bringing to full fruition a symbiotic relationship that was remarkably slow in developing.[57] Ownership ties between the two industries date back to the late nineteenth century when the Edison Company had a leading role in both. But Edison left the movie business in 1917 and the record business in 1929. The Pathé company, based in France, followed a similar pattern of rise and fall. Movie studios' financial ties to the music industry in the late twenties were confined mostly to writers and publishers, although Warner Brothers did own Brunswick Records from 1929 to 1938. RCA (which owned NBC) merged with (i.e., absorbed) the Victor record and phonograph company in 1929 after having formed RKO in 1928 out of several existing film and entertainment companies, including the remnants of Pathé's film enterprises. RCA gradually withdrew from RKO and sold its last holdings in that company in 1943.

According to Erik Barnouw, "[e]arly corporate links such as those between CBS and Paramount [which ended before CBS acquired Columbia Records in 1938], and between RCA and RKO, had . . . almost no effect on [radio] programming."[58] The effect of corporate ties on the content of recordings was also negligible. The pacesetter in recording industry exploitation of the film-music symbiosis turned out to be a company with no movie studio affiliation—Decca, the U.S. branch of which was founded in 1934. Read and Welch describe Decca as

[c]oncentrating on recording and pressing records rather than producing radios or phonographs. . . . By focusing its attention on the popular record market and cultivating Hollywood talent for their mushrooming juke box business, this company avoided most of the headaches being experienced by others. . . . The success of Decca and its ace, Bing Crosby, whom this company had lured away from Columbia, was one of the influences which prompted Metro-Goldwyn-Mayer to attempt to do much the same thing. . . .[59]

MGM established its record company in 1946 as "an outlet for movie sound tracks,"[60] but quickly branched out to become a major label covering many different types of music. Other film companies eventually followed suit, including ABC-Paramount (1955), United Artists (1957), Warner Brothers (1958), and Columbia (Colpix Records, founded 1959). In addition, Disney, Twentieth-Century-Fox, MCA/Universal, and Metromedia have all had one or more record labels. Warner Brothers emerged in the 1960s as the most important of the film-based record companies and acquired two major independent labels, Atlantic and Elektra.[61] The Warner-Elektra-Atlantic complex became one of the major components of the Warner Communications conglomerate.

The corporate conglomeration of film and popular music did not have any highly visible effect on the content of either until the recent wave of song plugging. This was ushered in by a minor soundtrack upsurge which started around 1977 with *Saturday Night Fever* and began to subside after *Urban Cowboy* in 1980. Then came MTV, which gave a strong incentive to film producers to put potential hit songs in their movies—music video clips could then be used to promote both the record and the movie. This is exactly what happened with *Flashdance*, which took in $210 million at the box office and spawned two number one hits.[62] In 1984 and 1985 soundtrack albums and hit songs from films dominated the record charts as never before and it became conventional wisdom in the film industry that a hit theme song could add millions of dollars to a film's receipts. As of the mid–1980s, "every record company has a film division and every movie company has its music division. Sometimes the lines blur, as with Universal and MCA, Warner Brothers (film division) and Warner Brothers (music division)"[63]

STYLES AND GENRES OF INTERACTION

The symbiosis of film and popular music has taken place in many different ways which can be better understood from an examination of genres and themes. It seems necessary to approach genre from three separate directions: record genres, music genres, and musical film subgenres. Themes include the functions of music in film and the idea of artistic integration.

Record genres include the soundtrack album, the single, and the cover version. A soundtrack album includes a large selection of music from a film, performed by the same artists heard in the film. The soundtrack is different from an original cast album, which presents music recorded by the cast of a play. A single is a 45-rpm record with two sides, at least one of which in this case would be from a film soundtrack. The record company designates one side of the single as the "plug side" for radio airplay. A cover version is a recording of a song somebody else first recorded. These are still common, but were most important in film music from about the twenties to the forties.

The two major genres of film music emphasized in this survey have been mainstream pop from the Tin Pan Alley tradition, and rock/rock and roll. Similar patterns are nevertheless evident in other genres including jazz,[64] rhythm and blues,[65] and country and western. An interesting development beginning in the 1970s was the mainstreaming of genres previously confined to the fringes of film music. *Nashville* (1975), *Coal Miner's Daughter* (1979), and *Urban Cowboy* did this for country and western, which since the earliest cowboy musicals such as *The Wagon Master* (1929)[66] had been heard mainly in the films of the singing cowboys: Ken Maynard, Gene Autry, Tex Ritter, and Roy Rogers. *2001: A Space Odyssey* (1968), *Deliverance* (1972), and *The Sting* (1973) made hit songs out of classical, bluegrass, and ragtime music, respectively.

Within the film musical genre there are numerous subgenres. One of the most basic distinctions often made is between the original and the adaptation. Originals have generally had an aura of experimentation and of an organic affinity to the film medium. They are presumably less "stagey" than adaptations are, but this varies widely. "Adaptation" refers mainly to films based on Broadway musicals, most of which fit in the category of musical comedy or "book shows." A book show has two main components—the musical numbers and the "book," meaning spoken dialogue.

Irene Kahn Atkins makes a distinction between the book show and the back-stage musical, calling these the "two types of film musicals."[67] The backstage musical generally has a plot that involves entertainers "putting on a show." The show business setting provides a plausible reason for characters to sing and dance. The book show, on the other hand, is "a kind of cinematic operetta . . . in which the music is an integral part of the drama, and singers burst into song spontaneously, with the orchestral accompaniment coming from nowhere, without the slightest attempt to justify the source of that accompaniment."[68] Atkins' system of categorization is problematic for two reasons. First, backstage musicals do have a book, or dialogue, so the backstage-book dichotomy is somewhat confusing. Second, Atkins has a very inclusive definition of film operetta, which in the usage of other writers may mean not merely a book show, but one that has a lush, romantic flavor, is set in a distant time or place, and features singers with a quasi-operatic style.

Opera itself is represented in the popular musical primarily through the rock opera, but also through occasional pop examples such as *The Umbrellas of Cherbourg*. In film opera, there is no "book." All the lines are sung, not spoken.

Another subgenre which includes little or no speaking is the music video, which takes a record as its starting point. Music video generally includes no talking except for occasional "framing" segments at the beginning and end. Most music videos are a mixture of "concept" and performance footage. In the former, the singer usually portrays a character, as in opera or operetta. In the latter, the singer appears as himself/herself, usually in concert.

A film consisting entirely of performance footage is a musical documentary. This category also includes films that mix performance footage with interviews and other nonmusical material. Many musical documentaries are about rock musicians and are therefore called rockumentaries. A precursor of musical do-cumentaries was the revue film of the twenties and thirties, which presented entertainers playing themselves or acting in vaudeville-type skits.

Musical films may also be categorized as singer's films or dancer's films, depending on which they emphasize. In either type, a consistent trend has been the employment of film as a "star vehicle," that is, a custom-made showcase for a singer or dancer's abilities.

Miscellaneous subgenres of musical film include the animated musical, the biopic, and the narrative film based on a song lyric. Animated musicals are often merely animated versions of other subgenres—for example, *Yellow Submarine* was an animated star vehicle for the Beatles. Biopics (biographical films) include many films about musical celebrities (e.g., *Yankee Doodle Dandy*, *The Great Caruso*, *Coal Miner's Daughter*). These are similar to the backstage musical in that characters can sing and dance without appearing to step outside the bound-aries of reasonable behavior. Narrative films based on song lyrics are rare but enjoyed a minor vogue with the mainstreaming of country and western music in the 1970s. Many country and western lyrics tell stories, occasionally with enough detail to provide the basis for a film. *Ode to Billy Joe* (1976) was one of the first examples.

Film music can also be classified according to the function it serves. Incidental or background music has been used since the earliest days of silent film to provide mood and pacing. The leitmotif, or recurring theme, is used in back-ground music to identify a particular character or situation and give unity to the film.

In many cases, the background leitmotifs are variations on the film's theme song. Traditionally, this song has come at the beginning or end of a film, to accompany the credits, provide summation, and tie the film to the promotional mechanisms of the music industry. However, it has become quite common for a theme song to be used as an interlude in the middle of a film, and for films to contain more than one song (making it difficult in some cases to single out one as the "theme song").

Nowadays theme songs are in many cases records by somebody other than the film star and are seldom tied to performance footage in the film. In contrast, theme songs in classical Hollywood musicals were often production numbers featuring a performance by one of the film's stars. Recent uses of the theme song have blurred the formerly clear distinction between it and background music.

One interesting way to interpret this is in the light of the theory of the "integrated musical," which refers mainly to the integration of music and plot. Placing theme songs in the background makes the sound background more noticeable but also removes the need to see, and therefore integrate into the plot, any singing or dancing. Replacing this is a more general need to conform the visual and musical elements. With the rise of record plugging and the spread of the music video aesthetic, music increasingly determines images but does not demand performance footage as it once did. Integration remains a widely accepted goal but is being approached from a new direction, resulting in the intrusion of popular music into TV shows of all types and otherwise standard Hollywood films. These hybrids, regardless of whether one likes them, represent the elevation of music, as both an art and an industry, to a more powerful position than it has held for many years in the cultural pecking order. There is no sign yet that the trend has peaked. It appears instead that music will exert ever greater influence in the next several years on production and reception in the media we have traditionally thought of as visual.

NOTES

1. My account of the early history of the phonograph relies on Roland Gelatt. *The Fabulous Phonograph, 1877–1977*, 2d rev. ed. (New York: Macmillan; London: Collier Macmillan, 1977); and Oliver Read and Walter L. Welch, *From Tin Foil to Stereo: Evolution of the Phonograph*, 2d ed. (Indianapolis: Howard W. Sams/Bobbs-Merrill, 1976).

2. Quoted in Gelatt, *The Fabulous Phonograph*, p. 21.

3. Reprinted in Gelatt, *The Fabulous Phonograph*, p. 29.

4. Ibid.

5. "Motion Picture Caveat I," repr. in Gordon Hendricks, *The Edison Motion Picture Myth* (Berkeley: University of California Press, 1961); repr. with *The Kinetoscope* and *Beginnings of the Biograph* as *Origins of the American Film* (New York: Arno Press & The New York Times, 1972), pp. 158–61, quote on p. 158.

6. Ibid., p. 159.

7. Gordon Hendricks, *The Kinetoscope: America's First Commercially Successful Motion Picture Exhibitor* (New York: The Beginnings of American Film, 1966); repr. with *The Edison Motion Picture Myth* and *Beginnings of the Biograph* as *Origins of the American Film* (New York: Arno Press & The New York Times, 1972), pp. 118–25.

8. Charles Hofmann, *Sounds for Silents* (New York: DBS Publications/Drama Book Specialists, 1970), p. 7.

9. My account of early film music relies on Charles Merrell Berg, *An Investigation of the Motives for and Realization of Music to Accompany the American Silent Film, 1896–1927* (Ph.D. diss., University of Iowa, 1973; repr. New York: Arno Press, 1976; hereafter cited as *Investigation*); Roger Manvell and John Huntley, *The Technique of Film Music* (London: Focal Press, 1957); and Kenneth Macgowan, *Behind the Screen: The History and Techniques of the Motion Picture* (1965; repr. New York: Dell, 1965).

10. Berg, *Investigation*, p. 52.

11. Ibid., pp. 39–40.

12. John W. Landon, *Behold the Mighty Wurlitzer: The History of the Theatre Pipe Organ* (Westport, Conn.: Greenwood Press, 1983), p. 4.

13. Ibid., p. 33.

14. Ibid., p. 15.

15. Berg, *Investigation*, pp. 82–83.

16. This and other cue sheets are reprinted in Berg, *Investigation*, pp. 103ff.

17. See Cyril Ehrlich, *The Piano: A History* (London: J. M. Dent & Sons, 1976), especially pp. 92–93.

18. Joseph Murrells, *Million Selling Records from the 1900s to the 1980s: An Illustrated Directory* (London: B. T. Batsford, 1984), pp. 14–15.

19. George W. Beynon, *Musical Presentation of Motion Pictures* (New York: G. Schirmer, 1921), p. 7.

20. Berg, *Investigation*, pp. 88–89.

21. Ibid.

22. Ibid., p. 253.

23. Irene Kahn Atkins, *Source Music in Motion Pictures* (Rutherford, N.J.: Fairleigh Dickinson University Press; London: Associated University Presses, 1983), p. 30.

24. Hofmann, *Sounds for Silents*, [pp. 42–43].

25. Maurice Fenton, "The Births of the Theme Song," *Photoplay*, November 1929; repr. in *The Movie Musical from Vitaphone to 42nd Street: As Reported in a Great Fan Magazine*, ed. Miles Kreuger (New York: Dover Publications, 1975), pp. 340–41, quote on p. 340.

26. See Alexander Walker, *The Shattered Silents: How the Talkies Came to Stay* (New York: William Morrow, 1979), pp. 1–3.

27. Ibid., p. 30.

28. Ivor Montagu, *Film World: A Guide to Cinema* (Baltimore: Penguin Books, 1964), p. 62 (Montagu's emphasis).

29. Columns for October 1929 to October 1930 are reprinted in *The Movie Musical from Vitaphone to 42nd Street*, ed. Kreuger, pp. 338–52.

30. Berg, *Investigation*, p. 274.

31. Manvell and Huntley, *The Technique of Film Music*, p. 24.

32. Berg, *Investigation*, p. 272.

33. Jerry Hoffman, "Westward the Course of Tin-Pan Alley," *Photoplay*, September 1929; repr. *The Movie Musical from Vitaphone to 42nd Street*, ed. Kreuger, pp. 56–59.

34. Walker, *The Shattered Silents*, p. 82.

35. Jane Feuer, *The Hollywood Musical* (Bloomington: Indiana University Press, 1982), p. 51.

36. John Kobal, *Gotta Sing Gotta Dance: A Pictorial History of Film Musicals* (London: Hamlyn, 1971), p. 9.

37. Philip K. Eberly, *Music in the Air: America's Changing Tastes in Popular Music, 1920–1980* (New York: Hastings House, 1982), p. 102.

38. Allen L. Woll, *The Hollywood Musical Goes to War* (Chicago: Nelson-Hall, 1983), p. 31.

39. Kobal, *Gotta Sing Gotta Dance*, p. 202.

40. Jerome Delamater, "Performing Arts: The Musical," in *American Film Genres: Approaches to a Critical Theory of Popular Film*, ed. Stuart M. Kaminsky, repr. (1974; New York: Dell, 1977), pp. 155–79, quote on p. 168. Freed was actually the associate producer of *The Wizard of Oz*.

41. Delamater, "Performing Arts: The Musical," p. 170.

42. See ibid., pp. 166–73; and Stanley J. Solomon, *Beyond Formula: American Film Genres* (New York: Harcourt Brace Jovanovich, 1976.), pp. 70–78.

43. Kobal, *Gotta Sing Gotta Dance*, p. 260.

44. Ibid., p. 204.

45. For further information on war-related musicals, see Woll, *The Hollywood Musical Goes to War*.

46. Clive Hirschhorn, *The Hollywood Musical* (New York: Crown, 1981), p. 16.

47. My account of rock in film relies on Fred Dellar, *The NME Guide to Rock Cinema* (Feltham, Middlesex, England: Hamlyn Paperbacks, 1981); David Ehrenstein and Bill Reed, *Rock on Film* (New York: Delilah Books, 1982); Jan Stacy and Ryder Syvertsen, *Rockin' Reels: An Illustrated History of Rock & Roll Movies* (Chicago: Contemporary Books, 1984); and especially Philip Jenkinson and Alan Warner, *Celluloid Rock: Twenty Years of Movie Rock* (London: Lorrimer Publishing, 1974).

48. Charles Hamm, *Yesterdays: Popular Song in America* (New York: W. W. Norton, 1979), p. 337.

49. Ehrlich, *The Piano: A History*, pp. 184–85.

50. See Erik Barnouw, *The Golden Web: A History of Broadcasting in the United States, Volume II—1933 to 1953* (New York: Oxford University Press, 1968), pp. 109, 217–18.

51. Jenkinson and Warner, *Celluloid Rock*, pp. 19–20.

52. Joel Whitburn, comp., *Top LP's, 1945–1972* (Menomonee Falls, Wisc.: Record Research, 1973), pp. 165–68.

53. Mark Evans, *Soundtrack: The Music of the Movies* (New York: Hopkinson and Blake, 1975; repr. New York: Da Capo Press, 1979), p. 192.

54. Ibid., pp. 194, 199.

55. Jenkinson and Warner, *Celluloid Rock*, p. 61.

56. See Michael Shore, *The Rolling Stone Book of Rock Video* (New York: Quill, 1984), pp. 21–22.

57. My account of early connections between the film and recording industries relies on Gelatt, *The Fabulous Phonograph*; Betty Lasky, *RKO: The Biggest Little Major of Them All* (Englewood Cliffs, N.J.: Prentice-Hall, 1984); Janet Wasko, *Movies and Money: Financing the American Film Industry* (Norwood, N.J.: Ablex Publishing, 1982); and Erik Barnouw, *A Tower in Babel: A History of Broadcasting in the United States, Volume 1—to 1933* (New York: Oxford University Press, 1966).

58. Barnouw, *The Golden Web*, p. 103.

59. Read and Welch, *From Tin Foil to Stereo*, p. 405.

60. Steve Chapple and Reebee Garofalo, *Rock 'n' Roll is Here to Pay: The History and Politics of the Music Industry* (Chicago: Nelson-Hall, 1977), p. 17.

61. For an excellent diagram of "Conglomerates in the Music Business" as of 1969, prepared by the American Guild of Authors & Composers, see Hans W. Heinsheimer, "Music from the Conglomerates," *Saturday Review* 52, no. 8 (February 22, 1969): 61–64, 77, diagram on 62–63.

62. Rob Tannenbaum, "Soundtracks Thrived in Summer of '85," *Rolling Stone*, no. 461 (November 21, 1985): 15–17, statistics on 15.

63. Richard Harrington, "The Saga of the Sound Tracks," *Washington Post* 12 January 1986: K1, K10-K11, quote on K11.

64. See David Meeker, *Jazz in the Movies: A Guide to Jazz Musicians, 1917–1977* (New Rochelle, N.Y.: Arlington House, 1977).

65. See Phil Beauchamp, "Black Vocal Groups in Motion Pictures," *Time Barrier Express*, no. 22 (March-April 1977): 7–11.

66. See C. A. Schicke, *Revolution in Sound: A Biography of the Recording Industry* (Boston: Little, Brown, 1974), p. 89.

67. Atkins, *Source Music in Motion Pictures*, p. 15.

68. Ibid.

SELECTED BIBLIOGRAPHY

There are three good histories of the recording industry: Gelatt, Read and Welch, and Schicke. Rock film is covered in four books: Jenkinson and Warner is the best history; Ehrenstein and Reed, Dellar, and Stacy and Syvertsen are useful as reference books. The best single source on silent film music is Berg. Hirschhorn is a comprehensive reference work on film musicals. The Shapiro volumes provide an exhaustive listing, by title, of songs popular each year from 1920 to 1969. If the song was featured in a movie, Shapiro so indicates, but the volumes are designed for the reader interested in music, not film. Pollock updates the Shapiro series to 1979. The following are useful discographies: Murrells, Rust, Pitts and Harrison, Whitburn, Osborne, and Meeker.

Atkins, Irene Kahn. *Source Music in Motion Pictures*. Rutherford, N.J.: Fairleigh Dickinson University Press; London: Associated University Press, 1983.

Barnouw, Erik. *The Golden Web: A History of Broadcasting in the United States, Volume II—1933 to 1953*. New York: Oxford University Press, 1968.

———. *A Tower in Babel: A History of Broadcasting in the United States, Volume I— to 1933*. New York: Oxford University Press, 1966.

Beauchamp, Phil. "Black Vocal Groups in Motion Pictures." *Time Barrier Express*, no. 22 (March-April 1977): 7–11.

Berg, Charles Merrell. *An Investigation of the Motives for and Realization of Music to Accompany the American Silent Film, 1896–1927*. Ph.D. diss., University of Iowa, 1973; repr. New York: Arno Press, 1976.

Beynon, George W. *Musical Presentation of Motion Pictures*. New York: G. Schirmer, 1921.

Chapple, Steve and Reebee Garofalo. *Rock 'n' Roll Is Here to Pay: The History and Politics of the Music Industry*. Chicago: Nelson-Hall, 1977.

Delamater, Jerome. "Performing Arts: The Musical." In *American Film Genres: Approaches to a Critical Theory of Popular Film*. Ed. Stuart M. Kaminsky. 1974; repr. New York: Dell, 1977: 155–79.

Dellar, Fred. *The NME Guide to Rock Cinema*. Feltham, Middlesex, England: Hamlyn Paperbacks, 1981.

Eberly, Philip K. *Music in the Air: America's Changing Tastes in Popular Music, 1920–1980*. New York: Hastings House, 1982.

Ehrenstein, David and Bill Reed. *Rock on Film*. New York: Delilah Books, 1982.

Ehrlich, Cyril. *The Piano: A History*. London: J. M. Dent & Sons, 1976.

Evans, Mark. *Soundtrack: The Music of the Movies*. New York: Hopkinson and Blake, 1975; repr. New York: Da Capo Press, 1979.

Fenton, Maurice. "The Birth of the Theme Song." *Photoplay*, November 1929. Repr. in *The Movie Musical from Vitaphone to 42nd Street: As Reported in a Great Fan Magazine*. Ed. Miles Kreuger. New York: Dover Publications, 1975: 340–41.

Feuer, Jane. *The Hollywood Musical*. Bloomington: Indiana University Press, 1982.

Gelatt, Roland. *The Fabulous Phonograph, 1877–1977*. 2d rev. ed. New York: Macmillan; London: Collier Macmillan, 1977.

Hamm, Charles. *Yesterdays: Popular Song in America*. New York: W. W. Norton, 1979.

Harrington, Richard. "The Saga of the Sound Tracks." *Washington Post* 12 January 1986: K1, K10-K11.

Heinsheimer, Hans W. "Music from the Conglomerates." *Saturday Review* 52, no. 8 (February 22, 1969): 61–64, 77.

Hendricks, Gordon. *The Edison Motion Picture Myth*. Berkeley: University of California Press, 1961. Repr. with *The Kinetoscope* and *Beginnings of the Biograph* as *Origins of the American Film*. New York: Arno Press & The New York Times, 1972.

———. *The Kinetoscope: America's First Commercially Successful Motion Picture Exhibitor*. New York: The Beginnings of the American Film, 1966. Repr. with *The Edison Motion Picture Myth* and *Beginnings of the Biograph* as *Origins of the American Film*. New York: Arno Press & The New York Times, 1972.

Hirschhorn, Clive. *The Hollywood Musical*. New York: Crown, 1981.

Hoffman, Jerry. "Westward the Course of Tin-Pan Alley." *Photoplay*, September 1929. Repr. in *The Movie Musical from Vitaphone to 42nd Street: As Reported in a Great Fan Magazine*. Ed. Miles Kreuger. New York: Dover Publications, 1975: 56–59.

Hofmann, Charles. *Sounds for Silents*. New York: DBS Publications/Drama Book Specialists, 1970.

Jenkinson, Philip and Alan Warner. *Celluloid Rock: Twenty Years of Movie Rock*. London: Lorrimer Publishing, 1974.

Kobal, John. *Gotta Sing Gotta Dance: A Pictorial History of Film Musicals*. London: Hamlyn, 1971.

Kreuger, Miles, ed. *The Movie Musical from Vitaphone to 42nd Street: As Reported in a Great Fan Magazine*. New York: Dover Publications, 1975.

Landon, John W. *Behind the Mighty Wurlitzer: The History of the Theatre Pipe Organ*. Westport, Conn.: Greenwood Press, 1983.

Lasky, Betty. *RKO: The Biggest Little Major of Them All*. Englewood Cliffs, N.J.: Prentice-Hall, 1984.

Macgowan, Kenneth. *Behind the Screen: The History and Techniques of the Motion Picture*. 1965; repr. New York: Dell, 1965.

Manvell, Roger and John Huntley. *The Technique of Film Music*. London: Focal Press, 1957.

Meeker, David. *Jazz in the Movies: A Guide to Jazz Musicians, 1917–1977*. New Rochelle, N.Y.: Arlington House, 1977.

Montagu, Ivor. *Film World: A Guide to Cinema*. Baltimore: Penguin Books, 1964.

Murrells, Joseph. *Million Selling Records from the 1900s to the 1980s: An Illustrated Directory*. London: B. T. Batsford, 1984.

Osborn, Jerry, comp. *Soundtracks & Original Cast*. Phoenix, Ariz.: O'Sullivan Woodside, 1981.

Pitts, Michael R. and Louis H. Harrison. *Hollywood on Record: The Film Stars' Discography*. Metuchen, N.J.: Scarecrow Press, Inc., 1978.

Pollock, Bruce, ed. *Popular Music: An Annotated Index of American Popular Songs*, vols. 7 and 8. Detroit: Gale Research, 1984.

Reed, Oliver and Walter L. Welch. *From Tin Foil to Stereo: Evolution of the Phonograph*. 2d ed. Indianapolis: Howard W. Sams/Bobbs-Merrill, 1976.

Rust, Brian, with Allen G. Debus. *The Complete Entertainment Discography, from the mid–1890s to 1942*. New Rochelle, N.Y.: Arlington House, 1973.

Schicke, C. A. *Revolution in Sound: A Biography of the Recording Industry*. Boston: Little, Brown, 1974.

Shapiro, Nat, ed. *Popular Music: An Annotated Index of American Popular Songs*, 8 vols. (vols. 1–6 ed. by Shapiro). New York: Adrian Press, 1965–1973 (publication dates for vols. 1–6 only; vol. 1 is 2nd ed.).

Shore, Michael. *The Rolling Stone Book of Rock Video*. New York: Quill, 1984.

Solomon, Stanley J. *Beyond Formula: American Film Genres*. New York: Harcourt Brace Jovanovich, 1976.

Stacy, Jan and Ryder Syvertsen. *Rockin' Reels: An Illustrated History of Rock & Roll Movies*. Chicago: Contemporary Books, 1984.

Tannenbaum, Rob. "Soundtracks Thrived in Summer of '85." *Rolling Stone*, no. 461 (November 21, 1985): 15–17.

Walker, Alexander. *The Shattered Silents: How the Talkies Came to Stay*. New York: William Morrow, 1979.

Wasko, Janet. *Movies and Money: Financing the American Film Industry*. Norwood, N.J.: Ablex Publishing, 1982.

Whitburn, Joel, comp. *Top LP's, 1945–1972*. Menomonee Falls, Wisc.: Record Research, 1973.

Woll, Allen L. *The Hollywood Musical Goes to War*. Chicago: Nelson-Hall, 1983.

SELECTED FILMOGRAPHY

My thanks to Andrew Pogue for his assistance in compiling the following information.

Alexander's Ragtime Band (USA 1938). Twentieth-Century-Fox. Produced by Darryl F. Zanuck. Directed by Henry King. With Alice Faye and Ethel Merman.

American Graffiti (USA 1973). Universal. Directed by George Lucas.

An American in Paris (USA 1951). MGM. Produced by Arthur Freed. Directed by Vincente Minnelli. Choreographed by Gene Kelly. With Gene Kelly and Leslie Caron.

American Musicals: Famous Production Numbers (USA 1929–1935). Compilation film distributed by the Museum of Modern Art in New York with selections from

Sunny Side Up (1929), *42nd Street* (1933), *Flying Down to Rio* (1933), *Gold Diggers of 1933* (1933), and *Gold Diggers of 1935* (1935).

American Pop (USA 1981). Columbia. Directed by Ralph Bakshi.

Around the World in 80 Days (USA 1956), United Artists. Produced by Michael Todd. Directed by Michael Anderson. With David Niven.

The Assassination of the Duke of Guise (L'Assassinat du Duc de Guise) (France 1908). Film d'Art. Directed by Charles Le Bargy and André Calmettes.

Babes in Arms (USA 1939). MGM. Produced by Arthur Freed. Directed by Busby Berkeley. With Mickey Rooney and Judy Garland.

The Band Wagon (USA 1953). MGM. Produced by Arthur Freed. Directed by Vincente Minelli. With Fred Astaire and Cyd Charisse.

The Barkleys of Broadway (USA 1949). MGM. Produced by Arthur Freed. Directed by Charles Waters. With Fred Astaire and Ginger Rogers.

The Big Broadcast (USA 1932). Paramount. Directed by Frank Tuttle. With Bing Crosby.

The Big Chill (USA 1983). Columbia. Directed by Lawrence Kasden.

The Birth of a Nation. (USA 1915). Epoch/Reliance–Majestic/Mutual. Directed by D. W. Griffith. With Lillian Gish and Mae Marsh.

Blackboard Jungle (USA 1955). MGM. Directed by Richard Brooks. With Glenn Ford.

The Broadway Melody (USA 1929). MGM. Directed by Harry Beaumont.

Butch Cassidy and the Sundance Kid (USA 1969). Twentieth-Century-Fox. Directed by George Roy Hill. With Paul Newman and Robert Redford.

Coal Miner's Daughter (USA 1980). Universal. Directed by Michael Apted. With Sissy Spacek.

Coming Home (USA 1978). United Artists. Directed by Hal Ashby. With Jane Fonda and John Voight.

Deliverance (USA 1972). Warner Brothers. Produced and Directed by John Boorman.

The Desert Song (USA 1929). Warner Brothers. Directed by Roy Del Ruth.

Doctor Zhivago (USA 1965). MGM. Directed by David Lean.

Don Juan (USA 1926). Warner Brothers. Directed by Alan Crosland.

Down Argentine Way (USA 1940). Twentieth-Century-Fox. Produced by Darryl F. Zanuck. Directed by Irving Cummings. With Betty Grable, Don Ameche, and Carmen Miranda.

Easy Rider (USA 1969). Columbia. Directed by Dennis Hopper.

Fantasia (USA 1940). Disney/RKO. Production Supervisor was Ben Sharpsteen.

Flashdance (USA 1983). Paramount. Directed by Adrian Lyne. With Jennifer Beals.

Flying Down to Rio. (USA 1933). RKO. Directed by Thornton Freeland. With Fred Astaire, Ginger Rogers, and Dolores Del Rio.

Footlight Parade (USA 1933). Warner Brothers. Directed by Lloyd Bacon. Choreographed by Busby Berkeley. With James Cagney and Joan Blondell.

42nd Street (USA 1933). Warner Brothers. Produced by Darryl F. Zanuck. Directed by Lloyd Bacon. Choreographed by Busby Berkeley. With Ruby Keeler and Dick Powell.

Gentlemen Prefer Blondes (USA 1953). Twentieth-Century-Fox. Directed by Howard Hawks. With Marilyn Monroe and Jane Russell.

Gigi (USA 1958). MGM. Produced by Arthur Freed. Directed by Vincente Minnelli. With Leslie Caron and Maurice Chevalier.

Gimme Shelter (USA 1970). Cinema V. Directed by David Maysles, Albert Maysles, and Charlotte Zwerin. With the Rolling Stones.

Gold Diggers of 1933 (USA 1933). Warner Brothers. Directed by Mervyn Leroy. Choreographed by Busby Berkeley. With Dick Powell and Ruby Keeler.

Gold Diggers of 1935 (USA 1935). Warner Brothers. Directed by Busby Berkeley. With Dick Powell and Adolphe Menjou.

Goldfinger (UK 1964). United Artists. Directed by Guy Hamilton.

The Good, the Bad, and the Ugly (Il Buono, Il Brutto, Il Cattivo) (Italy 1966). Produzioni Europee Associate/United Artists. Directed by Sergio Leone.

The Graduate (USA 1967). Avco Embassy. Directed by Mike Nichols.

The Great Caruso (USA 1951). MGM. Produced by Joe Pasternak. Directed by Richard Thorpe. With Mario Lanza.

Guys and Dolls (USA 1955). MGM. Produced by Samuel Goldwyn. Directed by Joseph L. Mankiewicz. With Marlon Brando, Jean Simmons, and Frank Sinatra.

A Hard Day's Night (UK 1964). United Artists. Directed by Richard Lester. With the Beatles.

Heavy Traffic (USA 1973). American International. Directed by Ralph Bakshi.

The Hollywood Revue of 1929 (USA 1929). MGM. Directed by Charles F. Riesner. With Jack Benny and Conrad Nagel.

I Married an Angel (USA 1942). MGM. Directed by W. S. Van Dyke. With Jeanette MacDonald and Nelson Eddy.

Jailhouse Rock (USA 1957). MGM. Directed by Richard Thorpe. With Elvis Presley.

The Jazz Singer (USA 1927). Warner Brothers. Directed by Alan Crosland. With Al Jolson.

Jesus Christ Superstar (USA 1973). Universal. Produced and Directed by Norman Jewison. With Ted Neeley, Carl Anderson, and Yvonne Elliman.

King of Jazz (USA 1930) Universal. Directed by John Murray Anderson. With Bing Crosby and Paul Whiteman.

Lights of New York (USA 1928). Warner Brothers. Directed by Bryan Foy.

Little Miss Marker (a.k.a. *The Girl in Pawn)* (USA 1934). Paramount. Directed by Alexander Hall. With Shirley Temple.

Love Me Tender. (USA 1956). Twentieth-Century-Fox. Directed by Robert Webb. With Elvis Presley.

Love Me Tonight (USA 1932). Paramount. Produced and Directed by Rouben Mamoulian. With Maurice Chevalier and Jeanette MacDonald.

The Love Parade (USA 1929). Paramount. Produced and Directed by Ernest Lubitsch. With Maurice Chevalier and Jeanette MacDonald.

Love Story (USA 1970). Paramount. Directed by Arthur Hiller.

Mary Poppins (USA 1964). Disney/Buena Vista. Directed by Robert Stevenson. With Dick Van Dyke and Julie Andrews.

Meet Me in St. Louis. (USA 1944). MGM. Produced by Arthur Freed. Directed by Vincente Minelli. With Judy Garland.

The Merry Widow (a.k.a. *The Lady Dances)* (USA 1934). MGM. Directed by Ernest Lubitsch. With Maurice Chevalier and Jeanette MacDonald.

Mickey (USA 1918). Paramount. Produced by Mack Sennett. Directed by F. Richard Jones. With Mabel Normand.

Monterey Pop (USA 1969). Foundation–Leacock/Pennebaker. Produced and Directed by D. A. Pennebaker. With Janis Joplin and the Jefferson Airplane.

Nashville (USA 1975). Paramount. Produced and Directed by Robert Altman. With Lily Tomlin and Shelley Duvall.

Naughty Marietta (USA 1935). MGM. Directed by W. S. Van Dyke. With Jeanette MacDonald and Nelson Eddy.

Ode to Billy Joe (USA 1976). Warner Brothers. Directed by Max Baer.

Oklahoma! (USA 1955). Magna Theatre Corporation. Directed by Fred Zinnemann. With Gordon MacRae and Shirley Jones.

On the Town (USA 1949). MGM. Produced by Arthur Freed. Directed by Gene Kelly and Stanley Donen. With Gene Kelly and Frank Sinatra.

Paramount on Parade (USA 1930). Paramount. Eleven directors with Elsie Janis as Production Supervisor.

Pinocchio (USA 1940). Disney/RKO. Directed by Ben Sharpsteen and Hamilton Luske.

Poor Little Rich Girl (USA 1936). Twentieth-Century-Fox. Produced by Darryl F. Zanuck. Directed by Irving Cummings. With Shirley Temple and Alice Faye.

Ramona (USA 1928) United Artists. Directed by Edward Carewe. With Dolores Del Rio and Warner Baxter.

The Road to Hong Kong (USA 1962). United Artists. Produced and Directed by Norman Panama and Melvin Frank. With Bing Crosby, Bob Hope, Dorothy Lamour, and Joan Collins.

Road to Singapore (USA 1940). Paramount. Directed by Victor Schertzinger. With Bing Crosby, Bob Hope, and Dorothy Lamour.

Rock Around the Clock (USA 1956). Columbia. Directed by Fred F. Sears. With Alan Freed, and Bill Haley and His Comets.

Saturday Night Fever (USA 1977). Paramount. Produced by Robert Stigwood. Directed by John Badham. Choreographed by Lester Wilson. With John Travolta.

Seventh Heaven (USA 1927). Twentieth-Century-Fox. Directed by Frank Borzage. With Janet Gaynor and Charles Farrell.

The Show of Shows (USA 1929). Warner Brothers. Directed by John Adolfi.

Singin' in the Rain (USA 1952). MGM. Produced by Arthur Freed. Directed by Gene Kelly and Stanley Donen. Choreographed by Gene Kelly. With Gene Kelly, Debbie Reynolds, and Donald O'Connor.

Snow White and the Seven Dwarfs (USA 1938). Disney/RKO. Supervising Director was David Hand.

The Sound of Music (USA 1965). Twentieth-Century-Fox. Produced and Directed by Robert Wise. With Julie Andrews and Christopher Plummer.

South Pacific (USA 1958). Twentieth-Century-Fox. Directed by Joshua Logan. With Rosano Brazzi and Mitzi Gaynor.

A Star Is Born (USA 1954). Warner Brothers. Directed by George Cukor. With Judy Garland and James Mason.

Steamboat Willie (USA 1928). Disney. Directed by Walt Disney. Animation by Ub Iwerks.

The Sting (USA 1973). Universal. Directed by George Roy Hill. With Paul Newman and Robert Redford.

The T.A.M.I. Show (a.k.a. *Gather No Moss*) (USA 1964). American International. Directed by Steve Binder. With the Rolling Stones and Chuck Berry.

The Three Little Pigs (USA 1933). Disney. Directed by Burt Gillett.

Three Smart Girls (USA 1936). Universal. Produced by Joseph Pasternak. Directed by Henry Koster. With Deanna Durbin.

Tommy (USA 1975). Columbia. Produced by Robert Stigwood. Directed by Ken Russell. With Roger Daltry, Ann-Margaret, and Elton John.

2001: A Space Odyssey (USA 1968). MGM. Directed by Stanley Kubrick.

The Umbrellas of Cherbourg (Les Parapluies de Cherbourg) (France 1964). Parc Film/ Madeleine Films. Produced by Jacques Demy. With Catherine Deneuve.

Urban Cowboy (USA 1980). Paramount. Directed by James Bridges. With John Travolta and Debra Winger.

The Wagon Master (USA 1929). Universal. Directed by Harry J. Brown. With Ken Maynard.

Walt Disney's Milestones in Animation (USA 1928–1937). Disney. This compilation film includes *Steamboat Willie* (1928), *The Skeleton Dance* (1928), *Flowers and Trees* (1932), *The Three Little Pigs* (1933), *The Old Mill* (1937) in their entirety.

West Side Story (USA 1961). United Artists. Produced by Robert Wise. Directed by Robert Wise and Jerome Robbins. With Natalie Wood and Richard Beymer.

What Price Glory? (USA 1926). Fox. Directed by Raoul Walsh. With Victor McLaghlin, Edmund Lowe, and Dolores Del Rio.

The Wizard of Oz (USA 1939). MGM. Produced by Mervyn LeRoy. Directed by Victor Fleming (and King Vidor uncredited). With Judy Garland, Bert Lahr, and Jack Haley.

Woodstock (USA 1970). Directed by Michael Wadleigh. With The Who, Santana, Sly and the Family Stone, and Joe Cocker.

Words and Music (USA 1948). MGM. Produced by Arthur Freed. Directed by Norman Taurog. With Mickey Rooney and Tom Drake.

Yankee Doodle Dandy (USA 1942). Warner Brothers. Directed by Michael Curtiz. With James Cagney.

Yellow Submarine (UK 1968). Directed by George Dunning. With the Beatles in animation.

9

FILM AND RADIO

GARY R. EDGERTON

INTRODUCTION

Radio and motion pictures in America have closely co-acted and intertwined throughout most of the twentieth century. This chapter will investigate this interaction from four standpoints: technology; business and economics; art and culture; and regulation and social control. Of all the symbiotic unions examined in this book, the relationship between film and radio is presently one of the least acknowledged and explored pairings by media historians and critics. The reason for this oversight probably has something to do with past tradition in higher education which typically separates the study of broadcasting (especially radio) and motion pictures, as well as the fact that the process of mass media symbiosis between these two communication arts matured and peaked nearly three decades ago. In point of fact, however, the involvement of radio and movies has persisted in a reciprocal pattern for more than ninety years, albeit the period between 1920 and 1950 was clearly the most vital and intense era of interaction. Still, the changing functions and operations of these two media and the very longevity of their relationship allow a privileged view into how time and the evolving nature of not only film and radio, but ultimately television, affected and shaped the path that each medium took in respect to the other mass media as a technology, industry, art form, and social force. The specific case of radio and motion pictures also offers general insights into the way different media interrelate on distinct levels at various phases of their symbiotic association; how they assert their unique and distinguishable means of framing reality; and in turn, how they merge with and alter the seemingly invisible and dynamic communication environment that today engulfs all of America.

HISTORICAL DEVELOPMENT

The Symbiotic Prehistory: 1895–1919

In Paris on 28 December 1895, Auguste and Louis Lumière were the initial constructor-entrepreneurs to exhibit motion pictures to a paying public; several months earlier, Guglielmo Marconi also set a pivotal precedent in the early technical development of radio by being the first inventor to successfully send wireless messages on his family estate near Bologna, Italy. During these final years of the nineteenth century, the growth of movies was slightly ahead of the emergence of the wireless: the film medium had not only unfolded on the technical front during the past half century, but now it was affirming itself in the commercial sector. The groundwork for radio communication was, in comparison, just being realized on the technical level. Technology, in fact, was really the sole meeting point between the two media during this embryonic period for the wireless.

The only similarities that appeared between radio and motion pictures were those that manifested themselves in scientific laboratories in Europe and America. Sound discoveries for the wireless and sound-on-film techniques developed simultaneously in the aural treatises and experiments that emerged from the scientific community in the early and mid-nineteenth century.[1] The possibilities of combining sound and picture first intrigued an Edison employee, Eugene Lauste, in 1888. By 1906 the technical roots of both radio and the talkies were firmly wedded in Lee De Forest's invention of the "audion," or vacuum tube amplifier. From that point until 1919, several research concerns, including General Electric and American Telephone and Telegraph (AT&T), continued to perfect sound amplification techniques. The use of the wireless in worldwide maritime affairs spurred on these experiments until the end of World War I. In turn, this continuing process of research and technical development also held long-range implications for the eventual development of both domestic radio and American talking pictures.[2]

Marketplace Beginnings: 1920–1933

In 1920 Westinghouse's KDKA in Pittsburgh began to explore the commercial aspects of radio communication by broadcasting the presidential election returns between Harding and Cox on November 2; less than two years later, AT&T's WEAF in New York became the first station to employ commercials by introducing the method of "toll" broadcasting. In contrast, "by 1922, the Motion Picture Industry had become the largest and most widespread commercial entertainment form the world had ever seen."[3] The identity of silent movies was clearly established as Hollywood rapidly became part of the national consciousness. Radio and "talkies," on the other hand, were still considered to be experimental media and were relatively unknown commodities. Each medium had to begin the trial and error process of becoming, which manifests itself both technically and economically during this period.

It is curious to note that although radio and sound-on-film techniques developed concurrently, the identities of the two media always remained separate in the minds of their developers and users. (Talkies existed in experimental form as disc-and-film systems as early as 1894, and sound-on-film systems by the end of World War I.)[4] In a differing fashion, television, frequently referred to as "radio movies" throughout its 1920–1940 embryonic period, was continually being meshed with the other two media before it emerged as a distinct medium.[5] Consequently, the apparent technical independence of radio from the talkies points to the fact that the two media would eventually provide the American public with distinctly dissimilar, although related, services.

Although Hollywood demonstrated apprehension and animosity toward radio in the late 1920s and early 1930s, the movie industry's initial fear of competition proved to be unfounded. In fact, the aural, private, and intimate experience of radio and the principally visual, aural, and more public gestalt of the movies actually complemented each other, giving rise to an America that was eagerly cultivating multiple media interests.

This trend toward mutualism, however, was not without its growing pains. Prior to 1928, the only apparent link between film and radio was the use of wireless communication in the directing of spectacular battle scenes on Hollywood sets.[6] Still, in the fall of 1922, and again in the spring and summer of 1927, there came a drop of truly alarming proportions in public attendance at films.[7] As a result, Hollywood went looking for scapegoats; and radio, just beginning its astronomical station and network growth, emerged as a prime target. Bosley Crowther manifests this point of view:

The illusions of soundless movies had prevailed as entertainment and as art so long as the public was accustomed to being stimulated by mechanical music and voice. But as soon as the public's ears were opened by the device of the radio, as they were, during the mid–1920s, to an extent that was profound, and people's minds were stimulated to create images to match what they heard, a vague sense of the lack of aural content in motion pictures began to be felt. A subtle psychological rejection of the incongruity of the silent screen occurred.[8]

Be that as it may, historical statistics compiled by the U.S. Department of Commerce still leave some question as to the accuracy of Crowther's analysis.[9] In all actuality, weekly attendance and movie box-office receipts continued to rise in a steady, gradual growth pattern throughout the 1920s despite the two downturns mentioned earlier; in fact, these two indicators doubled in output from 1922 to 1930. No doubt Hollywood wasn't matching its meteoric growth rate of the teens or expanding at the scale of the newly established radio industry which actually expanded from 30 to 618 stations nationwide during the same time frame. Nevertheless, radio was much smaller than the movie business by 1930; and in turn, it might be safe to say that Hollywood remained relatively stable, if not nearly unaffected by the immense growth of radio throughout the decade.

Both film and broadcast historians have traditionally recounted that Hollywood reacted to the radio boom by either ignoring the new medium or acting antagonistically toward it. Actually, this supposition is only partially true. The problem with most general media histories is that they tend to view media symbiosis primarily on the programming level. Hollywood did indeed actively resist radio from the perspective of talent and content. "Motion picture studios limited the appearance of their contract actors on radio for fear of both overexposure and competition."[10] From an economic perspective, however, Hollywood neither disregarded nor resisted the new medium.

Several of the major movie companies purchased individual radio stations; for instance, Warner Brothers owned and operated KFWB in Los Angeles.[11] Paramount, the dominant American studio in the 1920s, made numerous attempts to acquire a controlling amount of CBS stock throughout the latter end of radio's period of enchantment. It was only Paramount's precarious financial situation and eventual bankruptcy caused by internal graft during the 1929–1933 period, and the hard-nosed business dealings of young CBS executive William S. Paley, that kept Paramount from absorbing and directing the future of the network.[12]

In October 1928 one film-broadcasting merger actually was consummated. At the time, Radio-Keith-Orpheum (RKO) Corporation signed a contractual agreement with the Radio Corporation of America (RCA).[13] RKO not only had studios, but it also had an elaborate network for distributing and exhibiting motion pictures. Likewise, RCA had a sound-on-film system that it planned to use with the RKO network. Although this merger was the only major commercial union between the broadcast and movie industries in the late 1920s–early 1930s period, the trend toward economic symbiosis between film and radio was clear. Motion pictures first set out to protect themselves from radio by pursuing financial arrangements which would leave the movies in a position of dominance over radio. Essentially, the motion picture industry employed this sort of financial maneuvering as a means of preserving the status quo as much as possible. The intensity to which film provoked economic symbiosis reflects just how much it considered the newer medium a threat. In retrospect, radio was never really an economic threat to the movies.

This is not to say that the motion picture industry was not frightened by radio. In a business world operating on a competitive ethic, suspicion is a typical reaction to any potential rival. Hollywood's talent ban indeed indicates its fear of radio. On the other hand, Hollywood's apprehension can also be interpreted as an overreaction. From 1928 to 1931, as networks grew, so did movie profits. Actually, it took a general nationwide recession in 1932 to temporarily curb both Hollywood and radio's financial well-being.

A Maturing Symbiosis: 1934–1940

"As the crisis deepened in 1932, Walter Gifford, the head of President Hoover's Organization on Unemployment Relief, was quoted as saying, 'the movies were a necessity to be ranked just behind food and clothing.' "[14] In volume 2 of his history of broadcasting trilogy, Erik Barnouw describes radio use with similar urgency: "According to social workers, destitute families that had to give up an icebox or furniture or bedding, still clung to the radio as to a last link with humanity.''[15] "To a great extent, film and radio complemented one another in the 1930s—fulfilling related but not duplicated interests and needs of their audiences.''[16] The necessity for both media to contribute in calming the shaken morale of Depression America is evident in how both industries flourished in the 1930s. One critic called Hollywood "more stable than steel, housing or power.''[17]

During the 1940s, one of the pioneering examples of uses and gratification research uncovered the concept of multiple media interests.[18] This term refers to the fact that people who are frequent users of one medium tend to also utilize other media. This was certainly the case with the growing popularity of both radio and sound film during the Depression. Hollywood and its movies provided escape and the chance to participate in the public rituals evident in the rises and popularity of many American film genres.

Network radio soon developed its own generic variations as well; and moreover, this programming could be enjoyed in the privacy of one's home.

With radio you didn't have to go out for entertainment in particular, you didn't have to go into the dirty, crime-ridden, alien downtown districts where the opera houses, orchestra halls, legitimate theaters, museums and first-run movie houses were located. You could listen in your bathrobe or other informal attire at any time of the day, in any kind of weather, at minimal additional cost (for electric current) beyond the original purchase price. While enjoying radio you could cook, clean, read, talk, exchange glances with family or friends, lie in bed; you could turn it on and off, adjust the volume, change stations at will.[19]

Radio also provided more than narrative entertainment; news, music, and talk shows all could be found on the broadcast band. Consequently, film and radio together were establishing themselves as vital and intricate parts of American life.

Not only were Hollywood and radio incapable of competing for the exclusive attention of the American public, but both media also approached commercialism from different angles. Broadcasting in the United States is obviously financed by advertising. Particularly during the 1928–1932 period, Madison Avenue began molding the eventual shape and structure of network radio. In contrast, Hollywood commercialism was never structured in the same way. Besides industrial films, advertising agencies were not to sponsor the production of any movies in the 1930s.[20] Radio's real competitors were newspapers and magazines which unquestionably felt the pressure of "advertising competition" and feared the "usurpation of newspaper news functions by radio.''[21] Although hostilities peaked during the so-called Press-Radio War of 1934, newspapers and radio especially suffered through intermittent public relations skirmishes throughout the next decade.[22]

Hollywood and broadcasting were actually allies in many ways. In 1933 both industries joined forces to short-circuit socialist Upton Sinclair's try for the California governorship. Even the Hollywood "talent ban," which all the major studios except RKO had adopted by 1932, would soon erode.[23] "N.B.C., for example, sent out its first broadcast in 1932 from Hollywood. In 1937 there were about 700" broadcasts, with a good deal of this time utilized by movie-based talent.[24] In April 1938, CBS opened an impressive new Hollywood center and production facility.[25] NBC next followed suit in October of that same year with the inauguration of its own "Hollywood Radio City."[26]

The prospects of merging the programming potentials of film and radio were originally pursued by advertising agencies eager to employ motion picture talent.[27] The movie industry consented because of the publicity value of radio programs that featured film stars. On 14 October 1934 the Lever Brothers' soap empire took an interesting and expensive gamble by developing "Lux Radio Theater" through the J. Walter Thompson agency. This program soon became a prime-time, Monday night fixture by employing most of the biggest names in the movies, including Clark Gable, in dramatic adaptations of current motion pictures and plays.[28] Similar programming fare subsequently appeared, such as NBC's "Photoplay" and "Forty-Five Minutes in Hollywood," which promoted "films, stars, companies, and Hollywood as an institution."[29]

In the late 1920s and early 1930s, radio also borrowed heavily from the narrative traditions of the movies in developing its serials. In fact, radio was just beginning to establish its own specific programming identity by 1930. Like all new media, there was an identifiable lag time during most of the 1920s and into the 1930s when radio had yet to find its own unique mode of expression. One critic lamented:

A word which recurs constantly when one is discussing the film and the other arts is radio. Actually of course radio is not an art at all but a transmitter of art like the phonograph. It touches the cinema really not on the artistic but on the industrial plane. And on the industrial plane the movie brings vampire charges against the radio.[30]

It wasn't long, however, before Hollywood stopped labeling radio as a vampire or parasite. Movies employed a familiar radio format and many broadcast personalities in its first film from the Big Broadcast series in 1932. Although occasional examples of film content from the early 1930s were already displaying radio's influence, this particular series is significant because its form and content are so thoroughly rooted in the conventions of radio: radio stars, songs, comedy routines, and a narrative structure in the form of a big broadcast. Successful sequels in 1936, 1937, and 1938 followed the original.

By 1935 critic A. M. Sullivan spoke of radio finally developing "a vision of an armchair, instead of a circus, stage or classroom."[31] Programming symbiosis had now come full circle. This process began at the prodding of radio, which at the time was seeking further financial and aesthetic improvement. Later, motion pictures benefited aesthetically as well as financially. Hollywood flourished with the input of new talent and funds. Radio exposure helped film personalities and vice versa. Stars became multimedia personalities, and the production of both movies and radio became almost exclusively centered in Hollywood. "Since the middle of last month [October 1937], Hollywood has originated 90 percent of the personality programs that travel over the NBC and Columbia air lanes."[32] As 1937 came to an end, "the rise of Hollywood radio poured funds into the film community, but enriched the networks even more."[33]

"Hollywood in 1938 was at the apex of its career as a controlled market. Eight companies collaborating closely ruled the industry—its production, distribution, and exhibition."[34] Ten years of litigation by the Justice Department would bring about the 1948 Paramount decision in which the eight "majors" were found guilty of antitrust violations. Eventually this decision would have repercussions for the broadcasting industry as well.[35]

Of all four areas of media symbiosis—technology, business and economics, art and culture, and regulation and social control—the last category proves the most difficult to specifically define. Essentially, when motion pictures were being pressured on the predominant regulatory issue of the period, radio usually experienced similar tensions soon afterwards. Moreover, film, the more established medium at the time, was typically the first to come under attack, with the results of such an investigation and eventual litigation setting the precedent to be forced on the broadcasting industry as well.

The history of motion picture regulation is dominated by two major issues: antitrust and censorship. Both legal issues had been amply established as points of contention prior to 1920. At first, the Motion Picture Patents Company (MPPC) legally harassed independent producers, distributors and exhibitors. Then, in 1915, the MPPC was dissolved by court ruling. In the late teens and early twenties, the Federal Trade Commission also was trying out its wings by issuing complaints against block booking and other questionable or illegal trade practices.

Spurred by ever-frequent public condemnations of film content, a newer movie hierarchy made a slightly bolder move toward self-regulation with the formation of the Hays Office in 1922. Five years later, concern over power and frequency allocations, as well as monopoly and censorship issues, also led to the establishment in 1927 of the Federal Radio Commission. Throughout the early and mid–1920s, both the motion picture and the radio industries were gathered politically under a similar umbrella at the Department of Commerce under the watchful eye of then secretary Herbert Hoover.

During the 1920s and into the 1930s, the morality of Hollywood's product was coming under continual scrutiny. By 1934 "the combination of the influential power of the Catholic Legion of Decency and the quasi-legal authority of the Production Code had forced the motion picture industry to modify its content."[36] Interestingly enough, broadcast regulation from 1927 through the 1930s also was primarily concerned with cleaning up content by attacking irresponsible and profane programming, illegal lotteries, advice programs, and fraudulent advertising. Advertisers, who came to dominate the broadcast industry in the late

1920s and early 1930s, actually did a more effective job in regulating appropriate content and conduct than the newly devised code of the National Association of Broadcasters (NAB), since most advertisers would not risk making a single enemy through offensive or controversial programming.[37] Nevertheless, the NAB had adopted a code of ethics and a table of standards of commercial practice at their annual meeting in Chicago during March 1929. Consequently, radio as well as motion pictures had developed effective and established guidelines by the mid–1930s because of social and commercial pressures.[38]

Both media also felt antitrust overtures in the late 1920s and early 1930s. However, the 1933 National Recovery Act gave a brief reprieve to the "questionable" practices of these communication industries to promote the nation's floundering business picture. Trust-busting again touched Hollywood in 1938 with the beginnings of litigation that eventually led to the 1948 Paramount decision; 1938 was also the year that the FCC began similar probes that ended five years later with *U.S. v. NBC* in which the Supreme Court broke up NBC's red and blue networks. It appears, then, that actual media symbiosis between radio and motion pictures occurred on only three levels: technology, business, and programming. Still, both media with such close associations learned to expect similar and nearly simultaneous regulatory pressures.

The Symbiotic Apogee: 1941–1947

There is generally a cultural lag from when a new medium emerges until the time that the unique aesthetic potential of that communication art begins to be fully realized. By the early 1940s, radio was clearly recognized as a potent and sophisticated cultural force. During the war years, media symbiosis between motion pictures and radio was finally realized. Both media were essentially autonomous in structure and operations, while at the same time technically cooperating, creatively sharing talent and themes, and financially enriching the industrial prospects of the other. "In fact, the ratio of actual to potential audience for motion pictures doubled in the decade 1935–1945 despite the growth of radio and wartime circumstances."[39] Moreover, the motion picture and radio industries enjoyed economic rebounds during the early and mid–1940s after the severe depression and recession woes of the 1930s.

Program sharing was no longer unusual as Bing Crosby, a longtime radio performer, became the biggest star in Hollywood in 1943. He, of course, was not the only longtime radio star to be under contract to a major movie studio; since the late 1930s, this list had included Bob Hope, Jack Benny, Fibber McGee and Molly, and George Burns and Gracie Allen, to name just a few. Radio also continued to borrow movie talent for "Hollywood Star Theater," "Silver Theater," "Screen Guild Theater," and the aforementioned "Lux Radio Theater" which remained popular throughout the 1940s. By 1940 Orson Welles actually began adapting the sound techniques he had previously developed at CBS's "Mercury Theater on the Air" to the aural experimentation he was devising in his early RKO films, *Citizen Kane* (1941) and *The Magnificent Ambersons* (1942). Radio was finally providing the necessary talent and input to expand the boundaries of film grammar from the point of view of sound aesthetics. In retrospect, therefore, this process of symbiosis had indeed flourished for both motion pictures and radio in many complex and unexpected ways.

Radio had matured as an industry and social force by the 1940s, and it was now being taken seriously by all facets of society. The five years that led to *U.S. v. NBC* point to apparent governmental and regulatory fears that broadcasting was now a big business, a competitor on a scale with the nation's other large industries. The new social importance of radio was also demonstrated by a dramatic rise in the number of textbooks and magazine articles on the subject. No longer were broadcast matters hidden within the confines of a few scientific journals. By the 1940s, social, cultural, and political researchers and critics were producing books and essays concerning the history, theory, criticism, and effects of radio.

Film and radio far from satisfied the media needs of all America. Radio was consistently accused of lowering the speech standard of the country.[40] Many other critics had a hard time deciding whether the typical movie was more banal than the average radio program.[41] Nevertheless, the years between 1941 and 1947 were very optimistic and profitable for both Hollywood and radio. The two media, in many ways drawn together by World War II, responded enthusiastically to the national crisis. After a quarter-century of commercial broadcasting, 1944 proved to be radio's peak year for profits. In 1946 Hollywood set its all-time box-office records. Little did either medium expect or anticipate the changes each would be forced into for survival in the subsequent decade with the full-fledged arrival of television.

Symbiosis Between Film and Radio in the Television Age: 1948–Present

The last year in which motion pictures and radio reigned together as the most authoritative and effectual mass media in the United States was 1948. Movies and radio not only affected and enriched each other, but both media were also dominant factors in the changes in development and content that were occurring in the newspaper, magazine, and recording industries. Radio substantially cut into the advertising income of the print-based media between 1935 and 1948, just as an increase in the number of photographs as well as stories about entertainment personalities were flooding into and altering the look and agenda of American magazines and newspapers. Moreover, radio and movies during this period also affected popular music trends, especially jazz and swing, as musicians from around the country became exposed to more regional and ethnic sounds and blended these styles into their own repertoires; this pattern, in turn, stimulated the record business in the United States. At no other time in our century had

252 Film and the Arts

two mass media so easily shared the cutting edge of economic, social, and cultural influence for mass communications in America.

This symbiotic peak and parity between film and radio, however, did not last into the next decade. The industrial structure and cultural functions of both radio and movies changed radically with the onset of the age of television. In the ensuing process, these two media pulled far apart from each other over the next five years, as TV became the central focus of interaction for both radio and motion pictures.

The first full prime-time television season was 1948–1949. From this point throughout the 1950s, radio devolved from a national advertising and entertainment medium to one that was more locally based. TV of course usurped radio's network model as the older medium's organizational focus decentralized more towards the municipal or regional market. Radio's programming strategies also shifted dramatically away from storytelling and comedy; in the place of these generic types, newer variations of an older format were substituted which highlighted exclusive combinations of music and talk by disc jockeys.

Although occasional predictions by industry insiders concerning the eventual demise of radio were indeed exaggerations, the older medium was clearly forced to make room in the media marketplace for the economic vitality and cultural pervasiveness of television. In the decade between 1949 and 1958, total U.S. advertiser expenditures on television commercials skyrocketed from $58 million to $1.387 billion; in contrast, radio's advertising income of $571 to $620 million during the same time frame remained relatively stagnant in scale.[42] Radio as a sponsored medium actually declined from 11 percent to 6 percent of all U.S. advertising dollars in those ten years following 1949, while TV grew from 1 percent to 13 percent.[43] Television evidently emerged out of and then quickly subsumed the network operations, financial support structure, and prime-time entertainment function of its electronic precursor.

Radio, for its part, did grow slowly during this difficult transition period. The number of total AM and FM stations nationwide leaped from 930 in 1945 to 3,500 in 1960 to over 8,400 today, despite a corresponding loss in national influence and advertising income. Still, radio has done especially well financially during the last two decades after changing its identity in response to television's explosive appearance and subsequent challenge in the late 1940s and early 1950s.

The motion picture industry also adapted to the onslaught of TV by weathering an adjustment period from 1948 through the early 1960s. To compound matters, Hollywood was concurrently under scrutiny at the time by the U.S. Department of Justice for antitrust violations, and by Congress for suspected infiltration by Communists. As a result, 25 percent of all the movie theaters in America closed by 1954, while a progressively shrinking demand for theatrical films from the American consumer forced the major movie studios to slash their total annual supply by nearly one-half by 1963.[44] As it had with radio, television simply assumed motion picture's function of providing the United States with its tame, family-oriented, mass entertainment. In turn, Hollywood sought alternative ways of conducting business to accommodate the presence of such a formidable media competitor.

Actually, the means by which the film community abated this downward slide was by encouraging programming symbiosis with its newest electronic rival. The movie was first initiated in the early 1950s by some of Hollywood's smaller independent companies, like Ziv and Screen Gems. These outfits began producing low-cost television programming on film as a way to assuage the seemingly insatiable appetite of TV. By mid-decade, though, most of the major movie studios were also contemplating similar strategies. Disney, a mini-major company, signed with ABC in April 1954, and began producing its "Disneyland" series. The next year, ABC garnered another coup by entering into an agreement with Warner Brothers, a traditional Hollywood major, to supply more prime-time programming for this network.

After Warner Brothers made the transition to television, Hollywood's other elites, MGM, Twentieth Century-Fox, and Paramount, soon followed suit during the next two years. In 1948 there had existed a split in the locations where movies and TV series were made in America: the overall majority of feature films at this juncture were being shot in Hollywood, while most television production was centered in New York. By the 1957–1958 TV season, however, programming symbiosis between motion pictures and television was solidly developing, as the setting, technology, and talent for both media were, for the most part, brought together in southern California. By the early 1960s, Hollywood was producing more films than ever, but this time for TV and theatrical movies combined.

Throughout the 1950s, therefore, motion pictures and radio learned to direct their respective attentions away from each other, and towards TV for matters of survival. In the subsequent process, television simultaneously supplanted both of these media as the primary and defining mass communication force in the United States. What then has been the extent of the symbiotic union between film and radio since 1950?

The media symbiosis involving motion pictures and radio has actually been quite peripheral over the past thirty-five years, and mostly tied into the crosswise connection between films, radio, and the recording industry with respect to the production and sale of hit movies, records, and live acts, usually relating in some way or another to the new style of rock and roll. Hollywood, of course, had been promoting popular theme songs as corresponding media tie-ins to their theatrical releases ever since the 1927 coming of sound. With the emergence of the 1950s youth culture and rock and roll, however, this cross-media marketing strategy became much more frequently employed and pronounced.

The first emphatic example of this freshly cultivated nexus point between the movies, radio, and records came in 1955 with the combined success of *The Blackboard Jungle* and Bill Haley's "(We're Gonna) Rock Around the Clock." Bill Haley and his band, the Comets, first recorded the single a year earlier, but the song was only a mild success. "Rock Around the Clock" had actually stalled and then disappeared from the charts before Richard Brooks decided to insert it under the opening titles of his new production in late 1954. *The Blackboard Jungle* was released in the spring of 1955, starring Glenn Ford as a high school teacher confronted by violent and delinquent students. The film created a subsequent sensation, as a backlash from certain segments of the older generation branded the picture as immoral, and in turn brought teenagers to the movie theaters in droves. Haley's song was soon rereleased, and the tune became the first rock and roll record ever to reach the number one spot on the *Billboard* chart. "The rock era had (officially) begun. In 1956, movie producer Sam Katzman signed Haley and the Comets to star in a film titled *Rock Around the Clock*. It established a new trend in marrying rock and roll with the silver screen."[45]

The simultaneous emergence of Elvis Presley, and the long-term popularity of his subsequent film career, crystallized this pattern of meshing America's mass communication arts in the distribution and promotion of these new multimedia recording stars. The rapid rise of Elvis's first number one single during the winter and spring of 1956 launched Presley beyond radio airplay to successive prime-time television appearances on Tommy and Jimmy Dorsey's "Stage Show" and the "Milton Berle Show."[46] Moreover, "even before his first RCA original release, 'Heartbreak Hotel,' went to number one, Elvis flew to Hollywood for a screen test with Hal Wallis at Paramount Pictures."[47] The direction of Presley's career from 1956 through 1972 was now set in place; he starred in thirty-four tailor-made vehicles which were inevitably accompanied by the cross-fertilization of a movie soundtrack, hit 45s, and top–40 radio. The complex, symbiotic relationship between motion pictures and radio had taken another turn in the television age.

The list of popular music personalities and acts that blended their successful hit-making careers with appearances in Hollywood movies over the last three decades is clearly too lengthy to mention in its entirety. The number includes scores of recording artists from Pat Boone to the Beatles to Dolly Parton and most recently Prince. Popular songs have also been used from time to time in a nondiegetic context in Hollywood feature films. This tactic, in fact, was most prevalent during the late 1960s and early 1970s: Simon and Garfunkel's "Mrs. Robinson" from *The Graduate* (1967) and B. J. Thomas's "Raindrops Keep Fallin' on My Head" from *Butch Cassidy and the Sundance Kid* (1969) are successful examples of this strategy. In any event, popular songs on radio enhance and publicize those movies in which they are heard, and vice versa. In addition, this tendency towards cross-media promotion involving motion pictures, radio, and various other media has accelerated multifold over the past two decades.

One certifiable highwater mark in this new and developing relationship between radio and film was the experience of entertainment magnate, Robert Stigwood of RSO (Robert Stigwood Organization), and then-Paramount chairman, Barry Diller, with their innovations in advertising and marketing *Saturday Night Fever* in 1977 and 1978. Stigwood and Diller essentially sold *Saturday Night*

Fever to the public by a method that had previously been employed only in the recording industry. Through his experience as a record producer, Robert Stigwood decided to try marketing his movie by a strategy that was similar to the way the music business promotes an album. He commissioned the Bee Gees, a group that he managed and represented, to compose a handful of disco-styled songs for a story that he had just secured the film rights to about a blue-collar worker who "came alive" while dancing on Saturday nights. Stigwood also signed television actor and personality John Travolta to a three-picture contract, and then approached Barry Diller of Paramount Pictures in the hopes of selling the distribution rights of this movie package in return for receiving additional financing from the studio for production, advertising, and marketing costs. Diller eventually agreed, although at first his sense was that *Saturday Night Fever*'s potential was only as a "small cult film with an unproven TV star, that might catch on with the disco crowd."[48] What ultimately catapulted this motion picture into one of the top-ten, all-time box-office champions at the time, were the specific procedures that were used in selling the picture to the American public.

Barry Diller gambled $3 million in promotional fees alone on Stigwood's idea that the movie, *Saturday Night Fever*, could be marketed like a record album. In other words, each single from the film's soundtrack, as well as the soundtrack itself, was issued intermittently and strategically to help promote one another, with the overall intention being that every one of these songs would also increase the public's recognition for the upcoming movie. Each hit record, therefore, functioned as a kind of advertisement for the next single, which in turn created additional anticipation for the eventual release of *Saturday Night Fever* and the accompanying soundtrack.

Specifically, the first 45, "How Deep Is Your Love," was issued thirty days before the release of the album, and sixty days prior to the film's premiere. By the time the soundtrack was released, "How Deep Is Your Love" was number two in the country.[49] In this process, frequent radio airplay was crucial as disc jockeys around the country informed their respective listeners day after day that "How Deep Is Your Love" was taken from the soon-to-be-released *Saturday Night Fever* and its companion album. This free promotion obviously primed the public for the arrival of the soundtrack and the eventual opening of the movie.

The album was next issued in mid-November 1977, while a second single, "Staying Alive," was released a week later. By the time the movie premiered on December 16, "How Deep Is Your Love" was the number one song in the country, "Staying Alive" was in the top ten, and the soundtrack had already sold one million copies. Radio was now functioning as the key cog in alerting the public to the film's release, albeit no motion picture could be successfully promoted in this manner unless both the music and the movie were popular enough to stand on their own. In other words, no advertising and marketing strategy alone can ever make a film a hit; it can, however, greatly maximize a movie's potential. In this way, Stigwood and Diller's experiment paid off as both the motion picture and the soundtrack became enormously successful beyond anyone's wildest dreams as each item grossed more than $100 million worldwide. As then-president of RSO records, Al Coury, explained in January 1979, "We did not know what would happen, but we were prepared for it, and the single has laid the groundwork for the LP and the film."[50]

The entire motion picture industry learned a valuable lesson during the case of *Saturday Night Fever* about the potential for cross-fertilization between the communication arts in the United States. Paramount and RSO actually outdistanced themselves six months later by employing the same techniques in their selling of *Grease* (1978), which became the highest-grossing musical in film history. The radio airplay surrounding two enormously successful, number one singles, "You're the One That I Want" and "Grease," propelled the movie and the accompanying soundtrack to a comparable replay of *Saturday Night Fever*'s record-breaking success. These two films, along with their soundtracks and single recordings, now indicated once and for all to even the most skeptical industry insiders that the motion picture industry was no longer an isolated segment of the American media, but an integral component among all segments of America's mass entertainment industries.

The popularity of both *Saturday Night Fever* and *Grease* started with the sophisticated interplay between radio, records, and the movies, but eventually extended into television specials and printed materials based on these motion pictures as well. Following RSO and Paramount's lead, the other major movie companies began experimenting with and formalizing similar cross-media advertising and marketing techniques in the release of their own motion pictures. By the early 1980s, in fact, television replaced radio as the starting point for much of the promotion that involved popular music. The reason for this usurpation was the birth of MTV on 1 August 1981.

Examples of movie themes had always been evident in the earliest music videos on TV. Still, television didn't really become more important than radio in the promotional process of new feature films and their accompanying soundtracks and videos until the massively successful selling of *Flashdance* that occurred during the spring of 1983. This time the MTV airplay of Irene Cara's "Flashdance . . . What a Feeling" and Michael Sambello's "Maniac" was only supplemented by concomitant radio exposure. The following year, *Footloose*, *Against All Odds*, *Purple Rain*, *Ghostbusters*, and *The Woman in Red*, just to name the most successful examples, all used MTV as the central linchpin in their respective marketing campaigns that ultimately touched upon television, radio, movies, records, and print.

In this sense, the symbiotic union between motion pictures and radio in the 1980s is growing ever more peripheral as the decade slowly comes to an end. Being merely two of several interlocking media parts that make up these complex promotional techniques is by itself a far cry from the fluid and multileveled symbiosis that radio and the movies shared during their heyday together in the 1930s and the 1940s.

STYLES AND GENRES OF INTERACTION

On the levels of technology and aesthetics, film and radio have as many similarities as differences. Motion pictures can almost be thought of as a bridge between the older mechanical technologies which are grounded in the methods and substance of the nineteenth-century industrial revolution, and the newer electronic world of our present information age. From the outset, movies offered society an effective and powerful means of recording human experience which, more often than not, was shaped and conveyed to respective audiences in the form of a drama or story. These filmed narratives are characteristically experienced out of the home in a public grouping, and have the dual dimension of affecting both a socially ritualized response as well as an appeal to our own individualized projections and fantasies. The essence of moviegoing for most persons in the United States has always been a situation which is typically framed in a communal forum within an entertainment context that occurs anywhere from a semiweekly to a special occasion basis.

Radio, on the other hand, has generally been much more accessible. This technology has been comparatively more manageable and sometimes even portable. The fact that radio has invariably been a part of the American home since the 1920s has obviously affected the way people have thought about and used the medium. The technology has been less noticeable and more taken for granted than motion pictures. With its spread in popularity, especially with the influx of the transistor model since the 1950s, radio is now more omnipresent and ubiquitous than ever. Rudolf Arnheim suggested in his theoretical exploration, *Radio*, back in the 1930s that the aesthetic strengths of this medium are its intimacy, immediacy, and ability to force the listener to experience the visceral and primitive quality of sound by itself.[51] Likewise, radio creates more of an invisible environment than the cinema, while theatrical movies remain high profile, although the film-viewing experience can be, and usually is, simultaneously public and personal in nature.

As technologies, though, radio and motion pictures share the dimension that they can either record or transmit other media, arts, or information. Both technologies, therefore, have the capacity to translate various modes, materials, and styles of communication other than what might be thought of as distinctly their own. In so doing, film and radio also alter the nature of the aesthetics, personalities, plots, and experiences that are being filtered through their respective technologies and, in the process, transform this content into something uniquely new and different.

For example, music via radio or movies is a vastly transfigured and modified version from a comparable live performance, although always related ontologically to the original source. More specifically, a pop song undergoes numerous transformations when seen and heard in person as opposed to its aesthetic and presentational style in a movie theater, over AM or FM radio, on record/audiotape/CD, or even on MTV. Changes in volume, pitch, and harmonics, as well as in appearance and dramatics, are, of course, directly derivative of the imprint of these media arts themselves, and these changes are what set film and radio apart from other means of artistic expression. These communication arts are more than mere conduits of human expression, however; for nearly a century now, radio and the movies have offered fine, popular, and folk artists and performers two additional art forms and outlets in which they can expand, refine, and develop their sensibilities and talents.

Motion pictures and radio are additionally referred to as popular arts, primarily because of the commercial dimension of each. The production of radio programming and feature films demands the mobilization of vast industrial, economic, and human resources. This condition, of course, is why society and culture have had such a difficult time accepting movies and radio as arts in the first place. The idea that a concern for money always debases the art object, as well as the assumption that genuine human creativity is next to impossible when its generation is dependent on large social organizations interacting with machines, are two attitudes that are firmly grounded in nineteenth-century Romantic notions about the nobility of the solitary artist and the correct relationship between human beings and their natural environment. Our conception of what exactly is "human" and "natural" has, of course, radically changed during the last one hundred years, as have opinions about what is art, what are its various functions, and what is the relationship between a personal and a public artistic vision.

Both radio and movies have generally preferred the broad, public view and interpretation of the human condition, rather than a more select and individualized version. This tendency, no doubt, has much to do with the financial structure and commercialized nature of these two mass media. Although film and radio have typically been used for separate, though complementary, reasons in different settings and contexts by the American public, these technologies do, in fact, share the inclination of all the popular arts towards shaping their content into predictable structures and styles. Moreover, this desire to capture patterns that are familiar and popular is a key reason why programming symbiosis has been so fertile and long-standing between these two media in particular, as well as with all the other communication arts in general.

In the 1920s, for instance, radio programming resembled vaudeville, as nearly three-quarters of an average station's schedule was made up primarily of music, talent nights, and variety shows. Sports and some news were also evident over the airwaves during this decade, although radio drama was merely a minor programming concern. Beginning in the 1930s, however, radio comedy and storytelling would grow to prominence, according more opportunities for motion pictures and radio to share content ideas, styles, and genres.

At the start of this decade, radio made great strides in building its own viable traditions in the situation comedy, the "woman's story" or soap opera, as well as the detective and the Western genres.[52] Ad agency and network programmers borrowed heavily from the popular formulas already established in print, on stage, and especially at the movies. As mentioned earlier in this chapter, radio's use of Hollywood plots and talent would become all the more overt with a trend of programming, started in 1934 with the premiere of "Forty-five Minutes in Hollywood," that was specifically designed to promote movie stars and their latest-breaking films. Although lower in profile and less enthusiastic at first about such crossover material, the movie colony was actually employing radio talent and conventions concomitantly with the aesthetic and cultural symbiosis that was then being initiated by the broadcast industry.

The first multimedia performer to bridge highly prosperous careers in both film and radio, and an anomaly because of the unusually early date at which this intersection began, is Will Rogers. He started as an immensely popular vaudeville performer in the teens and made his movie debut in 1918. Despite the fact that Rogers appeared in fifteen silent motion pictures, this comic entertainer needed to talk to be most successful. Radio, of course, was an ideal vehicle for the humorist, as Rogers's place on the medium grew concurrently with networking during the second half of the 1920s.

By 1929 Will Rogers's film career was revitalized with the advent of sound movies, while his role as the nation's best-known sociopolitical humorist was once and for all confirmed through his hosting of a regular radio program beginning in early 1930. Will Rogers's talents also embraced print where he wrote a widely syndicated newspaper column. The cowboy philosopher remained a national celebrity and a star attraction in print, on the screen, and over the airwaves until his untimely death in a plane crash during the summer of 1935.[53] Overall, Will Rogers is the quintessential case in point of what was now possible because of the birth and maturation of America's mass communication arts: the media star as symbol and personality could now be replicated as easily as the story formula since the most prominent aspect and essence of these new electronic technologies was, and still is, the performer.

Fueled by this growing symbiosis between radio and motion pictures, the multimedia star phenomenon abounded in the 1930s, far beyond previous proportions. Two telling examples include Eddie Cantor and Orson Welles. Eddie Cantor, the comedian with the "banjo eyes," is emblematic of the vital and exuberant lowbrow traditions that livened the aesthetic and cultural maturation of both film and radio. Cantor first came to prominence in American popular culture as a vaudeville and burlesque entertainer in the teens; his forte was musical comedy, and he became a star with the Ziegfeld revues and on Broadway. There he developed a style of comedy that was made popular in vaudeville: fast-paced, urban, gag-oriented, and a little bit risqué.

Eddie Cantor's initial brush with the media arts was in a series of generally forgettable motion pictures that began with *Kid Boots* in 1926. His early movie career, however, failed to exploit either his experienced stage presence or his unique speech pattern. These signatures of personality, which were well-tempered through his years in vaudeville, did not strike a responsive chord with a mass audience until he began hosting his own network radio program in September 1931. At this juncture, Cantor's more earthy and modern brand of humor revolutionized the corny and homey style that was then characteristic of most radio comedy. His show quickly skyrocketed into radio's top ten and remained there for the rest of the decade.

That Eddie Cantor influenced the future of radio was clearly demonstrated the next year as producers found in similar vaudeville comedians the personalities they needed to revive radio. That year marked the debut for such comedy series as those of Jack Benny, Burns and Allen, Ed Wynn, Jack Pearl, Joe Penner, Fred Allen, and the Marx Brothers. With this inundation of funny men and women, the domination of radio by the comedians had begun.[54]

Moreover, Eddie Cantor's success on radio reinvigorated his lackluster movie career. Although none of his subsequent pictures matched the quality of other fellow vaudevillians, such as W. C. Fields and the Marx Brothers, Cantor's comic persona was finally exploited to the utmost in films like *Roman Scandals* (1933) and *Kid Millions* (1934).[55] The verbal, gag-dominant vaudeville style had also reinterpreted motion picture comedy in the early 1930s. Despite the fact that Eddie Cantor's legacy to radio far surpasses his efforts in screen humor, he is nonetheless representative of a comedic cultural tradition that is raucous, ribald, and nonreflexive, and which ably transformed the evolution of a key genre across the decade's two most influential and pervasive mass communication arts. Consequently, the aesthetic and cultural symbiosis between radio and the cinema had its share of profound and enduring contributions from what is typically considered the lowbrow end of the popular culture continuum; for the most part, this is where entertainers like Eddie Cantor flourished.

In contrast, other multimedia performers crossed over to radio and film from influences that can be considered both elite and popular. The broadcast and motion picture work of Orson Welles is a prime example of the injection of more highbrow impulses into the growing confluence between the two media in the 1930s and 1940s. Welles, a true prodigy and original, found prominence both on Broadway and over the radio airwaves beginning in 1935, when he was only twenty years of age. Although his theatrical career was nearly five years old at this point, Welles's creative imagination and considerable dramatic talents came to full fruition that year when he teamed up with John Houseman to help launch the Federal Theatre in New York.

During the next three years, Welles became the most successful, versatile, and controversial actor-director in New York, as he and Houseman produced popular renditions for their WPA unit of such classics as *Dr. Faustus* and an all-black casting of *Macbeth* set in Haiti. He simultaneously averaged a salary of between $1,000 and $1,700 a week portraying the lead character, Lamont Cranston, on the prime-time radio hit "The Shadow." Welles really enjoyed the best of both worlds for a time, and his genius spurred him to conceive of novel ways to blend the seemingly contradictory traditions of the elite and the popular arts together.[56]

Orson Welles genuinely loved the more European and time-honored customs and practices of the experimental or art theatre. He and John Houseman, in fact, created their own repertory company, the Mercury Theater, in 1937, as a reaction against the government's attempted censorship of their production of Marc Blitzstein's *The Cradle Will Rock* because of the play's obvious left-wing sentiments. With the Mercury troupe, Welles continued his golden touch with renowned and influential presentations of *Heartbreak House*, *Shoemakers's Holiday*, *Danton's Death*, and *Julius Caesar* in business suits and a modern setting. All the while, Welles not only continued his lucrative relations with radio as "The Shadow, whose sinister voice sent cold chills down the backs of countless potential criminals, but also as the occasional voice on the "March of Time" series and in various radio commercials.[57]

An important point to consider is that Orson Welles's growing reputation during the second half of the 1930s was no doubt just as dependent on his propensity for stuntmaking and controversy as it was for his interpretive genius in directing and staging the classics. In other words, he had an intuitive aptitude for public relations which in this century usually translates into an effective sense of how and when to use the mass media to best advantage. For example,

When the WPA production of *The Cradle Will Rock* was ordered canceled on opening night by Washington—on political grounds—Welles defied the government. He and his theatrical company led the customers through the streets to an empty theater. The play became an enormous success, and CBS invited the prodigy of show business to broadcast a one-hour drama from the network's Studio One each Sunday evening at 8 p.m.[58]

Welles obviously was never above popularizing himself or his more classical pursuits. On 9 May 1938 Orson Welles's audacious theatrical exploits placed him squarely on *Time*'s cover, just three days after his twenty-third birthday. Less than six months later, this boy wonder–enfant terrible of American drama and entertainment became a household name across the United States because of what should have been just another in a long line of innovative stunts: the "War of the Worlds" broadcast was indeed set apart, however, because of the fact that now Orson Welles was directing the imagination and energies of his Mercury Theater ensemble through the mass electronic forum of network radio.

The Columbia Broadcasting System and station WABC in New York premiered the "Mercury Theater on the Air" on 11 July 1938. Not surprisingly, the program was at first picked up only on a sustaining basis by CBS, since no sponsor was then interested in the apparently highbrow intentions of Orson Welles and John Houseman. From the outset, Welles believed "that radio is a medium preeminently suited to the storytelling art," as he reaffirmed his commitment with this series for adapting classic and challenging works from the stage and literature to the aesthetics of the airwaves.[59] What initially resulted, in turn, were minuscule ratings against radio's most popular show at the time, "The Chase and Sanborn Hour," starring Edgar Bergen and Charlie McCarthy.

Although it is a coincidence that Chase and Sanborn was also the sponsor of Eddie Cantor, the ease with which acts like Cantor and Edgar Bergen received backing from sponsors and advertising agencies, as opposed to more serious dramatists like Welles, Norman Corwin, Archibald MacLeish, Arch Oboler, and Irving Reis of the "Columbia Workshop," who all began their radio careers on a sustaining basis, is a telling indicator that assimilation into the media arts is usually slower and more tentative for those cultural strains that are traditionally considered more elite. The case of Orson Welles and others nevertheless illustrates in an emphatic way that a mass communication art like radio eventually borrows from and integrates all of society's cultural impulses when symbiotically sharing with other arts and media, and developing aesthetically itself. Welles, particularly, hurried along his acceptance by the radio establishment and its mass audience by exercising a combination of his own talent for technical innovation as well as his ability to court the bright lights of publicity and controversy.

The story of the "War of the Worlds" broadcast and its subsequent effect on its audience is well documented in countless sources, especially in *The Panic Broadcast* by the radio show's scriptwriter, Howard Koch, and in Hadley Cantril's *The Invasion from Mars*.[60] For our purposes, let it suffice to quote the lead *New York Times* article from the following day to give some sense of the frenzy and excitement that occurred when the Mercury troupe updated H. G. Wells's story, moved the location to northern New Jersey, and fitted the structure and style of presentation to approximate the emerging conventions of radio news and documentary programming. Because of the resulting consternation and alarm that it caused, people today tend to forget that the play itself remains a remarkable structural and aesthetic achievement:

A wave of mass hysteria seized thousands of radio listeners throughout the nation between 8:15 and 9:30 o'clock last night when a broadcast of a dramatization of H. G. Wells's fantasy, "The War of the Worlds," led thousands to believe that an interplanetary conflict had started with invading Martians spreading wide death and destruction in New Jersey and New York. The broadcast, which disrupted households, interrupted religious services, created traffic jams and clogged communication systems, was made by Orson Welles, who as the radio character, "The Shadow," used to give "the creeps" to countless child listeners. This time at least a score of adults required medical treatment for shock and hysteria.[61]

At the time the "Mercury Theater on the Air" broadcast its "War of the Worlds" adaptation on Halloween Eve 1938, this anthology program was being predictably and consistently pummeled in the ratings by the "Chase and Sanborn Hour" with an average of about 3 percent of the total possible audience as opposed to 35 percent for the variety show. Although the "Mercury Theater on the Air" would never seriously challenge its rival's popularity on NBC Red, Welles actually succeeded in garnering a substantial improvement in his program's audience share after the notoriety of the "panic broadcast."

Granted, this development was not his intention, nor does it appear from the memoirs and records that remain that he ever expected the "War of the Worlds" broadcast to cause anywhere near the kind of stir that it did. Be that as it may, Orson Welles's special talent for calling the mass media's attention to whatever happened to be his latest project indeed facilitated a quicker popular acceptance of his radio series than anyone could have expected.

Directly after the "panic broadcast," the Campbell Soup Company offered sponsorship to the performers at the "Mercury Theater on the Air," and then renamed the troupe and their new anthology program "Orson Welles's Campbell Playhouse." This show was designed specifically to be a series of book dramatizations. Next, CBS moved the offering the following March to a more propitious time on Friday evenings, as "the radio program" quickly became "one of the most popular current radio attractions."[62] In the final analysis, Orson Welles's sense of brazen showmanship was as important a factor as his considerable dramatic talents in fostering the assimilation of his more classical roots into the maturing aesthetic and cultural conventions of radio.

Welles, of course, would replay this pattern again when he entered Hollywood in 1940: *Citizen Kane* (1941) was an unqualified structural and technical tour de force, while at the same time being a source of great controversy because it presented a certain parallel to the life of newspaper tycoon William Randolph Hearst. In reaction, Hearst objected vociferously to the movie, and attempted to use his influence and leverage to suppress the film's distribution. That elements of politics, sociology, business, and culture accompany innovations in technology and aesthetics becomes evident in an analysis of the contributions of Orson Welles to both motion pictures or radio. Therefore, tracing the eclectic origins, sources, and traditions of any of America's mass communication arts, whether the line of investigation begins with a popular artist like Eddie Cantor or an Orson Welles, demands the acknowledgment of each of the media's many dimensions, not just what is readily apparent on the screen or over the airwaves.

Moreover, the cases of Will Rogers, Eddie Cantor, and Orson Welles all point to the emergence of the multimedia star in twentieth-century America. As the number of communication arts has proliferated with the invention of television and video, so too has the phenomenon of the multimedia entertainer become increasingly more common. Orson Welles is also an example of a crossover performer, or a player who is able to mix styles and genres of presentation in the same communication art. For instance, Welles had the ability to play in a highbrow Shakespearean adaptation on radio, a middlebrow adventure series like "The Shadow," or a lowbrow commercial. In addition, musical performers of today, such as Wynton Marsalis or Richard Stoltzman, may cross over easily in either direction between classical and more popular genres on records, radio, or television.

As referred to earlier in the history part of this chapter, Orson Welles's radio technique also carried over and influenced his innovative use of sound in both *Citizen Kane* and *The Magnificent Ambersons*. Although it is usually assumed that radio benefited much more from the subsequent interchange of programming, talent, and aesthetics that occurred between itself and the movies, the process of symbiosis has, in fact, been mutual and long-standing. Besides the already mentioned Big Broadcast series from Paramount, the strategy of using a behind-the-scenes setting at a radio station as a basis for a movie has intermittently spanned more than forty years from *International House* (1933), with W. C. Fields and Cab Calloway, to Clint Eastwood's *Play Misty for Me* (1971).

Radio personalities and their gimmicks have also populated the world of films ever since the repartee between Charlie McCarthy and W. C. Fields was re-created in *You Can't Cheat an Honest Man* (1939), or the Jack Benny versus Fred Allen feud became *Love Thy Neighbor* (1940) on the big screen. This trend occasionally manifests itself in contemporary motion pictures as well, as it did in *American Graffiti* (1973) with the depiction of gravel-voiced Wolfman Jack broadcasting from his Mexican station, XERB, to young teen audiences in California.

Radio programs also became source material for a number of motion pictures over the years. *Sorry Wrong Number*, for instance, started life as the May 25, 1943, episode of "Suspense" starring Agnes Moorehead; five years later, Barbara Stanwyck re-created the role on film with *Sorry Wrong Number* (1948). On the other hand, scores of Hollywood classics from *Stagecoach* (1939) to *It's a Wonderful Life* (1946) to *Shane* (1952) were all performed later as radio plays with many of the original talents replaying their roles behind the microphone, including John Wayne, Claire Trevor, Jimmy Stewart, Alan Ladd, and Van Heflin. This tradition actually continues into the 1980s as Mark Hamill reprised his role as Luke Skywalker for National Public Radio in its thirteen-part adaptation of *Star Wars* in 1982.

As also developed in the history section of this chapter, motion pictures and radio's major point of interaction for more than three decades has indeed been the nexus created in the marketing and presentation of popular music in America. Today, when instances of media symbiosis are observed, it is nearly impossible to think in terms of only two communication arts; and this is certainly the case with radio and film in the 1980s. Now the number of media involved in the selling of most popular artists and their respective works has escalated; and in turn, the process of symbiosis itself has become much more multifaceted and complex than it has ever been in the past.

One of the key reasons why so many media arts are involved with the same artists performing identical material is the trend towards conglomeration and diversification that has been so much a part of the business and industry of mass communication in the United States since the late 1950s. As was the case with the promotion of *Saturday Night Fever* and *Grease* in 1977 and 1978, Paramount's parent corporation Gulf & Western owned 193 companies at the time, which included motion pictures, radio, television, music recording, and book publishing and retailing. These interrelationships under the same corporate umbrella ensured a conscious and orchestrated blending of the media for the dual purpose of creating the same popular stars and symbols, as well as maximizing total income.

Undoubtedly, this tendency toward cross-media fertilization has always been a part of mass communication in the United States, but the pattern has never been as prominent, efficient, or sophisticated as it is today. This development also points to the ever-growing need for a more highly tuned, critical awareness on the part of the average media consumer, or the level of advertising and marketing that presently exists will more and more assume the role as the major arbiter of style and taste in American popular art.

NOTES

1. For further development on radio's prehistory, see Arthur Edwin Krows, *The Talkies* (New York: Henry Krows, 1930), pp. 77–85.

2. For further elaboration on the technical development of both radio and the "talkies," see Kenneth Macgowan, *Behind the Screen: The History and Technique of the Motion Pictures* (New York: Dell, 1965), pp. 275–86.

3. Garth Jowett, *Film: The Democratic Art* (Boston: Little, Brown, 1976), p. 139.

4. The coming of sound is well documented in Macgowan, chap. 19, "The Inventive Struggle, 1906–1926."

5. In 1925 *Science* magazine cited an early example in television experimentation which found a way to replace a mechanical TV system with an electric one: "Motion pictures have already been sent and received by radio." See "Radio Movies," *Science* 17 April 1925: xii of supplement.

6. W. F. Crosby, "Radio and the Motion Pictures," *St. Nicholas Magazine* February 1927: 308–10.

7. Robert Sklar, *Movie-Made America: A Cultural History of the Movies* (New York: Random House, 1975), p. 272.

8. Bosley Crowther, *The Lion's Share: The Story of an Entertainment Empire* (New York: E. P. Dutton, 1957), p. 42.

9. Ibid., p. 43.

10. Christopher H. Sterling and John M. Kittross, *Stay Tuned: A Concise History of American Broadcasting* (Belmont, Calif.: Wadsworth, 1978), p. 133.

11. Sol Taishoff, *The First 50 Years of Broadcasting* (Washington, D.C.: Broadcasting Publications, 1982), p. 25.

12. "Talkie Money," *Business Week* 24 September 1933: 22; and Erik Barnouw, *The Golden Web: A History of Broadcasting in the United States, 1933–1953* (New York: Oxford University Press, 1968), pp. 58–59.

13. "A Merger in Entertainment," *Literary Digest* 3 November 1928: 12.

14. Andrew Bergman, *We're in the Money* (New York: New York University Press, 1971), p. xii.

15. Barnouw, *The Golden Web*, p. 6.

16. Sterling and Kittross, *Stay Tuned*, p. 133.

17. James Rorty, "Dream Factory," *Forbes* September 1935: 162.

18. See Paul F. Lazarsfield and Patricia L. Kendall, *Radio Listening in America: The People Look At Radio—Again* (New York: Prentice-Hall, 1948), chap. 1.

19. Jowett, *Film*, p. 270.

20. "Talkies Adopt Radio Methods in New Sponsored Programs," *Business Weekly* 20 July 1939: 8.

21. "The Newspapers' Radio Rival," *Literary Digest* 9 May 1931: 11.

22. Sammy R. Danna, "The Press-Radio War," in *American Broadcasting: A Source Book on the History of Radio and Television*, ed. Lawrence W. Lichty and Malachi C. Topping (New York: Hastings House, 1975), pp. 344–50.

23. Barnouw, *The Golden Web*, p. 103.

24. "Hollywood and Radio," *Business Week* 6 November 1937: 27.

25. David Glickman, "CBS Dedicates New Hollywood Center," *Broadcasting* 1 May 1938: 27.

26. "Hollywood Radio City Ideal Plant," *Broadcasting* 1 November 1938: 22–23.

27. Barnouw, *The Golden Web*, pp. 103–104.

28. "Movies and Soap," *Newsweek* 24 October 1949: 50.

29. Barnouw, *The Golden Web*, p. 104.

30. Margaret Farrand Thorp, *America at the Movies* (New Haven, Conn.: Yale University Press, 1939), p. 267.

31. A. M. Sullivan, "Radio and Vaudeville Culture," *Commonweal* 13 December 1935: 178.

32. "Hollywood Makes New Broadcasting Center with 'Good News'," *Newsweek* 15 November 1937: 25.

33. Barnouw, *The Golden Web*, p. 107.

34. Ibid., p. 105.

35. Gary Edgerton and Cathy Pratt, "The Influence of the Paramount Decision on Network Television in America," *Quarterly Review of Film Studies* 8, no. 3 (Summer 1983): 9–23.

36. Jowett, *Film*, p. 281.

37. Commission on Freedom of the Press, *A Free and Responsible Press* (Chicago: University of Chicago Press, 1947).

38. "Movies and Radio Join Varied Brood of Blue Eagle," *Newsweek* 9 December 1933: 34.

39. Sklar, *Movie-Made America*, p. 270.

40. Francis T. S. Powell, "Radio and Language," *Commonweal* 10 April 1929: 653.

41. Leo C. Rosten, *Hollywood* (New York: Harcourt, Brace, 1941), p. 28; and Sidonie M. Gruenberg, "New Voices Speak to Our Children," *Parents* June 1941: 23, 40, 42, and 78.

42. Christopher H. Sterling and Timothy R. Haight, *The Mass Media: Aspen Institute Guide to Communication Industry Trends* (New York: Praeger, 1978), pp. 124–26.

43. Ibid., pp. 130–31.

44. Karen A. Libbett, ed., *Encyclopedia of Exhibition* (New York: National Association of Theatre Owners, 1980), p. 33.

45. Fred Bronson, *The Billboard Book of Number One Hits* (New York: Billboard Publications, 1985), p. 1.

46. Ibid., p. 10.

47. Ibid., p. 15.

48. "Robert Stigwood and RSO Productions," *Newsweek* 31 July 1978: 41.

49. Bronson, *The Billboard Book*, p. 476.

50. "The Selling of *Saturday Night Fever*," *Variety* 3 January 1979: 223–24.

51. Rudolf Arnheim, *Radio* (New York: Arno Press, 1971).

52. See J. Fred MacDonald, *Don't Touch That Dial! Radio Programming in American Life, 1920 to 1960* (Chicago: Nelson-Hall, 1979).

53. "Cowboy Philosopher," *New Republic* 28 August 1935: 62; "Fans Want Their Idol Kept Immortal on the Screen," *Newsweek* 14 September 1935: 28; "Last Film Role ...," *Literary Digest* 30 November 1935: 24; and "New 'Ah, Wilderness!' Cast Headed by Will Rogers," *Newsweek* 12 May 1934: 23.

54. MacDonald, *Don't Touch That Dial!*, p. 115.

55. Eddie Cantor, "You Oughta Be In Pictures," *Saturday Evening Post* 20 October 1934: 29 and 65.

56. "Marvelous Boy," *Time* 9 May 1938: 27–34.

57. "Orson Welles," *Current Biography 1941* (New York: H. W. Wilson, 1941), pp. 909–912.

58. William Manchester, *The Glory and the Dream* (New York: Bantam, 1974), p. 190.

59. " 'First Person Singular': Welles, Innovator on Stage, Experiments on the Air," *Newsweek* 11 June 1938: 25–26.

60. Howard Koch, *The Panic Broadcast* (New York: Avon, 1970); and Hadley Cantril, Hazel Gaudet, and Herta Herzog, *The Invasion from Mars: A Study in the Psychology of Panic* (Princeton, N.J.: Princeton University Press, 1940).

61. "Radio Listeners Panic, Taking War Drama as Fact," *New York Times* 31 October 1938: 1, 4.

62. "Orson Welles Begins Radio Book Series," *Publishers Weekly* 4 March 1939: 956.

SELECTED BIBLIOGRAPHY

The amount of research and writing that specifically addresses the symbiotic relationship between radio and motion pictures is sparse indeed. Unlike the plethora of materials that exists on the multileveled interchange between film and television, movies and radio have never been accorded the same substantial degree of historical and critical attention.

There are probably a number of sound reasons for this apparent oversight: first, the structural makeup of each mass media industry was more separate and discrete during the so-called golden ages of both radio and the movies. Most insiders and observers of the business of mass communication in America no doubt thought of Hollywood and network radio in those days as distinct unto themselves; in this way, their symbiosis was less involved and complex than what analysts have come to expect in the era of conglomeration.

There is also an important second reason: the symbiotic peak between radio and film from 1941 through 1947 predates the explosion of media studies in American higher education. It is an unfortunate coincidence that as the publication of broadcasting and motion picture–related materials accelerated astronomically in the 1960s and 1970s, no longer was the symbiotic union between motion pictures and radio as immediate an agenda item as those relationships that involved television in some way.

Last, it cannot be overlooked that even today the academic tradition in radio-television-film and mass media studies has typically encouraged individuals to specialize in one medium over the others. Although this tendency has been somewhat breaking down lately, allegiances are still characteristically fostered for cinema studies, as opposed to telecommunications, etc., to the virtual exclusion of all the other communication arts. Now may be the time to increasingly consider those points of contact, as well as those levels of interaction which link all the mass media together, along with the symbolic environment they help create.

Consequently, the sources that follow are meant to be an introduction to studying the symbiotic relationship between film and radio; therefore, works are included that may only acknowledge the crossover between radio and the movies in a peripheral way. Hopefully, more research and publication will be forthcoming in the near future to help outline and better understand this important, though largely uncharted, research area.

Books and Articles

Archer, Gleason L. *History of Radio to 1926*. New York: Arno Press, 1971.

Arnheim, Rudolf. *Radio*. New York: Arno Press, 1971.

Barnouw, Erik. *A History of Broadcasting in the United States*. New York: Oxford University Press. Volume I - *To 1933: A Tower in Babel*. 1966. Volume II - *1933 to 1953: The Golden Web*. 1968. Volume III – *From 1953: The Image Empire*. 1970.

Bergman, Andrew. *We're in the Money*. New York: New York University Press, 1971.

Bohn, Thomas W. and Richard L. Stromgren with Daniel H. Johnson. *Light & Shadows: A History of Motion Pictures*. 2d ed. Sherman Oaks, Calif.: Alfred, 1978.

Bronson, Fred. *The Billboard Book of Number One Hits*. New York: Billboard Publications, 1985.

Brown, Les, ed. *Channels of Communication: The Essential 1986 Field Guide to the Electronic Environment*. New York: C. C. Publishing, 1986.

Buxton, Frank and Bill Owen. *The Big Broadcast, 1920–1950*. New York: Viking, 1972.

Cantril, Hadley, Hazel Gaudet, and Herta Herzog. *The Invasion from Mars: A Study in the Psychology of Panic*. Princeton, N.J.: Princeton University Press, 1940.

Compaine, Benjamin M., Christopher H. Sterling, Thomas Guback, and J. Kendrick Noble, Jr. *Anatomy of the Communications Industry: Who Owns the Media?* White Plains, N.Y.: Knowledge Industry Publications, 1983.

Crowther, Bosley. *The Lion's Share: The Story of an Entertainment Empire*. New York: E. P. Dutton, 1957.

Czitrom, Daniel J. *Media and the American Mind: From Morse to McLuhan*. Chapel Hill: University of North Carolina Press, 1982.

DeLong, Thomas A. *The Mighty Music Box*. Los Angeles: Amber Crest Books, 1980.

Dunning, John. *Tune In Yesterday: The Ultimate Encyclopedia of Old-Time Radio, 1925–1976*. Englewood Cliffs, N.J.: Prentice-Hall, 1976.

Havig, Alan R., guest ed. *Journal of Popular Culture: In-Depth Radio*. XII: 2. Bowling Green, Ohio: Popular Press, 1979.

Jowett, Garth. *Film: The Democratic Art*. Boston: Little, Brown, 1976.

Koch, Howard. *The Panic Broadcast*. New York: Avon, 1970.

Krows, Arthur Edwin. *The Talkies*. New York: Henry Krows, 1930.

Landry, Robert J. *This Fascinating Radio Business*. Indianapolis, Ind.: Bobbs-Merrill, 1946.

Lazarsfeld, Paul F. and Harry Field. *The People Look At Radio*. Chapel Hill: University of North Carolina Press, 1946.

Lazarsfeld, Paul F. and Patricia L. Kendall. *Radio Listening in America: The People Look At Radio—Again*. New York: Prentice-Hall, 1948.

Lichty, Lawrence W. and Malachi C. Topping, eds. *American Broadcasting: A Source Book on the History of Radio and Television*. New York: Hastings House, 1975.

MacDonald, J. Fred. *Don't Touch That Dial! Radio Programming in American Life, 1920–1960*. Chicago: Nelson-Hall, 1979.

Macgowan, Kenneth. *Behind the Screen: The History and Technique of the Motion Pictures*. New York: Dell, 1965.

McLuhan, Marshall. *Understanding Media: The Extensions of Man*. New York: New American Library, 1964.

Settel, Irving. *A Pictorial History of Radio*. New York: Grosset & Dunlap, 1960.

Siepman, Charles A. *Radio's Second Chance*. Boston: Little, Brown, 1946.

Smart, James R. *Radio Broadcasts in the Library of Congress 1924–1941: A Catalog of Recordings*. Washington, D.C.: Library of Congress, 1982.

Sklar, Robert. *Movie-Made America: A Cultural History of American Movies*. New York: Random House, 1975.

Sterling, Christopher H. and Timothy R. Haight. *The Mass Media: Aspen Institute Guide to Communication Industry Trends*. New York: Praeger, 1978.

Sterling, Christopher H. and John M. Kittross. *Stay Tuned: A Concise History of American Broadcasting*. Belmont, Calif.: Wadsworth, 1978.

Summers, Harrison B. *A Thirty-Year History of Programs Carried on National Radio Networks in the United States, 1926–1956*. New York: Arno Press, 1971.

Taishoff, Sol. *The First 50 Years of Broadcasting*. Washington, D.C.: Broadcasting Publications, 1982.

Thorp, Margaret Farrand. *America at the Movies*. New Haven, Conn.: Yale University Press, 1939.

Wertheim, Arthur Frank. *Radio Comedy*. New York: Oxford University Press, 1979.

White, Llewellyn. *The American Radio*. Chicago: University of Chicago Press, 1947.

Wilkerson, Tichi and Marcia Borie. *The Hollywood Reporter: The Golden Years*. New York: Coward-McCann, 1984.

SELECTED FILMOGRAPHY

An exploratory chapter on the relationship between radio and motion pictures would certainly be remiss to ignore the availability of old radio dramas when citing their counterparts in film. Although there exists a handful of commercial distributors of vintage radio shows, two companies presently stand out from the rest in quantity of selection, quality of recording, and price. These companies are Adventures in Cassettes, Department R–520, 1401-B West River Road N., Minneapolis, MN 55411 (800) 328–0108; and Radio Yesteryear, Box C, Sandy Hook, CT 06482 (800) 243–0987. Catalogs with extensive listings are available from both companies.

Moreover, most of the radio programs cited in this chapter can be obtained from these outlets. There is a large selection of shows by individual entertainers (such as Will Rogers, Eddie Cantor, Orson Welles, Edgar Bergen, Charlie McCarthy and W. C. Fields, etc.), as well as specific episodes (the "Mercury Theater on the Air" broadcast of "War of the Worlds," "Sorry Wrong Number" from "Suspense," etc.) and series ("The Shadow," "Lux Radio Theatre," "Forty-Five Minutes in Hollywood," "The Chase and

Sanborn Hour,'' etc.). What follows is a selected list of comparable motion pictures that are distinguished in some way by their symbiotic link to radio.

American Graffiti (USA 1973). Universal. Directed by George Lucas. Screenplay by George Lucas, Gloria Katz, and Willard Huyak. With Richard Dreyfuss, Ronny Howard, Paul le Mat, Charlie Martin Smith, Cindy Williams, Candy Clark, and Mackenzie Philips.

The Big Broadcast (USA 1932). Paramount. Directed by Frank Tuttle. Screenplay by George Marion, Jr. With Bing Crosby, Kate Smith, Cab Calloway, and the Mills Brothers.

The Big Broadcast of 1936 (USA 1935). Paramount. Directed by Norman Taurog. Screenplay by Walter de Leon, Francis Martin, and Ralph Spence. With Jack Oakie, George Burns, Gracie Allen, and Bing Crosby.

The Big Broadcast of 1937 (USA 1936). Paramount. Directed by Mitchell Leisen. Screenplay by Walter de Leon and Francis Martin. With Jack Benny, George Burns, Gracie Allen, Martha Raye, Ray Milland, and Benny Goodman.

The Big Broadcast of 1938 (USA 1937). Paramount. Directed by Mitchell Leisen. Screenplay by Walter de Leon, Francis Martin, and Ken England. With W. C. Fields, Bob Hope, Dorothy Lamour, Martha Raye, and Leif Erikson.

Blackboard Jungle (USA 1955). MGM. Directed by Richard Brooks. Screenplay by Richard Brooks. Music by Bill Haley and the Comets. With Glenn Ford, Sidney Poitier, Anne Francis, and Louis Calhern.

Butch Cassidy and the Sundance Kid (USA 1969). Twentieth Century-Fox. Directed by George Roy Hill. Screenplay by William Goldman. With Paul Newman, Robert Redford, and Katharine Ross.

Citizen Kane (USA 1941). RKO. Directed by Orson Welles. Screenplay by Orson Welles and Herman Mankiewicz. With Orson Welles, Joseph Cotten, Dorothy Comingore, Ruth Warrick, Ray Collins, and Everett Sloane.

Flashdance (USA 1983). Paramount. Directed by Adrian Lyne. Screenplay by Tom Hedley and Joe Eszterhas. Music by Giorgio Moroder. With Jennifer Beals and Michael Nouri.

Going My Way (USA 1944). Paramount. Directed by Leo McCarey. Screenplay by Frank Butler, Frank Cavett, and Leo McCarey. With Bing Crosby, Barry Fitzgerald, and Frank McHugh.

The Graduate (USA 1967). United Artists/Embassy. Directed by Mike Nichols. Screenplay by Calder Willingham and Buck Henry. With Dustin Hoffman, Anne Bancroft, and Katharine Ross.

Grease (USA 1978). Paramount/RSO. Directed by Randal Kleiser. Screenplay by Bronte Woodard. With John Travolta, Olivia Newton-John, and Stockard Channing.

International House (USA 1933). Paramount. Directed by A. Edward Sutherland. Screenplay by Francis Martin, Walter de Leon, Lou Heifetz, and Neil Brant. With W. C. Fields, George Burns, Gracie Allen, Bela Lugosi, Rose Marie, Rudy Vallee, and Cab Calloway.

Jailhouse Rock (USA 1957). MGM. Directed by Richard Thorpe. Screenplay by Guy Trosper. With Elvis Presley, Judy Tyler, and Dean Jones.

Love Thy Neighbor (USA 1940). Paramount. Directed by Mark Sandrich. With Jack Benny, Fred Allen, Mary Martin, and Eddie ''Rochester'' Anderson.

The Magnificent Ambersons (USA 1942). RKO. Directed by Orson Welles. Screenplay by Orson Welles. With Joseph Cotten, Tim Holt, Anne Baxter, Agnes Moorehead, and Ray Collins.

Play Misty for Me (USA 1971). Universal/Malpaso. Directed by Clint Eastwood. Screenplay by Jo Heims and Dean Reisner. With Clint Eastwood, Jessica Walter, and Donna Mills.

Roman Scandals (USA 1933). Samuel Goldwyn. Directed by Frank Tuttle. Screenplay by William Anthony McGuire, George Oppenheimer, Arthur Sheekman, and Nat Perrin from a story by George S. Kaufman and Robert E. Sherwood. Music by Alfred Newman. Choreography by Busby Berkeley. With Eddie Cantor.

Saturday Night Fever (USA 1977). Paramount/RSO. Directed by John Badham. Screenplay by Norman Wexler. With John Travolta and Karen Lynn Gorney.

Sorry Wrong Number (USA 1948). Paramount. Directed by Anatole Litvak. Screenplay by Lucille Fletcher from her stage play. With Barbara Stanwyck and Burt Lancaster.

Star Wars (USA 1977). Twentieth Century-Fox. Directed by George Lucas. Screenplay by George Lucas. With Mark Hamill, Harrison Ford, Carrie Fisher, and Alec Guinness.

Steamboat Around the Bend (USA 1935). Twentieth Century-Fox. Directed by John Ford. Screenplay by Dudley Nichols and Lamar Trotti. With Will Rogers.

You Can't Cheat an Honest Man (USA 1939). Universal. Directed by George Marshall. Screenplay by George Marion, Jr., Richard Mack, and Everett Freeman from a story by W. C. Fields. With W. C. Fields and Edgar Bergen with Charlie McCarthy and Mortimer Snerd.

10

FILM AND TELEVISION

WILLIAM LAFFERTY

INTRODUCTION

To examine fully the symbiotic relationship between film and television, it is necessary to recognize this relationship as bipartite in nature: on one hand there exist the particular economic and technological foundations which predicate film and television as industries, while on the other hand there are the products of these industries, motion pictures and television programming, manifesting shared and individual aesthetic and formal aspects. Recognizing this dual relationship, this chapter focuses primarily upon the era during which the television and film industries forged the bases of their extensive symbiotic relation, roughly the decades between 1940 and 1960.

Contrary to conventional wisdom, the economic relationship between film and television has a lengthy history, beginning with the initial relationship between the Hollywood motion picture industry and the American radio broadcasting industry, discussed in chapter 9 of this book. During the 1920s Hollywood actively entered radio broadcasting, and during the 1930s the major film studios took seriously the potential of television broadcasting, both as lucrative opportunity and economic threat. Although the Federal Communications Commission approved commercial telecasting in 1941, World War II interrupted what technical advances and little program development had occurred. Immediately following the war, however, commercial American television underwent one of the most phenomenal periods of industrial growth ever experienced by the American economy. The film industry reacted to this rapid growth of a formidable entertainment competitor in several ways. Initially, Hollywood withheld its substantial library of feature films from the television industry, while exploring avenues by which the film industry could capitalize upon the growing popularity of television. Studio activity centered about developing theater television and the acquisition of television stations, with Twentieth Century-Fox and Paramount particularly active. Technical problems, distribution difficulties, and shifting audience demand prevented theater television from becoming a viable proposition, while governmental prejudice against the major studios, spawned by antitrust judgments, withheld station licenses from the major film firms.

Although the "majors" declined any extensive participation in either film distribution or production, the periphery of established Hollywood and legions of independent, nontheatrical filmmakers eagerly greeted the opportunities afforded by television. While television remained in its prewar, formative years, the broadcasting industry generally assumed that television would follow the basic model of network radio, with a number of interconnected stations broadcasting live, network-originated programming. However, after World War II it quickly became apparent that a large portion of television programming would be film: the medium's almost insatiable appetite for programming coupled with the slow progress of a nationwide coaxial cable network created an intense demand for both available theatrical features and made-for-television films. Throughout the late 1940s and into the 1950s, independent producers and the "B" film studios of Hollywood offered their inventories to help fill the burgeoning demand by television for older feature films which had quickly established themselves as popular television fare. These minor Hollywood studios, industrial filmmakers, and newly created television film firms engaged in the production of films expressly for television, both for network telecasting and syndication. By the mid–1950s the major Hollywood studios had reexamined their positions on television. For a variety of reasons, primarily concerning the diminishing value of their libraries relative to what television was prepared to pay, the major studios opened their film vaults to both individual stations and the networks, and entered into full-scale production for television. By the mid– to late–1950s, the symbiotic economic relationship which exists today between the film and television industries had been forged.

Throughout the 1960s and 1970s, recent Hollywood features played an important role in prime-time network programming, while the major Hollywood studios, themselves mostly absorbed by diversified conglomerates, concentrated heavily upon continued television production, and the advent of cable television and new video technologies afforded new, often radical, possibilities in the production and distribution of Hollywood's product, a concern addressed elsewhere in this volume.

While the economic structures of the film and television industries ultimately assumed a very evident symbiotic relationship, a similar relationship evolved between the media's aesthetic bases. Early in television's commercial life it was correctly assumed that television production would borrow heavily from motion picture technique. As television progressed, its programming heavily dependent upon film, television film production techniques and technology came to influence motion picture production, especially by the 1960s as creative personnel schooled in television moved into the Hollywood film industry. Whereas early television technique, both in live origination and film production, consciously adhered to the Hollywood model of the "well-made film," the particular limitations imposed by the television screen and program time restrictions, as well as the technology of television itself, helped to create a different, more succinct visual language, which eventually the Hollywood industry, to varying degrees, appropriated.

HISTORY AND DEVELOPMENT

At least in its formative stages, television enjoyed a technological history nearly as old as that of motion pictures. Basic scientific concepts governing the transmission of images through electrical means were advanced as early as 1839 when Alexandre Edmond Becquerel demonstrated the electrochemical effects of light, spawning the technical basis of the photocell and, ultimately, the direct physical correlation between modulated electrical current and variable intensities of light, which serve as the foundation of the television system. Several years later telegraphic facsimile devices appeared which utilized the principles of sequential scanning and transmitter-receiver synchronization, anticipating the technical bases for television transmission. During the late nineteenth century, coincident with the appearance of the first practical projected motion pictures and wireless radio transmission, experiments in mechanical scanning by German and British innovators produced the basis for the mechanical television systems which would dominate video experimentation until the 1930s; shortly after the turn of the century advances in cathode ray tube design and construction in Germany and Russia provided the foundations for today's electronic television systems, which superseded mechanical systems.[1] It is interesting to note that, in very broad terms, the technical development of television paralleled that of motion pictures, although displaced by almost fifty years. The formation of both the technological and commercial base of the motion picture industry progressed through distinct stages, ranging from the discrete though related scientifically motivated experiments of individual investigators, from Janssen to Marey to Muybridge, to what Michael Chanan has termed the bricolage stage, wherein various entrepreneurs like Friese-Greene and Thomas Armat individually sought to improve technically cinematic apparatuses with an eye toward commercial exploitation.[2] With the appearance of organizations strong in both capital and technical skills, such as the Edison and Lumière interests, the actual beginnings of both the technological and commercial foundations of the film industry had evolved. Television underwent the same transformation, its initial technical beginnings founded within scientific inquiry, progressing into a period of sophisticated bricolage through the innovations of J. L. Baird, C. Francis Jenkins, and others, until, by the 1930s, mammoth, vastly capitalized electrical firms like RCA and Fernseh AG developed the technological foundation for modern television, while organizations like the BBC, Reichs-Rundfunkgesellschaft, and NBC set about to realize the commercial potential of that technology, achieved soon after World War II.

As discussed in chapter 9, the motion picture industry had at first kept a wary eye on the development of commercial radio broadcasting, using radio primarily as a means of promoting Hollywood's product, but by the late 1920s several of the major studios had actively entered radio. Hollywood first evinced interest in the potential benefits and threats of television relatively early, about the time that C. Francis Jenkins, a leading American innovator in motion picture technology, began demonstrating his rudimentary mechanical-scanning apparatus for the transmission of what he labeled ''radio-movies''; in 1924 the Motion Picture Producers and Distributors Association (MPPDA) issued its members a report on Jenkins's experiments, and in 1928 the MPPDA issued another report dealing with the general status of television technology.[3] As with radio the decade before, the Hollywood industry kept track of the progress of a potentially awesome competitor. Apparently, in public, Hollywood scoffed at the notion that television could be perfected to a degree capable of competing with the local movie theater, but within the industry, especially after General Electric's demonstration of theater television in 1930, there existed widespread speculation that a technically viable television system capable of providing free entertainment within the home might be imminent.[4] Publicly, the president of NBC claimed that Hollywood had little to fear from video, since advertisers could never support costs for entertainment rivaling a feature film.[5] Amid growing public interest in television, the MPPDA conducted another survey focusing upon the relation between television and the film industry. Completed in 1937, the report cited advances in coaxial technology, the promising alliance between RCA and NBC in technology and programming, and the interest of the Radio Manufacturers Association (RMA) in promulgating technical standards for reconciling the various competing television systems. The report recommended that the film industry either actively engage in broadcasting by acquiring radio and television stations, or even entire networks; and it admonished Hollywood that ''It must prepare now for this new industry which is certain to become an important part of American life.''[6] Meanwhile, the film industry came to the realization that films would conceivably comprise a large segment of future television programming, primarily because of projected difficulties in establishing a nationwide coaxial cable network.[7] Indeed, as early as 1931 pioneer broadcast engineer John V. L. Hogan predicated that future television would necessarily rely heavily upon syndicated film programs.[8] While the studios began to recognize the probable importance film might wield in video programming, the established broadcasters then experimenting with television, particularly NBC, sought to diminish that importance, primarily out of self-interest. Broadcasters generally assumed that television would follow the paradigm of radio, with live programming sent out over cable to a network of interconnected stations; the major radio networks banned the use of recorded (or ''transcribed'') material over their lines since syndicated, recorded programming threatened the networks' oligopoly over the distribution of programming. If recorded entertainment could be syndicated, station by station, by a sponsor, the entire economic justification of the network would not exist. Although the broadcasters assumed that recorded (that is, filmed) programming would also be banned from television network use, the inherent complex and costly differences between video programming and relatively inexpensive radio programming pointed towards the eventual widespread use of film in television, an issue the studios realized. In its 1939 report on the status of television, the MPPDA stated that

[f]or the time being television needs us, and very badly. But most television people hope to relegate film to a minor position and bring the direct pick-up into all programs. In fact if networks were now possible they might adopt the policy of excluding films as they excluded for years the transcribed radio programs. There being no networks, film will start unopposed and as an essential factor. . . . [9]

By the late 1930s, based upon the current development of television and its own assessments of video's future, the Hollywood film industry's nascent symbiotic relation to television centered about four major avenues open to Hollywood in meeting the challenge of television:

1. Direct investment in television and radio broadcasting stations and networks as a means of controlling the competing media's development and realizing a financial return on that development;
2. the exploitation of theater television, by which the ''immediacy'' of television could be exploited within the basic model of motion picture exhibition;
3. the vending of the studios' vast film libraries to television broadcasters; and,
4. the production of films specifically for television.

During the next two decades, the film industry would pursue each of these avenues, with varying degrees of success.

In terms of direct entry into television broadcasting, Paramount Pictures proved to be by far the industry's leader. After already exhibiting a deep interest in broadcasting through its partial ownership of CBS earlier in the decade, Paramount in 1938 acquired a sizable interest in the Allen B. DuMont Laboratories, an early television broadcaster and manufacturer of electronic television equipment, intending to secure a position within both the telecasting and television equipment markets.[10] Paramount justified its interest in DuMont by reaffirming Hollywood's belief that film would ultimately become a major factor in video programming, by claiming that the film industry risked being excluded from the potential of television by the radio network ''monopoly'' in broadcasting, and by citing Paramount's desire to perfect a theater television system.[11] Meanwhile, RCA, suddenly confronted with a major Hollywood studio in the television industry sponsoring a video system in competition with its own, countered that Paramount's interest in DuMont existed solely so that Paramount could lobby the RMA and FCC to adopt what RCA termed the DuMont system's ''inferior'' technical standards; RCA claimed that Paramount's investment in DuMont was ''primarily for the purpose 'of protecting' their larger interest in the theatre and movie industry and not to develop the new art of television.''[12] With the FCC's adoption of the RMA's National Television Standards Committee recommendations on video standards (to which DuMont reluctantly acceded), any ploy by Paramount to sabotage commercial television by pushing for inferior standards would no longer be feasible.[13] Throughout the next ten years, Paramount exhibited an active role in developing the resources of DuMont.

Other studios made movies to enter television broadcasting, but compared to those of Paramount, their actions were minimal. Towards the close of World War II and afterwards, Warner Brothers, already active in radio, sought video licenses for stations in the nation's largest urban areas, as did Twentieth Century-Fox, MGM (which, through parent company Loew's, already was involved in radio), and even Walt Disney Studios.[14] By 1948 even the larger independent movie theater operators sought television stations of their own.[15] In the years immediately following the war, it appeared that the major Hollywood studios would succeed in realizing their first option in dealing with both the threat and promise of television by buying into the burgeoning but young television industry. However, several events prevented Hollywood from ever maintaining major control of television broadcasting.

Coincident with Hollywood's interest in buying into television came a federal district court decision in 1946, ruling the major Hollywood studios in violation of the Sherman Antitrust Act, and two years later the Supreme Court ordered divestiture of the studios' exhibition outlets as a means of correcting what the court viewed as Hollywood's monopolistic practices.[16] This decision severely prejudiced the studios' requests for television broadcasting licenses. During the late 1930s Congress investigated the monopolistic tendency of network radio broadcasting, leading to new restrictions on station ownership and the severing of the NBC Blue network from RCA (becoming, in 1944, ABC); the FCC, wary of any antitrust implications, held in abeyance all decisions on granting television licenses to applicants allied with the motion picture industry, an industry which, reflected by the 1948 Supreme Court decision, had exhibited "monopolistic tendencies." With the FCC prejudiced against Hollywood applicants, the studios felt little hope that they could secure telecasting properties and establish themselves within the television industry, and by 1950 most studio license applications had been withdrawn.[17] Other, perhaps less compelling, obstacles interfered with Hollywood's quest for television station ownership. In the two years following World War II, CBS and NBC promoted competing color television systems; confusion as to the FCC's ultimate action on the competition prompted some would-be Hollywood broadcasters (like Disney, whose films were virtually all in color) to withdraw their applications until settlement of the color question.[18] A more pressing problem occurred in September 1948 when the FCC, beset by technical problems involving television channel interference, announced a freeze on the processing of applications for new stations while new allocation patterns could be determined.[19] As a result, some studios, like Warner Brothers, declined to pursue license applications, unsure of the delay and unwilling to tie up capital for an indeterminate period.[20] As a result of this combination of factors, particularly the FCC's reluctance to issue telecasting licenses to the major studios because of the onus of monopolistic tendencies, the Hollywood film industry found itself effectively removed from buying its way into television broadcasting.

Well before the events which stymied Hollywood's attempts at acquiring television broadcast properties, the film industry anticipated a second option in dealing with television: theater television. Various proposals for theater television projection systems had been advanced early in television's technical development, with the most intensive research centered in Great Britain and Europe.[21] Theater television found use in Germany in telecasting the 1936 Olympics, and by 1939 its first commercial use in London proved extremely popular when also used to televise sporting events.[22] During the 1930s in the United States, General Electric, as part of the RCA group, and RCA itself exhibited various versions of large-screen television, while British interests, Baird Television and Scophony, announced plans by the end of the decade to move into the American market.[23] The motion picture industry saw theater television as a logical means by which to meet the challenge of television, a way in which a prime attraction of television, its immediacy, could be introduced into the industry's standard exhibition practice at a period when home television, in terms of both receivers and programming, was limited. By exploiting theater television, not only would the film industry as a whole benefit, but particularly the exhibitors, logically concerned about the inroads home (or ''free'') television might make on theater attendance, could still maintain a box-office draw. Shortly before World War II, the film industry seemed on the brink of investing heavily in the large-screen systems of RCA and Scophony; while research leading to technical improvements in the systems was suspended for the duration, the film industry made moves to challenge RCA in the theater television field when Paramount and Twentieth Century-Fox, through a major Fox stockholder, General Precision Equipment Corporation, acquired an interest in Scophony, fueling predictions that, after the war, there would be a struggle between the electronics and film industries for control of theater television.[24]

After the war, interest in theater television flourished within Hollywood, with claims that the new medium would be incorporated into all new theater construction, that it would lower labor costs by reducing the number of projectionist positions, and that, ultimately, films would merely be transmitted like television programs to the theaters themselves, eliminating print and distribution costs.[25] Warner Brothers, in addition to Paramount and Twentieth Century-Fox, announced plans to pursue theater television installations for their theaters and the development of programming to serve them, and joined RCA with Fox to develop RCA's system.[26] Although other systems promoted by other studios and manufacturers, including Fox's Swiss-derived Eidophor process and systems by General Precision and Century-Reeves, the RCA and Paramount apparatuses became the industry's leaders after the war, with over a hundred theaters equipped with their large-screen television systems by 1952.[27] By the early 1950s hundreds of events, mostly sporting contests, had been broadcast live to individual theaters over specially routed coaxial cables.[28] However, as with the studios' attempt to acquire their own broadcasting stations, the push for theater television encountered problems, again with the FCC.

To supply programming economically to theatres, both the Motion Picture Association of America (successor to the MPPDA) and the Society of Motion Picture Engineers advocated that the FCC reserve special frequencies within the television broadcast spectrum, providing theaters a cheaper and more efficacious alternative to the costly land lines of AT&T, lines which often could not be cleared for nationwide or even regional transmission of events to some theaters.[29] During the early 1950s opposition to this plan built: AT&T and Western Union argued that such frequencies would be a duplication of services offered by common carriers (that is, themselves), while other groups, such as the Fair Television Practices Committee, claimed that such frequencies would be illegal in that they would be inaccessible to the public at large, thus defying the Communications Act of 1934.[30] The film industry's previous antitrust problems compounded this opposition. Indeed, Paramount and Twentieth Century-Fox had been charged in late 1945 by the Justice Department with purposely inhibiting the progress of theater television; that litigation continued until the defendants entered into a consent decree in 1949, but the additional charges of antitrust made the film industry's task in convincing the FCC of its worth to own television licenses or be assigned special theater television frequencies virtually impossible.[31] The interminable hearings on the film industry's request for theater television frequencies, frequently conducted amid veiled animosity toward Hollywood, concluded in the spring of 1953, with FCC chairman Paul Walker concerned that if the request of the film industry for these special frequencies were granted, the FCC might be "unwittingly used to perpetuate a monopoly on news and sporting events that the public has had access to through home TV."[32] In the summer of 1953 the FCC rendered its final decision, denying the frequencies, claiming that such an allocation "was essentially a service which should be performed by communications common carriers," and that any decision concerning applications to use such common carrier frequencies would depend on "whether they meet the standards of public interest, convenience or necessity."[33] By the time the FCC rendered this decision, effectively ending any hopes of the industry for widespread theater television, the luster had begun to wear from the promising future theater television had at first promised. The industry's leader in television theater exhibition, United Paramount Theatres (the divested exhibition branch of Paramount), revealed in 1952 that its Chicago Balaban & Katz chain had consistently lost money on its theater television programs, and that it had no intention of installing any more units within its circuit.[34] Except for MGM, the majors' divestiture of their exhibition outlets had been accomplished by early 1953, meaning the studios had little incentive to encourage television's invasion of the theaters where Hollywood's product was consumed.[35] The changing demographics and leisure time activities of Americans, not to mention home television, probably contributed to diminishing the attraction of theater attendance. With the decline of theater television, the studios focused their attention on new film technologies including wide-screen and three-dimensional processes to entice audiences into theaters.[36]

Thus, primarily because of the taint of "monopolistic tendencies," the FCC had by the early 1950s thwarted the two options which would have provided the film industry with direct entry into television broadcasting, the acquisition of television stations and the development of theater television. Those options that remained, the film industry's release of its film libraries and its producing new filmed programming for television, provided the bases upon which the true symbiotic relation between the film and television industries exists.

From the very origins of what can be considered modern American television broadcasting during the 1930s, feature films played a major role in programming. From the day RCA's experimental New York station W2XBS conducted its first program transmission in July 1936, films, particularly features, would serve as a mainstay of that and other experimental stations' programming.[37] For early experimental television, reaching few viewers and carrying no advertising, the acquisition of films for telecasting posed no serious problem for the handful of operating stations; but as television's technical progress evolved, gaining more and more public visibility, acquiring suitable films for broadcasting became increasingly difficult. In 1939 NBC attempted to secure films from the Hollywood industry, but all the major studios, including NBC's own corporate affiliate RKO, refused, considering television to be a potential competitor and, most important, unable to pay the rentals the studios' films could earn in regular release and reissue.[38] NBC could secure only twenty-five hours of film programming, culled mainly from peripheral Hollywood studios and British producers, a prescient indication of where television would obtain most of its feature film fare over the next fifteen years.[39] NBC president Lenox Lohr downplayed NBC's inability at the time to obtain more feature film programming, but following World War II televised features, despite their age or quality, became a popular and economical aspect of early television programming.[40]

With virtually all telecasting in abeyance for the duration of World War II, the problems associated with obtaining film programming for television did not fully manifest themselves until the television industry underwent almost exponential growth following the war. The number of stations hitting the air between the end of the war and the first full year following the lifting of the freeze, 1953, increased from 6 to 125, while the number of American families owning television sets jumped from but 8,000 to well over 20 million during the same period.[41] In 1946 new station applications indicated that broadcasters intended to devote nearly half their broadcast hours to film, primarily as means of providing economical programming to fill ever-lengthening broadcast days.[42] Shortly after World War II, with the completion of a nationwide coaxial cable able to provide live network programming still several years away and the cost of producing live television programming, particularly for smaller television broadcasters, prohibitive, film offered an attractive option to station programmers.

Logically, early video programming contained a surfeit of educational, documentary, and promotional films which could be rented outside the established Hollywood industry for little more than shipping charges and for which, importantly, telecasting rights could be secured. Although the use of such films coincided with findings of the CBS Television Institute indicating that viewers of early television ranked educational service as an important expectation of the new medium, such uninspired programming drew predictable response: in 1946 Worthington Minor, as producer of live television at CBS his opinion perhaps jaundiced, stated unequivocally that "Of the films available to television, only about one in ten is really interesting."[43] The difficulties involved in ascertaining the broadcast rights to films posed a serious problem. By early 1946 *Variety* reported that the supply of available, inexpensive government films had been practically exhausted, and that confusion about the assignment of broadcast rights to the films' ASCAP soundtracks threatened their continued use in television.[44] The clearance of telecasting rights for films, particularly features, would remain a vexing problem for television broadcasters for the next decade.

In the several years following the war, as the demand for more sophisticated, higher quality filmed programming grew and advertising dollars became more available, local stations eagerly sought any and all Hollywood products for which television rights could be assigned and which could be economically acquired. The major Hollywood studios, of course, refused telecasters access to their film libraries. Although television's obvious position as a competitor to Hollywood undoubtedly influenced the studios' decision, the simple economic fact that the industry's films, almost regardless of age, could still earn much more in theatrical release than the fledgling television was prepared to pay emerged as the primary reason for Hollywood's attitude.[45] Another, more subliminal but as pervasive reason for the studios' reluctance centered around the assignment of their films' television rights. In the absence of any clear-cut legal precedent after the war, the studios found themselves responsible for the arduous and expensive task of clearing all video rights to their films before those films could be freed for broadcasting, necessitating a process of negotiation with virtually all the creative personnel and craft unions involved in a particular film's production.[46] From this problem with rights assignment arose an issue which would play a major determining role in the growth of films on television, centering about the relations among Hollywood, the young television industry, and powerful labor groups like the American Federation of Musicians (AFM) and Screen Actors Guild (SAG).

In the decade before television's postwar commercial blossoming, the AFM wreaked havoc within the broadcasting and recording industries with its varying and extreme demands concerning the employment and compensation of union musicians. With the ascension of James Petrillo to the federation's presidency in 1940, the union's attitude towards the technological displacement of musicians became more militant, anchored in Petrillo's belief that "musicians play themselves out of jobs when their performances can be repeated without their appearance."[47] While television remained experimental, the AFM set a minimal scale for video use of union musicians, but in 1945 Petrillo banned all use of federation members in television.[48] In 1946 the AFM, as part of a lucrative new contract with the eight major Hollywood studios, prohibited the release to television of those studios' films produced after 1946 containing union-produced soundtracks.[49] The broadcasting industry suspected collusion between the MPPA and AFM: as a payoff to the AFM for banning video use of musicians, inhibiting the entertainment value of early live television, the studios agreed to withhold their films. With television lacking both live music and recent feature films, the AFM and Hollywood placed themselves in a mutually advantageous position for future bargaining.[50] Spurred by the AFM action, the Screen Actors Guild in its 1947 agreement with the major studios banned television use of films released after 1 August 1948.[51]

As a result of the machinations between the major studios and the unions, the films available to telecasters consisted, according to *Sponsor* magazine, of "a motley collection of Westerns, grade B comedies and melodramas, serialized adventures, cartoons, shorts, a small supply of Grade A features, and some foreign films," the output of producers not signatories to any American labor agreements nor beholden to mainsteam Hollywood.[52] Television stations initially used these generally undistinguished films to fill broadcast hours, with little hope that they could establish wide audiences. However, this "motley assortment" achieved respectable, and at times spectacular, ratings. Early surveys of video viewership revealed that audiences very much enjoyed these feature films.[53] After the adoption of the standard radio ratings services to television, the popularity of these old features appeared indisputable.[54] Advertiser interest in sponsoring feature film presentations, especially during daytime and late-night "off-hours" when airtime was inexpensive, surged between 1947 and 1950. However, by 1950 some markets, like Los Angeles, Chicago, and Cincinnati, had already exhausted the supply of films released for broadcast.[55] As a result, station and network film programmers scrambled to find all available feature film, and those producers unaligned with the MPAA began to release more and more film to satisfy the demand, generating significant income for themselves.

As early as 1938 United Artists (UA), distributor of independent features, had supplied films for television on a station-by-station basis; in 1942 UA joined several small independent producers already active in the field in releasing 162 features and 52 shorter Westerns to television.[56] In 1948 UA leased a package of 38 features and 44 shorts to New York's WPIX-TV, which earlier had acquired 24 British films from the Korda organization.[57] Late in 1948 minor Hollywood studio Eagle-Lion leased 51 features to CBS.[58] By 1949 the market appeared so lucrative that a major Hollywood studio, Universal, anticipated releasing some of its considerable library of Westerns for television broadcasting. However, the AFM claimed soundtrack rights, and insisted that Universal completely rescore all films intended for video release using union musicians; Universal deemed that the costs in rerecording the nearly fifty films, around $2,300 per film, would make their video release unprofitable, and scrapped the idea.[59] By 1950 foreign films, especially recent British productions but also subtitled, newly released Italian films which had experienced but limited American theatrical release, became a staple of major market television stations.[60]

By 1951, with the majors still not entering the television film market and the supply of features in precariously short supply, financially strapped "B" studios like Monogram and Republic reached accords with the AFM for the television release of all their films, agreeing to rescore the films using union musicians and to deposit 5 percent of the studios' realized profits into a union trust; as testimony to the increased prices paid by television for any feature films, Monogram, shut down by striking musicians before the agreement and realizing depressed revenue on theatrical rentals, nevertheless recorded a gain in earnings for the year, despite the costs involved in readying the films for video release.[61] With the ever-increasing demand for films by television, producers could demand sizable prices for television release of their films, reflected by the $2 million received by major Hollywood independent David Selznick for twelve features.[62] Some minor distribution firms, like Quality Films which sold a package of twenty-six aged features to Du Mont for $1.8 million in 1951, realized windfall profits from television; these organizations had purchased from the studios negatives of films considered beyond their commercial viability before television created such demand for features, originally intending to release them within the non-theatrical, 16-mm market.[63] Meanwhile, the overall decrease in movie theatre attendance only accelerated the minor studios' sale of features to television. By the early 1950s, the "B" movie market finished, smaller studios and independents like Republic had little recourse but to sell to television, an option their lack of union obligations allowed them to do.[64]

As more and more television stations hit the air following the lifting of the freeze in 1951, the demand for feature film programming, established as popular with viewers, became even more intense. As a result, the major Hollywood studios could finally command the prices which they believed their film libraries worth by the mid–1950s. In 1955 both Twentieth Century-Fox and Paramount sold packages of older features to television; later that year, with the breakup of RKO following its sale to General Teleradio, a huge portion of the RKO film library—over 700 features including post–1948 films—was sold to the C & C Super Corporation for over $15 million.[65] General Teleradio, with no interest in pursuing filmmaking, considered RKO's film library a source of quick cash to underwrite other activities; by 1957 C & C Super had realized an estimated $25 million gross in leasing its RKO films.[66] Fearing that the RKO films would flood the market, reducing the potential value of their own features' television release, other major studios, including Columbia, Warner Brothers, and Universal, soon began offering pre–1948 titles from their previously unavailable libraries, while studios like Republic and Fox, which had previously offered only a limited number of older features, now made more recent "A" features available.[67]

In placating the SAG, the agreement between RKO and C & C Super stipulated that C & C had to negotiate with the actors union over compensation for the telecasting of features made after 1 August 1948, the date cited in the SAG contract with the MPAA; C & C paid the guild $715,000 in late 1956 to clear a package of eighty-two features for video release.[68] Of course, studios like Republic and distributors like United Artists (which released thirty-nine post–1948 features to television in 1956), not signatories of the SAG agreement, remained free to dispose of their films without dickering with the unions.[69] The AFM, however, claimed that any pre–1948 films had to be rescored using union musicians, a demand that the studios ignored and Petrillo did not pursue, evidently because of such a demand's tenuous legality.[70] By late 1956 the MPAA began negotiations with virtually all Hollywood craft unions in order to work out an industry-wide agreement on the release of post–1948 films; since no agreement materialized, pre–1948 features and British films remained the staple of local film programming and the networks' infrequent attempts at running prime-time features, as with ABC's "Famous Film Festival" in 1955.[71] The networks by 1960 wished to televise post–1948 films in prime time as a programming ploy to boost sagging viewership, necessitating negotiations which eventually led to a strike of the SAG membership in 1960.[72] After the SAG won major concessions from the studios, NBC on 23 September 1961 premiered "NBC Saturday Night at the Movies" with *How To Marry a Millionaire* (1953), part of a $25 million package purchased from Twentieth Century-Fox.[73] Envious of NBC's ratings success with "NBC Saturday Night at the Movies," ABC followed suit, purchasing a block of United Artists post–1948 features, axing several hour-long adventure dramas, and launching "Hollywood Special" in April 1962.[74] CBS, the industry's leading network bolstered by a stable of strong situation comedies, did not add a prime-time feature film program until the fall of 1965, intending to strengthen a weak Thursday night lineup.[75]

Two studios, however, did not exhibit the initial eagerness of the other majors to release their libraries to television. Paramount, among its previously described television ventures, maintained an interest in developing subscription television, beginning in 1951 with its acquisition of a half-interest in International Telemeter.[76] However, persistent opposition to pay-TV within the broadcast industry and difficulties in obtaining suitable pay programming frustrated Paramount's plans; after withholding its films from television release, believing that they could be profitably used in its subscription television plan, Paramount in 1958 finally sold its pre–1948 library to MCA for television release.[77] Meanwhile, other attempts to launch home pay-TV, including Zenith Radio's Phonevision system and Skiatron's Subscribervision, encountered the same problems as did Telemeter, particularly resistance by most studios to release feature films to the services.[78] Loew's, parent of MGM, did not begin distribution of its extremely valuable film library to television until late 1956, and used that library as a tool with which to gain the station ownership denied the industry by the FCC several years earlier. Feature films for television had become so profitable for the studios that MGM traded use of its features for part ownership in the stations using the films, acquiring quarter interests in stations in Los Angeles, Denver, and Minneapolis.[79]

By the mid–1960s, then, a standard aspect of today's network (and cable) television programming had evolved, the use of recently released feature films, especially in prime time. Indeed, as the pool of available features diminished and the prices for those available features rose steadily, the television industry, often in cooperation with the studios, undertook the production of its own features, the made-for-television film, a staple of contemporary television programming.[80] Beginning with NBC's *See How They Run* in 1964, the "made-for-TV movie" capped the formation of an important, early symbiotic relation between film and television, representing Hollywood's fourth option in dealing with the promise and threat of video: the production of films exclusively for television.

Early in television's commercial development, while it still appeared that television would assume the model of network radio emphasizing live origination, programming filmed specifically for video received scant attention. Especially as World War II drew to a close, though, it became increasingly evident that the prohibitive costs of staging live programming, the projected difficulties in obtaining filmed products from Hollywood, and the unlikelihood that a nationwide coaxial network could be quickly constructed, would lead to a potentially lucrative market for television films.[81] Some studios made limited and tentative efforts to enter such a production market: MGM formed a television department in 1943 but did not enter into any production until well into the next decade, while RKO launched RKO Television Corporation in 1944, producing by 1947 only a series of quiz films edited from newsreels.[82] After the war the Hollywood majors closed ranks in denying the use of their contract players and creative personnel in the production of films for television.[83]

In 1944 former Universal executive Arch Heath, reflecting a growing consensus within the film industry, maintained that films would necessarily become a mainstay of postwar video programming, adding that "[s]ince probably no one has produced a good professional film, or series of films, for television, sponsored by a reputable advertiser, the field is open."[84] Heath maintained that the traditional Hollywood methods of filmmaking would prove far too expensive for sponsors, and advocated that television film producers "forget about the 'so-called' essential cost of movies, and start from scratch on their own system of motion picture production."[85] Heath's observations would prove prophetic, as filmmakers, often from the periphery of the established film industry, sought new methods to finance and produce films to satisfy television's voracious appetite for programming.

In the five years following World War II, *Newsweek* magazine estimated that over 800 film producers had entered the television film market, hoping to capitalize upon the needs of new stations for programming, but that "[m]ost of them had closed up shop with the first rent bill."[86] Early television film producers encountered a number of problems which served to eliminate all but the largest and most resourceful from competition. As with the Hollywood studios, labor demands made by the musicians threatened; by late 1949 Petrillo and the AFM had issued guidelines for the use of union music in television films, but the wage scales demanded, according to *Televiser* magazine, placed "the production of low-cost television films in a restrictive vise, forcing many small producers out of business."[87] Other craft unions and guilds, including the SAG, made claims regarding television films, further complicating the situation, especially for marginal producers. Meanwhile, the FCC freeze on granting new station applications stymied the phenomenal growth that had been anticipated, with too many television film producers competing for sales to too few stations.[88] As a result, unless a producer had an established reputation or a signed contract from a sponsor in hand, financing for filmed television programming proved virtually impossible.[89]

During the late 1940s two general methods evolved by which television film producers attempted to market their product to the television industry. The first method involved effecting severe scales of economies in production so that little production capital would be needed and the package price could be met by individual stations. Jerry Fairbanks, first among these early producers and who by 1952 had eight filmed series in syndication ranging from cartoons (*Crusader Rabbit*) to sports (*Ringside with the Rasslers*), proved the industry's innovator in developing low-cost production techniques.[90] At the heart of Fairbanks's production scheme at his Los Angeles studio was a simultaneous three-camera shooting method, dubbed "Multicam," designed to capture efficiently and economically a multitude of camera setups and angles, themselves all precisely preplanned and rehearsed before filming and intended to provide the editor with a variety of choices when assembling the final cut.[91] Other cost-saving measures included the use of 16-mm film (cheaper to process and making prints more economical to ship) and specially built cameras, magazines, and lighting systems, all designed to reduce typical film shooting schedules by 500 percent.[92] However, difficulties encountered in 1948 by the Fairbanks organization in the production of its most ambitious series, "Public Prosecutor," reflected the problems being felt throughout the burgeoning television film industry. The series, accorded a $150,000 budget and backed by promised NBC syndication, was to consist of twenty-six seventeen-and-a-half-minute programs.[93] As was standard practice in syndication, stations in large markets like New York City's NBC affiliate would be charged $1,500 per segment, with the prices graduated according to market size, with WOI-TV in Ames, Iowa, charged the minimum $100.[94] By the fall of 1948, though, Fairbanks announced that production of "Public Prosecutor" had been discontinued, the cost of each segment totaling more than $10,000 (approximating the cost of staging the live, hour-long "Philco Playhouse") because of Hollywood guild wage demands.[95] By the time the FCC announced the freeze, the completed episodes of "Public Prosecutor" had not found one buyer; the series finally reached the air over the Du Mont network during the 1951–1952 season.[96] Fairbanks attributed his problems with "Public Prosecutor" to the high costs involved in Hollywood production, and cautioned that only through producers' forgoing any expectations of immediate profits and the guilds and crafts setting a lower scale for television films could the fledgling television film industry survive.[97] Some producers tried filming abroad to avoid costs associated with Hollywood production, but to no avail. Sheldon Reynolds's "Foreign Intrigue" series shot in Europe, despite being shown in thirty markets during the 1951–1952 season, nevertheless lost $100,000.[98]

The experiences of Fairbanks and other television film producers proved convincingly that new methods of financing and distributing television films were needed in addition to the rationalization of film production. For example, CBS and IMPPRO co-produced "The Cases of Eddie Drake" in 1949, to be offered to a CBS sponsor first at considerably below its $7,500 per episode production cost, then syndicated nationwide; CBS and IMPPRO would then participate equally in all profits above production, syndication, and promotion costs over the series' commercial life.[99] The pattern developed in financing television film by one of broadcasting's largest sponsors, Procter & Gamble, quickly became the industry standard: Procter & Gamble entered an agreement with Frank Wisbar Productions in 1949 to produce the "Fireside Theatre" drama anthology series for showing Tuesdays over NBC. Procter & Gamble paid only about 70 percent of each episode's production costs, with the rights reverting to Wisbar and his syndicator after the network run; the series proved a ratings winner on NBC, and in subsequent off-network syndication, under different titles like "Strange Adventure" and "Royal Playhouse," the series earned considerable revenue for Wisbar.[100] In an effort to broaden their market, some syndicators began what would become an important aspect of American television distribution, the exploitation of foreign markets; in 1952 CBS Television Film Sales placed "Gene Autry" with the first Italian television stations and the musical series "Holiday in Paris" on Brazilian television.[101] By the summer of 1951 fifty filmed programs had been placed in syndication, accounting for twenty programming hours weekly, with another eight hours broadcast weekly over the networks.[102] But, until the lifting of the freeze and the further proliferation of television stations, the production of films for television remained a tenuous enterprise for most participants.

During the embryonic period of television film production, the most successful firms were, understandably, those who brought to the field the most experience and the highest visibility. For example, Cincinnati's Frederick W. Ziv Company had been radio's preeminent producer and syndicator of radio programming when it entered television in 1946; by 1952 Ziv Television Programs, backed by a large and efficient sales force experienced in radio syndication, had grossed over $20 million by producing and syndicating direct to sponsors such programs as "The Cisco Kid," shot in color in anticipation of color television and still in heavy distribution today.[103] Realizing that syndication profits only came in the "long run," Ziv and his associates advocated spending money for quality productions rather than concentrate on production shortcuts, insuring continued audience interest in the product.[104] The potential of filmed television also attracted interest within the established motion picture industry. Hal Roach Studios, under the supervision of Hal Roach, Jr., had been transformed from a moribund operation on the margins of the Hollywood industry into the world's largest television film production center, with an output of almost 800 half-hour series episodes, 53 pilot films, 4 hour-long featurettes, and over 500 commercials between 1949 and 1953.[105]

The entry of Roach into television production during the late 1940s signaled the beginnings of Hollywood's active participation in television film production. As early as 1948 Twentieth Century-Fox and Universal produced and distributed newsreels and shorts to television.[106] By 1950 a number of major studios, including Fox, Universal, RKO, and Columbia, produced filmed commercials through East Coast subsidiaries.[107] The studios' first major effort at supplying film programming to television occurred in 1950 when Paramount's KTLA began the "kinescoping" and syndication of four programs, including Hollywood animator Bob Clampett's popular children's show "Time for Beany," to forty-two markets nationwide.[108] Following Eastman Kodak's 1947 announcement of its kinescope recording system, allowing programs originated live to be recorded on film off a television monitor, kinescoping, despite the process's frequently poor image quality, became vital to the distribution of network programming to those markets not provided with coaxial cable service; by 1948 NBC, CBS, and Du Mont recorded twenty hours of programming weekly, representing twenty-eight different programs, for immediate shipment to affiliates, while by 1949 NBC produced by kinescoping 50 percent more filmed entertainment yearly than all the Hollywood studios combined.[109] By 1950 Republic, already active in distributing its features to television, announced its plunge into the television film industry with the production of *Commando Cody, Sky Marshall of the Universe*.[110] By 1952 a number of smaller Hollywood studios, including Republic, Eagle-Lion, General Service, and Goldwyn, had devoted their production facilities to independent television film producers, marking the end of those studios' direct involvement in theatrical production.[111]

Also in 1952 Columbia, through its Screen Gems subsidiary, began production of thirty-nine half-hour films for the previously live "Ford Theater" on NBC, signaling the first full-scale production of film for television by a major studio; although Columbia intended to use top-name Hollywood talent, complaints from exhibitor organizations prevented this.[112] Late in 1952 Columbia and Universal signed agreements with SAG, entitling the union's members to "residuals" based upon subsequent showings of the studios' made-for-television films, creating an important labor precedent which endures today.[113] Within two years, between 1954 and 1956, Columbia's subsidiary Screen Gems expanded its production budget to $9 million, producing some of television's most popular shows, including "Father Knows Best" and "Rin Tin Tin."[114] By 1954, several years following the lifting of the FCC freeze and amid the rapid but orderly growth in the number of television stations and the resultant market for television films, the major Hollywood studios actively pursued full-scale television film production, estimating the gross on that production to be in excess of $130 million.[115]

That year Walt Disney and ABC, which had been absorbed by Paramount's divested exhibition branch, United Paramount Theatres, agreed to produce a weekly filmed show, "Disneyland," which quickly became a consistent ratings winner.[116] Other studios soon followed the lead of Columbia and Disney. In 1955 Warner Brothers premiered its "Warner Brothers Presents," an hour-long "umbrella" series which alternated three programs, all loosely based on popular Warner Brothers features, *Casablanca*, *Cheyenne*, and *King's Row*.[117] Indeed, like the Disney program, the Warners production existed primarily to publicize soon-to-be-released feature films.[118] Twentieth Century-Fox that year produced "The Twentieth Century-Fox Hour" for CBS, featuring stories often based upon the studio's more popular features.[119] MGM also entered prime time with its "MGM Parade" on ABC, which suffered the same self-promotion emphases as the Warners program. After 1956, though, the major studios, especially Warners, Universal, Columbia, and Fox, jettisoned the promotional aspect of their films for television, and set their television filmmaking into profitable and proven paths, primarily the production of half-hour situation comedies, hour-long action-adventure shows, and, ultimately, made-for-television features, consistently the most popular program types. By 1964 the major studios accounted for thirty-five hours of prime-time programming and realized almost a third of their revenue from television; today, the film business relies on television production, the release of features to television, and syndication for half its revenue.[120]

In many ways, then, the American television and motion picture industries had achieved a remarkable level of symbiotic interaction within the first decade of commercial television's full emergence following World War II. Although conventional wisdom often assumes that the Hollywood film industry greeted the arrival of television as a threatening competitor, suspicious and disdainful of the young medium, historical evidence suggests instead that the motion picture industry had long maintained a substantial interest in the economic potential of television. The Hollywood industry's attempts at exploiting that potential focused upon four distinct areas: direct investment in television broadcasting stations and networks, the pursuit of theater television, the release of the major studios' considerable film libraries for television broadcast, and the production of films specifically for television. The onus of monopolistic business practices, resulting from the Paramount decision, prevented the studios from extensive, direct investment in television broadcasting properties, while government enmity towards Hollywood resulting from these practices and shifting theater attendance patterns rendered theater television a stillborn concept almost from its inception. However, as the exhibition value of the major studios' films declined in value, the films' revenue potential through telecasting increased during the 1950s; with the thorny problems involving union and guild reimbursement for the telecasting of the majors' films generally solved by mid-decade, feature films became an increasingly important aspect of television programming (initially locally, then at the network level) and a major source of revenue for the studios. Finally, as the production of films for television, as pioneered by independent producers and marginal Hollywood studios, became a prosperous industry, especially following the lifting of the FCC freeze on new stations, the major Hollywood studios began to embrace fully television film production as a lucrative pursuit compensating for the decline in the theatrical film market. By the mid–1950s, in response to the profound changes in the economic structure of Hollywood beginning after World War II, the economic relationship between television and Hollywood, far from being antagonistic, had become fully symbiotic.

STYLES AND GENRES OF INTERACTION

Early in the medium's technical and commercial development, a tacit assumption generally held throughout the American broadcasting industry maintained that television would ultimately follow the paradigm of network radio: a "chain" of interconnected stations broadcasting live, network-originated entertainment. This assumption arose from two distinct attitudes: a predisposition within early video practice which held that only through live origination which exploited the so-called essential nature of television, its ability to transmit instantaneously images and sound, could the aesthetic potential of television be realized, and, at a more pragmatic level previously discussed, the belief that recorded programming destroyed the economic justification for a network. For many critics and practitioners of early video, that essential nature of the medium, its "immediacy," was a nature diametrically different from the "recorded" nature of film. Echoing this attitude in their 1951 production manual *The Television Program*, Edward Stasheff and Rudy Bretz argued that

[i]f television is to find itself, then, it should accentuate its differences from film. It should make the most of its frequently described power of "immediacy," which is its ability to transport the audience to the site of events taking place elsewhere at the same moment—whether these events occur in a studio or at a remote location.[121]

However, during the first two decades of commercial television's development, live program origination would not become the "essential" element of television, with film, as previously discussed, becoming an increasingly vital aspect of television programming and production. As film became a more and more important part of television, there developed a fertile exchange of generic forms and production techniques between the two media.

Early television programming, logically, inherited virtually all its program types from radio broadcasting: situation comedies, soap operas, mystery and crime shows, comedy-variety programs, all these genres had their immediate origins in radio, but as those in the fledgling television industry readily admitted, the formation of these genres had been determined by a number of different influences.[122] Early in the development of commercial video, television producers consciously attempted to adapt popular radio programs to television, with ABC a leader in the trend, the network believing that "by using shows with a good audio foundation and by giving them proper visual presentation we should have good television shows."[123] As a result, a good deal of early television programming originated live, being "visualized" renditions of network radio programs, with game shows, audience participation shows, and variety shows especially prevalent because they lent themselves to easy "visualization" and were relatively cheap to produce. Individual stations used this approach in devising their own local programming. However, as described in the preceding section, economic and logistic problems encountered during television's rapid initial growth precluded television from fully assuming the radio network paradigm, emphasizing live origination of programming among interconnected stations, leading to the development of a variety of filmed dramatic formats for network and syndicated presentation, formats which drew heavily from established motion picture genres. For example, the ubiquitous Western, a staple of both radio and motion pictures, became equally important in early television as both recycled theatrical releases and as filmed television programming, leading *Sponsor* magazine to claim that television had "literally grown on a foundation of Western programming."[124] Meanwhile, successful radio properties like "My Friend Irma" and "The Life of Riley" underwent metamorphoses into almost concurrent television series and motion picture adaptations, while successful films like *I Remember Mama* (1948) spawned successful television programs, a trend which continues today with the video transpositions ranging from *M*A*S*H* to *Fast Times at Ridgemont High*. As live television drama began to garner critical acclaim during the 1950s, the Hollywood industry began producing theatrical versions of successful teleplays, including *Marty* (1955), *Visit to a Small Planet* (1960), *Twelve Angry Men* (1957), *The Miracle Worker* (1962), *Judgment at Nuremberg* (1961), and *Days of Wine and Roses* (1962). Meanwhile, Hollywood also absorbed television drama's best and brightest, with actors like Paul Newman, Jack Lemmon, James Dean, and Eva Marie Saint, writers like Reginald Rose, Gore Vidal, Rod Serling, and Horton Foote, and directors like Arthur Penn, Franklin Schaffner, and George Roy Hill making the transition from the small to the large screen.[125] Of course, the exchange of talent flowed from Hollywood into television as well. With the burgeoning of filmed television during the early 1950s, personnel established within Hollywood, often among the smaller studios falling on hard times, turned to television for their livelihoods. Some film directors like George Archainbaud easily made the transition from directing "B" Westerns to half-hour episodes of "Hopalong Cassidy" and "Gene Autry"; by the mid–1950s "B" film directors considered trade journeymen at the time but now revered by cinema aficionados, like Jacques Tourneur, John Brahm, and Joseph H. Lewis, had made the transition to television, followed by more visible industry craftsmen like Lewis Milestone, Mitchell Leisen, and Tay Garnett.[126] Indeed, by 1955 NBC presented a half-hour drama anthology, "Screen Director's Playhouse," featuring work by top Hollywood names like John Ford and Fred Zinnemann, while the same year Alfred Hitchcock devoted most of his energy to his CBS series.[127] Accompanied by other technical and creative personnel from the Hollywood industry, especially cinematographers, these directors brought to early filmed television a sense of the Hollywood craft and technique conditioned by the particular constraints of television, while, during the 1950s and into the 1960s, as most filmed television progressed from half-hour anthologies to hour-long Westerns and, ultimately, to the made-for-television movie, a generation of future Hollywood directors honed their film-making skills by toiling within the television film industry. The direction and writing of episodes of Western and action series during the 1950s gave people like Robert Altman, Blake Edwards, Arthur Hiller, and Sam Peckinpah their entry into mainstream Hollywood.[128]

The interchange of creative talent between the media affected both the production techniques of Hollywood film and television. In the production of both live and filmed programming, the television industry early assumed that video production technique would borrow heavily from established motion picture technique, primarily since the television audience had gained its "visual literacy" from the formal and narrative methods of Hollywood. In 1944 one industry observer succinctly recognized what would become a general philosophy towards video production, stating that "in spite of all that has been said about television's spontaneity, immediacy and intimacy . . . television in your home is really a motion picture and what makes a motion picture interesting should also attract and hold the television audience."[129] While the producer of the early filmed television program "Your Show Time" (1949) maintained that "Techniques required for TV production are largely variations of the known techniques in the theatrical motion picture field," another producer of early television film cautioned that "The idea that Hollywood in its generic sense, can transfer its technical talents to TV with little or no effort is a myth."[130] The young television film industry realized that essential differences in the technological bases and modes of program distribution between the two media would necessarily lead to a modification of film technique for television purposes, leading to leaner and more economical narratives.[131] Ultimately, this improved technique included overcoming the time constraints imposed by television, the medium's substantially smaller screen size compared to theatrical films, and problems involved in the transmission and reception of the video signal.

A good idea of how motion picture technique came to be adapted for television is given by Jerry Fairbanks's description of his allowances for producing "Public Prosecutor," as already discussed among the first filmed television series. At the scenario level, the structure of each episode eliminated the insertion of commercials which, it was feared, could frustrate the viewer's apprehension of the narrative; the advertisements appeared at the very beginning and ending of the episode, keeping the narrative intact.[132] For video, the melding of radio and motion picture scripting was conscious:

Scripts should be prepared in such a way so that the viewer can follow the plot by listening, and not be required to remain glued to the set at all times to follow the action.

On the other hand, the dialog should not explain every happening. In short, television-film writing should be a careful blending of radio and motion picture scripting.[133]

A number of technical limitations had to be surmounted during the early days of television film production, involving new lighting methods and proper contrast ratios, reflecting the image's ultimate delivery over a small, cathode ray tube (as opposed to a theater's large screen).[134] Industry producers cautioned that the extremely small size of contemporary receiver viewing tubes, around ten inches diagonal, required the avoidance of long shots, wherein detail would be lost. As a result, "Public Prosecutor" and other filmed programs of the era contained mostly close-ups and medium shots. According to Fairbanks,

Close grouping of actors is a must because of the smallness of video screens. If large, sharp images and facial reactions are to be clearly received on video sets, players must remain closely grouped. Half figures are the rule, not the exception.[135]

Realizing that this reliance on tight, close shots could become visually monotonous, Fairbanks cautioned that "[p]an and dolly shots should be emphasized."[136] As a further concession to the receiver's limitations, Fairbanks believed "the camera must be carefully centered on the players and action because of the curvature of the screen. Any action on the edge of the picture is likely to be distorted because of this curve."[137]

Early film production for television suffered from various technical limitations. Some early producers, like Fairbanks, relied on 16-mm film for shooting because of its relative inexpensiveness compared to 35-mm; other producers (as is current practice) favored 35-mm to ensure good image quality. However, because of available projection facilities at individual stations and lower shipping costs, in distribution virtually all prints were 16-mm, perhaps leading to the outcry of early critics and audiences over the perceived inferior quality of filmed television.[138] Through wartime advances in fine-grain emulsions in aerial photography and the appearance of relatively sophisticated 16-mm equipment after the war, release prints in the smaller gauge film delivered acceptable image quality, but for a variety of reasons, the sound generated by those prints was often inferior.[139] Inexperience in processing and printing 16-mm soundtracks at laboratories, the inherent technical inferiority of the small 16-mm soundtrack on release prints, and the broadcasting of the resulting poor sound over the superior FM audio channel in television transmission combined to irritate early television viewers, perhaps expecting high-quality sound from years of radio exposure, and to denigrate the overall quality of television film.[140] This situation led the television film industry to adopt the cost and quality benefits afforded magnetic sound recording well before the major Hollywood studios did so.[141] By 1950 the sound quality of broadcast film had increased substantially through improved laboratory procedures and new equipment.[142] Meanwhile, some blamed the viewer's inability to tune the receiver and the broadcaster's poor projection habits for continued complaints about the quality of film transmission.[143]

By 1950, amid advances in filmmaking technology and the appearance of a more experienced work force, the production of the ubiquitous filmed, half-hour television program had become standardized. By the late 1940s and early 1950s, through the use of kinescopic recording, there occurred a merging of motion picture production technique and live television production technique (already anticipated with Fairbanks's Multicam system), whereby programs were staged in a studio using multiple video cameras and a switcher for live broadcast, but also recorded off a monitor as produced for subsequent distribution or syndication.[144] In 1950 with the appearance of the Vidicam system and, later, the Electronicam system, truly integrated television-film methods appeared: mounted alongside the standard television camera and aligned to compensate for parallax was a motion picture camera, which would run while, in typical live television procedure, a director chose the appropriate shots from each video camera which were simultaneously filmed. The resulting program, composed of already "edited" film using live television techniques but accomplished in a minimum of time, could then be distributed, error-free (as opposed to live origination or kinescopes), since the director always had the option of doing retakes.[145] By the late 1950s, the appearance of videotape technology challenged film as the primary medium for television recording, with tape generally used for time-delay rebroadcast and, ultimately, news and program production, but film enduring as the medium of choice for most dramatic television production.[146] By the late 1950s, with improvements in video production technology and technique, as well as vastly improved receivers, so-called Hollywood techniques became standard aspects of live television drama, including deep-focus and long-shot compositions and sophisticated editing rhythms, while the advent of videotape technology afforded television producers the flexibility of film without the cost, but still imparted an aura of "liveness" to the telecast production.[147]

As discussed above, the standard techniques of film production, especially as practiced in Hollywood, had to make concessions to the limitations of the television screen and the constraints of time. As a result, though, of this crossover of production talent from both live and filmed television into the Hollywood film industry, the look of feature films changed: television had a strong effect upon Hollywood filmmaking technique and practice. Particularly time constraints, as already described, played a large role in defining the practice of television-film (and, of course, live) production, while speed and cost of production dictated the adoption of new technologies. From the 1950s and into the 1960s, television directors and editors developed techniques which let them visually and aurally present a maximum of narrative information within a short amount of time: the use of rack-focus to direct attention or segment conversations, the overlapping of sound from one scene to the next as an efficacious transitional device, mismatched presence of synchronous sound with accompanying image (often to hide dialogue looping), these devices and others became regularly employed in television practice but were in direct opposition to the accepted Hollywood style of filmmaking as evolved during the 1930s and 1940s. A good example is reflected by the relative depiction and placement of opening credits: the credits of virtually all Hollywood films until well into the 1960s consisted of initial titles against a fairly static background; following these opening titles, generally segmented by a dissolve, the narrative would begin. However, in television practice where the viewer must be immediately "hooked" (lest he or she change the channel for something more interesting) and time is limited for diegetic unfolding, the period generally occupied by credits in features was sacrificed to the narrative. As a result, in television films credits began to be superimposed over action, judiciously placed at lapses in action during the program's first few minutes, or even deferred until following the first commercial break. Following the rise of this technique in television practice, Hollywood soon followed.[148]

Television assumed its own technological devices as well, which also altered style, perhaps best exemplified by the zoom lens. Introduced into live television production on 21 July 1947 to televise a Giants-Reds baseball game, Dr. Frank Back's "Zoomar" zoom lens quickly became the standard video camera lens, replacing the cumbersome three prime-lens turret and enabling a studio camera to range fluidly from close-up to long shots within one take; the lens achieved such widespread television use that Ernie Kovacs titled his 1956 comic novel about television *Zoomar*.[149] However, the zoom lens had been among Hollywood's tools since at least 1932 with the introduction of the B & H Cooke Varo Lens, used by RKO, Columbia, Warners, and Fox; however, it never achieved any widespread popularity in the Hollywood industry, cinematographers relying upon prime lenses and decrying the zoom lens's apparent "distortion" of space which was inconsistent with accepted Hollywood technique.[150] By the 1960s, though, the formal characteristics achieved through the zoom lens had strongly influenced traditional Hollywood filmmaking, as the device accompanied into feature film production generations of directors schooled in television technique, including Robert Altman, Robert Mulligan, Sydney Pollack, and Steven Spielberg, and even graduates from television commercials, like Stan Dragoti, and television news documentary, like William Friedkin. By the early 1970s various aspects of Hollywood and television had commingled to the point where they achieved a coalescence with the "made-for-TV movie," a genre that combined the topicality and distinctive narrative structures and production techniques of television with the basic formal concerns of Hollywood melodrama, while further advancements in video and filmmaking technologies, including the influence of computer-aided production, resulted by the 1980s in a remarkable degree of integration between video and film production techniques, especially in special effects.[151]

Of course, not all film shown on television consisted of made-for-television programs; as already discussed, theatrical feature films played a huge role in early television programming, and the telecasting of these films posed unique problems. The most pressing problem concerned the films' irregular running times, preventing them from being used in discrete segments of broadcast time unless edited. As *Sponsor* magazine asked, "how to fit an 80-minute picture into a 55-minute slot?"[152] Depending on the hour the films were used, some stations opted to show the entire feature, but with "Class A" advertising time at a premium, most films were cut. The procedure used by most stations, according to *Sponsor*, was to "eliminate all dark scenes that won't show up on a TV tube, then all the long-shots in which distant objects get lost," leading to reducing a film's running length by as much as 30 percent and, undoubtedly, causing some narrative confusion as well.[153] Some in the industry claimed such editing actually improved many films; the director of programs and production for Du Mont maintained that such editing, rather than harming the audience's ability to follow the story, actually increased its enjoyment through the edited film's quicker pacing.[154] As with filmed programs, the insertion of commercials posed a problem, and how stations elected to resolve that problem indicates some of the early assumptions about early television audiences:

In foreign movies, which seem to attract a more intelligent audience, Mindy Brown [WOR-TV editor] looks for a quiet point where nothing much is happening. Grant Theis, film director for WCBS-TV, favors splicing in commercials just after a fadeout indicating the passage of time. On Westerns, the cliff-hanger type of break is most common. . . . Since adults don't get so personally involved in Westerns as in grade A dramas, it's safe to break in at a high point.[155]

Foreign films posed additional problems for programmers. As already discussed, foreign releases, often recent, figured prominently in early film programming since their rights could easily be obtained. When New York's WPIX ran British films on its "Premiere Theatre," its sponsor became disappointed with the results, claiming that because "the people attracted to grade A British films are too 'high class,' " they resented commercials.[156] In fact, according to *Television* magazine, "British films earned a unanimous raspberry" with film programmers, claiming that sponsors refused to run them; one film distributor who acquired a block of British films spent $150,000 to rerecord them, claiming that he would "accept a cockney accent only when it was used by a cop or taxi driver."[157] Foreign films offered another complication: unencumbered by the Hays Code, the American film-industry's self-censorship guidelines, foreign films, warned an attorney, "often have a carefree, if bawdy, attitude toward sex," which "could result in difficulties with the FCC, imperiling [a station's] license."[158] With the eventual release of the major studios' films to television during the 1960s, features posed an additional problem in telecasting: wide-screen films needed to be "scanned," their negatives especially printed to remove anamorphic distortion while maintaining the major center of activity of each frame, so that the telecast prints would be comprehensible.[159]

The initial video use of feature films had subtle but profound effects upon the ultimate nature of television programming and advertising. The problem of attracting daytime viewers confronted station programmers who realized that sponsorship during the daytime hours would be crucial if overall station operation were to be profitable. Before the opening of the coast-to-coast network, the cost of imitating radio's most popular daytime fare, soap operas, was too high for individual stations, while filling those hours with alternative local live or syndicated film programming would also be expensive. At Philadelphia's WPTZ, a pioneer in East Coast telecasting, programmers reasoned that if 70,000 people regularly attended movie house matinees, there must be a substantial daytime audiences for feature films on television, as well.[160] In the spring of 1950, using Eagle-Lion and Monogram features made between 1938 and 1946, WPTZ launched the hour-long "Hollywood Playhouse."[161] The program proved an immediate success; its ratings not only placed it as the most popular daytime television program anywhere in the country, but adjusting for the number of television sets versus radio sets in the Philadelphia market, the program would have placed among the top ten Philadelphia *radio* programs.[162] According to *Television* magazine, WPTZ's experiment proved conclusively that, in the words of WPTZ's president, "Daytime television is a sound and valuable advertising period," who added that he expected to see "the same thing done by WPTZ in Philadelphia duplicated in every market in the land."[163]

Part of WPTZ's plan for "Hollywood Playhouse" involved the sale of "participation" time to sponsors; that is, rather than one sponsor footing the bill for the entire program, all costs would be divided among several advertisers, giving each effective television advertising time but at a price far less than it would be if the individual advertiser sponsored an entire program. The participation scheme had been used by other stations to sell time, particularly for lengthy programs like films or sports which, if sponsored individually, would be too expensive for most sponsors. However, participation represented a profound departure from radio and, later, television's standard of individual sponsorship and ownership of a program by an advertiser, particularly at the network level. By the mid–1950s, the "magazine concept," based upon early television's participation method, would become more and more prevalent at the network level, with a number of sponsors, rather than one, supporting individual programs. The television and advertising industries justified the magazine concept (so dubbed because of a printed magazine's containing many different advertisements from many different advertisers) so that more sponsors could gain access to the finite number of prime-time hours, but ultimately the concept served to diminish the program control of sponsors while securing the television networks both control and lucrative ownership of original programming, something the networks lacked during the radio era.[164] By the early 1950s, then, the use of feature films in programming led both to the discovery of a daytime audience and the implementation of an advertising pattern which endures today.

Although initially the fledgling television industry assumed that television would follow the model of network radio, exclusively emphasizing live program origination, a variety of factors led to the integration into television of large amounts of filmed programming. Assuming generic forms borrowed from both radio and feature films, most of this early filmed programming, as previously discussed, originated within the periphery of the established Hollywood motion picture industry, and by the mid–1950s the major Hollywood studios had enthusiastically embraced film production for television. As a result, there occurred a particularly fruitful exchange of production techniques between motion pictures and television: while the Hollywood approach to filmmaking, represented by the industry professionals who early entered video, imparted to the newer medium basic narrative and stylistic skills and a sense of craftsmanship, the rigors and constraints of television production in turn modified and augmented the classic Hollywood style of filmmaking, manifest in a variety of new formal and narrative techniques integrated into feature film production by filmmakers who had begun within the television industry. Ultimately, through advances in both video and filmmaking technology, there would arise by the 1970s a virtual melding of film and television techniques.

NOTES

1. For a brief discussion of the distant scientific antecedents of modern television, see Joseph H. Udelson, *The Great Television Race, A History of the American Television Industry 1925–1941* (University: University of Alabama Press, 1982), pp. 13–24. See also selections in Raymond Fielding, ed., *A Technological History of Motion Pictures and Television* (Berkeley and Los Angeles: University of California Press, 1967), particularly L. R. Lankes, "Historical Sketch of Television's Progress," pp. 227–29; and A. G. Jensen, "The Evolution of Modern Television," pp. 235–49. A useful summary of historical sources concerning the technological prehistory and history of television can be found in Udelson, pp. 187–92.

2. Michael Chanan, *The Dream That Kicks: The Prehistory and Early Years of Cinema in Britain* (London: Routledge & Kegan Paul, 1980), p. 51. Chanan borrows the term from Lévi-Strauss, using it to signify a "cultural practice which is distinguished from engineering proper."

3. "Television vs. Theatre," *Variety* 3 May 1939: 30, cited in Allan David Larson, "Integration and Attempted Integration Between the Motion Picture and Television Industries Through 1956" (Ph.D. diss., Ohio University, 1979), p. 36.

4. Larson, "Integration and Attempted Integration," pp. 27–29.

5. "Radio Is Movies' Best Friend—Aylesworth," *Broadcasting* 11 (1 August 1936): 9.

6. "Film Industry Advised to Grab Television," *Broadcasting* 12 (15 June 1937): 7.

7. See, for example, the prognosis of Lee de Forest in *Television Today and Tomorrow* (New York: Dial Press, 1942), pp. 33–43, 111–15; and Paramount's plan to "bicycle" prints to form a video network, in David Glickman, "Television Activity Is Spurred as Paramount Acquires Rights," *Broadcasting and Broadcast Advertising* 15 (15 November 1938): 17.

8. John V. L. Hogan, "Recorded Programs for Television," *Radio News* 13 (July 1931): 15.

9. "Television vs. Theatre," p. 3, cited in Larson, "Integration and Attempted Integration," p. 36.

10. Gary Newton Hess, "An Historical Study of the Du Mont Television Network" (Ph.D. diss., Northwestern University, 1960), p. 92.

11. Glickman, p. 17; "Paul Raibourn of Par Stresses Why Film Co. Bought into Du Mont," *Variety* 1 May 1940: 4.

12. "Du Mont Attacked on Movie Capital," *New York Times*, 9 May 1940, sec. 1, p. 18, cited in Larson, "Integration and Attempted Integration," p. 46.

13. Udelson, *The Great Television Race*, pp. 151–58.

14. Larson, "Integration and Attempted Integration," pp. 73–74.

15. "Warners, Fabian, Schines Bid for TV Station Grants," *Variety* 21 April 1948: 23.

16. A full discussion of the studios' antitrust experiences can be found in Michael Conant, *Antitrust in the Motion Picture Industry: Economic and Legal Analysis* (Berkeley and Los Angeles: University of California Press, 1960).

17. Douglas Gomery, "Failed Opportunities: The Integration of the U.S. Motion Picture and Television Industries," *Quarterly Review of Film Studies* 9 (Summer 1984): 225–26.

18. "Disney Pulls Out of Black and White," *Variety* 24 April 1946: 28.

19. Harry Castleman and Walter J. Podrazik, *Watching TV: Four Decades of American Television* (New York: McGraw-Hill, 1982), p. 37.

20. Larson, "Integration and Attempted Integration," p. 122.

21. T. M. C. Lance, "Some Aspects of Large Screen Television," *Journal of the Television Society* 4, no. 4 (December 1944): 82–89.

22. "Fernsehen bei den Olympischen Spielen 1936," *Fernsehen und Tonfilm* 7, no. 8 (August 1936): 57–59; Ben Kaufman, "Television for Theaters," *Television* 1 no. 2 (Fall 1944): 23.

23. Larson, "Integration and Attempted Integration," p. 51.

24. Ibid., pp. 55–56.

25. Ibid., p. 165.

26. John E. McCoy and Harry P. Warner, "Theatre Television Today, Part I," *Hollywood Quarterly* 4, no. 2 (Winter 1949): 162.

27. "GPL's 'Videofilm' System for Theater TV," *International Projectionist* 25, no. 11 (November 1950): 15; "Century-Reeves Big-Screen TV," *International Projectionist* 25, no. 4 (April 1950): 27; Douglas Gomery, "Theatre Television: The Missing Link of Technological Change in the U.S. Motion Picture Industry," *Velvet Light Trap*, no. 21 (1985): 58.

28. Gomery, "Theatre Television," p. 59.

29. Ibid.

30. Larson, p. 189.

31. "Raibourn Denies Anti-Trust Charges," *Broadcasting-Telecasting* 29 (24 December 1945): 75.

32. "Expect FCC Skepticism Won't Deter Current Hearings on Theatre TV," *Variety* 4 February 1953: 4, 18; "FCC Halts Theatre Tele Hearings To See If Useful Purpose Is Served," *Variety* 11 February 1953: 2, 54.

33. *19th Annual Report of the Federal Communications Commission. Fiscal Year Ended June 30, 1953* (Washington D.C.: U.S. Government Printing Office, 1954), p. 34.

34. "B&K Theatre TV 'Downbeat' May Hurt Trade Bids," *Variety* 12 March 1952: 4, 15.

35. Conant, *Antitrust*, pp. 107–109.

36. Gomery, "Theatre Television," p. 59.

37. Castleman and Podrazik, p. 9; Eric Smoodin, "Motion Pictures and Television, 1930–1945: A Pre-History of the Relations Between the Two Media," *Journal of the University Film and Video Association* 34, no. 3 (Summer 1982): 5; Udelson, p. 135.

38. "NBC Studies Use of Film in Video," *Broadcasting-Broadcast Advertising* 16 (15 January 1939): 25; "NBC Has Telecast Rights to 15 Films but Distribs Mostly Balk at Small Rentals Involved," *Variety* 5 July 1939: 35.

39. "NBC Studies Use of Films in Video," p. 25.

40. Larson, "Integration and Attempted Integration," p. 38.

41. U.S. Bureau of the Census, "Radio and Television Stations, Sets Produced, and Families with Sets: 1921 to 1956," *Historical Statistics of the United States. Colonial Times to 1957* (Washington, D.C.: U.S. Government Printing Office, 1960), p. 491.

42. "*Televiser*'s Film Survey Results: Rentals and Production Costs," *Televiser* 4, no. 4 (July-August 1947): 9.

43. Henry Clay Gibson, "Educational Films and Television," *Television* 2 (May 1945): 13; Sydney R. Lane, "Films as a Source for Programming," *Television* 2 (May 1946): 14.

44. Abel Green, "Video Faces Years of Decision With Many an 'X' Twixt Ichon and Eye," *Variety* 20 March 1946: 46.

45. Tino Balio, ed., *The American Film Industry* (Madison: University of Wisconsin Press, 1976), p. 320.

46. Jackson Dube, "Report on Films for Television: Programming," *Television* 5, no. 3 (March 1948): 20–21.

47. "Petrillo—Words and Music," *Television* 10, no. 10 (October 1953): 52.

48. Robert D. Leiter, *The Musicians and Petrillo* (New York: Bookman Associates, 1953; repr. New York: Octagon Books, 1974), p. 172; James Petrillo, "Why Members of the American Federation of Musicians Are Not Working for Television and Frequency Modulation Radio," *Official Proceedings of the 49th Annual Convention* (New York: American Federation of Musicians, 1946), p. 91.

49. Joseph Dermer, "Television and Union Music," *Televiser* 7, no. 9 (November 1950): 15.

50. "Petrillo—Words and Music," p. 54.

51. Larson, "Integration and Attempted Integration," p. 87.

52. "Sensational but Scarce," *Sponsor* 4 (2 June 1950): 31.

53. "TV," *Sponsor* 2 (April 1948): 92; "TV," *Sponsor* 1 (September 1947): 82.

54. See, for example, "Film Programming," *Television* 6, no. 8 (August 1949): 42; Mary Gannon, "Television: The Local Businessman's Most Powerful Sales Medium," *Television* 7, no. 2 (February 1950): 25.

55. "Sensational but Scarce," p. 31.

56. "Trade Studies New UA-Indie Pact on Video," *Variety* 1 January 1947: 3; Larson, "Integration and Attempted Integration," p. 39.

57. Larson, "Integration and Attempted Integration," p. 90.

58. Ibid., p. 91.

59. "U Found It too Costly to Bridge Music So Its Pix for Video Are Nix," *Variety* 4 May 1949: 26.

60. "Sensational but Scarce," pp. 31, 54; "Headquarters for TV Feature Films [advertisement]," *Sponsor* 4 (2 June 1950): 54.

61. Larson, "Integration and Attempted Integration," p. 138.

62. "Video's Big Coin Lures 'A' Pix," *Variety* 28 November 1951: 1.

63. Larson, "Integration and Attempted Integration," p. 140.

64. Thomas M. Pryor, "Movie Chief Urges Speedy Video Tie," *New York Times* 4 September 1953: 11, cited in Larson, "Integration and Attempted Integration," p. 224.

65. Larson, "Integration and Attempted Integration," p. 241; Douglas Gomery, "*Brian's Song*: Television, Hollywood, and the Evolution of the Movie Made for Television," in *American History/American Television: Interpreting the Video Past,* ed. John E. O'Connor (New York: Frederick Ungar, 1983), p. 212. General Teleradio sold RKO's lot to Desilu, one of the leading producers of film for television.

66. Gomery, "*Brian's Song,*" p. 212.

67. Larson, "Integration and Attempted Integration," pp. 244–45.

68. Ibid., p. 247.

69. "UA's Post-'48 Features Into TV Despite Lack of Residual Formula," *Variety* 14 November 1956: 33.

70. Larson, "Integration and Attempted Integration," pp. 246–47.

71. "Post-'48 Movies," *Broadcasting-Telecasting* 51 (10 September 1956): 35; Gomery, "*Brian's Song,*" p. 213; Castleman and Podrazik, *Watching TV,* p. 149. The 1946 AFM agreement with the studios included a clause which diverted 5 percent of the gross realized by television release of post–1946 films into the union's performance trust fund.

72. Gomery, "*Brian's Song,*" p. 213; Castleman and Podrazik, *Watching TV,* p. 14g.

73. Gomery, "*Brian's Song,*" p. 213; Castleman and Podrazik, *Watching TV,* p. 149.

74. Castleman and Podrazik, *Watching TV,* p. 149; Alex McNeil, *Total Television: A Comprehensive Guide to Programming from 1948 to the Present* (New York: Penguin Books, 1984), pp. 795–96.

75. Castleman and Podrazik, *Watching TV,* p. 182.

76. "Special Theatre TV Shows Probably to Comprise Initial Telemeter Pickups," *Variety* 11 April 1951: p. 3.

77. Gomery, "*Brian's Song,*" pp. 212–13. In 1965, from the profits it amassed from distributing its Paramount films, MCA acquired Universal Studios.

78. "Fee TV: Is It a Threat to Advertisers?" *Sponsor* 6 (19 May 1952): 40–41, 74, 76. A complete description of the tribulations encountered by Zenith in pioneering subscription television can be found in Edward A. Spray, "The Concept, Development, and Testing of Phonevision" (M.A. thesis, Indiana University, 1969), especially pp. 102–117.

79. Larson, "Integration and Attempted Integration," p. 249.

80. Gomery, "*Brian's Song,*" p. 214.

81. George T. Shupert, "The Place of Films in Television," *Television* 1 (Spring 1944): 40–42.

82. Larson, "Integration and Attempted Integration," p. 60; "*Televiser's* Film Survey Results," p. 10.

83. "WB, Metro Remain Firm Vs. Their Stars on TV," *Variety* 30 December 1951: 71.

84. Arch B. Heath and J. Raymond Hutchinson, "Making Motion Pictures for Television," *Televiser* 1, no. 3 (Spring 1944): 29.

85. Ibid.

86. "Filmed TV," *Newsweek* 12 February 1951: 78. An indication of the reasons for the initial optimism surrounding the filmed television market can be found in Jerry

Fairbanks, "Films for Television," *Journal of the Society of Motion Picture Engineers* 51 (December 1948): 590.

87. "Discord in Music for TV Films," *Televiser* 6, no. 8 (November 1949): 10.

88. "Fairbanks Charges TV 'Mediocrity' Due To 'Viewer-Go-Hang' Attitude," *Variety* 26 March 1952: 22.

89. "Commercial Producers Look With Caution on Packaged Programs for Television," *Business Screen* 10, no. 3 (May 1949): 10, 30.

90. "Programs: A Cross-Section of Video Films on the Air Now or Available for Sale," *Sponsor* 5 (10 March 1952): 98–99, 101.

91. Jerry Fairbanks, "Motion Picture Production for Television," *Journal of the Society of Motion Picture and Television Engineers* 55 (December 1950): 568–69.

92. Jerry Fairbanks, "New Low-Cost TV Film Technique," *Television* 6, no. 11 (November 1949): 23, 28.

93. Thomas F. Brady, "Hollywood Agenda," *New York Times* (19 October 1947), sec. 2, p. 5; McNeil, *Total Television*, p. 528.

94. Brady, "Hollywood Agenda," p. 5.

95. Sidney Lohman, "News of TV and Radio," *New York Times* (24 October 1948), sec. 2, p. 11.

96. Ibid.; McNeil, *Total Television*, pp. 528–29.

97. Mary Gannon, "Hollywood and TV Try New Financial Patterns," *Television* 5, no. 11 (November 1948): 32.

98. "Shooting in Europe Is No Film Bargain," *Television* 9, no. 7 (July 1952): 19.

99. Gannon, "Television: The Local Businessman's Most Powerful Sales Medium," p. 18. Unfortunately, the CBS series suffered the same fate as Fairbanks's "Public Prosecutor": the series was not picked up by a CBS sponsor, filming was halted after nine episodes were completed, and only when Du Mont picked it up during the 1952 season were the next four episodes shot; see McNeil, *Total Television*, p. 119.

100. Fred Kugel, "The Economics of Film," *Television* 8, no. 7 (July 1951): 11–12.

101. Fred Kugel, "TV Film: $100,000,000 a Year Industry," *Television* 9, no. 7 (July 1952): 46.

102. Kugel, "The Economics of Film," p. 12.

103. "Syndicated Film," *Television* 9, no. 7 (July 1952): 27; "The Men Who Make and Sell TV Film," *Television* 10, no. 7 (July 1953): 19.

104. "Syndicated Film," p. 27.

105. "The Men Who Make and Sell TV Film," p. 18.

106. "Movietone News," *Televiser* 5, no. 3 (15 March 1948): 22; "Hollywood Report," *Television* 5, no. 8 (August 1948): 55.

107. Larson, "Integration and Attempted Integration," p. 152.

108. "KTLA Has Private 'Kine' Network," *Variety* 29 November 1950: 30.

109. "Kodak's Video Film Recorder Makes Its Debut," *Televiser* 4, no. 6 (November-December 1947): 28; "Report on Film Recordings," *Television* 6, no. 1 (January 1949): 22–23; Herman Brandschain, "Kinescoping," *Broadcasting-Telecasting* 36 (28 March 1949): 54-C.

110. Larson, "Integration and Attempted Integration," p. 154.

111. "Producers," *Sponsor* 6 (14 July 1952): 192.

112. Larson, "Integration and Attempted Integration," p. 155.

113. Ibid., p. 156.

114. "SG's $9,000,000 Vidpix Budget," *Variety* 17 November 1954: 49.

115. Larson, "Integration and Attempted Integration," p. 230.

116. "ABC, Disney Set Weekly TV Series," *Broadcasting-Telecasting* 46 (5 April 1954): 31; McNeil, pp. 899–90.

117. McNeil, *Total Television*, p. 700. Only "Cheyenne" survived the first season, alternating after that with "Sugarfoot" and "Bronco," indicating a renaissance of sorts in television Westerns.

118. Larson, "Integration and Attempted Integration," p. 233.

119. Ibid.; McNeil, *Total Television*, p. 679.

120. Robert Vianello, "The Rise of the Telefilm and the Networks' Hegemony Over the Motion Picture Industry," *Quarterly Review of Film Studies* 8 (Summer 1984): 206–207.

121. Edward Stasheff and Rudy Bretz, *The Television Program: Its Writing, Direction, and Production* (New York: A. A. Wyn, 1951), p. 22.

122. See, for example, Seymour Mintz, "Mr. Sponsor Asks . . . Is TV Developing any Distinctive, Popular Program Types of Its Own?" *Sponsor* 3 (10 October 1949): 33.

123. Harvey Marlowe, "Turning Sound Programs Into Good Video," *Televiser* 4, no. 1 (January-February 1947): 16.

124. "Wild-West Fever: Will It Sell for You?" *Sponsor* 4 (25 September 1950): 28.

125. Michael Kerbel, "The Golden Age of TV Drama," in *Television: The Critical Eye*, ed. Horace Newcombe, 3d ed. (New York: Oxford University Press, 1982), pp. 48–49.

126. Christopher Wicking and Tise Vahimagi, *The American Vein: Directors and Directions in Television* (New York: E. P. Dutton, 1979), pp. 117–18, 120, 125, 131, 133, 139.

127. Castleman and Podrazik, *Watching TV*, pp. 101, 107–108.

128. Frederick Foster, "The Big Switch Is to TV!" *American Cinematographer* 36, no. 1 (January 1955): 27, 38–40; Wicking and Vahimagi, *The American Vein*, pp. 85, 89, 96, 102.

129. Shupert, "The Place of Films," p. 41.

130. Norman Elzer, "The Lucky Strike Series," *Television* 6, no. 8 (August 1949): 14; Brewster Morgan, "To Film or Not To Film," *Television* 7, no. 8 (August 1950): 23.

131. Heath and Hutchinson, "Making Motion Pictures," p. 29.

132. Fairbanks, "Films for Television," p. 593.

133. Ibid.

134. Jerry Albert, "Film Facts," *Televiser* 7, no. 8 (October 1950): 22; Fairbanks, "Films for Television," p. 592; Elzer, "The Lucky Strike Series," p. 14.

135. Fairbanks, "Films for Television," p. 592.

136. Ibid.

137. Ibid.

138. Andrew Hamilton, "Making New Movies—for TV," *Science Digest* 29, no. 1 (January 1951): 62.

139. John Flory, "Importance of 16-MM Film in Television," *Television* 1 (Fall 1944): 48; John Maurer, "16 mm in TV," *Television* 6, no. 8 (August 1949): 31–41.

140. Hazard E. Reeves, "Sound in TV Films," *Television* 6, no. 8 (August 1949): 33.

141. Don Harrold, "Magnetic Recording Boon to Budget Film Production," *American Cinematographer* 31 (March 1950): 84; Loren L. Ryder, "Editing Magnetic Sound," *American Cinematographer* 32 (April 1951): 157.

142. R. M. Paskow, "TV Film Making Progress Despite Hollywood's Lethargy,"

Televiser 7, no. 2 (February 1950): 9; "16-MM Film TV," *Broadcasting-Telecasting* 36 (10 January 1949): 58.

143. "The Selling Is Furious But Pricing Lacks System," *Sponsor* 5 (10 March 1952): 93.

144. George Shupert, "TV's Closed-Circuit Pre-Filming Technique Offers Low-Cost Shows," *Television* 6, no. 8 (August 1949): 22–23.

145. Larry Gordon, "Half-Hour Film Produced in 60 Seconds," *Televiser* 7, no. 4 (May 1950): 6–7; " 'Electronicam'—DuMont's New Dual Recording TV-Film Camera," *American Cinematographer* 36, no. 5 (May 1955): 280, 290–92.

146. "Videotape: The Revolution Is Now," *Television* 14 (July 1957): 46.

147. Kerbel, "The Golden Age," pp. 53–57.

148. For example, an early 1960s hour-long dramatic series, "Route 66," invariably opened with the program's two protagonists driving their Corvette and talking to one another; their conversation served to establish the base for the succeeding narrative. The credits were squeezed into establishing shots during the dialogue. By 1979, onscreen credits had been completely eliminated in Francis Ford Coppola's theatrical release of *Apocalypse Now*.

149. "Zoomar Zooms Tele Along," *Variety* 23 July 1947: 33; "The Zoom in Television," *Fortune* (May 1952): p. 213; Ernie Kovacs, *Zoomar* (Garden City, N.Y.: Doubleday, 1957).

150. "Distinctive Shots Are Obtained with the B & H Cooke Varo Lens," *American Cinematographer*, "Bell & Howell Supplement" 14, no. 7 (November 1933): S–4; John Belton, "The Bionic Eye: Zoom Esthetics," *Cineaste* 11, no. 1 (Winter 1980–1981): 21.

151. For an overview of the merging of these media's production bases, see Richard Patterson and Dana White, eds., *Electronic Production Techniques* (Hollywood: American Society of Cinematographers, 1985).

152. "How To Use TV Films Effectively," *Sponsor* 5 (10 March 1952): 33.

153. Ibid.

154. Ibid.

155. Ibid., p. 56.

156. Ibid.

157. Abby Rand, "Feature Films," *Television* 9, no. 7 (July 1952): 49, 52.

158. Samuel Spring, "Legal Traps of Film: Censorship, Copyright," *Television* 9, no. 7 (July 1952): 14.

159. "How Wide-Screen Movies Fit the 21-inch Tube," *Broadcasting* 71 (3 October 1966): 27.

160. "Hollywood Films Pay Off in High Ratings!" *Television* 7, no. 5 (May 1950): 20.

161. Ibid.; "Sensational But Scarce," p. 30.

162. Ibid.

163. Ibid., p. 22.

164. Fairfax M. Cone, "The Magazine Concept Must Win Out," *Television* 10, no. 12 (December 1953): 19.

SELECTED BIBLIOGRAPHY

As reflected in the accompanying notes for the preceding two sections, the literature describing aspects of the symbiotic relationship between motion pictures and television

is plentiful, with the most valuable divided into roughly three types: university dissertations; periodical articles, within both the scholarly and the trade presses; and reference
works. Since the documentation for the preceding sections is quite complete, the reader
is advised to consult those cited sources which refer to the reader's specific area of
interest. Also, before undertaking research into the historical relation between the broadcasting and motion picture industries, one should be aware of three books which would
aid such research:

Allen, Robert C. and Douglas Gomery. *Film History: Theory and Practice*. New York:
    Alfred A. Knopf, 1985. This book gives a comprehensive survey of the historio-
    graphic issues and methodologies involved in the researching and writing of film
    history, which can be fruitfully applied to broadcasting history as well.

Schreibman, Faye C. "Searching for Television's History." In *Broadcasting Research
    Methods*. Ed. Joseph R. Dominick and James E. Fletcher. Boston: Allyn and
    Bacon, 1985. This chapter gives an overview of the methods and sources for
    locating examples of television programming and information on that program-
    ming; the "Reference Appendix," pp. 37–41, is particularly helpful.

Slide, Anthony, ed. *International Film, Radio, and Television Journals*. Westport, Conn.:
    Greenwood Press, 1985. This volume comprises essays devoted to hundreds of
    the world's most important media periodicals, including overviews of editorial
    emphasis and location sources.

There exist a number of titles within each area which can provide the reader with broad
introductions to aspects of the media's symbiotic relationships. In the absence to date of
any published book devoted to the relation between the film and television industries,
the most fruitful and comprehensive sources are recent dissertations (available in hard
copy or microfilm from University Microfilms, Ann Arbor, Michigan):

Dombkowski, Dennis Joseph. "Film and Television: An Analytical History of Economic
    and Creative Integration." Ph.D. diss., University of Illinois at Urbana-Cham-
    paign, 1982.

Larson, Allan David. "Integration and Attempted Integration Between the Motion Picture
    and Television Industries Through 1956." Ph.D. diss., Ohio University, Athens,
    Ohio, 1979.

These dissertations are the most complete discussions particularly of the economic
relationship between film and television. Although in many respects they cover similar
ground, each makes good use of important source material, especially trade publications,
while the Dombkowski work extends the discussion beyond Larson's 1956 cutoff date,
dealing with, among other issues, the rise of American television in foreign markets and
regulatory issues during the 1960s and 1970s. Other dissertations of interest include

Hoffman, Earl Kenneth, Jr. "The Impact of Television Production on Motion Picture
    Production." Ph.D. diss., New York University, New York, 1983. This study is
    a rather general analysis of the technological impact of new video production
    techniques on contemporary filmmaking.

Moore, Barbara Ann. "Syndication of First-Run Television Programming: Its Devel-
    opment and Current Status." Ph.D. diss., Ohio University, Athens, Ohio, 1979.
    This study focuses upon the rise of filmed, syndicated television programming;
    its first chapter, "Development of First-Run Syndication," gives a useful overview
    of the relation between film and television in this field.

Rouse, Morleen Getz. "A History of the F. W. Ziv Radio and Television Companies:
    1930–1960." Ph.D. diss., University of Michigan, Ann Arbor, Michigan, 1976.

A complete study of television's first and foremost independent producer and syndicator of television films, this dissertation draws from Ziv's own files and details the early days of film production for television.

Schnapper, Amy. "The Distribution of Theatrical Feature Films to Television." Ph.D. diss., University of Wisconsin, 1975. This dissertation is a study of the economic factors which determined the release of Hollywood's features to television.

As evinced by the sources cited both in this chapter and in the dissertations listed above, the film and television trade press provides the basic source for primary material on the relationship between the industries. Two invaluable publications are generally available in most research libraries and on microfilm. These include

Broadcasting. Washington, D.C., 1930– . An indispensable resource for historical study of the American broadcasting industry, this biweekly, then weekly, magazine devoted particular attention to the integration of film into telecasting; by the early 1950s a special section entitled "Film" had been added, detailing developments in the television film industry, including news on both feature film and film for television.

Variety. New York, 1906– . The "show-biz bible," weekly *Variety* provides a remarkably impartial viewpoint about the developments between the film and television industries from as early as the late 1920s.

A number of other journals are also important sources of data on the relationship between film and television, including *Television Age* (later *Television/Radio Age*), *Television* (New York), *Journal of the Society of Motion Picture (and Television) Engineers* (later *SMPTE Journal*), *American Cinematographer*, *Millimeter*, *Sponsor*, *Advertising Age*, *Printer's Ink*, and *TV Guide*. Unfortunately, there exists virtually no comprehensive index to most of these periodicals except *TV Guide*, but one is advised, especially for older citations, to consult *Readers' Guide to Periodical Literature*, *Public Affairs Index Service (P.A.I.S.)*, and *The Engineering Index*. Since the early 1970s, most major periodicals in the field have been indexed in *Film Literature Index*, *FIAF International Index to Film (and Television) Periodicals*, *Access*, and *The Magazine Index*. Within academia, journals such as *Cinema Journal*, *Journal of Film and Video*, *The Velvet Light Trap*, *Journal of Popular Film and Television*, *Quarterly Review of Film Studies*, and *Screen* (all indexed through FIAF and *Film Literature Index*) have carried scholarly articles concerning the relationship between film and television. The following are of particular interest:

Quarterly Review of Film Studies, Summer 1984. A special issue devoted to the film-television relation, including articles entitled "Thinking It Differently: Television and the Film Industry," "The Rise of the Telefilm and the Networks' Hegemony Over the Motion Picture Industry," and "Failed Opportunities: The Integration of the U.S. Motion Picture and Television Industries."

Journal of Film and Video, Summer 1985. A special issue devoted to "Methods of Television Study," including an article entitled "The Coming of Television and the 'Lost' Motion Picture Audience."

Boddy, William. "The Studios Move into Prime Time: Hollywood and the Television Industry in the 1950s." *Cinema Journal* 24 (Summer 1985): 23–37. A concise rendition of many of the same points made in this chapter.

Useful reference works (detailed more extensively in Schreibman, cited above) include the following:

Brooks, Tim and Earl Marsh. *The Complete Directory to Prime Time Network TV Shows:*

1946–Present. 3d ed. New York: Ballantine Books, 1985. A comprehensive compendium of virtually all prime-time programming carried on American television.

McNeil, Alex. *Total Television: A Comprehensive Guide to Programming from 1948 to the Present.* New York: Penguin Books, 1984. Similar to the above but also containing nonnetwork syndicated programming.

Marill, Alvin H. *Movies Made for Television.* New York: Da Capo Press, 1980. A listing and credits for made-for-television films.

Wicking, Christopher and Tise Vahimagi. *The American Vein: Directors and Directions in Television.* New York: E. P. Dutton, 1979. A neo-auteurist approach to filmed television drama, including brief appraisals of various directors' video work and credit listings for each.

Finally, a book which gives a fairly complete overview of the development of the American television industry, including its relations with Hollywood, is

Castleman, Harry and Walter J. Podrazik. *Watching TV: Four Decades of American Television.* New York: McGraw-Hill, 1982.

SELECTED FILMOGRAPHY/VIDEOGRAPHY

It is difficult to cite individual films which illustrate the development of a symbiotic relationship between the motion picture and the television industries, since the essence of this union was primarily at the economic level. Still, there do exist examples of both feature films and television programming which reflect shifting aesthetic, formal, and even economic concerns between these two media. Several examples of these motion picture and TV offerings follow.

Filmography

Brian's Song (USA 1971). Screen Gems. Directed by Buzz Kulik. With James Caan and Billy Dee Williams.

Days of Wine and Roses (USA 1962). Warner Brothers. Directed by Blake Edwards. With Jack Lemmon and Lee Remick.

How to Marry a Millionaire (USA 1953). Twentieth Century-Fox. Directed by Jean Negulesco. With Betty Grable, Marilyn Monroe, and Lauren Bacall.

Judgment at Nuremberg (USA 1961). United Artists. Directed by Stanley Kramer. With Spencer Tracy and Maximilian Schell.

Marty (USA 1955). United Artists. Directed by Delbert Mann. With Ernest Borgnine and Betsy Blair.

M*A*S*H (USA 1970). Twentieth Century-Fox. Directed by Robert Altman. With Elliott Gould and Donald Sutherland.

The Miracle Worker (USA 1962). United Artists. Directed by Arthur Penn. With Anne Bancroft and Patty Duke.

Network (USA 1976). United Artists. Directed by Sidney Lumet. Screenplay by Paddy Chayefsky. With Faye Dunaway, William Holden, and Peter Finch.

Patterns (USA 1956). United Artists. Directed by Fielder Cook. Screenplay by Rod Serling.

Requiem for a Heavyweight (USA 1962). Columbia. Directed by Ralph Nelson. Screenplay by Rod Serling. With Anthony Quinn and Jackie Gleason.

Twelve Angry Men (USA 1957). United Artists. Directed by Sidney Lumet. Screenplay by Reginald Rose. With Henry Fonda and E. G. Marshall.

Visit to a Small Planet (USA 1960). Paramount. Directed by Norman Taurog. With Jerry Lewis.

Videography

The Comedian (USA February 14, 1957). CBS. Playhouse 90. Directed by Bohn Frankenheimer. Screenplay by Rod Serling. With Mickey Rooney, Mel Torme, Kim Hunter, and Edmund O'Brien.

Fireside Theatre (USA 1950–1954). NBC. Frank Wisbar Productions.

Marty (USA May 24, 1953). NBC. Goodyear TV Playhouse. Produced by Fred Coe. Screenplay by Paddy Chayefsky. With Rod Steiger and Nancy Marchand.

No Time for Sergeants (USA March 15, 1955). ABC. The U.S. Steel Hour. Directed by Alex Segal. Screeplay by Ira Levin. With Andy Griffith.

Public Prosecutor (USA 1948, 1951–1952). Du Mont. Produced by Jerry Fairbanks.

The Three Musketeers (USA 1949; November 24, 1950). CBS. The Magnovox Theatre. Produced by Hal Roach, Jr. (at his studio). Directed by Budd Boetticher.

To Have and Have Not (USA January 17, 1957). NBC. The Lux Video Theatre. Screenplay by William Faulkner. With Edmond O'Brien and Beverly Garland.

11

FILM AND VIDEO ART

EDWARD SMALL

INTRODUCTION

To posit a symbiotic relationship between art and two inextricably related media—film and video—is itself neither revolutionary nor problematic. On the one
hand, film and video history has exhibited so much aesthetic merit that one no
longer invites serious consternation through simple reference to, say, "film art."
(Though I would paraphrase Christian Metz to contend that whereas few films
exhibit no art, fewer still exhibit a great deal; the matter is one of considerable
degree.)[1] On the other hand, the postulate that an advantageous union now exists,
and has historically existed, between the theory and practice of the fine arts (viz.
painting and sculpture) and classic film cum contemporary video has received
considerable scholarly attention over the past two decades. It is this latter premise
which will occupy the focus of this chapter. Further, by surveying extant scholarly
data and insights, I will seek to develop two related and somewhat more novel
theses: first, that film and video exhibit an intrinsic similarity (i.e., unlike their
extrinsic relationship to, say, theater or the novel, their relationship to each other
is intrinsic and their demonstrable dissimilarities are clearly matters of degree
and not kind); second, that the same aesthetic impetus which historically motivated practitioners of the fine arts, today also drives those film and video artists
devoted to that major genre usually termed "experimental" or "avant-garde."
Finally, the systematic reflexivity of contemporary experimental film/video constitutes the clearest and best-developed defense of these same theses.

STYLES AND GENRES OF INTERACTION

The Question of Genre

The very discussion of experimental/avant-garde production as a major genre
derives from rather revisionist genre theory which elevates the use of the term
and concept "genre" to major structural groupings (in contradistinction to more

traditional genre theory, which only strives to segment select subcategories of
the fictive feature into such theatrical narratives as "musicals" or "Westerns").
The remarkable familiarity of the fictive feature, however, makes it an excellent
ground against which other major genres can be figured. Cinema's "royal road,"
it is what people usually think of when they discuss film (just as the term "video"
unfortunately can too readily call to mind only popular programming in broadcast
television).

One familiar major genre which is better understood by such configuration
with fictive features is the documentary or actuality film (cf. "nonfiction" and
"factual" as alternate, though not always synonymous, labels). If one considers
early Lumière production, its origins are probably as old as cinema itself, although conscious distinction appears pronounced no earlier than the 1920s, with
the productions of both Robert Flaherty and John Grierson. Today, the more
than half-century-old tradition of the actuality film subordinates a rich complex
of subtypes: newsreels, educational/industrial productions, travelogues, anthro-
pologic/ethnographic works, propaganda documentaries, and cinéma vérité.
These are typically films about fact, not fiction; and their subjects are often real-
people-in-real-places. Thus, contradistinction to fictive features is classic and
far more familiar than that major genre which will constitute the core concern
of this chapter—experimental/avant-garde production.

Eight Characteristics of the Genre

Today's major genre of avant-garde production is progressively synthetic—
consolidating both mechochemical (i.e., film) and electronic (i.e., video) constructions. I will deal with this recent amalgamation in detail later in this chapter.
For the moment, however, a historical perspective privileges the cinematic component because, like the aforementioned actuality genre, early endeavors date
from the 1920s. Yet for both components, a number of technostructural characteristics should directly aid definition and help frame distinctions which separate this genre not only from actuality work but fictive features as well.

1. Economic Independence

The first characteristic gains primacy in homage to David Curtis's 1971 study,
Experimental Cinema, which detailed his concept of economic independence:
works made outside commercial channels.[2] While many fictive and documentary
works are comparably independent, the situation of the experimental/avant-garde
genre is so thoroughly disassociated from industry financing and distribution, as
well as from related structural and stylistic demands, that this distinction rests
upon matters far more consequential than those of degree; indeed, matters interwoven with the entire issue of film and video art. To be sure, painters and
sculptors have generally produced exemplary art under the simultaneous support
and constraints of political, personal, or institutional patronage. But when we
examine more modern periods, periods which chronologically parallel the very

advent of photography and the motion picture, we are rather drawn to a prototype of pronounced independence. Think of the many modern painters like Matisse, Rousseau, Rouault, Kandinsky, Mondrian, Monet, Manet, Modigliani, Cézanne, Seurat, Van Gogh, Gauguin, Renoir, and Picasso to obtain some sense of the analogous independence at once suffered and enjoyed by experimental film and video artists. Filmmaker Stan Brakhage provides the perfect prototype of an artistically successful avant-garde career independent of box-office rewards, financed by an almost monastic poverty, and thus free from any conceptual constraints. Further, Brakhage's often controversial subject matter and initially idiosyncratic (though today highly influential) forms have no real counterpart in either documentary or fictive productions.

2. Noncollaborative Construction

Related is characteristic number two: noncollaborative construction. In this age of auteur concerns, only the experimental/avant-garde genre evidences uncontestable, quintessential auteur controls. For these are works often crafted by just one or perhaps two artists—their concept, funding, and total production. Recall Alexandre Astruc's 1948 "La Caméra-Stylo" contention that the cinema will become an art only when its materials are as inexpensive as a writer's pencils and pads.[3] For experimental filmmakers like Brakhage or Maya Deren (whose 1943 *Meshes of the Afternoon* may have been known to Astruc), such precise economic equivalence was of course never truly realized. Still, post–World War II availability of 16-mm hardware and film stock greatly increased accessibility of materials for individual artists who sought free expression for their creativity, expression unhampered by industrial economics and its concomitant, intricate ensemble strategies. Whereas a typical fictive feature—regardless of "auteur" directorship—employs writers, cinematographers, editors, sound and lighting technicians, etc. (and the list is an extensive one), all of whom perforce contribute their own creative talents along with their execution of stipulated tasks, the typical experimental artist is comparatively quite autonomous. By way of example, consider Brakhage's 1963 production of *Mothlight*. The original concept and related "scripting" were Brakhage's. All funding for materials came from his purse. All of the construction (here an innovative form of cameraless animation employing fragments of moth wings as found objects, literally sandwiched between two adhesive mylar strips having precise 16-mm registration for printing and projection) including editing and the choice of a silent soundtrack were Brakhage's tasks. Finally, the film's distribution (and economic expectations) rested with the artist. Thus Brakhage is as much the "auteur" of this four-minute work as Picasso was the auteur of a painting like *Three Dancers*, about four decades earlier.

3. Brevity

The especially terse length of *Mothlight*, a technostructural aspect directly related to Curtis's concept of economic independence, exemplifies characteristic number three—brevity. Though select experimental productions can be found which match or exceed feature length, brevity becomes a hallmark of this major genre. To be sure, some subtypes of documentary production are also brief (e.g., newsreels). And such an alternate major genre as the television advertising commercial is paradigmatically terse. Nonetheless, due to economic constraints as well as an artistic preference for structural strategies which offer high re-playability, typical running times for experimental works are far closer to *Moth-light*'s than to fictive features or to typical documentary productions. Kenneth Anger's legendary *Scorpio Rising* (1963) runs almost one half-hour, but his *Kustom Kar Kommandos* (1965) runs only three and one-half minutes. Bruce Baillie's *Quixote* (1964–1965) runs forty-five minutes, but his better-known *Castro Street* (1966) runs ten. Jordan Belson's prize-winning *Allures* (1961) is nine minutes long, Bruce Conner's very popular *Cosmic Ray* (1961) is four minutes, Marie Menken's silent *Lights* (1964–1966) runs for eight and a half minutes—and such times are the rule, with something like Michael Snow's *La Région Centrale* (1970–1971) being exceptional due to its 190-minute projection. Again, a brief experimental work often operates like a phonograph record by bearing the expectation of high replayability. Whereas even a particularly pleasing fictive feature may call for no more than two or three reviewings, an experimental film like Norman McLaren's *Begone Dull Care* (1949) remains fresh after literally hundreds of viewings, in part due to its abandon of any hint of recallable story (and its rapid barrage of handpainted and often abstract images).

4. Nonnarrative Construction

This same telling lack of story brings us to characteristic number four—nonnarrative constructions. While exceptions abound, especially if one considers even a slender hint of story as evidence for narrativity, by and large these are works intentionally and theoretically opposed to that commonplace and remarkably formulistic narrative construction which is so essential to the entire history of the fictive feature, from *Birth of a Nation* through this year's Academy Award winners. With its "classical continuity," the fictive motion picture is marked by precise cinematographic and editing patterns (e.g., matched action, no jump cuts, axis lines) which traditionally have come to embody broader narrative elements—elements shared by the cinematically influential classic novel (i.e., characterization, point of view, and a clear presentation of diegetic time: a fictive differential between the film's running time and the story's chronology).[4] The coordinate major genre of actuality/documentary work shares such constructions only in part (relying more upon a spoken word soundtrack—literally "narration"—for its typical narrativity). But it is only the experimental genre which eschews them for doctrinaire purposes. As we will see, even the earliest experimental artists of the European avant-garde sought cinema's essence outside its chance bonding with the nineteenth-century novel. Indeed, experimental films like Hans Richter's *Rhythmus 21* (1921) or Brakhage's *Mothlight* are so removed from narrative concerns that they "play" equally well if projected in forward or reverse modes. Further, this same nonnarrative characteristic initially embraced strategies and structures closer to lyric poetry, painting, or music.

5. Mental Imagery

This tendency also realized a devotion to altered states of consciousness, which thus presents characteristic number five—a penchant for the phenomenology of mental images. To be sure, a particular documentary could address a related subject (such as current psychological research on mental images resulting from biofeedback guidance of theta EEG modes, for example), and some of the earliest fictive films (such as Porter's 1906 *Dream of a Rarebit Fiend*) manifest a concern with dreams, as part of the narrative, that remains strong today. Yet the emphasis upon mental imagery exhibited by the experimental avant-garde genre is clearly a difference of kind, not degree. For by and large, both the actuality and fictive genres rest their aesthetic upon what theorist André Bazin called "The Ontology of the Photographic Image."[5] Whether mechochemical or electronic devices are used, they are directed to depict—or from Bazin and Siegfried Kracauer's perspective to "capture"—objective phenomena, our consensual realm of external perceptions. Consider Kracauer's explicit thesis: "Films come into their own when they record and reveal physical reality."[6] Indeed for Kracauer, experimental film's affinity for interior realms flies in the face of a "medium which gravitates toward the veracious representation of the external world."[7] In contrast, a mental image, by definition, is an experience independent of external stimuli (or with the exception of such stimulus agents as drugs, hypnotic commands, or pressure upon the closed eyelids.) While film/video surrogates of mental images rest upon aesthetic assumptions distinct from Kracauer's or Bazin's, they continue to manifest themselves in the face of such critiques. The variety of mental imagery types which came to dominate aesthetic strategies throughout the history of the experimental film are particularly extensive. Deren's *Meshes*, for example, depicts dreams within dreams. Conner's (1975) *Take the 5:10 to Dreamland* appears devoted to a phenomenology of hypnogogic images—those which preface the dreaming state and which are experienced briefly between actual waking states and true sleep. Belson's numerous films like *Mandala* (1953), *Allures* (1961), *Samadhi* (1967), *Meditation* (1971), and *Chakra* (1972) are explicit attempts to realize surrogates of that particular body of imagery experienced in states of deep meditation, states which are better detailed in Asian psychology than in our own Western traditions. But it is probably Brakhage who offers the clearest example of an experimental artist tending to carefully structure much of his production to imitate what his extensive writings have termed "closed eye vision" experiences.[8] His fairly well-known "Prelude" to *Dog Star Man* (1961), for example, provides a veritable catalog of mental images defined and labeled by such contemporary psychologists as Peter Sheehan.[9] Hallucination, dream, memory, eidetic and entoptic forms are exclusively interwoven throughout this twenty-five-minute, nonnarrative, noncollaborative, independent experimental film. The work is also silent.

6. Avoiding Verbal Language

Mental imagery, as presented above, is a nonverbal cognitive phenomenon (which may or may not be accompanied by, or interspersed with, subvocalization). Perhaps as an intuitive aesthetic strategy which would augment audience experience of mental image modes, a great number of experimental works simply eschew words—written, spoken as dialogue, or narrated. While this at times manifests itself as silence, I prefer to entitle this sixth characteristic an avoidance of verbal language. Even before the 1930s advent of sound, early avant-garde production evidenced less use of intertitles than actuality or fictive works from the same period. And once sound became available, clearly the greater proportion of experimental/avant-garde films (and, later, videos) employed a soundtrack of either music or effects in opposition to the fictive feature's characteristic dialogue or the documentary's hallmark of voice-over narration. Well before current psychological theories of cortical asymmetry, experimental artists seemed to have grasped the psychophysiological divorce between left and right hemispheric functions, providing the right brain hemisphere's "specialization" for imagery, and an isolation from any competition with the left brain hemisphere's specialization for verbal language. Most experimental works are thus "right brain" works.[10] An extreme but telling exemplification of this rests upon the extraordinary number of extant silent experimental film/video productions, after sound had come to almost dominate the fictive and actuality genres. Of course, the experimental genre's striking independence from industry funding and collaborative construction signals a special style of economic, and thus technological, poverty throughout its history. Yet such economic influences only partly explain this aesthetic of silence. Probably the one American experimental artist whose work has so consistently and so considerably avoided sound is Brakhage. While he began his film work in Colorado in the 1950s, burdened by the shoestring economics of independent production and some technical naiveté that may have originally dictated lack of soundtracks (by then commonplace in 16-mm formats), even a simple survey of his extensive theoretical writings reveals that his continued concern for silence is clearly a matter of design. Further, a great number of experimental artists continue that same choice, even today when inexpensive, easy-to-use, small-format video equipment makes any such avoidance of sound the technological trick. Video sound costs nothing extra, in contrast to film sound, yet this chapter will later survey a number of silent avant-garde video works which chose to reject that technologic resource.

7. Technologic Innovation

Such rejection, however, is generically anomalous, as our seventh characteristic is a particular affinity for technologic innovation. Far more than its coordinate, contradistinct genres of documentary and fictive productions, the experimental genre cleaves to resources like distortion lenses, animation, step-optical printing, and computerized images. The genre's use of animation provides a concise example of this. Animation itself is a technique—the technique of stop-action or single-frame cinematography—not a genre. Like any other technical resource (cf. lighting), it is transgeneric. The animated models of *2001*, the animated maps in documentary's *Why We Fight* series, and the vast use of animation in television advertising commercials clearly demonstrate this point. Whereas a brief Warner Brothers cartoon or fictive feature-length classic like *Snow White* should receive generic distinction, animation's use by experimental artists must rather be regarded as but another technostructural resource, albeit a particularly prominent one. An excellent book-length insight into this intertransformational interweave of experimental structure and animation techniques is Robert Russett and Cecile Starr's *Experimental Animation*.[11] For example, their discussion of Mary Ellen Bute's "early use of electronics for drawing," which led in the 1950s to very sophisticated applications of cathode ray tube technology, raises profound theoretical questions regarding the complex interrelationships between classic cinematographic single-framing and contemporary computerized/video animation devices.[12] It becomes clear that much of experimental film/video's embrace of technological development springs from its (previously described) desire to somehow construct accurate surrogates of many an artist's fleeting phantom "mental image phenomenology." But this same "technologic" embrace also serves as our eighth and final generic characteristic: reflexivity.

8. Reflexivity

Reflexivity is a core concern of so much contemporary art that it is at once commonplace enough to suggest ready definition and complex enough to confound such suggestion. Further, it is an international concern which Metz, for example, refers to as "*autoréflexivité*," after French film theory.[13] Formally, it manifests itself as structural strategies which uncover or reveal the construction of a given work—painting, film, etc. Let us examine the fine arts for some examples. John Chamberlain's 1960 metal sculpture *Essex* clearly exhibits its automotive and other found-object metal parts as metal parts (rather than sculpting the parts in such a fashion that their original identity is obscured for the sake of having them look like something else, such as a human face or figure). A better-known and earlier example from painting is Georges Rouault's *The Old King* (1916), which comparably exhibits its brush strokes and pigments in its less radical depiction of the subject's torso and profile. The function of these formal elements also serves theoretical considerations. For by exhibiting the stuff-and-substance of its construction, a given work of art helps answer classic questions as to the essence of its media and modes. A contrast between the classical-continuity editing of fictive features and one of Bruce Conner's experimental compilation films should help clarify this point. A feature such as *Gone With the Wind* (1939) strives to disguise its junctures, its editing, to the extent that this strategy (which continues today) is aptly termed "invisible editing." In contrast, Conner's (1957) *A Movie*—made up of bits and snippets of found footage from old newsreels, cartoons, commercials, etc.—strives to exhibit these junctures, calls attention to its compilation, to its essential construction. As signaled by its very title, the Conner film is highly reflexive. Indeed its real subject is "editing" (or montage) rather than any story or philosophical theme (outside this extremely philosophical aesthetic consideration). Thus experimental production is often a type of extant, manifest, immediate theory—direct theory sans the intervention of a separate semiotic system such as the verbal discourse predicated upon the printed prose which you, the reader, now process (clearly Conner's cinematic constructions are semiotically closer to his subject—editing—than any prose or even verse could ever be).[14] Of course reflexivity can be found in varying degrees in the fictive and actuality genres as well, but hardly to the extent seen throughout the entire history of experimental/avant-garde work. This final characteristic—reflexivity—will progressively come to dominate our historical overview, which follows. There we will see a growing artistic exploration of film/video essence, an ongoing attempt to detect and exhibit elements independent of literary and dramatic influence (and, more recently, the very experimental influences of painting and music as well).

Media Specificity

No one of these eight characteristics can be considered either necessary or sufficient for a working definition of this major genre. Conversely, it would be a rare experimental work which exhibited all of them. Still, when a cluster of such characteristics can apply to a given film or video work, the generic distinction is likely. The labels for precise subcategorization are, as we will see, diverse and largely predicated upon historical and/or geographical trends. These trends have been variously termed "avant-garde," "underground," "visionary," "expanded," and even—most appropriate to this chapter—"art films." But I suggest that all these labels are inappropriate for truly contemporary productions which typically have been influenced by the international, continuing confluence between mechochemical and electronic constructions of moving images to the point where their similarities are more interesting and instructive than are their differences. (Paradoxically, this point is more fully framed by select video artists who seek reflexive exhibition of videographic essence.) For film and video bear an intrinsic bonding to each other far different from either's extrinsic attachment to, say, the novel or the essay or the theater. While the groundwork for this same insight dates from the earliest experimental theory and production of the European avant-garde, I believe that any accurate and systematic examination of media-specific elements can offer more empirical evidence. One such system which may be most insightful is Metz's *grande syntagmatique*.

The French cinesemiotician Christian Metz's theoretical writings have enjoyed remarkable popularity and demonstrable influence in the United States since the 1974 publication of his *Film Language: A Semiotics of the Cinema*. In his *Film Language* chapter "Problems of Denotation in the Fiction Film," Metz presents his *grande syntagmatique* under the section entitled "The Large Syntagmatic

Category of the Image Track.''[15] Here he offers eight ''syntagmatic'' editing
configurations which are designed to cover both narrative and nonnarrative montage patterns (of shot organization). The *grande syntagmatique* seeks to be
definitive while remaining open to revision and/or additions. More significant,
each syntagmatic type is precisely, systemically defined in commutable contradistinction to the other seven. That is, an ''autonomous shot'' is definitively
distinct from a ''scene,'' both of which are in turn distinct from a ''sequence''
or ''bracket syntagma,'' etc. Further, a good number of studies have demonstrated the system's applicability to (first) film and (later) video.[16] In telling
contrast, any attempt to apply the *grande syntagmatique* to a play or a poem or
a novel or an essay or a painting would be directly, and informatively, frustrated.
The system is doubtless medium-specific, and its ability to encompass both film's
mechochemical and video's electronic constructions (of images) strongly suggests that we are thus dealing with an intrinsic bonding, one which I would like
to label with the metaterm ''cinevideo.'' What follows, then, is a brief historical
overview of the evolution of this major genre, ''Experimental Cinevideo,'' and
its symbiotic relationships to concomitant developments in the fine arts, especially painting. As we shall discover, no other major genre has ever evidenced
any comparable degree of such an interrelationship.

HISTORY AND DEVELOPMENT

Experimental Cinevideo begins in Europe in the 1920s, migrates to the United
States during the international Depression of the 1930s, flourishes in America
during the late 1950s, and returns to international scope after the 1960s,—a
scope it retains today, while it extends a penchant for new technologies into the
realms of video and computers. Its earliest auteurs were established fine-artists
who sought new freedom of expression for their creativity in the (then) fairly
new technostructural resource of motion pictures. Thus painters like Fernand
Léger initially built upon structures and conventions familiar to their fine art
production for their construction of avant-garde films. Such influence served two
purposes. First, it provided the artist ready nonnarrative prototypes for the new
medium; second, it provided the medium itself reflexive insight into a number
of popular (but hardly intrinsic) structures for the organization of its images
(and, later, sounds). John Hanhardt's essay ''The Medium Viewed'' helps detail
many combinations of intuitive and doctrinaire premises which marked this initial
body of experimental theory and production: the European avant-garde.

The term ''avant-garde'' links the films to which it refers with advanced art and ideas in
other media and disciplines, and, by definition, with a view of film which is neither
traditional nor orthodox. Because most people share a traditional notion of what constitutes
a film, films are generally expected to conform to certain conventions. . . . The best-
known type of film is the feature-length, commercial entertainment film. . . . Film appreciation in general (and in particular its historiography and criticism) has supported this

type of film by according it the preeminence it enjoys today while attempting, in the process, to balance its mass entertainment with its justification as art. . . .[17]

Hanhardt's survey of avant-garde ideology recognizes the essential links between avant-garde personalities and productions in the fine arts and related—if not, more accurately, "derived"—constructions, which came to characterize a primary subordinate to our major genre of Experimental Cinevideo.

The avant-garde films of Europe of the 1920s, and in America with increasing activity since the early 1940s, aspired to a radical otherness from the conventions of filmmaking. . . . Thus these independent films . . . involve the filmmaker directly through a tactile, "hands on" approach or an assertive point of view that is the expression of an artist engaged in such vanguard aesthetic movements as surrealism, cubism, abstract expressionism or minimalism. This cinema subverts cinematic convention by exploring the medium and its properties and materials, and in the process creates its own history separate from that of the classical narrative cinema.[18]

As we shall see, such initial and continued building upon insights derive from various fine arts like painting, while fruitful, historically came to be regarded as something of a dead end. Current film/video reflexive strategies seek far more unadulterated media essence. Still the same sensibilities which motivated men and women in earlier eras to turn to canvas and brush and paint, today motivate related attention to the distinct, and I think far more versatile, resources of film and video. Moreover, so much of the original European avant-garde ideology continues to influence these sensibilities, that aesthetic appreciation is still predicated upon a kind of running comparison between experimental production and more popular cinema (and television)—what Hanhardt calls the "history of the world's cinema."

The successive phrases in the history of the world's cinema are taken as a loosening of the techniques of filmmaking and story-telling from the restraints of theatrical models to seeking allegiance to the predominant traditional literature, and, to a much larger extent, and primarily in Europe, to the modernist novel and criticism. Film is not permitted, in this view, to transcend the narrative model of traditional literary forms but must instead carry on the tradition of the popular novel.[19]

The material which follows is a historical overview of the complex development of the one major genre clearly outside this popular history, a genre that thus provided the particular conceptual vantage which has allowed critics and historians like Hanhardt to detect the prejudicial, myopic, but popular position that he calmly castigates. Each period of the genre contributes its distinct insights and, often, entertains distinct premises. Always, each period explores then current technological innovation and consequential structural possibilities. Throughout, the influence from—and, at times, upon—the fine arts shall be a core concern of our survey.

The European Avant-Garde

Clearly the best examination of the interrelationship between the experimental film of the 1920s and early twentieth-century painting is Standish D. Lawder's *The Cubist Cinema*.[20] This book-length study provides precise comparisons—through both its prose and illustrations—between personalities and productions in the fine arts and the European avant-garde: "it focuses on the interrelationships between film and modern art, predominantly painting, from 1895 to about 1925; that is to say, from the inception of film to that moment when Cubism and its derivative styles began to lose supremacy within the tradition of European modernism."[21] Lawder's regard for these interrelationships emphasizes reciprocity. That is, paintings of the period at once influence and are influenced by certain films.

Again, the major proportion of such films are today categorized under that label, used by such historians as David Curtis, the European avant-garde (EAG). While all such generic boundaries are contemporary divisions rather than conscious categorization from the actual period, today the EAG is regarded as the origin of that larger genre which we have examined as Experimental Film and Video.

Lawder's examination of Hans Richter's *Rhythmus 21*, one of the earliest and today best-preserved (and thus best-known) EAG productions (released in the year 1921), bears out this complex of influences and heritage.

Richter's first film, *Rhythm 21*, was a kinetic composition of rectangular forms of black, grey, and white. Perhaps more than in any other avant-garde film, it uses the movie screen as a direct substitute for the painter's canvas, as a framed rectangular surface on which a kinetic organization of purely plastic forms was composed. For, normally, the movie screen is perceived as a kind of window . . . behind which an illusion of space appears; in *Rhythm 21*, by contrast, it is a planar surface activated by the forms upon it.[22]

With the privileged perspective of hindsight, *Rhythmus 21* bears remarkable resemblance to the form of both earlier and later paintings by the Dutch artist Piet Mondrian (1872–1944). As H. W. Janson writes, "by the early 1920s Mondrian had developed . . . a completely non-representational style that he called Neo-plasticism . . . "[23] Whereas early Cubist compositions by Mondrian (such as his 1912 *Flowering Trees*) prefigure form and function of a film like *Rhythmus 21*, his more mature, later paintings like *Composition with Red, Blue, and Yellow* are—with the exception of the painting's color and the film's movement—so similar to *Rhythm 21* that reciprocal influence seems uncontestable.

But the EAG was hardly limited to Cubist strategies. Surrealism, Dada, and Futurism all had mutual manifestation in both paintings and experimental films of this period. Salvador Dalí and Luis Buñuel's capstone of the EAG movement, their very well-preserved and well-known *Un Chien Andalou* (1929), draws as much upon André Breton's "Surrealist Manifesto" as do earlier and later canvases by such painters as Max Ernst. Indeed, Dalí remains today the major surrealist artist representing the movement, and his expression in both painting and film is indicative of our thesis. Lawder's key example, however, is rather *Ballet Mécanique*, a 1924 EAG production of the French painter-filmmaker Fernand Léger. Through illustrations drawn from Léger's cubist/futurist/dadist paintings (e.g., 1924 *Contraste de Forms*; 1925 *Éléments Mécaniques*) and frame enlargements from this classic avant-garde film, Lawder directly details comparable expression of form and function in both media.

Early U.S. Developments

The European avant-garde was to close with the coming of sound and the international Great Depression. During the same period, however, rather separate and distinct experimental film production enjoyed a smaller movement in the United States where Charles Sheeler and Paul Strand's 1921 *Manhatta* is considered as the initial, surviving production. In contrast to the EAG works, *Manhatta* owes influence more to poetry (*viz.* Walt Whitman) than painting. While exceptions can be presented, this same independence from painting marks most of these few avant-garde films which allowed the United States to continue the tradition begun in Europe in the 1920s. Maya Deren's 1943 *Meshes of the Afternoon* is a good example of this. *Meshes* is a very powerful, very successful, and very experimental film (having most of our eight generic characteristics). However, while likely influenced by the more painterly EAG work which preceded it, *Meshes* retains a distinctly independent quality. "In structure the film is close to the French Surrealist genre, but Deren replaces the deliberately arbitrary treatment of time and location that characterizes Surrealist works with a precisely calculated technique. . . . [Further] in her writing . . . Deren rejects all inference of symbolism in her work."[24] Nonetheless, select U.S. films from this period often do exhibit an interweave with both personalities and/or productions from the fine arts, though to be sure they are far less doctrinaire in that fabric. The German-born Oskar Fischinger provides pertinent example. Influenced by the EAG, he began his abstract experimental animations in Europe and continued his synaesthetic address of form-and-color correspondences (to light classical music) in America after a mid–1930s invitation to Hollywood. His 1940 *An American March* is largely a cinematographic interpretation of Sousa's famous "Stars and Stripes," but given frames look a great deal like post-Cubist paintings.

More exemplary is the experimental animation of the American illustrator Douglass Crockwell, whose silent cinematic abstractions of the 1940s at once recall and to some extent prefigure the abstract expressionism of a painter like the American Jackson Pollock (1912–1956). Pollock's "Action Painting" was predicated upon chance bondings of pigment to canvas. As Janson suggests, Pollock "relinquished" the "strict control" of earlier painters to chip and spatter paint upon his canvas in such a way as to insure that the resulting shapes were "largely determined by the internal dynamics of his material and his process: the viscosity of the paint," etc.[25] Likewise, Crockwell's *Long Bodies* (1946–1947) depends upon somewhat random relationships of material—relationships predicated upon how multicolored, melted fragments of wax bond together. His technique was to form a solid (three-by-four-inch) block of these colored waxes, then to slice off tissue-thin layers upon one face, recording the careful cross-sectioning with an animation camera. The result often looks like a Pollock painting in motion, as does a work from Canada: *Begone Dull Care*. Completed in 1949 by the National Film Board animator Norman McLaren, *Begone Dull Care* is at once a Fischinger-like attempt to realize graphic correspondences to music (by the Oscar Peterson Jazz Quartet) and to bypass the use of a camera for experimental animation. By painting directly onto film—at times ignoring the frame lines—both representationally and (more often) abstractly, McLaren realized a marvelous medley of color, line, and form that is remarkably akin to countless Pollock paintings from its period.

U.S. Underground Film

It would be the 1950s, however, which would finally experience the true flourish of experimental film in the land it had migrated to after the demise of the EAG. Often called "underground" films because of independent financing and distribution, many of these works were more directly influenced by poetry than painting. Indeed, as Curtis documents, the famous avant-garde critic-artist Jonas Mekas came to entitle many such productions "experimental poetic films."[26] Still, other works, like Kenneth Anger's *Eaux d'Artifice* (1953), seem to be really more reflexive, addressing experimental film's far more prestigious foil—the Hollywood cinema—rather than either poetry or painting.

I believe that the best book-length study on the films of this period is Sheldon Renan's now classic *An Introduction to the American Underground Film*.[27] Tracing the origins of his subject back to the work of the EAG, Renan also recognizes the essential reflexivity of experimental films and filmmakers which his book documents. To be sure, these productions of the 1950s and the 1960s reveal—for Renan—diverse subject matter: portraiture, protest, sexuality, etc. But when Renan addresses "cineplastics" to mention Tony Conrad's (1965) *The Flicker* (constructed entirely from intercut pure black or white frames) or Brakhage's very bionic attention to "the physiological and philosophical aspects of seeing," or the work of Andy Warhol, Robert Breer, and Nam June Paik toward answering questions as to the essential nature of film, such works operate more purely, more reflexively, and therefore stand in contradistinction to other underground productions such as the "rare" narratives or the "uneasy category" of the aforementioned "film poems," which Renan also discusses.[28]

Thus this period exhibits only occasional, or in turn geographically limited, interrelationships to established fine arts, like painting. It is Renan's category of "The West Coast Abstract School" which in fact may prove the greatest heritage from the period with demonstrable links to the theories and constructions of classic or contemporaneous painters. From that same "school" comes James Whitney's *Yantra* (1950–1955), for example, an animated extension of Indo-Asian mandala paintings. The West Coast painter Jordan Belson employed similar tools and similar subject matter in such films as *Allures* (1960), the concentric and symmetric mandalas of which are quintessential Jungian archetypes.

More singularly, such underground filmmakers as Robert Breer exhibit both a background in painting and a regard for the cinematographic image as a kind of canvas. Breer graduated from Stanford in 1949 with a degree in painting and in the 1950s began his highly innovative, animated "time paintings" employing very rapid exchanges of found objects and his own, often abstract, drawings or paintings. To quote Renan: "Thus as a painter approaching cinema, he has chosen to define one unit of cinema as the viewing of a painting for 1/24 of a second, and to define a motion picture as several of these units viewed in sequence. The idea of lifelike continuity does not exist in his definition or in many of his movies."[29]

I must add, however, that Breer's very use of animation's single-frame technique to relate disparate images (often giving but one frame to each image) is a highly reflexive strategy as well, one which depends upon contradistinction to more popular animation—such as Disney's—for its reflexive value and quite theoretical posture. Comparably, the sculptor Bruce Conner's compilation works—such as *A Movie* (1958) or *Cosmic Ray* (1961), both made up of "found footage" fragments of originally unrelated films—exemplify essentially underground reflexivity, what I have termed "manifest theory" (here, on the cine-video-specific resource of montage). And Andy Warhol's rather notorious work from this period—while doubtless an extension of his painting—also maintains such a classic (though converse) theoretical subject for its reflexive focus: the reductio ad absurdum revelation of Bazin's post–World War II castigation of montage, and his unqualified celebration of a "cinema of duration." *Sleep* (1963), for example, allows Warhol to show a man sleeping for six hours, a clever theoretical challenge to audience patience and participation.

Other underground filmmakers with roots in painting could be identified, such as the late Stan Van Der Beek or the San Francisco painter Robert Nelson or Ed Emshwiller (who began his career as comic book illustrator), but clearly the larger thrust of the underground period is rather divorced from painting. Marie Menken's work is exemplary for this concern. While her 1963 "exploration" of Mondrian's famous painting *Broadway Boogie Woogie* clearly reveals interrelationships to the fine arts, other films by her are quite independent of any such liaison—whether to painting, dance, drama, or narrative. The very reflexive *Light* (ca. 1965), for example, is a handheld-yet-animated (because single frames are used) study of urban electric illumination which is at once a wonderful visual experience and a comment. In part, it comments on the bionic differences and similarities between cinematic recording and the phenomenology of (human) vision; but it also examines Breer's questions regarding the issues of single-frame cinematography and popular notions of "animation." Thus such an aesthetic complex can best be studied as a diachronic extension of a fine artist's sensibilities and strategies beyond paint-and-canvas into film-and-camera, rather than any synchronic symbiotic construction.

Expanded Cinema

Renan's 1967 study concludes with an introduction to a "whole new area of film and film-like art," which he terms "expanded cinema."[30] Much of this same newness for Renan depended upon then infant technostructural innovations which were to provide even greater extensions for artistic sensibilities seeking to go beyond the confines of paint and canvas:

Expanded cinema is not the name of a particular style of filmmaking. It is a name for a spirit of inquiry that is leading in many different directions. It is cinema expanded to include many different projectors in the showing of one work. It is cinema expanded to include computer-generated images and the electronic manipulation of images on television. It is cinema expanded to the point at which the effect of film may be produced without the use of film at all.[31]

When Renan composed these lines, he could also write that "videotape is fairly new, the first such recorder having been developed in 1956 by Ampex."[32] I would today add that the same painterly impetus for imagery which photography exhibited was technologically transformed first into cinema's (eventual) amalgam of sound and image, and more recently into video's more purely electronic constructions. This current evolution of cathode ray tube (CRT) technology is within the lived experience of most readers. The 1950s were the decade of live broadcast television, structures transformed by the 1960s advent of video tape recorders, transformed again by the portable video equipment that resulted from the 1970s introduction of videocassettes. And indeed the decade of the 1980s seems marked by the marriage of microcomputers to CRT displays.

However, the book-length study which chose Renan's phrase—some three years later—for its title, placed only partial emphasis upon such technostructural innovation. Indeed, Gene Youngblood's (1970) *Expanded Cinema*, with its long introduction by Buckminster Fuller, begins with an explicit thesis: "when we say expanded cinema we actually mean expanded consciousness."[33]

Today, *Expanded Cinema*'s survey is best addressed as the logical extension of what Renan had already categorized as "The West Coast Abstract School." Covering the period of the late 1960s through the early 1970s, Youngblood's emphasis came to bear upon the great number of complex constructions which California artists (for the most part) were crafting through such technostructural resources as cinematic step-optical printers plus cinematic amalgamations which drew upon video technology or then quite new computer systems. Woven into this same survey is a philosophical optimism for "expanded consciousness."

Marshall McLuhan's influence is evident here, but Youngblood was also so-phisticated enough to trace his philosophical notions back to McLuhan's own source—the Jesuit theologian Pierre Teilhard de Chardin's concept of the noo-sphere. Calling "Expanded Cinema" a new tool, Youngblood wrote that

This tool is what Teilhard de Chardin has called the *noosphere*, the film of organized intelligence that encircles the planet, superposed on the living layer of the biosphere and the lifeless layer of inorganic material, the lithosphere. The minds of three-and-a-half billion humans—twenty-five percent of all humans who ever lived—currently nourish the noosphere; distributed around the globe by the intermedia network, it becomes a new "technology" that may prove to be one of the most powerful tools in man's history.[34]

Hoping that this "intermedia network" would "finally [liberate] cinema from its umbilical to theatre and literature," Youngblood regarded the works he sur-veyed as (reflexive) arts in themselves rather than extensions of any other art form.[35] "The notion of experimental art, therefore, is meaningless. All art is experimental or it isn't art."[36]

While *Expanded Cinema* begins with the rather underground heritage of Brak-hage's work, its real value today is its more specialized analyses of such Ex-perimental Cinevideo artists as Patrick O'Neill, whose *7362* (the title being, reflexively, the stock's emulsion number) provided a very abstract, dynamic step-optical printer-product which Youngblood implicitly relates to the work of painters like Frank Stella, but which he clearly argues transcends the earlier medium. "All the visual arts are moving toward the cinema."[37] Appropriately, the best written chapter in the book may be "The Cosmic Cinema of Jordan Belson," focusing on an artist who began as a painter but whose cinematic, metamorphic mandala images break the boundaries of a painter's traditional tools.[38]

However, *Expanded Cinema*'s cover employs a frame from Scott Bartlett's *OFFON* (1967), and it is this particular work which I believe best exemplifies Youngblood's most valuable contribution to our own interests. For *OFFON* has a reflexive purity which at once separates it from literary, poetic, dramatic, and even painterly positions while emphasizing the essential commonality between cinematographic and videographic constructions—what I have called "cinevi-deo."

Winner of many international awards, *OFFON* . . . was the first videographic film whose existence was equally the result of cinema and video disciplines. Like all true videographic cinema, *OFFON* is not filmed TV, in the way that most movies are filmed theatre. Rather, it's a metamorphosis of technologies. . . . The basic source of video information was in the form of twenty film loops that Bartlett and [Tom] De Witt had . . . made for a mul-tiprojection light concert. . . . [and which] were fed through a color film chain in [a] television control room. . . . Simultaneously, other loops and portions of Glen McKay's light show were rear-projected onto a screen on the studio floor, which was . . . a second video source. Both video sources were routed into one monitor. . . . [and] a special [motion picture] camera was set up [to record the composite imagery].[39]

For my own purposes, I have come to employ the term "cinevideo" to encompass two complementary designations: one is to label such synthetic film/ video constructions like *OFFON*; two is to recall the ongoing, greater confluence of mechochemical and electronic constructions for moving images which has come to characterize the entire discipline of film/video, as well as this special genre. Youngblood's period of "expanded cinema" contributed a great deal to both senses of the term. Yet the dazzling, rapidly paced, and subtly superimposed constructions which he documented were not without foil. Indeed, Youngblood's *Expanded Cinema* chapter "Synaesthetic Cinema and Extra-Objective Reality" briefly glances at distinct works like Michael Snow's *Wavelength* to offer some indication that aesthetically different experimental production was taking place and gaining prominence on America's other coast.

Minimalist-Structuralist Work

While a great number of West Coast experimental cinevideo artists of the late 1960s and early 1970s were originally painters, their later attention to film and video can best be regarded as an attempt to transcend paint-and-canvas's classic concerns. In return they inherited a separate and very complex goal which had its origins in the EAG work a half century earlier: reflexive exhibition of cinevideo essence. A greater number of East Coast artists, on the other hand, came to film (and only much later video) in a fashion more directly linked to their earlier media. Building on the current "less is more" aesthetic of the minimalist painting of the period, in hindsight they also appear greatly influenced by the often notorious films of pop-art painter Andy Warhol. While their West Coast counterparts may be said to evidence some concern with painterly "op art" strategies (for cinevideo works like *OFFON* do reveal a pronounced concern with op's perceptual play, in such strategies as rapid intercutting of positive and negative shots of otherwise identical images), the extent of East Coast homage to painterly fashions is far more pertinent to this chapter's comparisons.

This is not to say that the minimalist-structuralist experimental works which began as an East Coast counterpoint to West Coast abstraction cum technologic virtuosity have no sense of reflexivity. On the contrary, the basic motivation for minimalist restrictions and reductions can wisely be judged as an almost empirical examination of variables that could aid attempts to answer reflexivity's perennial questions regarding a given medium's extrinsic and intrinsic elements. But this somewhat scientific motivation was by no means explicit at the time. What was explicit, however, was a very influential essay by P. Adams Sitney which constituted the final chapter of his 1974 publication *Visionary Film*.[40]

Sitney's *Visionary Film* is, historically, an insightful counterpart to Youngblood's earlier study. Each book details distinct directions in the experimental genre, distinctions that are bound up with the geographic separations of the American coasts. For instance, both works deal with Stan Brakhage. But whereas Youngblood addresses Brakhage's interest in mental imagery as an extension of his own notions of expanded consciousness, Sitney also correlates Brakhage's "closed eye vision" with particular parameters of contemporary painting, much in the way Lawder would elaborate *The Cubist Cinema*, the following year. Two illustrations in Sitney's chapter "The Lyrical Film" bear this out. One is a frame from Brakhage's film *Thigh Line Lyre Triangular*, the other a black-and-white reproduction of Willem de Kooning's painting *Woman with a Green and Beige Background*.[41] Both are presented as examples of "abstract expressionist space," though unlike Lawder's arguments for Léger, Sitney sees no evidence for doctrinaire design in Brakhage's intention. Indeed, he contends that while "the resulting version of space corresponds to that of Abstract Expressionism, whose motivations are away from the physical eye, [this] seems not to have occurred to Brakhage."[42] Further, in contradistinction to Lawder's later book (though more complementary to Youngblood's earlier one), Sitney seeks to correlate the films he examines with contemporary consciousness: "If, as I have claimed, the great unacknowledged aspiration of the American avant-garde film has been the cinematic reproduction of the human mind, then the structural film approaches the condition of meditation and evokes states of consciousness without meditation; that is, with the sole mediation of the camera."[43]

But this concern with consciousness has a quality distinct from Youngblood's; and the largely East Coast minimalist-structuralist films again have qualities distinct from previously examined West Coast productions of this period. Further, Sitney's very influential chapter-essay "The Structural Film" came to describe such qualities and—like other insightful and influential criticism—prescribe a kind of prototype for structural films which would follow his publication.

Speaking of such experimental filmmakers as Michael Snow, a Canadian painter whose 1967 *Wavelength* became perhaps the watershed film for the movement described, Sitney wrote that "theirs is a cinema of structure in which the shape of the whole film is predetermined and simplified, and it is that shape which is the primal impression of the film.'"[44] Moreover, Sitney clearly delineated specific characteristics of works like *Wavelength*, a forty-five-minute-long zoom, shot in a New York City loft.

Four characteristics of the structural film are its fixed camera position (fixed frame from the viewer's perspective), the flicker effect, loop printing, and rephotography off the screen. Very seldom will one find all four characteristics in a single film, and there are structural films which modify these usual elements.[45]

Whereas the painterly movement of Abstract Expressionism (to paraphrase Harold Rosenberg's famous insight) realized compositions which were rather records-of-an-event than pictures-of-an-object (the event of the construction itself), the later movement of minimalism was far less dependent upon the reflexivity of randomness for its structural exhibition. For example, Bob Law's early 1970s *Black Paintings* were an installation of a number of pure black canvases upon pure white museum walls to the effect of reducing both frame and canvas to entities of such restriction that the viewer is forced to focus upon painting's most basic, most elementary structures. Such work is not without pedagogic purpose and, thus, its true audience is likely fellow painters curious about structural essentials often overlooked or ignored when more complex subjects are chosen. Compare an "expanded" cinevideo like *OFFON*, which provides a very complex admixture of structures and concomitant visual-aural effects to the extent that the work has the quality of a technologic tour de force, dazzling its audience with remarkable metamorphoses of abstract and representational images, full of electronic colors, rapid montage, and layered collage. Snow's *Wavelength*, in contrast, largely reduces its variations to a single, highly reflexive subject: the nature of a "zoom." That is, *Wavelength*'s particular perspective play of a (slow) exchange of focal lengths (from wide-angle through normal to telephoto, over a forty-five-minute period) runs in implicit contradistinction to the type of perspective variation resulting from (say) a simple cut or—more comparably—a dolly-shot (where the camera physically moves through the space). Indeed, the subject of Snow's film is as much Sitney's first characteristic ("fixed camera position") as the simple loft and meager events which his camera captures, while zooming toward a windowed wall.

As we shall see, Sitney's well-defined movement continued beyond his 1974 essay as the film-video confluence which marked West Coast work came to encompass all experimental production, both in the United States and abroad. For the resources of video were too attractive to long remain ignored by experimental artists, many of whom looked toward these very strategies of Minimalism-Structuralism for their increased attention to reflexivity.

Experimental Video

In his 1977 book *Video Visions*, Jonathan Price wrote that "historically, American video art begins in the late sixties within and around the studios made available in educational stations in Boston, San Francisco, and New York, thanks to charitable grants. . . ."[46] Detailing the influential work of such video artists as the Korean-born Nam June Paik or the American Michael Shamberg (whose own book *Guerilla TV* allowed a grass-roots introduction to rapid technological changes in progressively less and less expensive video technology), Price's study is today one of many which begin to document the very recent advent of experimental video.

From the view of this chapter, experimental video is a logical technostructural extension of the previous patterns and premises that marked the longer history of experimental film. Indeed, I believe the resulting amalgam is aptly entitled "Experimental Cinevideo." To substantiate this regard, one need only review the technological changes in the work of multidecade careers, artists like Van

Der Beek or Emshwiller whose production began cinematographically only to transform into more electronic directions with the coming of inexpensive video hardware. Exceptions in such reviews, like the work of Brakhage, also abound, of course. In order to help offset them I would also ask the reader to recall our initial eight characteristics in regard to the prototypic personality and production of one video artist: Nam June Paik.

Calling Paik a "Day-glow Godfather," Jonathan Price notes a background in music rather than painting (especially the influence of John Cage), making the Korean immigrant seemingly removed from many of the painterly influences this chapter has surveyed.[47] However, most of Paik's earliest video works were so Dadaist in posture that he is more rightly regarded as a child of this same culture, albeit one who skipped the step of painting. Still, it is Paik's skills with electronics that figure most prominently in his development. Indeed, in 1970 Paik was to "invent" one of the first video-synthesizers (with Japan's Shuya Abe):

[Paik] proposed a machine to generate TV pictures by itself, to transform any pictures from a camera and to make and mix its own. . . . [Later] Paik boasted [that] "this will enable us to shape the TV screen canvas as precisely as Leonardo, as freely as Picasso, as colorfully as Renoir, as profoundly as Mondrian, as violently as Pollock, and as lyrically as Jasper Johns."[48]

The international fame and flourish of Paik's career which followed effectively exemplify our eight generic characteristics. Technical innovation is perhaps foremost, but Paik's varied creations typically are nonnarrative and highly reflexive as well. Although he is often collaborative, he has always retained the experimental artist's auteur control as well as related economic independence. Because video is cheaper than film, many of his works do lack brevity, but his synthetic works especially seem devoted to electronic surrogates of mental images, often avoiding (or at times confounding) verbal language.

Other contemporary video artists also clearly exemplify our eight characteristics. Peter Campus's *Three Short Tapes* (1974) are brief (five, thirteen, and eleven minutes), highly reflexive works which explore such videographically specific characteristics as chromakey-matting, video feedback, and video color. *R-G-B*, for example is a mirror-like feedback regress, a real time self-portrait of Campus as he places colored filters before his camera's lens—all in natural sound sans even one spoken word. The video is noncollaborative, independent, and only minimally narrative. To be sure, the work is also a good example of Minimalism-Structuralism in experimental video production. Barbara Buckner's perfectly silent *Hearts* (1979) uses technologically innovative synthetic images in a very nonnarrative twelve-minute independent production. Nan Hoover's (1978) *Impressions* is a nine-and-three-quarter-minute single take (a popular minimalist-structuralist format) recording the slow movements of a human hand to an identical "soundtrack" of chosen silence, and with comparable disregard for narrative.

There are today probably hundreds of experimental videos which embody our key characteristics. Stephen Beck's exemplary constructions, many of which came from his special invention—the Direct Video Synthesizer—are quintessential confirmations of these specific links. His *Video Weavings* (1976) is about ten minutes long, largely noncollaborative, independent, rich in the intrinsic reflexivity of technical innovation, and totally nonnarrative, being an almost Fischinger-like interpretation of a music track. The synthetic patterns recall Navaho tapestry and metamorphose colors and forms into stunning surrogates of mental imagery. Both *Video Weavings* and Ed Emshwiller's more recent (1984) *Skin Matrix* (which also evidences almost all of the eight characteristics) further display the CRT-specific quality of a stained-glass aesthetic. As McLuhan pointed out two decades ago, the mode of the film image is predicated upon light reflected off a screen, while video depends upon light projected through a screen, at the viewer.[49] Thus while works like *Matrix* or *Weaver* help confirm our compound genre—Experimental Cinevideo—their particular reflexivity paradoxically frames the subtle distinctions between these two confluent media, as well.

It is important to point out, to underscore the scholarly handicaps which come from experimental video's very youth, however. Whereas the cinematic prototypes it derives from are—by virtue of their historic remove—fairly well documented today, I know of no single, book-length study on experimental video which could provide an effective analogue to, say, Renan's survey of underground film or Lawder's study of the EAG. Thus the suggestions mentioned in my review of the literature (below) must be accepted as provisional. Even Price's (already cited) *Video Visions* bears the particular handicap of its date (1977). The truly explosive development and accessibility of portable video technology have realized such a flourish of activity by a countless number of practicing and potential artists that only the scholarly hindsight of future decades will allow proper perspective for the period we now witness. Thus I suggest that interested researchers turn to the current catalogs of experimental video distributors—such as New York City's Electronic Arts Intermix (EAI)—to acquire some sense of both early, established artists and the ever-changing influx of new constructions, based upon new technology, from new artists. But no catalog nor critical description can capture the essential experience of actually viewing these experimental video extensions of the earlier experimental film evolution.

Which experimental video artists, from the perspective of the present writing, seem most established and worthy of extended regard? This is a difficult question to answer, in part because our major genre—Experimental Cinevideo, which began in Europe only temporarily sheltered its early development within the confines of the United States—has again returned to international scope. Artists in England or Japan compete with American counterparts for the fragile posterity of critical and scholarly recognition. For example, a 1980 Canadian, trilingual introduction to then current video work entitled *Canada Video* informally documents the theories and productions of Calvin Campbell, Tom Sherman, Lisa

Steele, and others.[50] But even were we to retain focus on only U.S. work, any hope to list pertinent artists would be very incomplete while very lengthy. John Alpert, Kit Fitzgerald, John Sanborn, John Reilly, Woody Vasulka, Bill Viola, and Jud Yalkut are all represented by EAI. We've alreay mentioned other EAI artists like Beck, Buckner, Campus, Emshwiller, Hoover, Paik, and Van Der Beek.

Further complications come from the subtle but substantial links that our major genre of experimental cinevideo has with such coordinate genres as the television advertising commercial (TVC). This is not to say that the interweave between the fine arts and, say, advertising is a new phenomenon. Let the reader only recall the now priceless "posters" produced by the French post-impressionist painter Henri de Toulouse-Lautrec, whose styles still mark contemporary commercial art. Today we also witness the extended use of modern technostructural resources like three-dimensional computer-generated animation and motion-control-graphics in such already classic commercials as Abel's (1973) Seven-Up "Butterfly" series.

The TVC lacks enough of our eight key characteristics to make it really a coordinate, rather than subordinate, genre to Experimental Cinevideo. Such ubiquitous constructions are decidedly dependent upon industry economics, for example. They are also usually highly collaborative, often narrative, and often predicated upon verbal language to a degree far removed from Experimental Cinevideo work. On the other hand, they share such characteristics as brevity and technical innovation with our major genre; and when they are not narrative they sometimes evidence concerns with mental imagery. Finally, a few recent TVCs begin to evidence a quiet reflexivity. This admixture of characteristics is so intricate that one could contend an instructive premise: only within Madison Avenue's product do we find the most popular, pragmatic, and profitable application of these almost laboratory-like developments called Experimental Cinevideo.

Other industrial or institutional video work also evidences remarkable links to our major genre. Offspring to our West Coast Optical School's Whitney family is John Whitney, Jr.—now head of Digital Productions, which employs multi-million dollar Cray "super-computer" technology to construct special (video-based) effects for commercial motion pictures. Fine artist David Em's industry-supported work for the Xerox Corporation has realized a number of mandala-rich computerized video pieces which—with the exception of such funding—neatly fit our key characteristics. And James Blinn's clever surface-mapping-algorithm-software serves a number of constructions which can easily be labeled "experimental video" in spite of the fact that they are direct products of Jet Propulsion Laboratory/National Aeronautics and Space Administration (JPL/NASA) resources.

Still, I believe it more fitting to conclude this chapter with discussion of at least one contemporary video artist whose constructions directly exhibit the key characteristics with which this same chapter began. Bill Viola is singularly a video artist. To the best of my knowledge he has no background in film, let alone painting. Born 1951 in Flushing, New York, he once commented that he had "a seven-channel childhood," and indeed greater New York City's (pre-CATV) broad provision of telecast fare can at once be credited as his major mentor and aesthetic incentive.

Viola has been a particularly successful video artist. His (1979) *Chott el-Djerid* (Arabic: "a portrait of light and heat") won Grand Prize at the Portopia International Video Art Festival held in Kobe, Japan (1981). The following year he was to stay in Japan under visiting-artist funding from the Sony Corporation. There, at Sony's Atsugi Plant, he completed *Hatsu Yume* (Japanese: "first dream"). He currently works out of Los Angeles, California.

Viola has completed a great many other video works, now distributed by such organizations as EAI. His *Information* (1973), for example, is a half-hour investigation of video reflexivity. But his central concerns—in both his fine writings and major video productions—are the very aesthetic issues of perception and related cognitive modes like memory. I remind the reader that the Greek etymology of "aesthetics" indicates a protoempirical regard for matters of "sensation/perception." (I have joined two contemporary terms with a slash, here, because I do not believe our current distinction between them was ever envisioned in centuries past.) We have not totally lost this sense of "aesthetic" as is clear in such modern terms as "anaesthetic" (literally, no sensation/perception) or "synaesthetic" (from psychology: sensory crossovers). But still, to employ "aesthetic" with that meaning today is quite revisionist. Since Baumgarten's *Aesthetica* (1750), the term has instead come to designate prescriptive issues of values or norms in the arts, as well as oft-related hermeneutic (i.e., interpretive) considerations.

Nonetheless, to speak of "aesthetics" in regard to Viola, one has to embrace that same revisionist and ancient "sense" (literally) of the term. *Chott el-Djerid*, for example, is a modern minimalist, half-hour study of Sahara mirages, the real subject of which is human perception (or, reflexively, the differences and similarities between video records and our phenomenology of perception). The work's subtle, direct sound makes it seem almost silent as the nonnarrative, slow montage excludes left-brain affinities for words and numbers. The videography is exquisite, and the resulting mood and emotion really too ineffable for critical capture. Likewise, *Hatsu Yume* is difficult to properly describe. As signaled by its title, the work's address has the quality of a remembered dream. In spite of Sony support, all videography, sound (subtle, direct, almost wordless), and editing (including temporally ambiguous "slow motion") are from Viola's hand, Viola's eye. The colors are incomparable captures-or-constructions, quietly bespeaking the artist's perfect grasp of his equipment. Throughout we are a disembodied eye and a progressively sensitive ear enjoying a dreamlike, nonnarrative tour of Japan's resorts, markets, cities, and lush bamboo groves— the texture so rich one synaesthetically "feels" the very fabric of Viola's (ultimately) electronic leaves and stalks.

In an article on "Video as Art" published in a 1984 issue of the *Journal of Film and Video*, Viola came to quote the Persian sage Rumi on perception, in a fashion that recalls the painter Klee's more contemporary and more western contention that art does not reproduce what we see but rather makes us see: "New organs of perception come into being as a result of necessity. Therefore, we should increase our necessity so that we may increase our perception."[51] I believe that, for Viola, video is basically a device which can (wisely used) increase our sensory necessity in just such a precisely aesthetic manner. Such sensory increase has always been art's primary purpose; hence the original, diachronic meaning of the term "aesthetic" for the fine arts. In this fashion, Viola's writing also addresses experimental video's at times symbiotic, at times transcendent, link to the fine arts.

Video art cannot be regarded separately from the artistic tradition. It is the latest connection in the long, long thread of inspiration stretching back through experimental film, photography, painting, sculpture, right to the roots of art history. With every new videotape, artists are participating in linking this cultural chain to our ever-moving present. What should be understood is that this artistic tradition is not the property of artists alone—it belongs to all of us and remains open and available to any creative effort, regardless of the role-label attached to the person making it.[52]

Just as Hanhardt framed the implicit and explicit comparisons which reciprocally reflect the distinct aesthetic premises of experimental film and popular fictive features, Viola regards much of the very value of experimental video in continued contrast to broadcast television, the dramatic series of which are but electronic extensions of the same classical continuity structures which have always dominated fictive features:

Video art is far more than the abstract color patterns and electronic palate painting most people think of when they hear the term. In our time it can come to represent more than even the specialized modern art tradition it has grown out of. Human imagination is all too often the limiting factor in the use of technology. A cursory glance at TV will strongly testify to this fact. As the media explosion continues, video professionals need to explode along with it, or else be left with the most advanced communications system in history but nothing to say on it.[53]

The ever-increasing aesthetic insights resulting from reflexivity's classic and contemporary investigations lead me to share Viola's optimism for the possibility of eventual transcendence over not only popular television but even the "specialized modern art tradition." Nonetheless, this chapter has demonstrated that no other genre ever evidenced even a comparable degree of interweave with the traditional fine arts that Experimental Cinevideo has. Thus it builds upon this base, employing its sophisticated advantage to ever-increasing insights into its distinct essence, its intrinsic potentials.

Nevertheless, especially over the past two decades—a period precisely connected to major developments in electronic means for constructing moving images—we have seen a pronounced reduction of the direct link between personalities and productions in the fine arts and Experimental Cinevideo. Instead we have witnessed an increased attention to new artistic tools like portable (and even studio) video technology by the same sensibilities which were, in earlier periods, drawn to the simpler "technologies" of paint and canvas. Allow me, then, to conclude this chapter with the related contention that only the impetus remained the same; that the same sensibilities which gave earlier societies a Modigliani or a Cézanne now manifest as a Paik or a Viola.

But this is not to say that such an exchange of technologies is independent of structural changes. Just as form/content can only retain its essential bond, there can be no exchange of tools without a perhaps concomitant, perhaps causal exchange of structure. For structure is the interrelationship of the parts to the whole; and because in structure all real change is intermutational, technostructural exchanges will always be one of the commutable components of that aesthetic reality. Consequently, our major genre of Experimental Cinevideo will continue to provide us a harbinger and exploration of an otherwise unpredictable aesthetic future, a future that is today attendant upon a degree of technologic invention so distinct in the history of all the fine arts that it is truly an especially promising, especially exciting, difference in kind.

NOTES

1. Christian Metz, *Film Language: A Semiotics of the Cinema* (New York: Oxford University Press, 1974), p. 77.

2. David Curtis, *Experimental Cinema* (New York: Universe, 1971).

3. Alexandre Astruc, "La Caméra-stylo," in *The New Wave*, ed. Peter Graham (Garden City, N.Y.: Doubleday, 1968).

4. Metz calls these "the time of the telling" and "the time of the thing told"; *Film Language*, p. 18.

5. André Bazin, *What is Cinema?* (Berkeley: University of California Press, 1967).

6. Siegfried Kracauer, *Theory of Film* (New York: Oxford University Press, 1960), p. ix.

7. Ibid., p. 79.

8. "Metaphors on Vision," Film Culture No. 30, 1964.

9. Cf. *The Function and Nature of Imagery* (New York: Academic Press, 1972).

10. A great many texts are available which detail cortical asymmetry research. One classic introduction would be A. Paivo's *Imagery and Verbal Processes* (New York: Holt, Rinehart & Winston, 1971).

11. Robert Russett and Cecile Starr, *Experimental Animation* (New York: Van Nostrand Reinhold, 1976).

12. Ibid., p. 105.

13. Personal letter; Paris 7–1–85.

14. As Metz wrote, however, while experimental film and video are indeed "forms of theory," they are a peculiar form "which cannot replace the written theory, but cannot be replaced by it either." Ibid.

15. Metz, *Film Language*, pp. 119ff.

16. A great number of applications are extant such as Peter Wollen's on *Citizen Kane*, Peter Koch's on *Persona*, Roth's on *Leone*, Lawrence on television commercials, Silverstone on British TV, and Porter on U.S. television.

17. John Hanhardt, "The Medium Viewed: The American Avant Garde Film," in *A History of the American Avant-Garde Cinema* (New York: AFA, 1976), p. 20.

18. Ibid., p. 21.

19. Ibid., p. 17.

20. Standish D. Lawder, *The Cubist Cinema* (New York: New York University Press, 1975).

21. Ibid., p. vii.

22. Ibid., p. 49.

23. H. W. Janson, *History of Art* (Englewood Cliffs, N.J.: Prentice-Hall, 1978), p. 657.

24. Curtis, *Experimental Cinema*, pp. 50–51.

25. Janson, *History of Art*, p. 663.

26. Curtis, *Experimental Cinema*, p. 62.

27. Sheldon Renan, *An Introduction to the American Underground Film* (New York: Dutton, 1967).

28. Ibid., pp. 25–35.

29. Ibid., p. 129.

30. Ibid., p. 227.

31. Ibid.

32. Ibid., p. 244.

33. Gene Youngblood, *Expanded Cinema* (New York: Dutton, 1970), p. 41.

34. Ibid., p. 57.

35. Ibid., p. 58.

36. Ibid., p. 65.

37. Ibid., p. 99.

38. Ibid., pp. 157ff.

39. Ibid., p. 319.

40. P. Adams Sitney, *Visionary Film: The American Avant-Garde* (New York: Oxford University Press, 1974).

41. Ibid., p. 190.

42. Ibid., p. 188.

43. Ibid., p. 408.

44. Ibid., p. 407.

45. Ibid., p. 408.

46. Jonathan Price, *Video Visions* (New York: New American Library, 1977), p. 92.

47. Ibid., pp. 127ff.

48. Ibid., pp. 139–40.

49. Marshall McLuhan, *Understanding Media: The Extensions of Man* (New York: McGraw-Hill, 1965), p. 313.

50. Available from the Publishing Division of the National Museums of Canada, Ottawa K1AOMB.

51. Bill Viola, "Video as Art," *Journal of Film and Video* 36, no. 1 (Winter 1984): 41.

52. Ibid., pp. 37–38.
53. Ibid., p. 41.

SELECTED BIBLIOGRAPHY

The following book-length studies constitute a select bibliography which should serve any reader seeking substantial background in the major genre of Experimental Cinevideo. While I have annotated this same bibliography, almost all of the books have so marked this chapter's explications that long annotations would be redundant.

American Federation of Arts. *A History of the American Avant-Garde Cinema*. New York: AFA, 1976. While devoted to U.S. work, this basic text does detail early European influences as well. Further it was designed to accompany a fine, seven-program package of thirty-seven U.S. experimental films (which includes such artists as Deren, Anger, Brakhage, Conrad, Menken, Snow, et al.), available for rental from AFA (41 East 65th St., New York City).

Curtis, David. *Experimental Cinema*. New York: Universe, 1971. Subtitled "a fifty-year evolution," Curtis's study is one of the best overviews of the historical evolution of international experimental film.

Lawder, Standish D. *The Cubist Cinema*. New York: New York University Press, 1975. This is an excellent, in-depth insight into EAG work and its interrelationships with the fine arts.

Le Grice, Malcolm. *Abstract Film and Beyond*. Cambridge: MIT Press, 1977. This highly theoretical text traces the entire evolution of experimental film and is especially valuable for its particular attention to recent British and European productions.

Price, Jonathan. *Video-Visions: A Medium Discovers Itself*. New York: New American Library, 1977. One of the few studies available on experimental video, Price's emphasis upon reflexivity is clear in his subtitle.

Renan, Sheldon. *An Introduction to the American Underground Film*. New York: Dutton, 1967. One of the first "texts" available on experimental film (with some attention to early video, as well), Renan's study is very valuable for U.S. production into the mid–1960s.

Russett, Robert and Cecile Starr. *Experimental Animation*. New York: Van Nostrand Reinhold, 1976. A well-illustrated insight into the intricate interrelationship between the technique of animation and the major genre of Experimental Cinevideo.

Sitney, P. Adams. *Visionary Film: The American Avant-Garde*. New York: Oxford University Press, 1974. Sitney's attention is directed to a number of subjects, but this work's major resource remains Sitney's material on structuralist aesthetics and production.

Youngblood, Gene. *Expanded Cinema*. New York: Dutton, 1970. This is the best study of late 1960s work growing out of the West Coast Abstract School, and does provide some attention to video.

SELECTED FILMOGRAPHY/VIDEOGRAPHY

Filmography

Allures (USA 1961). Made by Jordan Belson.
Ballet Mécanique (France 1924). Made by Fernand Léger. Cinematography by Dudley Murphy.

Begone Dull Care (Canada 1949). Made by Norman McLaren and Evelyn Lambart.

B'way Boogie Woogie (*Mood Mondrian*) (USA 1963). Made by Marie Menken.

Castro Street (USA 1966). Made by Bruce Baillie.

Un Chien Andalou (France 1929). Directed by Luis Buñuel. Screenplay by Salvador Dalí and Luis Buñuel.

Cosmic Ray (USA 1961). Made by Bruce Conner.

Eaux D'Artifice (USA 1953). Made by Kenneth Anger.

The Flickers (USA 1966). Made by Tony Conrad.

Kustom Kar Kommandos (USA 1965). Made by Kenneth Anger.

Lights (USA 1964–1966). Made by Marie Menken.

The Long Bodies (USA 1947). Made by Douglass Crockwell.

Manhatta (USA 1921). Made by Paul Strand and Charles Sheeler.

Meshes of the Afternoon (USA 1943). Made by Maya Deren with Alexander Hammid.

Mothlight (USA 1963). Made by Stan Brakhage.

A Movie (USA 1958). Made by Bruce Conner.

OFFON (USA 1967). Made by Scott Bartlett with Tom DeWitt.

Prelude: Dog Star Man (USA 1961). Made by Stan Brakhage.

Quixote (USA 1964–1965). Made by Bruce Baillie.

La Région Centrale (Canada 1971). Made by Michael Snow.

Rhythmus 21 (Germany 1921). Made by Hans Richter.

7362 (USA 1965–67). Made by Patrick O'Neill.

Scorpio Rising (USA 1963). Made by Kenneth Anger.

Take the 5:10 to Dreamland (USA 1976). Made by Bruce Conner.

Thigh Line Lyre Tringular (USA 1961). Made by Stan Brakhage.

Wavelength (Canada 1967). Made by Michael Snow with Hollis Frampton.

Videography

Chott el-Djerid (USA 1979). Made by Bill Viola.

Hatsu Yume (USA/Japan 1981). Made by Bill Viola.

Hearts (USA 1979–1981). Made by Barbara Buckner.

Impressions (USA 1978). Made by Nan Hoover.

Information (USA 1973). Made by Bill Viola.

Skin Matrix (USA 1984). Made by Ed Emshwiller.

Three Short Tapes (USA 1973–1974). Made by Peter Campus.

Video Weavings (USA 1976). Made by Stephen Beck.

12

FILM AND THE NEW MEDIA

BRUCE AUSTIN

INTRODUCTION

"New" is a relative term. Often, it seems, what we mean by "new" is "new to *us*." Cable television, for instance, is hardly new since it has existed virtually as long as broadcast TV. What is new about the new media, though, is their entrepreneurial development, exploitation, diffusion, and audience adoption. And it is in this sense that the "nowness" of the new media presents a heuristic challenge to scholars. What is new, too, is the way we think about and how we define film. The symbiotic process between the new media and film has irrevocably changed the compartmentalized methods by which we have traditionally defined film and other media.

Yrjo Littunen et al. remind us that "every innovation in communications technology has turned out to be less overwhelming in its impact than was initially predicted with the exception of printing."[1] While perhaps not cataclysmic, the introduction of the new media has provoked changes in the production process of moviemaking, the economics of film, the context of cinema consumption, and the way movies are viewed by audiences. Not all new media are discussed here. Omitted are such new technologies as videotex, teletext, electronic mail, cellular radio, fiber optics, and other largely linear, static, and information-oriented media. The focus here is on pay-television and home video, especially, with brief mention of other new media still at their birth or infancy stage. These media comprise the "population" of symbiotically related forms. The new media environment, it is important to note, is extremely volatile; upswings and downturns characterize both the fiscal support among agencies which exploit them and audiences which adopt them. While such volatility makes precise predictions difficult, a symbiosis map can be reasonably constructed by referring to the new media. As the chapter's title indicates, this is not a pairwise analysis of media symbiosis. This inquiry discusses how these new media have symbiotically interacted with motion pictures at four levels: technology, business, society, and, to a lesser extent, art.

HISTORICAL DEVELOPMENT

Craftsmanship and Technology

Although nearly a dozen new media are presently changing the meaning of motion pictures as a technology, a business, a sociocultural force, and an art form, the oldest of the new media is subscription television (STV). STV marks the introduction of pay-TV. STV uses the electromagnetic spectrum as do other broadcasters with the difference that, as its name states, users are charged a fee for services and the signal is scrambled to prevent free viewing. Signal scrambling was first used in 1947 by Zenith with its Phonevision system in Chicago. However, rather than over-the-air transmission, Phonevision, as its name indicates, employed telephone lines. Movie mogul Samuel Goldwyn championed this system as having "the greatest" potential for generating revenues for the movie industry.[2] For here was a technology that moved the box office from Main Street into each audience member's home. The technological and economic benefits of STV were directly tested by Paramount Pictures when, in 1953, it implemented a system called Telemeter in Palm Springs. This experiment, along with one in Etobicoke, Canada, in 1960, failed, as did Henry Griffing's, a movie exhibitor who tested a system in Bartlesville, Oklahoma, in 1957.[3] Best known among the STV entrepreneurs was former NBC president Sylvester L. (Pat) Weaver. Heavily financed, supported by several major corporations and a number of entertainment industry personalities, Weaver introduced his Subscription Television company to Los Angeles and, briefly, to San Francisco in mid–1964. It, too, was a failure in large part due to an emotionally loaded campaign, launched by movie exhibitors, which placed the STV issue on the California ballot as a public referendum.[4]

Although STV was the first, the dominant—although certainly not the only—force in pay-television is cable TV. Without question, cable is the most widespread and mature of all the new media, interrelating with film on all four levels of symbiosis. Beginning in the late 1940s, community antenna television (CATV), as it was then known, was designed primarily as a method for delivering broadcast TV signals to geographic areas of the country which up until then had been unable to receive TV clearly due to signal interference or their distance from TV transmitters. Relatively unsophisticated technologically, in its early development cable simply involved placing a master antenna on the highest elevation possible and running wires to individual homes. Later, inventive amateurs and enterprising electronic experts designed methods to extend the web of wires by developing a booster transmitter to ensure signal strength.

More important for symbiosis than the simple introduction of cable was pay-cable. Until 1975 cable TV was more or less simply an earthbound means of retransmitting ordinary television signals. In 1975 Time Inc.'s Home Box Office (HBO) began using a Satcom I transponder to deliver programming. HBO had begun in November 1972 with an audience of 365 homes in Wilkes-Barre,

Pennsylvania, without attracting much attention. The decision to lease space on a satellite and, on 30 September 1975, offer the Ali-Frazier "Thriller in Manila" fight, was profound. The coupling of satellite technology and earth station distribution via cable systems created a new two-tiered system of pay-television: basic and premium. For film, this meant that now an entirely new method of distribution was possible, along with a new source of revenue. Additionally, satellite technology offers the possibility—yet to be implemented—of eliminating middlemen. Conceivably, movie producers can manufacture their product and distribute it directly to audiences. Direct Broadcast Satellite (DBS) offers the means for transmitting information directly from its producer, to the transponder of a geosynchronous orbit satellite, and then to the downlink microwave dish placed, e.g., on an individual's rooftop. (HBO, of course, is not alone. Cinemax, Showtime, the Movie Channel, the Disney Channel, and others all act as movie distributors now.)

Two forms of home video, videodiscs and videocassettes, predominate among the new media as symbiotic with film. Emerging at virtually the same time as satellite-delivered HBO was Sony's introduction of its Betamax videocassette recorder. Earlier, though, was the development of videodiscs in the late 1960s. While pay-TV offers strictly a method for film distribution (albeit limited to the TV screen), cassettes and discs provide a new *form* of, and medium for recording, motion pictures. That is, the technical difference between cable and broadcast transmission of movies (or any other visual) was largely negligible; cassettes and discs, by virtue of how information is initially encoded, offer a discernible difference—the information does not "go" through the air. Videodiscs, first developed by Phillips, with their potential to store 108,000 frames of information, were heralded as the premiere method for data storage and retrieval. Moving images, too, as well as stereo sound were possible. In addition to avoiding the signal interference possibilities and hardware necessities of broadcasting, satellite, and cable transmission, then, videodiscs possessed two special advantages for movies: fewer duplications of the original (i.e., one step, or generation, from film negative to videodisc), resulting in a sharper, higher-resolution image, and enhanced high-fidelity sound. The chief drawbacks, however, were also two: images were still locked into the three-by-five aspect ratio of low-resolution TV, and varying disc formats. The videodisc was separately manufactured using three incompatible formats: the reflective laser optical disc, the capacitance electronic disc, and the video high-density disc.

Unlike the videodisc, home videocassette recorders (VCR) have but two—at present, mainstream—incompatible formats: Beta and Video Home Systems (VHS). Within a year of Sony's November 1975 introduction of its Betamax, Matsushita introduced its VHS unit through Quasar. More recently, another format has entered the VCR technology: the 8-mm format. And by 1987 we see enhanced image quality of "super VCRs." Both disc and tape, as with satellites, offer new means for movie distribution and viewing. Perhaps more important, both media are new raw materials for recording moving images.

On the level of technology a few lesser players might also be noted. Multipoint Distribution Service (MDS), begun in 1975, employs an omnidirectional microwave signal with an effective radius of no more than 25 miles. In addition to its limited range, MDS is also hampered by easy signal disturbance since it requires an unbroken line of sight between sending and receiving units. A spin-off of MDS is multichannel MDS (MMDS) which provides for four or more channels by one operator, unlike MDS's one-channel capacity. Low power television (LPTV) operates like a "regular" TV outlet, but with less power, resulting in an effective signal radius of about 15 miles. The first LPTV operation initiated service in December 1981, and by mid–1985 more than 125 LPTV stations were in operation. A final new technology of interest, yet to be implemented, is high definition (or density) television (HDTV). Rather than being an information distribution system, HDTV is a means for image enhancement. By increasing the number of TV scanning lines from the present U.S. standard of 525 to as many as 1,125, HDTV image resolution approximates that of 35-mm film.

In terms of technological symbiosis, MDS, MMDS, LPTV, and HDTV are all footnotes to the dominant players: pay-television and home video. Videotape, especially, offers a new way of manufacturing movies. And, as will be discussed in the next section, these players all offer new ways of distributing movies and generating revenues.

Business and Economics

The strength of the symbiotic union between the new media and film varies from level to level. On a technological level there are many possibilities, not all of which have come to fruition. On the level of business and economics, the Hollywood film establishment has a long history of being confronted by the influx of newer media which were first viewed as competitors. Typically, Hollywood's response has been to view such changes in its economic environment as revolutionary rather than evolutionary. Like the military-industrial establishment, Hollywood has been fully prepared to fight and win the previous war. Nevertheless, thus far, by tinkering with the technology and negotiating with the corporation first viewed as competitors, Hollywood has managed to adapt and adjust to change and has remained prolific, prosperous, and profitable. The introduction of first radio, and a quarter-century later television, caused economic realignments in the movie industry without provoking long-lasting structural dislocation. The new media's symbiosis with film is following a similar pattern. Maxwell E. McCombs and Chaim H. Eyal's analysis of Americans' spending on the mass media between 1968 and 1977 concluded that "in terms of manifest behaviors as well as the underlying motivations and gratifications, [society's use of mass communications] seems remarkably resilient in the face of rapid technological change." In particular, these authors reported, movies showed extraordinary economic stability during this period.[5]

As an overview of the business-economic level of symbiosis it may be profitable to chart changes in the series of film exhibition windows between 1965 and 1985. Generally, in 1965 movies moved through a distribution system beginning with a theatrical run, followed by exhibition on network television, and, finally, syndicated and local TV. By 1986 the new media had interposed themselves between the theatrical and network TV windows resulting in a model in which movies begin their exhibition in movie theaters, then travel to pay-television, home video (discs and tapes), network television, and finally syndication/ local TV. It is clear that, from the symbiosis perspective, different styles of interaction occur between different industrial sectors, and here the focus is sharpest on distribution and exhibition.

As business partners and/or product consumers, the dominant new media are pay-TV and videocassettes. STV, despite its long history, appears to be virtually on its last legs. With decreasing numbers of subscribers, operators, and revenues, STV's future is grim. This dismal outlook is largely due to increased operating costs, the fact that it can offer only one program at a time (unlike cable), nonpaying customers, and increased profitability during advertiser-supported hours.[6] Drop-ins (additional VHF television stations) have been largely neglected by both the FCC and business; DBS development has largely been put on hold due to its expense for consumer and operator; and LPTV, while growing in number of operators, has yet to prove itself as a medium that will attract viewers.

Pay-TV, in all its various forms including MDS, MMDS, Satellite Master Antenna TV (SMATV), and especially cable TV, is a significant economic arena in which symbiosis is occurring. The move from one- to four-channel MMDS in 1984 enhanced its viability as a consumer-exhibitor of motion pictures. At about the same time, the viability of SMATV was underscored by Showtime/ The Movie Channel's move to provide programming to such "private" cable systems; until mid–1984 large-scale pay programming services had boycotted SMATV.[7] Further, in this example we see a symbiotic union forming on three levels: between Hollywood, a pay-cable service, and a hybrid satellite-wire technology.

Because the new media discussed in this chapter are essentially distribution systems, they compel the movie companies (e.g., Paramount, Columbia, etc.) to become producers for them. This creates a business environment of economic interdependency between the new media and Hollywood. Among premium cable operators it is now commonplace to participate in and produce movies. HBO, the dominant service, buys some 200 movies annually and began the close symbiotic link with Hollywood, followed by other services, with $3.5 million in "participation" money for *On Golden Pond* (1981).[8] Without this cash the picture may not have been produced; with the money, HBO was guaranteed sole pay-TV rights for the film over a specified period of time—the equivalent of what used to be known theatrically as an exclusive run. Likewise, Paramount Pictures, at the close of 1983, sold Showtime/The Movie Channel, the second-ranked pay service, exclusive access to some seventy-five of its movies over the next five years, a deal worth an estimated $500 million.[9] And although some in

Hollywood feel as though a giant such as HBO has unfairly placed the industry over a financial barrel due to its dominance in the pay-TV market,[10] there is no denying that while control is a point of consternation, cash creates the reality of production.

By 1982 pay-cable fees amounted to 17.4 percent of all movie studio revenues—some $500 to $600 million—the second largest source of revenue for the industry, for the first time exceeding revenues from foreign sales.[11] Pay-TV and home video mean new markets and new profit sectors for Hollywood. And this is true not only domestically, but on an international level, too. For just as the U.S. film industry came to dominate the world's trade in theatrical motion pictures, so too is this occurring overseas for movies presented on new media.[12] And in addition to demands for current product, pay-TV, videocassettes, and, to a lesser extent, discs, have also increased the value of the movie studios' film libraries.[13]

While interest in and sales of video discs were initially promising, they have failed to catch on appreciably. Despite their visual superiority when compared to tape and pay-TV, consumer adoption has been slow due to the three incompatible formats, the high price for both player and software, and the fact that they are restricted to a playback-only format. Perhaps most telling is RCA's action in April 1984 when it announced that, after taking a $580 million loss on its capacitance disc system, it was getting out of the market.[14] Greater business activity and closer economic ties are found between the studios and the VCR industry. Videocassettes are an attractive medium for film producers on both a rental and outright sales basis. According to some observers, the high penetration of VCRs makes this market appear more profitable for movie producers than pay-cable since 20 percent of the wholesale price returns to the copyright owner— a return greater than that from cable TV.[15] Further, as David Waterman notes, "prerecorded home video successfully competes as a delivery system by offering distributors more efficient methods of pricing programs to consumers."[16] In 1983, 12 percent of all movie industry revenues were earned from videotapes; one year later, $1.6 billion in sales and rentals of prerecorded tapes were racked up (two-thirds of all tapes sold are movies).[17]

The film industry is historically characterized by an exceptionally high degree of concentration, and current indications suggest tight-knit symbiosis between film producers and the new media. Thomas Guback reports that in the 1970s the film industry majors accounted for between 70 and 89 percent of revenues from films earning more than $1 million in rentals. Waterman found that six companies accounted for 89 percent of all domestic theatrical rentals in 1983. Douglas Gomery reports similar data to Guback and, further, notes that the domination of the medium is in fact a "bilateral oligopoly": the few major movie companies control the production sector and sell to an exhibition sector largely controlled by a few exhibition chains.[18] In April 1980 a movies-only pay-TV service, named Premiere, designed to compete with HBO was formed involving the Getty Oil Company, Columbia Pictures, MCA Inc. (parent to Universal

Studios), Paramount Pictures, and Twentieth Century-Fox. Although this venture ultimately failed, it was a clear harbinger of things to come; following a Justice Department inquiry and allegation of price fixing and conspiracy to create a monopoly, a U.S. District Court found the partnership in violation of the Sherman Anti-Trust Act and issued an injunction to halt operation of service on 31 December 1980 (service had been scheduled to begin on 2 January 1981). In January 1983 two premium cable services, Showtime and The Movie Channel, merged; as initially formulated, the deal would have ultimately brought together MCA, Paramount, Warner Brothers, Viacom International (which owned Showtime), and American Express (The Movie Channel was a joint venture of Warner Communications and American Express) but ran afoul of the Justice Department.[19] By mid–1983 Tri-Star Pictures, formed by HBO, Columbia, and CBS, was in operation and had released its first feature in early 1984. While such developments may raise eyebrows among antitrust scholars and hark back to the pre–1948 consent decree days when the film industry was a vertically integrated oligopoly, the trend toward increased concentration and—formal or informal—merger of new and old media continues unabated.

A relatively recent development suggests the growing interdependence among these industries. On 17 January 1984, TeleFirst, an ABC subsidiary, began broadcasting recent movies to VCR owners in the Chicago market using a scrambled signal. TeleFirst represented symbiosis among traditional network television, over-the-air scrambling transmission technology, film producer-distributors, and video cassette recorder owners (since subscribers needed to own a VCR to record the transmissions). Early reports indicated that TeleFirst planned to offer some thirty-three movies monthly in addition to nonmovie programming. Initial indications of the popularity of TeleFirst, however, were not favorable. There were no more than 4,000 subscribers after two months of operation, and it was estimated that 100,000 subscribers were needed for the service to reach a profit. Indeed, six months after inception, ABC announced that TeleFirst would end operations on 30 June 1984. Losses for ABC were estimated at $15 million and ABC Video Enterprises president Herbert Granath cited competing pay TV alternatives and confusion among TeleFirst subscribers as to how to use the service as key reasons for its demise.[20]

A final note to this section concerns theatrical exhibition of movies. While more fully developed in the third section of this chapter (styles and genres), here we can simply note that the close, amiable business relationship which exists between film producers and the new media is not shared once theaters are introduced for consideration. With increasing revenues being earned nontheatrically, film producers find less economic incentive to attend to what was formerly their primary market. Indeed, what may be occurring, despite the recent increase in the number of screens, is a reversal of nomenclature: what were ancillary markets (pay-TV) have become primary markets and vice versa.

If the past is even a modestly accurate predictor for the future, the new media are harbingers of increased profitability for the film industry. The advent of radio and television did not result in replacing the old medium (i.e., motion pictures) with the new. Instead, new forms served as the impetus for realignment, reassessment, and redistribution of effort and energy for the film industry. In short, although it may not be business as usual for the film industry as it meets the new media, largely, it seems, it will be business as *if* usual. James Monaco notes that "no matter how people eventually receive their audiovisual entertainment . . . and no matter where they consume it . . . the American film industry will most likely be the source of the programming." He concludes, therefore, that "Hollywood is in the best position ever to control audiovisual entertainment."[21]

Society and Culture

On this level of symbiosis we are concerned with how audiences use their leisure time to pursue media activities. Broadly considered, motion pictures enjoyed nearly four decades as the mass medium virtually unrivaled as a leisure pastime. The introduction of commercial radio broadcasting in the 1920s caused barely a dent in the average weekly film attendance of Americans. As Leo Handel reported in 1946, one mass medium tended to stimulate audience consumption for other media.[22] Not until the introduction of television did frequency of attendance at movies drop off. And as we have seen, on the levels of technology and business, compatibility among the new media and film exists. But when we consider the new media and film behaviorally—i.e., movie attendance at theaters—in relationship to the time people spend with the new media, we find a (perhaps even sharper) replay of what occurred when television was introduced: theatrical audiences were siphoned off by TV. Important to note, however, is that despite the shift in the audiences' physical location—from theater to livingroom—the content consumed was frequently film.

Cable and premium cable TV have seen enormous growth in audience adoption since their inception. Almost half of all U.S. households today subscribe to cable. Placed in a historical context, in 1952 only .1 percent of all homes had cable, accounting for only 14,000 subscribers served by some seventy cable systems. With the introduction of satellite-distributed HBO in 1975, these figures rose to greater than 15 percent cable penetration, nearly 11 million subscribers, and more than 3,600 systems. By 1983 there were more than 33 million subscribers served by some 6,200 cable systems.[23] Present estimates for the rate of cable adoption range from 250,000 to nearly 400,000 households a month.[24] Cable consultant Paul Kagen estimates that by 1993 there will be 104 million pay-TV subscribers and 60 million homes with cable.[25] Moreover, premium cable's adoption rate rivals that of basic cable's (of course one must first have basic in order to receive premium). From a mid–1977 estimate of some 700,000 HBO subscribers, this, the giant among the premium services, now has more than 14 million.[26] A 1982 study found that 38 percent of those cable subscribers who have the option of picking up premium cable did so; a study published the following year reported that the figure had increased to 60 percent.[27]

The "smaller" pay-TV players generally have not experienced the same growth patterns as has cable. Neither MDS, STV, nor SMATV has been able to crack and hold subscription levels above one million. While perhaps they, and other new media such as DBS, may one day find their niche, at present their number of subscribers is negligible. Indeed, the present, as well as the projected, growth rate for basic and premium cable is such that these other pay-TV forms may very well be left either in the dust or forced to "pick up" populations ignored for one reason or another by cable operators.[28]

Initial interest in and sales of videodiscs were promising. Media consultant David Butterfield estimated that by 1990 discs would become a $6.75 billion industry.[29] For reasons identified earlier, such grandiose visions have been severely revised: only about 400,000 players had been sold by 1984 and generous estimates of 1990 penetration levels indicate only 5 to 10 percent ownership in the United States.[30] Today the only realistic glimmers of hope for videodisc consumer adoption are the technological developments enabling disc players to interface with personal computers and high-fidelity compact audio discs.

Far more significant than videodiscs are VCRs. Within less than a decade, more than thirteen million VCRs have been purchased, and by 1990 VCR penetration in U.S. households should reach 51 percent—a figure exceeding that expected for cable. Indeed, the adoption rate for VCRs parallels the growth of color TV in the United States virtually unit for unit.[31] The United States is the world's largest market for VCRs—accounting for more than one-third of all sales—and increased adoption can be anticipated as a result of steadily falling prices, the introduction of high-fidelity stereo sound capability, and, more recently, the introduction of an 8-mm format.

Demographically, cable subscribers, VCR owners, and persons attending movie theaters are hardly dissimilar. Little difference is found between cable subscribers and VCR owners since a significant motive for VCR purchases is to record premium cable offerings. Persons in all three groups tend to be younger, better educated, earn higher than average incomes, hold professional or managerial jobs, and reside in urban areas.[32] According to Paramount's marketing president, Gordon Weaver, moviegoers and videocassette buyers "are not separate and distinct audiences[;] they seem to complement each other."[33] J. Patrick O'Connor reported that in 1983, premium cable subscribers paid some "$2.4 billion to watch movies at home" compared to the $3.5 billion generated in box office revenues.[34]

Beyond demographics are motivational and behavioral issues. Again, the pattern that unfolds reveals a distinct overlap of the interests, reasons for adoption, and viewing patterns among cable subscribers, VCR owners, and people who attend movies at theaters. Even for the "fringe" videodisc medium, the overlap persists: despite the high cost of discs, disc owners purchase as many as thirty a year, virtually all of them movies.[35] Research shows that the most important reason for cable subscription is to receive more movies and that once people are cable "connected," their amount of movie viewing increases. While people may have myriad motives for subscribing to basic cable, the reason for premium cable subscription is without ambiguity: movies.[36] Furthermore, the greatest amount of time subscribers spend with pay-cable is actually watching movies, followed at a great distance by viewing sports and entertainment specials. Thus, movies are not only the overwhelming incentive for cable and premium cable subscription, they are also the type of programming which is overwhelmingly viewed. This, of course, can most easily be accounted for by examining the scheduling patterns of cable, which consist largely of movies, and concluding that the menu equals the diet: the programming which is most frequently offered is that which is most frequently consumed. This information further underscores the notion that audiences are not so much giving up motion pictures as they are the form of exhibition and viewing context.

Research on owners' use of their VCRs indicates that recording movies is the most frequent activity. Further, movies account for the most frequently played back recordings, and movies, along with cultural programs, form the core program material for videotape libraries.[37] Research conducted in 1980 found that use of prerecorded tapes (purchase or rental) was infrequent.[38] No doubt this finding is explained by both the higher cost of prerecorded tapes and the smaller number of tape rental establishments at the time. More recent reports indicate that more than four-fifths of all VCR owners buy or rent tapes—mostly movies— and that of the ten million prerecorded tapes sold in 1983, most were movies.[39]

VCRs, more so than cable, have—and will most likely continue to have— the closest symbiotic union with theatrical film. Since they are an in-home medium featuring direct control by users, program timing and selection is not only convenient, it is possible, unlike cable. For some films, VCRs may actually boost theatrical attendance. Paramount Pictures, for instance, reported that the videocassette release of *Flashdance* (1983) increased theatrical receipts.[40] Still earlier, a 1981 Newspaper Advertising Bureau study found that individuals who preferred seeing movies in theaters were also the most likely to purchase a VCR in the future: "this suggests that many people like movies and like to see them so well that they like to see them in theaters *and* at home."[41]

Art

As has been documented above, the new media and film clearly interact on several levels. Thus far, technological, industrial, economic, and social issues have taken precedence over artistic and aesthetic concerns. In this regard, the present chapter differs from the others in this volume insofar as a close, critical analysis of programming symbiosis is not as feasible since the symbiotic union simply is not mature enough yet. Although symbiosis on the level of art has been alluded to at several points, in large part its omission is due to the shuffling of resources, efforts, and economics of the industries involved. With industrial stabilization, broadly defined, absent among the constituents (including those which are present, those still to come, and those which will no longer be), content-programming symbiosis remains in flux and in a state of uncertainty. Issues of art must wait until the industries' restructuring activities have stabilized.[42]

A review of the history of Hollywood's interaction with previous new media—radio and broadcast TV—indicates that external technological "threats" have resulted in internal technological advances on an aesthetic level. For instance, the impetus for such important innovations as sound, color, and various wide-screen (e.g., CinemaScope, Cinerama) processes is largely attributable to broadcasting. These technical and aesthetic advances in the cinema came as a result not of invention at the time of radio or TV's introduction, but rather due to exploitation of existing technology in the face of competition and as a means for either mimicking or outdoing the new technology.[43] Thus, today we find extended use of videotape in the film industry for rehearsals, side by side with film (for instant playback, thereby reducing the number of takes printed), and for editing. Director Francis Ford Coppola rehearsed and preshot *One from the Heart* (1982) and *Rumblefish* (1983) on videotape and is perhaps best known for adopting similar technical innovations.[44] Other examples of Hollywood's turn to new technologies include wireless microphones, use of radio to synchronize camera and audiotape recording, the Steadicam and Skycam, computer-assisted special effects generators, and improved film stocks and lens optics.[45] Moreover, as they learned to do with broadcast TV, moviemakers have begun using the new media to promote and sell their pictures. A recent development, for instance, is offering music videos derived from a film to MTV, "Night Tracks," and so on.

Beyond the issue of film production are the aesthetics of theatrical film exhibition and viewing. Clearly this level overlaps considerably with the business and economic level, yet must be noted within any discussion of art and programming. Theatrical film exhibitors may increasingly turn to new media and new technologies as an aid to their business. Not necessarily the same media and technologies, of course, but a judicious selection from among those available in order to provide viewers with brighter and sharper screen images.

On a purely economic level, theaters have begun renting and selling video-cassettes in their lobbies of the movies they are showing on their screen; plans for using automatic teller machines to issue and bill for discount movie theater tickets have also been suggested.[46] Aesthetically, however, exhibitors may be initially reluctant to implement conversions to projection systems such as Show-scan or to equip their theaters for satellite reception of high-definition images due to the expenses involved. Historically, exhibitors have, as a group, been skeptical of and slow to adopt new technological innovations, especially those which they perceive as simply adding to expenses without substantially increasing revenues. Henry B. Aldridge has traced this pattern of behavior back to the introduction of sound. Contemporary reports indicate that this pattern is being broken.[47]

Perhaps the most interesting development among exhibitors is "electronic cinema." Broadly defined, electronic cinema includes the production of theatrical films on videotape as well as their distribution (by, e.g., satellite), and exhibition.[48] Clearly, some of these technological innovations will have to await refinement until they are adopted. Speakers at a 1984 international Tape/Disc Association seminar, including representatives from Sony and General Electric, predicted that satellite-fed video distribution of movies would occur by 1990.[49] Likewise, large-screen film is biding its time. "Large-screen film differs from wide screen in that it encompasses nearly all of an individual's field of vision."[50] Imax, Omnivision, Dynavision, Envirovision, and Showscan are all large-screen processes which are either presently or nearly available. Showscan, for instance, which is available and has been audience tested, is 70-mm film projected at sixty frames a second; it more than doubles the standard frame size and projection speed. Showscan's developer, Douglas Trumball, reported that physiological tests of viewers watching Showscan movies revealed heart rate and galvanic skin response "far exceeding the normal level." However, he also noted the studios' reluctance to commit the money to produce Showscan movies and exhibitors' reluctance to purchase the new equipment necessary to show the movies.[51] Martin Polon wrote that with research and development, "the motion picture industry can dominate the very technologies that seem to menace it."[52] The production and distribution sectors have taken the lead in this regard; it is likely that the exhibition branch will not be far behind.

Conclusion

Despite the mutual fertilizing and benefits of symbiosis between film and the new media, some points of contention remain. From an economic and business perspective, film today faces a full frontal assault by these myriad new media, each vying for the same slice of leisure time cut out for *theatrical* movies. Earlier changes in film's media environment conveniently occurred one at a time and with temporal breathing (or recovery) spells of considerable duration in between; for example, the introduction of radio and, a quarter of a century later, "movies-in-the-home," or television. Today film is confronted with the concomitant confluence of multiple new media innovations. Contemporary observers assert that we are in the midst of a "communications revolution," which they variously label an explosion, a wave, or a new age. Moreover, although some new media may take considerable time before they fully mature, it is clear that, by and large, they will not simply go away. Nor will dish nights, Bingo, double features, stereoscopic and smelly movies, or casual complacency force them to leave. And while it is clear that whatever the strategies taken, history documents Hollywood's skill or luck in adapting to previous technological innovations, we must ask what of today's technologies? The large number of new media acronyms which confront the motion picture medium is numbing. Indeed, the contemporary catchword is technology—or, more to the point, television—of abundance. More-over, virtually all of the new media were introduced nearly simultaneously. Thus, both the absolute number of new media and the simultaneity of their diffusion/adoption press questions and demand answers.

STYLES AND GENRES OF INTERACTION

The ramifications of the symbiosis between theatrical film and the new media give rise to numerous issues and questions. Clearly, one such effect is very simply the way we talk about film: with the formation of such operations as Tri-Star, for instance, the new media have become part of the mainstream film industry, and the movie business has become part of the pay-TV and home video industries. By definition, symbiosis results in a blurring of definitions and func-tions. The symbiosis considered in this chapter is relatively recent. Despite the long roots, which may be traced back to the 1940s, it has been only over the past decade that we have seen any appreciable growth and maturity among the new media. One consequence of this is that not all the important issues and questions can be raised or answered. This section attempts to sketch an outline for further thought and analysis on a few issues. We begin by examining eco-nomic concerns, followed by issues of audience, and lastly, aesthetics.

A rather traditional response to the introduction of new media forms has been optimism and blue-sky rhetoric. First radio, then broadcast TV, and most recently cable, have been heralded as the means by which democracy and universal education might truly be achieved. Neither occurred, of course. The rhetoric about the new media was once filled with grandiose visions—and to a limited extent, actual implementation—of a proliferation of services with differing iden-tities, each offering audiences multiple, distinct program options; as with the balderdash concerning the civic possibilities of TV, this narrow-casting function of the new media has given way to the realities of capitalist economics. Rather than diversity, what we are seeing is increasing concentration of ownership and a rather uniform set of business procedures with the further consequence of homogeneity of programming and diminished audience choices. For instance, by 1979 more than one-third of all cable subscribers were served by the ten largest cable organizations.[53] This is perhaps the most serious, meaningful, and important "downside" to the symbiosis among media. Symbiosis, it should be remembered, is akin to concentration, which on some levels we may wish to applaud but on others we rightfully fear. And, not surprisingly, media success is determined by majorities, not minorities—the larger the audiences, the greater the success.

The movie industry's history unambiguously reveals its proclivity to strive toward and embrace oligopoly. First there was the MPPC, more honestly known as "the Trust," a combine of companies unified to control the patents, produc-tion, and distribution of film. The Trust was broken by independents such as

Carl Laemmle who, rather promptly, proceeded to form their own cartel under the aegis of the MPPDA. International issues of concern to the film industry were assuaged by the Webb-Pomerene Export Trade Act, which gave legislative sanction to monopoly and collusive actions as long as they occurred outside of the United States. Today, the symbiosis between the new media and Hollywood can portend only more of the same. Conglomeration (e.g., the ill-fated Premiere venture and the up-and-running Tri-Star) reduces the economic threats to all by spreading risk across several markets. Although the new media have and will continue to cut into theatrical box-office revenues, the new media are sure to provide more than equivalent compensation to film producers. Moreover, as Janet Wasko has noted, the "de facto protectionism" which has long existed largely closes the United States as an import market to foreigners, thereby lowering—if not eliminating—concerns of external competition.[54] Thus, the continued strength and survival of the Hollywood–new media symbiosis is ensured; indeed, not only does the symbiosis result in a systemically intact structure, but the structure is reinforced and enhanced. With the flourishing myriad of new technological delivery systems, producers find themselves in the comfortable position of being able to pick, choose, and refuse projects. The uniform economic mindset suggests increased homogeneity of products and visual ideas.[55]

Only one "player" in the symbiotic process appears to have much to lose economically: theatrical exhibitors. Despite their adoption of high-fidelity sound reproduction systems, enhanced screen technologies, and the like, exhibitors are faced with a closing window between theatrical and nontheatrical release, increased ticket prices that may inhibit attendance, and audience research indicating that although the average amount of time spent at the cinema may remain constant, theatrical movies will account for the least amount of total media consumption. Whether showmanship, by itself, including the glitzy, gauche gimmicks of Hollywood hype so popular in the 1950s and 1960s, can turn the tide against such threats is doubtful. Viewed at this level of analysis are issues of the way messages are presented and the behavioral patterns of message consumption. While production profits as a result of symbiosis, on other levels the forecast is less rosy. For exhibitors, it is confluence of many new media that offers the greatest concern since they find themselves having to compete for audiences with not just radio, or television, or redistribution of the population from urban to suburban areas. Rather, one-at-a-time competition has given way to all-at-once confrontation.

One response to this concern has been to assert that the box-office performance of a movie during theatrical exhibition is the criterion by which fee schedules for other forms of release are determined. Indeed this might be true if all the various distributors are truly independent of one another and the market is truly competitive. Such is not the case—as symbiosis illustrates; symbiosis suggests cooperation, not competition. By 1985 dozens of made-for-pay-TV movies had been produced by a number of services. Thus, what may have initially been the conventional wisdom of theatrical release as a barometer for the commercial value of a film did not deter HBO from producing the first made-for-cable movie, *The Terry Fox Story*, and offering it to subscribers on May 22, 1983. Moreover, many of the exhibition windows are presold—often even prior to the actual production of a film.

The negative consequences of symbiosis are limited not only to movie exhibitors. They extend to issues of audiences and aesthetics. For example, one clear impact of the introduction of multiple forms of competition is that the window between theatrical and nontheatrical release is closing. The smaller the window, the less the opportunity for some (perhaps most) films to demonstrate their legs, or box-office strength. That is, a movie which needs time to generate positive word-of-mouth may suffer by virtue of "small" opening week returns. Anything short of a blockbuster may well be relegated to "marginal" or "failure" status. Such a film was the Oscar-winning *Tender Mercies* (1983). This movie was partially financed by HBO with the stipulation that HBO would have exclusive rights to the picture for one year after theatrical release. Allegations were raised, especially after the Academy Awards ceremony, that the film had a slow audience build and had not exhausted its theatrical audience. Thus, according to the movie businesspeople, not only were exhibitors shortchanged, so too were audiences who were deprived of the theatrical experience of viewing the film due to HBO's unceremonious demand that contractual obligations be fulfilled.

The rather gloomy portrait being painted thus far—with the exception of the production-distribution sector—extends still further. With the certainty of symbiosis we must ask, too, what kinds of visual entertainment will and will not be produced? What sorts of stories will and will not be told? Who will view movies, under what kinds of circumstances, and for what reasons? It is unquestionable that the broader the base of the medium the greater the tendency for the content to drift toward the lowest common denominator. This pattern is especially clear when we watch prime-time broadcast TV. The jewels of television are identifiable as such simply because they are so very different from the usual offerings. Too, the tendency to imitate and copy crosses media: John Sayle made a small-budget film, *Return of the Secaucus Seven* (1980), and Lawrence Kasden spent more money to follow up on this theme with *The Big Chill* (1983). The success of the latter no doubt helped make possible another theatrical film, *St. Elmo's Fire* (1985) (or *The Little Chill*, as it has been called), for the younger set, and then CBS television offered *Hometown* during their fall 1985 schedule. Are there really many meaningful differences among these? As symbiosis strengthens and matures, the determining factor for what is produced increasingly becomes profitability. And, while there is nothing new about profit potential as the foremost concern among producers, symbiosis may escalate the prominence of this beyond present levels with the result being an even greater emphasis on repetition and formula.

Of course, new technologies also provide the means for a new, and perhaps improved, aesthetic experience. We are appreciative of Dolby and stereo sound, the use of computer-generated imaging, and the development of the Steadicam and Skycam. But in one sense, these developments bear a striking similarity to the gimmick of the 1950s, for example, 3-D, Smell-O-Vision, AromaRama. Do these technological advances compensate for what might be missing in the way of narrative? Each of us must decide the answer to this question individually. The unfortunate part, though, is that regardless of how we may feel about this issue, we do not play a role in the production process. That is, the decision will be made for us and we can only react.

Lastly, the prominence of TV technologies has meaning with regard to how movies are viewed. By the early 1970s the trend toward multiplex theatrical exhibition had become well established. Along with multiplexing came a diminishing screen size which nurtured an audience that conceives of and is accustomed to the movie experience as virtually identical in form to television— albeit, in most cases, without commercial interruption (though commercials on movie screens are becoming common). As Home Box Office attracts more and more subscribers, movies on the small screen become the movie experience for many. The excitement and the aesthetic sense of specialness engendered by the large-screen format may well be on their way to becoming extinct. A new movie audience generation now conceptualizes movies as run through their home monitor, taped and played back by their home VCR, rented from the video store, and, on special occasions, reproduced in stereo by their videodisc player or hi-fi VCR.

We have seen that the established film organizations have been active in developing programming for the new media. Indeed, the newer organizations have come to take an important place among the established producers. Just as the Disney organization has entered the cable-TV arena, so too has HBO entered the theatrical market via Tri-Star. Moreover, HBO, to take perhaps the most visible example, produces original programming for its service. Yet to be answered are questions concerning the form and content of new media programming and the way such programming compares to theatrical film. Clearly, there are no definitive answers to such questions—at least not yet. The trend toward hybridized movie production may suggest the possibility of movies which are aesthetically appealing regardless of the means of exhibition. With the development of HDTV and such processes as Showscan it is conceivable that previous aesthetic notions of what TV and film are aesthetically about may go by the wayside or need serious rethinking. For instance, up until the present television was considered a producer's and a close-up medium; film was considered a director's and a long-shot medium. How, if at all, will this change as the new media matures? The future of the videodisc also remains unclear. If this technology persists as a means for presenting moving visual entertainment (as opposed to instruction and information storage and retrieval), what does this suggest about form and content? When the audience becomes the "programmer"—for selecting, structuring, and manipulating information—does this make a significant difference to the program, the viewing environment, and the viewing experience? It will be important to examine and trace the aesthetic patterns as the symbiotic process evolves.

As was suggested earlier, the dynamic evolutionary steps between industries, within one industry, and among audiences are still quite fluid. While it is quite clear that our definitions for motion pictures and the new media have shifted with growth and development, the final, definitive posture has yet to be established. Similarly, issues of audiences have blurred. Still in the process is a sorting out of the theatrical window for movies, video, pay-television, and the like. Answers to questions of audience-industry adjustment to the symbiotic process remain and, at present, are somewhat speculative.

All of these issuees, and more, give us pause to reconsider how we define film. What, in the age of new media, does film mean? Just as questions about the future of videodiscs can be raised, so too are there questions about film. Indeed, perhaps the name best associated with film, Eastman Kodak, is now fully geared up for production of videotape. In the symbiotic process between motion pictures and the new media we are seeing the intentions, goals, and dividing lines being diluted by one another. The final arrangement has yet to occur. One thing, however, is clear: there has not been and will not be a vote taken on any of these issues; they will be decided for us. The consequences of symbiosis, for better or worse, are determined by a small group of influential businesspeople. The larger group of audiences will have an opportunity only to endorse or to reject changes and even here, only in the most obscure and imprecise fashion. What film will become is being determined largely on the basis of profitability. Surely the use of this one criterion overlooks the fullness of the symbiotic process.

NOTES

1. Yrjo Littunen, with Pertti Hemanus, Kaarle Nordenstreng, and Tapio Varis, "Cultural Problems of Direct Satellite Broadcasting," *International Social Science Journal* 32 (1980): 283.

2. Samuel Goldwyn, "Hollywood in the Television Age," *New York Times Magazine* 13 February 1949: 15, 44, 47. See also Lynne Schafer Gross, *The New Television Technologies* (Dubuque, Iowa: Wm. C. Brown, 1983), p. 70.

3. Gross, *The New Television Technologies*, p. 70.

4. See ibid., p. 71; and David H. Ostroff, "A History of STV, Inc. and the 1964 California Vote Against Pay Television," *Journal of Broadcasting* 27 (Fall 1983): 371–86.

5. Maxwell E. McCombs and Chaim H. Eyal, "Spending on Mass Media," *Journal of Communication* 30 (Winter 1980): 157–58.

6. See Sydney W. Head with Christopher H. Sterling, *Broadcasting in America* (Boston: Houghton Mifflin, 1982), pp. 318–20; Watson S. James, "The New Electronic Media: An Overview," *Journal of Advertising Research* 23 (August-September 1983):

34; Julie Talen, "STV: Going, Going . . . ," *Channels* 3 (November-December 1983): 33; "Viewers Turn Off Subscription TV," *Business Week* 16 May 1983: 28–29.

7. See James Traub, "SMATV: Private Cable at Ease," *Channels* 4 (November-December 1984): 36.

8. Sonny Kleinfield, "Time Inc. is Everything," *Rolling Stone* 27 October 1983: 51.

9. Howard Polskin, "Paramount Deal with Showtime Shakes Pay-TV," *TV Guide* 31 December 1983: A–1.

10. Tom Nicholson with Janet Huck and Peter McAlevey, "HBO Versus the Studios," *Newsweek* 15 November 1982: 83.

11. See Peter Caranicas, "Hollywood Wakes Up and Smells the Coffee," *Channels* (July-August 1983): 44; and Todd Gitlin, *Inside Prime Time* (New York: Pantheon Books, 1983), p. 329.

12. For history on this, see Thomas Guback, *The International Film Industry: Western Europe and America Since 1945* (Bloomington: Indiana University Press, 1969); for contemporary information, see "Pay-TV: An InterMedia Survey," *InterMedia* 10 (January 1982): 1–16.

13. Michael Schwarz, "A New World: Hollywood," *Channels* 2 (February-March 1982): 26–28.

14. David Pauley and Connie Leslie, "The Videodisc Strikes Out," *Newsweek* 16 April 1984: 69.

15. David Lachenbruch, "The VCR is Changing the Whole TV Picture," *Channels* 4 (March-April 1984): 16.

16. David Waterman, "Videocassettes, Videodiscs, and the Role of Theatrical Distribution" (Paper presented at the Columbia University Research Program in Telecommunications and Information Policy Conference, New York City, March 1984).

17. Steve Behrens, "Video Software: Home at the Bijou," *Channels* 4 (November-December 1984): 10; see pp. 10–12 for information on the impact of rentals on loss of revenues to the studios due to the First Sale Doctrine of copyright law.

18. Thomas Guback, "Theatrical Film," in *Who Owns the Media*, ed. Benjamin M. Compaine (White Plains, N.Y.: Knowledge Industries Publications, 1979), p. 221; Waterman, "Videocassettes, Videodiscs, and the Role of Theatrical Distribution"; Douglas Gomery, "The American Film Industry of the 1970's: Stasis in the 'New Hollywood,' " *Wide Angle* 5, 4 (1983): 54.

19. See Sharon Rosenthal, "Snapping Back at the Crocodile That Ate Hollywood," *TV Guide* 3 March 1984: 4–8; Stephen J. Sansweet, "Pay TV's Showtime and Movie Channel Agree to Merge in Five-Company Venture," *Wall Street Journal* 10 January 1983: 4; Peggy Ziegler and Joe Boyle, "Three Studios Buy into Movie Channel," *Multichannel News* 17 November 1982: 1, 139.

20. See P. J. Bednarski, "Living with Tele1st," *Channels* 4 (March-April 1984): 55–56; Howard Polskin, "ABC to Telecast Recent Movies to VCR Owners," *TV Guide* 14 January 1984: A–1; Howard Polskin, "Few Subscribers to Wee-Hour Pay-TV Service," *TV Guide* 14 April 1984: A–1; Howard Polskin, "ABC Folds TeleFirst," *TV Guide* 23 June 1984: A–1.

21. James Monaco, "The Silver Screen Under Glass," *Channels* 1 (August-September 1981): 50, 52.

22. Leo Handel, "Radio, Movies, Publications Increase Each Other's Audience," *Printers' Ink* 19 July 1946: 42–43.

23. Christopher H. Sterling and Timothy R. Haight, *The Mass Media* (New York: Praeger Publishers, 1978), p. 56; see too A. C. Nielson Company, *1983 Annual Report*, p. 6; Les Brown, "Cable TV: Wiring for Abundance," *Channels* 3 (November-December 1983): 25; Kenneth R. Clark, "The Making of a Giant: How Cable Changed America," *Chicago Tribune* 30 October 1983, sec. 4, p. 1.

24. The lower estimate is reported by Robert D. Kahn, "More Messages from the Medium," *Technology Review* 86 (January 1983): 49; the higher estimate is reported by Howard Polskin, "What You Can Expect from Cable Now," *TV Guide* 2 June 1984: 3.

25. Cited in Laura Landro, "Pay-TV Industry Facing Problems After Misjudging Market Demand," *Wall Street Journal* 29 June 1983: 37.

26. Sterling and Haight, *The Mass Media*, p. 107; "Satellite Channels: A Guide," *Channels* (November-December 1984): 53–62.

27. James, "The New Electronic Media," p. 33; Dean M. Krugman and Donald Eckrich, "Differences in Cable and Pay-Cable Audiences," *Journal of Advertising Research* (August-September 1982): 23.

28. See Jack T. Pottle, "Pay Television: A Primer on Competition," *Satellite Communications* 6 (November 1982): 26–30.

29. Cited in Steve Behrens, "Shortcut to the Home," *Channels* 3 (March-April 1984): 30.

30. James, "The New Electronic Media," pp. 35–36.

31. See David Lachenbruch, "Home Video: Home Is Where the Action Is," *Channels* (November-December 1983): 42; and David Lachenbruch, "VCRs: The Hottest Thing Since Television," *Channels* 4 (November-December 1984): 6.

32. For data on cable subscribers, see Krugman and Eckrich, "Differences in Cable and Pay-Cable Audiences," pp. 23–29; Stanley Marcus, "The Viewers' Verdict So Far—On Cable TV," *Panorama* 1 (October 1980): 42–45; James T. Rothe, Michael G. Harvey, and George C. Michael, "The Impact of Cable Television on Subscriber and Non-Subscriber Behavior," *Journal of Advertising Research* 23 (August-September 1983): 15–23; and James G. Webster, "The Impact of Cable and Pay Cable Television on Local Audiences," *Journal of Broadcasting* 27 (Spring 1983): 119–26. For data on VCR owners, see Mark R. Levy's four reports: "Program Playback Preferences in VCR Households," *Journal of Broadcasting* 24 (Summer 1980): 327–36; "Home Video Recorders: A User Survey," *Journal of Communication* 30 (Autumn 1980): 23–27; "Home Video Recorders and Time Shifting," *Journalism Quarterly* 58 (Fall 1981): 401–405; "The Time-Shifting Use of Home Video Recorders," *Journal of Broadcasting* 27 (Summer 1983): 263–68.

33. Quoted in Gregg Kilday, "Ninth Annual Grosses Gloss," *Film Comment* 2 (March-April 1984): 62.

34. J. Patrick O'Connor, "Cable Viewers: How to Pick the Right Channel for You," *TV Guide* 29 October 1983: 20.

35. See Lachenbruch, "Home Video," p. 43; Gross, *The New Television Technologies*, p. 105.

36. See Richard V. Ducey, Dean M. Krugman, and Donald Eckrich, "Predicting Market Segments in the Cable Industry: The Basic and Pay Subscribers," *Journal of Broadcasting* 27 (Spring 1983): pp. 155–61; Leo W. Jeffres, "Cable TV and Viewer Selectivity," *Journal of Broadcasting* 22 (Spring 1978): 167–77; Krugman and Eckrich, "Differences in Cable and Pay-Cable Audiences," pp. 23–29; Gale D. Metzger, "Cable Television Audiences," *Journal of Advertising Research* 23 (August-September 1983): 41–47; Edward Mink, "Why the Networks Will Survive Cable," *Atlantic Monthly* 252

(December 1983): 63–68; Rothe et al., "The Impact of Cable Television on Subscriber and Non-Subscriber Behavior," pp. 15–23.

37. See Donald E. Agostino, Herbert A. Terry, and Rolland C. Johnson, "Home Video Recorders: Rights and Ratings," *Journal of Communication* 30 (Autumn 1980): 28–35 and Levy's research reported in note 32 above.

38. See Levy, "Program Playback Preferences in VCR Households;" and "Home Video Recorders: A User Survey."

39. Lachenbruch, "Home Video," p. 42.

40. Tony Seidman, "Homevid Aids Cinema B.O. for Two Pics," *Variety* 26 October 1983: 1, 396.

41. Newspaper Advertising Bureau (NAB), *Movie-Going in the United States and Canada* (New York: NAB, 1981), p. 41, emphasis in original.

42. See Alison F. Alexander and James E. Owers, "The Restructuring of the Communications Industry" (Paper presented at the Eastern Communications Association Conference, Providence, RI, 3 May 1985).

43. An interesting twist on the typical direction of which medium responds to which other medium's technological advance is stereo television. Motion pictures, as well as radio, have for years used stereo sound; although several years off, TV will soon be broadcasting in stereo (see David Lachenbruch, "Hear Ye! Hear Ye! Stereo Comes to TV," *TV Guide* 9 June 1984: 41–44).

44. See Raymond Fielding, "Recent Electronic Innovations in Professional Motion Picture Production," *Journal of Film and Video* 36 (Spring 1984): 43–49, 72; Judy E. Klein, "Coppola Makes 'Rumble Fish'—The Coppola Way," *Boxoffice* 119 (November 1983): 10–11.

45. See Garrett Brown, "It's a Bird . . . It's a Plane . . . It's a . . . Camera!" *American Film* 6 (September 1983): 59–61; Martin Polon, "Future Technologies in Motion Pictures," in *The Movie Business Book*, ed. Jason E. Squire (Englewood Cliffs, N.J.: Prentice-Hall, 1983), pp. 389–90.

46. See Alexander Auerbach, "Big Screen + Little Screen = Big Money," *Boxoffice* 120 (May 1984): 6; and Gary Fisher, "Computers in the Theatre," *Boxoffice* 120 (March 1984): 44–46.

47. Henry B. Aldridge, "New York Theatres and Film Exhibition in America" (Paper presented at the Society for Cinema Studies Conference, New York City, April 1981); Karen Stabiner, "The Shape of Theatres to Come," *American Film* 5 (September 1982): 51–56.

48. Michael Nielsen, "Hollywood's High Frontier: The Emergence of Electronic Cinema," *Journal of Film and Video* 36 (Spring 1984): 31–42, 72.

49. "Say Vid Exhibition 5 Years in Future," *Variety* 14 (April 1984): 7.

50. Allen Stegman, "The Large-Screen Film: A Viable Entertainment Alternative to High Definition Television," *Journal of Film and Video* 36 (Spring 1984): 23.

51. See David Crook, "Movie House: A Trip to Infinity," *Los Angeles Times* 18 June 1981: 1, 14; Pat Dowell and Ray Heinrich, "Bigger than Life," *American Film* 8 (May 1984): 49–53; Phoebe Hoban, "Fast Films," *American Film* 8 (February 1984): 100; Bill Krohn and Harley Lond, "Showscan: A New Type of Exhibition for a Revolutionary Film Process," *Boxoffice* 120 (February 1984): 10–11; Stabiner, "The Shape of Theaters to Come"; Stegman, "The Large-Screen Film."

52. Polon, "Future Technologies in Motion Pictures," p. 402.

53. For a discussion of the trend toward dominance by multiple-system operators, see

Herbert H. Howard, "Ownership Trends in Cable Television: 1972–1979," *Journalism Quarterly* 58 (Summer 1981): 288–91.

54. Janet Wasko, "Hollywood, New Technologies and International Banking: A Formula for Financial Success," in *Current Research in Film: Audiences, Economics, and Law*, ed. Bruce A. Austin, vol. 1 (Norwood, N.J.: Ablex Publishing, 1985), p. 102.

55. For more information on monopoly/oligopoly, concentration, and conglomeration see, for instance, Guback, "Theatrical Film," pp. 179–249.

SELECTED BIBLIOGRAPHY

In addition to the materials presented in the preceding notes, the following items should prove instructive to readers interested in the symbiosis of new media and film. The listing is brief and readers are encouraged to make use of the notes for additional analyses.

The rate with which literature on the new media is being published is phenomenal. Simply keeping up with the pace is a full-time job. Indeed, it is easily conceivable that readers will have available to them twice the number of publications which were available when the present chapter was written (December 1985). Perhaps of more help than the articles which follow are sources where information on this chapter's topic may be found.

A useful, selected guide to "Articles on Mass Communication in U.S. and Foreign Journals" is published in each issue of *Journalism Quarterly*. Brief annotations for most entries are provided. Also published quarterly is *Communication Abstracts*. *Communication Booknotes* is a monthly publication which offers reviews of mostly book-length treatments on a variety of communication topics. *Media Information Australia* provides reviews and annotations of both books and articles.

Popular periodicals should not be overlooked. *Time*, *Newsweek*, *TV Guide*, and others regularly report on the new media. The bimonthly *Channels of Communication* is especially valuable. The expense of subscribing to the many newsstand and trade publications can be enormous. Check university and larger public libraries for the following: *Advertising Age*, *Boxoffice*, *Broadcasting*, *Cable Vision*, *Daily Variety*, *Hollywood Reporter*, *Pay TV Newsletter*, *Television Digest*, and *Variety*.

Auerbach, Alexander. "Pay Cable Helps Theatre Boxoffice, Market Study Shows." *Boxoffice* 119, 7 (July 1983): 20–21.

Beville, Hugh M., Jr. "The Audience Potential of the New Technologies: 1985–1990." *Journal of Advertising Research* 25, 2 (April-May 1985): RC–3–RC–10.

"Cable Execs, Film Exhibitors Pass Small Peace Pipe at NATO." *Variety* 310, 45, (9 November 1983): 27.

Carey, James W. "Changing Communications Technology and the Nature of the Audience." *Journal of Advertising* 9, no. 2 (1980): 3–9, 43.

Colvin, Geoffrey, "The Crowded New World of TV." *Fortune* 110, 6, (17 September 1984): 156–66.

Gelman, Eric et al. "The Video Revolution." *Newsweek* CII, 34 (6 August 1984): 50–57.

Hartshorn, David J. "Children and Video-films at Home." *Educational Studies* 9, 2 (1983): 145–49.

Ivre, Ivar. "Mass Media: Costs, Choices and Freedom." *InterMedia* 9, 5 (September 1981): 26–31.

Jassem, Harvey C. and Roger Jon Desmond. "Theory Construction and Research in Mass Communication: The Implications of New Technologies." Paper presented at the Eastern Communications Association Conference, Philadelphia, PA, March 1984.

Komatsuzaki, Seisuke. "Social Impacts of New Communications Media: The Japanese Experience." *Telecommunications Policy* 6, 4 (December 1982): 269–75.

Luther, Rodney. "Television and the Future of Motion Picture Exhibition." *Hollywood Quarterly* 5, 2 (1951): 164–77.

Margulies, Lee. "Will Movie Theaters Survive Video?" *Home Video* 3, 11 (November 1982): 50–53.

Nadel, Mark and Eli Noam, eds. *The Economics of Physical Distribution: Video Cassettes/ Discs and Movie Theater, an Anthology.* New York: Columbia University, Research Program in Telecommunications and Information Policy, 1983.

Nelson, Richard Alan. "Entering a Brave New World: The Impact of the New Information and Telecommunications Technologies." *Journal of the University Film and Video Association* 35, 4 (Fall 1983): 23–34.

Nicholson, Tom, with David T. Friendly and Peter McAlevey. "Hollywood's Play for the Pay-TV Crowd." *Newsweek* C1, 8 (21 February 1983): 66.

Nielsen, Arthur C., Jr. "The Outlook for Electronic Media." *Journal of Advertising Research* 2, 6 (December 1982–January 1983): 9–16.

Pauley, David, with David T. Friendly and Michael Reese. "Big Bucks for the Big Screens." *Newsweek* CIII, 22 (28 May 1984): 63.

Polskin, Howard. "Your Push-Button, Pay-Per-View Movies Should be Here Shortly." *TV Guide* (13 July 1985): 32–34.

Schwarz, Michael. "Turning Movie Houses Into Video Houses." *Channels* 2, 2 (April-May 1982): 29–30.

Silverman, Syd. "Entertainment in the Satellite Era." *Variety* 310, 43 (26 October 1983): 13, 99.

Turan, Kenneth. "Two Porcupines About to Embrace." *TV Guide* (14 July 1984): 37–40.

U.S. Senate, Committee on the Judiciary, 97th Congress, 1st and 2d Sessions. *Copyright Infringements (Audio and Video Recorders).* Serial No. J–97–84. Washington, D.C.: U.S. Government Printing Office. 1982.

Williams, Wenmouth, Jr., and Mitchell E. Shapiro. "A Study of the Effects In-Home Entertainment Alternatives Have on Film Attendance." In *Current Research in Film: Audiences, Economics, and Law.* Ed. Bruce A. Austin. vol. 1. Norwood, N.J.: Ablex Publishing, 1985.

SELECTED FILMOGRAPHY

Movies made specifically for the new media are a relatively recent phenomenon. While *The Terry Fox Story* is usually credited as the first made-for-cable film (see above), it was actually preceded by an obscure Showtime movie, *Falcon's Gold.* Listed below are a few made-for-cable movies and one miniseries. If it continues to be updated, an especially useful source of information on such films is Alvin H. Marill's *Movies Made for Television* (New York: Zoetrope, 1984).

Between Friends (USA September 15, 1983). HBO. Produced by Jonathan Estrin and Shelley List. Directed by Lou Antonio. Screenplay by Jonathan Estrin and Shelly List. With Elizabeth Taylor, Carol Burnett, and Barbara Bush.

To Catch a King (USA February 12, 1984). HBO. Produced by Alfred Kelman, Mark

Monnet, Thomas Johnston, and William Storke. Directed by Clive Donner. Screenplay by Roger Hirson. With Robert Wagner and Teri Garr.

The Cold Room (USA March 24, 1984). HBO. Produced by Bob Weis and Mark Forstater. Directed and Screenplay by James Dearden. With George Segal and Amanda Pays.

Draw! (USA July 15, 1984). HBO. Produced by Ronald Cohen. Directed by Steven Hilliard. Screenplay by Stanley Mann. With Kirk Douglas and James Coburn.

The Far Pavilions (USA April 22–24, 1984). HBO. Produced by Geoffrey Reeve. Directed by Peter Duffell. Screenplay by Julian Bond. With Ben Cross, Amy Irving, and Omar Sharif.

Prisoners of the Lost Universe (USA August 15, 1983). Showtime. Produced by Harry Robertson. Directed by Terry Marcel. Screenplay by Harry Robertson and Terry Marcel. With Richard Hatch, Kay Lenz, and John Saxon.

Right of Way (USA November 21, 1983). HBO. Produced by George Schaefer and Philip Parslow. Directed by George Schaefer. Screenplay by Richard Lee. With Bette Davis, James Stewart, and Melinda Dillon.

Robin Hood and the Sorcerer (USA January 15, 1984). Showtime. Produced by Paul Knight. Directed and Screenplay by Ian Sharp. With Michael Praed, Anthony Valentine, and Judi Trott.

Sakharov (USA June 20, 1984). HBO. Produced by Robert ''Buzz'' Berger. Directed by Jack Gould. Screenplay by David W. Rintels. With Jason Robards, Glenda Jackson, and Nicol Williamson.

The Terry Fox Story (USA May 22, 1983). HBO. Produced by Robert Cooper. Directed by Ralph Thomas. Screenplay by Edward Hume. With Eric Fryer, Robert Duvall, and Chris Makepeace.

FILM INDEX

SUBJECT INDEX

Hitchcock, Alfred: Milton Caniff and, 74; Salvador Dali and, 36–37; Bernard Herrmann and, 181, 182, 196, 198, 199, 205; stage plays as source material for early sound films, 150; television work, 292. Works: *Blackmail*, 150; *Juno and the Paycock*, 150; *Man Who Knew Too Much, The*, 205; *North by Northwest*, 22, 181, 196; *Paradine Case, The*, 36; *Psycho*, 181, 194, 196, 197–98, 199; *Rebecca*, 36, 185, 186, 187; *Spellbound*, 36–37, 186, 196; *Thirty-Nine Steps, The*, 202; *Torn Curtain*, 182, 198; *Vertigo*, 181, 196, 197

Hoffman, Dustin, 152

Hofmann, Josef, 218

Hogan, John V. L., 276

Hogarth, Burne, 74

Holiday (play), 149

Holiday in Paris (TV program), 288

Hollywood Playhouse (TV program), 298

Hollywood Star Theater (radio program), 250

Holst, Gustav, 185

Home Box Office (HBO), 340–41, 343, 344, 346, 353, 354

Hometown (TV program), 353

Honegger, Arthur, 174, 175

Hoover, Nan, 330

Hopalong Cassidy (TV program), 292

Hope, Bob, 227, 250

Hopper, Dennis, 115

Hopper, Edward, 41

Horne, Lena, 218

Horner, James, 179

Houseman, John, 107, 260, 261

House Un-American Activities Committee (HUAC), 106, 108

Howard, Sidney, 147, 149

"How Deep Is Your Love?" (song), 255

Hoyt, Charles, 53

HUAC, 106, 108

Hudson, Rock, 109

Huelsenbeck, Richard, 33

Hulk, The (comic book), 73

Humanity (play), 142

Hunter, Kim, 152

Hurd, Earl, 68, 78

Hurt, William, 152

Hurwitz, Leo, 57

Huston, John, 37, 71, 117

Hyatt, Donald, 56

Ibsen, Henrik, 150

Imax, 350

Immortal One, The (play), 142

IMPPRO, 288

Impressionism, 21, 23–25

Impressions (video art), 330

In Celebration (play), 153

Information (video art), 333

Inge, William, 152

"Internationale, L' " (song), 175

International Film Service, 69

"In the Hall of the Mountain King," by Grieg (musical composition), 171, 206

Intruder in the Dust (literary work), 107

Ippolotov-Ivanov, Mikhail, 174

Irving, Henry, 141

Irwin, May, 136

Ivens, Joris, 28, 56

Ives, Charles Edward, 175

Ives, James M., 40

Iwerks, Ub, 68

Jackson, Glenda, 153

Jaffe, Herb, 113

James, Henry, 5, 7, 109

James, William, 5

Jannings, Emil, 142

Jansen, Pierre, 190, 199

Jarre, Maurice, 208

Jaws (literary work), 113

Jenkins, C. Francis, 275, 276

Jessua, Alain, 177

Jesus Christ Superstar (album), 229

Johns, Jasper, 330

Johnson, Nunnally, 103

Jolson, Al, 145, 221, 222

Jones, James, 106

Jungle Jim (comic strip), 70

Juno and the Paycock (play), 150

Kahles, C. W., 75

Kaiser, Georg, 142

Kandinsky, Vasily, 41, 313

ABOUT THE
CONTRIBUTORS

CAROLYN ANDERSON is Assistant Professor in the Department of Communication at the University of Massachusetts at Amherst. Her research and teaching interests include film and television history and criticism.

BRUCE AUSTIN is Associate Professor in the College of Liberal Arts and Chairperson of the degree program in Professional and Technical Communication, Rochester Institute of Technology. He is editor of the annual publication, *Current Research in Film: Audiences, Economics, and Law* (Ablex) and is writing a book on movie audience research for Wadsworth.

CHARLES BERG, Director of Film Studies and Associate Professor in the Department of Theatre and Media Arts at the University of Kansas, is a widely published scholar–critic whose work has appeared in *Cinema Journal, Speech Monographs, Journal of Popular Film, Hollwood Reporter, Down Beat*, and *Jazz Times* among others. Along with teaching and writing, he is a jazz saxophonist/flutist and leader of the Chuck Berg Quartet.

ROYAL BROWN is Associate Professor and Chairman of the Film Studies Program at Queens College in the City University of New York. He is also a faculty member of the Ph.D. Program in French at the City University's Graduate Center. He has published extensively on film and music, and has written regularly on film music recordings for *High Fidelity* and, most recently, *Fanfare*.

GARY BURNS is Assistant Professor in the Department of Speech at the University of Missouri–St. Louis. He received his Ph.D. in Radio, Television, and Film from Northwestern University in 1981.

GARY R. EDGERTON is Associate Professor and Chairperson of the Communication Department at Goucher College. He is Associate Editor of the *Journal of Popular Film and Television*, and the author of *American Film Exhibition*

(Garland, 1983). He also has published numerous articles on film and broadcasting in such journals as *Quarterly Review of Film Studies*, *Journal of Film and Video*, *Journal of Popular Film and Television*, and *Journal of Popular Culture*.

WILLIAM LAFFERTY is Associate Professor in the Department of Theatre Arts at Wright State University in Dayton. He received his Ph.D. in Radio, Television, and Film from Northwestern University. His primary research interest is the evolution of American television, and he has published in such journals as *American Cinematographer*, *Cinema Journal*, and *SMPTE Journal*. In 1985 he won the Broadcast Education Association History Competition with his essay on technological innovation in British and American radio broadcasting.

MARTIN NORDEN teaches film as an Associate Professor of Communication at the University of Massachusetts at Amherst. He has published dozens of articles on film and television in anthologies such as Greenwood Press's *TV Genres* and *Eros in the Mind's Eye* and in such journals as *Wide Angle*, *Journal of Popular Film and Television*, *Journal of Film and Video*, *Film and History*, and *Journal of Communication*.

RICHARD SHALE is Associate Professor of English at Youngstown State University in Ohio. A Phi Beta Kappa graduate of Ohio Wesleyan University, he earned his M.A. and Ph.D. in American Culture at the University of Michigan. He is the author of *Donald Duck Joins Up: The Walt Disney Studio During World War II* and *Academy Awards: An Ungar Reference Index* as well as numerous articles on film and other aspects of popular culture.

EDWARD SMALL is Associate Professor of Radio-TV-Film at the University of Missouri–Columbia, where he has been Director of Film Studies since 1983. His scholarly specializations include film-video theory and experimental (avant-garde) works, which he also produces as an independent artist. He is currently Associate Editor for the *Journal of Film and Video* and was Executive Vice President for the University Film and Video Association through 1985. The research for his chapter was partially funded by a Travel to Collections Grant from the National Endowment for the Humanities (RY–20471–84).

GREGORY WALLER teaches courses in film and popular culture at the University of Kentucky. His publications include *The Stage/Screen Debate: A Study in Popular Aesthetics* and *The Living and the Undead: From Stoker's "Dracula" to Romero's "Dawn of the Dead."*